Bankruptcy:
Law and Practice

Bankruptcy: Law and Practice

Christopher Berry

Solicitor
Edwin Coe & Calder Woods
Lincoln's Inn, WC2

Edward Bailey, MA, LLB (Cantab)

Barrister
Temple EC4

Foreword by

The Right Hon Sir Nicolas Browne-Wilkinson,

Vice-Chancellor

London
Butterworths
1987

United Kingdom	Butterworth & Co (Publishers) Ltd, 88 Kingsway, LONDON WC2B 6AB and 61A North Castle Street, EDINBURGH EH2 3LJ
Australia	Butterworths Pty Ltd, SYDNEY, MELBOURNE, BRISBANE, ADELAIDE, PERTH, CANBERRA and HOBART
Canada	Butterworths. A division of Reed Inc., TORONTO and VANCOUVER
New Zealand	Butterworths of New Zealand Ltd, WELLINGTON and AUCKLAND
Singapore	Butterworth & Co (Asia) Pte Ltd, SINGAPORE
South Africa	Butterworth Publishers (Pty) Ltd, DURBAN and PRETORIA
USA	Butterworth Legal Publishers, ST PAUL, Minnesota, SEATTLE, Washington, BOSTON, Massachusetts, AUSTIN, Texas and D & S Publishers, CLEARWATER, Florida

British Library of Cataloguing in Publication Data

Berry, Christopher
Bankruptcy: law and practice.
1. Bankruptcy—England
I. Title II. Bailey, Edward
344.206′78 KD2149

ISBN 0 406 52610 9

Typeset by Phoenix Photosetting, Chatham, Kent
Printed and bound in Great Britain by
Mackays of Chatham Ltd, Kent

Foreword

The coming into force of the Insolvency Act 1986, presents all those involved in personal insolvency matters with formidable problems. Some wholly new concepts are introduced by the new Act. Moreover the voluminous new rules made under the Act were only published at a very late date. Never has there been a more pressing need for a book which produces order out of a statutory maze.

I welcome this book for that reason. Not only is it published when the need is greatest, but also it renders intelligible much that is made obscure by the statutory drafting. I have found particularly instructive the introduction to the new law in Chapter 1 which explains the basic concepts underlying the law before going on to the necessary detailed consideration in Part 2.

The book will be especially useful because it contains, in one volume, both the old law and the new. One of the unhappier features of the new legislation is that the old bankruptcy law will continue to apply to all cases in which the petition was presented before 29 December 1986. Thus, for many years bankruptcy practitioners will be concerned with two different systems, the old and the new. This book, containing as it does clear and concise statements of both systems, will be invaluable.

Finally, the last part of the book deals under separate headings with various problems commonly encountered in connection with bankruptcy, notably the effect of bankruptcy on rights in the matrimonial home. I am not aware of any other text book which provides this useful service.

I have no doubt that lawyers, accountants and the courts will all find this book a most useful aid in seeking to discover and apply the new law. I wish it well.

Nicolas Browne-Wilkinson V-C
February 1987

Preface

Until the advent of the Insolvency Act 1986 the law relating to bankruptcy had undergone relatively little change for a century. The Bankruptcy Act 1914 (still the framework for the majority of bankruptcies for at least a couple of years to come) was itself based on the Act of 1883.

Over the years there were numerous calls for reform. The one which ultimately provoked a legislative response was that contained in the final Report of the Review Committee on Insolvency Law and Practice chaired by Sir Kenneth Cork. The Insolvency Act 1985 was passed containing substantial alterations not only in the law relating to individual insolvency but also in relation to corporate insolvencies. The Companies Act 1985 having been passed not long previously it was decided to consolidate all bankruptcy legislation with the exception of the Bankruptcy Act 1914. That Act will gradually fade out of use over the next few years until all individual insolvencies or bankruptcies will operate under the new legislation. Thus, as part of the consolidation process the Insolvency Act 1986 takes over from the 1985 Act before any of the bankruptcy parts of the 1985 Act come into effect. In many respects the provisions of the new legislation falls short of the Review Committee's proposals. Even so the implementation of the change will have taken almost ten years from the appointment of Sir Kenneth Cork's committee.

Many of the basic principles of bankruptcy law and practice are changed by the Insolvency Act 1986. These are dealt with by way of introduction in ch 1 and in detail thereafter and it would be superfluous to summarise them here.

In 1984, according to the Department of Trade and Industry's General Annual Report on Bankruptcy for that year there were 7,726 bankruptcy cases, compared with 6,576 in 1983. The estimated liabilities in these failures amounted in total to about £563m compared with about £232m in 1983. With assets to a value of about £106m (£56m) there was therefore an overall estimated deficiency of some £457m. By easing and speeding the process by which a person may be made bankrupt and by streamlining the procedure once a bankruptcy order is made, it is to be hoped that a significant improvement in that overall deficiency might be achieved.

What cannot be foreseen at present is the extent by which the number of people undergoing the bankruptcy process will increase by virtue of the streamlining of the procedures. The new statutory demand procedure could result in a dramatic increase in bankruptcy petitions.

Overhead costs accounted for 64.5% of recoveries in cases administered by the official receiver in 1984, and about 53% of recoveries in cases where 'private' trustees were appointed (since basic administration expenses remain about the same for each case, the official receiver's net recovery appears rather better than the 'private' cases, given that the official receiver is almost invariably left with the smaller cases). The real test of the new legislation will be whether or not these figures are improved over the forthcoming years.

This book was originally conceived, at a time when it seemed that the Cork Report would follow the fate of the Report of The Blagden Committee and other such reports, as needed to fill the gap existing between the authoritative *Williams & Muir Hunter on Bankruptcy* and the handbooks and short summaries of the law available on the market. Because of its format as an annotated statute some understanding and appreciation of the subject was thought desirable in order to achieve the best use of *Williams & Muir Hunter*.

However, the Command Paper 'A Revised Framework for Insolvency Law' (Cmnd 9175) unexpectedly contained provisions with far reaching effect not only on corporate insolvency but also upon bankruptcy. The concept of this book has therefore been expanded to attempt a comprehensive guide to both the 'old' and the 'new' law together with a commentary on the effect of bankruptcy on other areas of the law, though without attempting the fine detail required of a specialist practitioner's textbook. The aims of this book are essentially practical although hopes that tables and precedent forms could be included for all aspects of bankruptcy work have necessarily been dashed because of the very considerable delay after the passing of the Insolvency Act in the finalisation of the Rules and the relevant statutory instruments.

Much more 'law' is contained in the Rules than was the case in Bankruptcy Rules of 1952, which are almost wholly procedural. It is not possible, as this book is published for immediate use under New Law, to accumulate sufficient indications of how the new procedures will operate to include tables and precedents attached to each subject. This has been done in Part 1 of the book which deals with the Old Bankruptcy Law, and hopefully that system will be achieved for later editions as the New Law unfolds in practice.

Our thanks go in particular to Sidney Pearlman, now retired, a solicitor with enormous practical knowledge and understanding of the Old Bankruptcy Law and without whom we should not have been asked to undertake this task.

For their patience in deciphering our manuscripts and coping with the usual temperamental outbursts of modern word processors in their own time we are enormously grateful to Millicent Russell, Nicola Strickland and to Jill Graham.

And finally, of course, to our wives Jan and Claire, both for assisting with the work (Claire From contributed ch 30) and for those lost weekends and evenings while we produced what it is hoped is a statement of the Law of Bankruptcy at the commencement of the Insolvency Act 1986.

December 1986

C.R.B.
E.H.B.

Contents

Table of Statutes

References in this Table to Statutes are to Halsbury's Statutes of England Fourth Edition, showing the volume and page at which the annotated text of the Act may be found.
Paragraph and page references printed in bold type indicate where the section of an Act is set out in part or in full.
References in italic type refer to pages of the appendices.

Table of Rules and Regulations

Paragraph and page references printed in bold type indicate where the rule or regulation is set out in part or in full. References in italic type refer to pages of the appendices.

Table of Cases

G

H

PARA

M

S

T

PARA

U

V

W

CHAPTER 1

Introduction and Explanation of Transitional Stages

1.1 INTRODUCTION

1.1.1 For several years to come two systems of bankruptcy, or individual insolvency, law will run side by side. Throughout this book the system which continues under the Bankruptcy Act 1914 will be referred to as the 'Old Bankruptcy Law' while cases operating under the Insolvency Act 1986 will be referred to as operating under the 'New Law'.

1.1.2 It is obviously of critical importance for any person involved in bankruptcy, or for anyone advising others involved, to decide whether the Old Bankruptcy Law or the New Law applies to the case in question.

1.1.3 At the outset, the Old Bankruptcy Law applies. It continues to apply to all bankruptcy cases in which by 29 December 1986, a petition had already been presented to the court or in which a receiving order or adjudication order had already been made.

As time goes by, the New Law cases will come in and, particularly after three years from 29 December 1986,[1] the balance of numbers will shift to a majority being conducted under the New Law.

[1] Because of the discharge provisions explained in ch 10 below.

1.1.4 This book must, of course, deal with both systems. Rather than trying to balance each topic by a discussion both of Old Bankruptcy and New Law, the authors have divided the book into three parts.

Parts I and II are statements of the Old and New respectively while Part III deals with those matters which can conveniently, and in some cases must, be dealt with as single topics under both the Old Bankruptcy Law and the New Law.

1.1.5 Since after 29 December 1986 no new petitions under the Old

Bankruptcy Law will be presented, no detailed attention is given to the petition under the Old Law nor to the acts of bankruptcy on which such a petition might have been based. However, since an understanding of the concept of the act of bankruptcy is relevant to many continuing aspects of the Old Bankruptcy Law, a summary of the concept of the act of bankruptcy is contained in this chapter and, thus, Part I of the book starts with defences to petitions already filed. Part I of the book will, over the years, become of less and less practical use as the numerous petitions on court files around the country are disposed of, by dismissal or receiving order.

1.1.6 There are important transitional provisions[1] in the Insolvency Act 1986 which are summarised in para 1.4 below, but all of which are covered under the relevant subject matter dealt with in later chapters. Finally, by way of initial introduction, the concept behind the New Law (as set out in Part II) is summarised in para 1.5.

[1] In the Insolvency Act 1986, Sch 11, Part II.

1.2 THE OLD BANKRUPTCY LAW CONCEPT

1.2.1 Bankruptcy proceedings start by the presentation of a petition to the court (not the issue of a bankruptcy notice), the date of that step being the test for whether a bankruptcy proceeds under the Old Bankruptcy Law or the New Law.

1.2.2 A debtor's own petition simply alleges that he is unable to pay his presently payable debts.[1] The court has virtually no discretion on a debtor's petition other than to make a receiving order[2] so that, in practical effect, there will be very few, if any, debtors' petitions overlapping the Old Bankruptcy Law and the New Law. Since no one need be served with a debtor's petition most courts appoint an immediate hearing before the registrar, that is to say as soon as the petition is presented.[3]

[1] Bankruptcy Act 1914, s 6.
[2] On a debtor's own petition the court almost invariably makes an order of adjudication as well as a receiving order.
[3] See chs 5 and 8 below for the difference between receiving orders and adjudication orders.

1.2.3 A creditor's petition must have been based upon at least one available act of bankruptcy.

The existence of an act of bankruptcy amounts to a statutory recognition of the fact that a debtor is either insolvent or unwilling to pay his proper creditors.

1.2.4 Almost invariably the relevant act of bankruptcy for many years has been the failure to comply with a bankruptcy notice. One or two of the others, particularly execution being levied, have been useful to creditors as available acts of bankruptcy on which to base a petition. Others simply fell into disuse over the years. All available acts of bankruptcy are set out below.

1.2.5 If an available act of bankruptcy was committed by a debtor then that act of bankruptcy was available to any creditor for use as a foundation for the presentation of a petition against that debtor, so long as the petition was presented within three months of the act of bankruptcy relied on. In ch 2 below consideration is given to the various areas in which there may be problems for petitioning creditors in relation to the petition and, therefore, defences or, at least arguments, available to debtors and their advisors.

1.2.6 The receiving order and its effect are considered in detail in ch 3 below. Generally, its effect is to protect the debtor from further action against him, but, more importantly in practice, to vest control of his assets in the official receiver. Subsequent to a receiving order there comes an order of adjudication (ch 6 below) which is the order which has the effect of transferring ownership as well as control of the debtor's assets.

1.2.7 Part I of the book deals with the various stages and options available in an Old Bankruptcy Law case, and no summary is included here. It is, however, plainly necessary to set out the various acts of bankruptcy on which an Old Bankruptcy Law case might still proceed.

1.3 THE ACTS OF BANKRUPTCY

1.3.1 By far the most common act of bankruptcy relied upon was the non-compliance with a bankruptcy notice.

Of the remaining available acts of bankruptcy most fell into complete disuse because they were of no practical assistance.

Others which were, or should have been, useful aids to creditors concerned to move quickly to protect a debtor's estate for creditors generally, faded out of use. With the advent of the Mareva injunction[1] creditors of the more sophisticated, but dishonest, debtor learned they could often get quicker, and more effective, assistance from a Mareva injunction than by trying to rely on one of the old acts of bankruptcy originally formulated to prevent concealment by a debtor.

1 [1975] 2 Ll L Rep 509.

1.3.2 The Bankruptcy Act 1914, s 1(1) defines most of the acts of bankruptcy. The 1914 Act contains one act of bankruptcy other than in s 1, at s 107(4), and more recent legislation has introduced two more, the making of a criminal bankruptcy order, under the Powers of Criminal Courts Act 1973, and failure to make payment required by administration order under the Insolvency Act 1976, s 11(5). However, the acts of bankruptcy outside s 1(1) are not effectively 'available' acts for the general body of creditors.

1.3.3 Non-compliance with a bankruptcy notice[1] is dealt with separately below, while the making of a criminal bankruptcy order is discussed in ch 23 below.

1 Under the Bankruptcy Act 1914, s 1(1)(g).

1.3.4 The Bankruptcy Act 1914 provided that an act of bankruptcy was committed by a debtor in each of the following cases:

(a) Section 1(1)(a). If in England or elsewhere he made a conveyance or assignment of his property to a trustee or trustees for the benefit of his creditors generally.

(b) Section 1(1)(b). If in England or elsewhere he made a fraudulent conveyance, gift, delivery, or transfer of his property, or of any part thereof.

(c) Section 1(1)(c). If in England or elsewhere he made any conveyance or transfer of his property or any part thereof, or created any charge thereon, which would under this or any other Act have been void as a fraudulent preference if he were adjudged bankrupt.

(d) Section 1(1)(d). If with intent to defeat or delay his creditors he did any of the following things, namely, departed out of England, or being out of England, remained out of England, or departed from his dwelling house, or otherwise absented himself, or began to keep house.[1]

(e) Section 1(1)(e). If execution against him had been levied by seizure of his goods under process in any action in any court, or in any civil proceedings in the High Court, and the goods had been either sold or held by the sheriff for 21 days.

(f) Section 1(1)(f). If he filed in the court a declaration of his inability to pay his debts or presents a bankruptcy petition against himself.

(g) Section 1(1)(g). Non-compliance with bankruptcy notice (see below).

(h) Section 1(1)(h). If the debtor gave notice to any of his creditors that he had suspended, or that he was about to suspend, payment of his debts.

[1] This is an act of bankruptcy which can be traced back to a bankruptcy law passed in 1542 and was expressed to be aimed at debtors who: '. . . craftily obtaining into their hands great substance of other men's goods, do suddenly flee to parts unknown, or keep their houses, not minding to pay or restore to any of their creditors their duties, but at their own wills and pleasures consume debts and the substance obtained by credit of other men, for their own pleasure and delicate living, against all reason, equity and good conscience.'

1.3.5 Non-compliance with a bankruptcy notice apart, the most useful of the acts of bankruptcy listed above was under s 1(1)(e), the levy of execution. Levy included a levy under a walking possession agreement with the sheriff and time began to run with effect from such an agreement.

1.3.6 The act of bankruptcy was committed on the expiry of the 21 days from seizure or sale. The available act was not a continuing act and, to be relied upon as an available act for a petition, the three-month time limit had to be calculated to run from the end of the 21-day period referred to in the subsection.[1]

The great advantage of this act of bankruptcy was that goods seized in an execution by one creditor could be held and thus made available for the general body of creditors.[2]

[1] See Bankruptcy Rules 1952, r 139(2); *Re a debtor (No 6864 of 1980), exp Debtor v Slater Walker* [1981] 2 All ER 987.
[2] See para 8.2 below, 'The doctrine of relation back'.

The bankruptcy notice

1.3.7 Section 1(1)(g) of the Bankruptcy Act 1914 defines non-compliance with a bankruptcy notice as follows:

> 'If a creditor has obtained a final judgment or final order against him for any amount, and, execution thereon not having been stayed, has served on him in England or by leave of the court, elsewhere, a bankruptcy notice under this Act, and he does not, within ten days[1] after service of the notice, in case the service is effected in England, and in case the service is effected elsewhere, then within the time limited in that behalf by the order giving leave to effect the service, either comply with the requirements of the notice or satisfy the court that he has a counterclaim set off or cross demand which equals or exceeds the amount of the judgment debt or sum ordered to be paid, and which he could not set up in the action in which the judgment was obtained, or the proceedings in which the order was obtained:
>
> For the purposes of this paragraph and of section two of this Act, any person who is, for the time being, entitled to enforce a final judgment or final order, shall be deemed to be a creditor who has obtained a final judgment or final order.'

Because of what are, in effect, the penal consequences of failure to comply with a bankruptcy notice, the notice itself is strictly construed[2] and a bankruptcy notice must not be in a form calculated to puzzle, perplex or mislead.[3] If it is in the prescribed statutory form, it will suffice, despite recent criticism of that form by Megarry V-C.[4]

As with all the s 1 acts of bankruptcy, non-compliance with a bankruptcy notice is an act of bankruptcy which is available (within the three-month time limit) to any creditor who is qualified to petition. The right to petition was not limited to the creditor issuing and serving the notice nor did it lapse if that creditor's debt was paid outside the time limit of the notice.[5]

The Rules relating to the service of a bankruptcy notice and a petition were the same.[5] The Rules provide that a bankruptcy notice must be served personally or, with the leave of the court, by substituted service in some way directed by the court.

A solicitor may not accept service of a bankruptcy notice on behalf of a debtor although the court could, and often did, order substituted service by posting the notice to the debtor care of his solicitor.

The bankruptcy notice had to be served within two months of its issue.[6] If it was not, the creditor applied ex parte for an extension and the notice was endorsed with the extension order. The debtor did not have to be notified at the time of any extensions.[7]

The bankruptcy notice served before 29 December 1986 may be treated as a statutory demand (see para 13.3 below) for the purposes of the New Law so long as the debt has not been paid, the date for complying with the notice was not more than three months before the presentation of the petition, and no petition has already been presented.[8]

[1] Period extended by Insolvency Act 1976, s 4.
[2] *Re a Judgment Debtor* No 530 of 1908 [1908] 2 KB 474.
[3] *Re a Judgment Debtor* No 75 of 1982 [1983] 3 All ER 545.
[4] See *Re Debtor (No 75 of 1982), ex p Debtor v National Westminster Bank plc* [1983] 3 All ER 545 at 560 and its sequel *Re a Debtor* No 75 of 1982 (No 2) Vol 127 Sol Journal p 783.
[5] Bankruptcy Rules 1952, SI 1952/2113, r 141, and rr 153 to 156.
[6] Ibid, r 140 as amended by SI 1982/441.
[7] *Re a Debtor (No 4 of 1942)* [1943] 1 All ER 125.
[8] Individual Insolvency Rules 1986, r 6.36.

1.3.8 The Old Bankruptcy Law contains many provisions relating to how a debtor might comply with a bankruptcy notice or obtain extensions of time for complying with it but since, as a result of the transitional provisions in the Insolvency Act 1986, the New Law takes over (save in cases where a petition is already filed), there is no practical point in reciting those provisions here.

1.4 THE TRANSITION

1.4.1 Subject to the exceptions set out in the Insolvency Act 1986, Sch 11, Part II and summarised below, the Old Bankruptcy Law, that is as under the Bankruptcy Act 1914 as amended, applies to all existing bankruptcies, that is to say cases in which, as at 29 December 1986 a bankruptcy petition has been presented or a receiving order or adjudication order made.

1.4.2 There are only five areas in which transitional provisions speed up the process of change. They are as follows:

(i) In relation to discharge.[1] One of the most far-reaching of the changes in bankruptcy law is the provision for automatic discharge after two or three years.

Ch 10 below explains the discharge and its effects and sets out the three types of discharge available in Old Bankruptcy Law cases.

The new provisions are much more 'automatic' than those generally described as automatic under the Insolvency Act 1976.

In the vast majority of cases (unless the bankrupt has failed to comply with his own obligations, for example as to his statement of affairs) a bankrupt under the Old Bankruptcy Law or the New Law will simply 'serve' his two or three years. See chs 10 and 18 below.

[1] Sch 11, para 13.

(ii) The release of the trustee.[1] In this respect the New Law simply takes over from the Old Bankruptcy Law, unless the trustee has by 29 December

1986 already applied for a release under the Bankruptcy Act 1914, s 93: para 4.10 below.

1 Sch 11, para 14.

(iii) Employment of solicitors by trustees.[1] Under the New Law, with effect from 29 December 1986 a trustee may employ a solicitor without the need for a resolution of his committee of inspection: see ch 26 below.

1 Sch 11, para 14(6).

(iv) Setting aside preferences.[1] The law relating to the giving of preference or the making of assignments or other transactions entered into before 29 December 1986 is the law in force at the date of the relevant transaction.

Thus, even in a New Law bankruptcy, the Old Bankruptcy Law applies to transactions entered into before 29 December 1986: See chs 8, 19 and 20 below.

1 Sch 11, para 17.

(v) Bankruptcy offences.[1] Even if a person against whom a bankruptcy order is made under the New Law has committed an offence under the New Law, he shall not be guilty of any offence if it was committed before the commencement date under the Insolvency Act 1986, i e before 29 December 1986.

However, the provisions of the Bankruptcy Act 1914 are deemed to remain in force in connection with the bankruptcy offences (see chs 4, 7 and 19 below) and, despite the fact that his bankruptcy proceeds under the New Law, a debtor can still be found to have committed an Old Bankruptcy Law offence if the circumstances would have justified a case under the Bankruptcy Act 1914.

If it is decided to proceed against a debtor in respect of an Old Bankruptcy Law offence, notwithstanding that it is a New Law bankruptcy, then the provisions of the Insolvency Act 1986, s 350(3) apply[2] even though the offence complained of is an Old Bankruptcy Law offence.

1 Sch 11, para 18.
2 See chs 14 and 17 below.

1.5 THE NEW LAW CONCEPT

1.5.1 The New Law is based upon the Command Paper 'A Revised Framework for Insolvency Law' (Cmnd 9175) which itself was the government's response to the final report of the Review Committee on Insolvency Law and Practice, chaired by Sir Kenneth Cork, which was presented in 1982. In the words of the Command Paper the main purposes, so far as they affect proposed insolvency were:

'(a) To curb the irresponsible and unprofessional activities of certain liquidators and receivers, whose failings have weakened confidence in insolvency procedures by providing for the establishment of professionally qualified or licensed insolvency practitioners who will be required to take out insurance cover against negligence and malpractice.

(b) To simplify wherever possible corporate and personal insolvency procedures.

(c) To perform voluntary corporate and personal insolvency procedures in order to encourage their use so as to reduce non-essential demands on public resources and to relieve insolvent companies and individuals of unnecessary involvement with the courts and the insolvency service.

(d) To make changes in the role of the insolvency service to allow official receivers to concentrate on protective and investigative work.'

1.5.2 The Insolvency Act 1986 contains provisions aimed at meeting all the above proposals. While no express charge of 'irresponsible and unprofessional activities' is laid at the door of trustees in bankruptcy in the Command Paper, in future only an authorised insolvency practitioner may act as a trustee in bankruptcy. Before the Insolvency Act no formal qualifications were necessary, although the majority of trustees had one of various accountancy qualifications. The expressed scheme of the Act was that intending insolvency practitioners would apply to the Secretary of State for an authorisation certificate enabling them to practise as liquidators or trustees under the Act. During the passage of the Bill through Parliament the government bowed to pressure from the accountancy professional associations to allow them to undertake a certification procedure for their own members. Accordingly there are two ways in which an individual may become an authorised insolvency practitioner. First he may be authorised to act by a recognised professional body. Second he may apply for and obtain an individual authorisation from the 'relevant authority'. In the first instance the recognised professional bodies will be the accountancy professional associations, The Law Society, and The Insolvency Practitioners Association. These bodies have agreed to work together on establishing common criteria for authorising individual members to act as insolvency practitioners. The relevant authority for individual applications is the Secretary of State or any body to whom he delegates the statutory authorising system. The government indicated in debate that only persons with lengthy experience of insolvency procedures need apply. There has been a widespread call for higher ethical standards to be observed by trustees in bankruptcy. Whether these provisions will in fact achieve the desired aim remains to be seen.

1.5.3 The simplification of personal insolvency procedures was long overdue. The Insolvency Act 1986 brings personal insolvency procedures more into line with those of corporate insolvency. The concept of the need for an act of bankruptcy is abolished and a single bankruptcy order replaces the receiving and adjudication orders under the Old Bankruptcy Law.

The new bankruptcy order is sought by the presentation of a petition by any creditor, the debtor himself, or the supervisor or any party to a composition or scheme made by the debtor under the Act. The creditor's petition involves an interesting development, for one of the grounds on which it may be presented is that the debtor has no reasonable prospect of being able to pay a future debt over the bankruptcy level, set initially at £750.

The requirements for such a petition are that the creditor must first serve a notice in the prescribed form on the debtor requiring him to establish to the satisfaction of the creditor that there is a reasonable prospect that the future debt will be paid when it falls due. The prospective debtor has three weeks to comply with the demand or to apply to set it aside.

This is a radical departure from present procedures particularly as the creditor may present a petition within the three-week period if there is a serious possibility that the debtor's property will be significantly diminished during that period: see para 13.2 below.

1.5.4 With the removal of the receiving order the debtor's property is automatically protected from the date on which the petition is presented. Any disposition by the debtor after that date is void unless the court's consent or ratification is obtained. Any legal proceedings may be stayed either by the bankruptcy court or the court in which those proceedings are pending.

1.5.5 After the bankruptcy order and the appointment of an insolvency practitioner as trustee in bankruptcy, the burdens of administering the estate are lessened to a certain degree by the trustee being given greater discretion than under the 1914 Act, and by the removal of the Old Bankruptcy Law provision to the effect that after 'acquired property' should not automatically vest in the trustee. This change does, however, place additional importance on the bankrupt properly fulfilling his statutory duty to make a complete statement of affairs within 21 days of the commencement of the bankruptcy and to give full information to the trustee of any later acquisition of property or income.

The 'reputed ownership' provisions are not re-enacted.

1.5.6 The categories of debts on distribution of the estate to creditors have also been simplified. The New Law takes into account the greater importance of interest in today's commercial life, in comparison with 1914, and a proper rate of interest can now be claimed on all debts. However, in seeking to afford some protection to the ordinary creditor's position, preferential debts are to be distributed before ordinary debts but not the interest on such debts. All interest claims rank pari passu, and rank in preference after ordinary debts. The bankrupt's spouse is treated as a deferred creditor entering in priority after the interest claims.

As noted above, the discharge provisions under the New Law are rather more automatic than before. In the ordinary case a bankrupt is discharged after three years from the commencement of his bankruptcy. The official receiver may, however, apply to the court to extend the duration of the bankruptcy on the grounds that the bankrupt has failed to comply with his obligations under the Act. Where a bankrupt has been bankrupt during the 15 years prior to the commencement of the bankruptcy, or when he has been made criminally bankrupt, he may only be discharged by order of the court and he must wait five years before applying for his discharge.

1.5.7 Understandably, in view of the public expense involved and pressure upon the official receiver, the government is anxious to encourage voluntary arrangements. In an attempt to place some statutory force behind 'arrangements' the 1986 Act introduces the interim order. Under an interim order any proceedings against the debtor may be stayed (including a bankruptcy petition) and an insolvency practitioner is appointed to advise the court whether it would be appropriate to hold a statutory creditors' meeting.

Should such a meeting be called, the creditors have an opportunity to consider any proposals the debtor may make for a voluntary arrangement or to propose alterations to those proposals. Where the meeting approves a scheme, all the creditors of the debtor, irrespective of whether they voted for the scheme or attended the meeting, are bound by the scheme. This is an important departure from the Old Bankruptcy Law relating to schemes and compositions.

The scheme is then carried into effect under the control of a 'supervisor' who must be an insolvency practitioner and will presumably be the insolvency practitioner who advised the court under the interim order. The supervisor acts ultimately under the control of the court.

1.5.8 There would appear, from the number of insolvency-related financial scandals in recent years, that there is a great need for protective and investigative work on the part of the official receiver's department. The Command Paper states that 'the government wishes to see insolvency-related offences prosecuted wherever possible'. In 1984 there were only 143 convictions (and no acquittals) of bankrupts under the Bankruptcy Acts.[1] It remains to be seen whether the official receiver's workload will be reduced under the New Law, for example by virtue of the automatic discharge provisions and the probable reduction in public examinations, or whether his duties in connection with every compulsory winding up, and what will probably be a significant increase in the number of bankruptcies, will in fact have the opposite effect.

With public expenditure severely restricted, there must be some doubt at the outset of the new insolvency provisions whether the official receiver's workload will in the result be sufficiently reduced to enable a proper investigative service to be undertaken; if it is not so reduced, public and parliamentary disquiet with the 'system' will remain.

[1] See Department of Trade General Annual Report on Bankruptcy for 1984.

1.5.9 The New Law was initially enacted in the Insolvency Act 1985. As well as changing the law relating to bankruptcy and instituting the requirement that insolvency practitioners should be qualified, this statute also contained a number of provisions concerning company liquidations. The majority of the provisions of the Insolvency Act 1985, including those parts directly concerned with bankruptcy, never effectively came into force. In order to consolidate the enactments relating to company insolvency and winding up the Insolvency Act 1986 was enacted and the New Law originally contained in the Insolvency Act 1985 forms Parts VIII to XI ('the second group of parts') and, together with miscellaneous matters bearing on both company and individual insolvency, Parts XII to XIX ('the third group of parts') of the Insolvency Act 1986. On the commencement date, 29 December 1986, the Insolvency Act 1985 came into force by order made under the Insolvency Act 1985, s 236(2). Immediately thereafter, by virtue of the Insolvency Act 1986, s 443, the 1986 Act came into force and in consequence of the provisions of Schedule 12 to the 1986 Act most (but not all) of the Insolvency Act 1985 was updated. For practical purposes therefore the New Law is to be found in the Insolvency Act 1986. It should be noted that the 1986 Act is not a simple re-enactment of the New Law as in the 1985 Act. The parliamentary criticism during its passage that the 1985 Bill was being carried with too much haste appears to have been vindicated. For while there are no substantive changes in the New Law provisions as they appear in the Insolvency Act 1986, the draftsman has taken the opportunity to tidy up the wording of the Act and the distribution of the material between the sections.

PART 1

The Old Bankruptcy Law

CHAPTER 2

Defences to a Petition under the Old Bankruptcy Law

2.1 INTRODUCTION

2.1.1 Since the Insolvency Act 1986 provides[1] that the Old Bankruptcy Law applies to petitions already presented to the Court by 29 December 1986 it is still important to examine what defences may be available to a debtor. Numerous petitions will be on various court files for many months.

[1] Insolvency Act 1986, Sch 11, para 10.

2.1.2 Apart from defending a petition it may be that a debtor can avoid bankruptcy if he can obtain a reasonable amount of time to put his affairs in order.

The bankruptcy court has an expressed discretionary power to adjourn proceedings before it on such terms, if any, as it may think fit to impose.[1]

Such power may be invoked by or on behalf of a debtor whose affairs may be at such a stage as to justify the grant of a suitable period of time to enable him, for example, to pay his debts in full[2] or to conclude a deal or complete a recovery which will allow him to avoid bankruptcy.

The court has a complete discretion but it is a discretion which must be exercised judicially and the exercise of which is susceptible to appeal.[3]

If an adjournment is granted the reason for it must be stated in the Order.[4]

[1] Bankruptcy Act 1914, s 109(2).
[2] *Re a debtor ex Petitioning Creditor* (1920) 89 LJKB 432.
[3] See *Re a Debtor (No 12 of 1970), ex p Official Receiver v Debtor* [1971] 1 All ER 504.
[4] Bankruptcy Rules 1952, r 173(2).

2.1.3 There are three heads which must be examined by a debtor wishing to defend a petition presented against him under the Old Bankruptcy Law. They are as follows:

(a) the jurisdiction and power of the court;
(b) the statutory factual matters requiring proof by the petitioning creditor; and
(c) the discretionary factors.

If the debtor wishes to defend the proceedings because he takes issue with a statement in the petition then he must:

(a) file a notice with the court specifying which statement in the petition he denies and disputes; and
(b) at least three days before the day fixed for the hearing of the petition send a copy of this notice to the petitioning creditor and his solicitor.[1]

Such a notice is required in relation not only to the three statutory factual matters requiring proof at the hearing (see para 2.3 below) but to any statement of fact alleged in the petition.

[1] Bankruptcy Rules 1952, r 166.

2.2 THE JURISDICTION AND POWER OF THE COURT

2.2.1 Since not all county courts have bankruptcy jurisdiction the question of whether the right court has been chosen should be checked. This should have been done by the court itself on presentation but, on the other hand, the court accepts the accuracy of the statements made in the petition, for example as to the address or place of business of the debtor, without any sort of check.

2.2.2 No county court without bankruptcy jurisdiction should accept a petition and, in any event, the fact that the wrong court is chosen by the petitioning creditor does not, of itself, invalidate the proceedings. So long as the court which hears the petition has bankruptcy jurisdiction, it has power to make a receiving order.[1]

However, a mistake by the petitioning creditor in this respect could help a debtor buy valuable time.

[1] Bankruptcy Act 1914, s 100(2).

2.2.3 One of the bases on which the court can entertain a petition is a carrying on of business by the debtor for an appropriate time in the area of the court.

If the alleged carrying on of business is the only basis upon which the court has jurisdiction over the debtor, that is to say that if the debtor is domiciled elsewhere and there is no residential qualification, then the debtor might be in a position to challenge whether he has carried on business at all.

The carrying on of business has been given a relatively wide interpretation in recent years and has been extended to managing a group of companies[1] and performing on the West End stage.[2]

However, even if in complete control, as a shareholder and a director, a person is not carrying on business if he is 'running his companies' businesses'.[1] There must be some personal element involving the debtor. This can continue even if the business relied on is not actually trading but, for example, where the debtor still had unpaid debts relating to it.[3]

1 *Re Brauch (a debtor), ex p Brittanic Securities and Investments Ltd* [1978] Ch 316.
2 *Re Debtor (No 1975 of 1970)* (unreported).
3 *Theophile v Solr-General* [1950] AC 186; *Re Bird, ex p Debtor v IRC* [1962] 2 All ER 406.

2.2.4 Ordinary residence is another of the bases on which a petitioner can rely for jurisdictional purposes.

It is not necessary to establish that the debtor resided at a specified address or a number of specified addresses[1] but the petitioning creditor must do more than establish casual or extraordinary visits. However, the residence may be temporary, or only for a particular purpose. 'A long sojourn is not a sine qua non.'[2] Essentially it boils down to a question to be decided on a common sense view of the facts.

1 *Re Brauch (a debtor), ex p Brittanic Securities and Investments Ltd* [1978] Ch 316.
2 *Re Bright, ex p Bright* (1903) 19 TLR 203.

2.3 THE 'FACTUAL' MATTERS TO BE PROVED TO THE COURT

2.3.1 The Bankruptcy Act 1914, s 5(2) and (3) provide:

> '(2) At the hearing the court shall require proof of the debt of the petitioning creditor, of the service of the petition, and of the act of bankruptcy, or, if more than one act of bankruptcy is alleged in the petition, of some one of the alleged acts of bankruptcy and, if satisfied with the proof, may make a receiving order in pursuance of the petition.
> (3) If the court is not satisfied with the proof of the petitioning creditor's debt, or of the act of bankruptcy, or of the service of the petition, or is satisfied by the debtor that he is able to pay his debts, or that for other sufficient cause no order ought to be made, the court may dismiss the petition.'

The prospect of the debtor being able to pay his debts and the 'other sufficient cause' element of sub-s (3) are discussed in para 2.4 below.

The other requirements of the subsection fall into three parts, 1 the petitioning creditor's debt, 2 the act of bankruptcy relied on, and 3 the service of the petition.

1 The petitioning creditor's debt

2.3.2 The debt must be proved as still subsisting at the hearing. This is usually done by means of an affidavit of continuing debt sworn shortly before the hearing.

The court is required to examine the debt relied upon by the petitioning creditor. It can question the consideration for a judgment debt and, in effect, look behind the judgment at the original debt.[1]

1 *Re Onslow, ex p Kibble* [1875] 10 Ch App 373.

2.3.3 The debt itself must be at least £200, both at the date of presentation of the petition and at the date of the hearing,[1] although two or more creditors can join forces to make up the required amount if necessary.[2] The debt must be a liquidated or ascertained debt which is legally due.[3]

[1] *Re Patel* [1986] 1 All ER 522. (If a debt on which the petition is based is a county court judgment and payment is made into court, Ord 22 r 9(2) of the County Court Rules 1981 provide machinery whereby the petitioning creditor can stop the court from accepting a part payment into court.)
[2] Bankruptcy Act 1914, s 110.
[3] *Re Snowden, ex p Snowden* [1881] 17 Ch D 44.

2.3.4 Legal recoverability is the most effective test for ascertaining whether or not a debt can be used as the basis for a bankruptcy petition.

Thus, for example, none of the following are sufficient debts for a petition presented under the Old Bankruptcy Law: a judgment debt which has expired by effluxion of time; [1] a contingent liability before it has accrued due;[2] a bill of exchange which has not fallen due;[3] and costs, ordered, but not taxed.[4]

[1] *Re Tynte, ex p Tynte* (1880) 15 Ch D 125.
[2] *Re Snowden, ex p Snowden* (1881) 17 Ch D 44.
[3] *Re Hayward, ex p Hayward* (1871) 6 Ch App 546; *Re Barr, ex p Wolfe* [1896] 1QB 616.
[4] *Re Debtor (No 20 of 1953) ex p Debtor v Scott* [1954] 3 All ER 74; *Re Noble, ex p Bankrupt v Official Receiver* [1965] Ch 129.

2.3.5 Because of the doctrine of relation back (as to which see ch 8 below), it may well be that a creditor should refuse to accept a tender of the amount of his debt from the debtor. It is not, therefore, a defence for a debtor to claim that he has offered to discharge the petitioner's claim. Indeed, even actual payment of the petitioner's debt will not necessarily suffice to defend a petition, although, if the petitioning creditor has been paid, and if no other creditor seeks substitution,[1] there should be no difficulty in the petitioner's obtaining leave to withdraw his petition under the Bankruptcy Act 1914, s 5(7).

[1] Bankruptcy Act 1914, s 111.

2 The act of bankruptcy

2.3.6 Plainly the court must satisfy itself over the act of bankruptcy. The act of bankruptcy must have been committed within three months of the presentation of the petition.[1] If the petition recites an 'out of date' act of bankruptcy, and the court has nevertheless allowed its presentation, or if the debtor can establish that the date recited is inaccurate and that, in fact, there either has been no act of bankruptcy or there was one but that it was committed more than three months before the petition was presented, then the debtor has a complete defence on that petition.

[1] Bankruptcy Act 1914, s 4(1)(c).

2.3.7 If, as is usually the case, the act of bankruptcy is the non-compliance with a bankruptcy notice the fact that an appeal is pending against a refusal to set aside the bankruptcy notice is not a ground for resisting the making of a receiving order,[1] although plainly it may provide a persuasive reason for seeking an adjournment of the petition.

[1] *Re Debtor (No 44 of 1978), ex p Debtor v Chantry Mount and Hawthorns* [1979] 3 All ER 265.

3 Service of petition

2.3.8 Service of the petition must be strictly proved. If the debtor denies service (which in the nature of things is unusual if the debtor is at the hearing of the petition itself) then the court will hear evidence from both sides.

It is more usual for disputes over service to arise on applications to rescind the receiving order under the Bankruptcy Act 1914, s 10(1).[1]

However if the point is taken at the hearing of the petition itself then the usual course taken by the court, if it finds that the petition is not properly served, is to adjourn it to another date to allow for service, rather than to dismiss the petition outright.[2]

[1] See *Re Brace, ex p Debtor v Gabriel and Official Receiver* [1966] 2 All ER 38.
[2] *Re Debtor (No 441 of 1938)* [1939] Ch 251.

2.4 THE DISCRETIONARY STATUTORY FACTORS

2.4.1 Strictly speaking, the question of whether or not a debtor can pay his debts may be a factual question rather than one on which the court can really be said to have a discretion. However, in practical effect, a court will not dismiss a petition, with a petitioning creditor unpaid, solely on this ground. The debt having been established (as is required – see para 2.3 above) the court is likely to adjourn the petition so that payment can be made followed by an application for withdrawal under the Bankruptcy Act 1914, s 5.[1] If a creditor has refused to accept a tender, the court can supervise payment before making an order for dismissal.

[1] *Theophile v Solr-General* [1950] AC 186.

2.4.2 In *Re a Debtor (No 17 of 1966)*,[1] the court annulled a receiving order which should not have been made, when the debtor was able to pay the instalments ordered on a judgment debt but not the whole of the debt itself. The Divisional Court indicated that the petition should have been dismissed on this head alone. This petition was also held an abuse of the process.

[1] *Re Debtor (No 17 of 1966)* [1967] 1 All ER 668.

'Other sufficient cause'

2.4.3 The discretion under the Bankruptcy Act 1914 is very wide and enables the court, if it thinks fit, to dismiss a petition if it concludes that no purpose could be served by a receiving order being made or, perhaps more clearly, if it is obvious that disadvantage to the creditors as a whole might result.[1]

However, the fear that advantage is unlikely to accrue to creditors, or that the receiving order will only benefit one creditor, to the disadvantage of a greater number of persons, will not suffice.[2]

[1] *Re Otway, ex p Otway* [1895] 1QB 812.
[2] See *Re Jubb, ex p Burman and Greenwood* [1897] 1 QB 641; *Re Hequard, ex p Hacquard* (1890) 24 QBD 71; *Re Scott, ex p Paris-Orleans Rly Co* (1913) 58 Sol Jo 11.

2.4.4 If a debtor has no assets at all then that should be sufficient cause to dismiss a petition against him. However, this idea has been said to be 'hedged about by important precautions'. 'A man may indeed be too poor to be made bankrupt but the burden of proof is heavy'[1] and it must be clear on the evidence available at the hearing of the petition that an investigation by the official receiver or a trustee could not be of any benefit. But see ch 5 below, on an application to rescind on this ground after the official receiver has had an opportunity to investigate the debtor's estate.

In one of the leading cases, *Re Otway*,[2] it is significant to note that, apart from the argument by the debtor that his one asset would be destroyed by the making of a receiving order, he was also assisted by the fact that the petitioning creditor was found by the court to have been guilty of extortion in relation to the proceedings. In the other leading case, *Re Betts*,[3] the debtor was already an undischarged bankrupt, and the creditor had proved for a prior debt in the first bankruptcy, in which only a small dividend had been paid.

[1] *Re Field* [1978] Ch 371 per Megarry V-C.
[2] *Re Otway, ex p Otway* [1895] 1 QB 812.
[3] *Re Betts, ex p Betts* [1897] 1 QB 50.

2.4.5 Connivance by the creditor at the act of bankruptcy relied upon disqualifies a person from presenting a petition and might prevent reliance on the act of bankruptcy recited in the petition.

2.4.6 Quite apart from its power to dismiss a petition for what it considers 'sufficient cause', the court will use its inherent power to dispose of the proceedings before it if it appears that a party is abusing the process of the court.

In *Re Otway*[1] the petitioning creditor demanded £25 for himself to consent to an adjournment (but there were other relevant factors in that case).

[1] *Re Otway, ex p Otway* [1895] 1 QB 812.

2.4.7 The most concise summary of the courts' approach was given, relatively recently (in 'Old Bankruptcy Law' terms), by Evershed MR as follows:

> 'The court will always look strictly at the conduct of a creditor using the bankruptcy proceedings and if it concludes that the creditor has used or threatened such proceedings at all oppressively the court will not hesitate to declare the creditor's conduct extortionate and will not allow him to make use of the process which he has abused.'[1]

[1] *Re Marjory, ex p Debtor v FA Dumont Ltd* [1955] Ch 600.

CHAPTER 3

The Receiving Order

3.1 INTRODUCTION

3.1.1 At the outset, a receiving order must be compared and contrasted with an adjudication order (as to which see ch 6 below). The receiving order is, according to the Bankruptcy Act 1914 made 'for the protection of the Estate'[1] and it takes immediate effect. It is effective from the earliest moment of the date on which it is made,[2] although the registrar invariably notes the precise time on which he makes the order.

[1] Bankruptcy Act 1914, s 3.
[2] *Re Warren, ex p Wheeler v Trustee in Bankruptcy* [1938] Ch 725.

3.1.2 The receiving order does not operate to divest the debtor of his property. It merely passes control, rather than ownership, of that property to the official receiver.[1] It is the adjudication which operates, in due course, as a transfer of the title to the debtor's property.[2]

[1] *Re Berry, Duffield v Williams* [1896] 1 Ch 939.
[2] See *Rhodes v Dawson* (1886) 16 QBD 548.

3.2 THE ORDER

3.2.1 When a receiving order is made on a creditor's petition it must give details of any act of bankruptcy on which it is made.[1]

[1] Bankruptcy Rules 1952, r 175(1).

3.2.2 The order requires the debtor to attend before the official receiver[1] who arranges for service of the perfected order on the debtor.[2]

[1] Bankruptcy Rules 1952, r 175(2).
[2] Ibid, r 176.

3.2.3 Subject to any order staying advertisement, the order is advertised in the *London Gazette*, by the Department of Trade under whose auspices the official receiver operates, and in such local paper as the Department of Trade, or the official receiver, thinks fit.[1]

The court is empowered to stay advertisement of the receiving order under its general powers to stay any of its proceedings in bankruptcy.[2] In an appropriate case, for example where the debtor has indicated that he has grounds for and that he will appeal against the court's decision and when advertising the receiving order could be very harmful to the debtor, the receiving order itself can contain the stay of advertisement.[3]

[1] Bankruptcy Rules 1952, r 178(1)(b).
[2] Bankruptcy Act 1914, s 113 and see ch 21 below.
[3] Bankruptcy Rules 1952, r 180.

3.2.4 The 'drawing up' of a draft receiving order for perfection by the court is the last step which a creditor is required to take in the process of making his debtor 'bankrupt'. If adjudication follows, as it usually does, it does so almost invariably as a result of an application by the official receiver (see ch 6 below).

3.3 THE EFFECT OF THE RECEIVING ORDER

3.3.1 Immediately upon the making of a receiving order an official receiver is, by the order itself, constituted receiver of the property of the debtor.[1]

Thus, legal ownership of the debtor's property remains in the debtor (and this does not change until adjudication) but in practical effect, by virtue of the appointment of the official receiver, he loses control over it.

The official receiver remains the person who is receiver of the debtor's property until adjudication[2] when he may, in default of the appointment of any other person, become trustee.[3]

[1] Bankruptcy Act 1914, s 7(1).
[2] Ibid, s 18.
[3] Ibid, s 53(1).

3.3.2 No creditor can proceed against 'the property or person of the debtor' in respect of his debt and no legal proceedings can be commenced against the debtor without leave of the court.[1]

If any creditor tries to continue with existing proceedings, to enforce a judgment, or to commence proceedings, either the court in question or the bankruptcy court itself can order an appropriate stay.[2]

However, the making of a receiving order against him does not terminate a debtor's responsibility to maintain his wife, even if he is separated from her.[3]

The Bankruptcy Act 1914 also gives specific exemption to a secured creditor who is permitted 'to realise or otherwise deal with his security'[4] and to a landlord who is permitted to levy distress for rent due from the bankrupt at any time before or after the commencement of the bankruptcy proceedings. However, in respect of a distress levied after the commencement of the bankruptcy, the distress is only available for six months prior to adjudication and it will not run after the date on which it is levied.[5]

1 Bankruptcy Act 1914, s 7(1).
2 Ibid, s 9(1).
3 Supplementary Benefit Act 1966, s 22 and see *London Borough of Hounslow v Peake* [1974] 1 All ER 688.
4 Bankruptcy Act 1914, s 7(2).
5 Ibid, s 35(1).

3.3.3 At any time after a receiving order has been made the official receiver may apply to the court for an order for the redirection of the debtor's post to himself or to some other person on his behalf, or if after adjudication, to the trustee.[1]

1 Bankruptcy Act 1914, s 24.

3.3.4 The Bankruptcy Act 1914[1] prohibits a person against whom a receiving order has been made from acting or continuing to act as a trustee in bankruptcy. However, it is not the Bankruptcy Act 1914 which invokes the other well known disqualifications. The relevant statutes do not refer to the making of a receiving order, but to a person being or becoming a 'bankrupt'. It seems clear that a person is not a bankrupt, properly so called under the Old Bankruptcy Law, until an adjudication order is made.[2] That distinction was either not appreciated by the draftsmen of the relevant statutes or Parliament decided that the disqualifications should not 'bite' until adjudication.

Thus, the disqualifications from, for example, acting as a company director or being a member of Parliament or practising as a solicitor and others (which are dealt with in ch 6 below) are not applicable during the period between receiving order and adjudication.

1 Bankruptcy Act 1914, s 94.
2 Although this does not explain why the Bankruptcy Act 1914 refers separately to 'a bankrupt', 'an undischarged bankrupt' and 'a person who has been adjudged bankrupt'.

3.3.5 However, during the period between receiving order and adjudication it is a criminal offence for the debtor to do any of the acts set out in the Bankruptcy Act 1914, s 154. Since the section is long and detailed and since it would be dangerous to summarise it (and since it is relevant to other sections of this book) the whole of s 154 is set out in full at para 3.9 below.

The activities prohibited by s 154 are, in general terms, the concealment, removal, gift, or transfer of property, and the destruction, falsification or disposal of books of account or documents of record.

Activities which are rendered illegal during this period but which are not set out in the Bankruptcy Act 1914, s 154 are, basically, those of absconding with property or quitting or making 'preparation to quit England'[1] and contributing to or increasing the extent of the debtor's insolvency by gambling or hazardous speculation.[2]

1 Bankruptcy Act 1914, s 159.
2 See ibid, s 157.

3.4 THE DUTIES AND OBLIGATIONS OF THE DEBTOR AFTER RECEIVING ORDER

3.4.1 The receiving order itself requires the debtor to attend before the official receiver.[1] In practice, when the debtor himself attends the hearing of a petition he is invited to attend before the official receiver's staff immediately after the hearing and before the receiving order itself has been drawn up and served upon him.

At the initial attendance before the official receiver the debtor will be interviewed by an examiner in the official receiver's department and will be furnished with instructions for the preparation of his statement of affairs.[2] This is called the preliminary examination and is based on an official receiver's questionaire, OR 7.

1 Bankruptcy Rules 1952, r 175(2).
2 Ibid, r 186(1).

3.4.2 At this initial interview the debtor will give a statement of the background and events leading up to the making of the receiving order, and the reasons he attributes to his insolvency. This, effectively, amounts to a 'proof of evidence' for the official receiver at the debtor's public examination, as to which see ch 7 below.

3.4.3 *Statement of affairs* As described above the official receiver is obliged to give the debtor instructions on the preparation of his statement of affairs. The Bankruptcy Act 1914 requires that the statement of affairs, a prescribed form, must be submitted on a debtor's petition within three days of the receiving order and on a creditor's petition within seven days of the receiving order.[1]

Whilst the court can and does extend time for the statement of affairs in cases where 'special reasons' exist, the time limits are very short and are not always strictly complied with. However, it is important that the statement of affairs is completed in good time before the first meeting of creditors. It should always been borne in mind that if the debtor fails to comply with the requirement to prepare and file a statement of affairs, he can be adjudicated bankrupt on this ground alone.[2]

Obviously the debtor's statement of affairs must be strictly accurate. If he makes a material omission in it he is guilty of a criminal offence unless he can prove that he had no intent to defraud by that omission.[3]

Where the affairs of the debtor are sufficiently complex, or for other reasons, the debtor cannot prepare a proper statement himself, the official receiver is empowered to employ someone, such as an accountant, to assist in its preparation at the expense of the estate.[4]

The form of statement of affairs is at Form 34 of the prescribed forms in the Bankruptcy Rules 1952. It is in printed form and its length and format preclude its reproduction here.

[1] Bankruptcy Act 1914, s 14(2).
[2] Ibid, s 14(3).
[3] Ibid, s 154(6).
[4] Ibid, s 74(2) proviso.

3.4.4 *The first meeting of creditors* The Bankruptcy Act 1914 requires that 'as soon as may be' after the receiving order the first meeting of creditors shall be held.[1]

The expressed purpose of the first meeting of creditors is to consider whether a proposal for composition or a scheme of arrangement shall be accepted by the creditors or whether he should be adjudged bankrupt 'and generally as to the mode of dealing with the debtor's property'.[1]

The meeting is summoned by the official receiver for a date not later than 14 days after the receiving order, unless the court authorises a later date.

Notice is given as soon as 'practicable' to each creditor recited in the debtor's statement of affairs, and by advertisement in a local newspaper and, giving at least six days' notice, in the *London Gazette*.

The notice should contain a summary of the debtor's statement of affairs and any observations the official receiver thinks fit to make.[2]

A person may not vote as a creditor at a meeting of creditors unless he has lodged his proof of debt before the time appointed for the meeting. Proofs of debt, and a discussion of what debts are provable in bankruptcy, are considered in ch 9 below (and the relevant Schedule to the Bankruptcy Act 1914 is set out at para 9.9 below).

[1] Bankruptcy Act 1914, s 13(1).
[2] Ibid, Sch 1 (see para 3.8 below).

3.4.5 The Bankruptcy Act 1914, s 22 sets out in full the duties of the debtor in relation to the discovery and realisation of his property and provides that 'wilful' failure to perform the duties imposed on him by the section amounts to a contempt of court.[1]

In particular the debtor is required:

(i) 'unless prevented by sickness or other sufficient cause' to attend the first meeting of creditors;[2] and
(ii) to do all which is 'reasonably required' by the official receiver, trustee, or the court to assist in the examination of his affairs and, specifically, he must give an inventory of his property, list and quantify his debtors and creditors, and execute all necessary instruments as reasonably required

by the official receiver. Wilful failure by a debtor to comply with these obligations is a contempt of court.[3]

[1] Bankruptcy Rules 1952, r 175(1).
[2] Bankruptcy Act 1914, s 22(1) although in practice he is often not called into the meeting itself, but attends in case he is required.
[3] Bankruptcy Act 1914, s 22(4).

3.4.6 In due course the debtor will, unless an order is made under the Insolvency Act 1976, s 6, be required to attend his public examination.

The public examination is dealt with separately at ch 7 below along with circumstances in which it might be dispensed with .

3.4.7 Quite apart from the first meeting of creditors described above, the trustee, or the official receiver if the debtor has not been adjudicated, is empowered to summon general meetings of creditors and the debtor is obliged to attend such meetings if required.[1]

[1] Bankruptcy Act 1914, s 22(2).

3.5 SPECIAL MANAGER

The official receiver is receiver and manager of the estate until a trustee is appointed.[1] He is empowered, however, if one or more creditors make application to him and if he is satisfied that the nature of the debtor's estate or business justifies it, to appoint a special manager who will act as such until a trustee is appointed[2] and he always has an absolute discretion as to whether or not to appoint a special manager[3] ie whether or not creditors make an application to him for such an appointment.

The special manager may have such powers as the official receiver shall entrust to him[2] and the debtor is obliged to co-operate and assist a special manager just as if he were the official receiver.[4]

There is no theoretical reason why the debtor himself should not be appointed special manager of his own estate and be remunerated by the official receiver for assistance rendered in the management of the estate.[5]

The special manager must, if directed, give security[6] and is remunerated according to resolution of the creditors at a creditors' meeting.[7] He can be removed at any time the official receiver thinks expedient and must be removed if the creditors require it by special resolution.[8]

[1] Bankruptcy Act 1914, s 74(1).
[2] Ibid, s 10.
[3] *Re Whitaker* (1884) 1 Morr 36.
[4] Bankruptcy Act 1914, s 22(2).
[5] See Bankruptcy Rules 1952, r 313(2).
[6] Bankruptcy Act 1914, s 10.
[7] See Bankruptcy Act 1914, s 10(3).
[8] See Bankruptcy Rules 1952, r 319.

3.6 PROCEDURAL TABLES

3.6.1 A. Application for stay of advertisement of receiving order

1. Debtor applies on motion supported by affidavit: s 113
2. Registrar (i) Fixes date for hearing.
(ii) If he thinks fit gives notice to official receiver to attend

3. Parties attend when registrar may stay advertisement on such terms as he thinks fit, e g as to filing statement of affairs, or the giving of notice to certain creditors or backers
(NOTE If made at the time of the making of a receiving order the receiving order itself can contain the stay of advertisement: s 113)

3.6.2 B. Receiving order to first meeting of creditors

Steps to be Taken	Bankruptcy Act 1914	Bankruptcy Rules 1952
1. Debtor attends official receiver at his office, as instructed by receiving order. He must do this at once, for the statement of affairs must be prepared and submitted within a matter of days.		see r 175
2. Official receiver furnishes debtor with instructions for the preparation of his statement of affairs. TIME: Forthwith on receiving notice that he has been appointed to an estate.		rr 186(I), 312(a)
3. Official receiver or one of his examiners causes debtor to be interviewed for the purpose of investigating his affairs and determining whether the estate should be administered in a summary manner.	see s 129	r 312(b)
TIME: Forthwith on receiving notice that he has been appointed to an estate.		r 312(b)
4. IF NECESSARY: Official receiver may employ at the expense of the estate some person or persons to assist the debtor in the preparation of his statement of affairs.	s 74(2) proviso	
5. Debtor who requires extension of time for submitting statement of affairs applies for extension either: (1) to the official receiver, who may, if he thinks fit, give a written certificate extending the time; or		r 187
(2) to the court, on notice to the official receiver	s 14(2)	
FEE ON APPLICATION: £5 Time will be extended only for special reasons.	s 14(2)	

Steps to be Taken	Bankruptcy Act 1914	Bankruptcy Rules 1952
6. Debtor makes out and submits to official receiver statement of affairs giving full particulars of his assets, debts and liabilities, and of his secured and unsecured creditors, by lodging with him: (1) 2 copies of statement of affairs; (2) affidavit verifying one copy of statement of affairs.	s 14(1)	r 186(2)
TIME: (1) If receiving order was made on debtor's petition: within 3 days from date of receiving order;	s 14(2)(i)	
(2) If receiving order was made on creditor's petition: within 7 days from date of receiving order.	s 14(2)(ii)	
If the receiving order is against a firm the debtors must submit a joint statement of their partnership affairs, and each debtor must also submit a statement of his personal affairs.		r 287
If the debtor wishes to propose a composition or scheme he must do so within 4 days after submitting the statement of affairs	s 16(1)	
On the official receiver's request the debtor must furnish the official receiver with trading and profit and loss accounts, and a cash and goods account, for such period not exceeding 2 years immediately preceding the date of the receiving order as the official receiver directs.		r 329(1)
The court may direct an account for a longer period.		r 329(1) proviso
If the debtor fails to supply accounts the official receiver must report the failure to the court, and the court may take such action thereon as it thinks just.		r 329(2)
7. Official receiver: (1) Files in court the verified statement of affairs.		r 186(3)
(2) Prepares summary of statement of affairs. (3) Sends summary of statement of affairs to each creditor mentioned therein, including the cause of debtor's failure and any observations he sees fit to make.	Sch 1, para 3	
TIME: When notice of first meeting of creditors is sent.	Sch 1, para 3	

Steps to be Taken	Bankruptcy Act 1914	Bankruptcy Rules 1952
8. Any person stating himself in writing to the official receiver to be a creditor may personally or by agent inspect statement of affairs at all reasonable times and take any copy or extract from it.	s 14(4)	
Any person untruthfully so stating himself to be a creditor is guilty of contempt.	see s 14(4)	r 80
9. Official receiver fixes time and place for first meeting of creditors.	s 13(1)	r 239(1)
TIME: The first meeting must be summoned for a day not later than 14 days after the date of the receiving order, unless the court otherwise orders for any special reason.	Sch 1, para 1	
Official receiver may apply for extention of time.		
The meeting must be held at the place which is, in the Official receiver's opinion, the most convenient for the majority of the creditors.	Sch 1, para 4	
No meeting can be summoned so long as advertisement of the receiving order is stayed.		
10. Official receiver summons meeting by:		
(1) Gazetting and advertising in a local newspaper notice of the time and place of the meeting	Sch 1, para 2	
TIME: Not less than 6 clear days before the date of the meeting	Sch 1, para 2	
(2) Sending to each creditor mentioned in debtor's statement of affairs; (i) notice of the time and place of the meeting; and (ii) a summary of the debtor's statement of affairs (including the cause of his failure and any observations he sees fit to make).	Sch 1, para 3	
TIME: As soon as practicable, but before the meeting.	Sch 1, para 3	
(3) Sending notice to debtor of the time and place of the meeting		r 239(2)
TIME: Not less than 3 days before the date of the meeting		r 239(2)
The sending of the notices may be proved by a certificate by the official receiver or his clerk or by an affidavit by the trustee or his solicitor or the clerk of either of them.		r 17

Steps to be Taken	Bankruptcy Act 1914	Bankruptcy Rules 1952
Unless the court otherwise orders, the proceedings at the meeting are valid notwithstanding that some creditors have not received the notice summoning the meeting.		r 242
The debtor is under a duty to attend the first meeting of creditors.	s 22(1)	
This duty is not absolved by failure of the official receiver to send him, or his failure to receive, notice of the meeting.		r 239(2) proviso

3.7 FORMS

APPLICATION to Official Receiver for appointment of special manager

IN THE [HIGH COURT OF JUSTICE *or* . . . . COUNTY COURT]
In Bankruptcy No. . . . of 19 . . .
Re A B

We, the undersigned creditors in the above estate, do, on the grounds hereafter set forth, apply to the Official Receiver to appoint a special manager of the above-named Debtor's [estate *or* business]. The Debtor carries on the business of a . . . . at (*addres*), and, unless such business receives the constant personal attention of a person acquainted with businesses of that type until such time as the said business can be profitably sold, there will be a considerable loss of assets to the estate.

DATED this . . . . day of . . . . 19 . . .

(*Creditors' signatures*)

ORDER of Official Receiver appointing special manager

IN THE [HIGH COURT OF JUSTICE *or* . . . . COUNTY COURT]
In Bankruptcy No. . . . of 19 . . .
Re A B [*add, after adjudication*, a Bankrupt]

UPON READING this application, and being of opinion that there are sufficient grounds for the application, I appoint (subject to the provisions of the Bankruptcy Act 1914 and of the Rules made thereunder) S M of (*address*) to be Special Manager of the [estate *or* business] of the above-named Debtor, until the first meeting of creditors, or until such further time as I may then direct, on his giving security to my satisfaction for £. . . .

The remuneration of the said Special Manager is, subject to any resolution of the creditors, agreed at £. . . . provided there are sufficient assets in the estate, after the payment of prior claims, to pay such remuneration; but he shall otherwise have no claim against any person or persons in respect thereof.

The powers entrusted to the said Special Manager are [to carry on the Debtor's business of a . . . ., at (*address*), with authority to retain the services of such of the employees as he may deem necessary, and to engage not more than . . . . additional employees, and to employ the Debtor at a salary not exceeding £. . . . per week].

The said Special Manager shall pay over to me all money belonging to the [estate *or* business] of the said Debtor which may come to his hands, of which money a statement shall be brought in to me by the said Special Manager weekly, and any money which may be required for current expenditure and disbursements shall be paid out of money to be provided by me from time to time, not exceeding the amount so paid in by the Special Manager as aforesaid and available for such purpose, and an account of such expenditure, together with the vouchers, shall be delivered to me weekly. The Special Manager shall not under any circumstances pledge my credit to any liabilities which may be incurred by him.

The accounts of the said Special Manager shall be verified by affidavit (*s*) as and when required by me.

DATED this . . . . day of . . . . 19 . . .

(*Signature*)
Official Receiver

RECEIVING ORDER on debtor's petition

IN THE [HIGH COURT OF JUSTICE *or* . . . . COUNTY COURT]
In Bankruptcy No . . . . of 19 . . .

Re A B

ON THE PETITION of the Debtor himself filed . . . . 19 . . . and numbered . . . . of 19 . . . a Reciving Order is hereby made against A B (*state name, address and description of debtor as set out in petition*) and [the Official Receiver *or* O R an Official Receiver] of this Court is hereby constituted Receiver of the estate of the said Debtor

DATED . . . . o'clock in the [forenoon] this . . . . day of . . . . 19 . . .

By the Court
Registrar

NOTE The above-named Debtor is required immediately after the service of this Order upon him to attend the Official Receiver of the Court at his offices at (*address*).

The Official Receiver's offices are open (except on holidays) every weekday from . . . am to . . . pm except . . . . days when they close at . . . . pm.

INDORSEMENT ON ORDER

The name and address of the Solicitor (if any) to the Debtor are (*name and address*).

RECEIVING ORDER on creditor's petition

IN THE [HIGH COURT OF JUSTICE *or* . . . . COUNTY COURT]
In Bankruptcy No. . . . . of 19 . . . .

Re A B

ON THE PETITION (dated . . . . 19 . . . . and numbered . . . . of 19 . . . .) of C D of (*address*) a Creditor filed . . . . 19 . . . . and on reading . . . . and on hearing . . . . and it appearing to the Court that the following act or acts of bankruptcy has or have been committed namely (*set out the nature and dates of the acts of bankruptcy on which the order is made*).

A Receiving Order is hereby made against [A B *or* A B & Co *or if a firm or firm name, or if so stated in petition*, A B and J K trading together in partnership as A B & Co *or as the case may be*] (*give name, address and description of debtor*

as set out in petition) and [the Official Receiver *or* O R an Official Receiver] of this Court is hereby constituted Receiver of the estate of the said Debtor
DATED . . . . o'clock in the [forenoon] this . . . . day of . . . . 19. . . .

By the Court
Registrar

NOTE The above-named Debtor is required immediately after the service of this Order upon him to attend the Official Receiver of the Court at his offices at (*address*).

The Official Receiver's offices are open (except on holidays) every weekday from . . . . am to . . . . pm, except . . . . days when they close at . . . . pm.

INDORSEMENT ON ORDER

The name and address of the Solicitor to the Petitioning Creditor are (*name and address*).

RECEIVING ORDER with stay of advertisement and proceedings

IN THE [HIGH COURT OF JUSTICE *or* . . . . COUNTY COURT]

In Bankruptcy No. . . . of 19 . . . .

Re A B [*add, after adjudication,* a Bankrupt]

ON THE PETITION (dated . . . . 19 . . . ' and numbered . . . . of 19 . . . .) of C D of (*address*) a Creditor filed . . . . . 19 . . . . and on reading . . . . and on hearing . . . . and it appearing to the Court that the following act or acts of bankruptcy has or have been committed namely (*set out the nature and dates of the acts of bankruptcy on which the order is made.*

A Receiving Order is hereby made against (A B *or* A B & Co *or, if a firm or firm name, or if so stated in petition,* A B and J K trading together in partnership as A B & Co *or as the case may be*] (*give name, address and description of debtor as set out in petition*) and [the Official Receiver *or* O R an Official Receiver] of this Court is hereby constituted Receiver of the estate of the said Debtor

AND IT IS FURTHER ORDERED that the advertisement of this Order [and all proceedings thereunder] shall be stayed for . . . . days from this date and that if an appeal be entered within that time the stay be continued over the hearing of the said appeal the Debtor [personally *or* by his [Counsel *or* Solicitor]] undertaking to attend forthwith on the Official Receiver and give the name of his Banker
DATED . . . . o'clock in the [forenoon] this . . . . day of . . . . 19 . . . .

By the Court
Registrar

NOTE The above-named Debtor is required immediately after the service of this Order upon him to attend the Official Receiver of the Court at his offices at (*address*).

The Official Receiver's offices are open (except on holidays) every weekday from . . . . am to . . . . pm, except . . . . days when they close at . . . . pm.

INDORSEMENT ON ORDER

The name and address of the Solicitor to the Petitioning Creditor are (*name and address*).

ORDER for stay of advertisement of receiving order and proceedings

IN THE [HIGH COURT OF JUSTICE *or* . . . . COUNTY COURT]

In Bankruptcy No. . . . of 19 . . . .

Re A B [*add, after adjudication*, a Bankrupt]

UPON THE APPLICATION of . . . . for an order staying the advertisement of [and all proceedings under] the Receiving Order made herein on . . . . 19 . . . . to enable the above-named Debtor to lodge [an application to rescind the said Receiving Order on the ground that [all his debts have been paid in full *or as the case may be*] *or* an appeal against the said Receiving Order] and the Debtor undertaking [to attend on the Official Receiver as and when required and to file a statement of his affairs]

IT IS ORDERED that the insertion of the advertisement in the 'London Gazette' local papers and all public notices of the Receiving Order made herein on . . . . 19 . . . [and all proceedings thereunder] be stayed over . . . . 19 . . . .

AND if an [application to rescind the said Receiving Order [on the ground of payment in full *or as the case may be*] be lodged *or* appeal be entered] within that time then the stay shall be continued pending the hearing of the said [application *or* appeal] and it is ordered that the Debtor do attend forthwith on the Official Receiver and give the name of his Banker

DATED this . . . . day of . . . . 19 . . . .

By the Court
Registrar

3.8 FIRST MEETING OF CREDITORS: BANKRUPTCY ACT 1914, SCH 1

1. The first meeting of creditors shall be summoned for a day not later than fourteen days after the date of the receiving order, unless the court for any special reason deem it expedient that the meeting be summoned for a later day.

2. The official receiver shall summon the meeting by giving not less than six clear days' notice of the time and place thereof in the *London Gazette* and in a local paper.

3. The official receiver shall also, as soon as practicable, send to each creditor mentioned in the debtor's statement of affairs, a notice of the time and place of the first meeting of creditors, accompanied by a summary of the debtor's statement of affairs, including the cause of his failure, and any observations thereon which the official receiver may think fit to make; but the proceedings at the first meeting shall not be invalidated by reason of any such notice or summary not having been sent or received before the meeting.

4. The meeting shall be held at such place as is in the opinion of the official receiver most convenient for the majority of the creditors.

5. The official receiver or the trustee may at any time summon a meeting of creditors, and shall do so whenever so directed by the court, or so requested by a creditor in accordance with the provisions of this Act.

6. Meetings subsequent to the first meeting shall be summoned by sending notice of the time and place thereof to each creditor at the address given in his proof, or if he has not proved, at the address given in the debtor's statement of affairs, or at such other address as may be known to the person summoning the meeting.

7. The official receiver, or some person nominated by him shall be the chairman at the first meeting. The chairman at subsequent meetings shall be such person as the meeting by resolution appoint.

8. A person shall not be entitled to vote as a creditor at the first or any other meeting of creditors unless he has duly proved a debt provable in bankruptcy to be due to him from the debtor, and the proof has been duly lodged before the time appointed for the meeting.

9. A creditor shall not vote at any such meeting in respect of any unliquidated or contingent debt, or any debt the value of which is not ascertained.

10. For the purpose of voting, a secured creditor shall, unless he surrenders his security, state in his proof the particulars of his security, the date when it was given, and the value at which he assess it, and shall be entitled to vote only in respect of the

balance (if any) due to him, after deducting the value of his security. If he votes in respect of his whole debt he shall be deemed to have surrendered his security unless the court on application is satisfied that the omission to value the security has arisen from inadvertence.

11. A creditor shall not vote in respect of any debt on or secured by a current bill of exchange or promissory note held by him, unless he is willing to treat the liability to him thereon of every person who is liable thereon antecedently to the debtor, and against whom a receiving order has not been made, as a security in his hands, and to estimate the value thereof, and for the purposes of voting, but not for the purposes of dividend, to deduct it from his proof.

12. It shall be competent to the trustee or to the official receiver, within twenty-eight days after a proof estimating the value of a security as aforesaid has been made use of in voting at any meeting, to require the creditor to give up the security for the benefit of the creditors generally on payment of the value so estimated, with an addition thereto of twenty per centum: Provided that where a creditor has put a value on such security, he may, at any time before he has been required to give up such security as aforesaid, correct such valuation by a new proof, and deduct such new value from his debt, but in that case such addition of twenty per centum shall not be made if the trustee requires the security to be given up.

13. If a receiving order is made against one partner of a firm, any creditor to whom that partner is indebted jointly with the other partners of the firm, or any of them, may prove his debt for the purpose of voting at any meeting of creditors, and shall be entitled to vote thereat.

14. The chairman of a meeting shall have power to admit or reject a proof for the purpose of voting, but his decision shall be subject to appeal to the court. If he is in doubt whether the proof of a creditor should be admitted or rejected he shall mark the proof as objected to and shall allow the creditor to vote, subject to the vote being declared invalid in the event of the objection being sustained.

15. A creditor may vote either in person or by proxy.

16. Every instrument of proxy shall be in the prescribed form, and shall be issued by the official receiver of the debtor's estate, or by some other official receiver, or, after the appointment of a trustee, by the trustee, and every insertion therein shall be in the handwriting of the person giving the proxy or of any manager or clerk, or other person in his regular employment, or of any commissioner to administer oaths in the Supreme Court.

17. General and special forms of proxy shall be sent to the creditors, together with a notice summoning a meeting of creditors, and neither the name nor the description of the official receiver, or of any other person, shall be printed or inserted in the body of any instrument of proxy before it is so sent.

18. A creditor may give a general proxy to his manager or clerk, or any other person in his regular employment. In such case the instrument of proxy shall state the relation in which the person to act thereunder stands to the creditor.

19. A creditor may give a special proxy to any person to vote at any specified meeting or adjournment thereof on all or any of the following matters:—

(a) For or against any specific proposal for a composition or scheme of arrangement;

(b) For or against the appointment of any specified person as trustee at a specified rate of remuneration, or as member of the committee of inspection, or for or against the continuance in office of any specified person as trustee or member of a committee of inspection;

(c) On all questions relating to any matter other than those above referred to, arising at any specified meeting or adjournment thereof.

20. A proxy shall not be used unless it is deposited with the official receiver or trustee before the meeting at which it is to be used.

21. Where it appears to the satisfaction of the court that any solicitation has been

used by or on behalf of a trustee or receiver in obtaining proxies, or in procuring the trusteeship or receivership, except by the direction of a meeting of creditors, the court shall have power, if it thinks fit, to order that no remuneration shall be allowed to the person by whom or on whose behalf such solicitation may have been exercised, notwithstanding any resolution of the committee of inspection or of the creditors to the contrary.

22. A creditor may appoint the official receiver of the debtor's estate to act in manner prescribed as his general or special proxy.

23. The chairman of a meeting may, with the consent of the meeting, adjourn the meeting from time to time and from place to place.

24. A meeting shall not be competent to act for any purpose, except the election of a chairman, the proving of debts, and the adjournment of the meeting, unless there are present, or represented thereat, at least three creditors, or all the creditors if their number does not exceed three.

25. If within half an hour from the time appointed for the meeting a quorum of creditors is not present or represented, the meeting shall be adjourned to the same day in the following week at the same time and place, or to such other day as the chairman may appoint, not being less than seven nor more than twenty-one days.

26. The chairman of every meeting shall cause minutes of the proceedings at the meeting to be drawn up and fairly entered in a book kept for that purpose, and the minutes shall be signed by him or by the chairman of the next ensuing meeting.

27. No person acting either under a general or special proxy shall vote in favour of any resolution which would directly or indirectly place himself, his partner or employer, in a position to receive any remuneration out of the estate of the debtor otherwise than as a creditor rateably with the other creditors of the debtor: Provided that where any person holds special proxies to vote for the appointment of himself as trustee he may use the said proxies and vote accordingly.

28. The vote of the trustee, or of his partner, clerk, solicitor, or solicitor's clerk, either as creditor or as proxy for a creditor, shall not be reckoned in the majority required for passing any resolution affecting the remuneration or conduct of the trustee.

3.9 THE OLD BANKRUPTCY LAW OFFENCES: BANKRUPTCY ACT 1914, s 154

(See paras 3.3.5 above and 7.6 below)

154 Any person who has been adjudged bankrupt or in respect of whose estate a receiving order has been made shall in each of the cases following be guilty of a misdemeanour:

(1) If he does not to the best of his knowledge and belief fully and truly discover to the trustee all his property, real and personal, and how and to whom and for what consideration and when he disposed of any part thereof except such part as has been disposed of in the ordinary way of his trade (if any) or laid out in the ordinary expense of his family, unless he proves that he had no intent to defraud:

(2) If he does not deliver up to the trustee, or as he directs, all such part of his real and personal property as is in his custody or under his control, and which he is required by law to deliver up, unless he proves that he had no intent to defraud:

(3) If he does not deliver up to the trustee, or as he directs, all books, documents, papers, and writings in his custody or under his control relating to his property or affairs unless he proves that he had no intent to defaud:

(4) If, after the presentation of a bankruptcy petition by or against him, or within six months next before such presentation, he conceals any part of his property to the

value of ten pounds or upwards, or conceals any debt due to or from him, unless he proves that he had no intent to defraud:

(5) If, after the presentation of a bankruptcy petition by or against him, or within six months next before such presentation, he fraudulently removes any part of his property to the value of ten pounds or upwards:

(6) If he makes any material omission in any statement relating to his affairs unless he proves that he had no intent to defraud:

(7) If, knowing or believing that a false debt has been proved by any person under the bankruptcy, he fails for the period of a month to inform the trustee thereof:

(8) If, after the presentation of a bankruptcy petition by or against him, he prevents the production of any book, document, paper, or writing affecting or relating to his property or affairs, unless he proves that he had no intent to conceal the state of his affairs or to defeat the law:

(9) If, after the presentation of a bankruptcy petition by or against him, or within six months next before such presentation, he conceals, destroys, mutilates, or falsifies, or is privy to the concealment, destruction, mutilation or falsification of any book or document affecting or relating to his property or affairs, unless he proves that he had no intent to conceal the state of his affairs or to defeat the law:

(10) If, after the presentation of a bankruptcy petition by or against him, or within six months next before such presentation, he makes or is privy to the making of any false entry in any book or document affecting or relating to his property or affairs, unless he proves that he had no intent to conceal the state of his affairs or to defeat the law:

(11) If, after the presentation of a bankruptcy petition by or against him, or within six months next before such presentation, he fraudulently parts with, alters, or makes any omission in, or is privy to the fraudulently parting with, altering, or making any omission in, any document affecting or relating to his property or affairs:

(12) If, after the presentation of a bankruptcy petition by or against him, or at any meeting of his creditors within six months next before such presentation, he attempts to account for any part of his property by fictitious losses or expenses:

(13) If, within six months next before the presentation of a bankruptcy petition by or against him, or, in the case of a receiving order made under section one hundred and seven of this Act, before the date of the order, or after the presentation of a bankruptcy petition and before the making of a receiving order, he, by any false representation or other fraud, has obtained any property on credit and has not paid for the same:

(14) If, within six months next before the presentation of a bankruptcy petition by or against him, or, in the case of a receiving order made under section one hundred and seven of this Act, before the date of the order, or after the presentation of a bankruptcy petition and before the making of a receiving order, he obtains under the false pretence of carrying on business, and, if a trader, of dealing in the ordinary way of his trade, any property on credit and has not paid for the same, unless he proves that he had no intent to defraud:

(15) If, within six months next before the presentation of a bankruptcy petition by or against him, or, in the case of a receiving order made under section one hundred and seven of this Act, before the date of the order, or after the presentation of a bankrutpcy petition and before the making of a receiving order, he pawns, pledges, or disposes of any property which he has obtained on credit and has not paid for, unless, in the case of a trader, such pawning, pledging, or disposing is in the ordinary way of his trade, and unless in any case he proves that he had no intent to defraud:

(16) If he is guilty of any false representation or other fraud for the purpose of obtaining the consent of his creditors or any of them to an agreement with reference to his affairs or to his bankruptcy.

For the purpose of this section, the expression 'trustee' means the official receiver of the debtor's estate or trustee administering his estate for the benefit of his creditors.

CHAPTER 4

The Official Receiver and the Trustee

4.1 INTRODUCTION

4.1.1. The Insolvency Act 1986 introduces the 'Insolvency Practitioner'[1] for cases proceeding under the New Law. However, the requirement for a specially qualified person does not extend back to cases proceeding under the Old Bankruptcy Law.

Chapter 15 below deals with the new-type of trustee in bankruptcy and this chapter (as does the whole of Part I) concentrates on the responsibilities and duties of the official receiver and of the trustee in bankruptcy in Old Bankruptcy Law cases.

[1] Bankruptcy Act 1914, s 1.

4.1.2 The official receiver's duties in Old Bankruptcy Law cases fall into the following four categories:

(a) To act as interim receiver, if such an appointment is made.[1]

(b) To act as receiver and manager of the debtor's estate between receiving order and adjudication.[2]

(c) To act as trustee in bankruptcy when the debtor is adjudicated and when no other person is appointed[3] and to assume trusteeship if, for any reason, that office becomes vacant.[4]

(d) To investigate and report to the court on the conduct of the debtor both before, and after, the receiving order.[5]

[1] Under Bankruptcy Act 1914, s 8, as to which see ch 3 above.
[2] Bankruptcy Act 1914, s 7(1).

[3] Ibid, s 53(1).
[4] Ibid, s 74(1)(g) and 78(4).
[5] Ibid, s 72(1).

4.1.3 The official receiver is entitled at all times, that is to say whether or not he has become trustee, to have access to, and facilities for, inspecting the bankrupt's books and documents. A trustee in bankruptcy is obliged to give the official receiver such aid as may reasonably be required to allow the official receiver to perform his statutory duties.[1]

Similarly, the official receiver must give a trustee such information concerning the debtor's estate as may be required to enable the trustee to perform his duties.[2]

[1] Bankruptcy Act 1914, s 72(4).
[2] Bankruptcy Rules 1952, r 351 (4).

4.2 THE OFFICIAL RECEIVER IN RELATION TO THE DEBTOR'S CONDUCT

4.2.1 It is the official receiver's duty to investigate the conduct of the debtor up to the receiving order and to observe and report on his conduct throughout the bankruptcy.

In practice, the investigation into his conduct up to the receiving order is conducted at the initial interview which takes place immediately after the receiving order has been made (see para 3.4 above) and at the subsequent public examination. The official receiver has power to follow up enquiries, both by requiring the debtor's assistance[1] and by the examination of other persons, as to which see ch 8 below.

[1] See Bankruptcy Act 1914, s 22(2).

4.2.2 Whilst he *must* report on criminal conduct by the debtor[1] the debtor's conduct or behaviour throughout the bankruptcy is only formally reported upon when the debtor's application for discharge comes before the court (see ch 10 below).

[1] Bankruptcy Act 1914, s 73(a).

4.2.3 When the official receiver does report on the debtor's conduct his reports are not only privileged but, for the most part, are also prima facie evidence of what is said in them.[1]

[1] See Bankruptcy Rules 1952, rr 321 and 311.

4.3 THE OFFICIAL RECEIVER AS TRUSTEE

As explained in more detail in ch 6 below immediately on a debtor being adjudged bankrupt his property vests in his trustee. Until a trustee is appointed the official receiver 'shall be Trustee'.[1] Thus, the official receiver's role changes from that of interim receiver to trustee of the debtor's property and his powers therefore also alter.[2] If for any reason the trustee's office is vacated the official receiver must act as trustee during that vacancy.[3] The official receiver is thus, in effect, trustee in default of any other appointee and save for special cases, e g small bankruptcies as defined in the Act, he is expressly prohibited from being appointed trustee.[4] However, when he is trustee he is in exactly the same position as any other trustee.[5]

1 Bankruptcy Act 1914, s 53(1).
2 See *Re Berry, Duffield v Williams* [1896] 1 Ch 939.
3 Bankruptcy Act 1914, ss 74(1)(g) and 78(4).
4 Ibid, s 19(5).
5 See *Re Duncan, ex p Official Receiver* [1892] 1 QB 879 and *Turquand v Board of Trade* (1886) 11 App Cas 286.

4.4 THE OFFICIAL RECEIVER'S ACCOUNTABILITY AND LIABILITY

4.4.1 The official receiver must keep a record book[1] and a cash book[2] and must account to the Department of Trade and Industry.[3] He is obliged to supply a list of creditors, with the amount due to each creditor to any creditor who demands it.[4] If one-sixth of the creditors require it, the official receiver is obliged to furnish a statement of account up to the date of the requisition.[5]

1 In which all committee of inspection resolutions are recorded: Bankruptcy Rules 1952, r 362.
2 Bankruptcy Rules 1952, r 363.
3 Bankruptcy Act 1914, s 74(3).
4 Ibid, s 84.
5 Ibid, s 85.

4.4.2 The official receiver, in his capacity as trustee, or otherwise, is immune from personal liability if he disposes of property in the possession, or on the premises, of the debtor against whom a receiving order has been made so long as he is without notice of a claim by any person in respect of that property, even if it transpires that the property in question is not the property of the debtor. However, if the court is of the opinion that the official receiver was negligent in respect of his actions, then he may nevertheless be personally liable.[1]

1 Bankruptcy Act 1914, s 61.

4.4.3 When an action is brought against the official receiver (or a trustee) representing the estate of the debtor, or where the official receiver is made a party to proceedings, he is not liable for any costs of such proceedings unless the court otherwise directs.[1] Similarly, he is not liable for costs personally if he unsuccessfully resists appeal against the rejection of a proof of debt.[2]

1 Bankruptcy Rules 1952, r 92(3).
2 Ibid, r 262.

4.4.4 The Bankruptcy Rules 1952, r 330 sets out in detail the official receiver's liability for costs expenses and damages. In summary, when acting pursuant to the provisions of the Bankruptcy Act 1914, or in the bona fide and reasonable belief that he is doing so, damages awarded against him are payable out of the estate of the debtor so long as he has reported the proceedings to the Department of Trade and Industry and the Department has determined that the proceedings be resisted. He should apply to adjourn any proceedings where the result of the Department of Trade and Industry's deliberations are awaited.

4.4.5 If a debtor against whom a receiving order has been made has no available assets the official receiver need not incur any expense in relation to the estate unless the Department of Trade and Industry directs otherwise.[1]

[1] Bankruptcy Rules 1952, r 324.

4.4.6 Subject to any order of the court, the assets remaining after payment of expenses properly incurred in preserving, realising or getting in any of the assets of the debtor are available, in the first place, to reimburse the actual expenses of the official receiver in protecting the property or assets of the debtor and the expenses incurred by him in carrying on the debtor's business.[1]

[1] Bankruptcy Rules 1952, r 115(1). For order of distribution in detail see ch 9 below.

4.5 THE TRUSTEE'S QUALIFICATIONS APPOINTMENT AND REMOVAL

4.5.1 The trustee is appointed either by the creditors in general meeting or, if the creditors in general meeting have so delegated the task, by the committee of inspection.

4.5.2 If appointment is by the creditors in general meeting, as it almost invariably is, then it is usually made at the first meeting of creditors. The appointment is by ordinary resolution, that is to say by a simple majority *in value* of the creditors voting. The voting may be effected personally by the creditor attending, or by proxy.

4.5.3 It is available to the creditors to appoint more than one person to be trustee[1] so that two or more trustees can act and hold property jointly. The creditors can also define what acts are to be done by a particular trustee. However, such appointments are rare and occur only in exceptional cases where, for example, one trustee might deal with a bankrupt's business assets while another deals with his personal property.

[1] Bankruptcy Act 1914, s 77(1).

4.5.4 Similarly, the creditors can, if they think fit, appoint persons to act as trustees in succession if one or more of the persons first nominated decline to accept the office.[1] Again, in practice, this is rare as it is usually known in advance whether or not a particular person will accept the appointment.

1 Bankruptcy Act 1914, s 77(2).

4.5.5 The trustee's appointment takes effect[1] only from the date of a certificate which is required to be issued by the Department of Trade and Industry to the effect that the Department is satisfied concerning the trustee's security (as to which see below).

This requirement gives the Department of Trade and Industry the opportunity of objecting to the appointment of a particular trustee on any of the following grounds:

(a) that it has not been made in good faith by a majority of the creditors voting;

(b) that the nominee is not fit to act as trustee; or

(c) that the nominee's connection with, or relation to, the bankrupt or a creditor is such that he cannot act with impartiality in the interest of the creditors generally.[2]

If the Department raises any of the above objections, then, if a majority in value of the creditors wish it, it must notify its objection to the High Court, which then decides on the validity of the objection.[3]

1 Bankruptcy Act 1914, s 19(5).
2 Ibid, s 19(2).
3 Ibid, s 19(3).

4.5.6 The proposed trustee must give security in a manner and to the satisfaction of the Department of Trade and Industry.[1] Security does not need to be given separately in respect of each bankrupt's estate in respect of which he accepts appointment, but may be given generally and be available for any bankruptcy in which he is appointed.[2]

Security is usually given by a fidelity insurance bond for which a premium is paid. Trustees who regularly act as such carry permanent cover in this respect.

1 Bankruptcy Act 1914, s 19(2).
2 Bankruptcy Rules 1952, r 355(1).

4.5.7 If, for any reason, a vacancy occurs in the office of a trustee of a bankrupt's estate, the official receiver acts as trustee until the vacancy is filled.[1] As with the appointment in the first place, it lies with the creditors in general meeting to fill the vacancy or direct the committee of inspection to do so and the official receiver must, on the request of any creditor, call a meeting of creditors for the purpose of filling the vacancy.[2]

If the creditors have not, within three weeks of the vacancy occurring, appointed a successor to the trustee the official receiver must report to the

Department of Trade which may itself appoint a trustee to fill the vacancy until the creditors make their own appointment.[2]

[1] Bankruptcy Act 1914, ss 53(1), 71(1)(g) and 78(4).
[2] Ibid, s 78.

4.5.8 A trustee may resign his appointment but is required to call a meeting of creditors giving at least seven days' notice, 'to consider whether his resignation shall be accepted'.[1] If a trustee resigns he is still subject to the same requirements, concerning his release, as he would have been had he completed his trusteeship (see below).

His resignation is not effective until he has handed over all books papers and documents to his successor or to the official receiver, and the order of release (see below) will not be effective until he has done so.[2]

[1] Bankruptcy Rules 1952, r 336.
[2] Ibid, rr 343 and 344.

4.5.9 A trustee may be removed by the creditors or by the Department of Trade and Industry:

1 Removal by creditors

The passing of an ordinary resolution of creditors is all that is required to remove a trustee. The meeting must have been convened on seven days' notice and the Bankruptcy Act 1914 expressly provides that the resolution is to be passed 'at a meeting specially called for that purpose'.[1]

The trustee may from time to time summon general meetings of creditors for the purpose of ascertaining their wishes.[2] He may not wish to do so if the creditors wish to remove him. However, he, or the official receiver, is bound to call a general meeting if a creditor 'with the concurrence of one-sixth in value of the creditors (including himself)' request that such a meeting be convened.[2] The person requiring a general meeting to be summoned must deposit a sum sufficient to pay the costs of summoning the meeting.[3]

[1] Bankruptcy Act 1914, s 95(1).
[2] Ibid, s 79(2).
[3] Ibid, proviso.

2 Removal by the Department of Trade

The Department of Trade is charged by the Bankruptcy Act 1914 to 'take cognizance of the conduct of trustees, and to investigate any apparent breach of duty'.[1] It is entitled to require a trustee to answer questions and even to examine a trustee (or any other person concerning the bankruptcy) on oath[2] or direct an investigation of the trustee's books and vouchers.[3]

Whether or not it has conducted such an investigation the Department may remove a trustee from office if it is of the opinion:[4]

(a) that he has been guilty of misconduct or has failed to perform his duties under the Bankruptcy Act 1914;
(b) that his trusteeship is being needlessly protracted without any probable advantage to creditors;

(c) that he is incapable of performing his duties by reason of absence or for medical reasons; or
(d) that he is unable to act with impartiality because of a connection with the bankrupt or his estate or with a particular creditor.

The procedure is very rarely carried out and no procedural table is included for the process, but see the Bankruptcy Rules 1952, r 339.

1 Bankruptcy Act 1914, s 81(1).
2 Ibid, s 81(2).
3 Ibid, s 81(3).
4 Ibid, s 95(2).

4.6 THE TRUSTEE'S DUTIES AND RESPONSIBILITIES

4.6.1 The Bankruptcy Act 1914 or the Bankruptcy Rules 1952, require that the trustee shall do the following;

(i) He must take possession of all deeds, books and accounts of the bankrupt and 'all other parts of his property capable of manual delivery'.[1]
(ii) He must summon a general meeting of creditors if required by one sixth in value of the creditors.[2]
(iii) He must keep proper books in which he must make entries or minutes of proceedings at meetings and of such other matters as may be prescribed, and any creditor may, subject to the control of the court, personally or by his agent, inspect any such books.[3]
(iv) He must keep a record book in which to record minutes of proceedings at general meetings of creditors and of the committee of inspection.[4]
(v) He must keep a cash book in such form as the Department of Trade and Industry may direct[5] and when he carries on the business previously run by the bankrupt he must keep a distinct account of the trading.[6]
(vi) Not less than twice a year the trustee should send to the Department of Trade an account of his receipts and payments as trustee[7] and, once a year, a statement showing 'the proceedings in the bankruptcy'.

NOTE (iii)–(vi) above give the basic outline of the trustee's duties in relation to his records and responsibility to account to the Department of Trade and Industry. For the prescribed form in which he must account and report and for auditing and more detailed provisions see the Bankruptcy Act 1914, ss 84–92 and the Bankruptcy Rules 1952, rr 362–373.

1 Bankruptcy Act 1914, s 48(1).
2 Ibid, s 95(2).
3 Ibid, s 86.
4 Bankruptcy Rules 1952, r 362.
5 See Bankruptcy Rules 1952, rr 363–364.
6 Bankruptcy Rules 1952, r 364(1).
7 Bankruptcy Act 1914, s 92(1) and (2).

4.6.2 The trustee's basic duty of course, whatever the detailed provisions of the Bankruptcy Act 1914 and the Bankruptcy Rules 1952, is to administer the bankrupt's estate. The requirement of the Bankruptcy Act 1914 in this respect is to a certain extent tucked away in the part of the Act entitled 'Distribution of Property'.

Section 62(1) provides:

> 'Subject to the retention of such sums as may be necessary for the costs of administration, or otherwise, the Trustee shall, with all convenient speed, declare and distribute dividends amongst the creditors who have proved their debts.'

4.7 THE TRUSTEE'S POWERS

4.7.1 The Bankruptcy Act 1914 sets out, in s 55, the trustee's powers to deal with property of the bankrupt. The section is as follows:

> '**55** Subject to the provisions of this Act, the trustee may do all or any of the following things:
>
> (1) Sell all or any part of the property of the bankrupt (including the goodwill of the business, if any, and the book debts due or growing due to the bankrupt), by public auction or private contract, with power to transfer the whole thereof to any person or company, or to sell the same in parcels;
>
> (2) Give receipts for any money received by him, which receipts shall effectually discharge the person paying the money from all responsibility in respect of the application thereof;
>
> (3) Prove, rank, claim, and draw a dividend in respect of any debt due to the bankrupt;
>
> (4) Exercise any powers, the capacity to exercise which is vested in the trustee under this Act, and execute any powers of attorney, deeds and other instruments, for the purpose of carrying into effect the provisions of this Act;
>
> (5) Deal with any property to which the bankrupt is beneficially entitled as tenant in tail in the same manner as the bankrupt might have dealt with it; and sections 56 to 73 of the Fines and Recoveries Act, 1833, shall extend and apply to proceedings under this Act as if those sections were herein re-enacted and in terms made applicable to those proceedings.'

4.7.2 Sections 56, 57 and 58 set out the powers exercisable by a trustee in relation to the bankrupt's estate, but only with the permission of the committee of inspection. Again, because it cannot usefully be summarised, the provisions of the Act are set out in full;

> '**56** The trustee may, with the permission of the committee of inspection, do all or any of the following things:
>
> (1) Carry on the business of the bankrupt, so far as may be necessary for the beneficial winding up of the same;
>
> (2) Bring, institute, or defend any action or other legal proceeding relating to the property of the bankrupt;
>
> (3) Employ a solicitor or other agent to take any proceedings or do any business which may be sanctioned by the committee of inspection;[1]
>
> (4) Accept as the consideration for the sale of any property of the bankrupt a sum of money payable at a future time subject to such stipulations as to security and otherwise as the committee think fit;
>
> (5) Mortgage or pledge any part of the property of the bankrupt for the purpose of raising money for the payment of his debt;
>
> (6) Refer any dispute to arbitration, compromise any debts, claims and liabilities, whether present or future, certain or contingent, liquidated or unliquidated, subsisting or supposed to subsist between the bankrupt and any person who may have incurred any liability to the bankrupt, on the receipt of

such sums, payable at such times, and generally on such terms as may be agreed on;

(7) Make such compromise or other arrangement as may be thought expedient with creditors, or persons claiming to be creditors, in respect of any debts provable under the bankruptcy;

(8) Make such compromise or other arrangement as may be thought expedient with respect to any claim arising out of or incidental to the property of the bankrupt, made or capable of being made on the trustee by any person or by the trustee on any person;

(9) Divide in its existing form amongst the creditors, according to its estimated value, any property which from its peculiar nature or other special circumstances cannot be readily or advantageously sold.

The permission given for the purposes of this section shall not be a general permission to do all or any of the above-mentioned things, but shall only be a permission to do the particular thing or things for which permission is sought in the specified case or cases.'

Section 57 permits the trustee to allow the bankrupt to manage or superintend his property while s 58 permits him to make an allowance to the bankrupt for his and his family's support or in consideration of services rendered by the bankrupt in the winding up of his estate.

If there is no committee of inspection permission is given, if appropriate, by the Department of Trade.[2]

1 The transitional provisions in the Insolvency Act 1986 have affected the trustee's ability to employ solicitors. See ch 26 below concerning the employment of solicitors by trustees.

2 Bankruptcy Act 1914, s 20(10), *Re Duncan, ex p Duncan* [1892] 1 QB 331.

Power to disclaim onerous contracts

4.7.3 When a trustee finds that the estate of a bankrupt is bound by a contract entered into with the bankrupt before his adjudication, or that a bankrupt's property is affected by rights or obligations which render the contract unprofitable, or the property is onerous, or unsaleable, he is able to rely on the provisions of the Bankruptcy Act 1914, s 54 to disclaim the relevant contract or obligation. Since it is a long section and it is important not to oversimplify it it is set out in full, like ss 55 and 56 above, but in the Appendix to this chapter (para 4.11).

4.7.4 A trustee's disclaimer need not be in any special form but must be in writing and signed by him. He is not entitled to disclaim a lease, however, unless he has obtained the leave of the court to do so.[1] A trustee may disclaim at any time within 12 months of the first appointment of a trustee[2] but thereafter he needs the leave of the court to do so. A party who is affected by any delay by the trustee in coming to a decision can force the trustee into a decision by serving a notice requiring him to elect whether or not he proposes to disclaim. If the trustee does not give notice of disclaimer within 28 days he is deemed to have adopted the contract.[3] This period may be extended by the court on an application by the trustee.

1 Bankruptcy Act 1914, s 54(3) and Bankruptcy Rules 1952, r 278(2).

2 Bankruptcy Act 1914, s 54(1).

3 Bankruptcy Act 1914, s 54(4).

4.7.5 A disclaimer acts as a determination of the relevant contractual position. Thus, by extinguishing the primary liability, guarantors can benefit since, from the date of the disclaimer, their own obligations will also cease.[1]

[1] *Stacey v Hill* [1901] 1 KB 660.

4.8 THE TRUSTEE'S LIABILITIES

4.8.1 A trustee is under the theoretical control of the committee of inspection in that he must have regard to directions given by a resolution of the creditors at a general meeting or by the committee of inspection.[1]

Apart from this provision, however, the trustee must use his own discretion in the management of the estate.[2] If he is in serious doubt about what course of action to follow the trustee may apply to the court for directions[3] as to how to overcome his difficulty. In such an application the court may direct a trustee to disregard the directions of the creditors or committee of inspection[4] but the court is not bound to give directions if it does not think it appropriate to do so.[5]

[1] Bankruptcy Act 1914, s 79(1) (where such directions conflict those of the creditors in general meeting override those of the committee of inspection).
[2] Bankruptcy Act 1914, s 79(4).
[3] Ibid, s 79(3).
[4] *Re Poole, ex p Cocks* (1882) 21 Ch D 397.
[5] See *Re Webb & Sons, ex p Webb & Sons* (1887) 4 Morr 52, *Re Harrison and Ingram, ex p Whinney* (1905) 54 WR 203; *Re Pilling, ex p Salaman* (1906) 13 Mans 229.

4.8.2 If the official receiver or a trustee in bankruptcy seizes or disposes of the property in the possession of a debtor, or on his premises, after a receiving order has been made, and he does so without notice of any claim in respect of that property, but it subsequently transpires that the property in question was not, at the date of the receiving order, the property of the debtor, the trustee or official receiver is not personally liable in respect of any loss suffered as a result of the seizure or disposal unless it can be established that he acted negligently.[1]

[1] Bankruptcy Act 1914, s 61.

4.8.3 Similarly if an action is brought against a trustee in bankruptcy in that capacity, or if he is made a party to any sort of action on the application of a third party, he is not liable for the costs of that action unless the court otherwise directs.[1]

[1] Bankruptcy Rules 1952, r 92(3).

4.8.4 If a trustee in bankruptcy carries on the business of the bankrupt he may be treated as a person accountable for value added tax in respect of that carrying on of business.[1]

[1] Value Added Tax Act 1983, s 31(4); VAT (General) Regulations 1985, SI 1985/886.

4.9 THE TRUSTEE'S REMUNERATION

4.9.1 The amount of a trustee's remuneration must be in the nature of a commission or be a percentage of both realisations and distributions.[1] The realisations element in the calculation is arrived at after the deduction of sums due to secured creditors out of their security. The rate of percentage or commission to be paid is fixed by ordinary resolution of the creditors or, if the creditors resolve, by the committee of inspection.[1]

When fixing the trustee's remuneration the creditors, or the committee of inspection if appropriate, must distinguish between the remuneration payable on realisations and that payable on distributions.[2] It must also express what expenses the remuneration is to cover so that the estate of the bankrupt is not charged with those expenses.[3] The percentage remuneration on the realisations by a trustee are calculated only on the amount actually realised by the trustee.[4]

If the creditors fail to fix a trustee's remuneration, for example by failing to attend meetings called for the purpose, then the court has power, using the provisions of the Bankruptcy Act 1914, s 105, to fix the trustee's remuneration.[5]

1 Bankruptcy Act 1914, s 82(1).
2 Bankruptcy Rules 1952, r 335.
3 Bankruptcy Act 1914, s 82(3).
4 See *Re Christie, ex p Christie* [1900] 1 QB 5.
5 *Re Colgate, ex p Trustee of Property of bankrupt* [1986] 1 All ER 419.

4.9.2 A trustee must not under any circumstances whatever accept any form of remuneration, gift, commission or benefit of any sort beyond the remuneration fixed by the creditors and payable out of the estate of the bankrupt.[1]

Similarly he must not make any arrangement to give up any part of his remuneration to the bankrupt or any solicitor or other person 'that may be employed about a bankruptcy'[2] nor must he make a charge for a payment made to a person who carries out duties which are required to be performed by the trustee himself.[3]

1 Bankruptcy Rules 1952, r 336.
2 Bankruptcy Act 1914, s 82(5).
3 Ibid, s 83(1).

4.9.3 The practical result of the provisions outlined above is that since he can only be remunerated from a percentage of realisations and distributions, a trustee will seldom be found to act in cases where the assets for realisation are small in value. Whilst there is nothing in the statute or rules to prevent a trustee acting without remuneration, and indeed the Bankruptcy Act 1914 provides for cases where a trustee receives his expenses only,[1] the reality is that, save in exceptional cases, where there are few or no assets the official receiver invariably remains the trustee.

When a trustee is appointed he usually calculates what he considers to be a reasonable remuneration and the percentage or commission calculations are then carried out afterwards and put to the creditors for approval. If a fourth (in number or value) of the creditors dissent from a resolution fixing the trustee's remuneration, or if the bankrupt himself persuades the Department of Trade that the trustee's remuneration is too high the Department of Trade itself fixes the remuneration to be paid.

[1] Bankruptcy Act 1914, s 82(2).

4.10 THE TRUSTEE'S RELEASE

4.10.1 Once he has realised all the property of the bankrupt, or as much as he can without, in his opinion, protracting the bankruptcy needlessly, and has distributed a final dividend the trustee applies for his release to the Department of Trade and Industry.[1]

[1] Bankruptcy Act 1914, s 93(1).

4.10.2 The Bankruptcy Act 1914, s 93 sets out the Department of Trade's powers on this application. They are not recited here because of the transitional provisions in the Insolvency Act 1986 in connection with the release of a trustee in an Old Bankruptcy Law case.[1]

[1] Sch 11, para 14(3).

4.10.3 In an Old Bankruptcy Law case, where a trustee in bankruptcy has not applied for his release under the Bankruptcy Act 1914, s 93 then the provisions of the New Law apply, as to which see chs 15 and 16.

4.11 APPENDIX TO CHAPTER 4: BANKRUPTCY ACT 1914, s 54

54(1) Where any part of the property of the bankrupt consists of land of any tenure burdened with onerous covenants, of shares or stock in companies, of unprofitable contracts, or of any other property that is unsaleable, or not readily saleable, by reason of its binding the possessor thereof to the performance of any onerous act, or to the payment of any sum of money, the trustee, notwithstanding that he has endeavoured to sell or has taken possession of the property, or exercised any act of ownership in relation thereto, but subject to the provisions of this section, may, by writing signed by him, at any time within twelve months after the first appointment of a trustee or such extended period as may be allowed by the court, disclaim the property;

Provided that, where any such property has not come to the knowledge of the trustee within one month after such appointment, he may disclaim such property at any time within twelve months after he has become aware thereof or such extended period as may be allowed by the court.

(2) The disclaimer shall operate to determine, as from the date of disclaimer, the rights, interests and liabilities of the bankrupt and his property in or in respect of the property disclaimed, and shall also discharge the trustee from all personal liability in respect of the property disclaimed as from the date when the property vested in him, but shall not, except so far as is necessary for the purpose of releasing the bankrupt and his property and the trustee from liability, affect the rights or liabilities of any other person.

(3) A trustee shall not be entitled to disclaim a lease without the leave of the court, except in any cases which may be prescribed by general rules, and the court may, before or on granting such leave, require such notices to be given to persons

interested, and impose such terms as a condition of granting leave, and make such orders with respect to fixtures, tenant's improvements, and other matters arising out of the tenancy, as the court thinks just.

(4) The trustee shall not be entitled to disclaim any property in pursuance of this section in any case where an application in writing has been made to the trustee by any person interested in the property requiring him to decide whether he will disclaim or not, and the trustee has for a period of twenty-eight days after the receipt of the application, or such extended period as may be allowed by the court, declined or neglected to give notice whether he disclaims the property or not; and, in the case of a contract, if the trustee, after such application as aforesaid, does not within the said period or extended period disclaim the contract, he shall be deemed to have adopted it.

(5) The court may, on the application of any person who is, as against the trustee, entitled to the benefit or subject to the burden of a contract made with the bankrupt, make an order rescinding the contract on such terms as to payment by or to either party of damages for the non-performance of the contract, or otherwise, as to the court may seem equitable, and any damages payable under the order to any such person may be proved by him as a debt under the bankruptcy.

(6) The court may, on application by any person either claiming any interest in any disclaimed property or under any liability not discharged by this Act in respect of any disclaimed property, and on hearing such persons as it thinks fit, make an order for the vesting of the property in or delivery thereof to any person entitled thereto, or to whom it may seem just that the same should be delivered by way of compensation for such liability as aforesaid, or a trustee for him, and on such terms as the court thinks just; and on any such vesting order being made, the property comprised therein shall vest accordingly in the person therein named in that behalf without any conveyance or assignment for the purpose:

Provided that, where the property disclaimed is of a leasehold nature, the court shall not make a vesting order in favour of any person claiming under the bankrupt, whether as underlessee or as mortgagee by demise except upon the terms of making that person–

(a) subject to the same liabilities and obligations as the bankrupt was subject to under the lease in respect of the property at the date when the bankruptcy petition was filed; or
(b) if the court thinks fit, subject only to the same liabilities and obligations as if the lease had been assigned to that person at that date;

and in either event (if the case so requires) as if the lease had comprised only the property comprised in the vesting order; and any mortgagee or under-lessee declining to accept a vesting order upon such terms shall be excluded from all interest in and security upon the property, and, if there is no person claiming under the bankrupt who is willing to accept an order upon such terms, the court shall have power to vest the bankrupt's estate and interest in the property in any person liable either personally or in a representative character, and either alone or jointly with the bankrupt to perform the lessee's covenants in the lease, freed and discharged from all estates, incumbrances, and interests created therein by the bankrupt.

(7) Where, on the release removal resignation or death of a trustee in bankruptcy, an official receiver is acting as trustee, he may disclaim any property which might be disclaimed by a trustee under the foregoing provisions, notwithstanding that the time prescribed by this section for such disclaimer has expired, but such power of disclaimer shall be exerciseable only within twelve months after the official receiver has become trustee in the circumstances aforesaid, or has become aware of the existence of such property whichever period may last expire.

(8) Any person injured by the operation of a disclaimer under this section shall be deemed to be a creditor of the bankrupt to the extent of the injury, and may accordingly prove the same as a debt under the bankruptcy.

CHAPTER 5

Rescission

5.1 INTRODUCTION

The part of the Bankruptcy Act 1914[1] which deals with the annulment of an order of adjudication does not provide that, automatically upon an annulment being granted, the receiving order is rescinded. Therefore an application for rescission of the receiving order is invariably included, separately, in an application for an annulment of adjudication.[2]

1 Bankruptcy Act 1914, s 29.
2 See ch 11 below and *Re Noble, ex p Bankrupt v Official Receiver* [1965] Ch 129.

5.2 THE COURT'S POWER TO RESCIND A RECEIVING ORDER

5.2.1 All courts exercising bankruptcy jurisdiction have the power to 'review, rescind or vary' any of their bankruptcy orders[1] (see ch 21 below). Therefore, the first step in securing a rescission of the receiving order is to invite the court which made it to rescind.

1 Bankruptcy Act 1914, s 108.

5.2.2 The grounds for an application are essentially the same as for an application to annul an adjudication order (see ch 11 below) namely, either (a) that the order should not have been made, or (b) that the debtor can pay his debts in full.

A third ground exists, not strictly for a rescission, but for a discharge of the receiving order[1] on the ground that a composition or scheme of arrangement has been accepted and approved under the Bankruptcy Act 1914, s 16. (Compositions and schemes under the Old Bankruptcy Law are not covered by this book.)

1 See Bankruptcy Rules 1952, r 208(1).

5.3 THE EXERCISE OF THE POWER TO RESCIND

5.3.1 In deciding whether or not it should rescind its own receiving order the court must exercise its discretion, having regard to the fact that the order which is the subject of review is still in effect. This means that it is by no means sufficient that the debtor and the petitioning creditor simply apply for rescission, if there are no proper grounds. It is not enough, for example, that the petitioning creditor has simply changed his mind. There must be appropriate grounds upon which the court can act[1] and even then, the court has a wide discretion.

Even if it can be shown by the debtor that the petitioner's debt was bad, his receiving order will not be rescinded if the debtor is hopelessly insolvent and, for the protection of the creditors generally, it would not be reasonable to order rescission.[2]

Thus, whereas effective grounds might have existed for an appeal from the receiving order, when time for appeal has passed, these same grounds will not necessarily suffice for an application to rescind.

1 See *Re Hester, ex p Hester* (1889) 22 QBD 632.
2 See *Re Noble, ex p Bankrupt v Official Receiver* [1965] Ch 129.

5.3.2 No hard and fast rules can be established for when the court will rescind a receiving order on the ground that it should not have been made. The court's discretion will be exercised taking all relevant considerations into account. Examples of the way the court's discretion has been exercised on such matters in the past are given in the notes.[1]

1 *Re Davenport, ex p Bankrupt v Eric Street Properties Ltd* [1963] 2 All ER 850; *Re Heyl, ex p D P Morgan Ltd* [1918] 1 KB 452; *Re Fairleigh* (1905) 21 TLR 198; *Re Betts, ex p Official Receiver* [1901] 2 KB 39; *Re Izod, ex p Official Receiver* [1898] 1QB 241; *Re Flatau, ex p Official Receiver* [1893] 2 QB 219; *Re Bond* (1888) 21 QBD 17.

5.3.3 The usual ground for an application for rescission is that the debtor's debts have been, or can be, paid in full. If, as it appears, there is a close analogy between rescission of the receiving order and annulment of adjudication, then the court, in the exercise of its discretion could, in an extreme case, probably refuse a rescission even if all debts have been paid in full[1] but such a course would be very unusual.

1 See *Re Hester, ex p Hester* (1889) 22 QBD 632.

5.3.4 A relatively recent decision of the court indicates that the benefit of hindsight can be used in order to found a recission application on grounds that it has *become* clear that the receiving order should not have been made.

In *Re Field, ex p Debtor v H and J Quick Ltd*[1] Megarry V.C. said:

> 'If after Receiving Order has been made the Official Receiver were to be satisfied that the debtor had no assets and no prospect of ever having any so that to continue the process of bankruptcy would merely be to pile up costs which would never be paid, I think that he could and should support an application by the debtor to have the Receiving Order rescinded, even if he has no duty to make such an application himself.'

1 [1978] Ch 371.

5.3.5 The above passage suggests that the official receiver should support an application of the sort envisaged. In fact there appears to be no reason why the official receiver should not initiate a rescission application himself, although it has been suggested that the official receiver only has a right to apply where an abuse of the process of the court is alleged.[1]

[1] See note to 3 Halsbury's Laws (4th edn) para 421.

5.3.6 Whether or not he is the originator of the application, the official receiver must, when the application is based upon payment in full, report to the court, not less than four days before the hearing of the application, on the conduct of the debtor during the proceedings and upon his affairs generally.[1]

[1] Bankruptcy Rules 1952, r 184(1).

5.3.7 The court can hear any creditor on the application and can direct that any creditor in the debtor's statement of affairs should be served with the application and any such creditor can file evidence for use in the application.[1]

[1] Bankruptcy Rules 1952, r 184(2) and (3).

5.4 PROCEDURAL TABLE

Steps to be taken	Bankruptcy Act 1914	Bankruptcy Rules 1952
1. Debtor or any person interested in the proceedings (eg a creditor) applies by ex parte motion to fix date for hearing of application to rescind receiving order, and files affidavit in support.	s 108(1)	
Fee on application on the ground that debts are paid in full: £4.		
The debtor will be the applicant in most cases.		
The debtor may be required to enter into a bond to provide for debts he disputes.	see s 29(4)	
NOTE: An application to rescind a receiving order is usually preceded by an application to stay advertisement of the receiving order, if advertisement has not already taken place.		
2. Registrar:		
(1) Fixes date for hearing;		
(2) Gives notice to official receiver of intended application and sends supporting affidavit with notice.		r 183(1)
TIME: Not less than 7 clear days before the hearing.		r 183(1)

Steps to be Taken	Bankruptcy Act 1914	Bankruptcy Rules 1952
3. If applicant is a 'person interested' in the proceedings: applicant serves notice of motion on debtor.		
4. If application is on the ground that the receiving order ought not to have been made: Debtor files and serves notice of motion for rescission, together with supporting affidavit, on: (1) Petitioning creditor; and (2) Official receiver. Further evidence may be filed.		
5. If the application is on the ground of payment in full: Official receiver files a report as to conduct and affairs of debtor, including his conduct during the proceedings.		r 184(1)
TIME: Not less than 4 days before day appointed for the hearing. The debtor is not entitled to be served with a copy of the official receiver's report but it is normally made available to him.		r 184(1)
6. Registrar may order notice of the application to be served on any creditor shown in the statement of affairs or who has notified official receiver or trustee that he has, or at the date of the receiving order had, a claim against the debtor.		r 184(2)
7. Any respondent or creditor who has been served with notice or appears with leave of the court may adduce evidence or may by affidavit object. Then:		r 184(3)
8. Parties attend hearing, where registrar considers report, any objections and evidence, and may make an order: (1) Rescinding the receiving order and dismissing the petition; or (2) When the application is on the ground that the receiving order ought not to have been made: Rescinding the receiving order and adjourning the petition; or (3) Dismissing the applicant; or (4) Adjourning the application.	s 108(1)	
If order is made rescinding receiving order:		

Steps to be Taken	Bankruptcy Act 1914	Bankruptcy Rules 1952
9. Registrar: (1) Makes order permitting vacation of the registration of the receiving order in the register of writs and orders affecting land;		r 185
(2) May make order (unless Registrar otherwise directs, the order must be made) permitting vacation of the registration of the petition as a pending action.		r 171 r 185
10. Chief Bankruptcy Registrar forthwith gives notice of order of rescission to Department of Trade and Industry to be gazetted.		r 5 r 358(1)
11. Official receiver advertises rescission of receiving order in local papers if original receiving order was so advertised.	s 74(1)(f)	

5.5 FORMS

APPLICATION to fix day to hear application to rescind receiving order

IN THE [HIGH COURT OF JUSTICE *or* . . . . COUNTY COURT]

In Bankruptcy No. . . . of 19 . . . .

Re A B [*add, after adjudication*, a Bankrupt]

Ex parte [the Debtor *or* the Bankrupt *or* C D a Creditor *or* the Official Receiver *or* the Trustee *or as the case may be*]

APPLICATION is hereby made for a day to be appointed to hear the application of the above-named Debtor for an order rescinding the Receiving Order made herein on . . . . 19 . . . . [on the ground that [the debts have been paid in full *or* it ought not to have been made] *or* under Section 108 of the Bankruptcy Act 1914].

(*Signature*), of (*address*), [Agents for (*name*), of (*address*),] Solicitors for the [Debtor *or* Bankrupt *or* Trustee *or* Judgment Creditor *or* Petitioning Creditor *or as the case may be*]

AFFIDAVIT supporting application to rescind receiving order

IN THE [HIGH COURT OF JUSTICE *or* . . . . COUNTY COURT]

In Bankruptcy No. . . . of 19 . . . .

Re A B [*add, after adjudication*, a Bankrupt]

I, A B of (*residence and description*), the above-named Debtor, make oath and say as follows:

[*Either, if payment has been made in full:*

1. On . . . . 19 . . . . a Petition was filed against me in this Court upon which on . . . . 19 . . . . a Receiving Order was made.

2. On . . . . 19 . . . . I filed a Statement of my Affairs setting out the whole of my assets and liabilities.

3. [On . . . . 19 . . . . I provided the Official Receiver with a sum of money sufficient to pay all my debts in full as set out in my said Statement of Affairs and the costs of the Petitioning Creditor and the costs, charges and expenses of the Official Receiver *or* I have lodged with the Official Receiver receipts for the debts owing by me as set out in my said Statement of Affairs, the whole of which have been paid in full, including the costs of the Petitioning Creditor, and I also undertake to pay any sum payable to the Official Receiver under the said Receiving Order.]

4. I therefore respectfully ask that the said Receiving Order may be rescinded and that the said Petition may be dismissed.

Or, if the receiving order ought not to have been made:

1. For the reasons hereinafter appearing I say that the Receiving Order made against me on the Petition of the above-named Petitioning Creditor ought not to have been made.

2. On . . . . 19 . . . ., the day prior to the day fixed for the hearing of the said Petition, a friend of mine, Mr L M, of (*address and description*), interviewed the Petitioning Creditor on my behalf and offered to pay to the Petitioning Creditor out of his own money the amount of my indebtedness as set out in the said Petition together with the taxed or agreed costs of the said Petition as to £. . . . forthwith and the balance within seven days of the dismissal of the said Petition. I was present at the said interview.

3. The Petitioning Creditor agreed to accept the said offer, and the said L M thereupon paid him the said sum of £. . . ., and the Petitioning Creditor undertook to inform his Solicitor of the said terms and to request him to ask this Honourable Court to dismiss the said Petition by consent.

4. Relying upon the said terms and the said undertaking of the Petitioning Creditor, I did not attend the hearing of the said Petition, nor was I represented thereat, and I believed that the said Petition would be dismissed.

5. I have since ascertained that the said Receiving Order was made against me owing to the fact that the Petitioning Creditor left London for the Continent immediately after the said interview, with the result that, owing to inadvertence on the part of the Petitioning Creditor, his Solicitor received no instructions from him prior to the hearing of the said petition and in my absence applied for a Receiving Order to be made against me.

6. The Petitioning Creditor returned to London on . . . . 19 . . ., and I had an interview with him on . . . . 19 . . . ., and he informed me that he had then for the first time heard of the making of the said Receiving Order and instructed his Solicitor to see me and take such steps as were possible to obtain the rescission thereof, which as aforesaid was made entirely owing to the aforesaid reason.

7. I therefore respectfully ask that the said Receiving Order should be rescinded and that the said Petition should be dismissed.]

SWORN at (*address*) this . . . . day of . . . .
19 . . . . before me,
(*Signature*)
A Commissioner for Oaths

(*Deponent's signature*)

NOTICE to Official Receiver of application for rescission of receiving order on payment of debts in full

IN THE [HIGH COURT OF JUSTICE *or* . . . . COUNTY COURT]
In Bankruptcy No. . . . of 19 . . . .
Re A B [*add, after adjudication*, a Bankrupt]

The Debtor having applied to the Court for rescission of the Receiving Order made against him on the ground that he has paid his debts in full, the Court has fixed . . . . 19 . . . . at . . . . o'clock in the [forenoon] for hearing the application.
DATED this . . . . day of . . . . 19 . . . .

(*Signature*)
Registrar

To the Official Receiver

NOTICE of application for rescission of receiving order on ground that it ought not to have been made

IN THE [HIGH COURT OF JUSTICE *or* . . . . COUNTRY COURT]
In Bankruptcy No. . . . of 19 . . . .
Re A B [*add, after adjudication,* a Bankrupt]

TAKE NOTICE that the Court has appointed the . . . . day of . . . . 19 . . . . at . . . . o'clock in the [forenoon] before [Mr Registrar . . . .] at (*address*) to hear the application of the above-named Debtor that the Receiving Order made against him on . . . . 19 . . . . on the petition of B D may be rescinded [on the ground that it ought not to have been made] or otherwise under the powers contained in Secton 108 of the Bankruptcy Act 1914.

The [affidavit of the Debtor], a copy of which is served herewith, will be read in support hereof.

To C D, of (*address*), the [Petitioning Creditor]
and to G H, of (*address*), his Solicitor,
and to the Official Receiver.

ORDER rescinding receiving order

IN THE [HIGH COURT OF JUSTICE *or* . . . . COUNTY COURT]
In Bankruptcy No. . . . of 19 . . . .
Re A B [*add, after adjudication,* a Bankrupt]

UPON THE APPLICATION OF A B of (*address*)
AND UPON READING [the report of the Official Receiver and the affidavit of . . . . filed . . . . 19 . . . .]
AND UPON HEARING [Counsel] *or* the Solicitor] for A B and for . . . .
[AND it appearing to the Court that [all the debts herein have been paid in full *or* the Receiving Order herein ought not to have been made] *or* AND the Court exercising its discretion under Section 108 of the Bankruptcy Act 1914]
IT IS ORDERED that the Receiving Order dated . . . . 19 . . . . against A B (*state name, address and description as in receiving order*) be and the same is hereby rescinded and that the Petition dated . . . . 19 . . . . be and the same is hereby dismissed

AND IT IS FURTHER ORDERED that any balance [remaining in the hands of the

Official Receiver after audit by the Department of Trade and Industry *or* in the Official Receiver's hands after charging a sum of £. . . . to be credited to the Bankruptcy Estates Account in respect of the Official Receiver's services under the Receiving Order and after audit by the Department of Trade and Industry] be paid out to the Debtor or to E F his Solicitor

AND IT IS FURTHER ORDERED that the registration of the Petition as a pending action at the Land Charges Department of HM Land Registry on . . . . 19 . . . . under Reference No . . . . and of the Receiving Order in the register of Writs and Orders affecting land at the said Department on . . . . 19 . . . . under Reference No . . . . be vacated upon application duly made in that behalf by the Debtor under the Land Charges Rules 1974.

DATED this . . . . day of . . . . 19 . . . .

By the Court
Registrar

CHAPTER 6

Adjudication

6.1 INTRODUCTION

6.1.1 It is only after adjudication that the debtor becomes 'the bankrupt'. After a receiving order has been made, but before adjudication, he is able to hold certain offices from which he becomes disqualified on adjudication.

6.1.2 In other respects the adjudication must be contrasted and compared with the receiving order. No order of adjudication can be made unless there has been a receiving order but the effects of each are very different.

6.1.3 Theoretically, several classes of persons can apply for an order of adjudication but, in creditors' petitions, it is almost invariably the official receiver who actually does so.

6.1.4 There is no requirement to give notice of an application for an order of adjudication to the debtor[1] although it is usually given, save in cases where in practice this is impossible, as where, for example, a debtor has absconded.[2]

1 Bankruptcy Act 1914, s 94.
2 See Bankruptcy Rules 1952, r 32(1).

6.1.5 The making of an adjudication order must be advertised by the Department of Trade and Industry in the *London Gazette* and in a local newspaper.[1] The production of a copy of the *London Gazette* containing notice of the order is conclusive evidence in all legal proceedings of the order having been made.[2]

1 Bankruptcy Act 1914, s 18(2).
2 Bankruptcy Act 1914, s 137(2).

6.2 GROUNDS

6.2.1 The official receiver, or any creditor, may apply to the court to adjudge the debtor bankrupt at any time after the receiving order has been made.

The grounds upon which the application may be made are:

(a) that the debtor has absconded;[1]

(b) that the debtor has failed, without reasonable cause, to submit a statement of affairs;[2]

(c) that the debtor does not intend to propose a composition or scheme;[3]

(d) that the creditors have not met;[4]

(e) that a quorum of creditors did not attend the first meeting of creditors or any adjournment of the first meeting of creditors;[5]

(f) that the creditors at the first meeting of creditors or an adjournment of it, by ordinary resolution, resolved that the debtor be adjudged bankrupt, or, that at the meeting they passed no resolution;[6]

(g) that a composition or scheme was not accepted by the creditors at the first meeting of creditors or at any adjournment of it;[7]

(h) that no composition or scheme has been approved by the court within 14 days after the conclusion of the public examination or such further time as the court may allow;[8]

(i) that the court's approval to a sanction or scheme was
  (i) obtained by fraud
  or
  (ii) that a composition or scheme cannot work satisfactorily
  or
  (iii) that default has been made in the payment of an instalment due under a composition or scheme;[9] and

(j) where the public examination of the debtor is adjourned sine die.[10]

1 Bankruptcy Rules 1952, r 218(2)(b).
2 Bankruptcy Act 1914, s 14(3) and Bankruptcy Rules 1952, r 218(2)(c).
3 Bankruptcy Rules 1952, r 218(2).
4 Bankruptcy Act 1914, s 18(1) and Bankruptcy Rules 1952, r 218(2)(c).
5 Bankruptcy Act 1914, Sch 1 para 24 and Bankruptcy Rules 1952, r 218(2)(a).
6 Bankruptcy Act 1914, s 18(1) and Bankruptcy Rules 1952, r 218(2)(c).
7 Bankruptcy Rules 1952, r 219.
8 Bankruptcy Act 1914, s 18(1) and Bankruptcy Rules 1952, r 218(2)(c).
9 Bankruptcy Act 1914, ss 16(16), 21(3) and Bankruptcy Rules 1952, r 218(2)(c).
10 Bankruptcy Rules 1952, r 220.

6.2.2 Even though mandatory words are used in the Bankruptcy Act 1914, it has in fact been held[1] that the court may refuse to adjudicate immediately and can adjourn the proceedings for further enquiries or investigation.

1 *Re Lord Thurlow, ex p Official Receiver* [1895] 1QB 724.

6.2.3 The debtor may consent to the adjudication in which case the official receiver applies ex parte. Alternatively, the debtor may apply himself. If the debtor applies for his own adjudication he may do so orally and without notice[1] and, if he is himself the petitioner, usually does so, or is invited to do so, at the hearing of the petition itself. Thus on the debtor's own petition, he is almost invariably adjudicated at the same time as the receiving order is made.

[1] Bankruptcy Rules 1952, r 217(2).

6.3 THE CONSEQUENCES OF AN ORDER OF ADJUDICATION

6.3.1 Upon the making of an order adjudging the debtor bankrupt his property 'shall become divisible among his creditors and shall vest in a trustee'.[1]

'Property' for the Bankruptcy Act 1914 generally is defined as including:

> 'money, goods, things in action, land and every description of property, whether real or personal and whether situate in England or elsewhere, also obligations, easements, and every description of estate, interest, and profit, present or future, vested or contingent, arising out of or incident to property as above defined.'[2]

The Bankruptcy Act 1914, s 38 refers to 'property' (as defined above) but it recites that, for these purposes, property shall also comprise:

> (a) 'all such property as may belong to or be vested in the bankrupt at the commencement of the bankruptcy or may be acquired by or devolve on him before his discharge', and
> (b) 'all goods being, at the commencement of the bankruptcy, in the possession order or disposition of the bankrupt in his trade or business, by the consent and permission of the true owner, under such circumstances that he is the reputed owner thereof . . .' (the doctrine of reputed ownership).

However, s 38 specifically excludes from this automatic vesting in the trustee the following:

(i) property held by the bankrupt on trust for any other person; and
(ii) tools of trade, clothing and bedding for the bankrupt and his wife and family to a total value of £250.

In fact this last provision is, in reality, not strictly construed and, save in exceptional circumstances, a bankrupt is seldom required to surrender his personal clothing or personal possessions of modest value to his trustee whether the trustee is the official receiver or some other person.

The bankrupt is also entitled to retain his personal earnings up to a reasonable limit required for his maintenance.

[1] Bankruptcy Act 1914, s 18(1).
[2] Bankruptcy Act 1914, s 167.

The doctrine of relation back

6.3.2 Although also dealt with in ch 8 below (Recovery of Assets) it is well to mention this important principle when dealing with adjudication generally. The Bankruptcy Act 1914 provides in effect, that the bankruptcy of a debtor is deemed to relate back to and commence at the time of the act of bankruptcy relied upon or, if there is more than one act of bankruptcy, to the time of the earliest of them which is proved to have been committed within three months of the presentation of the bankruptcy petition.[1]

The property of the bankrupt which is divisible among his creditors comprises, inter alia, all such property as may belong to or be vested in the bankrupt at the commencement of the bankruptcy.[2]

Thus, in practice, the effective date under the Old Bankruptcy Law at which the bankrupt's assets as a whole, become available for his creditors is often many months earlier than the adjudication order. (This is so though it is clearly only the adjudication which can be said to make the debtor 'bankrupt'.)

1 Bankruptcy Act 1914, s 37(1).
2 Ibid, s 38(a).

The doctrine of reputed ownership

6.3.3 The provision in the Bankruptcy Act 1914, 38(c) that the property of the bankrupt includes

> 'all goods being, at the commencement of the bankruptcy, in the possession order and disposition of the bankrupt, in his trade or business, by the consent and permission of the true owner, under such circumstances that he is the reputed owner thereof'

can be traced back as a provision of English law for some 300 years. It was thought desirable, in order to discourage a debtor from being enabled, by means of the possession of the goods of another, 'to obtain false credit'.[1]

As long ago as 1848[2] the court observed that 'the bankrupt law was originally made when commerce was in a very different state' and recent legislation has specifically excluded the sort of items which might commonly be found in a bankrupt's possession, but with 'the permission of the true owner', in a modern business context, for example goods on hire purchase or acquired under a conditional sale agreement.[3]

1 *Re Florence, Ex p Wingfield* (1879) 10 Ch D 591.
2 *Belcher v Bellamy* (1848) 2 Ex Ch 303.
3 The Consumer Credit Act 1974 (Commencement No 8) Order 1983, SI 1983/1551 introduced a new s 38A to the Bankruptcy Act 1914 with effect from 15 May 1985.

Property excluded from the effect of adjudication

6.3.4 Property held by the bankrupt in trust is not property divisible among his creditors and does not vest in the trustee.

When a bankrupt is a trustee, formally so appointed, and where the trust fund in question is clearly identifiable and separate from the bankrupt's estate, no problems should arise. However, the doctrine of reputed ownership (see para 6.3.3 above) can result in an assumption against the bankrupt to the effect that property in his possession at the commencement of the bankruptcy has vested in the trustee. It is necessary in such circumstances to examine the facts in order to ascertain whether the property in question can be established to be trust property or not.

In such circumstances

> 'the Courts of Equity are very astute in distinguishing and tracing trust funds however much their character or nature may be altered, provided that what is found in the possession of the bankrupt trustee can be clearly identified.'[1]

[1] *Williams & Muir Hunter* (19th edn) p 260 citing *Re Strachan, ex p Cooke* (1876) 4 Ch D 123. See also *Re Diplock, Diplock v Wintle* [1948] Ch 465.

6.3.5 If it becomes necessary to trace trust monies then there is a presumption, in examining expenditure upon himself by the bankrupt, that he has expended his own monies rather than any trust money he may be holding.[1] Thus, the rule in *Clayton's* case (which need not be discussed here) is supervened by this approach to an examination of trust funds held by a bankrupt.

[1] *Re Hallet's Estate, Knatchbull v Hallett* (1879) 13 Ch D 696.

6.3.6 By far the most commonly held trusteeship held by a bankrupt is that relating to the trust for sale on which his matrimonial home is held. Chapter 22 below deals specifically with the matrimonial home.

6.3.7 The Bankruptcy Act 1914 provides[1] that certain pensions and salaries be retained by the bankrupt and do not pass to the trustee.

[1] Bankruptcy Act 1914, ss 50 and 51.

6.3.8 That part of the bankrupt's personal earnings which he needs for his own support, and that of his wife and family, do not pass to the trustee but any earnings, even after adjudication, in excess of his personal needs do vest in the trustee and should be handed over to the trustee by the bankrupt.[1] On the other hand the profits of a business carried on by the bankrupt are treated differently and should theoretically pass to the trustee without deduction.[2] In practice, under the Old Bankruptcy Law, trustees very seldom pursue bankrupts in respect of the bankrupt's earnings after adjudication. However, the question of whether or not a bankrupt has made voluntary payments to his trustees throughout the bankruptcy, is often very relevant when the court comes to consider an application by the bankrupt for his discharge (see ch 10 below).

[1] *Re Roberts* [1900] 1 QB 122.
[2] *Re Rogers, ex p Collins* [1894] 1 QB 425.

6.3.9 Certain causes of action do not vest in the trustee. In summary, a cause of action, whether in contract or tort, will not vest if it is personal to the bankrupt in that it affects his physical person[1] or his feelings[2] or reputation.

If a cause of action is available both for the benefit of the estate of the bankrupt and for his personal benefit, it must be split between the two, as for example in a claim for damages following an accident when the general damages for pain and suffering will not pass but the special damages for loss of earnings will.[3]

[1] Eg damages for assault, *Beckham v Drake* (1849) 2 HL Cas 579.
[2] *Wilson v United Counties Bank Ltd* [1920] AC 102.
[3] *Wilson v United Counties Bank Ltd* (supra). Where damages for negligence in running the bankrupt's business vested in trustee but damages for bankrupt's injured reputation did not.

6.3.10 As indicated above the £250 limit on value of tools of bankrupt's trade is not strictly enforced. In fact it increased from £20 under the Bankruptcy Act 1914 to £250 as a result of an amendment made by the Insolvency Act 1976. Nevertheless, inflation has made the current figure unrealistic.

Papers and documents cannot be said to be 'tools of trade'[1] but it has been suggested[2] that a 'writer's typewriter or dictating machine' could. The Old Bankruptcy Law moved slowly and, over the years, with the Insolvency Act 1986 in force, it will become of academic interest only. The court has not yet had to consider the typewriter and it remains to be seen whether the calculator or computer will be put to the test in deciding whether or not they can be 'tools of trade'.

[1] *Re Sherman* (1915) 32 TLR 231.
[2] *Williams & Muir Hunter* (19th edn) p 280.

6.4 THE DISQUALIFICATIONS

6.4.1 The Bankruptcy Act 1914 is the only statute which imposes an automatic disqualification of any sort upon the making of a receiving order. It provides that a person against whom a receiving order has been made cannot be a trustee in bankruptcy.[1]

All the other statutes (including parts of an earlier Bankruptcy Act still in force today) impose their various disqualifications upon a person being or becoming a 'bankrupt', that is to say, upon his being adjudicated bankrupt.

[1] Bankruptcy Act 1914, s 94.

6.4.2 The most important such disqualifications are:

6.4.2.1 *Company directors.* It is a criminal offence for a bankrupt to act, whether formally appointed or not, as a director of a company or, directly or indirectly, be concerned in the management of any company, save with the leave of the court.[1] The court empowered to give such leave is the court by which he was adjudged bankrupt and notice of any such application must be given to the official receiver, who must report to the court, and, if he is of the opinion that it is contrary to the public interest that the application be granted, attend the hearing and oppose it. The bankrupt must be served with a copy of the official receiver's report not less than seven days before the date fixed for the hearing of the application.[2]

[1] Company Directors Disqualification Act 1986, s 11.
[2] Bankruptcy Rules 1952, r 238.

6.4.2.2 *Receivers.* It is a criminal offence for an undischarged bankrupt to act as a receiver or manager of the property of a company without leave of the court.[1]

[1] Company Directors Disqualification Act 1986, s 11.

6.4.2.3 *Solicitors.* An adjudication in bankruptcy of a solicitor operates immediately to suspend the solicitor's practising certificate.[1] The suspension continues until the practising certificate expires, annually in the ordinary way, or until the adjudication is annulled and the order of annulment served on The Law Society.[2] Adjudication of a solicitor is also a ground for The Law Society to 'intervene' in a solicitor's practice by the appointment of an agent.[3]

After a receiving order is made, but before adjudication, The Law Society has a discretion with respect to the issue of a practising certificate but any existing certificate remains in force until renewal is applied for.[4]

[1] Solicitors Act 1974, s 15(1).
[2] Solicitors Act 1974, s 16.
[3] See Solicitors Act 1974, s 35 and Schedule 1.
[4] Solicitors Act 1974, s 12.

6.4.2.4 *Elected officers.* An undischarged bankrupt cannot be elected to, nor act as a member of a local authority or be elected to sit or vote in either House of Parliament.[1]

[1] Local Government Act 1972, s 80(1)(6).

6.4.2.5 *JP.* An undischarged bankrupt is disqualified from being appointed or acting as a justice of the peace.[1]

[1] Bankruptcy Act 1883, s 32(1)(a) and (b).

6.5 THE APPOINTMENT OF TRUSTEE IN BANKRUPTCY AND THE COMMITTEE OF INSPECTION

6.5.1 Chapter 4 deals with the trustee in bankruptcy but it is necessary to record here that when a debtor is adjudged bankrupt the creditors may, by ordinary resolution, appoint 'some fit person' to fill the office of trustee.[1] If no one is so appointed, the official receiver automatically becomes trustee.[2]

[1] Bankruptcy Act 1914, s 19.
[2] Ibid, s 53(1).

6.5.2 In fact the appointment of the trustee need not be made by the creditors. They can delegate the appointment to the committee of inspection.[1] However, the committee of inspection itself is appointed by the creditors. The Bankruptcy Act 1914, s 20(1) provides:

> 'The Creditors qualified to vote may, at their first or any subsequent meeting, by resolution appoint a Committee of Inspection for the purposes of superintending the administration of the bankrupt's property by the Trustee.'

[1] Bankruptcy Act 1914, s 19(1).

6.5.3 The appointment of a committee of inspection is not a necessity although it usually happens if a trustee other than the official receiver is appointed. If no committee of inspection is formed, the Department of Trade performs the functions which would otherwise be exercised by such committee.[1] In practice, the Department of Trade delegates the function to the official receiver.[2]

[1] Bankruptcy Act 1914, s 20(10).
[2] Bankruptcy Rules 1952, r 328.

6.5.4 The Bankruptcy Act 1914, s 20 provides that, in relation to a committee of inspection:
(a) that it shall consist of not less than three nor more than five members;
(b) to qualify as a member, a person must be a creditor or hold a general proxy or power of attorney from a creditor. (The creditor's proof must have been admitted); and
(c) that it should act by the majority attending the meeting but that it shall not act at all unless a majority of the committee attend a meeting.

6.5.5 Members of a committee of inspection may not, without the court's leave, profit in any way from the estate of the bankrupt nor may they, without the leave of the court, purchase any part of the estate.

The committee member is in a fiduciary position.[1] Thus, if there is any question of solicitors or agents of a creditor acting for a trustee in bankruptcy, then that solicitor or agent should not be an attorney or proxy nominated by a creditor to sit on the committee of inspection.

The functions of the committee of inspection are:
(a) to sanction those acts done by the trustee which require such sanction, namely:
  (i) carrying on business;
  (ii) taking or defending or settling litigation or an arbitration;
  (iii) compounding with a creditor or person claiming to be a creditor;
  (iv) distributing in specie;
  (v) allowing the bankrupt to manage his own property or making the bankrupt an allowance; and
  (vi) opening a bank account other than with the Bank of England; and
(b) to inspect and audit the trustee's accounts.[2]

[1] Bankruptcy Rules 1952, rr 349, 350; *Re Bulmer, ex p Greaves* [1937] Ch 499.
[2] Bankruptcy Rules 1952, rr 364, 367 and 368.

6.5.6 The trustee may summon meetings when he thinks fit (as can a committee member).[1] In practice, although the Bankruptcy Act 1914 provides for monthly meetings in default of the committee fixing dates, meetings are usually only convened when a trustee needs sanction for a particular course of action requiring sanction.

[1] Bankruptcy Act 1914, s 20(3).

6.5.7 The creditors in general meeting can overrule a committee decision[1] and can remove a committee member.[2]

[1] *Re Ridgeway, ex p Hurlbatt* (1889) 6 TLR 21.
[2] See Bankruptcy Act 1914, s 20(7).

CHAPTER 7

The Public Examination and Conduct of the Bankrupt

7.1 INTRODUCTION

7.1.1 The principle behind the public examination is that it gives an opportunity for the official receiver, the trustee (if appointed by then) and the creditors to obtain information about the bankrupt, his estate, his conduct and dealings generally in the relevant periods leading up to the commencement of his bankruptcy.

7.1.2 A useful outline summary of the court's role in relation to the public examination has been given as follows:

> 'The Public Examination is held before an Officer of the Court for the purpose and the sole purpose of the debtor being examined. Nothing is to be determined or concluded against him or for him upon the examination. The Court is only collecting from him evidence upon which it may afterwards act with regard to him in such manner as it thinks fit. The examination is a mere mode of obtaining evidence from the bankrupt himself. The registrar is to control the examination; but he has no power to call witnesses. He has only to sit there and control the examination and to collect the answers of the debtor to the questions put to him. The Registrar must no doubt determine whether the questions which it is proposed to put to the debtor are proper questions or whether they are or are not put in a proper form. The Registrar has to regulate the examination – to determine what questions are properly put and what questions cannot be put and to enforce upon the debtor, as far as he can, at that time, in that place, and for that purpose, his obligation to answer; but it is a mere mode of collecting evidence.'[1]

1 *Re Cronmire, ex p Cronmire* [1894] 2 QB 246.

7.2 THE INSOLVENCY ACT 1976, s 6

7.2.1 If the official receiver applies for such an order[1] the court may direct that the public examination of a bankrupt should be dispensed with .[2]

1 Insolvency Act 1976, s 6(2).
2 If an order is made that the public examination be dispensed with the various provisions of the legislation which provide for things to be done before or after the conclusion of the public examination shall be deemed to relate to the date on which such an order is made.

7.2.2 In deciding whether or not it should make such an order, the court is required to have regard to the following circumstances of the bankrupt's case;[1]

(a) whether he has made a full disclosure of his affairs;
(b) whether he has been bankrupt before;
(c) the number and nature of his debts; and
(d) whether or not the bankruptcy would be a matter of public concern.

[1] Insolvency Act 1976, s 6(1)(a) and (d).

7.2.3 The fact that it is the official receiver who must apply for an order means that, in practice, certain criteria are applied in deciding which cases are considered relevant for such applications. No guidelines are published but it is generally recognised that different tests apply in different parts of the country.

In the High Court (that is to say, generally, for London cases) the view is taken that there is 'public concern' in any case in which the Inland Revenue or the Commissioners of Customs and Excise are creditors.[1] In practice, this means that in High Court cases, the official receiver applies for dispensation in relatively few cases.

In other parts of the country the practice varies widely. In a busy area such as, for example, Croydon, Surrey, there is a significant proportion of cases in which such applications are made. No reliable guidelines can be recorded but it is thought that public examinations are dispensed with in over three-quarters of cases outside London. In London, they are seldom dispensed with at all.

[1] And it should be borne in mind that the Crown has the privilege of being able to present all its petitions in the High Court.

7.2.4 The court's power to review or rescind any of its own orders[1] is expressly retained in connection with the provisions of the Insolvency Act 1976, s 6. However, since it is only the official receiver who can apply for an order dispensing with the public examination, an effective review can only take place after the official receiver has thought it appropriate to apply for dispensation in the first place.

Thus, the bankrupt might apply for a review under the Bankruptcy Act 1914, s 108 if the official receiver's application is refused and a creditor or the trustee may apply for a review if the public examination is dispensed with. However, if the official receiver does not even think it appropriate to apply in the first place, no review or appeal appears to be available.

[1] See Bankruptcy Act 1914, s 108(1).

7.3 CALLING THE MEETING AND THE BANKRUPT'S ATTENDANCE

7.3.1 The Act provides[1] that the public examination shall be held 'as soon as conveniently may be after the expiration of the time for the submission of the debtor's statement of affairs'. Since that time expires, in the case of the debtor's own petition, after three days and, in the case of a creditor's petition, after seven days, from the making of the receiving order,[2] the theory is that the public examination should take place very early on in the bankruptcy and probably before adjudication.

In practice, however, save in very simple cases, few debtors get their statement of affairs finalised in the time allotted and most public examinations take place several weeks, or months, after the receiving order is made. Practice, in this respect, differs in different parts of England and Wales.

[1] Bankruptcy Act 1914, s 15(2).
[2] Ibid, s 14(2).

7.3.2 The official receiver liaises with the court over the fixing of a date and time for the public examination and it is the official receiver's duty to notify the debtor, the creditors and the Department of Trade of the time, date and place fixed. He must also advertise the hearing in a local newspaper.[1]

[1] Bankruptcy Rules 1952, rr 188 and 189.

7.3.3 The court may issue a warrant for the arrest of the bankrupt, or order a seizure of any of his books, papers, money or goods for safe keeping, if 'without good cause shown' he fails to attend his public examination.[1]

[1] Bankruptcy Act 1914, s 23(1)(d).

7.3.4 In the High Court, it is invariably (and in the county court almost invariably) the registrar of the court who holds the public examination.[1]

[1] See Bankruptcy Act 1914, s 102(2)(b).

7.3.5 Apart from the provisions of the Insolvency Act 1976, power is given to the court to dispense with the public examination if the bankrupt suffers from a mental or physical affliction or disability which justifies dispensing with it. It can also direct that the public examination takes place on such terms and in such manner as it thinks expedient in all the cirumstances,[1] for example, at the bankrupt's home or at some other venue.

If the court decides to dispense with the public examination it can, nevertheless, order a private examination under the provisions of Bankruptcy Act 1914, s 25.

[1] Bankruptcy Act 1914, s 15(10).

7.4 THE HEARING

7.4.1 The public examination proceeds in open court.[1] The official receiver, appearing in person,[2] and the trustee, if one has been appointed by this stage, and all creditors who have proved, being entitled to attend in person and put questions, or be represented by a person 'authorised in writing'. In a criminal bankruptcy, the official petitioner may attend.[3] Attendance is usually by solicitors or counsel[4] but is not necessarily so.

[1] Bankruptcy Rules 1952, r 8(1)(a).
[2] He has power to employ solicitors and counsel if authorised by the Department of Trade. Bankruptcy Act 1914, s 15(5).
[3] See ch 23 below.
[4] See Bankruptcy Act 1914, s 15(4).

7.4.2 The bankrupt is examined on oath and the court keeps such notes of the examination as it thinks proper. There is usually a shorthand writer. These notes must, at the conclusion of the examination, or at some later date, must be read over to, or read by, the bankrupt who must sign them.[1] The signed notes must be open to inspection by the creditors at all reasonable times.[1] They are kept on the court file.

[1] Bankruptcy Act 1914, s 15(8).

7.4.3 The bankrupt has no right to refuse to answer a question on the grounds that it might incriminate him.[1] He must answer all questions unless they are disallowed by the court.

In general a question will only be disallowed if the court is satisfied that the answer could not secure any further assets or rights for the estate.[2] Thus, a bankrupt may be forced to provide details of a secret formula or disclose hitherto secret sources of information or profits.[3]

[1] See *Re Paget* [1927] 2 Ch 85; *Re Jawett* [1929] 1 Ch 108; *R v Erdheim* [1896] 2 QB 260.
[2] *Re Paget, ex p Official Receiver* [1927] 2 Ch 85.
[3] *Re Keene* [1922] 2 Ch 475; *Re Jawett* [1929] 1 Ch 108.

7.4.4 The usual practice of the official receiver is to put to the bankrupt, in question and answer form, the information, if it is relevant, which his staff has already obtained at the preliminary examination which took place immediately or soon after the receiving order was made. He is not confined to this information but the preliminary examination notes are an obvious 'proof of evidence' for the purpose of the public examination.

7.4.5 The public examination cannot be concluded until after the first meeting of the creditors.[1] Thus, questions of the bankrupt which may arise as a result of the proceedings at the first meeting of creditors can be put to the bankrupt.

Similarly, the public examination must be concluded before an application to approve a composition or scheme of arrangement can be heard.[2] Thus, creditors have an opportunity of making whatever enquiries they think appropriate of the bankrupt before deciding whether to support a scheme or composition.

[1] Bankruptcy Act 1914, s 159; *Re Williams* (1884) 1 Morr 91.
[2] Bankruptcy Act 1914, s 16(6).

7.4.6 When the court is satisfied that the bankrupt's affairs have been investigated sufficiently, it must order that the public examination be concluded.[1]

It has power to adjourn the public examination as often as is necessary to ensure a sufficient investigation.[2] It can also adjourn the public examination sine die, as it does for example where the debtor fails to attend and cannot be found. One consequence of such an adjournment is that it is a ground, in itself, for an application for an order of adjudication. Another consequence of an adjournment sine die is that it prevents the bankrupt applying for a discharge.[3]

1 *Re Cronmire, ex p Cronmire* [1894] 2 QB 246 and Bankruptcy Act 1914, s 15(9).
2 Bankruptcy Act 1914, s 16(3).
3 See ch 10 below.

7.4.7 At the conclusion of the public examination, the court may make an order directing that the bankrupt shall enjoy an automatic discharge.[1]

1 See ch 10 below.

7.5 THE EFFECT OF THE BANKRUPT'S EVIDENCE

7.5.1 The most practical use for the notes taken at a public examination is for the official receiver when he is reviewing the bankruptcy as a whole for the purpose of his report under the Bankruptcy Act 1914, s 26 on an application by the bankrupt for discharge.[1]

1 See ch 10 below.

7.5.2 The evidence given by the bankrupt at his public examination may be used against him and, indeed, is admissable against him even in criminal proceedings.[1] However, it is not admissable against other parties, even in proceedings in the bankruptcy.[2]

1 *Re Robinson* (1867) LR 1 CCR 80.
2 *Re Brunner* (1887) 19 QBD 572.

7.6 THE CONDUCT OF THE BANKRUPT

7.6.1 Certain of the 'offences', that is to say criminal offences, which arise in bankruptcy can be committed in respect of activities which took place before the bankruptcy petition itself was presented. These activities become relevant for these purposes if a receiving order is subsequently made against the debtor. They are set out in the Bankruptcy Act 1914, s 154. It would be dangerous to try and summarise some 16 different criminal offences and the whole of the Bankruptcy Act 1914, s 154 is therefore set out in para 3.9 above. In general terms the s 154 offences are the concealment, removal, gift or transfer of property and the destruction, falsification or disposal of books of account or documents of record.

7.6.2 The debtor's responsibilities and duties on the making of the receiving order against him have already been discussed in para 3.4 above.

7.6.3 In addition to these duties, the Bankruptcy Act 1914 imposes a specific duty on the bankrupt to do the utmost in his power to assist the official receiver or his trustee in the realisation of his property and its distribution among his creditors.[1]

It is a contempt of court on the part of the bankrupt if he wilfully fails to perform his duty.[2] It has even been suggested[3] that the duty imposed on the bankrupt extends to a requirement that the bankrupt should, if necessary, release his solicitor, or former solicitor, from the solicitor's duty of privilege in respect of the bankrupt's affairs.

[1] Bankruptcy Act 1914, s 22(3).
[2] Ibid, s 22(4).
[3] See *Williams & Muir Hunter* (19th edn) p 108 and *The Law Society's Guide to Professional Conduct of Solicitors* (1974) para 11.2(g).

7.6.4 In order to assist in the provision of a satisfactory explanation of the manner in which any loss has been suffered, the official receiver is entitled to request the bankrupt to furnish trading and profit and loss accounts and a cash and goods account for a period of up to two years preceding the receiving order.[1] The court may order such an account to be prepared. This is often ordered at the hearing of the public examination if it is clear from the answers given by the bankrupt that an explanation will not emerge without such an order.

[1] Bankruptcy Rules 1952, r 329.

7.6.5 It is an offence[1] for the bankrupt to fail to give a satisfactory explanation of the manner in which a loss, or any substantial part of it, was suffered within a year preceding the bankruptcy petition. This is an absolute offence for which the bankrupt may be convicted even if he has used his best endeavours to offer an explanation.[2]

[1] Bankruptcy Act 1914, s 157(c).
[2] *R v Salter* [1968] 2 QB 793.

7.6.6 *Obtaining credit.* The disqualifications which are suffered by a bankrupt are set out in para 6.4 above. These disqualifications necessarily affect the conduct of a certain, small, number of persons who go bankrupt.

However, by far the single most significant restraint on the conduct and way of life of a bankrupt is that concerning his ability to enjoy credit. Whereas much of the Old Bankruptcy Law is still directed at a system of trading and commerce which simply no longer exists, the restriction on obtaining credit is, in practical effect, much more inhibiting than it used to be. In the day of the credit card and bank overdraft, it can be surprisingly difficult *not* to obtain credit, even unwittingly and the offence[1] is an absolute offence, and is committed even if the bankrupt does not know that he has obtained credit.[2]

Under the Bankruptcy Act 1914, s 155, an undischarged bankrupt will be guilty of an offence if, alone or jointly with another person, he obtains £50 without disclosing to the person from whom he obtains such credit that he is an undischarged bankrupt. The disclosure of the bankrupt's state need only be notified to the person once; it need not be reiterated whenever credit is obtained.[3]

Despite the absence of any mens rea requirement in s 155, and the court's decisions concerning the absolute nature of the offence, it is clear from more recent decisions that the bankrupt has to do something to obtain the credit, even if it is only to establish a trading relationship with a person as a result of which credit is given.

'Credit' is given a fairly wide interpretation. For example, a bankrupt obtains credit if he takes a letting of property on the basis that rent is paid in arrears.

For a variety of cases on this subject see the notes below.[4] Of the 276 different offences for which 153 prosecutions were taken to conviction (with no acquittals) in 1984, 151 were charges under the Bankruptcy Act 1914, s 155.[5]

1 Under the Bankruptcy Act 1914, s 155.
2 *R v Duke of Leinster* [1924] 1 KB 311.
3 *R v Zeitlin* (1932) 23 Cr App Rep 163.
4 *R v Hayat* (1976) 120 Sol Jo 434; *R v Juy* (1886) 55 LT 788; *R v Hartley* [1972] 2 QB 1; *R v Fryer* (1912) 7 Cr App Rep 183; *Fisher v Raven* [1964] AC 210; *R v Smith* (1915) 11 Cr App Rep 81; *De Choisy v Hynes* [1937] 4 All ER 54.
5 141 convictions were under s 155(a) (obtaining credit) and 10 were for undischarged bankrupts trading under another name (*Department of Trade General Annual Report for the Year 1984*).

7.6.7 *Engaging in trade.* It is an offence for an undischarged bankrupt to engage in any trade or business under a name other than that under which he was adjudicated bankrupt without disclosing to all those with whom he transacts business the name under which he was adjudicated.[1]

1 Bankruptcy Act 1914, s 155(1); and see *R v Doubleday* (1964) 49 Cr App Rep 62.

7.6.8 Sections 156 (as amended), (disposal or concealment of property to defraud creditors), 157 (rash or hazardous speculation or gambling), 158 (failure to keep proper accounts) and 159 (absconding with property) are the other statutory offences in the Bankruptcy Act 1914, Part VII.

In respect of these, or any of the other bankruptcy offences, the procedure is[1] that the official receiver, or trustee, reports to any court exercising jurisdiction in bankruptcy that, in his opinion, a bankrupt or a debtor against whom a receiving order has been made, has been guilty of an offence under the Bankruptcy Act 1914. Alternatively, a creditor or member of the committee of inspection may apply. In this case, he must persuade the court that there is ground to believe that an offence has been committed.

In either case the bankruptcy court must order prosecution if there is a reasonable possibility that the debtor will be convicted and if the circumstances are such as to render a prosecution desirable. When a prosecution is ordered by the court, it must be instituted and carried on by the Director of Public Prosecutions[2] except where the order is based on the report of the official receiver and has been applied for by him, when the Department of Trade, or the official receiver himself, may institute and carry on the proceedings (so long as they are before a court of summary jurisdiction and nothing renders it desirable to the Department of Trade that the proceedings be in the hands of the Director of Public Prosecutions).[2]

[1] Bankruptcy Act 1914, s 161 (as amended by Bankruptcy (Amendment) Act 1926).
[2] Bankruptcy Act 1914, s 165.

7.6.9 In the majority of bankruptcies of course, criminal behaviour has not taken place. However, the conduct of the bankrupt is or may be relevant to any application made by the bankrupt, particularly where the discretion of the court is to be exercised. The most common example of such an application is the application for discharge under the Old Bankruptcy Law at which the official receiver has to report to the court, not only on the s 26 facts, but on the course of the bankruptcy generally.[1]

In other applications, however, for example for leave to act as a director of a limited company,[2] it can only assist the court for the official receiver or trustee to be able to report that the bankrupt has been co-operative and helpful throughout the proceedings.

[1] See ch 10 below.
[2] Company Directors Disqualification Act 1986, s 11.

CHAPTER 8

Recovery of Assets

8.1 INTRODUCTION

8.1.1 The appointment of the trustee in bankruptcy is dealt with in ch 4 above while the manner in which the bankrupt's property vests in him as trustee is covered under 'Adjudication' in ch 6 above.

8.1.2 One of the principal assets in most bankruptcies is the bankrupt's home, usually properly described as the matrimonial home. The law in that connection is discussed as a separate subject in ch 22 below.

8.1.3 The case of *Re Condon, ex p James*[1] should always be borne in mind if a set of unusual circumstances arises in which it appears that unfairly, or unreasonably, a trustee is seeking to make a recovery which, in all the circumstances, a 'high minded and honourable person' would not.[2] In essence, the case should prohibit a trustee from taking advantage of a right, if to do so, it would be inconsistent with natural justice.[3]

1 (1874) 9 Ch App 609.
2 *Re Tyler, ex p Official Receiver* [1907] 1 KB 865.
3 *Re Wigzell, ex p Hart* [1921] 2 KB 835.

8.2 THE DOCTRINE OF RELATION BACK

8.2.1 The trustee in bankruptcy's title to the property of the bankrupt relates back to, and commences from the time of the commission of the act of bankruptcy on which the receiving order, leading to the adjudication, is made.

If the bankrupt has committed more than one act of bankruptcy, the date of commencement is the time of the first act of bankruptcy within three months preceding the presentation of the bankruptcy petition.[1]

[1] Bankruptcy Act 1914, s 37.

8.2.2 In consequence, dealings with the bankrupt's property between the date of the act of bankruptcy and the bankrupt's adjudication, when the property of the bankrupt vests in the trustee (be it the official receiver or separate trustee) are ineffective and invalid against the trustee. Thus, the trustee is able to upset the transaction in question and regain for the estate the property concerned.

8.2.3 One of the important applications of the doctrine of relation back (and perhaps the most common mistake made by creditors or their advisers who overlook it) is that it enables the trustee to recover payments made by the bankrupt to his petitioning creditor during the period in which, hoping he might avoid bankruptcy, he makes part payments in reduction of his debt. Most creditors are content to accept payments on account but are very unhappy to find that such 'recoveries' must come back into the estate for the benefit of the creditors as a whole[1] if they proceed to pursue the debtor into bankruptcy.

The principle, quite simply, is that a man who has committed an act of bankruptcy is not entitled to deal with his estate.[2] He may, however, put his solicitor in funds for the purpose of defending or opposing the bankruptcy proceedings themselves. This is discussed in more detail in ch 26 'Solicitors acting in bankruptcy matters' below.

[1] See for example, *Re Ashwell, ex p Salaman* [1912] 1 KB 390.
[2] *See Ponsford Baker & Co v Union of London and Smiths Bank Ltd* [1906] 2 Ch 444.

8.2.4 The court will, in appropriate cases, assist a trustee in the recovery of assets. By way of example, the court will rescind a previous dismissal of a prior petition (exercising its powers under the Bankruptcy Act 1914, s 108(1)) and thus extend the period available for the application of the doctrine of relation back, thus enabling a trustee to recover funds paid over to that original petitioning creditor.[1]

[1] *Re Thomas, ex p IRC v Falconer* [1984] 1 WLR 232.

8.3 EXCEPTIONS TO THE DOCTRINE OF RELATION BACK

8.3.1 As long as the transaction in question takes place before the date of the receiving order[1] and the other party to the transaction did not, at the time of the transaction, have notice of any available act of bankruptcy committed by the bankrupt before that time[2] the following are excluded from the effects of the doctrine of relation back:

(a) payments by the bankrupt to any of his creditors;[3]
(b) any deliveries or payments *to* the bankrupt;[4]
(c) any conveyance or assignment by the bankrupt for valuable consideration;[5] and
(d) any contract dealing or transaction by or with the bankrupt for valuable consideration.[6]

If a purchaser of real property takes a conveyance from the bankrupt with notice of an act of bankruptcy he is, nevertheless caught by the doctrine of relation back even if the *contract* for that conveyance was made for valuable consideration at a time when he did not have notice.[7]

[1] Bankruptcy Act 1914, s 45, proviso (i).
[2] Ibid, s 45, proviso (ii).
[3] Ibid, s 45(a).
[4] Ibid, s 45(b).
[5] Ibid, s 45(c), and see *Re Wethered, ex p Salaman* [1926] Ch 167.
[6] Bankruptcy Act 1914, s 45(d).
[7] *Powell v Marshall, Parkes & Co* [1899] 1 QB 710.

8.3.2 An available act of bankruptcy is any act of bankruptcy available for the presentation of a petition at the date the actual petition was presented.[1]

Notice of an act of bankruptcy can be actual or constructive. When an act of bankruptcy has in fact been committed, any communication of it in a way in which a reasonable man would believe an act of bankruptcy had been committed is sufficient notice for these purposes.[2]

[1] See Bankruptcy Act 1914, s 167.
[2] *See Hope v Meek* (1855) 10 Exch 829.

8.3.3 Even with notice of an act of bankruptcy, a payment of money or delivery of property *to* a person who is subsequently adjudicated bankrupt, or his assignee, escapes application of the doctrine of relation back if it is made in the ordinary course of business or is otherwise bona fide[1] provided that it is made before the receiving order is made.[2]

[1] For an example of the application of 'otherwise bona fide' see *Re Dalton, ex p Herrington and Carmichael v Trustee* [1963] Ch 336.
[2] Bankruptcy Act 1914, s 46.

8.3.4 If a third person makes a payment of money or transfer of property belonging to the bankrupt to a third party after a receiving order has been made in circumstances in which, in normal course, the transfer is void against the trustee, then, so long as the transferor or payor was without notice of the making of the receiving order, the trustee in bankruptcy can only make recovery against the payor or transferor if he can satisfy the court that it is not reasonably practicable to make recovery from the person to whom it was paid or transferred.[1] The most practical application of this principle is the protection it affords to banks which pay out on cheques drawn by the bankrupt and which are presented for payment after the receiving order but before the bank has notice of it.

The exception is only available for the period up to the gazetting of the receiving order under the Bankruptcy Act 1914, s 11.

[1] Bankruptcy (Amendment) Act 1926, s 4.

8.3.5 All these exceptions to the doctrine of relation back are qualified by the requirement that the person claiming entitlement to the exception must have acted in good faith.

8.4 FRAUDULENT PREFERENCE

8.4.1 Theoretically payments or transfers which are technically fraudulent preferences are also, in themselves, available acts of bankruptcy[1] but in practice they were seldom ever relied on as such.

[1] Bankruptcy Act 1914, s 1(1)(c) and see ch 1 above.

8.4.2 In the first place it must be appreciated that despite the description invariably given to it, a fraudulent preference does not necessarily mean that the bankrupt, or the party receiving a payment or transfer from him, has behaved fraudulently, or even improperly. It has often been said that better expressions or titles for such transactions would be 'undue preference' or 'voidable preference'.[1] The relevant section[2] of the Bankruptcy Act 1914 merely says that such transactions shall 'be deemed fraudulent' whilst the expression has gone altogether in New Law cases: see ch 20 below.

If a transaction is deemed a fraudulent preference in an Old Law case, or where the Old Law continues to apply (see ch 20 below) then it is void against the trustee in bankruptcy.

[1] See *Re Patrick and Lyon Ltd* [1933] Ch 786.
[2] Bankruptcy Act 1914, s 44 (as amended).

8.4.3 Every transfer of property, payment or charge of property made by a debtor who is unable to pay his debts from his own money as they fall due, and made 'with a view' to giving the receiver of the payment or charge a preference over the debtor's other creditors, shall be void against a trustee in bankruptcy if the debtor is adjudged bankrupt on a bankruptcy petition presented within six months[1] after the date of the transfer, payment or charge.[2] The precise wording of s 44 extends to the bankrupt submitting to a judgment or incurring an obligation and to assisting a guarantor or surety.

[1] A month is a calendar month: Interpretation Act 1978, Sch 1.
[2] Bankruptcy Act 1914, s 44 (as amended).

8.4.4 In order to avoid a transaction as a fraudulent preference, and, therefore, to be able to recover the money or property transferred by the bankrupt, it is usually necessary for the trustee to show that the relationship of debtor and creditor existed between the bankrupt and the receiving party (unless the person who is designed to benefit is a guarantor).

8.4.5 If a transaction is to be avoided as a fraudulent preference it is necessary for the trustee to prove (and the onus is on him[1]) that it was carried out 'with a view' of giving the creditor a preference over the other creditors.

[1] *Re Marsden, ex p Lancaster* (1883) 25 Ch D 311; *Re Cohen, ex p Trustee* [1924] 2 Ch 515.

8.4.6 In deciding whether or not the bankrupt undertook the relevant transaction with such a view the court will decide what was his knowledge of his affairs and what were his intentions when the relevant payment was made. A payment is made 'with a view' of preferring the payee if the debtor/payor at the time of making the payment knew that he could not pay his debts as they arose, and intended to pay one of his creditors ahead of the others.[1] It matters not that he thought he might have been able to pay the others in due course. It is his knowledge and intention at the time of the payment which is crucial.[1]

On the other hand, even if in fact the debtor/payor could not pay his debts in full he does not commit a fraudulent preference if he is unaware of the fact at the time of making the payment or disposal and was and is not therefore making it 'with a view' of preferring the payee.[2]

[1] *Re FP and CH Matthews Ltd* [1982] Ch 257.
[2] *Re M Kushler Ltd* [1943] Ch 248.

8.4.7 Proving an intention by the payor is often difficult but it has been held that the court is entitled to draw the inference of an intention to prefer a creditor from the surrounding facts.[1]

[1] *Re Cutts, ex p Bognor Mutual Building Society v Trustee in Bankruptcy* [1956] 2 All ER 537.

8.4.8 At the time of entering into the transaction the bankrupt must have been unable to pay his debts as they became due, that is to say he must have been what is commonly regarded as insolvent. When this is in doubt the trustee can encounter some difficulty in proving the position. The exercise often requires a reconstruction of the bankrupt's financial position on a certain date, not always, in practice, very easy.

8.5 AVOIDANCE OF ASSIGNMENTS OF BOOK DEBTS[1]

8.5.1 Whenever it has been made, a trustee in bankruptcy may avoid an assignment by the bankrupt of any book debts which have not been paid at the commencement of the bankruptcy. He is entitled to avoid such an assignment if:
(a) the bankrupt was engaged in trade or business; and
(b) the assignment is not registered under the Bills of Sale Act 1878.

There is a proviso to protect a bona fide sale of a business, or a particular contract, or series of contracts in the business.[2]

[1] Bankruptcy Act 1914, s 43.
[2] Ibid, s 43(2).

8.5.2 This effective right of recovery extends to assignments by way of charge as well as to absolute assignments, although it would not appear to extend to the assignment of the benefit of a contingency as opposed to future book debt.[1]

[1] See *Re Brush Aggregates Ltd* (1983) 127 Sol Jo 285.

8.5.3 A trustee may make practical use of this provision when a bankrupt has in the course of his business, assigned his debts to a factoring company.

8.6 AVOIDANCE OF 'SETTLEMENTS'[1]

8.6.1 The provisions of the Bankruptcy Act 1914, s 42(1) are designed primarily to enable a trustee to frustrate attempts made by a bankrupt, in a fairly lengthy period leading up to the bankruptcy, to divest himself of assets in favour of his family or friends in an attempt to defeat his creditors.[2]

1 Bankruptcy Act 1914, s 42.
2 *Re Debtor, ex p Official Receiver Trustee of Property of Debtor v Morrison* [1965] 3 All ER 453.

8.6.2 Settlements of his property by a bankrupt are liable to attack by a trustee and, if the attack is successful, are 'void' if the settlor becomes bankrupt within ten years of the 'settlement' under attack. More stringent tests are applied by the court in respect of settlements made within two years of the bankruptcy.

The relevant section of the Bankruptcy Act 1914, s 42, refers to the time scale being computed from the settlor becoming bankrupt. This has been held to refer to the committing of the act of bankruptcy leading to the relevant receiving order.[1]

1 *Re Reis, ex p Clough* [1904] 1 KB 451.

8.6.3 'Settlement' for these purposes means any conveyance or transfer of property. It extends not only to real property but to any form of property, so long as there is a disposition of that property. Thus, an ordinary gift of money was not caught under this section[1] whereas a gift of jewellery[2] or of money used to buy a property[3] was.

If a bankrupt, in divorce proceedings, consents to an order that the matrimonial home be sold and the proceeds distributed in some way then the giving of that consent can be a settlement for the purposes of s 42.[4] However, the spouse who benefits from such an order may still be a purchaser for valuable consideration (see para 8.64 below) if he or she gives up a legal right to pursue a relevant claim in the divorce proceedings.[4]

1 *Re Player, ex p Harvey* (1885) 15 QBD 682.
2 *Re Vansittart, ex p Brown* [1893] 1 QB 181.
3 *Re debtor, ex p Official Receiver, Trustee of Property of Debtor v Morrison* [1965] 3 All ER 453.
4 *Re Abbott, ex p Trustee of Property of Bankrupt v Abbott* [1983] Ch 45 and see ch 22 below.

8.6.4 A settlement is not caught if either; (a) it is made before and in consideration of marriage (presumably the settlor's), unless made fraudulently; or (b) if it is 'in favour of a purchaser or encumbrancer in good faith and for valuable consideration'. In this respect the purchaser must act honestly and without any intent to defraud any person, whether or not the settlor, or donor, has also acted in good faith.[1]

To come within this exception the purchaser really needs to have given, in benefit to the bankrupt's estate, a commercial or reasonable value for what he has received by way of settlement.[2] There must be a commercial quid pro quo;[3] and see note 4 to para 8.6.3 above.

[1] *Mackintosh v Pogose* [1895] 1 Ch 505.
[2] *Re Debtor, ex p Official Receiver, Trustee of Property v Morrison* [1965] 3 All ER 453.
[3] *Re Windle, ex p Trustee of the Bankrupt v Windle* [1975] 3 All ER 987.

8.6.5 *Two years.* Unless the settlement falls within one of the excluded categories in para 8.6.4 above it will be void (or, realistically, voidable since the trustee is not *bound* to take steps to set it aside), if made within two years of the bankruptcy. This is the case whatever the state of solvency or otherwise of the bankrupt when he made the settlement.

8.6.6 *Ten years.* However, in a period of ten years prior to the bankruptcy until the start of the two-year period referred to in para 8.6.5 above, the settlement is voidable with the qualification that if the beneficiaries, or persons claiming under the settlement, can prove that the settlor/bankrupt, was at the time of making the settlement, able to pay all his debts without the aid of the property comprised in the settlement and 'that the interest of the settlor in such property passed to the trustee of such settlement upon the execution thereof'[1] then the settlement is not voidable.

[1] Bankruptcy Act 1914, s 42(1).

8.6.7 When a trustee succeeds in avoiding a settlement he has the right to follow the money or goods into the hands of the receiver or volunteer.[1]

[1] *Re Intended Action, Trustee of Rousou v Rousou* [1955] 2 All ER 169.

8.6.8 As indicated in para 8.6.1 above s 42(1) is intended to prevent property from being put in the hands of relatives to escape the claims of creditors. When valuable goods or chattels are involved which do not require any formal settlement or transfer documentation to record the transaction, for example in the case of furniture which a husband can easily claim was given by him to his wife, the court will look carefully at the 'delivery' of the chattel in order to satisfy itself that a gift was properly perfected.[1]

[1] See *Re Cole, ex p Trustee of Property of Bankrupt v Cole* [1963] Ch 175.

8.7 FRAUDULENT CONVEYANCES

8.7.1 The longest period prior to a bankruptcy during which the trustee can under the Bankruptcy Act 1914 attack transfers or settlements of property is, as indicated above, ten years. Under the Law of Property Act 1925, s 172 there is no such time limit so long as the trustee proceeds within the ordinary limitation period of 12 years,[1] although time does not begin to run until the fraud complained of is, or ought reasonably to be, discovered.[1]

The test in this respect is whether or not a conveyance was made with intent to defraud creditors. If it was, it is voidable at the instance of any person thereby prejudiced. A trustee in bankruptcy is a person thus prejudiced and, if he cannot proceed under the Bankruptcy Act 1914, s 42, he may be able to rely on the provisions of the Law of Property Act 1925, s 172.

[1] Limitation Act 1980.

8.7.2 A conveyance is not caught by this provision if it was: (a) for 'valuable' consideration and in good faith by the conveyor/bankrupt; or (b) if it was for 'good' consideration, similarly in good faith by the conveyor but also to a person who was without notice of any intent to defraud creditors.

The Law of Property Act defines 'valuable' consideration[1] and this includes marriage. 'Good' consideration in these circumstances is presumably therefore designed to extend to 'natural love and affection' so that such transactions would be protected so long as the receiver of the property conveyed was without notice of the conveyor's motives.

[1] Law of Property Act 1925, s 205.

8.7.3 The expression 'conveyance' for these purposes is not limited to a formal conveyancing document. It has been held to extend to a parol direction by the debtor as to how certain money should be applied[1] although it has been suggested[2] that a more recent decision throws doubt on this approach.[3]

[1] *Re Eicholz, Eicholz's Trustee v Eicholz* [1959] Ch 708.
[2] *Rye v Rye* [1962] AC 496.
[3] See *Williams & Muir Hunter* (19th edn) pp 336–337.

8.7.4 As with the Bankruptcy Act 1914, s 42, such a conveyance is only voidable and not void ab initio. If the relevant property is subsequently purchased for valuable consideration by a bona fide purchaser, without notice of any intent to defraud creditors, then that purchaser acquires a good title to the property in question.[1]

[1] *Harrods Ltd v Stanton* [1923] 1 KB 516.

8.7.5 The Law of Property Act 1925, s 172 is repealed by the Insolvency Act 1986, s 423 (as to which see ch 20 below) but only in respect of transactions entered into before its coming into force. The 'Old Law' remains effective (in all bankruptcies) in respect of transactions which took place before the commencement of the Insolvency Act 1986, ie 29 December 1986.

8.8 RECOVERY OF GOODS SEIZED IN EXECUTION

8.8.1 An act of bankruptcy was committed by a debtor if an execution was levied against him by the seizure of his goods and the goods were either sold or held by the sheriff for 21 days. This available act of bankruptcy used to be useful to a creditor concerned to preserve for the bankruptcy the very goods which had been seized by the sheriff. Preservation was possible because the Bankruptcy Act 1914 restricts the rights of execution creditors[1] if the execution was not completed before the date of the receiving order or before the execution creditor had notice of an available act of bankruptcy by the debtor.

1 Bankruptcy Act 1914, ss 40 and 41.

8.8.2 The execution creditor is only entitled to retain the benefit of his execution in such circumstances if the execution is completed and it is only completed by a seizure and sale.[1] If, before sale, or other completion of the execution,[2] the sheriff is served with a notice of the making of a receiving order he must deliver the goods, and any money seized or received in part satisfaction of the execution, to the official receiver.[3]

1 Bankruptcy Act 1914, s 40(2).
2 Defined in cases of attachments of debts and of possession of land in Bankruptcy Act 1914, s 40(2).
3 Bankruptcy Act 1914, s 41.

8.8.3 The sheriff was obliged, where goods are sold in an execution or where money is paid to him to avoid a sale, and where the execution was in enforcement of a judgment for more than £250 to retain the funds for 14 days in order to give other creditors an opportunity of presenting a petition under the Old Bankruptcy Law, or of giving him notice of a petition having been presented. If a receiving order is subsequently made against the debtor the sheriff must pay the funds he holds to the official receiver or trustee 'who shall be entitled to retain it as against the execution creditor'.[1]

1 Bankruptcy Act 1914, s 41(2).

8.8.4 The court has power,[1] in appropriate circumstances to override these provisions of the Bankruptcy Act. This power has only been applied in winding up rather than bankruptcy cases[2] but such applications are of guidance in bankruptcy cases. In general terms, the courts have been reluctant to exercise the power. An exceptional case would have to be made out to disturb the normal principles of the bankruptcy legislation.

1 Companies Act 1985, s 821.
2 See *Williams & Muir Hunter* (19th edn) p 317.

8.9 AFTER ACQUIRED ASSETS

8.9.1 As already explained in ch 6 above, the personal earnings of the bankrupt which are required for the support and maintenance of himself and his family are exempt from seizure by the trustee. This stems from the common law rather from any statutory provision.

The court may order the direct payment of a bankrupt's salary, or part of it, to the trustee but such orders are very rare.[1] Bankrupts with surplus earnings will usually be requested by the official receiver or trustee to make regular payments to the trustee. This invariably helps when the bankrupt's conduct is examined on an application for discharge (see ch 10 below).

With that exception, however, 'after acquired' property coming to the bankruptcy, that is to say coming to the bankrupt after his adjudication, vests in his trustee in bankruptcy, whatever the source of the acquisition, for example by inheritance, by luck, or the personal skill of the bankrupt. Thus even under the Old Bankruptcy Law the trustee is entitled to seize and realise such property for the benefit of the creditors. In practice trustees seldom take active steps to investigate the fortunes of the bankrupt after his adjudication. The New Law contains new provisions in this respect, as to which see para 16.2.3 below.

[1] Bankruptcy Act 1914, s 51.

8.9.2 However, there is one qualification to this rule which is potentially important in the early stages of bankruptcy.

All transactions by a bankrupt with a person dealing with him bona fide and for value in respect of 'after acquired' property of the bankrupt are valid against the trustee in bankruptcy if they are completed before any intervention by the trustee.[1] Thus the trustee cannot trace any assets 'lost' to the estate so long as they fall within this fairly narrow exclusion.

[1] Bankruptcy Act 1914, s 47.

8.10 EXAMINATIONS UNDER THE BANKRUPTCY ACT 1925, s 25

8.10.1 In many of the preceding paragraphs it has been clear that, before the trustee or the committee of inspection can reasonably decide what course to adopt in respect of property or transactions which are relevant for the purpose of recovering assets for the bankruptcy, information has to be gathered and considered. The solvency or otherwise of the bankrupt at a particular date, the bona fides of a third person, whether or not value was given, are only a few of the factors which have to be considered by a trustee and his committee of inspection.

To assist in such investigations, and to help the trustee trace assets or obtain other relevant information he may invoke the assistance of the Bankruptcy Act 1914, s 25.

8.10.2 In addition to assisting a trustee in bankruptcy with the recovery of assets the private examination under the Bankruptcy Act 1914, s 25 can also serve to help him to ascertain the validity of a creditor's claim.

8.10.3 The power to examine the bankrupt under s 25 is quite separate from the preliminary examination described in ch 3 above and the public examination described in ch 7 above. In the case of the bankrupt, or his or her spouse, the trustee is entitled to an order for a private examination. He will often think such an examination necessary if he is dissatisfied with the information informally offered by the bankrupt or if the bankrupt, or his wife, is positively uncooperative.

In the case of the bankrupt, or his wife, it is not necessary to show that there has been a default in providing information. The trustee is virtually entitled to the examination as of right.[1]

[1] *Re Bennett and Glave, ex p Close* (1877) 5 Ch D 145.

8.10.4 It is not only the bankrupt or his wife who is susceptible to such an examination. In the words of s 25 an order may be made against 'any person whom the court may deem capable of giving information respecting the debtor, his dealings or property'.[1] In the case of a third party, however, it is usually necessary for the applicant to show that enquiry has been made of the person to be examined and that, for some reason, the information supplied is insufficient or that the witness has failed to respond.[2]

[1] Bankruptcy Act 1914, s 25(1).
[2] See *Re Rolls Razor Ltd (No 2)* [1970] Ch 576.

8.10.5 Whilst s 25 only refers to applications by the official receiver or trustee, it is clear that, by implication, any interested party may apply for a private examination[1] and may do so at any time after a receiving order has been made, i e if appropriate before adjudication.[2]

[1] Bankruptcy Rules 1952, r 72(2).
[2] Bankruptcy Act 1914, s 25(1).

8.10.6 An application by the trustee or the official receiver must state its grounds but need not be supported by affidavit.

By implication an application by some other interested party should be supported by an affidavit setting out the grounds of the application.[1] The application is made ex parte.[2]

There must be no 'ulterior motive' by the applicant. For example the court will not allow a s 25 examination of a witness on matters over which the trustee has already started litigation against the witness.[3]

[1] Bankruptcy Rules 1952, r 72(2).
[2] Bankruptcy Rules 1952, r 68.
[3] *Re Franks, ex p Gittins* [1892] 1 QB 646.

8.10.7 The person to be examined may be required to produce any documents in his possession custody or power relating to the debtor, the debtor's property or dealings. If the witness refuses to come before the court, or refuses to produce documents ordered to be produced the court may authorise his arrest so that he may be brought forward for examination.[1] Any failure to attend is a contempt of court and may be dealt with accordingly.[2]

[1] Bankruptcy Act 1914, s 25(2).
[2] Bankruptcy Rules 1952, r 68.

8.10.8 The witness is entitled to reasonable conduct money[1] although, unlike a subpoena the order for attendance at a s 25 examination need not be served personally.[2]

[1] Bankruptcy Act 1914, s 25(2) and Bankruptcy Rules 1952, r 64.
[2] *Re Weinberg, ex p Official Receiver* (1907) 96 LT 790 and Bankruptcy Rules 1952, r 88.

8.10.9 If, for any reason, a full private examination is impossible, undesirable or unnecessary, then the applicant is entitled to request an order for a written reply, on oath to interrogatories.[1] This may be useful if the trustee needs a lot of technical or detailed information from a witness who could not reasonably be expected to supply it from the 'witness box' without a great deal of hearing time being occupied.

1 Bankruptcy Act 1914, s 25(3).

8.10.10 A person ordered to be privately examined may apply to the court to rescind the order if it is likely to cause injustice to him. Since the order is made ex parte, he does not appeal against the order but he applies on summons or motion to set it aside.[1]

The trustee may appeal from an order setting aside the original order[2] or from an order refusing his original application.[3]

1 *Re Debtor (No 3 of 1909)* [1917] 1 KB 558.
2 *Re Debtor (No 12 of 1958), ex p Trustee of Property of Debtor v Clegg* [1968] 2 All ER 425.
3 *Re Green, ex p Trustee* [1958] 2 All ER 57n.

8.10.11 The examination proceeds in private before a registrar. However, if a witness refuses to answer a question which is allowed by the registrar, he will report it to a judge of his court who will deal with the matter in the same manner as if the witness was in default of answering before the judge himself.[1]

1 Bankruptcy Rules 1952, r 83(1).

8.10.12 Although neither the Bankruptcy Act 1914 nor the Bankruptcy Rules 1952 allow for it, in practice a witness is allowed to be represented by solicitor and/or counsel at such an examination. However, he is not entitled to the cost of his representation nor is he entitled to be present, or represented, whilst third parties are examined.[1]

1 *Re Beall, ex p Beall* [1894] 2 QB 135.

8.10.13 As in the public examination the bankrupt may not refuse to answer a question on the ground that the answer may incriminate him but a witness, other than the bankrupt, is entitled to refuse to answer a question on that ground.[1]

As a general rule 'fishing' questions, that is to say questions on matters in respect of which there is no indication that the witness may be able to give relevant evidence, are not admitted.

1 *Re Firth, ex p Schofield* (1877) 6 Ch D 230.

8.10.14 The bankrupt's solicitor, or former solicitor, is not immune from examination under s 25. His position in respect of the bankrupt client's privilege is explained in ch 26 below.

8.10.15 The s 25 examination is not only useful to a trustee for the purposes of securing information. The section also contains 'teeth' in that, if a person being examined admits that he is indebted to the bankrupt, the court may order him to pay the admitted debt to the trustee or the official receiver with, or without, the costs of the examination itself.[1]

The court has to be sure that there is a 'crystal clear admission' of liability before making such an order under what has been described as this 'draconian' power.[2]

[1] Bankruptcy Act 1914, s 25(4).
[2] *Re Debtor (No 26 of 1982)* [1983] LS Gaz R 2997.

8.10.16 Until the shorthand notes of a private examination are filed on the court file they are privileged and not even the bankrupt is entitled to see them. Thereafter they are available for inspection unless the registrar of the court makes a 'stop' order.[1] He may do so where, for example, public scrutiny may jeopardise the overall purpose of the bankruptcy proceedings.[2]

[1] Bankruptcy Rules 1952, r 15.
[2] *Re Poulson, ex p Granada Television Ltd v Maudling* [1976] 2 All ER 1020.

8.11 SEIZURE OF THE BANKRUPT'S PROPERTY

8.11.1 In respect of certain property no 'seizure' is appropriate or required.

For example, a chose in action is deemed to have been duly assigned to the trustee[1] and where the bankrupt's property consists of stocks or shares or other 'property transferable in the books of any company office or person' the trustee is simply empowered to exercise the right to transfer that property as if the bankrupt himself exercised it.[2]

[1] Bankruptcy Act 1914, s 48(5).
[2] Ibid, s 48(3).

8.11.2 However, in other cases, a degree of co-operation is inevitably required by the bankrupt. The point has previously been made that, in practice, the matrimonial home is frequently the most significant asset to be realised in a bankruptcy. That subject is discussed as a separate matter in ch 22 below.

8.11.3 The debtor is obliged to give an inventory of his property to the official receiver[1] and he must, to the utmost of his power, assist in the realisation of that property.[2] If he fails to do either, he is guilty of contempt of court and may be punished accordingly.[3] These provisions have been discussed in more detail in chs 3, 4 and 6 above.

[1] Bankruptcy Act 1914, s 22(2).
[2] Ibid, s 22(3).
[3] Ibid, s 22(4).

8.11.4 However, the Bankruptcy Act 1914 also gives the trustee statutory support for the use of force in the seizure of the property of a bankrupt. A person acting under a warrant of the court may use force to break into premises in which there is property of the bankrupt and, in appropriate cases, the court will issue a search warrant to assist the trustee.[1] The trustee's protection against innocent seizure of the goods of someone other than the bankrupt is considered in ch 4 above.

[1] Bankruptcy Act 1914, s 49.

8.12 PROCEDURAL TABLES

Applications in respect of fraudulent preference, fraudulent transfer or avoidance of a settlement

Steps to be Taken	Bankruptcy Act 1914	Bankruptcy Rules 1952
1. The trustee in bankruptcy applies to court on motion for appropriate declaration and for order setting aside transfer or settlement, etc. **2.** Application is supported by affidavit setting out grounds for seeking appropriate declaration. **3.** Court officer fixes date for hearing of motion and files notice of motion or seals or sends to applicant for service on respondent or respondents. **4.** At first return date directions will be given for disposal of application. **5.** Judge considers application and may make declaration that transfer or settlement is void and make an order setting it aside.	ss 37(1) 42, 44	

Private examination under Bankruptcy Act 1914, s 25

Steps to be Taken	Bankruptcy Act 1914	Bankruptcy Rules 1952
1. Official receiver or trustee may submit to debtor his wife or person suspected of having dealings with debtor or his property a questionnaire setting out the matters on which information is required. This allows the person questioned an opportunity to answer without the necessity of a formal examination. A questionnaire is not the same thing as an interrogatory (for which a court order is required).		

Steps to be Taken	Bankruptcy Act 1914	Bankruptcy Rules 1952
2. If person questioned fails to answer or his answers are unsatisfactory: official receiver or trustee applies ex parte in writing to court supported by unsworn report, for order for private examination of person questioned.	ss 25(1)	r 72(1), (2)
The application must state shortly the ground on which it is made.		r 72(1)
The examination may be held on the application of a creditor. If the trustee declines to examine, and a creditor applies, he must show on affidavit a prima facie probability that some benefit will result to the estate or creditors. The creditor will be responsible for the costs of the examination unless the court otherwise directs. In practice the creditor usually applies for leave to use the trustee's name, on giving an indemnity against all costs and expenses for which the trustee may become liable in consequence of the examination.		
3. Registrar considers the application and may: (1) Fix date for hearing of private examination; (2) (i) issue a Summons to witness to attend for examination; or		r 65(1)
(ii) where witness is in prison for contempt of court; issue an order for his production; (3) Require witness to produce any documents in his custody or power relating to debtor, his dealings or property.	s 25(1)	
4. Official receiver or trustee serves summons on witness together with conduct money.	s 25(2)	
A certificate of service is indorsed on the summons. If witness fails to attend or produce relevant documents the court may issue a warrant for his arrest and he may be brought before the court for examination.	s 25(2)	see r 79
If it is wilfully shown that witness wilfully failed to attend or produce documents he may be committed for contempt of court.		r 68
Witness may apply to set aside the summons. Witness may apply for release from custody.		

Steps to be Taken	Bankruptcy Act 1914	Bankruptcy Rules 1952
5. Witness attends registrar, before whom he is examined usually by the trustee or his legal representatives. The examination is on oath, either by word of mouth or by written interrogatories.	s 25(3)	
If it is desired that the witness be examined before a special examiner, a common form application is made, supported by affidavit setting out the facts making the appointment necessary. A shorthand writer is appointed to take down the examination. The party at whose instance the order appointing the shorthand writer is made must pay his fees.		r 70
If witness refuses to answer any questions or produce any relevant documents registrar may report him to the judge who may commit him for contempt. The court may make an order seeking the aid of another court for holding the examination. An order seeking aid with a request to a court having bankruptcy jurisdiction in Scotland or Northern Ireland and British courts elsewhere is deemed sufficient to enable the court to exercise, in matters directed by the order, such jurisdiction as either the court making the request or the court to which the request is sent could exercise in regard to matters within their respective jurisdictions.	ss 25(6) 122	
Courts which may act in aid are: (1) The High Court; (2) The county courts; (3) The courts having jurisdiction in bankruptcy in Scotland and Northern Ireland; (4) Every British court elsewhere having jurisdiction in bankruptcy or insolvency.	s 122	
6. Witness attends court on date appointed to sign transcript of private examination. He may be ordered to sign it at another court.		

8.13 FORMS

APPLICATION for order for private examination and appointment of shorthand writer

IN THE [HIGH COURT OF JUSTICE *or* . . . . COUNTY COURT]
In Bankruptcy No. . . . of 19 . . . .
Re A B [*add, after adjudication*, a Bankrupt]
Ex parte [the Debtor *or* the Bankrupt *or* C D a Creditor *or* the Official Receiver *or* the Trustee *or as the case may be*]

APPLICATION is hereby made by T T for an order that B B of (*address*) be summoned for examination under Section 25 of the Bankruptcy Act 1914 on the grounds set out in the [report of the Trustee *or as the case may be*] filed herewith, and for a day to be appointed for such examination.

AND also for the appointment of [one of the shorthand writers of this Court] for the purpose of taking down in shorthand the evidence of the said B B and making a transcript of his notes thereof.

DATED this . . . . day of . . . . 19 . . . .

(*Signature*), of (*address*), [Agents for (*name*), of (*address*),] Solicitors for the [Debtor *or* Bankrupt *or* Trustee *or* Judgment Creditor *or* Petitioning Creditor *or as the case may be*]

APPLICATION for order for private examination, seeking aid of another court for holding examination

IN THE [HIGH COURT OF JUSTICE *or* . . . . COUNTY COURT]
In Bankruptcy No. . . . of 19 . . . .
Re A B [*add, after adjudication*, a Bankrupt]
Ex parte [the Debtor *or* the Bankrupt *or* C D a Creditor *or* the Official Receiver *or* the Trustee *or as the case may be*]

APPLICATION is hereby made for an order for the examination of B B of (*address*) under Section 25 of the Bankruptcy Act 1914, on the grounds set out in the report of the Trustee filed herewith, and that the [High Court of Justice in Bankruptcy *or* . . . . Country Court] be sought to act in aid of and be auxiliary to this Court pursuant to Section 122 of the Bankruptcy Act 1914 for the purpose of holding such examination.

DATED this . . . . day of . . . . 19 . . . .

(*Signature*), of (*address*), [Agents for (*name*), of (*address*),] Solicitors for the [Debtor *or* Bankrupt *or* Trustee *or* Judgment Creditor *or* Petitioning Creditor *or as the case may be*]

REPORT of trustee supporting application for private examination

IN THE [HIGH COURT OF JUSTICE *or* . . . . COUNTY COURT]
In Bankruptcy No. . . . of 19 . . . .
Re A B [*add, after adjudication*, a Bankrupt]

I, T T, of (*address and description*), the Trustee of the property of the above-named Debtor, hereby report to the Court as follows:

1. A Receiving Order was made against the above-named Debtor on . . . . 19 . . . ., and he was adjudicated bankrupt on . . . . . 19 . . . . At the [first] meeting of creditors held on . . . . . 19 . . . . I was appointed Trustee and my said appointment was confirmed by the Department of Trade and Industry on . . . . 19 . . . .

2. In the course of the investigation by me of the affairs of the Debtor as such Trustee I ascertained that on . . . . 19 . . . . he had effected an insurance on his life in the Z Assurance Company Limited, for the sum of £. . . ., the annual premium of £. . . . having been paid throughout by him. I have also ascertained that the surrender value of the policy relating to the said insurance is £. . . . and that the said policy is stated by him to have been handed by him to B B, his wife, by way of security for money lent by her to him amounting in all to £. . . ., on dates named by him.

3. I can find no entries in the Debtor's books relating to the alleged advances and I have asked the said B B to supply me with particulars thereof and to produce any cheques or other evidence in her possession relating thereto, but the said B B has not replied to my letters dated respectively . . . . and . . . . 19 . . . ., and she has failed to supply me with any information in regard to the alleged advances.

4. I therefore ask that an order be made for the examination of the said B B under Section 25 of the Bankruptcy Act 1914, she being in my submission a person capable of giving information respecting the Debtor, his dealings and property.

DATED this . . . . day of . . . . 19 . . . .

(*Signature*)
Trustee

SUMMONS to attend for private examination

IN THE [HIGH COURT OF JUSTICE *or* . . . . COUNTY COURT]

In Bankruptcy No. . . . of 19 . . . .

Re A B [*add, after adjudication*, a Bankrupt]

To B B, of (*address*)

You are hereby required to attend at the [High Court of Justice, *or* . . . . County Court] on . . . . 19 . . . . at . . . . o'clock in the [forenoon] to give evidence in the above matter, and then and there to have and produce [all ledgers and books of account, invoices, statements of account, letters, books, papers, and documents of every kind, in any manner relating to your dealings and transactions with A B, a Bankrupt, touching a debt alleged to be due by you to the said Bankrupt's estate amounting to the sum of £. . . .] whereof if you fail, having no lawful impediment to be then made known to the Court and allowed by it, the Court may by warrant cause you to be apprehended and brought up for examination.

DATED this . . . . day of . . . . 19 . . . .

(*Signature*)
Registrar

NOTE This summons is issued on the application of [the Official Receiver and Trustee], and take notice that if the sum of £. . . . stated to be due by you to this estate be paid to O R, Official Receiver, at (*address*), on or before . . . . 19 . . ., this summons will be discharged.

APPLICATION for warrant of seizure

IN THE [HIGH COURT OF JUSTICE *or* . . . . COUNTY COURT]
In Bankruptcy No. . . . of 19 . . . .
Re A B [*add, after adjudication*, a Bankrupt]
Ex parte [the Debtor *or* the Bankrupt *or* C D a Creditor *or* the Official Receiver *or* the Trustee *or as the case may be*]

APPLICATION is hereby made that a warrant of seizure be issued authorising forcible entry into the premises at (*address*) where the above-named Debtor resides and the seizure and removal of all the property, household goods, effects, and all other things whatsoever belonging to the Debtor thereat and therein found with the exception only of his necessary wearing apparel, bedding and tools as excepted by the Bankruptcy Act 1914.

Ex parte [the Debtor *or* the Bankrupt *or* C D a Creditor *or* the Official Receiver *or* the Trustee *or as the case may be*]
APPLICATION is hereby made for (*state relief claimed*)
DATED this . . . . day of . . . . 19 . . . .

(*Signature*), of (*address*), [Agents for (*name*), of (*address*),] Solicitors for the [Debtor *or* Bankrupt *or* Trustee *or* Judgment Creditor *or* Petitioning Creditor *or as the case may be*]

AFFIDAVIT supporting application for search warrant

IN THE [HIGH COURT OF JUSTICE *or* . . . . COUNTY COURT]
In Bankruptcy No. . . . of 19 . . . .
Re A B [*add, after adjudication*, a Bankrupt]
Ex parte [the Debtor *or* the Bankrupt *or* C D a Creditor *or* the Official Receiver *or* the Trustee *or as the case may be*]

I, T T, of (*residence and description*), the Trustee of the property of the above-named Debtor, make oath and say as follows:

1. As a result of inquiries I made in the course of my duties as Trustee, I have reason to suspect and believe that certain property of the Debtor, namely (*describe the property*), is concealed in the house of one L M, of (*address*), such house not belonging to the said Debtor.

2. I ask that a search warrant may issue in order that the said premises may be entered and search be made for the said property therein, and that if such property be found it may be seized and handed to me.

SWORN at (*address*), this . . . . day of . . . . 19 . . . . before me, (*Signature*) A Commissioner for Oaths } (*Deponent's signature*)

AFFIDAVIT supporting application for warrant of seizure

IN THE [HIGH COURT OF JUSTICE *or* . . . . COUNTY COURT]
In Bankruptcy No. . . . of 19 . . . .
Re A B [*add, after adjudication*, a Bankrupt]

I, T T, of (*residence and description*), make oath and say as follows:

1. It is desirable in the interests of the creditors that a warrant of seizure be issued in order that forcible entry may be made into the premises at (*address*)

where the Debtor resided, for the purpose of seizing and removing all his property, household goods, effects and all other things belonging to him thereat and therein, with the exception only of those articles and things excepted by the Bankruptcy Act 1914.

2. The warrant is necessary as the keys of the premises are in the Debtor's possession and he has not attended upon the Official Receiver or the Trustee and his whereabouts are unknown. He has not replied to letters sent to him at the said address by the Trustee; and the Trustee's agent attended at the said premises on . . . . 19 . . . . and also on . . . . 19 . . . ., but was unable to find anyone there or to obtain admission.

SWORN at (*address*), this . . . . day of . . . .
19 . . . . before me, } (*Deponent's signature*)
(*Signature*)
A Commissioner for Oaths

NOTICE OF MOTION to set aside transfer of property as fraudulent preference or by reason of relation back of trustee's title

IN THE HIGH COURT OF JUSTICE
Chancery Division No. . . . of 19 . . . .
In Bankruptcy

Re A B, a Bankrupt.
Ex parte The Trustee of the property
of the above-named Bankrupt Applicant
and
X Y Respondent

TAKE NOTICE that this Honourable Court will be moved before [the Judge sitting in Bankruptcy at the Royal Courts of Justice, Strand, London WC2 at the sitting of the Court *or, in a county court*, His Honour the Judge thereof at the sitting of the Court at (*address*)] on [Monday] the . . . . day of . . . . 19 . . . . or so soon thereafter as Counsel can be heard by Counsel on behalf of the above-named Applicant:

1. For a declaration that [a transfer made by the above-named Bankrupt to the Respondent of a motor-car registered number . . . . on . . . . 19 . . . . *or* a payment made by the above-named Bankrupt to the Respondent of £1,000 on . . . . 19 . . . . *or as the case may be*] is a fraudulent preference under the provisions of Section 44 of the Bankruptcy Act 1914, and an act of bankruptcy under the provisions of Section 1(1) thereof and is void as against the Applicant as such Trustee.

2. Further or alternatively for a declaration that the said [transfer *or* payment] is void against the Applicant as such Trustee under the provisions of Section 37(1) of the Bankruptcy Act 1914 in that it was made after the above-named Bankrupt had committed an act of bankruptcy to which the title of the Applicant as such Trustee relates back.

3. For an Order that the Respondent [do deliver the said motor car to the Applicant as such Trustee or pay to him the sum of £. . . . the value thereof or such sum as the Court shall deem just *or* do pay to the Applicant as such Trustee the said sum of £1,000].

AND FURTHER TAKE NOTICE that on the hearing of this motion and in support thereof these will be read the affidavits of the Applicant and J K, copies of which are delivered herewith [and that also there will be read a transcript of the shorthand note of the evidence given by the Respondent at his examination under Section 25 of the Bankruptcy Act 1914 on . . . ., 19 . . . .] [and that without further notice viva voce evidence will be adduced].

DATED this . . . . day of . . . . 19 . . . .

(*Signature*), of (*address*), [Agents for (*name*), of (*address*),] Solicitors for the [Debtor *or* Bankrupt *or* Trustee *or* Judgment Creditor *or* Petitioning Creditor *or as the case may be*]

To X Y of (*address*) and
to his Solicitors G H & Co,
of (*address*)

NOTICE OF MOTION to set aside payment made by bankrupt as voluntary settlement or transfer

IN THE HIGH COURT OF JUSTICE
Chancery Division No. . . . of 19 . . . .
In Bankruptcy

Re A B, a Bankrupt.
Ex parte The Trustee of the property
of the above-named Bankrupt Applicant
and
X Y Respondent

TAKE NOTICE that this Honourable Court will be moved before [the Judge sitting in Bankruptcy at the Royal Courts of Justice, Strand, London WC2 at the sitting of the Court *or, in a county court*, His Honour the Judge thereof at the sitting of the Court at (*address*)] on [Monday] the . . . . day of . . . . 19 . . . . or so soon thereafter as Counsel can be heard by Counsel on behalf of the above-named Applicant:

1. For a declaration that a payment of £. . . . made by the above-named Bankrupt to the Respondent on . . . . 19 . . . . constituted and was a voluntary settlement or transfer within the meaning of Section 42 of the Bankruptcy Act 1914 and as such is void against the Applicant as Trustee.
2. For an Order that the Respondent do pay the said sum of £. . . . to the Applicant as such Trustee.
3. For such further or other order as to the Court may seem meet.
4. For an order that the costs of this motion be paid by the Respondent.

AND FURTHER TAKE NOTICE that on the hearing of this motion there will be read an affidavit of the Applicant a copy of which is delivered herewith and that without further notice viva voce evidence will be adduced.

DATED this . . . . day of . . . . 19 . . . .

(*Signature*), of (*address*), [Agents for (*name*), of (*address*),] Solicitors for the [Debtor *or* Bankrupt *or* Trustee *or* Judgment Creditor *or* Petitioning Creditor *or as the case may be*]

To X Y of (*address*) and
to his Solicitors G H & Co,
of (*address*)

CHAPTER 9

Proofs of Debt and Distributions to Creditors

9.1 INTRODUCTION

9.1.1 The creditor of a person who is adjudicated bankrupt can only enjoy a distribution out of the bankrupt's estate in respect of any debt which is 'payable', as to which see below. If he has a provable debt he must lodge a claim with the official receiver, or the trustee in bankruptcy that written claim being the 'proof of debt'. This is required by all creditors except the petitioning creditor whose debt is proved by the evidence given, on the hearing of the petition.

9.1.2 The relevant date for the purpose of proof by a creditor is the date of the receiving order.

9.1.3 There is no obligation on a creditor to prove in his debtor's bankruptcy but he does not rank for dividend unless he has proved[1] and the fact that he does not prove does not alter the effect of a discharge (see ch 10 below) on the bankrupt's provable debts.

[1] See *Re Ward, ex p Hammond & Son v Official Receiver and Debtor* [1942] Ch 294.

9.2 PROVABLE DEBTS IN BANKRUPTCY

9.2.1 Subject to certain exclusions, which are set out below, the Bankruptcy Act 1914 defines as debts provable in bankruptcy, the following:

> 'All debts and liabilities present or future, certain or contingent, to which the debtor is subject at the date of the Receiving Order or to which he may become

subject before his discharge by reason of any obligation incurred before the date of the Receiving Order.'

Thus the language of the Act is wide and, understandably, seeks to cover the great majority of what may be regarded as the bankrupt's debts.

9.2.2 The reference to contingent liabilities means that provable debts extend, for example, to a bankrupt surety's liability on a principal debt even though his liability had not matured at the date of the receiving order.[1] In such case the principal creditor may prove for the whole of the debt.[2] Similarly, a co-surety may prove in the estate of the bankrupt for contribution to payment of the principal debt.[1]

[1] *Wolmershausen v Gullick* [1893] 2 Ch 514.
[2] *Re Parker, Morgan v Hill* [1894] 3 Ch 400.

9.2.3 Liability for interest is a further example of a contingent liability for which a proof of debt may be lodged. However, where, as is usually the case these days, the agreed rate of interest on a principal debt exceeds 5% then, in respect of interest accruing after the receiving order, only a claim calculated at the rate of 5% qualifies for dividend until after all other, and most deferred, claims have been paid. Thereafter, the further interest claimed may be paid out with other postponed or deferred claims (see para 9.4).[1] The New Law provisions with regard to interest are significantly different to those applicable in Old Bankruptcy Law cases.[2]

[1] Bankruptcy Act 1914, s 66, And see *Quartermaine's Case* [1892] 1 Ch 639 and *Re Browne v Wingrove, ex p Ador* [1891] 2 QB 574.
[2] See ch 16 below.

9.2.4 A third fairly common contingent claim provable in bankruptcy is a claim for costs ordered but not quantified by the date of the receiving order. Such costs are provable. However, this does not apply to the costs of the pursuit of a claim which itself is not provable until judgment is entered on it,[1] for example, a claim for damages in tort.

[1] *Re Newman, ex p Brooke* (1876) 3 Ch D 494.

Excluded claims

9.2.5 The following are excluded:

(a) unliquidated damages in tort cannot be proved for[1] but the fact that a claim lies in tort does not exclude it if it can properly be framed in some other way, for example, in breach of contract[2] or breach of trust;[3]

(b) a debt or liability incurred by the bankrupt with a person who had notice of an available act of bankruptcy by the bankrupt at the time of incurring that debt or liability is not provable[4] if the relevant bankruptcy petition was presented within three months of the debt or liability being incurred. Thus, a creditor is able to prove in a bankruptcy which is commenced more than three months after the relevant debt was incurred;

(c) a debt incurred after the date of the receiving order cannot be proved[5] whether or not the creditor had notice of the receiving order;
(d) a debt or liability which is incapable of being valued or fairly estimated may be deemed to be a debt provable in the bankruptcy if the court makes an order to that effect.[6] It is the trustee's duty to estimate the value of a contingent claim if for any reason, the value of it is not certain.[7] If the creditor is dissatisfied with the trustee's assessment, he may appeal to the court.[8] It is on such an application that the court may, if it thinks fit, declare that any part of the contingent claim which cannot be valued should be deemed not to be provable; and
(e) apart from the debts which are expressly excluded from proof, any debts which would not otherwise be enforceable against the bankrupt are excluded, for example, statute-barred claims[9] or claims which are founded on an illegal or immoral consideration or, being in that category of contract which has to be evidenced in writing,[10] are not so evidenced.

1 Bankruptcy Act 1914, s 30(1).
2 As in a professional negligence claim.
3 See *Tilley v Bowman Ltd* [1910] 1 KB 745.
4 Bankruptcy Act 1914, s 30(2).
5 Bankruptcy Act 1914, s 30(3).
6 Ibid, s 30(6).
7 Ibid, s 30(4).
8 Ibid, s 30(5).
9 The limitation period ceases to run after the receiving order. See *Re Coles, ex p Ross* (1827) 2 GL & J 330.
10 Eg Law of Property Act 1925, s 40, Statute of Frauds (1677), s 4.

9.2.6 Where there have been mutual dealings between a bankrupt and proving creditor, the creditor is, in general, permitted to set off his obligations to the bankrupt against the liability of the bankrupt to him and to prove for the balance[1] (or be liable for an adverse balance). Since this has the practical effect of allowing the creditor a considerable advantage over other creditors, who are not in a position to effect a set off, fairly strict rules apply, or have been developed. The Bankruptcy Act 1914 directs that an account is taken at the date of the receiving order[2] (so that the doctrine of relation back[3] is effectively excluded) and that the account is only taken in respect of *mutual* dealings, that is where the two parties dealt with each other as both debtor and creditor to one another. No set off is available to a creditor who allowed credit to a debtor at a time when he had notice of an available act of bankruptcy committed by the debtor.[4]

For a series of relevant decisions on mutuality and set off in bankruptcy see the cases referred to in the notes.[5]

1 Bankruptcy Act 1914, s 31.
2 See *Re Daintry, ex p Mant* [1900] 1 QB 546.
3 See ch 11 below.
4 Ibid, s 31.
5 *Forster v Wilson* (1843) 12 M & W 191; *Rolls Razor Ltd v Cox* [1967] 1 QB 552; *Re Gedney, Smith v Grummitt* [1908] 1 Ch 804; *Re debtor (No 82 of 1926)* [1927] 1 Ch 410; *Re DH Curtis (Builders) Ltd* [1978] Ch 162; *Tilley v Bowman Ltd* [1910] 1 KB 745.

9.3 THE PROOF OF DEBT

9.3.1 The Bankruptcy Act 1914 requires that a set of rules set out in its Second Schedule, must be observed.[1] The Schedule is concise and cannot usefully be summarised. It is therefore set out in full (as amended[2]) at para 9.9 below. As is clear from the Schedule, the claim must be in writing but, unless the trustee or official receiver requires it, need no longer be sworn.

[1] Bankruptcy Act 1914, s 32.
[2] By the Bankruptcy (Amendment) Act 1926, s 11; the Insolvency Act 1976, s 5(1)(2); the Social Security (Consequential Provisions) Act 1975, s 1(3), Sch 2, para 3; and the Social Security Pensions Act 1975, s 65(1), Sch 4, para 2.

9.3.2 If a creditor wishes to attend the first meeting of creditors and vote at that meeting he must have proved as a creditor[1] by not later than the time stipulated for that purpose in the notice convening the meeting. That time must not be earlier than midday on the day but one before, nor later than midday on the day before the appointed day.[2] In practice, the standard form used by the official receiver to convene the first meeting of creditors only stipulates for the latest time by which proofs (and proxies) must be lodged.

[1] Bankruptcy Act 1914, Sch I, para 8.
[2] Bankruptcy Rules 1952, r 252(1)(2).

9.3.3 The provision in the Second Schedule that all creditors who have proved may examine the proofs of other creditors before the first meeting of creditors enables the creditors to liaise with each other on the question of nomination for the office of trustee in bankruptcy and any other matters of mutual interest or concern.

9.3.4 The Second Schedule to the Bankruptcy Act 1914 draws a distinction between unsecured and secured creditors. In particular, the secured creditor is obliged, where he has not realised his security, nor surrendered it to the trustee or official receiver, to value and give full particulars of the security he holds. Armed with this information, the trustee may decide whether or not to exercise his right to redeem it, paying the creditor its assesssed value.[1] Because the security can be redeemed in this way, secured creditors must exercise care in valuing their security. They should not be tempted to value it on the low side, leaving them to prove as unsecured creditors for a greater amount than might otherwise be the case.

[1] Bankruptcy Act 1914, Sch 2, para 13(a).

9.3.5 If a creditor's debt is due in a foreign currency, it seems likely that the date for conversion of that debt into sterling is the date of the receiving order. In a company winding up case, it was held that the proper date was the date of the winding up order[1] and, by analogy, the corresponding date in bankruptcy should be the date of the receiving order.

[1] *Re Dynamics Corpn of America* [1976] 2 All ER 669.

9.4 DISPUTED CLAIMS

9.4.1 The trustee in bankruptcy is obliged, by the Second Schedule to the Bankruptcy Act 1914, having examined every proof and the grounds of the debt, to admit or reject it in whole or in part or he may require the creditor to produce further evidence in support of the claim.[1]

[1] Bankruptcy Act 1914, Sch 2, para 23 and see *Re debtor (No 819 of 1970), ex p Biart v Trustee of Property of Debtor* [1974] 3 All ER 502.

9.4.2 If he decides to reject a claim he must state his grounds in a written notice of rejection. Thereupon the creditor may within 21 days[1] apply to the court to reverse or vary the trustee's decision.[2]

[1] Bankruptcy Rules 1952, r 261.
[2] Bankruptcy Act 1914, Sch 2, para 25.

9.4.3 Similarly, if the trustee is of the opinion that a proof has been improperly admitted (perhaps by the official receiver or because of information which subsequently comes to light), he may apply to the court to have it expunged or reduced in amount.

9.4.4 The time limit of 21 days within which a creditor must appeal against the rejection of his proof may be extended but, in practice, will only be so extended in special circumstances. The trustee is heard on the application.[1]

[1] See *Re Vanbergen, ex p Trustee of Property of Bankrupt v Vanbergen* [1955] 1 All ER 40.

9.4.5 Any creditor is entitled to appeal a trustee's decision in relation to a proof.[1]

[1] Bankruptcy Act 1914, Sch 2, para 25.

9.4.6 A proof may be withdrawn. The notes in the procedural table at para 9.7 deal with the steps which should be taken in this respect.

9.5 THE ORDER OF DISTRIBUTION TO CREDITORS

9.5.1 Making an assumption, rare enough in practice, that the trustee in bankruptcy is able to realise sufficient funds to achieve a surplus in the estate for return to the bankrupt (who ranks, in effect as a creditor after all the creditors have been satisfied), the following are the main headings, in the order of preference, for payment:
(1) those entitled to payment of bankruptcy costs and charges;
(2) pre-preferential creditors;
(3) preferential creditors;
(4) ordinary creditors;
(5) postponed creditors; and
(6) the bankrupt.
These headings are discussed below:

1 Bankruptcy costs and charges

9.5.2 Once the direct expenses properly incurred in preserving, realising and getting in any of the assets of the debtor have been paid, the first priority is to pay the costs and charges of the bankruptcy. Since these are, themselves, in several different categories, an order of priority for these expenses is established[1] as follows:

(a) the official receiver, in respect of actual expenses incurred in protecting the property or assets of the debtor and any expenses or outlay incurred by him or by his authority in carrying on the bankrupt's business;[2]
(b) the official receiver, in respect of any fees, percentages, and charges payable to him and any other fees payable, or costs, charges and expenses incurred by or authorised by him;
(c) the petitioning creditor in respect of the deposit lodged by him on the petition, or subsequently for any particular purpose;
(d) the party lodging a deposit on any application for the appointment of an interim receiver, in respect of such deposit;
(e) the special manager, if any, in respect of his remuneration;
(f) the petitioner in respect of his taxed costs;
(g) the person if any, appointed to assist the debtor in the preparation of his statement of affairs, in respect of his remuneration and charges;
(h) the official receiver, in respect of any allowance made to the debtor or his family;
(i) any shorthand writer appointed by the court in respect of his taxed charges;
(j) the trustee, in respect of necessary disbursements other than actual expenses of preserving, realising and getting in the assets;
(k) any person properly employed by the trustee with the sanction of the committee of inspection in respect of his costs;
(l) the trustee in respect of any allowance made to the debtor with the sanction of the committee of inspection;
(m) the trustee for his remuneration; and
(n) the committee of inspection in respect of actual out-of-pocket expenses necessarily incurred, subject to the approval of the Department of Trade and Industry.

Thus, the trustee, who is charged with the distribution of the assets, may retain such sums as may be necessary to meet the costs of administration, that is, the costs referred to in the above list, before discharging any debts of the bankrupt.

1 Bankruptcy Rules 1952, r 115 as amended by SI 1967/371.
2 See Bankruptcy Act 1914, ss 53(1), 56.

2 Pre-preferential claims

9.5.3 Such claims are, in practice, rare. They are something of a relic of the past when more individuals traded in person rather than with the benefit of a limited liability company, and when apprenticeship was more common and premiums were paid for articles for a clerk.

The Bankruptcy Act 1914 provides that unpaid wages for an apprentice or a proportionate part of a premium paid for articles are pre-preferential claims in the bankruptcy of the apprentices' or articled clerks' principal.[1]

The Employment Protection Act 1975 now provides for reimbursement of such claims from the Redundancy Fund, (the Department of Employment then being subrogated to the employer's claim in the bankruptcy).[2]

1 Bankruptcy Act 1914, s 34.
2 Ibid, ss 64, 67.

9.5.4 There are special provisions for the trustees of friendly societies and in relation to the costs of deeds of arrangement, but the only other occasionally relevant pre-preferential claim is a claim for funeral expenses of a deceased who died insolvent, the estate being administered in bankruptcy.[1]

1 Bankruptcy Act 1914, s 130(6).

3 Preferential claims

9.5.5 Subject to the pre-preferential claims, of which there are very seldom any, preferential debts rank next for payment. They rank equally between themselves and must be paid in full in priority to all other debts.[1] If the assets realised are insufficient to cover all the preferential debts then they abate in equal proportions between themselves.[2]

1 Bankruptcy Act 1914, s 33(1).
2 Ibid, s 33(2).

9.5.6 The preferential debt should not be confused with the secured debt. A secured creditor has no priority in order of distribution; he may simply rely on his security, having no special priority if the security is insufficient to discharge his entire debt.[1]

If a secured creditor has a preferential and a non-preferential claim, he is entitled to appropriate the realisation of his security to the non-preferential debt thus allowing him to prove as a preferential creditor for that unpaid part of the bankrupt's liability to him.[2]

1 Bankruptcy Act 1914, Sch 2, para 10.
2 *Re William Hall (Contractors) Ltd* [1967] 2 All ER 1150.

9.5.7 The preferential claims are, basically:

(a) rates for one year prior to the receiving order;[1]

(b) tax for one year. Despite the strict terms of the Bankruptcy Act 1914,[2] it does not confine the Inland Revenue or Commissioners of Customs and Excise to the year preceding the receiving order or to the tax year preceding the receiving order but extends to any fiscal year before the date of the receiving order in respect of which tax is unpaid.[3] For different taxes, for example, income tax and capital gains tax, the Revenue may chose to prove for different years.[4]

This right extends to any sort of tax payable by the bankrupt, for example, it extends to value added tax,[5] car tax[6] and to betting and gaming duty;[7]

(c) class 4 national insurance contributions,[8] again for a period of one selected year prior to the making of the receiving order against the bankrupt;

(d) wages and salary of a clerk or servant[9] or of a labourer or workman,[10] in each case for a period not exceeding four months before the receiving order and not exceeding £800 in amount.[11] Whether or not a creditor is a clerk or servant on the one hand or a labourer or workman on the other, can usually be decided without difficulty but it is sometimes necessary to examine the relationship of the creditor with the bankrupt in order to see if the employer-employee relationship exists. By way of relevant examples, see the cases in the notes.[12] Since the establishment of the Redundancy Fund, employees, in practice, may make claims for redundancy and for unpaid remuneration on the Fund and the Secretary of State for Employment is subrogated to the rights of the employee in his employer's bankruptcy;[13] and

(e) Social Security contributions outstanding at the date of the receiving order.[14]

1 Bankruptcy Act 1914, s 33(1)(a).
2 See Bankruptcy Act 1914, s 33(1)(a).
3 *Re Pratt, ex p IRC v Phillips (Trustee)* [1951] Ch 225.
4 *Lord Advocate v Purvis Industries Ltd* (1958) 38 T C 155.
5 Value Added Tax Act 1983, Sch 7, para 12.
6 Car Tax Act 1983.
7 Betting and Gaming Duties Act 1981.
8 Bankruptcy Act 1914, s 33(1)(a) as amended by Social Security (Consequential Provisions) Act 1975, Part I.
9 Bankruptcy Act 1914, s 33(1)(b) as replaced by Bankruptcy Amendment Act 1926.
10 Bankruptcy Act 1914, s 33(1)(c).
11 Insolvency Act 1976, s 1(1).
12 *Re Newspaper Pty Syndicate Ltd, Hopkinson v Newspaper Pty Syndicate Ltd* [1900] 2 Ch 349; *Re Ashley & Smith Ltd, Ashley v The Company* [1918] 2 Ch 378; *Carney v Back* [1906] 2 KB 746; *Re Disney, ex p Allsop* (1875) 32 LT 433; *Re CW and AL Hughes Ltd* [1966] 2 All ER 702.
13 Employment Protection (Consolidation) Act 1978, s 106.
14 Bankruptcy Act 1914, s 33(1)(f) as amended in respect of debts specified in Social Security Act 1975, s 153(2) and Social Security Pensions Act 1975, Sch 3.

9.5.8 Preferential debts are required to be paid 'forthwith', subject to the realisation by the trustee of sufficient for the costs referred to above (para 9.4.1). Thus, preferential creditors can usually expect a much earlier dividend payment than other creditors.

4 Ordinary creditors

9.5.9 Creditors who have proved in the bankruptcy and who do not fall into any of the categories discussed above, and who have not become such creditors by way of subrogation, and are not deferred creditors (as to which see below) all rank equally together for the payment after those categories have been paid.[1] They abate equally if, as is usually the case, there are insufficient funds for payment in full.

1 Bankruptcy Act 1914, s 33(7).

5 Deferred or postponed creditors

9.5.10 *Interest.* Whilst the full amount of interest legally payable by a debtor prior to his receiving order may be proved for in full, interest at the rate of only 5% ranks for dividend with ordinary creditors until all the debts in the bankrupt's estate have been paid in full.[1] However, such interest ranks for payment ahead of other deferred or postponed debts.[2]

[1] Bankruptcy Act 1914, s 66(1).
[2] *Re Baughan, ex p Official Receiver v Bennett* [1947] Ch 313.

9.5.11 *Loans between husband and wife.* Where a husband is adjudicated bankrupt, his wife is a deferred creditor in respect of money or other property lent or entrusted to her husband.[1] However, if it is the wife who is adjudicated bankrupt then her husband is only a deferred creditor in respect of money or property lent for the purpose of use in the wife's trade or business.[2] Any other sort of loan ranks with the claims of other creditors.

A wife is not a postponed creditor if her loan was to a firm or partnership of which her husband was a member.[3]

[1] Bankruptcy Act 1914, s 36(2).
[2] Ibid, s 36(1).
[3] *Re Tuff, ex p Nottingham* (1887) 19 QBD 88.

9.5.12 *Loans to traders.* Where money was lent to a bankrupt who was in business, and where agreement for repayment had been reached whereby the lender would receive a share of the profits of that business or, if the rate of the interest payable on the loan varied with the profits of the business, then such a creditor is deferred until all the ordinary creditors have been paid in full.[1]

[1] Partnership Act 1890, s 3.

9.5.13 *Statutory interest.* Once all the above debts have been paid, any surplus must be applied in the payment of interest at the rate of 4% on the proved debts.[1] Such interest is calculated without rests from the date of the receiving order.

[1] Bankruptcy Act 1914, s 33(8).

9.5.14 *Claims under voidable settlements.* The last distribution, before a surplus exists for the bankrupt, is a claim by the beneficiary of a settlement made by the bankrupt but avoided by his trustee under one of the provisions discussed in ch 8 above.[1]

[1] Bankruptcy Act 1914, s 42(2), (3).

6 Surplus

9.5.15 The bankrupt is entitled to any surplus remaining after all the creditors who have proved in his bankruptcy, have been paid in full.[1]

[1] Bankruptcy Act 1914, s 69.

9.6 THE PAYMENT OF THE DIVIDEND

1 Time

9.6.1 The Bankruptcy Act 1914 obliges the trustee to declare a first dividend (if any) and to distribute it, within four months of the conclusion of the first meeting of creditors.[1] However, if he can satisfy his committee of inspection that there is 'sufficient reason' for postponing the declaration then he may do so.[1] Save in unusually straightforward cases, this period is almost invariably extended.

[1] Bankruptcy Act 1914, s 62(2).

9.6.2 Subsequent dividends should be made at intervals of not more than six months, again subject to sufficient reason to the contrary.[1] In practice, trustees will often argue that there are sufficient reasons to the contrary but if a trustee unreasonably delays payment, it is for the committee of inspection, or the creditors in general meeting, to require that he proceeds in accordance with the Bankruptcy Act 1914 or is removed (see ch 4 above).[2]

[1] Bankruptcy Act 1914, s 62(3).
[2] And see provisions of Bankruptcy Act 1914, s 68.

9.6.3 When he is in a position to declare a final dividend, the trustee must give notice[1] of his intention to do so by advertisement in the *Gazette*[2] and, in particular, by notice to every creditor who is named in the bankrupt's statement of affairs but who has not actually proved as a creditor. The notice[3] is designed to give creditors a last chance to prove as such. It gives the period (not less than 14 days) in which proofs may be lodged.

Similarly, the trustee must give notice in the prescribed manner[4] to creditors who have notified the trustee of claims but have not established them to his satisfaction. He gives notice to the effect that if they do not satisfy him with respect to their claims within the time specified in the notice, he will declare a final dividend without regard to their claims.[5]

[1] Bankruptcy Act 1914, s 62(4); Bankruptcy Rules 1952, r 267(1)(2).
[2] Effected by Department of Trade on receiving notice from the trustee.
[3] Bankruptcy Rules 1952, Form No 172, r 267.
[4] Ibid, Form No 173.
[5] Bankruptcy Act 1914, s 67; Bankruptcy Rules 1952, r 267.

9.6.4 The trustee's notice of dividend is in a form prescribed in the Bankruptcy Rules 1952[1] and is accompanied by a statement[2] giving particulars of the bankrupt's estate, including details of the trustee's own remuneration, and a notice of the creditor's right to have that remuneration fixed by the Department of Trade if a quarter, in number or value, of the creditors dissent from the resolution passed by the creditors in general meeting (or the committee of inspection as the case may be) approving it in the first place.[3]

[1] Form 175.
[2] Prescribed by Bankruptcy Rules 1952, Form 169.
[3] See para 9.6 above and Bankruptcy Act 1914, s 68.

2 Payment

9.6.5 The 'system' theoretically expects such creditor to call on the trustee personally in order to collect his dividend. Of course, in practice, the creditor requests payment by post[1] by completing and returning a form of authority on the notice of dividend described above.

[1] Bankruptcy Rules 1952, r 272.

3 Unclaimed dividends

9.6.6 Dividends unclaimed and undistributed, and any unclaimed or undistributed money in the hands of the trustee after payment of his final dividend, must be paid by the trustee to the Insolvency Services Account at the Bank of England. Claims against such sums may be made to the Department of Trade. A person dissatisfied with the Department's decision may apply to the High Court.[1]

[1] Bankruptcy Act 1914, s 153.

9.7 PROCEDURAL TABLES

A. Proof of debt

1. The creditor who claims in the bankruptcy proves his debt in a claim called the *proof of debt*. It must be in writing but may be unsworn, unless either the official receiver or trustee require it to be sworn (Bankruptcy Act 1914, Sch 2 para 2).

Steps to be Taken	Bankruptcy Act 1914	Bankruptcy Rules 1952
1. Proof of debt may be made by the creditor himself or someone authorised by him or on his behalf. If it is made by an authorised person it must state his authority and means of knowledge.	Sch 2, para 3	
It must contain or refer to a statement of account showing the particulars of the debt and should specify any vouchers by which it can be substantiated. The official receiver or trustee may call for production of the vouchers at any time.	Sch 3, para 4	
It must state whether or not the creditor is a secured creditor. Failure so to state by a secured creditor may result in surrender of the creditor's security unless the court is satisfied the omission arose from inadvertence in which case the court may allow amendment on such terms as it sees fit.	see Sch 2, para 5	

Steps to be Taken	Bankruptcy Act 1914	Bankruptcy Rules 1952
The creditor must deduct all trade discounts, but he need not deduct any cash discount not exceeding 5% on the net amount of his claim.	Sch 2, para 8	
The creditor bears the cost of proving his debt unless the court specifically orders otherwise.	Sch 2, para 6	
2. Creditor delivers (or sends by post) affidavit verifying the debt to official receiver or trustee.	Sch 2, para 2	
TIME:		
(1) If proof is intended to be used at first meeting of creditors it must be lodged: not later than the time mentioned for the meeting in the notice convening the meeting, which must be not earlier than midday on the day but one before, or later than midday on the day before, the day appointed for the meeting.		r 252(1)(2)
(2) If proof is intended to be used at an adjournment of first meeting of creditors and was not lodged in time for first meeting, it must be lodged: not less than 24 hours before time fixed for adjourned meeting.		r 252(3)
(3) If trustee has given notice of intention to declare a dividend proof must be lodged if debt is to rank for dividend: within the time specified in the notice of intention (which must be not less than 14 days from the date of the notice).		r 267(2)
Official receiver or trustee examines every proof and ground of debt and, in writing to creditor, may:	Sch 2, para 23	
(1) admit proof in whole or part;	Sch 2, para 23	
or		
(2) reject proof in whole or part;	Sch 2, para 23	
or		
(3) require further evidence in support of proof.	Sch 2, para 23	
If the proof is rejected he must state the grounds of rejection in writing.	Sch 2, para 23	
TIME for admitting or rejecting proofs:		
(1) If official receiver is acting as trustee: within 14 days from the latest date for lodging proofs mentioned in the notice of intention to declare a dividend.		r 258

Steps to be Taken	Bankruptcy Act 1914	Bankruptcy Rules 1952
(2) By trustee other than official receiver: within 28 days after receiving a proof which has not previously been dealt with by official receiver; or,		r 259
where trustee has given notice of intention to declare a dividend: within 14 days after the latest date mentioned in the notice for lodging proofs.		rr 259, proviso, 260(2)
If trustee fails to deal with a proof within the time limited he will be deemed to have admitted it.		see r 259
The court may extend the time for dealing with proofs.		r 389
Where a proof has been rejected on its merits it cannot be withdrawn and a fresh proof presented. A creditor may withdraw a proof which has not been used for the purposes of either voting or claiming a dividend without the consent either of the trustee or of the court. A proof which is rejected on technical grounds may be withdrawn and a fresh proof tendered; a proof rejected on its merits cannot be withdrawn but an appeal may be brought against the rejection within 21 days.	see Sch 1, para 10	see r 261
If a creditor votes in respect of his whole debt he is deemed to have surrendered his security unless the court, on application, is satisfied that the omission to value the security has arisen from inadvertence. Where a creditor's proof has been admitted the notice of dividend will be sufficient notification to the creditor of the admission.		r 260(1)
A creditor may release the debtor from his debt. When decision has been made admitting or rejecting proofs.		
3. If a trustee is appointed: official receiver: (1) makes a list of all proofs of debt which he has received; and		r 253(a)
(2) hands proofs over to trustee after taking, on the list, receipt from trustee.		r 253(b)
If a trustee other than the official receiver is not appointed: official receiver sends to registrar all proofs tendered in the proceedings with a certified list distinguishing proofs wholly or partly		

Steps to be Taken	Bankruptcy Act 1914	Bankruptcy Rules 1952
admitted and those wholly or partly rejected.		r 254
TIME: Forthwith after either: (1) final payment has been made in a composition or scheme approved by court, or		r 254(a)
(2) final dividend has been declared in the administration of the estate in bankruptcy.		r 254(b)
4. Where trustee is appointed: trustee: (1) Sends to registrar a certified list of all proofs received by him from official receiver or otherwise tendered during the preceding month, distinguishing those admitted, rejected and held over for further consideration; and		r 255(a)
(2) transmits all proofs admitted or rejected to registrar to be filed.		r 255(b)
5. If trustee thinks proof was improperly admitted: trustee or, if trustee declines to intervene, any creditor, applies by motion supported by affidavit for order to expunge proof or reduce its amount.	Sch 2, paras 24, 26	
6. Trustee or other applicant gives notice of application to creditor who made the proof.	Sch 2, para 24	
7. All parties having notice attend hearing, where court considers matter and may make order expunging or reducing the proof. Where the proof exceeds £200 the application is in open court before a judge; in other cases it is before a registrar in chambers.		r 8(1)(g) r 8(2)
If creditor assigned debt offer he proved in bankruptcy.		
8. Assignee applies to court, supported by affidavit, for leave to expunge assignor's proof and to file his own proof in substitution. The application is heard in chambers as there is no question of dispute. Machinery is, however, provided for the payment of dividends to a person other than the creditor who proved the debt.		see r 273
9. Court considers application and may by order expunge the assignor's proof and give assignee leave to file his proof in substitution.		
10. Assignee files proof as in Steps 1 and 2.		

B. Disputed claims

Steps to be Taken	Bankruptcy Act 1914	Bankruptcy Rules 1952
1. If the creditor is dissatisfied with rejection or partial rejection of his proof of debt he may appeal by motion supported by affidavit for order reversing or varying official receiver's or trustee's rejection.	Sch 2, para 25	r 268(1)
TIME: (1) Within 21 days from date of decision to reject proof		r 261
(2) Where the appeal is brought after latest date for lodging proofs mentioned in declaration of intention to pay dividend: within 7 days from date of notice of rejection against which appeal is made.		r 268(1)(a)
If no appeal is brought within the prescribed time the trustee must exclude the rejected proof from participation in the dividend.		r 268(2)
The official receiver or trustee must provide for the dividend payable upon the proof and probable costs of the appeal if the appeal succeeds.		r 268(1)(b)
2. Creditor: (1) serves notice of motion on official receiver or trustee; (2) files affidavit supporting motion.		r 268(1)(a)
TIME: As in Step 1.		r 268(1)(a)
3. Trustee files proof at court together with memorandum stating his reasons for rejection.		r 257(1)
TIME: Within 3 days of receiving notice of motion.		r 257(1)
The trustee may file an affidavit in opposition.		
4. Parties attend for hearing of application, where court may allow appeal in whole or in part, or dismiss it, reversing or varying trustee's decision.	Sch 2, para 25	
Where the rejected proof is for a sum greater than £200 application is to a judge in open court; in other cases it is to a registrar in chambers.		r 8(1)(g) r 8(2)
Where an appeal succeeds no costs may be ordered personally against the official receiver.		r 262

9.8 FORMS

NOTE: The official receiver provides forms of proof of debt without charge. Attached to the proof almost invariably is a form of proxy so that the creditor may appoint a proxy, very often the official receiver himself, to vote at the first meeting of creditors.

NOTICE to creditor of admission of proof where interest exceeding 5% is postponed or deferred

IN THE [HIGH COURT OF JUSTICE *or* . . . . COUNTY COURT]
In Bankruptcy No. . . . of 19 . . . .
Re A B [*add, after adjudication*, a Bankrupt]

TAKE NOTICE that, as [Official Receiever *or* Trustee] of the above estate, I have this day admitted your proof against such estate, but for the purpose of dividend I have marked it as allowed at the sum of £. . . . being £. . . . the amount remaining due in respect of principal and £. . . . interest, calculated at the rate of 5% per annum in accordance with Section 66 of the Bankruptcy Act 1914, without prejudice to your right to receive out of the estate any higher rate of interest to which you may be entitled after all debts proved on the estate have been paid in full.

AND FURTHER TAKE NOTICE that subject to the power of the Court to extend the time no application to reverse or vary my decision in so dealing with the proof for the purpose of dividend, will be entertained after the expiration of [21 *or* 7] days.

DATED this . . . . day of . . . . 19 . . . .

(*Signature*)
[Official Receiver *or* Trustee]

To C D, of (*address*)

NOTICE of rejection of proof of debt

IN THE [HIGH COURT OF JUSTICE *or* . . . . COUNTY COURT]
In Bankruptcy No. . . . of 19 . . . .
Re A B [*add, after adjudication*, a Bankrupt]

TAKE NOTICE that, as [Official Receiver *or* Trustee] of the above estate, I have this day rejected your claim against such estate [to the extent of £. . . .] on the following grounds:

[That the debt or liability of the Debtor to you was contracted by the Debtor after you had notice that he had committed the act of bankruptcy on which the Bankruptcy Petition herein was founded *or as the case may be*.]

AND FURTHER TAKE NOTICE that if you are dissatisfied with my decision in respect of your proof, you may apply to the Court to reverse or vary the same, but, subject to the power of the Court to extend the time, no application to reverse or vary my decision in rejecting your proof will be entertained after the expiration of [21 *or* 7] days from this date.

DATED this . . . . day of . . . . 19 . . . .

(*Signature*)
[Official Receiver *or* Trustee]

To C D, of (*address*)

NOTICE by trustee requiring further evidence in support of proof

(*Address and date*)

Re A B

TAKE NOTICE that as [Official Receiver *or* Trustee] of the property of the above-named Debtor I require further evidence in support of the proof of debt filed by you herein.

The evidence required by me is:

(1) Evidence of the alleged payment by you to the Debtor of the sum of £. . . . on . . . . 19 . . . .; if in writing, the Debtor's request for the said sum, and if not, how and when the request was made; the cheque drawn by you in respect of such sum; the receipt (if any) given by the Debtor.

(2) Evidence of the alleged case payment made by you to the Debtor on . . . . 19 . . . . stating the circumstances under which you allege the said payment was made; why it was made in cash and not by cheque; whether you drew a cheque for the said cash, and if so the production thereof; and if no cheque was drawn, the source of the said large sum of cash or how otherwise it came into your possession:

AND TAKE NOTICE that if you fail to supply the said evidence or fail to supply me with satisfactory reason of your inability to supply the same, or othewise fail to satisfy me as to your claim, I shall [reject your said proof in full *or as the case may be*].

DATED this . . . . day of . . . . 19 . . . .

(*Signature*)
[Official Receiver *or* Trustee]

To C D, of (*address*)

APPLICATION by trustee for extension of time for dealing with proof of debt

IN THE [HIGH COURT OF JUSTICE *or* . . . . COUNTY COURT]

In Bankruptcy No. . . . of 19 . . . .

Re A B [*add, after adjudication*, a Bankrupt]

Ex parte [the Debtor *or* the Bankrupt *or* C D a Creditor *or* the Official Receiver *or* the Trustee *or as the case may be*]

APPLICATION is hereby made on behalf of T T, the above-named Trustee, for an Order extending the time for . . . . days within which the Trustee may admit or reject the proof of debt of C D, lodged [herein *or* with the Official Receiver on . . . . 19 . . . .] upon the grounds set forth in the affidavit* of C D filed . . . . 19 . . . .

(*Signature*), of (*address*), [Agents for (*name*), of (*address*),] Solicitors for the [Debtor *or* Bankrupt *or* Trustee *or* Judgment Creditor *or* Petitioning Creditor *or as the case may be*]

* The affidavit should contain particulars of the alleged consideration for the debt alleged in the proof and the grounds on which the trustee requires his time for dealing with the proof to be extended; for example, that the creditor, although requested so to do, has failed to supply the trustee with all the necessary evidence in support of his claim, and that the trustee's time for dealing with the proof will expire before he will be in a position to deal with it.

NOTICE OF MOTION by trustee for order expunging proof on the ground that it has been improperly admitted

IN THE [HIGH COURT OF JUSTICE *or* . . . . COUNTY COURT]

In Bankruptcy No. . . . of 19 . . . .

Re A B, a Bankrupt

Ex parte the Trustee of the Property of the above-named Bankrupt Applicant

v

L M Respondent

TAKE NOTICE that this Honourable Court will be moved before [the Judge sitting in Bankruptcy at the Royal Courts of Justice, Strand, London WC2 at the sitting of the Court *or, in a county court*, His Honour the Judge thereof at the sitting of the Court at (*address*)] on [Monday] the . . . . day of . . . . 19 . . . . or so soon thereafter as Counsel can be heard by Counsel on behalf of the above-named Applicant.

(1) for an Order that the proof of debt sworn herein by the Respondent on . . . . 19 . . . . for the sum of £. . . . and admitted to rank for dividend on . . . . 19 . . . . be expunged;

(2) that such an Order as to the costs of and incidental to this application be made as to the Court may seem meet;

(3) that such further or other Order be made as to the Court may seem fit.

AND TAKE NOTICE that in support hereof the affidavit of the Applicant filed . . . . 19 . . . ., a copy of which is served herewith, will be read [and that if necessary viva voce evidence will be adduced].

DATED this . . . . day of . . . . 19 . . . .

(*Signature*), of (*address*), [Agents for (*name*), of (*address*),] Solicitors for the [Debtor *or* Bankrupt *or* Trustee *or* Judgment Creditor *or* Petitioning Creditor *or as the case may be*]

To L M, of (*address*), the Respondent, and to his solicitors Messrs G H & Co, of (*address*)

APPLICATION by assignee for leave to expunge assignor's proof and file proof in substitution

IN THE [HIGH COURT OF JUSTICE *or* . . . . COUNTY COURT]

In Bankruptcy No. . . . of 19 . . . .

Re A B [*add, after adjudication*, a Bankrupt]

Ex parte [the Debtor *or* the Bankrupt *or* C D a Creditor *or* the Official Receiver *or* the Trustee *or as the case may be*]

APPLICATION is hereby made on behalf of L M for an Order that the proof of debt filed herein by O P be expunged and that leave be given to the said L M to file a proof in substitution thereof and to receive such dividends as the said O P would have been entitled to receive on his said proof.

DATED this . . . . day of . . . . 19 . . . .

(*Signature*), of (*address*), [Agents for (*name*), of (*address*),] Solicitors for the [Debtor *or* Bankrupt *or* Trustee *or* Judgment Creditor *or* Petitioning Creditor *or as the case may be*]

9.9 PROOF OF DEBTS: BANKRUPTCY ACT 1914, Sch 2 (as amended)

9.9.1

Proof in ordinary cases

1. Every creditor shall prove his debt as soon as may be after the making of a receiving order.

2. A debt may be proved by delivering or sending through the post in a prepaid letter to the official receiver or, if a Trustee has been appointed, to the Trustee:–
(a) in any case in which the Official Receiver or Trustee so requires, an affidavit verifying the debt;
(b) in any other case, an unsworn claim to the debt.

3. The affidavit or claim may be made by the creditor himself or by some person authorised by or on behalf of the creditor. If made by a person so authorised, it shall state his authority and means of knowledge.

4. The affidavit or claim shall contain or refer to a statement of account showing the particulars of the debt, and shall specify the vouchers, if any, by which the same can be substantiated. The Official Receiver or Trustee may at any time call for the production of the vouchers.

5. The affidavit or claim shall state whether the creditor is or is not a secured creditor and if it is found at any time that the affidavit or claim made by or on behalf of a secured creditor has omitted to state that he is a secured creditor, the secured creditor shall surrender his security to the Official Receiver or Trustee for the general benefit of the creditors unless the Court on application is satisfied that the omission has arisen from inadvertence, and in that case the court may allow the affidavit or claim to be amended upon such terms as to the repayment of any dividends or otherwise as the court may consider to be just.

6. A creditor shall bear the cost of proving his debt, unless the Court otherwise specially orders.

7. Every creditor who has lodged a proof shall be entitled to see and examine the proofs of other creditors before the first meeting, and at all reasonable times.

8. A creditor proving his debt shall deduct therefrom all trade discounts, but he shall not be compelled to deduct any discount, not exceeding five per cent on the net amount of his claim, which he may have agreed to allow for payment in cash.

9. Formal proof of debts in respect of contributions payable under the Social Security Act 1975 or the Social Security (Northern Ireland) Act 1975, or of state scheme premiums payable under Part III of the Social Security Pensions Act 1975 or any corresponding provisions in force in Northern Ireland to which contributions and premiums priority is given by this Act shall not be required except where it may otherwise be provided by rules under this Act.

9.9.2

Proof by secured creditors

10. If a secured creditor realises his security, he may prove for the balance due to him, after deducting the net amount realised.

11. If a secured creditor surrenders his security to the Official Receiver or Trustee for the general benefit of the creditors, he may prove for his whole debt.

12. If a secured creditor does not either realise or surrender his security, he shall, before ranking for dividend, state in his proof the particulars of his security, the date when it was given, and the value at which he assesses it, and shall be entitled to receive a dividend only in respect of the balance due to him after deducting the value so assessed.

13. (a) Where a security is so valued, the Trustee may at any time redeem it on payment to the creditor of the assessed value.
(b) If the Trustee is dissatisfied with the value at which a security is assessed, he may require that the property comprised in any security so valued be offered for sale at such times and on such terms and conditions as may be agreed on between the creditor and the Trustee, or as, in default of such agreement, the Court may direct. If the sale be by public auction the creditor, or the Trustee on behalf of the estate, may bid or purchase.
(c) Provided that the creditor may at any time by notice in writing, require the Trustee to elect whether he will or will not exercise his power of redeeming the security or requiring it to be realised, and if the trustee does not, within six months after receiving the notice, signify in writing to the creditor his election to exercise the power, he shall not be entitled to exercise it; and the equity of redemption, or any other interest in the property comprised in the security which is vested in the Trustee, shall vest in the creditor, and the amount of his debt shall be reduced by the amount at which the security has been valued.

14. Where a creditor has so valued his security, he may at any time amend the valuation and proof on showing to the satisfaction of the Trustee, or the Court, that the valuation and proof were made bona fide on a mistaken estimate or that the security has diminished or increased in value since its previous valuation; but every such amendment shall be made at the cost of the creditor, and upon such terms as the Court shall order, unless the Trustee shall allow the amendment without application to the Court.

15. Where a valuation has been amended in accordance with the foregoing rule, the creditor shall forthwith repay any surplus dividend which he may have received in excess of that to which he would have been entitled on the amended valuation, or, as the case may be, shall be entitled to be paid out of any money, for the time being available for dividend, any dividend or share of dividend, which he may have failed to receive by reason of the inaccuracy of the original valuation, before that money is made applicable to the payment of any future dividend, but he shall not be entitled to disturb the distribution of any dividend declared before the date of the amendment.

16. If a creditor after having valued his security subsequently realises it, or if it is realised under the provisions of rule 13, the net amount realised shall be substituted for the amount of any valuation previously made by the creditor, and shall be treated in all respects as an amended valuation made by the creditor.

17. If a secured creditor does not comply with the foregoing rules he shall be excluded from all share in any dividend.

18. Subject to the provisions of rule 13, a creditor shall in no case receive more than one hundred pence in the pound, and interest as provided by this Act.

9.9.3

Proof in respect of distinct contracts

19. If a debtor was, at the date of the receiving order, liable in respect of distinct contracts as a member of two or more distinct firms, or as a sole contractor, and also as member of a firm, the circumstances that the firms are in whole or in part composed of the same individuals, or that the sole contractor is also one of the joint contractors, shall not prevent proof in respect of the contracts, against the properties respectively liable on the contracts.

9.9.4

Periodical payments

20. When any rent or other payment falls due at stated periods, and the receiving order is made at any time other than one of those periods, the person entitled to the rent or payment may prove for a proportionate part thereof up to the date of the order as if the rent or payment grew due from day to day.

9.9.5

Interest

21. On any debt or sum certain, payable at a certain time or otherwise, whereon interest is not reserved or agreed for, and which is overdue at the date of the receiving order and provable in bankruptcy, the creditor may prove for interest at a rate not exceeding four per cent per annum to the date of the order from the time when the debt or sum was payable, if the debt or sum is payable by virtue of a written instrument at a certain time, and if payable otherwise, then from the time when a demand in writing has been made giving the debtor notice that interest will be claimed from the date of the demand until the time of payment.

9.9.6

Debt payable at a future time

22. A creditor may prove for a debt not payable when the debtor committed an act of bankruptcy as if it were payable presently, and may receive dividends equally with the other creditors, deducting only thereout a rebate of interest at the rate of five pounds per centum per annum computed from the declaration of a dividend to the time when the debt would have become payable, according to the terms on which it was contracted.

9.9.7

Admission of rejection of proofs

23. The Trustee shall examine every proof and the grounds of the debt, and in writing admit or reject it, in whole or in part, or require further evidence in support of it. If he rejects a proof he shall state in writing to the creditor the grounds of the rejection.

24. If the Trustee thinks that a proof has been improperly admitted, the Court may, on the application of the Trustee, after notice to the creditor who made the proof, expunge the proof or reduce its amount.

25. If a creditor is dissatisfied with the decision of the Trustee in respect of a proof, the Court may, on the application of the creditor, reverse or vary the decision.

26. The Court may also expunge or reduce a proof upon the application of a creditor if the Trustee declines to interfere in the matter, or, in the case of a composition or scheme, upon the application of the debtor.

27. For the purpose of any of his duties in relation to proofs, the Trustee may administer oaths and take affidavits.

28. The Official Receiver, before the appointment of a Trustee, shall have all the powers of a Trustee with respect to the examination, admission, and rejection of proofs, and any act or decision of his in relation thereto shall be subject to the like appeal.

CHAPTER 10

Discharge

10.1 INTRODUCTION AND THE NEW LAW

10.1.1 An order of discharge must be contrasted with a rescission of the receiving order (ch 5 above) and an annulment of the adjudication order (ch 11 below).

The effects of such an order are described in more detail below. By way of introduction, it is sufficient to explain that a discharge effectively releases the bankrupt from his personal restrictions and disqualifications, for example the ability to obtain credit, or act as a company director, whilst, at the same time, he is relieved of his debts which, in effect, remain in his estate in bankruptcy. However, the bankruptcy still exists. It is only an annulment which can have the effect of setting aside the bankruptcy itself.

In particular, any assets still unrealised remain vested in the trustee in bankruptcy.

10.1.2 Whereas the Old Bankruptcy Law and the New Law will overlap in various fields for many years, in the very important subject of the discharge, that overlap will be limited.

In terms of space and words this chapter is largely devoted to what will be a diminishing number of applications made by bankrupts under the Bankruptcy Act 1914, s 26. In certain Old Bankruptcy Law cases the bankrupt may, for various reasons, not wish to wait for the simple effluxion of time which under the New Law will, in the main, enable him to achieve his discharge.

10.1.3 For a period of three years from 29 December 1986 there will be three types of discharge available to most bankrupts namely:

(i) under the New Bankruptcy Law;[1]
(ii) under the automatic provisions of the Insolvency Act 1976, ss 7 and 8; and
(iii) under the Bankruptcy Act 1914, s 26.

The complexity of these three types of discharge is in inverse proportion to their relevance these days but even the 'old' Bankruptcy Act 1914, s 26 type applications will be possible. They will be the only type available to certain bankrupts, for example to the person who has been adjudicated within 15 years before a second bankruptcy (see para 10.1.4 below).[2]

1 Insolvency Act 1986, Sch 11, para 13.
2 Also see ch 20 below and Insolvency Act 1986, s 278.

10.1.4 The Insolvency Act 1986, Sch 11, para 13[1] provides that where a person:

(a) was adjudged bankrupt before 29 December 1986 or is adjudged bankrupt on or after that date on a petition presented before that date; and
(b) that person was not an undischarged bankrupt at any time in the period of fifteen years ending with the adjudication

that person shall be deemed (if not previously discharged under the procedures explained below) to be discharged
(a) in the case of a person adjudged bankrupt before 29 December 1986 after three years from that date and
(b) in the case of a person adjudged bankrupt after 29 December 1986 but on a petition presented before that date, after three years from the date of his adjudication.'

1 See also ch 20, below.

10.1.5 However, on an application by the official receiver, the court may order that the three year discharge period shall cease to run, for such period as it shall direct, if it is satisfied that the bankrupt has failed or is failing to comply with any of his obligations under the Bankruptcy Act 1914 or any rules made thereunder.[1]

The court also has power to suspend the running of the discharge period until such time as the bankrupt shall have complied with any conditions imposed by the court.[1]

1 Insolvency Act 1986, Sch 11, para 13.

10.2 AUTOMATIC DISCHARGE AND THE INSOLVENCY ACT 1976

1 If the adjudication date was pre-1 October 1967

10.2.1 On 1 October 1977 all bankrupts who had been adjudicated before 1 October 1967 were absolutely discharged.[1]

1 Insolvency Act 1976, s 7(4).

2 If the adjudication date was between 1 October 1967 and 30 September 1972

10.2.2 A bankrupt who was adjudicated after 30 September 1967 and before 1 October 1972 became absolutely discharged after ten years from the date of his adjudication.[1]

[1] Insolvency Act 1976, s 7(4).

3 If the adjudication date was between 1 October 1972 and 30 September 1977

10.2.3 A bankrupt who was adjudicated after 1 October 1972 but before 1 October 1977 became entitled to have his bankruptcy made the subject of an automatic review by court. On the hearing of reviews many bankrupts have been granted a discharge. This 'quincenial' review[1] is discussed at para 10.2.6 below.

[1] Insolvency Act 1976, s 8.

4 If the adjudication date is after 1 October 1977

10.2.4 In cases where adjudication was after 1 October 1977 there are two categories of the 'automatic' procedure which might come into effect.

Unless an order of the type discussed at 10.2.5 below is made, then (if the bankrupt has not already applied for a discharge under the Bankruptcy Act 1914, s 26[1]) the official receiver must, within 12 months of the fifth anniversary of the adjudication, make an application to the court in respect of the adjudication.[2]

At the hearing of that 'review' the court may grant the bankrupt a discharge, absolutely or conditionally.

Applications for a discharge at such hearings are dealt with at para 10.2.6 below.

[1] See also para 10.3 below.
[2] Insolvency Act 1976, s 8(1)(d), (2).

5 The automatic discharge

10.2.5 The other type of case relevant to persons adjudicated bankrupt under the Old Bankruptcy Law after 1 October 1977 is the type of case generally referred to as the 'automatic discharge'.[1]

If a bankrupt's public examination has been dispensed with by the court[2] under the provisions of the Insolvency Act 1976, s 6,[3] or if it has been concluded, the court may, if it thinks fit, make an order to the effect that the bankrupt is discharged with effect from the fifth anniversary of his adjudication.

If made at all the order is either made at the same time as the order dispensing with the public examination or it is made on the conclusion of the hearing of the public examination.

The automatic discharge order may be rescinded before it takes effect[4] and it does not preclude the bankrupt from applying under the Bankruptcy

Act 1914, s 26 for an earlier discharge nor from applying for an annulment of the adjudication order.

[1] Insolvency Act 1976, s 7.
[2] See ch 7 above.
[3] Insolvency Act 1976, s 8(3).
[4] Ibid, s 7(3).

10.2.6 A review of adjudication under the Insolvency Act 1976, s 8 (see para 10.2.3 and 10.2.4 above) comes before the registrar of the court. Notice is given to the bankrupt at least 14 days before the hearing[1] but creditors are not notified.

As in an application for discharge under the Bankruptcy Act 1914, s 26 (see below) the court is required to take into consideration a report by the official receiver 'as to the bankrupts conduct and affairs, including a report as to the bankrupt's conduct during the proceedings under his bankruptcy'.[2]

The report is prima facie evidence of the statements it contains.[2]

[1] Insolvency Act 1976, s 8(3).
[2] Ibid, s 8(4).

10.2.7 The court's powers in relation to a discharge on the five-year review are effectively the same as those available to it under the Bankruptcy Act 1914, s 26, namely it is empowered:[1]

(a) to grant or refuse an absolute discharge;
(b) to suspend the discharge for such period as it thinks fit or until a dividend of 50p in the £ has been paid to creditors; or
(c) to require the bankrupt as a condition of his discharge to consent to judgment being entered against him by the official receiver or trustee for a sum not exceeding the balance of his provable debts such balance to be paid out of future earnings or after acquired property of the bankrupt and in such manner and subject to such conditions as the court may direct.

The effect of these provisions is identical to those relating to a discharge under the Bankruptcy Act 1914, s 26 and are discussed in more detail under that head at para 10.6 below.

[1] Insolvency Act 1976, s 8(6).

10.2.8 There are two important procedural differences between an application for discharge at the hearing of a five-year review and an application under the Bankruptcy Act 1914, s 26.

In the first place the bankrupt himself need not be present or presented at a five-yearly review.[1] This enables the backlog of dormant bankruptcies to be reduced without the need for co-operation by a bankrupt who might, for example, have moved away, or simply see no point in going to the hearing of his automatic review.

Second, as is explained at para 10.5 below, whilst a s 26 application is almost invariably treated as opposed and therefore before a judge (or registrar in the High Court), an application at a five-year review takes place before the registrar.

[1] Insolvency Act 1976, s 8(5).

10.2.9 If a discharge is granted to a bankrupt under the automatic review provisions of the Insolvency Act 1976, s 8 the consequences and effect of the order are the same if an order was granted under the Bankruptcy Act 1914, s 26.[1] These are discussed at para 10.6 below.

[1] Insolvency Act 1976, s 8(9).

10.3 THE APPLICATION UNDER THE BANKRUPTCY ACT 1914, s 26

10.3.1 The procedural table at para 10.7 below sets out the detailed steps required to bring a discharge application before the court and those steps are not repeated here. However, a couple of aspects regarding the timing of the application should particularly be borne in mind.

10.3.2 The official receiver is bound to report on the bankrupt's conduct and affairs and to file the report at court and serve it on the bankrupt at least seven days before the hearing of the application.[1] In practice, because of the pressure on the Official Receiver's Department and since a considerable amount of work is often required to compile the report, the bankrupt and his advisers seldom receive the report before the seven-day deadline.

The report deals with the bankruptcy, and the debtor and his affairs generally but, in particular, it reports on the 'Facts' recited in the Bankruptcy Act 1914 s 26, the details and significance of which are dealt with below. The s 26 Facts are of critical importance in a discharge application. Basically, the more of them, and the degree of seriousness in respect of each, found against a bankrupt the more difficult is his task in making a successful application, or in reducing the conditions or period of suspension imposed.

The point, for present purposes, is that the official receiver's report constitutes prima facie evidence of the statements in it, so that, if there are s 26 findings[2] with which the bankrupt seeks to quarrel the onus is on him to rebut the prima facie finding already made.

He is required, at least two days before the hearing of the discharge application, to serve a notice on the official receiver to the effect that a particular finding is challenged.[3]

This means that the bankrupt and his advisors have a theoretical period of only five days in which to consider the report and its findings and to consider the Facts (as seen by the bankrupt) and the available evidence in order to decide whether or not the report should be challenged.

[1] Bankruptcy Rules 1952, r 228.
[2] Bankruptcy Act 1914, s 26(6).
[3] Bankruptcy Rules 1952, r 229(1).

10.3.3 The official receiver invariably studies the transcript or signed notes of the bankrupt's public examination before deciding what s 26 Facts should be asserted and since this is usually the best available evidence it is sensible for a bankrupt or his advisors to obtain a copy of the public examination notes or be in a position to attend a court at short notice in order to study them, so that the official receiver's report can be considered properly. A bankrupt having the benefit of solicitors and counsel on his application should consider reserving a conference with counsel for a day or so after the official receiver's report is due, so that a view can be taken on its significance in good time before the counter-notice has to be given.

10.3.4 The other aspect of 'timing' which requires consideration is the timing of the application itself. A discharge cannot under s 26 (rather than under the provisions of the Insolvency Act 1976, see para 10.2 above) be heard until after the public examination of the bankrupt is concluded. Theoretically it can be made immediately after the public examination is concluded but such applications are rare unless the conclusion of the public examination is a formality, e g by the signing by the bankrupt of the notes or transcript.

10.3.5 Creditors who have proved are entitled to inspect the official receiver's report[1] and to oppose a bankrupt's application for discharge. A creditor's rights at the hearing are considered at para 10.5 below. In relation to the application he must, if he intends to rely on grounds other than those relied on in the official receiver's report, file a written notice of his intention at least two days before the hearing. He must give notice of the reasons he intends to rely upon for opposing the discharge and he must serve copies of his notice on the official receiver and the bankrupt.[2]

1 Bankruptcy Rules 1952, r 15.
2 Ibid, r 229(2).

10.4 THE S 26 FACTS

10.4.1 Since a finding against a bankrupt of any of the s 26 Facts prevents the court from granting an immediate unconditional order of discharge[1] and since the court is expressly required to take into account the official receiver's report[2] which inevitably deals with any question of a finding in respect of the Facts, it is obviously of critical importance for any person considering an application under the Old Bankruptcy Law for a s 26 discharge to consider whether any, or many of the Facts apply to his case.

1 Bankruptcy Act 1914, s 26 and see para 10.6 below.
2 See para 10.5 below.

10.4.2 The s 26 Facts are as follows:
(a) that the bankrupt's assets are not of a value equal to 50p in the pound on the amount of his unsecured liabilities, unless he satisfies the court that the fact that the assets are not of a value equal to 50p in the pound on the amount of his unsecured liabilities has arisen from circumstances for which he cannot justly be held responsible;
(b) that the bankrupt has omitted to keep such books of account as are usual and proper in the business carried on by him and as sufficiently disclose his business transactions and financial position within the three years immediately preceding his bankruptcy;

(c) that the bankrupt has continued to trade knowing himself to be insolvent;
(d) that the bankrupt has contracted any debt provable in the bankruptcy without having at the time of contracting it any reasonable or probable ground or expectation (proof whereof shall lie on him) of being able to pay it;
(e) that the bankrupt has failed to account satisfactorily for any loss of assets or for any deficiency of assets to meet his liabilities;
(f) that the bankrupt has brought on, or contributed to, his bankruptcy by rash and hazardous speculations, or by unjustifiable extravagance in living, or by gambling, or by culpable neglect of his business affairs;
(g) that the bankrupt has put any of his creditors to unnecessary expense by a frivolous or vexatious defence to any action properly brought against him;
(h) that the bankrupt has, within three months preceding the date of the receiving order, incurred unjustifiable expense by bringing a frivolous or vexatious action;
(i) that the bankrupt has within three months preceding the date of the receiving order, when unable to pay his debts as they become due, given an undue preference to any of his creditors;
(j) that the bankrupt has, within three months preceding the date of the receiving order, incurred liabilities with a view of making his assets equal to 50p in the pound on the amount of his unsecured liabilities;
(k) that the bankrupt has, on any previous occasion, been adjudged bankrupt, or made a composition or arrangement with his creditors; or
(l) that the bankrupt has been guilty of any fraud or fraudulent breach of trust.

10.4.3 The official receiver either immediately after the close of the bankrupt's public examination, or by study of its transcript prior to preparing his report for a discharge application, completes his own form OR 134 which is entitled 'Report on Facts under Sections 26 and 27, etc' This form gives a useful insight into the criteria applied by official receivers in preparing their reports.

Since many of the s 26 Facts recited above are self-explanatory there is no point in further comment here. The following observations however should be borne in mind.

10.4.4 *Fact (b) (failure to keep proper books of account).* The official receiver will form a view on the reason for any failure, eg neglect, incompetence or a possible desire to 'cover up'. The preliminary examination[1] will have recorded details of defects in the bankrupt's book-keeping.

[1] See chapter 3.

10.4.5 *Fact (c) (continuing to trade whilst insolvent).* During the course of his preliminary examination[1] the debtor will have been asked to admit a date by when he had knowledge of his insolvency. The official receiver will examine this date and compare it with, for example, dates on which he was sued, or had execution levied, or was subject to final demands by bankers or other creditors. From the bankrupt's statement of affairs, the official receiver can list liabilities still outstanding but incurred after the date at which the official receiver submits that the debtor admits (or must have known) of his insolvency.

A much quoted phrase in this connection is that of Comer J:

> 'The moment (a person) becomes insolvent, then he is no longer going on at his own risk in case of failure; he is going on at the risk of his creditors. . . . In my judgment he has no right to do that.'[2]

[1] See chapter 3.
[2] *Re Stainton, ex p Board of Trade* (1887) 4 Morr 242.

10.4.6 *Fact (d) (contracting debts without reasonable expectation of ability to pay).* Banks very frequently require directors who are also shareholders in a borrowing company to give personal guarantees of the borrowing company's liabilities. When a company's borrowing is substantial it often follows that, in the bankruptcy of a guarantor of such liabilities, this Fact is found. Whilst it may often be impossible to challenge the official receiver's inevitable conclusion that this fact should be found as proved against a bankrupt, it is, or ought to be, the case that where the lender himself knew, or ought to have known, of the fact when he took the guarantee, the creditor should not be heard to complain.[1]

[1] *Re Stern, ex p Keyser Ullman Ltd v The Bankrupt* [1982] 2 All ER 600: the claim against the bankrupt exceeded £118m. Whilst his larger creditors were heard at his discharge application under Fact 'f' they did not seek to raise Fact 'd'.

10.4.7 *Fact (f) (rash or hazardous speculation or unjustifiable extravagance, etc).* Mr Justice Comer's test[1] of whose capital was at risk is a relevant consideration in connection with this 'fact'.

If the official receiver proposes to rely on the offence of rash and hazardous speculation he should not merely assert such a finding but should specify which transaction or transactions he complains of.[2]

Whilst the opening words of Fact (f) are frequently quoted it should be borne in mind that this fact extends to the bankrupt's standard of living and refers to possible culpable neglect of his business.

[1] Para 10.4.5 above.
[2] See *Re John Brown & Co* (1906) 22 TLR 291.

10.4.8 *Facts (g) & (h) (vexatious or frivolous defence or bringing of an action).* In particular the official receiver will look for any evidence of litigation being conducted contrary to the advice of solicitors or counsel.[1]

[1] Also see *Re Wenlock* (1968) 112 Sol Jo 722.

10.4.9 *Fact (i) (undue preference within three months).* This 'offence' is not the same as a fraudulent preference by the bankrupt as described in para 8.4 above.[1] It is somewhat wider, although covering a period of only three months preceding the receiving order rather than six months preceding presentation of the petition.

Fact (i) of s 26 is relevant only in relation to the conduct of the bankrupt and has no bearing on the validity of the transaction itself.

It is the bankrupt's duty when on the eve of bankruptcy, not to interfere in any way whatever among his creditors.[2]

The official receiver will consider whether the creditor in question pressed for payment by legal process or otherwise and whether or not the creditor was a friend or relative of the bankrupt.

[1] Under the Bankruptcy Act 1914, s 44.
[2] *Re Skegg, ex p Skegg* (1890) 25 QBD 505.

10.4.10 *Fact (k) (fraud or fraudulent breach of trust).* Neither fraud nor fraudulent breach of trust are defined for these purposes. Clearly the court does not need to find that a criminal offence has been committed. Ordinary civil law definitions of fraud are sufficient.

A lack of honesty by the bankrupt, as in making false statements,[1] or selling goods purchased on credit at less than cost price[2] is sufficient for these purposes.

[1] *Re Duce and Duce, ex p Duce* (1889) 6 Morr 290.
[2] *Re Coleman, ex p Coleman* (1858) 3 De G & J 43.

10.5 THE HEARING OF AN APPLICATION UNDER S 26

10.5.1 The hearing is in open court.[1] Theoretically, the hearing is in chambers if unopposed[2] but, since the Bankruptcy Rules 1952 provide[3] that wherever s 26 Facts are found the application for discharge is deemed to be opposed, it follows that chambers applications are very rare. Seldom does the official receiver have the happy task of reporting an excess of 50p in the pound and an absence of any of the other facts.

In any event, since, in practice, the courts have to list applications well in advance of the seven-day deadline by which the official receiver's report under s 26 must be filed, the end result is always an assumption that the application is opposed for the purposes of r 227 and the hearing is therefore fixed to proceed in open court.

[1] Bankruptcy Act 1914, s 26(1); Bankruptcy Rules 1952, r 8(1)(c).
[2] Bankruptcy Rules 1952, r 8(1)(c).
[3] Bankruptcy Rules 1952, r 227.

10.5.2 Being an opposed application, even only technically so because of r 227, the hearing must be before a judge in the county courts[1] or, in the High Court before a Registrar in Bankruptcy.[2]

[1] Bankruptcy Act 1914, s 102(2)(c).
[2] Ibid, s 102(3).

10.5.3 The court is expressly required to take into consideration the official receiver's report 'as to the bankrupt's conduct and affairs, including a report as to the bankrupt's conduct during the proceedings under his bankruptcy'.[1] It is usually read at the commencement of the hearing.

The official receiver's report is prima facie evidence of the statements in it.[2] Whilst it is not conclusive[3] it invariably carries great weight in any discharge hearing.

Apart from its reference to the official receiver's conclusion in relation to the s 26 Facts, his report also sets out the general background to the bankruptcy for the court's benefit and it contains a statement showing the bankrupt's assets and liabilities as estimated in his statement of affairs and what has been realised. It also summarises the extent of the preferential debts[4] and give estimates in relation to dividends for preferential and other creditors.

1 Bankruptcy Act 1914, s 26(6).
2 See *Re Oswell, ex p Board of Trade* (1892) 9 Morr 202.
3 See ch 9 above.
4 See para 10.6 below.

10.5.4 Creditors may be heard on an application for discharge[1] although of course no creditor can be required to be present or represented at a discharge application.

Although opposing creditors have the right to appear at the discharge hearing, and make submissions to protect their own interests and, if appropriate, to protect others, there is no right for creditors to cross examine the bankrupt or call evidence in opposition to the bankrupt's application.[2]

1 Bankruptcy Act 1914, s 26(7).
2 *Re Stern (a bankrupt), ex p Keyser Ullmann Ltd v The Bankrupt* [1982] 2 All ER 600.

10.5.5 In most cases it is thought that the court will glean all necessary information from the official receiver's report and it will only occasionally be necessary for the court to be asked to exercise its discretion to allow creditors to adduce further evidence by way of cross-examination of the bankrupt or otherwise. The reason that no court has discretion in this respect is that it is thought likely that there could be considerable waste of money and time and general 'unfairness' if an opposing creditor 'possibly unaffected by the outcome and possibly activated by malice' was entitled to cross-examine as of right.[1]

1 Per Templeman LJ in *Re Stern (a bankrupt), ex p Keyser Ullmann Ltd v The Bankrupt* [1982] 2 All ER 600.

10.6 THE ORDER OF DISCHARGE AND ITS EFFECTS

10.6.1 In a case in which the bankrupt has committed any offence under the Bankruptcy Act 1914, or any 'misdemeanour connected with his bankruptcy', or where any of the s 26 Facts are proved, the court *cannot* grant an immediate and unconditional order of discharge.[1]

1 Bankruptcy Act 1914, s 26(2).

10.6.2 If any of the s 26 Facts are found then four alternatives are open to the Court; they are set out in s 26(2) itself and are as follows:

(i) to refuse the discharge;
(ii) to suspend the discharge for a period of not less than two years; (but see below)
(iii) to suspend the discharge until a dividend of not less than 50p in the £ has been paid to Creditors; or
(iv) to require the bankrupt, as a condition of his discharge, to consent to judgment being entered against him by the official receiver or trustee for the balance or part of any balance of the debts provable in the bankruptcy.

10.6.3 Where the only s 26 Fact found against the bankrupt is the fact that his assets are not of a value of 50p in the £ then the suspension under (iii) above may be for less than two years.

10.6.4 The judgment which may be entered against the bankrupt under (iv) above is designed to be for payment out of the future earnings or after acquired property of the bankrupt. The court may order that the judgment be paid subject to such conditions and in such manner as it may direct.[1] Execution may not be issued on such a judgment without leave of the court, 'which may be given on proof that the bankrupt has, since his discharge, acquired property or income available towards payment of his debts'.[1]

[1] Bankruptcy Act 1914, s 26(2)(iv).

10.6.5 It should be noted that it is not for the court to order the entry of a judgment. The court sets out the terms and conditions of the judgment it requires as a condition of granting a discharge. It is then for the bankrupt to decide whether or not he consents to the entry of such a judgment. If the bankrupt has not given his consent within one month of the making of the order the court may rescind the order and make such other order as it thinks fit.[1]

[1] Bankruptcy Rules 1952, r 231(4).

10.6.6 In practice, a debtor who is legally advised usually calculates the maximum he considers he can afford and offers it to the court. The court should not impose a condition that the bankrupt consents to judgment unless it is probable that there will be after acquired assets or a surplus of income which will enable him to satisfy it.[1]

[1] *Re Bullen, ex p Amaud* (1888) 5 Morr 243; *Re Gould, ex p Gould* (1890) 7 Morr 215.

10.6.7 The court has power both to suspend a discharge and attach conditions to it concurrently.[1] In that event the discharge only becomes effective when both suspension and satisfaction of the conditions are fulfilled.

If the relevant condition is the requirement of consent to the entry of a judgment against the debtor, it is, of course, the entry of the judgment which complies with the condition, and not its satisfaction.

[1] Bankruptcy Act 1914, s 26(8).

10.6.8 The order of discharge is effective from the date it is made and it bears that date, whenever perfected. Its operation, however, is suspended until it has been perfected.[1]

[1] Bankruptcy Rules 1952, r 232.

Principal effects of the order

10.6.9 The three principal effects of the order are:

(i) the removal of the disqualifications, most notably the restriction upon obtaining credit (see chs 3 and 6 above);

(ii) the ability of the bankrupt to acquire property (and income) without his trustee having the right to intervene and appropriate it; and

(iii) to release the provable debts in the bankruptcy.

As to (iii) above, apart from certain excepted debts and liabilities, an order of discharge has the effect of releasing the bankrupt from all debts *provable* in the bankruptcy.[1] The only relevant debts not released by discharge are those arising by means of fraud or fraudulent breach of trust to which the bankrupt was a party.[2] There are other excluded categories, but they are either extremely rare[3] or, now, defunct.[4]

[1] Bankruptcy Act 1914, s 28(2).
[2] Ibid, s 28(1)(b).
[3] A charge or recognisance chargeable for an offence against a statute relating to any breach of the Public Revenue (but not fines): Bankruptcy Act 1914, s 28(1)(a).
[4] Eg liability for a judgment against the bankrupt for damages for an action in seduction. (Bankruptcy Act 1914, s 28(1)(c)).

10.6.10 An order of discharge does not release any person who, at the date of the receiving order, was a partner or co-trustee with the bankrupt, or was jointly liable under contract with him. Similarly it does not in any way release a surety for him from that surety's liability to the creditor.

10.6.11 The Bankruptcy Act 1914 specifically provides for the defence of proceedings brought by creditor on a debt released by discharge. The Act provides[1] that an order of discharge shall be conclusive evidence of the bankruptcy, and its validity, and that in any proceedings against a bankrupt who has obtained his discharge, the bankrupt may simply plead that the cause of action occurred before his discharge.

[1] Bankruptcy Act 1914, s 28(3).

10.6.12 The salary or income of the bankrupt after discharge does not continue to be vested in his trustee.[1]

However, if the bankrupt's discharge was conditional upon his consenting to the entry of a judgment against him, such judgment being paid out of his future earnings or after acquired property, he must give the official receiver such information as the official receiver requests about his earnings and after acquired property, until such time as the judgment is satisfied.[2] He must also, not less than once a year file a statement, verified by affidavit, showing particulars of any property or income acquired by him after his discharge.[2]

[1] *Re Gold, ex p Gold* (1891) 8 Morr 45.
[2] Bankruptcy Rules 1952, r 236(1).

10.6.13 Notwithstanding the order of discharge (but presumably where the judgment entered following the bankrupt's consent on or after the hearing of his application remains unsatisfied) the official receiver or trustee may require the bankrupt to attend before the court to be examined on oath as to his earnings, income, after acquired property, or dealings, or to be examined on the statement filed in accordance with the procedure set out at para 10.6.12 above.[1]

If the bankrupt fails either to file such a statement or to attend for examination as required by the official receiver or the trustee then the court has power to rescind the order of discharge.[2]

[1] Bankruptcy Rules 1952, r 236(2).
[2] Ibid, r 236(2).

10.6.14 Quite apart from the provisions of the Bankruptcy Rules 1952, r 236 (para 10.6.13 above) the court's powers under the Bankruptcy Act 1914, s 25)[1] to examine persons under oath, extend to an examination of the bankrupt after he has obtained his discharge.[2] This may be necessary if it becomes clear that, for example, he secreted assets from his trustee and the court, and that the court did not have a proper picture of his financial position when it considered the application for discharge. The result of such an examination may cause an interested party to apply for a review of the order of discharge.[3]

[1] See ch 8 above.
[2] *Re Debtor (No 12 of 1958) ex p Trustee of Property of Debtor v Clegg* [1968] 2 All ER 425.
[3] Bankruptcy Act 1914, s 108(i).

10.7 CERTIFICATE OF MISFORTUNE

10.7.1 The certificate of misfortune is really ancillary to an order of discharge. The Bankruptcy Act 1914 provides that such a certificate may be issued if 'the bankruptcy was caused by misfortune without any misconduct' on the bankrupt's part.[1]

Such certificates were of potential relevance in the days before the 1914 Act when certain disqualifications from public office were, following an adjudication in bankruptcy, perpetual. The certificate of misfortune enabled the bankrupt to escape the disqualifications. Whilst a bankrupt is disqualified from holding certain public offices for a period of five years from obtaining a discharge, these days applications for certificate of misfortune are rare. They may be sought by bankrupts seeking to 'clear' their names or by professional men who may be disqualified from pursuing their chosen profession and who hope, probably reasonably, that such a certificate will ease the task of applying for restoration to the professional body charged with granting or refusing the bankrupt's right to practise his profession.

[1] Bankruptcy Act 1914, s 26(4).

10.7.2 The issue of such certificates is rare. A bankrupt must be able to show an absence of misconduct on his part. He must also show not only misfortune but circumstances in which his downfall, though caused by the misfortune, was so improbable that no prudent person would have taken it into consideration when adopting a certain course of action.[1]

[1] See *Re Lord Colin Campbell* (1888) 20 QBD 816.

10.7.3 Thus, where a senior partner who was, reasonably, trusted by his partners, caused the bankruptcy of his partners by rash and hazardous speculation without their knowledge,[1] and where a solicitor presented his own petition (and was presumably adjudicated on the same day) under the misapprehension that he was insolvent,[2] certificates of misfortune were granted.

On the other hand a bankrupt whose misfortune was the Stock Exchange's suspension of dealings in shares he held, was not entitled to a certificate as it was of his own doing that he had borrowed heavily against the shares subsequently suspended.[3]

[1] *Re Boulton Bros & Co* [1927] 1 Ch 79.
[2] *Re Thomas, (1962) December (Cardiff No 11 of 1958)* referred to in 3 Halsbury's Laws (4th edn) para 452, fn.
[3] *Re debtor (No 612 of 1960), ex p Debtor v Official Receiver* [1964] 2 All ER 165.

10.8 PROCEDURAL TABLE FOR S 26 APPLICATION

Application for discharge under the Bankruptcy Act 1914, s 26

Steps to be Taken	Bankruptcy Act 1914	Bankruptcy Rules 1952
1. Bankrupt requests official receiver to supply him with certificate specifying the number of his creditors of whom the official receiver has notice, whether they have proved or not.		r 225
2. Official receiver supplies bankrupt with certificate accordingly.		
3. Bankrupt applies to court to fix day for hearing application for discharge by lodging;	s 26(1)	
(1) application in writing and		
(2) official receiver's certificate as to number of creditors, which must be reduced to registrar.		r 225
TIME: Any time after adjudication but the application will not be heard until the public examination has been concluded, unless it has been dispensed with.	s 26(1)	see r 196
Fee on application in respect of each debtor; £67 plus 5p for each creditor to be notified.		

Steps to be Taken	Bankruptcy Act 1914	Bankruptcy Rules 1952
4. Registrar appoints time and place for hearing application, and notifies time and place appointed to official receiver and trustee.	s 26(7)	
TIME: Not less than 28 days before day appointed.		r 226(1)
5. Official receiver sends notice of time and place appointed for hearing to:		
(1) Department of Trade and Industry to be gazetted.		r 226(1)
Fee on gazetting £14.50		
TIME: Forthwith on receipt of notice from registrar		r 226(1)
(2) Each creditor who has proved or is mentioned in the statement of affairs.	s 26(7)	r 226(2)
TIME: Not less than 14 days before day appointed for hearing.		r 226(2)
The official receiver must file a certificate of the posting of the notice to the creditors.		
6. Official receiver:		
(1) files report as to bankrupt's conduct and affairs, including his conduct during the proceedings under his bankruptcy and	s 26(2)	r 228
(2) sends copy report to bankrupt by registered post or the recorded delivery service.		r 228
TIME: Not less than 7 days before day appointed for hearing.		r 228
The report is prima facie evidence of the statements contained in it.	s 26(6)	
If the official receiver reports to the court any fact, matter or circumstance which would justify its refusing an unconditional order of discharge, the application is deemed to be an opposed application and consequently must be heard, in a county court, by a judge.	s 102(2)(c), (3)	r 227
Any creditor who has proved or any person on his behalf may inspect the report.		r 15
7. If bankrupt intends to dispute any statement with regard to his conduct or affairs contained in official receiver's report; bankrupt:		
(1) files at the court notice in writing specifying the statements in the report which he proposes to dispute; and		
(2) serves copy notice on official receiver.		r 229(1)

Steps to be Taken	Bankruptcy Act 1914	Bankruptcy Rules 1952
TIME: Not less than 2 days before hearing of application.		r 229(1)
8. Any creditor who intends to oppose the discharge on grounds other than those mentioned in official receiver's report:		
(1) files in court notice in writing stating his intended opposition and ground of it;		
(2) serves copy notice on official receiver;		
(3) serves copy notice on bankrupt.		r 229(2)
TIME: not less than 2 days before hearing of application.		r 229(2)
9. Court hears application for discharge.		
TIME: Not until bankrupt's public examination is concluded.	s 26(1)	
The application is heard by a registrar in the High Court; in the country court it is heard by a registrar if unopposed but by a judge if opposed.	s 102(2)(c), (3)	r 227
The official receiver's report is read and must be taken into consideration at the hearing.	s 26(2)	
The court may hear the official receiver, the trustee in bankruptcy and any proving creditor, and may put such questions to the bankrupt and receive such evidence as it thinks fit.	s 27(7)	
A creditor may oppose the discharge but he will only be heard if he puts forward grounds which do not appear from the official receiver's report. The court has a discretion to allow an opposing creditor to cross examine the bankrupt.		
10. The court makes order.		
Either:		
(1) If any of the s 26 'Facts' are proved or if the bankrupt is found to have committed a bankruptcy offence (see ch 7 above) then the court must		
(i) refuse the discharge; or	s 26(2), first proviso, (i)	
(ii) suspend the discharge either:		
(a) for such period as the court thinks proper or	s 26(2), first proviso, (ii)	
(b) until a dividend of not less than 50p in the £ has been paid to creditors or	s 26(2), first proviso, (iii)	

Steps to be Taken	Bankruptcy Act 1914	Bankruptcy Rules 1952
(iii) discharge the bankrupt conditionally on his own consenting to the entry of judgment against him by official receiver or trustee in bankruptcy for any sum not exceeding the balance of the debts provable under the bankruptcy and which are unsatisfied at the date of discharge, such sum to be paid out of the future earnings or after-acquired property of bankrupt in such manner and subject to such conditions as court directs; but execution may not be issued in the judgment without leave, which may be given on proof that bankrupt has since his discharge acquired property or income available towards payment of his debts.	s 26(2), first proviso, (iv)	
or		
(2) Court may either:		
(i) grant absolute order of discharge; or	s 26(2)	
(ii) refuse absolute order of discharge; or	s 26(2)	
(iii) suspend operation of order for specified time; or	s 26(2)	
(iv) grant order of discharge subject to any conditions with respect of any earnings or income which may afterwards become due to bankrupt, or with respect to his after-acquired property;	s 26(2)	
The powers of suspending and of attaching conditions to a bankrupt's discharge may be exercised concurrently.	s 26(8)	
The order bears the date of and takes effect from the day on which it is made, but its operation is suspended until such time as it is drawn up and signed.		r 232
The order will not be delivered out until the time for appealing has expired or until any appeal entered has been determined.		r 233(1)
The bankrupt's costs of or incidental to his application for discharge are not allowed for out of his estate.		r 230
The court may in any case adjourn the application, or on the bankrupt's		

Steps to be Taken	Bankruptcy Act 1914	Bankruptcy Rules 1952
application, allow the application to be withdrawn. The bankrupt may wish to withdraw his application for discharge; once such an application has been dismissed it cannot be heard de novo, and the only course available is to apply for a review of the order of dismissal. The application to withdraw is by motion on affidavit.	s 108(1)	
The trustee or the Department of Trade and Industry may appeal against any order made on application for discharge.	s 26(9)	r 234
At any time after discharge the trustee or the official receiver may, notwithstanding the order for discharge, apply to revoke it.	s 26(9)	
11. Certificate of misfortune: court may, if it thinks fit grant certificate that bankruptcy was caused by misfortune without any misconduct on bankrupt's part.	s 26(4)	
They are usually made informally and without notice at the hearing of the application to discharge; if made subsequently, the application should be made by motion supported by an affidavit, making the official receiver a respondent.	s 102(3)	r 8(1)(c)
The bankrupt may appeal by motion against the refusal of such a certificate	s 26(4)	
If court grants order for discharge conditionally on bankrupt consenting to entry of judgment against him for balance or any part of balance of any part of balance of provable debts not satisfied at date of discharge.	s 26(2), first proviso, (iv)	
12. Bankrupt signs consent to entry of judgment		r 231(1)
TIME: within 1 month after making of order		r 231(4)
If consent is not given within one month the official receiver or trustee may apply for an order rescinding the order of discharge or making such other order as the court thinks fit.		r 231(4)
The order or discharge will not be signed, completed or delivered out until this consent has been given.		r 231(1)
The judgment cannot be executed without leave.	s 26(2) first proviso	

Steps to be Taken	Bankruptcy Act 1914	Bankruptcy Rules 1952
13. Official receiver or trustee enters judgment against bankrupt accordingly on register of judgments of appropriate court.		r 231(2)
The judgment must be entered in the court having jurisdiction in the bankruptcy (though in the High Court it will be entered in the Chancery Division).		r 231(2)
14. If judgment is entered in county court; county court registrar makes return of judgment to registrar of county court judgments at County Courts Branch of Lord Chancellor's Department.		r 231(3)
15. If order for discharge is made conditional on bankrupt submitting to judgment or upon conditions as to disposal of his after-acquired property: bankrupt must: (1) give official receiver all information required by him as to his earnings and after-acquired property; (2) not less than once a year file at the court a statement verified by affidavit, showing particulars of any property or income acquired by him after his discharge		r 236(1)
Failure to comply with these provisions may lead to bankrupt's examination on oath as to his dealings with the property, and to rescission of the order of discharge.		r 236(2)
16. If official receiver or trustee wishes to issue execution on any judgment entered pursuant to conditional order of discharge: official receiver or trustee files application in writing for leave to issue execution, stating shortly the grounds on which the application is made.	s 26(2), first proviso	r 235(1)
17. Registrar fixes time and place for hearing.		r 235(2)
18. Official receiver or trustee sends to bankrupt: (1) notice of hearing; (2) copy of application.		r 235(3)
TIME: Not less than 8 days before day appointed for hearing.		r 235(3)
19. Court hears application and on proof that bankrupt has since his discharge acquired property or income available towards payment of his debts may give leave for execution to issue on judgment. Then:	s 26(2), first proviso	

Steps to be Taken	Bankruptcy Act 1914	Bankruptcy Rules 1952
20. Registrar draws up and signs order discharging bankruptcy		r 40
TIME: (1) After expiration of time limited for appealing or if an appeal is entered after determination of appeal and		r 233(1)
(2) After bankrupt has given any necessary consent to a judgment as a condition of making of order.		r 231(1)
21. Registrar sends notice of order to Department of Trade and Industry to be gazetted		r 233(2)
TIME: Forthwith when time for appealing against order has expired or when appeal has been decided.		r 233(2)
Fee on gazetting: £14.50		
If bankrupt desires modification of conditional order of discharge because he cannot comply with its terms.		
22. Bankrupt applies in writing for order modifying conditional order of discharge	s 26(2), second proviso	r 237
TIME: After the expiration of 2 years from date of order	s 26(2), second proviso	r 237
Fee: £6.		
23. Registrar fixes day for hearing application.		
24. Bankrupt gives notice of day fixed for hearing application to official receiver and to all creditors who have proved.		r 237
TIME: At least 14 days before day fixed for hearing.		r 237
25. Court hears application and, if satisfied there is no reasonable probability of bankrupt's being in a position to comply with terms of order in such manner and on such conditions as it thinks fit.	s 26(2), second proviso	
If bankrupt desires review, rescission or variation of order of discharge:		
26. Bankrupt makes application in chambers, supported by affidavit, for review, rescission or variation of order	s 108(1)	
The registrar marks the application 'Fix a day. Notice to Official Receiver'.		
27. Bankrupt serves copy of application indorsed with time and place of hearing, and copy affidavit, on official receiver.		
28. If bankrupt shows prima facie case for varying order registrar:		
(1) Adjourns matter into court		

Steps to be Taken	Bankruptcy Act 1914	Bankruptcy Rules 1952
(2) Sends notice of adjournment to official receiver and trustee.		
29. Official receiver:		
(1) gives notice to Department of Trade and Industry to be gazetted;		
(2) gives notice to such creditors, if any, as court has directed to be served with notice;		
(3) files certificate of postage of notices.		
30. Court considers application and may make order reviewing rescinding or varying order of discharge	s 108(1)	

10.9 FORMS

CERTIFICATE of number of creditors

IN THE [HIGH COURT OF JUSTICE *or* . . . . COUNTY COURT]

In Bankruptcy No . . . . of 19 . . . .

Re A B [*add, after adjudication*, a Bankrupt]

I certify that the creditors of the above-named Bankrupt who require to be notified of his intention to apply for his discharge are . . . . in number.

DATED this . . . . day of . . . . 19 . . . .

(*Signature*)
Official Receiver

APPLICATION to fix day to hear application for discharge

IN THE [HIGH COURT OF JUSTICE *or* . . . . COUNTY COURT]

In Bankruptcy No . . . . of 19 . . . .

Re A B [*add, after adjudication*, a Bankrupt]

I, A B, of (*address*) having been adjudged bankrupt on . . . . 19 . . . . and being desirous of obtaining my discharge, hereby apply to the Court to fix a day for hearing my application.

My public examination was concluded on . . . . 19 . . . .

[There are no other Receiving Orders against me in this or in any other Court *or as the case may be stating any other receiving orders, with their results*].

Annexed hereto is the certificate of the Official Receiver certifying the number of my creditors.

DATED this . . . . day of . . . . 19 . . . .

(*Signature*)

To the Registrar of the . . . . Court.

NOTICE by bankrupt of intention to dispute statements in Official Receiver's report on application for discharge

IN THE [HIGH COURT OF JUSTICE *or* . . . . COUNTY COURT]
In Bankruptcy No. . . . of 19 . . . .
Re A B [*add, after adjudication*, a Bankrupt]

TAKE NOTICE that A B, the above-named Bankrupt, intends to dispute the undermentioned statements contained in the report of the Official Receiver dated . . . . 19 . . . . on the application of the Bankrupt for his discharge.
(*Set out in detail the statements disputed*)
DATED this . . . . day of . . . . 19 . . . .

(*Signature*), of (*address*), [Agents for (*name*), of (*address*),] Solicitors for the [Debtor *or* Bankrupt *or* Trustee or Judgment Creditor *or* Petitioning Creditor *or as the case may be*]

To the Registrar
and to the Official Receiver

NOTICE by creditor of intention to oppose discharge on grounds other than those contained in Official Receiver's report

IN THE [HIGH COURT OF JUSTICE *or* . . . . COUNTY COURT]
In Bankruptcy No. . . . of 19 . . . .
Re A B [*add, after adjudication*, a Bankrupt]
Ex parte [the Debtor *or* the Bankrupt *or* C D a Creditor *or* the Official Receiver *or* the Trustee *or as the case may be*]

TAKE NOTICE that CD, of (*address*), a creditor herein, intends to appear on the hearing of the above-named Bankrupt's application for discharge, fixed for . . . . 19 . . . ., and to oppose the granting of the same on the grounds set out in the report of the Official Receiver and also on grounds other than those contained therein as hereunder appears:
(*Set out grounds*)
DATED this . . . . day of . . . . 19 . . . .

(*Signature*), of (*address*), [Agents for (*name*), of (*address*),] Solicitors for the [Debtor *or* Bankrupt *or* Trustee *or* Judgment Creditor *or* Petitioning Creditor *or as the case may be*]

To the Registrar
and to the Official Receiver
and to the above-named Bankrupt.

ORDER suspending discharge

IN THE [HIGH COURT OF JUSTICE *or* . . . . COUNTY COURT]
In Bankruptcy No. . . . of 19 . . . .
Re A B [*add, after adjudication*, a Bankrupt]

UPON THE APPLICATION of A B of (*address*) adjudged bankrupt on . . . . 19 . . . . and upon taking into consideration the report of the Official Receiver as to the

Bankrupt's conduct and affairs including the Bankrupt's conduct during the proceedings under his bankruptcy
AND UPON HEARING the Official Receiver and C D and E F Creditors and T T the Trustee
AND WHEREAS [it has not been proved that the Bankrupt has committed any of the offences mentioned in Section 26 of the Bankruptcy Act 1914 *or* it has been proved that the Bankrupt has committed the following offences namely (*give particulars*) [and *or* but] proof bas been made of the following facts under [Section 26(3) as amended by Section 1 of the Bankruptcy (Amendment Act 1926] [and] [under Section 27 of the Bankruptcy Act 1914] namely (*give particulars*) [and that he has been guilty of misconduct in relation to his property and affairs namely (*give particulars*)]]
IT IS ORDERED that the Bankrupt's discharge be suspended [until a dividend of not less than 50p in the pound has been paid to the creditor with liberty to the Bankrupt at any time after the expiration of 2 years from the date of this Order to apply for a modification thereof pursuant of Section 26 *or* for . . . . [months]] and that he be discharged as from . . . . 19 . . . .
DATED this . . . . day of . . . . 19 . . . .

By the Court
Registrar

ORDER discharging bankrupt subject to period of suspension and conditionally on bankrupt making payments

IN THE [HIGH COURT OF JUSTICE *or* . . . . COUNTY COURT]
In Bankruptcy No. . . . of 19 . . . .
Re A B, a Bankrupt

UPON THE APPLICATION of A B of (*address*) adjudged bankrupt on . . . . 19 . . . . and upon taking into consideration the report of the Official Receiever as to the Bankrupt's conduct and affairs including the Bankrupt's conduct during the proceedings under his bankruptcy
AND UPON HEARING the Official Receiver and C D and E F Creditors and T T the Trustee
AND WHEREAS it has not been proved that the Bankrupt has committed any of the offences mentioned in Section 26 of the Bankruptcy Act 1914 but proof has been made of the following facts under [Section 26(3) as amended by Section 1 of the Bankruptcy (Amendment) Act 1926] [and] [under Section 27 of the Bankruptcy Act 1914) namely (*give particulars*) [and that he has been guilty of misconduct in relation to his property and affairs namely (*give particulars*)]]
IT IS ORDERED that the Bankrupt's discharge be suspended for . . . . [months] and that he be discharged as from . . . . 19 . . . . subject to the following conditions as to his future earnings after acquired property and income which conditions shall operate concurrently with the aforesaid suspension and shall continue to operate if necessary after . . . . 19 . . . . that is to say after setting aside the yearly sum of £. . . . for the support of himself his wife and family the Bankrupt shall pay the surplus (if any) of such earnings after-acquired property and income to the Trustee of his Bankruptcy T T for distribution among the creditors in the Bankruptcy. An account shall on the first day of every year (the first of such accounts to be filed on 1 January 19 . . . .) or within 14 days thereafter be filed in these proceedings by the Bankrupt setting forth a statement of his receipts from earnings after-acquired property and income during the year immediately preceding the said date and the surplus payable under this Order

shall be paid by the Bankrupt to the Trustee within 14 days of the filing of the said account until his creditors shall have received . . . . pence in the pound
DATED this . . . . day of . . . . 19 . . . .

By the Court
Registrar

CONSENT of bankrupt to judgment being entered for balance of provable debts

IN THE [HIGH COURT OF JUSTICE *or* . . . . COUNTY COURT]
In Bankruptcy No. . . . of 19 . . . .

Re A B, a Bankrupt

I, A B, of (*address*), the above-named Bankrupt, do hereby consent to Judgment being entered against me in the [Chancery Division of Her Majesty's High Court of Justice] by the [Official Receiver *or* Trustee] for the sum of £. . . . being the balance or part of the balance of the debts provable under my bankruptcy which is not satisfied at the date of my discharge; but this consent is subject to the provision contained in the Bankruptcy Act 1914 with regard to the issue of execution on such Judgment.
DATED this . . . . day of . . . . 19 . . . .

(*Signature*)

CHAPTER 11

Annulment

11.1 INTRODUCTION

11.1.1 The annulment of an adjudication in bankruptcy must be contrasted with an order of discharge, as to which see ch 10 above.

11.1.2 In one respect it is potentially less advantageous than a discharge in that, whereas a discharge releases the bankrupt from all provable debts, the annulment, having the effect of revesting any remaining assets in the debtor, allows a creditor who has not proved to pursue his debtor for the original debt. He cannot do this if he has proved[1] but he can pursue a debt which is not provable.

[1] *More v More* [1962] Ch 424.

11.1.3 An application for an annulment is invariably coupled with an application to rescind the receiving order and dismiss the petition. It was a lacuna in the old legislation that the order of annulment did not automatically affect the receiving order on which it was made.[1]

[1] See *Re Noble, ex p Bankrupt v Official Receiver* [1965] Ch 129.

11.1.4 In practice, the court almost invariably refuses to entertain an application to annul until after the debtor's public examination has been concluded but, theoretically, the court has a complete discretion and in the appropriate cases, where all debts have been paid and neither the official receiver nor the majority of creditors oppose the application, the adjudication could be annulled even without a public examination having taken place.[1]

[1] *Re Debtor (No 37 of 1976), ex p Taylor v Debtor* [1980] Ch 565.

11.2 WHO MAY APPLY

'Any person interested'[1] may apply for an order of annulment.

In practical effect, this can mean that even a creditor who may adversely be affected by the debtor's presentation of his own petition, (and inevitable adjudication), can apply.[2]

The debtor himself can plainly apply but his wife (on that ground alone) is not a 'person interested' for these purposes.[3]

[1] Bankruptcy Act 1914, s 29(1).
[2] *Re Debtor (No 17 of 1966)* [1967] Ch 590.
[3] *Re Beesley, ex p Beesley v Official Receiver* [1975] 1 All ER 385.

11.3 GROUND 1: WHERE IN THE OPINION OF THE COURT A DEBTOR OUGHT NOT TO HAVE BEEN ADJUDICATED BANKRUPT

11.3.1 This is the first of the only two grounds on which an application for annulment can be made[1] and despite the ground recited in the heading is, ultimately, in the discretion of the court.

[1] Bankruptcy Act 1914, s 29(1).

11.3.2 If, at the hearing of a petition, the petitioner, whether it be the debtor himself or a creditor, proves all which has to be proved to secure a receiving order, then it probably cannot be argued that there is a technical reason why the adjudication should not have been made.

The recent cases have, in general, been in respect of minors where, in one case, there turned out to be no legally enforceable debts[1] and, in another, the debt was an award of damages which was payable by instalments where the debtor could pay the instalments but not the whole debt.[2]

[1] *Re Davenport, ex p Bankrupt v Eric Street Properties Ltd* [1963] 2 All ER 850.
[2] *Re Debtor (No 17 of 1966)* [1967] Ch 590.

11.3.3 Chapter 2 above deals with the defence of a petition on the ground of an abuse of the process of the court. If facts are not available at the time of the petition, or, for example, the debtor is only able to marshall his case after adjudication has been ordered, then the debtor or any 'interested person' can use the same ground as would have been available for a defence in an application to annul.

11.3.4 Similarly, if for example, a debtor could *prove* that, despite the evidence available at the hearing of the petition, it was not properly served, and he did not know of the hearing of the petition, the receiving order should be annulled.

11.4 GROUND 2: WHERE IT IS PROVED TO THE SATISFACTION OF THE COURT THAT THE DEBTS OF THE BANKRUPT ARE PAID IN FULL

11.4.1 This is the only other ground for annulment.[1]

[1] *Re Gyll, ex p Board of Trade* (1888) 59 LT 778.

11.4.2 If the debtor disputes a debt he may enter into a bond in such sum and with such sureties as the court approves, pending the disposal of any proceedings concerning the disputed debt.[1]

[1] Bankruptcy Act 1914, s 29(4).

11.4.3 If a creditor cannot be found or identified the debt is considered paid in full if paid into court.[1]

[1] Bankruptcy Act 1914, s 29(4).

11.4.4 The power to annul is discretionary. If the debtors conduct is such as to justify refusal it will be refused even if the debts are paid in full.[1]

[1] See *Re Taylor, ex p Taylor* [1901] 1KB 744.

11.4.5 The release of a debt by the creditor, even under seal, does *not* suffice as payment for these purposes[1] if payment has not in fact been made. Payment in full means payment of 100p in the pound and, where there is a surplus of assets, interest at 4% from the date of the receiving order until payment.[2]

[1] *Re Keet* [1905] 2 KB 666.
[2] Bankruptcy Act 1914, s 33(8).

11.5 EFFECT OF ANNULMENT

11.5.1 The effect of the annulment of the adjudication is to 'remit the party whose bankruptcy is set aside to his original position or situation'.[1]

However, all dispositions, sales, payments and other acts done by the official receiver, trustee or other person acting under their authority shall be valid despite the order of annulment being made.[2]

[1] *Bailey v Johnson* (1872) LR 7 Exch 263.
[2] Bankruptcy Act 1914, s 29(2).

11.5.2 The court can order that any remaining property of the debtor shall vest in such person as it directs[1] or that it reverts to the debtor, thus effectively *re* vesting it in him after the period of adjudication.

[1] Bankruptcy Act 1914, s 29(2).

11.5.3 Despite the annulment of an adjudication, the trustee in bankruptcy still has to account to the Department of Trade.[1]

[1] Bankruptcy Rules 1952, r 223.

11.5.4 An annulment does not operate to prevent criminal proceedings from being brought on any bankruptcy offence.[1]

[1] *DPP v Ashley* [1955] Crim LR 565.

11.5.5 At the time of making an order of annulment the court will make an order permitting the vacation of the registration at the Land Charges Registry of the petition as a pending action and of the receiving order in the register of Writs and Orders affecting land.[1]

[1] Bankruptcy Rules 1952, r 224.

11.6 PROCEDURAL TABLE

Steps to be Taken	Bankruptcy Act 1914	Bankruptcy Rules 1952
1. Any person interested may apply for order annulling adjudication.	s 29(1)	
If a trustee in bankruptcy has been appointed as a result of the adjudication the trustee is a necessary party to the proceedings.		
2. Applicant for annulment serves on official receiver and trustee: (1) notice of motion for annulment; (2) a copy of affidavits in support.		r 183(1)
TIME: Not less than 7 clear days before hearing of application.		r 183(1)
3. Parties attend hearing, where registrar considers report, objections and evidence, and if satisfied either: (1) that the adjudication ought not to have been made; or (2) that the bankrupt's debts are paid in full, may make an order:	s 29	
(1) annulling the adjudication, rescinding and vacating registration of receiving order and dismissing the petition; or (2) annulling the adjudication but not rescinding the receiving order; or		r 224
(3) dismissing the application.		
4. Registrar gives notice of order of annulment to Department of Trade and Industry to be gazetted and advertised.	s 29(3)	

Steps to be Taken	Bankruptcy Act 1914	Bankruptcy Rules 1952
5. If interested person wishes annulled adjudication order to be restored: applicant may apply to fix a day to hear application for rescission of order annulling adjudication order.	s 108(1)	
6. Registrar appoints day for hearing application. **7.** Applicant serves on debtor and official receiver: (1) notice of intended application; and, (2) affidavit supporting the application. **8.** Parties attend hearing before registrar, who may make order rescinding order annulling adjudication order, and adjudging debtor bankrupt.	s 108(1)	

11.7 FORMS

APPLICATION to annul adjudication order

IN THE [HIGH COURT OF JUSTICE *or* . . . . COUNTY COURT]

In Bankruptcy No . . . . of 19 . . . .

Re A B [*add, after adjudication*, a Bankrupt]

Ex parte [the Debtor *or* the Bankrupt *or* C D a Creditor *or* the Official Receiver *or* the Trustee *or as the case may be*]

I, R S, of (*address*), being interested in this matter, do hereby make application to the Court that the Order of Adjudication against A B be annulied on the ground that [all the debts have been paid in full *or* it ought not to have been made].

DATED this . . . . day of . . . . 19 . . . .

(*Signature*)

APPLICATION to fix day to hear application to annul adjudication order

IN THE [HIGH COURT OF JUSTICE *or* . . . . COUNTY COURT]

In Bankruptcy No . . . . of 19 . . . .

Re A B [*add, after adjudication*, a Bankrupt]

Ex parte [the Debtor *or* the Bankrupt *or* C D a Creditor *or* the Official Receiver *or* the Trustee *or as the case may be*]

APPLICATION is hereby made for a day to be appointed to hear the application of the above-named Bankrupt for an order annulling the Adjudication Order made herein on . . . 19 . . . . on the ground that [all the debts have been paid in full *or* it ought not to have been made] and that the Receiving Order made herein and dated . . . . 19 . . . . be rescinded and the Petition be dismissed.

DATED this . . . . day of . . . . 19 . . . .

(*Signature*), of (*address*), [Agents for (*name*), of (*address*),] Solicitors for the [Debtor *or* Bankrupt *or* Trustee *or* Judgment Creditor *or* Petitioning Creditor *or as the case may be*]

NOTICE to Official Receiver and trustee of application for annulment of adjudication order on payment of debts in full

IN THE [HIGH COURT OF JUSTICE *or* . . . . COUNTY COURT]

In Bankruptcy No. . . . of 19 . . . .

Re A B [*add, after adjudication*, a Bankrupt]

The Bankrupt having applied to the Court for annulment of the Order of Adjudication made against him on the ground that he had paid his debts in full the Court has fixed . . . . 19 . . . . at . . . . o'clock in the [forenoon] at (*address*) for hearing the application.

DATED this . . . . day of . . . . 19 . . . .

(*Signature*)
Registrar

To the Official Receiver,
and to Mr T T, Trustee of the estate of the Bankrupt.

NOTICE of application for annulment of adjudication order on ground that it ought not to have been made

IN THE [HIGH COURT OF JUSTICE *or* . . . . COUNTY COURT]

In Bankruptcy No. . . . of 19 . . . .

Re A B [*add, after adjudication*, a Bankrupt]

TAKE NOTICE that the Court has appointed the . . . . day of . . . . 19 . . . . at . . . . o'clock in the [forenoon] before [Mr Registrar . . . .] at (*address*) to hear the application of the above-named Bankrupt that the Order of Adjudication made against him on . . . . 19 . . . . on the Petition of C D may be annulled on the ground that it ought not to have been made [and that the Receiving Order made herein and dated . . . . 19 . . . . be rescinded and that the Petition be dismissed].

The affidavit of the [Debtor], a copy of which is served herewith, will be read in support of this motion.

DATED this . . . . day of . . . . 19 . . . .

(*Signature*), of (*address*), [Agents for (*name*), of (*address*),] Solicitors for the [Debtor *or* Bankrupt *or* Trustee *or* Judgment Creditor *or* Petitioning Creditor *or as the case may be*]

To C D, of (*address*), the Petitioning Creditor,
and to G H, of (*address*), his Solicitor,
and to the Official Receiver,
and to Mr T T, the Trustee.

AFFIDAVIT supporting application to annul adjudication order on ground of payment of debts in full

IN THE [HIGH COURT OF JUSTICE *or* . . . . COUNTY COURT]

In Bankruptcy No. . . . of 19 . . . .

Re A B [*add, after adjudication*, a Bankrupt]

I, A B, of (*residence and description*), the above-named Bankrupt, make oath and say as follows:

1. On . . . . 19 . . . . a Petition was filed against me in this Court upon which . . . . 19 . . . . a Receiving Order was made, and on . . . . 19 . . . . I was adjudged bankrupt.

2. On . . . . 19 . . . . I filed a Statement of my Affairs setting out the whole of my assets and liabilities.
3. On . . . . 19 . . . . I provided the [Official Receiver *or* Trustee] with a sum of money sufficient to pay all my debts in full as set out in my said Statement of Affairs and the costs, charges and expenses under the said bankruptcy.
4. I respectfully ask that the said Order of Adjudication may be annulled, the said Receiving Order be rescinded and the Petition be dismissed.

SWORN at (*address*), this . . . . day of . . . .
19 . . . . before me, } (*Deponent's signature*)
(*Signature*)
A Commissioner for Oaths

ORDER annulling adjudication order

IN THE [HIGH COURT OF JUSTICE *or* . . . . COUNTY COURT]
In Bankruptcy No . . . . of 19 . . . .
Re A B [*add, after adjudication,* a Bankrupt]

UPON THE APPLICATION A B of (*address*)
AND UPON READING the report of O R filed . . . . 19. . . . and the affidavit of A B filed . . . . 19 . . . .
AND UPON HEARING . . . .
AND it appearing to the Court that [all the debts herein have been paid in full *or* the Order of Adjudication herein ought not to have been made]
IT IS ORDERED that the Order of Adjudication dated . . . . 19 . . . . against A B (*state name, address and description as in adjudication order*) be and the same is hereby annulled and that the Receiving Order dated . . . . 19 . . . . be and the same is hereby rescinded and that the Petition dated . . . . 19 . . . . be and the same is hereby dismissed
AND IT IS FURTHER ORDERED that any balance in the Official Receiver's hands [after charging a sum of £. . . . to be credited to the Bankruptcy Estates Account in respect of the Official Receiver's services under that Order of Adjudication and] after audit by the Department of Trade and Industry be paid out to the Debtor or to E F his Solicitor
AND IT IS FURTHER ORDERED that the registration of the Petition as a pending action at the Land Charges Department of HM Land Registry on . . . . 19. . . . under Reference No . . . . and of the Receiving Order in the register of Writs and Orders affecting land at the said Department on . . . . 19 . . . . under Reference No . . . . be vacated upon application duly made in that behalf by the Debtor under the Land Charges Rules 1974.
DATED this . . . . day of . . . . 19 . . . .

By the Court
Registrar

APPLICATION by creditor to fix day to hear application for rescission of order anulling adjudication order

IN THE [HIGH COURT OF JUSTICE *or* . . . . COUNTY COURT]
In Bankruptcy No . . . . of 19 . . . .
Re A B [*add, after adjudication,* a Bankrupt]
Ex parte [the Debtor *or* the Bankrupt *or* C D a Creditor *or* the Official Receiver *or* the Trustee *or as the case may be*]

APPLICATION is hereby made for a day to be appointed to hear an application on

behalf of C D, of (*address*), a Creditor of the above-named A B, that the application of the said A B, to annul the Order of Adjudication made against him on . . . . 19 . . . . may be re-heard and reviewed and that the Order dated . . . . 19 . . . . annulling the said Order of Adjudication may be rescinded and that the said A B may be adjudged bankrupt.
APPLICATION is hereby made for (*state relief claimed*)
DATED this . . . . day of . . . . 19 . . . .

(*Signature*), of (*address*), [Agents for (*name*), of (*address*),] Solicitors for the [Debtor *or* Bankrupt *or* Trustee *or* Judgment Creditor *or* Petitioning Creditor *or as the case may be*]

NOTICE of application by creditor for rescission of order annulling adjudication order

IN THE [HIGH COURT OF JUSTICE *or* . . . . COUNTY COURT]
In Bankruptcy No. . . . of 19 . . . .

Re A B
Ex parte C D, a Creditor

TAKE NOTICE that application will be made to this Court on . . . . 19 . . . . on behalf of the above-named C D that the application, notice of which is dated . . . . 19 . . . . to annul the Order of Adjudication made against the said A B on . . . . 19 . . . . may be re-heard and reviewed and that the Order dated . . . . 19 . . . . annulling the said Order of Adjudication may be rescinded and discharged and that the above-named A B may be adjudged bankrupt.
AND TAKE NOTICE that in support of this application there will be read the affidavit of the said C D, a copy of which is served herewith.
APPLICATION is hereby made for (*state relief*)
DATED this . . . . day of . . . . 19 . . . .

(*Signature*), of (*address*), [Agents for (*name*), of (*address*),] Solicitors for the [Debtor *or* Bankrupt *or* Trustee *or* Judgment Creditor *or* Petitioning Creditor *or as the case may be*]

PART 2

The New Bankruptcy Law

CHAPTER 12

Voluntary Arrangements

12.1 INTRODUCTION

12.1.1 In an attempt to reduce the number of bankruptcies the Review Committee[1] recommended the encouragement of voluntary arrangements by personal debtors with their creditors. This is effected in the Insolvency Act 1986 by the approved composition or scheme (a 'voluntary arrangement'). The approved composition or scheme of arrangement under the Act binds all creditors entitled to attend the creditors' meeting which approves the voluntary arrangement whether they attend or not and, if attending, whichever way the creditor votes.

This avoids the essential weakness of arrangements under the Deeds of Arrangement Act 1914 which could not prevent non-assenting creditors from petitioning for bankruptcy. Indeed, any creditor of the debtor could rely on the making of a deed of arrangement as an act of bankruptcy on which to base his petition.

Whether these provisions will attract greater use than the provisions of the Bankruptcy Act 1914[2] which enabled the court to approve a scheme or composition binding on all creditors with debts provable in any bankruptcy remains to be seen. Much may depend in practice upon the ability of individual debtors to meet insolvency practitioners, presumably through the offices of the debtor's professional advisers, with whom the debtor can prepare, propose and implement a scheme.

The main advantage of the New Law proposals appears to be that the debtor may initiate the procedure at any time whereas the Old Bankruptcy Law procedures followed a receiving order being made. There may be more incentive for a debtor to secure voluntary arrangements at an earlier stage of his financial difficulties than at a time when all may seem lost.

From the creditors' viewpoint the relatively substantial cost of bankruptcy proceedings will be an appreciable incentive to concur with proposals for a voluntary arrangement. However, insolvency practitioners will require payment for acting as nominee and so only estates with significant assets will be suitable for a composition or scheme approved under the Insolvency Act.

[1] Review Committee on Insolvency Law and Practice. See para 1.5 above.
[2] ss 16–21.

12.1.2 The provisions relating to approved voluntary arrangements apply not only to debtors who are not bankrupt but also to debtors who have been adjudicated bankrupt but have yet to obtain a discharge. The procedure is for the debtor or undischarged bankrupt (or his trustee in bankruptcy) or the official receiver to apply to the court for an interim order. While the application is pending and after any order is made, the court may stay any action, execution or other legal process against the debtor or his estate.

Under the interim order a creditors' meeting is called and held. The decision of this meeting approving or rejecting voluntary arrangements is reported to the court by the chairman of the meeting and, if the arrangements have been approved, the composition or scheme comes into effect subject to a right of challenge to the court which must be exercised within 28 days of the chairman's report to the court.

12.1.3 A debtor cannot, however, proceed to a voluntary arrangement on his own. He requires the assistance of an insolvency practitioner, styled for these purposes as 'the nominee', who must have a role defined in the arrangements proposed by the debtor supervising the implementation of the composition or scheme of arrangement. The Act provides that the nominee should act in relation to the composition or scheme 'either as trustee or otherwise' though no other capacity is specified.

12.1.4 The voluntary arrangements proposed by the debtor may be either a composition with creditors or a scheme of arrangement. There is no distinction under the Insolvency Act 1986 between compositions and schemes either as to procedure or effect of approval.

A 'composition' is an agreement between the debtor and his creditors whereby the compounding creditors agree with the debtor and between themselves to accept from the debtor payment of less than the respective amounts due to them in full satisfaction of the whole of their claim. Where a composition is approved in accordance with the provisions of the Act it is legally binding under the Act. Outside statutory provision the consideration which supports the agreement to accept part payment as a discharge of the whole debt is the mutual agreement of the other creditors to do likewise.

A 'scheme of arrangement' may take any form acceptable to the parties, but the usual method is by assignment by the debtor of his property or a specified part of his property to a trustee for realisation and distribution of the proceeds of sale amongst the creditors rateably or in such proportions as they agree.

The trusts under which the trustee holds the property will be agreed by the creditors and specified in a deed of assignment. It has been common for such deeds to appoint a committee of inspection to control the trustee's administration of the estate. Such a committee might be appointed in a scheme approved under the New Law, but the Insolvency Act 1986 enables any creditor dissatisfied with the performance of the nominee to apply to the court, so the appointment of a committee of inspection will not be a matter of any particular importance to the average creditor.

12.2 INTERIM ORDERS

12.2.1 Where an individual debtor wishes to make a proposal to his creditors for a composition in satisfaction of his debts or a scheme of arrangement of his affairs he must apply to the court for an interim order. While such an application is pending the court has a discretionary power to stay any action, execution or other legal process against the debtor or his property.[1] This power is exercisable by any court in which proceedings against the debtor are pending and enables that court to stay the proceedings or allow them to continue on such terms as the court considers fit.[2]

An application for an interim order may not be made while a bankruptcy petition presented by the debtor is pending where the court has decided to appoint an insolvency practitioner to prepare a report on the feasibility of the debtor entering into voluntary arrangements. In that event the court may if appropriate proceed to make an interim order without there being an application under the Insolvency Act 1986, s 253.[3]

1 Insolvency Act 1986, s 254(1).
2 Ibid, s 254(2).
3 Ibid, ss 253(5) and s 273(2).

12.2.2 The debtor must give at least two days' notice of his application to this intended nominee and to any creditor who to his knowledge has presented a bankruptcy petition against him.[1] In the case of an undischarged bankrupt the application for an interim order may be made by the bankrupt or his trustee or the official receiver. Whoever is the applicant must give notice to the other two and to the proposed nominee.[2] Any person to whom notice has been given may appear or be represented at the hearing of the application.[3] The application to the court for an interim order must be accompanied by an affidavit covering the following matters[4]:

(a) the reasons for making the application;
(b) particulars of any execution or other legal process which, to the debtor's knowledge, has been commenced against him;
(c) that he is an undischarged bankrupt or (as the case may be) that he is able to petition for his own bankruptcy;
(d) that no previous application for an interim order has been made by or in respect of the debtor in the period of 12 months ending with the date of the affidavit; and
(e) that the nominee under the proposal (naming him) is a person who is qualified to act as an insolvency practitioner in relation to the debtor, and is willing to act in relation to the proposal.

The affidavit should exhibit the copy of the notice to the intended nominee endorsed to the effect that he agrees to act.[5]

[1] Individual Insolvency Rules 1986, r 5.5(4)(b)(c). The notice to the intended nominee must be accompanied by the debtor's proposal document, see para 12.2.5 below.
[2] Insolvency Act 1986, s 253(4); Individual Insolvency Rules 1986, r 5.5(4)(a)(c).
[3] Individual Insolvency Rules 1986, r 5.6(1).
[4] Ibid, r 5.5(1).
[5] Ibid, r 5.5(2).

12.2.3 On the hearing of the application the court may make an interim order if it would be appropriate to do so for the purpose of facilitating consideration and implementation of the debtor's proposals and provided it is satisfied that:[1]
(a) the debtor intends to make a proposal for a voluntary arrangement;
(b) on the day of the making of the application the debtor was an undischarged bankrupt or was able to petition for his own bankruptcy;
(c) no previous application has been made by the debtor for an interim order during the 12 months preceding the application; and
(d) the nominee is a qualified insolvency practitioner[2] and is willing to act as nominee on the debtor's proposals. Should the debtor be an undischarged bankrupt, the order may contain provisions as to the conduct of the bankruptcy, including staying the bankruptcy proceedings and the administration of the estate while the order is in force. The court may not make provisions which have the effect of relaxing or removing any of the requirements of the Act or Rules of Court unless it is satisfied that the provision is unlikely to result in any significant diminution in the debtor's estate or its value.[3] An interim order leading to an approved scheme may also be made by the court when considering a debtor's petition for bankruptcy.[4]

[1] Insolvency Act 1986, s 253(4).
[2] As to which see ch 15 below.
[3] Insolvency Act 1986, s 255(3), (4) and (5).
[4] See para 13.5.3 below.

12.2.4 The interim order has the effect of preventing a bankruptcy petition being presented or proceeded with against the debtor, neither may any other proceedings or execution or other legal process be commenced or continued against the debtor without the leave of the court.[1] The interim order has a very short life. It ceases to have effect at the end of 14 days, beginning with the day after the order is made, unless it is an order made after the presentation of a debtor's petition in which event the court has power to determine the length of its validity.

[1] Insolvency Act 1986, s 252(2).

12.2.5 Within this 14-day period, the nominee has to submit a report to the court stating whether in his opinion a meeting of the debtor's creditors should be summoned to consider the proposal, and if so the date, time and place where that meeting should take place.[1] This short time limit is mitigated by the provision that the court may extend the period of the interim order on the application of the nominee.[2]

In order to enable the nominee to prepare his report the debtor must submit[3] (a) a document setting out the terms of his proposal[4] and (b) a statement of affairs giving particulars of his assets and liabilities together with other prescribed information.[5] The debtor must serve his proposal document with the written notice of proposal which he has to give to his intended nominee before applying for an interim order.[6] The statement of affairs is to be delivered within seven days of the proposal unless the nominee allows a longer period.[7] The nominee may require additional disclosure from the debtor.[8]

1 Insolvency Act 1986, s 256(1). The court is to fix a time for considering the nominee's report when making the interim order: Individual Insolvency Rules 1986, r 5.6(3). The nominee's report must be delivered to the court not less than two days before the interim order ceases to have effect: ibid, r 5.10(1).
2 Insolvency Act 1986, s 256(4).
3 Ibid, s 256(2).
4 A lengthy list of matters which must be dealt with in the proposal document is specified in the Individual Insolvency Rules 1986, r 5.3(2).
5 Individual Insolvency Rules 1986, r 5.8; however, a bankrupt applicant who has already delivered a statement of affairs need not prepare a further statement unless required to do so by the nominee.
6 Ibid, r 5.4.
7 Ibid, r 5.8(2).
8 Ibid, r 5.9.

12.2.6 On receiving the nominee's report the court, if satisfied that a creditors' meeting should be summoned to consider the proposal, directs that the interim order be extended for a specific specified period in order to allow the debtor's proposal to be considered by the creditors. The interim order may be discharged if the debtor fails to comply with his obligations to provide the nominee with information, or for any other reason it is considered to be inappropriate for the creditors' meeting to take place.

12.2.7 Should a nominee fail to submit his report, the debtor may apply to the court for a direction that the nominee be replaced by another insolvency practitioner and that the interim order should be extended for sufficient further period to enable the replacement nominee to submit his report.[1]

1 Insolvency Act 1986, s 256(3); Individual Insolvency Rules 1986, r 5.11.

12.3 CREDITORS' MEETING UNDER THE INSOLVENCY ACT 1986, s 258

12.3.1 The meeting is summoned in accordance with the details proposed in the report by the nominee, or where a debtor's petition has been presented, the person appointed by the court under the Insolvency Act 1986, s 273 ('the appointed person'). All creditors of whose claim and address the nominee or appointed person is aware must be notified of the meeting.[1] A 'creditor' is defined by reference to the commencement of a bankruptcy, and includes every person who is a creditor of the bankrupt in respect of a debt provable against the bankrupt's estate and every person who would be such a creditor if the bankruptcy commenced on the day on which notice of the meeting is given.[2] Therefore creditors of future and contingent debts as well as creditors with existing debts are included.

[1] Which must, be held not less than 14, nor more than 28, days from the filing of the nominee's report in Court; Individual Insolvency Rules 1986, r 5.13.
[2] Insolvency Act 1986, s 257.

12.3.2 The conduct of the meeting is governed by the Rules.[1] The meeting may approve the debtor's proposals or do so with modifications if the debtor consents to each modification. The meeting is expressly empowered to replace the nominee with another insolvency practitioner. No proposal or modification may affect the rights of a secured or preferential creditor without the consent of the creditor concerned. At the conclusion of the meeting the chairman is under a duty to report to the court and give notice of the result of the meeting to such persons as may be prescribed.[2] Should the meeting decline to approve the proposed composition or scheme the court may discharge the interim order.

[1] Insolvency Act 1986, s 258(6); Individual Insolvency Rules 1986, rr 5.14–5.20.
[2] Ibid, r 5.22.

12.3.3 Where the meeting approves the proposals, with or without modification, every creditor who had notice of the meeting and was entitled to vote under the rules is bound by the composition or scheme as if he were a party to it whether or not he attended the meeting or voted in support of the proposals.[1]

[1] Insolvency Act 1986, s 260(2). By s 260(3) the Deeds of Arrangement Act 1914 does not apply to an approved composition or scheme.

12.3.4 Following the approval of voluntary proposals made by an undischarged bankrupt the court may annul the bankruptcy order and, or alternatively, give directions for the administration of the bankrupt's estate in order to facilitate the implementation of the scheme. The bankruptcy order may not, however, be annulled before the expiry of 28 days from the date on which the chairman of the meeting reported to the court. This is to maintain the order in existence for a period to enable the meeting's decision to be challenged in court, and if a challenge is made the bankruptcy order continues in force until that application and any appeal is determined.

12.3.5 An interim order also continues in force for 28 days after the chairman's report to the court; it then lapses unless within that 28-day period a challenge is made to the meeting's approval of a scheme or composition and the court extends the applicability of the order pending determination of the challenge. A bankruptcy petition which has been stayed by an interim order is deemed to have been dismissed when the interim order ceases to have effect, unless the court orders otherwise.[1]

[1] Insolvency Act 1986, s 260(5).

12.3.6 An application[1] to challenge the meeting's approval of voluntary arrangements may be made on one or both of two grounds: namely (a) the interests of a creditor are unfairly prejudiced; and (b) that there has been some material irregularity at or in relation to the meeting.

Such an application must be made within 28 days after the chairman of the meeting's report to the court. This time limit is mandatory under the Act and apparently cannot be extended by the court even where a creditor is unaware of the meeting held to consider the composition or scheme proposed by the debtor, the details of the scheme or the decision of the meeting.[2]

The nominee is under no statutory duty to creditors to take reasonable steps to ascertain their identities and, in any event, will be heavily dependent on the debtor to make full disclosure of all his existing, future, and contingent creditors. The Act does not, within the context of approving voluntary arrangements, make provision to cover the position of a creditor whose existence is not made known to, or ascertained by, the nominee or approved person and who does not learn about the approval of a scheme within the 28-day period from the chairman's report to the court.[3] However, such a creditor has the sanction of being able to present a petition for bankruptcy if he can show that the debtor gave false or misleading information in any material particular or by any material omission in connection with his proposals for a voluntary arrangement.[4]

1 This application is made under Insolvency Act 1986, s 262, and see Individual Insolvency Rules 1986, r 5.25.
2 Insolvency Act 1986, s 262(3).
3 On the filing of a bankruptcy petition the court in which it is filed must notify the chief land registrar in order that notice of the petition be registered in the Register of Pending Actions. A creditor whose debt is for any purpose connected with any registered land in the debtor's estate is deemed to have actual notice of the petition when so registered: Law of Property Act 1925, s 198.
4 See para 13.5 below.

12.3.7 An application under s 262 to challenge the approval of a composition or scheme may be brought by: (i) the debtor; (ii) any creditor entitled to vote; (iii) the nominee or his replacement; and (iv) where the debtor is a bankrupt, the trustee of his estate or the official receiver.

On the making of a challenge application the court may revoke or suspend the meeting's approval, and may direct a specified person to summon a further meeting to consider the debtor's proposal or any revised proposal he may make. Where a further meeting is directed the court will have to extend or renew the interim order to protect the debtor's estate and is empowered to do so. The court further has power to make directions covering any acts done since the meeting under the approved composition or scheme, including acts which could not have been done with an interim order in force.

12.3.8 Unless a successful challenge application is made, an approval given to voluntary arrangements by a creditors' meeting shall be effective and may not be invalidated by any irregularity at or in relation to the meeting.[1] This provision safeguards the composition or scheme from technical attack on the grounds of procedual irregularity, and after 28 days have expired following the chairman's report to the court, the nominee may begin supervising the scheme with confidence that it cannot be overturned by an aggrieved creditor unless the debtor is shown to have provided false or misleading information (see above). It also emphasises the importance of this time limit for bringing challenge applications under the Insolvency Act 1986, s 262.

[1] Insolvency Act 1986, s 262(8).

12.4 IMPLEMENTATION

12.4.1 Upon the provisions of any approved composition or scheme coming into effect the nominee (or his replacement) or the appointed person becomes known as 'the supervisor' and is responsible for the implementation of the scheme.[1] The court may replace or order additional supervisors, but a supervisor must be a qualified insolvency practitioner.[2]

[1] See Individual Insolvency Rules 1986, rr 5.21, 5.27.
[2] Insolvency Act 1986, s 263 and see ch 15 below.

12.4.2 The supervisor is entitled to apply to the court for directions in relation to any particular matter arising under the composition or scheme.[1] Any person dissatisfied by an act omission or direction of the supervisor may apply to the court. On such application the court has a complete discretion to confirm, reverse or modify the matter complained of and to give the supervisor directions.

[1] Insolvency Act 1986, s 263(4).

12.4.3 *Register of voluntary arrangements.* The chairman of the creditors' meeting is required by the Rules[1] to report to the Secretary of State (a) the name and address of the debtor, (b) the date on which the arrangment was approved by the creditors, (c) the name and address of the supervisor, and (d) the court in which the chairman's report is filed. This report is to be given 'immediately' after the chairman files his report in court. The Secretary of State is to maintain a register of individual voluntary arrangements from these reports and keep this register open to public inspection.[2]

[1] Individual Insolvency Rules 1986, r 5.24.
[2] Ibid, r 5.23.

12.4.4 *Completion of voluntary arrangement.* Within 28 days of the final completion of the voluntary arrangement, the supervisor must send notice to the debtor, all creditors bound by the arrangement, and to the Secretary of State stating that the arrangement has been fully implemented.[1] The notice must be accompanied by a report summarising all receipts and payments made by the supervisor and explaining any difference between the actual implementation of the arrangment as compared with the proposal approved by the creditor's meeting.

[1] Individual Insolvency Rules 1986, r 5.29; the court may extend the 28-day period.

CHAPTER 13

Bankruptcy Orders

13.1 BANKRUPTCY PETITIONS

13.1.1 The scheme of the act is to abolish the concept of the act of bankruptcy and bring the procedure for initiating bankruptcy proceedings into line as far as possible with that for compulsory corporate winding up. Under the New Law bankruptcy proceedings are commenced by petition on which the court may make a bankruptcy order.[1] A petition may be presented against an individual ('the debtor') by:

(a) one or more of his creditors;
(b) the debtor himself;
(c) the supervisor of a composition or scheme under the Insolvency Act 1986, s 260[2] or any person other than the debtor who is bound by that composition or scheme; or
(d) the official petitioner or any person specified by the court under (3) the Powers of Criminal Courts Act 1973, s 39(3) as having suffered loss and damage where a criminal bankruptcy order has been made against the debtor.

Where a person is entitled to present a petition under two or more of the categories specified above, the petition is treated as a petition under such one of these paragraphs as is specified in the petition.

Once a petition has been presented it may not be withdrawn without the leave of the court.[3] This was the position under the previous law.[4] Under the Bankruptcy Act 1914, the court had to be informed of the facts of the case and proposed terms of withdrawal to ensure that the case was a proper one for withdrawal of the petition.[5] But where the petitioning creditor had been paid in full and then applied for leave to withdraw his petition, leave could not be refused unless there was another creditor qualified and willing to be substituted as petitioning creditor.[6] The proper practice was for the registrar to adjourn the petition to give an opportunity to other creditors to be substituted.[7] After withdrawal of his petition on terms which the debtor subsequently failed to honour, a second petition from the creditor was not an abuse of process.[8]

[1] Insolvency Act 1986, s 264.
[2] See ch 12 above.
[3] Insolvency Act 1986, s 266(2).
[4] Bankruptcy Act 1914, s 5(7).
[5] *Re Bebro* [1900] 2 QB 316; *Re Debtor (No 883 of 1927)* [1928] Ch 199.
[6] *Re Bebro* (above).
[7] *Re Mann, ex p Debtor v Harrods Ltd* [1958] 3 All ER 660.
[8] *Re Bebro* (above).

13.1.2 A petition may only be presented by a creditor or the debtor if, on the day on which the petition is presented, the debtor:[1]
(a) is domiciled in England and Wales; or
(b) is personally present in England or Wales; or
(c) has been ordinarily resident or has had a place of residence in England or Wales during the previous three years; or
(d) has carried on business in England and Wales during the previous three years.

Carrying on business includes (a) membership by the debtor of a firm or partnership which carries on business, and (b) carrying on a business by an agent or manager for the debtor or any firm or partnership in which the debtor is involved.

This phrase has been given a wide interpretation by the courts. Trading is not completed until the trader has performed all the obligations that the fact of trading has imposed upon him.[2] Accordingly, a debtor continues to carry on business for the purposes of bankruptcy law until he has paid all his trade debts and satisfied all his tax and customs liabilities notwithstanding the fact that he may have disposed of or otherwise ceased his business.[3] Therefore although the debtor may have apparently ceased to trade for over three years, a bankruptcy petition may still be presented against him in respect of unpaid trade debts provided they are not statute-barred. In this context, the extension of the one-year period under the previous law to three years under the Insolvency Act 1986 is of little practical significance.

[1] Insolvency Act 1986, s 265(1) and (2).
[2] See Lord Porter in *Theophile v Solr General* [1950] 1 All ER 405 at 411, quoting Vaughan Williams J in *Dagnall's Case* [1896] 2 QB 407.
[3] *Theophile v Solr General* (above); *Re Bird, ex p Debtor v IRC* [1962] 2 All ER 406, CA. In the latter case, Harman LJ (at 413) suggested that even a liability owed by the debtor to his accountants in respect of professional fees where no demand had been made would be a sufficient debt to support a bankruptcy petition.

13.1.3 The Act[1] gives the court a general power to dismiss or stay proceedings on a petition. This power may be exercised on the grounds that there has been a contravention of the rules or for any other reason. When staying a petition the court has a general discretion to impose terms and conditions.

[1] Insolvency Act 1986, s 266(3).

13.2 CREDITORS' PETITIONS

13.2.1 A creditor's petition may be presented by one or more creditors and in respect of one or more debts owed by the debtor, but the following conditions must be satisfied:[1]

(a) the amount of the debt or aggregate amounts of the debts must equal or exceed the bankruptcy level, which the Act sets at £750, subject to variation by the Secretary of State by statutory instrument;

(b) the debt, or each of them if more than one, must be for a liquidated sum due to one or more of the petitioning creditors payable either immediately or at some future time and must be unsecured;

(c) the debt or each of them, is a debt which the debtor appears either to be unable to pay or to have no reasonable prospect of being able to pay; and

(d) there must be no outstanding application to set aside a statutory demand to pay the debt or to satisfy the creditor that the debt will be paid when it falls due under the Insolvency Act 1986, s 268(1) or (2).

[1] Insolvency Act 1986, s 267(2).

13.2.2 The requirement under condition (b) above that any debt which forms the subject of a petition must be unsecured does not apply where either:

(i) the petition contains a statement by the person holding the right to enforce the security that he is prepared to release it to the benefit of all creditors, in the event that a bankruptcy order is made; or

(ii) the petition contains a statement by the creditor of the estimated value of the security at the date of the petition and is expressed not to be made in respect of the secured part of the debt. Where the amount of the debt exceeds the security the secured and unsecured parts of the debt are treated, for the purposes of a creditor's petition, as separate debts. A debt is not to be treated as a debt for a liquidated sum by reason only that it is quantified in a criminal bankruptcy order. A person who is specified in such an order as having suffered loss and damage under the Powers of Criminal Courts Act 1973 may not therefore present a petition as a creditor, he must do so under the separate category of petitioner authorised in respect of criminal bankruptcy orders.

13.2.3 The requirement under condition (c) above that the debt, or each debt, is one which the debtor appears unable to pay or to have no reasonable prospect of paying must be established formally, as follows:[1]

(i) a debtor 'appears to be unable to pay a debt' only where the debt is then due and either (a) a demand notice in the prescribed form has been served on the debtor requiring him to pay, or secure, or compound the debt to the creditor's satisfaction, and three weeks or more have elapsed since the notice was served without the demand being complied with or set aside in accordance with the rules,[2] or (b) execution or other process issued in respect of a judgment or court order in favour of the creditor in respect of the debt has been returned unsatisfied in whole or in part.

(ii) a debtor 'appears to have no reasonable prospect of being able to pay a debt' only where a demand notice in the prescribed form has been served on the debtor requiring him to establish to the satisfaction of the creditor that there is a reasonable prospect that the debt will be paid when it falls due and the debtor has neither complied with nor had the demand set aside under the rules[2] within three weeks.

Provided the debtor has made an application to set aside the demand within three weeks a petition may not be presented. The application to set aside the demand operates as a stay on the presentation of the petition until such time as the application is heard and determined.

1 Insolvency Act 1986, s 268(1) and (2).
2 See para 13.3 below, and see Individual Insolvency Rules 1986, r 6.4, and form 6.4.

13.2.4 A petition may, however, be presented before the end of the three-week period specified for a demand notice if there is a serious possibility that the debtor's property or the value of any of his property will be significantly diminished during that period. A statement to that effect must be contained in the petition.[1]

The court may not, however, make a bankruptcy order on the petition until at least three weeks have elapsed since the service of the demand notice.[2]

1 Insolvency Act 1986, s 270.
2 Ibid, s 271(2).

13.3 THE STATUTORY DEMAND

13.3.1 The provision for a statutory demand brings bankruptcy law into line with the standard practice in company liquidation. However, two important differences to company law will be noted:

(a) in bankruptcy the statutory demand is an essential prerequisite to a creditor's petition (except where execution on a court judgment or order has been returned unsatisfied – which is also a ground for winding up a company), whereas the demand under the Insolvency Act 1986, s 123 is merely one way of showing that the company is unable to pay its debts, albeit the way normally adopted by petitioning creditors; and

(b) the individual debtor may apply to set aside the statutory demand, a remedy that is not available to the company served with a demand under the Insolvency Act, 1986 s 123. This has at least two main ramifications. First, the alleged individual debtor can stifle the proposed bankruptcy proceedings by such an application. The alleged corporate debtor cannot do so, though in appropriate circumstances a company can obtain injunctive relief to restrain the advertising of a winding-up petition. Second, while the corporate debtor may oppose the petition when it is heard on the basis that there is a bona fide dispute as to the debt or that the company has a cross-demand which equals or exceeds the debt, the individual debtor is effectively forced to take the initiative and apply to set aside the demand where such grounds exist. For although the individual debtor is not precluded from resisting the petition on such grounds, as they are specifically available to him under the rules in an application to set aside the statutory demand he is likely to be penalised in costs if he makes no such application but allows the creditor to proceed with the issue and hearing of a petition.

The statutory demand will replace the Old Law bankruptcy notice as the usual way in which bankruptcy proceedings are initiated. By way of a transitional provision the Individual Insolvency Rules 1986, r 6.36 provides that a person who has served a valid bankruptcy notice under the Bankruptcy Act 1914 before the commencement date of the Insolvency Act 1986 may proceed on that notice after the commencement date as if it were a duly served statutory demand, provided no bankruptcy petition has been presented under the 1914 Act based on that notice. Where the debtor applies to set the bankruptcy notice aside under the 1914 Act, r 6.36(3) provides that the application is to be treated as one to set aside a statutory demand.

13.3.2 The Individual Insolvency Rules[1] require the statutory demand to be dated and signed by the creditor himself or a person stating himself to be the creditor's authorised agent. An affidavit of service of the statutory demand must be filed with the petition.[2] To be valid the statutory demand must comply with the following requirements:[3]

(i) It must specify whether it is made under the Insolvency Act 1986, s 268(1) (debt payable immediately) or the Insolvency Act 1986, s 268(2) (debt not payable immediately).

(ii) It must state the nature and amount of the debt and
- (a) if founded on a judgment or order of the court it must give details of the judgment or order; and
- (b) if made under the Insolvency Act 1986, s 268(2) it must state the grounds on which the creditor alleges that the debtor appears to have no reasonable prospect of paying the debt.

(iii) If interest not previously notified to the debtor as a liability of his or any other periodic charge is included in the demand it must be separately identified, limited to the date of the demand, and the grounds on which payment of it are claimed specified.

(iv) If the creditor holds any security in respect of the debt, the full amount of the debt is to be specified together with the nature of the security and the value put on it by the creditor at the date of demand. The demand may only claim payment of the balance after deducting the value of the security from the full amount of the debt.

(v) An explanation must be given to the debtor of the following matters:
- (a) the purpose of the demand and the consequences of non compliance;
- (b) the time within which the demand must be complied with (at least three weeks must be allowed);
- (c) the methods of compliance open to the debtor (these comprise not only payment but securing or compounding the debt to the satisfaction of the creditor); and
- (d) his right to apply to the court to set aside the statutory demand.

(vi) Information must be provided as to how the debtor may enter into communication with a named individual with a view either:
  (a) to securing or compounding the debt; or
  (b) to establishing that there is a reasonable prospect that the debt will be paid when it falls due.

[1] Individual Insolvency Rules 1986, r 6.1(1).
[2] Ibid, r 6.11(1). The affidavit of service must exhibit a copy of the demand as served: r 6.11(2).
[3] Ibid, rr 6.1(2)–(5) and 6.2, see Forms 6.1, 6.2, 6.3.

13.3.3 Service of the statutory demand should ordinarily be effected personally on the debtor. The requirements for the affidavit of service are contained in the Individual Insolvency Rules 1986, r 6.11, see appendix below. However, where the statutory demand is in respect of a judgment debt and the creditor knows or believes with reasonable cause (a) that the debtor has absconded or is avoiding service and (b) there is no real prospect of recovering the debt by execution, the demand may be advertised in one or more newspapers under r 6.3(3). No leave of the court is required.

A creditor's petition may only be presented on a total debt of £750.[1] However, more than one debt may be aggregated for the purposes of a petition and accordingly a statutory demand may be served in respect of any size of debt. A statutory demand which has not been complied with is effective for founding a petition for a period of four months after service. Thereafter the demand may be relied on but an affidavit explaining the reasons and circumstances of the delay in presenting the petition must be served with the petition.[2]

The total debt of at least £750 must remain due at the date of presentation of the petition. Accordingly the debtor may pay the debt or or bring it down to below £750 at any time before the petition is presented. In this respect creditors and their legal advisers should be careful to consider giving written instructions to any court where judgment or order for payment has been obtained against the debtor not to accept a part payment into court in reduction of the judgment debt.[3] Where a part payment reduces the outstanding balance to below £750, a bankruptcy petition may not be presented in respect of that debt.[4]

[1] Insolvency Act 1986, ss 267(2)(a) and (4).
[2] Individual Insolvency Rules 1986, r 6.12(7).
[3] County Court Rules 1981, Ord 22, r 9(2).
[4] *Re Patel, ex p Debtor v Dallomo* [1986] 1 All ER 522.

13.3.4 *Setting aside the statutory demand.* The debtor may apply to set aside the statutory demand within 18 days from the date of service on him,[1] or where demand is advertised in a newspaper, the date of first appearance of advertisement. The application is to 'the appropriate court' i e the court in which he would present his own bankruptcy petition.[2] The application must be supported with an affidavit specifying the date of service of the statutory demand and the grounds on which the debtor claims it should be set aside[3] and as from the date on which it is delivered to the court the time limited for compliance with the statutory demand ceases to run.[4]

On receipt of the application the court may dismiss it without notifying the creditor if satisfied that no sufficient cause is shown.[5] Otherwise, the court fixes a time and place for a hearing giving at least seven days' notice to the debtor and to the person named in the statutory demand as the individual with whom the debtor may enter into communication.[6] The court may grant the application if:[7]

(a) the debtor appears to have a counter-claim, set-off or cross-demand which equals or exceeds the amount of the debt or debts specified in the statutory demand;
(b) the debt is disputed on grounds which appear to the court to be substantial;
(c) the creditor appears to hold security for the debt and either has not complied with the requirement to specify and value it in his demand or the court considers that its value equals or exceeds the value of the demand; or
(d) satisfied on other grounds that the demand ought to be set aside.

The creditors may be required to amend a demand which undervalues a security without prejudice to the right to present a petition on that demand.[8] Where the court dismisses the application it may authorise the creditor to present a petition forthwith or after a specified date.[9]

[1] Individual Insolvency Rules 1986, r 6.4(1).
[2] Ibid, r 6.4(2), and see para 13.6.1 below.
[3] Individual Insolvency Rules 1986, r 6.4(4). The affidavit should exhibit the statutory demand.
[4] Ibid, r 6.4(3).
[5] Ibid, r 6.5(1).
[6] Ibid, r 6.5(2).
[7] Ibid, r 6.5(4) and see form 6.6.
[8] Ibid, r 6.5(5).
[9] Ibid, r 6.5(6).

13.3.5 That an application to set aside the statutory demand may be granted on bases (a) and (b) above introduces into bankruptcy law the practice of the Companies Court relating to disputed winding-up petitions following demands under the Insolvency Act 1986, s 123. For in company law the general principle is that an order for winding up will not be made where there is a bona fide dispute over the debt, i e a dispute based on substantial grounds[1] or where the debtor company has a set off or counterclaim based on a substantial ground.[2] Every case will turn on its own facts but the following points may be noted:

(i) the motive behind the proceeding, however venomous or ulterior does not, of itself, affect the matter;[3]
(ii) the court is not obliged to accept that there is a substantial dispute because unconditional leave to defend has been given in RSC Ord 14 proceedings. The court is entitled to investigate the evidence and reach its own conclusion[4] although plainly the granting of leave to defend will usually be highly persuasive;
(iii) the court need not prevent a petition proceeding because an appeal has been lodged against the judgment relied on[5] although provided the notice of appeal suggests that there is merit in an appeal, the court will usually be reluctant to allow a debtor to be made bankrupt before that appeal is determined;

(iv) the court may stand proceedings over where it is alleged that a judgment was obtained by fraud and impeachment proceedings are instituted;[6]

(v) however wealthy the Respondent may appear to be and whatever the prospect there may be in obtaining payment by other means, a party may not be prevented from exercising his rights to present a demand followed, if there is non-payment, by a petition.[7]

[1] See, eg *Re King's Cross Industrial Dwellings Co* (1870) LR 11 Eq 149; *Re The Imperial Anglo-German Bank* (1872) 25 LT 895; and *Re Welsh Brick Industries Ltd* [1946] 2 All ER 197.
[2] *Re LHF Wools Ltd* [1970] Ch 27.
[3] *Mann v Goldstein* [1968] 2 All ER 769.
[4] *Re Welsh Brick Industries Ltd* [1946] 2 All ER 197, CA.
[5] *Re Amalgamated Properties of Rhodesia (1913) Ltd* [1917] 2 Ch 115, CA.
[6] *Bowes v Directors of Hope Life Insurance & Guarantee Co* (1865) 11 HL Cas 389.
[7] *Cornhill Insurance plc v Improvement Services Ltd* [1986] 1 WLR 114.

13.4 DEBTORS' PETITIONS

13.4.1 An individual debtor may present a petition to the court on the sole ground that he is unable to pay his debts.[1] The petition must be accompanied by a statement of affairs containing particulars of creditors, debts, other liabilities and assets, as prescribed, together with any other information prescribed.[2]As with creditors' petitions the Act provides that a debtor's petition may not be withdrawn without leave of the court.[3] This restates the position under the Old Law, see the Bankruptcy Act 1914, s 6(2) and is designed to discourage abuse of the legal process of bankruptcy.

[1] Insolvency Act 1986, s 272(2).
[2] Individual Insolvency Rules 1986, r 6.68. The statement of affairs must be in form 6.28.
[3] Insolvency Act 1986, s 266(2).

13.5 PETITION IN CONNECTION WITH VOLUNTARY ARRANGEMENTS

13.5.1 Under the provisions of the Insolvency Act 1986[1] for voluntary arrangements, where a composition or scheme has been duly approved in creditors' meeting, it is binding on any creditor who was entitled to notice of and to vote at the meeting irrespective of his presence, representation or manner of voting at the meeting. Any such creditor or the supervisor of the scheme may present a petition for a bankruptcy order to be made on one of the following grounds, namely that;

(a) the debtor has failed to comply with his obligations under the composition or scheme in question;

(b) either the debtor's statement of affairs or other document supplied by the debtor to any person in connection with his proposals for voluntary arrangements, or information given at a creditors' meeting by the debtor, was false or misleading in a material particular or was subject to material omissions; or

(c) the debtor has failed to comply with the reasonable requirements of the supervisor of the composition or scheme.

[1] Insolvency Act 1986, s 276.

13.5.2 In the event that an order is made on such a petition any expenses properly incurred in the administration of the aborted composition or scheme shall be a first charge on the bankrupt's estate.

13.6 MAKING THE BANKRUPTCY ORDER

13.6.1 On a creditor's petition the Act provides[1] that the court shall not make a bankruptcy order unless satisfied that the debt, or one of the debts, on which the petition was presented has not been paid secured or compounded if due. In the case of a future debt the court must be satisfied that there is no reasonable prospect of it being paid when it falls due.

[1] Insolvency Act 1986, s 271(1).

13.6.1.1 In the case of debts already due the failure of the debtor to meet the formal demand or satisfy execution should be sufficient to satisfy the court. The debtor may, however, resist the petition and seek an order dismissing it on the grounds that either:
(a) he is able to pay all his debts, in the determination of which the court has to take into account the debtor's contingent and prospective liabilities; or
(b) he has made an offer to secure or compound the debt which if accepted would require the petition to be dismissed, but that the offer has been unreasonably refused by the petitioning creditor.

13.6.1.2 There are no statutory guidelines as to how the court should exercise this jurisdiction, which is expressly limited in scope to an unreasonable refusal of an offer to secure or compound the debt. Accordingly, this is in contrast to the provision under the Old Bankruptcy Law that a petition for a receiving order could be dismissed by the court not only on procedural grounds or on the basis that the debtor is able to pay his debts but also 'for other sufficient cause'. The defences to a petition for a receiving order under this head (see para 2.4.3 above) are of no relevance to the New Law. In giving the court discretion to dismiss a bankruptcy petition where the petitioner has unreasonably refused an offer of composition or security the Insolvency Act 1986 alters the position from that existing under the Old Bankruptcy Law where the fact that a majority of the debtor's creditors had assented to a deed of arrangement was not 'sufficient cause' to dismiss a petition for a receiving order.[1]

[1] *Re Dixon, ex p Dixon* (1884) 13 QBD 118.

13.6.1.3 Under the New Law the fact that the petitioning creditor is out of step with the majority of the creditors may be sufficient for the court to hold that his refusal to accept the proposal was unreasonable; or to hold that acceptance of the proposal would have required the dismissal of the petition and so dismiss the petition. Under these circumstances the more appropriate course for the debtor under the New Law seems to be to apply for an interim order under s 255 which would have the effect of staying the petition while the debtor's proposals are put to the test at a formal creditor's meeting. The failure of the debtor to make such an application could be relied on by the petitioner in upholding his petition. However an interim order cannot be made without an insolvency practitioner willing to act as nominee, and where the debtor has not yet been able to instruct an insolvency practitioner this ground of defence to a bankruptcy petition will be required.

This defence should also be appropriate where one or a few creditors are acting oppressively and are refusing to accept security from a debtor with temporary financial embarrassment but reasonable prospects of future solvency.

13.6.2 Where the petition is based on a future debt the court has to determine whether there is a reasonable prospect that the debtor will be able to pay the debt when it falls due. For this purpose the court is required to assume that the facts and other matters known to the creditor at the time that he entered into the relevant transaction gave rise to a reasonable prospect of repayment.[1] This affords some protection to undue harrassment of an individual whose debt is not yet payable from creditors who were aware of financial difficulties at the date they entered into the transaction with the debtor which gives rise to the future debt relied on in the petition.

Where the debtor was in financial difficulties at the date of that transaction, the onus will be on the petitioner to satisfy the court of the extent of his knowledge of those difficulties and that, by themselves alone, events since then have transformed the debtor's affairs from a state in which there were reasonable prospects of repayment into a position where no reasonable prospect of payment exists. Subject to this provision the court is free from statutory guidelines as to what constitutes a lack of reasonable prospect of payment.

1 Insolvency Act 1986, s 271(4), and note that s 436 'transaction' includes a gift agreement or arrangement.

13.6.3 On a debtor's petition, a bankruptcy order does not follow automatically.

The court must not make an order where it appears to the court that:[1]

(a) the total unsecured debts would be less than the small bankruptcy level;[2] and
(b) the value of the estate would be equal to or more than the minimum amount;[2] and
(c) during the five years prior to the presentation of the petition the debtor has not been adjudged bankrupt nor entered into a composition with his creditors or a scheme of arrangement of his affairs; and
(d) that it would be appropriate to appoint a person to prepare a report on the possibility of the debtor entering into voluntary arrangements.

In the event that the above conditions are met the court has a discretion to appoint an insolvency practitioner ('the appointed person') to inquire into the debtor's affairs and prepare a report. The report is to state whether the debtor is willing to enter into voluntary arrangements under the Act, and whether the insolvency practitioner concerned considers that a meeting of creditors should be summoned to consider the debtor's proposals and if so when and where he proposes that the meeting should be held.

The insolvency practitioner must send a copy of his report to the debtor so that he receives it not less than three working days before the date fixed for the court's consideration of the report.[3] The debtor is entitled to attend the hearing and make representations; he may indeed be required to attend.[4] The insolvency practitioner's remuneration for work done up to the time of the court's consideration of his report is paid by the official receiver from the deposit monies paid by the debtor.[5]

[1] Insolvency Act 1986, s 273.
[2] 'Small bankruptcy level' and 'minimum amount' are to be prescribed for these purposes from time to time: Insolvency Act 1986, s 273(1); see Insolvency Proceedings (Monetary Limits) Order 1986, SI 1986/1996 – small bankruptcy level is £20,000, minimum amount is £2,000.
[3] Individual Insolvency Rules 1986, r 6.44(2).
[4] Ibid, r 6.44(3).
[5] See Insolvency Fees Order 1986, SI 1986/2030, art. 9.

13.6.4 The court, on considering the report of the insolvency practitioner, may make an interim order under the Insolvency Act 1986, s 255 (see ch 12 above) or if this is thought inappropriate, a bankruptcy order. Should a bankruptcy order be made the court may, if it appears appropriate, issue a certificate for the summary administration of the bankrupt's estate.

13.6.5 On a petition arising out of default in connection with voluntary arrangements, the petitioner will have to make out one of the three specified grounds.[1] The extent and degree to which information from the debtor needs to be false or misleading or the materiality of omissions is not covered by the Act. The case of the creditor concealed, or perhaps overlooked by the debtor when disclosing his affairs to the nominee has been mentioned in para 12.3.6 above. In other cases where the false or misleading fact or omission relates to the debtor's affairs generally, to be material it will at least have to be sufficient to satisfy the court on a balance of probability that the meeting of creditors which approved the composition or scheme would not have done so had the true facts been known.

[1] Insolvency Act 1986, s 276.

13.6.6 The court has a statutory discretion, in accordance with the Rules, to authorise a creditor's petition to be amended by the omission of any creditor or debt and to be proceeded with as if the creditor or debt deleted had never been on the petition.[1] Where there is a joint petition, therefore, each petitioning creditor and debt may support the petition through to a bankruptcy order provided the debt is equal to or exceeds the bankruptcy level. The court has power to consolidate two or more bankruptcy petitions presented against the same debtor on such terms as it thinks fit.[2]

[1] Insolvency Act 1986, s 269(1); Individual Insolvency Rules 1986, r 6.22.
[2] Individual Insolvency Rules 1986, r 6.236.

13.7 PROCEDURE ON PETITION

13.7.1 The bankruptcy petition should be filed in the appropriate court as prescribed by the Rules.[1] The petition must contain sufficient information to establish that it is brought in the appropriate court.[2]

1 Individual Insolvency Rules 1986, r 6.9 (creditor's petition), r 6.40 (debtor's petition).
2 Ibid, r 6.9(5).

The county court

13.7.1.1 Not all county courts have a bankruptcy jurisdiction. The petition must be presented in that county court which has a bankruptcy jurisdiction for the county court area in which the debtor has resided or carried on business for the longest period during the six months prior to the date on which the petition is presented.[1] Where the debtor has resided in one insolvency district and carried on business in another, the appropriate court is the one in the area of which the debtor has carried on business. Where a debtor has carried on business during the six months preceding the petition in more than one insolvency district, the petition must be presented to the court for the insolvency district in which the debtor has, or has had for the longest time during that six months, his principal place of business.

1 For 'resided' or carried on business see para 2.2 above.

The High Court

13.7.1.2 A petition is presented in the High Court where:
(a) the debtor has resided or carried on business within the London insolvency district for the greater part of the six months immediately preceding the presentation of the petition, or for a longer time during those six months than anywhere else;
(b) the debtor is not resident in England and Wales;
(c) the petitioning creditor is unable to ascertain the residence or place of business of the debtor; or
(d) it is presented by a minister of the Crown or a government department.

13.7.2 Proceedings are not invalidated if they are brought in the wrong court. Every court having bankruptcy jurisdiction has jurisdiction throughout England and Wales, and therefore if the petition is presented in the wrong court the court may either transfer the petition to the correct court or proceed on the petition itself.[1] Where a point of law arises and both parties consent or the county court considers it appropriate on the application of one party, the court may transfer the proceedings to the High Court.[2] The High Court may order the transfer to it of proceedings pending in a County Court.[3]

1 Individual Insolvency Rules 1986, r 7.12.
2 Ibid, r 7.11(2).
3 Ibid, r 7.11(4).

13.7.3 The Individual Insolvency Rules[1] require that the Chief Land Registrar should be given notice by the court in which a petition is filed of the fact that petition has been presented against the debtor. The registrar of the court requests the Chief Land Registrar to register notice of the petition in the Register of Pending Actions so as to constitute notice of the petition to all persons and for all purposes connected with any registered land in the debtor's estate.[2] Where a petition is presented against a firm, the Chief Land Registrar will register pending action notices against all the partners. On dismissal or withdrawal of a petition, the court is to order the vacation of the registration of the petition as pending action.[3]

1 Individual Insolvency Rules 1986, r 6.13 (creditor's petition), r 6.43 (debtor's petition). The notice should be in form 6.14.
2 Law of Property Act 1925, s 198. These deeming provisions do not apply to unregistered land: Law of Property Act 1969, s 24.
3 Individual Insolvency Rules 1986, r 6.27, form 6.22.

13.7.4 *Form of creditor's petition.* The Rules[1] require that the petition shall contain sufficient information to establish that it is brought in the appropriate court, and further provides[2] that the petition shall state the following matters 'so far as they are within the petitioner's knowledge':

(a) the debtor's name, place of residence and occupation (if any);
(b) the name or names in which he carries on business if other than his true name, and whether he carries on any business of a specified nature alone or with others;
(c) the nature of the debtor's business and its address or addresses;
(d) any name or names other than his true name in which the debtor has carried on business at or after the time when the debt was incurred and whether he has done so alone or with others; and
(e) any address or addresses at which the debtor has resided or carried on business at or after the time when the debt was incurred and the nature of that business.

The petition must also identify the debt on which it is based.[3] The amount, the consideration for it and the fact that the debt is owed to the petitioner must be stated together with the date on which it was incurred. Where the debt includes interest not previously notified to the debtor or any other charge (e g a servicing charge) which accrues from time to time that fact must be specifically stated. The petition should also state either that the debt is for a liquidated sum due and the debtor appears unable to pay it, or that the debt is for a liquidated sum payable at some certain future time (giving the date) and the debtor appears to have no reasonable prospect of being able to pay it. Subject to the provisions of the Insolvency Act 1986, s 269(1) the petition should state that the debt is unsecured.

Where the debt is one for which, under the Insolvency Act 1986, s 267, a statutory demand must have been served on the debtor, details of the date and service of the demand must be given together with a statement that the debtor has neither complied with it or sought to set it aside.[4] Where the creditor relies on execution on a judgment being returned unsatisfied, the petition must specify the court from which execution issued and give particulars of the return.[5] Defects of form which are not defects of substance may be rectified by amendment.[6]

[1] Individual Insolvency Rules 1986, r 6.9(5). The petition should also give any alias used by the debtor which is known to the petitioner r 6.7(3).
[2] Ibid, r 6.7(1).
[3] Ibid, r 6.8(1).
[4] Ibid, r 6.8(2).
[5] Ibid, r 6.8(3).
[6] Ibid, r 7.55.

13.7.5 *Presentation and service of creditor's petition.*

13.7.5.1 The creditor delivers the petition to the appropriate court for filing together with two copies, one for service on the debtor and the other to be exhibited to the affidavit verifying service.[1] The petition must be verified by affidavit in accordance with the requirement of the Individual Insolvency Rules, r 6.12(1).[2] The court endorses the date and time of filing on the petition and the copies, and fixes a time and place for hearing the petition which is also endorsed on the petition and the copies.[3] Where the petition proceeds on a statutory demand, an affidavit proving service of the demand and exhibiting a copy of the demand must be filed with the petition.[4] If the service of the demand has been acknowledged in writing by the debtor or his authorised agent, the affidavit providing service may be sworn by the creditor or person acting on his behalf with the acknowledgment of service exhibited to the affidavit. Otherwise the affidavit must be sworn by the person who effected service of the demand. Where there is written acknowledgment or personal service, the rules provide that the creditor may take steps to bring the demand to the attention of the debtor (though public advertisement is not authorised) such as would be required to obtain an order for substituted service. If the court is satisfied on affidavit evidence that these steps were sufficient, it may allow the filing of the petition.[5] Where the creditor has taken advantage of r 6.3(3) which allows the advertising of the statutory demand in a newspaper the affidavit must specify (a) the means of the creditor's knowledge or belief that the debtor has absconded or is avoiding service and that the judgment debt is unlikely to be recovered by execution or other process and (b) the date or dates on which and the newspaper in which the statutory demand was advertised. The affidavit must be sworn by the creditor himself or by a person having direct personal knowledge of the circumstances.[6]

Rule 6.12 which requires verification of the petition by affidavit further provides:

(a) if the petition is based on debts due to two or more creditors, the debts to each creditor must be separately verified;
(b) the petition must be exhibited to the verification affidavit;
(c) the affidavit must be made by the petitioner or person with direct knowledge of the matters in question;
(d) where the maker of the affidavit is not the petitioner he must identify himself and state his capacity, authority and means of knowledge;
(e) when the petition is based on a statutory demand served more than four months before the presentation of the petition, the affidavit must state the reasons for the delay; and

(f) that the affidavit is prima facie evidence of the truth of the statements in the petition.

[1] Individual Insolvency Rules 1986, r 6.10(1) and (3); no petition may be filed unless a receipt for the deposit payable on presentation is produced, r 6.10(2).
[2] Ibid, r 6.10(1).
[3] Ibid, r 6.10(4) and (5).
[4] Ibid, r 6.11.
[5] Ibid, r 6.11(5) (6) and (9).
[6] Ibid, r 6.11(8).

13.7.5.2 Upon presentation of the petition, the petitioner must deposit the sum prescribed by the appropriate fees order.[1] The deposit is paid either to the official receiver or to the county court and a receipt given. No petition may be filed without the receipt for the deposit being produced.[2] The official receiver shall account to the petitioner or to the estate for the deposit and any money deposited is repaid to the petitioning creditor out of the estate as a first charge on the estate.[3] The deposit is repayable to the petitioner where the petition is dismissed, unless a bankruptcy order has been made or a fee is payable to an insolvency practitioner for preparing a report under the Insolvency Act 1986, s 274, or on annulment of the bankruptcy order unless it is required to pay the administration fee.[4]

[1] Insolvency Fees Order 1986, SI 1986/2030, art 9; the sum is £200 except in the case of a debtor's petition when it is £100.
[2] Individual Insolvency Rules, r 6.10(2).
[3] Ibid, r 6.224(1).
[4] Insolvency Fees Order 1986, art 11.

13.7.5.3 Service of the petition may be effected by an officer of the court, the petitioning creditor, his solicitor or service agent.[1] The court may order substituted service in such manner as it thinks fit if satisfied by affidavit or other evidence on oath that the debtor is keeping out of the way to avoid service.[2] Immediately following successful service of the petition an affidavit proving service and exhibiting a sealed copy of the petition shall be delivered to the court for filing.[3] Should a debtor die before service, the court may order service to be effected on the personal representatives or on such other person as it thinks fit.[4]

[1] Individual Insolvency Rules 1986, r 6.14(1).
[2] Ibid, r 6.14(2) and (3), forms 6.15 or 6.16.
[3] Ibid, r 6.15, forms 6.17 or 6.18.
[4] Ibid, r 6.16.

13.7.6 *Security for costs.* In the case only of a petition based upon a future liquidated debt under the Insolvency Act 1986, s 268(2) where the creditor alleges that the debtor has failed to establish that there is a reasonable prospect that he will pay the debt when it falls due, the debtor may apply for an order that the petitioning creditor give security for costs.[1] The Rules give the court a discretion as to the nature and amount of any security ordered. No guidelines are laid down as to the exercise of the discretion.

[1] Individual Insolvency Rules 1986, r 6.17.

13.7.7 *Hearing of creditor's petition*

13.7.7.1 The petition shall not be heard until at least 14 days after service on the debtor, unless the court is satisfied that the debtor has absconded or it is a proper case for an expedited hearing.[1] At the hearing, the petitioning creditor, the debtor and any creditor who has given notice under r 6.23 may appear. A debtor who intends to oppose the petition must file in court a notice specifying his grounds of objection to the making of a bankruptcy order and serve a copy of the notice on the petitioning creditor not later than seven days before the hearing date.[2] A creditor who intends to appear on the hearing of the petition must notify the petitioning creditor of his intention not later than 4.00pm on the third business day before the hearing. The court may, however, give leave to appear to a creditor who has failed to give the requisite notice.[3] The petitioning creditor is required to prepare a list containing the names and addresses of all creditors who have notified their intention to appear together with their solicitors, if any.[4] A petition against two or more debtors may be heard separately or collectively.[5]

[1] Individual Insolvency Rules 1986, r 6.18.
[2] Ibid, r 6.21. The notice should be in form 6.19.
[3] Ibid, r 6.23, form 6.20.
[4] Ibid, r 6.24, form 6.21.
[5] Ibid, r 6.19.

13.7.7.2 The Rules make no specific provision as to the conduct of the hearing of the petition. Under the previous law the hearing of the petition usually took place in chambers on affidavit evidence. There was power for the registrar to adjourn the matter to the judge, allow cross-examination and make orders for discovery. A similar procedure will presumably apply to the hearing of petitions under the Insolvency Act 1986.[1]

[1] For hearings of applications generally see Individual Insolvency Rules, r 7.6.

13.7.7.3 The petitioning creditor may apply to the court for an extension of time for hearing if the petition has not been served in sufficient time to allow the petition to proceed on the hearing date originally allocated.[1] The rules impose an obligation on the petitioning creditor to notify the debtor and any creditor who has given notice of intention to appear of any adjourned hearing date.[2] Should the petitioning creditor fail to appear on the hearing of the petition, he may not present another petition against the same debtor on the same debt, either alone or jointly with any other person, without the leave of the court to which the previous petition was presented.[3]

[1] Individual Insolvency Rules 1986, r 6.28.
[2] Ibid, r 6.29.
[3] Ibid, r 6.26.

13.7.7.4 On the hearing of the petition, the court may make a bankruptcy order if satisfied that the statements in the petition are true and that the debt has not been paid, secured or compounded.[1] Where the petition is preceded by a statutory demand, it may not be dismissed on the ground only that the amount of the debt was overstated in the demand unless the debtor gave notice to the creditor within the three weeks allowed for compliance with the demand that he disputed the validity of the notice on that basis.[2] A petition brought in respect of a judgment debt may be stayed or dismissed on the ground that an appeal is pending or execution has been stayed.[3]

[1] Individual Insolvency Rules 1986, r 6.25(1).
[2] Ibid, r 6.25(3).
[3] Ibid, r 6.25(2), form 6.22.

13.7.7.5 Where a bankruptcy order is made it is settled by the court. The order is to state the date of presentation of the petition, the date and time of making the order and must contain a notice requiring the bankrupt to attend forthwith on the official receiver at the place stated in the order.[1] The order should also be endorsed with the name, address, telephone number and reference of any solicitor representing the petitioning creditor.[2] It may also include a provision staying any action or proceeding against the debtor.[3]

[1] Individual Insolvency Rules 1986, r 6.33(1) and (2), form 6.25.
[2] Ibid, r 6.33(4).
[3] Ibid, r 6.33(3).

13.7.7.6 Following the making of the bankruptcy order, the court sends two sealed copies of the order to the official receiver who forwards one copy to the bankrupt.[1] Subject to an order of the court made on the application of the bankrupt or the creditor[2] the official receiver, on receipt of the bankruptcy order:[3]

(a) notifies the Chief Land Registrar for registration in the register of writs and orders affecting land;
(b) advertises the order in such local paper as he thinks fit; and
(c) causes the order to be gazetted.

[1] Individual Insolvency Rules 1986, r 6.34(1).
[2] Ibid, r 6.34(3). A person who has obtained an order must forthwith notify the official receiver: r 6.34(4).
[3] Individual Insolvency Rules 1986, r 6.34(2).

13.7.7.7 At any time after the making of a bankruptcy order, the official receiver or the trustee in bankruptcy may apply to the court for an order amending the full title of the proceedings.[1] If an order is made the official receiver must notify the Chief Land Registrar and, if so ordered by the court gazette the order or advertise it in a local newspaper.[2]

[1] Individual Insolvency Rules 1986, r 6.35(1).
[2] Ibid, r 6.35(2).

13.7.7.8 *Substitution of petitioner.* In the event that a creditor petitions and is found not to be entitled to an order, or a petitioner consents to withdrawal, dismissal or adjournment of his petition, or a petitioner fails either to appear at the hearing of his petition or to apply for a bankruptcy order, the court may order the substitution as petitioner of another creditor.[1] A substitution order may be made on such terms as it thinks just (eg as to payment of the deposit) in favour of a creditor who would have been qualified to present a petition on the date the petition was presented and who has given notice of his intention to appear at the hearing under r 6.23.[2] Such a creditor may indeed apply to the Court for an order giving him carriage of the petition in place of the petitioning creditor on the grounds that the petitioning creditor intends to secure the postponement or withdrawal of the petition or othewise does not intend to prosecute the petition diligently.[3] The court may not make a change of carriage order where the petitioning creditors's debt has been paid, secured or compounded.[4]

1 Individual Insolvency Rules, r 6.30(1).
2 Ibid, r 6.30(2).
3 Ibid, r 6.31(1)(2).
4 Ibid, r 6.31(3).

13.7.7.9 *Withdrawal of petition.* Should the petitioner wish to apply to the court for leave to withdraw the petition or for the petition to be dismissed he must file an affidavit specifying the grounds of the application and the reasons for it, unless the court otherwise orders.[1] The affidavit should refer to payments made to the petitioner and must state what dispositions of property have been made to secure or compound his debt, whether such property belonged to the debtor and if so, whether the disposition has been approved or ratified by the court.[2] The relevant court order should be specified. The court may not allow a petition to be withdrawn before it is heard.[3]

1 Individual Insolvency Rules, r 6.32(1).
2 Ibid, r 6.32(2).
3 Ibid, r 6.33(3).

Debtor's petition

13.7.8 The petition must identify the debtor[1] and must admit insolvency, requesting that a bankruptcy order be made against him.[2] Particulars must be given of any bankruptcy order, composition or scheme of arrangement made or entered into within five years of the date of the petition.[3] The petition must be accompanied by a statement of affairs.[4] The debtor must deliver to the court three copies of the petition and two copies of the statement of affairs together with a receipt for the deposit payable on presentation.[5] Once the copies of the petition have been endorsed with the time and place of hearing, one is returned to the debtor, one sent to the official receiver together with a copy of the statement of affairs and the remaining petition and statement of affairs are retained by the court to be sent to any insolvency practitioner appointed under the Insolvency Act 1986, s 273(2).[6] The Court may hear the petition immediately or fix a time and place for the hearing.[7]

The bankruptcy order is settled by the court and may include the certificate of summary administration, if issued by the court under the Insolvency Act 1986, s 275(1).[8] The court sends two sealed copies of the order to the official receiver who sends one forthwith to the bankrupt and notifies the Chief Land Registrar, advertises in a local paper and causes the order to be gazetted.[9]

1 Individual Insolvency Rules 1986, r 6.38.
2 Ibid, r 6.39(1).

[3] Ibid, r 6.39(2).
[4] Insolvency Act 1986, s 272(2); Individual Insolvency Rules 1986, r 6.41. For the content of the statement of affairs see form 6.28.
[5] Individual Insolvency Rules 1986, r 6.42(1).
[6] Ibid, r 6.42(3) and (4).
[7] Ibid, r 6.42(2).
[8] Ibid, rr 6.45(1) and 6.48, form 6.30.
[9] Ibid, r 6.46(1)(2) and form 6.26. The court may order the official receiver to suspend the publicising of the order on the application of the bankrupt or a creditor, r 6.46(3).

CHAPTER 14

The Bankrupt's Estate: Protection and Investigation

14.1 PROTECTION OF THE BANKRUPT'S ESTATE

14.1.1 The Insolvency Act 1986 abolishes the receiving order which, under the Old Bankruptcy Law served to protect the debtor's estate pending adjudication, and in place imposes protection provisions which apply automatically from the date on which the petition is presented. This is one of the measures in the Insolvency Act 1986 which brings individual insolvency law into line with corporate insolvency law.

14.1.2 The bankrupt's estate is defined in the Act[1] as:

(a) all property belonging to or vested in the bankrupt at the commencement of the bankruptcy; or

(b) any property which is or is treated as being comprised in the estate by virtue of the provisions of the second group of Parts of the Act.[2]

The following are excluded from the bankrupt's estate, for bankruptcy purposes:

(i) such tools, books, vehicles and other equipment as are necessary to the bankrupt for personal use by him in his employment business or vocation (subject to the trustee's right to replace any of these items at lower cost if this is reasonable[3]);

(ii) such clothing, bedding, furniture, household equipment and provisions as are necessary for satisfying the basic domestic needs of the bankrupt and his family;

(iii) property excluded from a bankrupt's estate by virtue of the provisions of other enactments;[4]

(iv) property held by the bankrupt on trust for any other person; and

(v) the right of nomination to a vacant ecclesiastical benefice.

'Property' includes any power exercisable by the bankrupt over or in respect of property. For the purposes of the bankrupt's estate the Insolvency Act 1986, s 283(4) provides that a power over or in respect of property is deemed to vest in the person entitled to it at the time of the transaction or event by virtue of which the power becomes exercisable. The fact that the power is not exercisable at the date of the commencement of a bankruptcy does not exclude it from vesting in the trustee.

A power over or in respect of property does not form part of the bankrupt's estate if the relevant property is not for the time being comprised in the bankrupt's estate and (a) is exercisable only after the trustee or the official receiver, if appropriate, has held the final meeting (see ch 16 below), and (b) cannot be exercised for the benefit of the bankrupt.

The property in the bankrupt's estate is, of course, held by the trustee subject to the right of any person other than the bankrupt in any such property. Any rights abandoned by a secured creditor when presenting his petition on which the bankrupt was ajudicated and any rights otherwise given up in accordance with the Rules are disregarded.

[1] Insolvency Act 1986, s 283.
[2] Eg After acquired property (s 307): see para 16.2.3 below; Interim payment under an Income payments order (s 310): see para 16.2.4 below; tools and clothes exceeding value of reasonable replacement (s 308); see para 16.2.2; charge on matrimonial home (s 313); see ch 22 below.
[3] Insolvency Act 1986, s 308(1).
[4] Ie social security, pensions and similar benefits under the National Insurance Acts, Family Allowances Acts and various enactments covering local government and public employees and members of the armed forces

14.1.3 From the date on which the petition is presented until the date on which the bankrupt's estate vests in the trustee, any disposition made by the bankrupt is void unless the court's consent or ratification is obtained to that disposition.[1]

'Disposition' includes a payment of money as well as a disposition of property and covers all dispositions made by the bankrupt irrespective of whether the property involved would form part of the bankrupt's estate. Where any payment of money is void because it was made between the date of the petition and the date of vesting in the trustee the person to whom it is paid holds the sum paid on behalf of the bankrupt as part of his estate. The Act does, however, protect the bona fide purchaser for value without notice of the petition and persons claiming title through such a purchaser. No remedy lies against such persons in respect of any disposition by the bankrupt.

A disposition by the bankrupt as trustee of trust property in this period is perfectly valid.

[1] Insolvency Act 1986, s 284.

14.1.4 Where a bankrupt incurs a debt to a banker or any other person by reason of a making of a payment which is void because it was made between the date of the petition and the date of vesting in the trustee after commencement of his bankruptcy that debt is deemed to have been incurred before commencement of the bankruptcy unless:

(a) that banker or person had notice of the bankruptcy before the debt was incurred; or
(b) it is not reasonably practicable for the sum paid to be recovered from the person to whom it was paid.[1]

The 'commencement of the bankruptcy' is the date on which the bankruptcy order was made.

[1] Insolvency Act 1986, s 284(5).

14.1.5 At any time when proceedings on a petition are pending the court may stay any action, execution or other legal process against the debtor or his property. As in the Old Bankruptcy Law such a stay may be ordered either by the Bankruptcy Court in which the petition is presented or by the court in which any other proceedings against the debtor are pending. This court has a discretion to impose a stay or allow the proceedings to continue on terms.[1]

[1] Insolvency Act 1986, s 285.

14.1.6 The restrictions on proceedings against the debtor or his property continue after an adjudication and the debtor is made bankrupt. The bankruptcy order operates as a complete bar to legal proceedings or execution, (subject to the exceptions listed below) and accordingly no creditor who has a debt provable in the bankruptcy has any remedy against the person or property of the bankrupt in respect of the debt beyond proof in the bankruptcy.

No legal proceedings may be commenced against the bankrupt before his discharge except with the leave of the court and on such terms as the court may impose.[1] 'Property' for these purposes includes all the bankrupt's property whether or not it is comprised in his estate.

There are two exceptions, namely:

(a) Enforcement procedures under s 346 of the Act. In the main these provisions are not, truly, exceptions to the rule that the bankruptcy order operates as a bar to proceedings or execution. They provide that a creditor who has issued execution against, or attached a debt of, the debtor before the commencement of the bankruptcy may only retain the benefit of the execution or attachment if it was completed before the bankruptcy order was made. The court is, however, given power to allow the creditor the benefit of his execution or attachment, albeit incompleted at the commencement of the bankruptcy, to such extent and on such terms as it thinks fit.

(b) Distress under the Insolvency Act 1986, s 347. This section allows a landlord, or any other person to whom rent is payable, to distrain upon the goods and chattels of an undischarged bankrupt but limited to a total of six months rent accrued due before the commencement of the bankruptcy.

[1] Insolvency Act 1986, s 285(3).

14.1.7 Secured creditors are not affected at least to the extent that they may enforce their security.[1] This is subject to the official receiver's rights in respect of goods of an undischarged bankrupt, held by way of pledge, pawn or charge, to inspect the goods after giving written notice of his intention to do so and, after inspection, to exercise the bankrupt's rights to redeem those goods. After receiving notice of an intent to inspect, the chargee is not entitled to realise his security without written leave of the court until the trustee has had a reasonable opportunity to inspect and redeem the goods.[2]

[1] Insolvency Act 1986, s 285(4).
[2] Insolvency Act 1986, s 285(5).

14.2 RECEIVERSHIP

Interim receiver

14.2.1 The court has power to appoint the official receiver to be interim receiver of the debtor's property at any time after the presentation of the petition and before the bankruptcy order is made.[1] Such appointment must be shown to be necessary for the protection of the debtor's property. An interim receiver may also be appointed by the court on the hearing of a debtor's petition in which event any insolvency practitioner may be appointed. Unless the interim receiver's powers are expressly limited by the court he has the same rights, powers, duties and immunities as a receiver and manager has after the bankruptcy order (as to which see para 14.2.6 below). An application to the court for the appointment of an interim receiver may be made by a creditor, debtor or insolvency practitioner appointed under the Insolvency Act 1986, s 273(2) at any time after the presentation of the petition.[2] The application must be supported by affidavit stating the grounds on which it is proposed that the interim receiver be appointed.[3] The official receiver and any appointed insolvency practitioner must be notified of the application and may attend and make representations.[4]

1 Insolvency Act 1986, s 286.
2 Individual Insolvency Rules 1986, r 6.51(1).
3 Ibid, r 6.51(2) and must estimate the value of the property over which the interim receiver may be appointed.
4 Ibid, r 6.51(3)–(6). An appointed insolvency practitioner may be appointed interim receiver. If such an appointment is sought, the affidavit under r 6.51(3) must state that he has consented to act.

14.2.2 The court order appointing any person to be an interim receiver must require that person to take immediate possession of all the debtor's property, or that part of the debtor's property to which the interim receiver's powers are limited. The order must state the nature and give a short description of the property of which the interim receiver is to take possession, and specify the duties to be performed by him with regard to the debtor's affairs.[1]

The interim receiver may require the debtor, to any reasonable extent, to give him an inventory of his property or provide him with any other information he needs or to attend upon him to provide such information as the receiver needs.[2] The order appointing the interim receiver may specify the duties to be performed by him.[3]

1 Individual Insolvency Rules 1986, r 6.52, form 6.32.
2 Insolvency Act 1986, s 286(5).
3 Individual Insolvency Rules 1986, r 6.52(1).

14.2.3 The applicant for the order appointing the official receiver as interim receiver must deposit with the official receiver such sum as the court directs to cover his fees and expenses.[1] Should the sum deposited subsequently prove insufficient the court may order an additional deposit on the application of the official receiver. Where this further deposit is not made within two working days of the service of the order, the court may discharge the order appointing the interim receiver.[2] Where an insolvency practitioner is appointed interim receiver, the appointment may be revoked if the appointee fails to provide the security required under the Insolvency Act 1986.[3] The appointee may be reimbursed out of the debtor's property if no bankruptcy order is subsequently made, or from the estate if it is.[4]

1 Individual Insolvency Rules 1986, r 6.53(1).
2 Ibid, r 6.53(2).
3 S 390(3).
4 Ibid, r 6.54(2).

14.2.4 The appointment of the interim receiver has the same effect as the making of a bankruptcy order as a bar to legal proceedings or execution against the person or property of the debtor, (see para 14.1.6 above). The interim receiver's remuneration is fixed by the court from time to time on his application.[1]

1 Individual Insolvency Rules 1986, r 6.56.

14.2.5 The interim receivership will come to an end and the person appointed will cease to be interim receiver of the debtor's property automatically if the bankruptcy petition against the debtor is dismissed or a bankruptcy order made.[1] In any other case the court terminates the appointment by order. This includes the case where an insolvency practitioner appointee fails to give or keep up his security.[2] The court may terminate the appointment on the application of the interim receiver, official receiver, the debtor or any creditors at any time.[3]

1 Insolvency Act 1986, s 286(7).
2 Individual Insolvency Rules 1986, r 6.55.
3 Ibid, r 6.57.

Receivership pending trustee's appointment

14.2.6 Between the date of the bankruptcy order and the date on which the bankrupt's estate vests in a trustee, the official receiver is automatically receiver and manager of the bankrupt's estate.[1] His function is to protect the estate and he has the same powers as a receiver or manager appointed by the High Court. He has express power to sell perishable goods or any other goods of the estate the value of which is likely to diminish if not disposed of speedily.

1 Insolvency Act 1986, s 287. NB This will not apply where the court orders summary administration of the estate of the bankrupt under s 297 as the official receiver becomes trustee immediately upon the court issuing a certificate for summary administration.

14.2.7 The official receiver is under a duty to take all steps that he considers fit to protect the estate. He need not, however, be required to do anything which involves incurring expenditure unless directed to do so by the Secretary of State. If he thinks it appropriate the official receiver may summon a general meeting of the bankrupt's creditors and he may be directed to do so by the court.

He is not liable to any person in respect of loss and damage resulting from the seizure or disposal of goods not belonging to the bankrupt, provided that he believes, on reasonable grounds, that he is entitled to seize or dispose of that particular property. He is, however, liable for loss caused by negligence. This protection of the official receiver has no effect on title to the goods, but the official receiver has a lien on any property or proceeds of sale for any expenses incurred in its seizure of disposal.

Special manager

14.2.8 On application to the court a special manager may be appointed where the official receiver has been appointed interim receiver of the debtor's property, or the debtor has been adjudicated bankrupt and his property has passed into the hands of the official receiver as receiver and manager, or his estate vested in a trustee.[1] An application may be made by the official receiver or the trustee in any case where it appears advisable because of the nature of the estate, property or business to have it managed by a person with particular expertise or that this is required in the general interest of the creditors. The court[2] specifies the powers to be entrusted to the special manager and may do so by directing that any particular provision of the Insolvency Act 1986, Second Group of Parts (i e the parts of the Act relating to individual insolvencies) which has effect in relation to the official receiver, an interim receiver or a trustee shall apply to the special manager. A special manager must give security and keep and produce accounts as prescribed in the Rules.[3]

It is to be noted the court appoints and defines the powers of a special manager and determines the length of his appointment, and that it is to the trustee that the special manager has his primary duty to produce accounts. This is in contrast with the Old Bankruptcy Law. Under the Bankruptcy Act 1914[4] the official receiver had power to appoint a special manager and define his powers on the application of any creditor. Where the official receiver declined to make an appointment the court would not involve itself with his decision.[5] Under the Insolvency Act 1986 creditors neither have the right to apply for the appointment of a special manager, nor need they initiate the procedure leading to appointment. Either the official receiver or the trustee in bankruptcy may apply of his own volition.[6]

Should the special manager fail to give or keep up his security the official receiver or trustee must report this failure to the court which may then discharge the appointment or remove the special manager.[7] The court should then give directions as to whether any, and if so what, steps should be taken to appoint a replacement.[8] The special manager's appointment terminates if the bankruptcy petition is dismissed, or if an interim receiver is discharged, or by order of the court on the application of the official receiver or trustee on the ground that his employment is no longer necessary or profitable for the estate.[9]

[1] Individual Insolvency Rules 1986, r 6.167. Insolvency Act 1986, s 370.
[2] Insolvency Act 1986, s 370(3).
[3] Insolvency Act 1986, s 370(5); Individual Insolvency Rules 1986, rr 6.168 and 6.170.
[4] S 10, and see s 74(1)(a).

5 *Re Whittaker* (1884) 50 LT 510.
6 1986 Act, s 370(2). This is equivalent to the procedure in company liquidation, see Insolvency Act 1986, s 177.
7 Individual Insolvency Rules, r 6.169(1)(2).
8 Ibid, r 6.169(3).
9 Ibid, r 6.171(1), (2). Nb the creditors may by resolution require the official receiver or trustee to apply to the court to terminate the special manager's employment.

14.3 INVESTIGATION OF THE BANKRUPT'S AFFAIRS

14.3.1 Where a petition has been presented other than by the debtor himself and a bankruptcy order is made, the bankrupt has 21 days from the commencement of the bankruptcy to submit a statement of affairs to the official receiver.[1] This period may be extended, or indeed the statement of affairs itself may be dispensed with, by direction of the official receiver if he thinks fit. The official receiver may act on his own volition to dispense with a statement of affairs or he may do so at the bankrupt's request.[2] Where a request is made by the bankrupt and refused by the official receiver, the bankrupt may apply to the court to exercise the power to release the bankrupt from his duty to submit a statement of his affairs or extend the 21-day period for him to do so.[3]

The official receiver may not revoke his release of the bankrupt from submitting a statement of affairs but may at any time require the bankrupt to submit further information or accounts[4] if directed to be verified by affidavit.[5] The bankrupt must bear his own costs of any application he makes to the court for an order that he be released from his duty to submit a statement of affairs or that his time for submission be extended.[6]

1 Insolvency Act 1986, s 288(1).
2 Individual Insolvency Rules 1986, r 6.62.
3 Insolvency Act 1986, s 288(3); for the procedure for the bankrupt's application see Individual Insolvency Rules, r 6.62(1) (release from duty to submit statement), r 6.62(2) (extension of time).
4 Individual Insolvency Rules 1986, r 6.66(1).
5 Ibid, r 6.66(2).
6 Ibid, r 6.62(7).

14.3.2 The information to be contained in the statement of affairs is prescribed in the Rules.[1] The Rules also provide[2] that the official receiver should furnish the bankrupt with instructions for preparing his statement of affairs and the necessary forms. The statement of affairs must be verified by affidavit.[3] Should the bankrupt be unable to prepare a proper statement of affairs, the official receiver may employ a person to assist in the preparation at the expense of the estate.[4] The bankrupt may himself request assistance and with the authority of the official receiver, employ a person to assist him at the expense of the estate.[5] The official receiver may require the bankrupt at any time to submit an amended statement of affairs[6] or trading accounts.[7] Trading accounts may not be required for any period earlier than three years before the date of presentation of the bankruptcy petition unless the court orders accounts for any earlier period.[8]

1 Individual Insolvency Rules 1986, r 6.59 (creditor's petition), r 6.68 (debtor's petition), which require the statement of affairs to be in form 6.33 or 6.28 respectively.

[2] Ibid, r 6.60(1).
[3] Ibid, r 6.60(2).
[4] Ibid, r 6.63(1) (creditor's petition), r 6.71(1) (debtor's petition, preparation of accounts only).
[5] Individual Insolvency Rules 1986, r 6.63(2) (creditor's petition).
NB r 6.63(3) provides that only a named person or firm may be authorised by the official receiver and r 6.63(4) that such authorisation may be subject to conditions. Similar provisions apply in the case of a debtor's petition, see r 6.71(2)–(4).
[6] Individual Insolvency Rules 1986, r 6.66 (creditor's petition), r 6.72 (debtor's petition).
[7] Individual Insolvency Rules 1986, r 6.64(1) (creditor's petition), r 6.69(1) (debtor's petition).
[8] Individual Insolvency Rules 1986, r 6.64(2) (creditor's petition), r 6.69(2) (debtor's petition). Accounts should be delivered in 21 days unless the official receiver allows a longer period rr 6.65, 6.70.

14.3.3 *Information to creditors.* Creditors have no express right to inspect the bankrupt's statement of affairs or trading accounts submitted by him. The official receiver is required by the Rules[1] to send to all creditors a report relating to the bankruptcy proceedings and the state of the bankrupt's affairs at least once after the making of the bankruptcy order. Where a statement of affairs has been lodged the official receiver must send a summary of the statement together with any observations he wishes to make, unless he has already reported to creditors and he has formed the opinion that the statement discloses no further matters which ought to be brought to the creditors' attention.[2] After the official receiver has released a bankrupt from the obligation to submit a statement he should send to creditors a report summarising the bankrupt's affairs, unless he considers this to be unnecessary in the light of a previous report to creditors.[3] The court may relieve the official receiver of the duty to send reports,[4] or make an order on the official receiver's application limiting the extent of disclosure.[5] For these purposes 'creditors' are creditors known to the official receiver or identified in the statement of affairs.[6] A creditor who wishes to obtain more information will have to seek it through the creditor's committee, if any, from the trustee if one is appointed, or seek an examination of the bankrupt.[7]

[1] Individual Insolvency Rules, r 6.73.
[2] Ibid, r 6.75.
[3] Ibid, r 6.76.
[4] Ibid, r 6.77.
[5] Ibid, r 6.61.
[6] Ibid, r 6.74.
[7] Ibid, rr 6.163. 6.172.

14.3.4 A bankrupt who fails to comply with his obligation to submit a statement of affairs or does so incorrectly is guilty of a contempt of court and is liable to be punished accordingly. He may also be guilty of the offence of failing to disclose all the property comprised in his estate or the offence of making a material omission in his statement of affairs[1] or other offences. Furthermore his prospects of an automatic discharge are severely affected. See ch 18 below. The fact that he may receive assistance in the preparation of his statement of affairs does not relieve him of his obligations.[2]

[1] Insolvency Act 1986, ss 353 and 356.
[2] Individual Insolvency Rules 1986, r 6.63(5) (creditor's petition), r 6.71(5) (debtor's petition).

14.3.5 The official receiver is under a duty to investigate the conduct and affairs of every bankrupt and report to the court if he thinks fit.[1] An exception arises where a certificate for summary administration is in force, in which event the official receiver has a discretion whether or not to investigate.[2] Accordingly the official receiver is under a statutory duty to become involved in every case of bankruptcy even where a trustee undertakes the responsibilities arising out of the administration of the estate.

The bankrupt is obliged to deliver both possession of his estate to the official receiver and all books, papers and other records of which he has possession or control and which relate to his affairs.[3] This includes documents to which there is legal professional privilege, though they remain privileged in the hands of the official receiver. Where delivery cannot be effected the bankrupt must take all reasonable steps required of him to protect the things or property involved. The official receiver may also require an inventory of the bankrupt's estate, information generally, and the attendance of the bankrupt, to such extent as is reasonable, both during the currency of the bankruptcy and also after the bankrupt obtains his discharge.

In addition to any criminal offence committed by failing to comply with his obligations to deliver up to the official receiver his estate, documents and records, etc or provide inventories or information or attend upon the official receiver, the bankrupt will be guilty of contempt of court and will be liable to be punished accordingly. As with his obligation in relation to the statement of affairs, his prospects of an automatic discharge are also seriously affected.

[1] Insolvency Act 1986, s 289.
[2] Ibid, s 289(5).
[3] Ibid, s 291. This duty of delivery up by the bankrupt does not apply where the bankrupt's estate vests in a trustee immediately on the making of the bankruptcy order under Insolvency Act 1986, s 297.

14.3.6 *Public examination of the bankrupt.* Public examination may be ordered by the court at any time between the bankruptcy order and discharge. Only the official receiver may apply but he must make an application if requested to do so by one-half in value of the creditors, unless the court orders otherwise.[1] Where the official receiver applies of his own motion, the court is obliged to order a public examination.[2] Where the application follows the intiative of the creditors, an order for public examination is discretionary.

The court appoints the day for examination on which any creditors may attend together with the official receiver and any trustee of special manager who has been appointed in connection with the bankruptcy.[3] The persons who are invited to question the bankrupt concerning his affairs, dealings and property or the causes of his failure are:[4]

(a) the official receiver and in criminal bankruptcy the official petitioner;
(b) the trustee in bankruptcy;
(c) any special manager who has been appointed; or
(d) any creditor who has tendered a proof of debt.

Failure by the bankrupt to attend for his public examination is a contempt of court.[5]

Should the bankrupt be suffering from any mental or physical disability which renders him unfit to be examined, the court may stay the order for examination or give directions as to the manner in which the examination should take place.[6] An application for a stay or for directions may be made by the official receiver, any person appointed by the court to manage the affairs of the bankrupt, or by a relative or friend of the bankrupt where considered by the court to be a proper person to make the application. The official receiver may make the application ex parte supported by evidence in the form of a report. Other applicants must give at least seven days' notice to the official receiver and any trustee of the bankrupt's estate and deposit with the official receiver such sum as the official receiver certifies to be necessary for the additional expenses of any examination that may be ordered on the application. Except where the bankrupt is a patient within the Mental Health Act 1983, the application must be supported by an affidavit of a registered medical practitioner as to the bankrupt's mental and physical condition.

1 Insolvency Act 1986, s 290(1), (2); Individual Insolvency Rules 1986, r 6.172 (order on application by official receiver), r 6.173 (order following request by creditors).
2 Insolvency Act 1986, s 290(3).
3 At least 14 days' notice of the hearing must be given: Individual Insolvency Rules 1986, r 6.172(3).
4 Insolvency Act 1986, s 290(4).
5 Ibid, s 290(5).
6 Individual Insolvency Rules 1986, r 6.174.

14.3.7 The law and practice in relation to the hearing of the public examination will broadly follow that applying to cases under the Bankruptcy Act 1914.[1] The Rules provide that the bankrupt must answer questions on oath and that the bankrupt and any person entitled to appear may appear by solicitor and counsel.[2] The notes of the examination should be read over to or read by the bankrupt and signed by him.[3] Thereafter the notes of the examination may be used in evidence against the bankrupt.[4] The court has a general power to adjourn the public examination[5] and should do so where criminal proceedings have been instituted against the bankrupt and the continuance of the examination might prejudice a fair trial.[6] Where an examination is adjourned generally the official receiver may there and then make an application under the Insolvency Act 1986, s 279(3) to suspend the automatic discharge provisions of the Act.[7] The expenses of a public examination will usually be payable out of the estate. But where the examination is ordered on a creditor's requisition, the court may instead order that the expenses or part of them be paid out of the deposit required from the creditors by way of security for such expenses.[8]

1 As to which see ch 7 above. Nb the court may order the Inland Revenue to produce any relevant document: Insolvency Act 1986, s 369; Individual Insolvency Rules 1986, rr 6.194–6.196.
2 Individual Insolvency Rules 1986, r 6.175(1), (2) and (3).
3 Ibid, r 6.175(4), form 6.58.
4 Ibid, r 6.175(5).
5 Ibid, r 6.176.
6 Ibid, r 6.175(6).
7 Ibid, r 6.176(4).

[8] Ibid, 6.177. The power of the court to order the requisitioning creditors to deposit security for the expenses of the hearing of the public examination is discretionary, and is contained in Individual Insolvency Rules 1986, r 6.173(2).

14.3.8 Where the bankrupt does not qualify for automatic discharge and makes an application to the court for his discharge from bankruptcy,[1] it is the duty of the official receiver to make a report to the court dealing with the matters prescribed by the Rules.[2] The official receiver's report is prima facie evidence of the facts stated in it, and the court must consider the report before deciding what order, if any, to make on the bankrupt's application for discharge. Such applications will not differ much in substance from similar applications under the Old Bankruptcy Law, as to which see ch 10 above.

[1] See chs 10 above and 18 below.
[2] Insolvency Act 1986, s 289(2); Individual Insolvency Rules 1986, r 6.218.

14.3.9 *Private examinations.* An examination of the bankrupt need not take place at a public examination under the Insolvency Act 1986, s 290. The Act contains powers, similar to those contained in the Bankruptcy Act 1914, s 25 for the private examination of the bankrupt or his or her spouse or former spouse.[1]

Sections 366 and 367 provide for the private examination of any person known or believed to have any property comprised in the bankrupt's estate or to be indebted to the bankrupt and to any person 'appearing to the court to be able to give information concerning the bankrupt or the bankrupt's dealings affairs or property.'[2]

The provisions of ss 366 and 367 are substantially the same as those under the Bankruptcy Act 1914, s 25 and which are discussed in para 8.10 above.

[1] Insolvency Act 1986, s 366(1)(a).
[2] Ibid, s 366(1)(b) and (c).

14.3.10 Application for a private examination may be made by the official receiver or the trustee in bankruptcy. He requests the court to summon the person from whom the information or property is required. The court may direct the person to submit an affidavit containing an account of his dealings with the bankrupt or to produce documents in his possession or under his control relating to the bankrupt or the bankrupt's dealings affairs or property.[1]

The procedure is in the Individual Insolvency Rules, 1986, Part 9. It provides for the application to be in writing ex parte and accompanied by a statement of the grounds upon which the application is made.[2]

[1] Insolvency Act 1986, s 366(1).
[2] Individual Insolvency Rules, r 9.2.

14.3.11 The procedure at the hearing is set out in the Individual Insolvency Rules, Part 9, rr 9.4, 9.5.[1] The examinee may be ordered to pay the costs of the examination if it appears to the court that the examination was made necessary because information had been unjustifiably refused by the person concerned.[2]

[1] See Appendix below.
[2] Individual Insolvency Rules 1986, r 9.6(1).

14.3.12 The Insolvency Act 1986, ss 366, 367 contain similar provisions to those in the Bankruptcy Act, s 25 concerning the court's power to order an examinee to make payment or deliver up property. These are discussed in para 8.10 above.

CHAPTER 15

The Trustee

15.1 INSOLVENCY PRACTITIONERS

15.1.1 Before the enactment of the Insolvency Act 1986 there were no formal qualifications required of a trustee in bankruptcy. In practice the official receiver was the trustee of the majority of bankrupt's estates, becoming trustee on adjudication and remaining the trustee throughout the bankruptcy as no other person was appointed.[1] In a few cases, however, trustees were appointed who misused their position to the detriment of creditors. There was, perhaps, greater concern with the activities of certain liquidators of insolvent companies than with trustees in bankruptcy, but the Review Committee[2] recommended that both in bankruptcy and corporate insolvency only persons authorised by the Secretary of State should be entitled to administer assets in insolvency. In line with this recommendation the Insolvency Act 1986 establishes the position of insolvency practitioner.

1 In 1984 official receivers completed the administration of 3,754 cases and non-official trustees completed 1,927 cases.
2 Chaired by Sir Kenneth Cork: see para 1.5 above.

15.1.2 As originally envisaged the New Law was to provide an entirely statutory system for regulating insolvency practitioners. Any person who wished to act as an insolvency practitioner in respect of corporate insolvency or personal bankruptcy, whatever professional qualification he held, was to apply to the Secretary of State for a certificate authorising him to act as an insolvency practitioner. The intention was that the Secretary of State would delegate his statutory powers to certain professional associations. In the course of the passage of the bill through Parliament strong representations were made to the government by these associations to the effect that the delegation of power on a comprehensively defined basis would inhibit the development and improvement of standards of expertise and conduct. The government was therefore asked to permit approved recognised professional bodies to undertake the entire certification procedure on a self-regulatory basis, allowing individuals to act as insolvency practitioners within the rules of whichever professional body the individual is a member or by which he is otherwise governed. The government acceded to this request, while maintaining a procedure whereby an individual who is not under the discipline of a professional body may apply for authorisation to act as an insolvency practitioner on his own behalf.

15.1.3 There are therefore two ways in which an individual, and only individuals may act as insolvency practitioners, may become an authorised insolvency practitioner. First he may be authorised by a recognised professional body. Second he may apply for and obtain an authorisation from the 'relevant authority'. Any person who acts as an insolvency practitioner without authorisation commits a criminal offence of strict liability. For the purpose of bankruptcy a person acts as an insolvency practitioner by acting (a) as trustee in bankruptcy, interim receiver or trustee in the sequestration of an estate, (b) as trustee under a deed of arrangement, (c) as supervisor of voluntary arrangements, or (d) as administrator of an insolvent estate.[1]

The official receiver is expressly exempted from all the statutory provisions relating to insolvency practitioners.

[1] Insolvency Act 1986, s 389.

15.1.4 *Recognised professional body.* The Secretary of State is empowered to make or revoke an order declaring a body to be a recognised professional body for the purposes of authorising individuals to act as insolvency practitioners.[1] The statutory criteria for recognition are that the body regulates the practice of a profession and maintains and enforces rules for securing that those of its members who are permitted to act as insolvency practitioners are fit and proper persons who meet acceptable requirements as to education, practical training and experience.

In the first instance the recognised bodies will be the three separate accountancy bodies, the Law Society and the Insolvency Practitioners Association.[2] These bodies are seeking to establish common criteria for authorising individual members to act as insolvency practitioners. Details of the criteria or respective criteria will have to be obtained from the professional bodies themselves.

[1] Insolvency Act 1986, s 391(1).
[2] Insolvency Practitioners (Recognised Professional Bodies) Order 1986, SI 1986/1764.

15.1.5 *Individual applications.* These are made to the 'relevant authority' which is the Secretary of State or any body to which he delegates the statutory authorising system.

The relevant authority is empowered[1] to make its own directions as to the manner of application, information required from the applicant, the prescribed fee on making the application, and the extent to and manner in which notice of the application is published. Directions governing, or requirements of, applicants need not be the same for every applicant or application. The same criteria as required of members of professional bodies govern the grant of authorisation by the relevant authority, though in debate the government indicated that applicants who were not members of professional bodies 'will be required to show a long and considerable experience of insolvency procedures, including work at a senior management level'.[2]

[1] Insolvency Act 1986, s 392.
[2] 467 HL Official Report (5th series) col 1105, and see Insolvency Practitioners Regulations 1986, SI 1986/1995.

15.1.6 The relevant authority. is to give written notice of the grant or proposed refusal of an authorisation, or in the case where it is proposed to withdraw an existing authorisation, notice of that proposal together with the date on which it is proposed that the withdrawal should take effect. On receiving notice of proposed refusal or notice of intended withdrawal of authorisation the applicant or practitioner may take advantage of a two-tier appeal procedure:

(a) within 14 days of the date of service of the notice he may make written representations to the relevant authority, to which the authority is required to have regard;[1] and
(b) within 28 days of either the date of service of the original notice, or, where written representations are made under (a) above, the date of service of a notice by the relevant authority that it does not propose to alter its decision in consequence of the representation, he may by notice in writing to the relevant authority require that his case be referred to the insolvency practitioners tribunal. Unless the authority then changes its decision it must refer the case to the tribunal.

Where the person concerned does not pursue either tier of the procedure the authority may proceed to give written notice of refusal or withdrawal of authorisation as appropriate.

[1] Insolvency Act 1986, s 395.

15.1.7 *Insolvency practitioner's tribunal.* This tribunal comprises a legal chairman, who must be a barrister or solicitor of not less than seven years' standing and two other members drawn from a panel of persons experienced in insolvency matters. It is subject to the supervision of the Council of Tribunals under the Tribunals and Inquiries Act 1971. On a reference by the relevant authority the tribunal investigates the case and makes a report to the authority stating, with reasons, what in their opinion is the appropriate decision in the matter. The authority is bound to decide the case in accordance with the tribunal's decision. The tribunal's report must be sent to the applicant or practitioner, and it may be published by the authority.

The procedure of the tribunal is governed by rules.[1] The tribunal must ensure that the person whose case is under investigation is given a reasonable opportunity to make representations.

[1] Insolvency Act 1986, Sch 7, para 4; Insolvency Practitioners Tribunal (Conduct of Investigations) Rules 1986, SI 1986/952.

15.1.8 *Qualification to act.* In order to be qualified to act as an insolvency practitioner an individual must not only be authorised by a recognised body or by the relevant authority as stated above, but he must also provide security meeting the prescribed requirements.[1]

This security for the proper performance of the insolvency practitioner's functions is for the protection of any person interested in the insolvency who suffers loss as a consequence of a breach by the practitioner of his duties. It will therefore be available to satisfy any order made by the court on an application under the Insolvency Act 1986, s 304.[2]

A person is not qualified to act as an insolvency practitioner at any time when (a) he is bankrupt or his estate sequestered, (b) an order disqualifying him from acting as company director, liquidator receiver or manager is in force, or (c) he is a patient under the Mental Health Act 1983, Part VII.

1 Insolvency Act 1986, s 390(3). Individual Insolvency Rules 1986, r 12.8; Insolvency Practitioners Regulations 1986, SI 1986/1995, Pt III.
2 See para 15.4 below.

15.1.9 In common with much of the Insolvency Act 1986, the details of practice relating to insolvency practitioners, e g appointment keeping accounts and the control by the courts, etc are contained in regulations.[1]

1 Insolvency Act 1986, s 419. See Insolvency Practitioners Regulations 1986, SI 1986/1995, Pt IV.

15.2 APPOINTMENT OF THE TRUSTEE

15.2.1 Upon the making of a bankruptcy order and until such time as the trustee is appointed and the estate is vested in him, the official receiver becomes the receiver and manager of the bankrupt's estate[1] subject to the powers and duties of any special manager appointed by the court under s 370 of the Act, see para 14.2.6 above.

The trustee may be appointed by (a) the bankrupt's creditors in general meeting, (b) the Secretary of State, or (c) the court.

1 Insolvency Act 1986, s 287.

Appointment by creditors

15.2.2 The appointment of a trustee will normally be made by the creditors in general meeting summoned by the official receiver.

Unless a certificate for the summary administration of the estate has been issued (see ch 20 below) or the court appoints the trustee (see para 15.2.6 below) the official receiver must decide whether to summon a general meeting of the bankrupt's creditors for the purpose of appointing a trustee 'as soon as practicable' within 12 weeks of the making of the bankruptcy order.[1] This discretion of the official receiver as to whether to call a meeting of creditors will be particularly useful where the assets available to the estate are insufficient to justify the appointment of a private trustee. In such cases, a formal creditors' meeting is likely to constitute unnecessary effort and expense.

1 Insolvency Act 1986, s 293.

15.2.3 If the official receiver decides against summoning a meeting he must, within the 12-week period, notify the court and every creditor known to the official receiver or identified in the bankrupt's statement of affairs.

From the date on which the court receives such notification the official receiver becomes the trustee.[1]

The need to notify the court and creditors is overtaken if any creditor requests the official receiver to summon a meeting for the purpose of appointing a trustee. By the Insolvency Act 1986, s 294 any creditor may make such a request where a general meeting has not yet been summoned and where there is no summary administration certificate in force. If the request is supported by not less than one-quarter, in value, of the bankrupt's creditors, including the creditor making the request, the official receiver is bound to summon a meeting.

[1] Insolvency Act 1986, s 293(3).

15.2.4 The Act does not seek to regulate the procedure at the general meeting of creditors. The procedure is left to the meeting itself, subject to the Rules.[1]

The trustee appointed must be a qualified insolvency practitioner who is not precluded under the Rules from acting in relation to the particular estate by reason of being an associate of the bankrupt or a creditor or otherwise. The creditors may, if they wish, appoint two or more insolvency practitioners to be joint trustees of the estate, but in such a case the creditors are required to make express provision in the appointment as to the circumstances in which the trustees must act together or may act individually.

The trustee's appointment by the creditors' meeting must be certified by the chairman of the meeting appointing him, but not before the appointee has provided the chairman with a written statement that he is a duly qualified insolvency practitioner and that he consents to act.[2] The certificate is sent to the official receiver (if he is not the chairman) who endorses it and files it in court, from which time the appointment of the trustee is effective.[3] As soon as may be after the certificate is filed at court the trustee must advertise his appointment 'in such newspaper as he thinks most appropriate for ensuring that it comes to the notice of the bankrupt's creditors'.[4]

[1] For the practice under the Old Bankruptcy Law see para 4.5 above. For the New Law see the Individual Insolvency Rules 1986, Part 6, Chapter 7.
[2] Individual Insolvency Rules 1986, r 6.120(2).
[3] Ibid, r 6.120(3)(4).
[4] Ibid, r 6.124.

Appointment by Secretary of State

15.2.5 There are three sets of circumstances in which the trustee in bankruptcy may be appointed by the Secretary of State:

(i) Where the creditors in general meeting fail to make an appointment. In this event the official receiver must decide whether or not to refer the need for an appointment to the Secretary of State.[1] If no reference is made the

official receiver notifies the court and becomes the trustee. Where the case is referred, the Secretary of State is free to make an appointment or decline to do so.[2] In either case the official receiver notifies the court and where the Secretary of State has declined to make an appointment the official receiver becomes trustee.[3]

(ii) On an application by the official receiver.[4] At any time when the official receiver is the trustee, except where he is trustee by virtue of the fact that that the petition was based on a criminal bankruptcy order, he may apply to the Secretary of State for the appointment of an alternative trustee. The Secretary of State may decline to make an appointment, but that does not prevent the official receiver making a subsequent application.[5] Where the Secretary of State does make an appointment the new trustee must notify all the creditors. In his notice the trustee must state whether he proposes to summon a general meeting for the purpose of establishing a committee of inspection or, if no general meeting is proposed, the trustee must set out the power of the creditors to require him to summon one.[6] The court may allow the new trustee to advertise his appointment in place of serving notice on creditors.

(iii) Where there is a vacancy in the office of trustee.[7] On the office becoming vacant for whatever reason the official receiver becomes trustee until the vacancy is filled. If the official receiver decides not to summon a general meeting of creditors to make an appointment to fill the vacancy he may refer the need for an appointment to the Secretary of State. The Secretary of State also has power to fill a vacancy where the original appointment was made by him.

1 Insolvency Act 1986, s 295.
2 Ibid, s 295(2).
3 Ibid, s 295(4).
4 Ibid, s 296 and see Individual Insolvency Rules 1986, r 6.122.
5 Ibid, s 296(3).
6 Ibid, s 296(5); Individual Insolvency Rules 1986, r 6.79. A request for a meeting is binding on the trustee if supported by one-tenth in value of the creditors.
7 Insolvency Act 1986, s 300.

Appointment by the court and special cases

15.2.6 Such appointments are made under the Insolvency Act 1986, s 297.

(i) Summary administration. On the issue of a certificate of summary administration of a bankrupt's estate, the official receiver becomes trustee. The court may, however, appoint an insolvency practitioner as trustee if it thinks fit.[1]

(ii) Criminal bankruptcy. Where the bankruptcy order is made on a petition based on a criminal bankruptcy order only the official receiver may be trustee.[2].

(iii) Debtor's petition. On the debtor's own petition, the court is required, in certain circumstances, to appoint an insolvency practitioner 'the appointed person' to report on the prospects of the debtor making voluntary arrangements under the Act (see para 13.5 3 above). In these circumstances in the event that a bankruptcy order is made but with no certificate for

summary administration, the court, if it thinks fit, may make the appointed person trustee of the bankrupt's estate.[3]

(iv) Bankruptcy after voluntary arrangements. Where a bankruptcy order is made after voluntary arrangements have been approved under the Act (see ch 12 above), the court may appoint the supervisor of the composition or scheme to be trustee.[4] Where the trustee is appointed by the court the official receiver is discharged from his duty to summon a general meeting or give notice to the creditors and the court of his decision not to do so.[5]

The court's order of appointment does not issue until the appointee files at court a statement that he is an insolvency practitioner duly qualified to act as trustee, and that he consents to act.[6]

The court appointed trustee gives notice to the creditors of his appointment and specifies in that notice either that he will summon a creditors' meeting or he must specify the creditors' powers to require a meeting.[7] If the court allows, the trustee may advertise his appointment as the court directs in lieu of giving notice to all the creditors.

1 Insolvency Act 1986, s 297(2) and (3).
2 Ibid, s 297(1).
3 Ibid, s 297(4).
4 Ibid, s 297(4).
5 Ibid, s 297(6).
6 Individual Insolvency Rules 1986, r 6.121, forms 6.42 or 6.43.
7 Insolvency Act 1986, s 297(7).

Vacancy

15.2.7 When a vacancy occurs in the office of trustee, for whatever reason, the official receiver becomes trustee.[1] The official receiver may summon a general meeting of the creditors or be required to do so by one-tenth in value of the creditors.[2] If no meeting has been held, or summoned in 28 days from the date on which the official receiver was aware of the vacancy and the official receiver does not propose to summon a meeting, he must refer the need for an appointment to the Secretary of State. Unless and until the Secretary of State makes an appointment the official receiver continues as trustee.

The office of trustee is deemed to be 'vacant' when it is necessary to revive the trusteeship after the final meeting or after the official receiver has given notice that the administration of the estate is complete (see para 15.5 below).

1 Insolvency Act 1986, s 300.
2 Ibid, s 314(7).

Objection by creditors

15.2.8 There appears to be no power under the Rules for the creditors to object to the trustee appointed to the bankrupt's estate. A procedure had been advocated whereby the majority in value of the creditors could apply to the court to consider their objections to the intended trustee. This procedure has not found its way into the Individual Insolvency Rules 1986, and creditors objecting to the trustee appointed will have to rely on their powers under the Insolvency Act 1986[1] to remove the trustee from office at a meeting summoned specially for that purpose. This power cannot, however, be exercised when a certificate for summary administration is in force, and is restricted where the official receiver is trustee or the trustee has been appointed by the Secretary of State or the Court.[2]

[1] S 298, see para 15.5 below.
[2] S 298(3)(4).

15.2.9 A copy of the order or certificate of the trustee's appointment may be adduced as proof that he is duly authorised to act as trustee to the estate in any proceedings.[1]

[1] Individual Insolvency Rules 1986, r 6.123.

Remuneration

15.2.10 The trustee's remuneration shall be fixed by the creditors' committee or if no such committee by the general meeting of creditors.[1] It will usually be fixed as a percentage of the assets realised but need not be, the creditors having a general discretion as to how the trustee should be paid. The trustee may have recourse to the final meeting of creditors[2] or to the court[3] to increase the amount of his remuneration. The trustee may charge when selling assets on behalf of a secured creditor an equivalent sum to that chargeable by the Official Receiver under general regulations.[4] Any creditor with the concurrence of at least 25% in value of the creditors may apply to the court for an order that the trustee's remuneration be reduced on the grounds that it is excessive in all the circumstances.[5]

[1] Individual Insolvency Rules 1986, r 6.138.
[2] Ibid, r 6.140.
[3] Ibid, r 6.141.
[4] Ibid, r 6.139; see Insolvency Regulations 1986, SI 1986/1994, regs 19–21.
[5] Ibid, r 6.142.

15.3 CONTROL OF THE TRUSTEE

15.3.1 A trustee other than the official receiver is obliged to have regard to any directions given to him by a general meeting of the creditors. In accordance with the Rules, the general meeting is authorised to establish a creditors' committee to exercise the creditors' powers of control over the trustee or any particular functions delegated to it.[1] Where no committee is established its powers are vested in the Secretary of State, subject to the provisions of the Rules.[2] This committee takes the place of the committee of inspection under the Bankruptcy Act 1914. The Review Committee considered that the designation 'committee of inspection' was inappropriate and suggested that the title 'trustee's committee' be used.[3] The Insolvency Bill used the title 'supervisory committee' but during debate the view prevailed that this title was not suitable in the light of the new provisions requiring all trustees in bankruptcy to be qualified insolvency practitioners.

The Insolvency Act 1985 avoided giving the committee a title, but the Insolvency Act 1986 and the Individual Insolvency Rules refer to the 'creditors' committee'.

1 Insolvency Act 1986, s 301(1); Individual Insolvency Rules 1986, Part 6, Chapter 11.
2 Insolvency Act 1986, s 302(2).
3 See Cork Report, para 932 and note ch 19 of the Report for a discussion of the role of creditors in the administration of the estate.

15.3.2 Any creditor may request the trustee to summon a general meeting at any time. The trustee is obliged to comply with the request if it is supported by at least one-tenth in value of the creditors including the creditor making the request.[1]

1 Insolvency Act 1986, s 314(7).

15.3.3 When the trustee is the official receiver the general meeting of creditors loses its functions. The powers of the supervisory committee become vested in the Secretary of State[1] subject to the Rules. The general meeting does, however, retain the function of appointing an insolvency practitioner as trustee in place of the official receiver.[2]

1 Insolvency Act 1986, s 302(1). Individual Insolvency Rules 1986, r 6.166.
2 Ibid, s 301(2).

15.3.4 There is an overall control by the court. The Insolvency Act 1986, s 303 enables the bankrupt, a creditor or 'any other person dissatisfied by any act, omission or decision of a trustee' to apply to the court. On such an application the court has a complete discrection to confirm, reverse or modify any act or decision of the trustee, give directions or make any other order it thinks fit. Additionally the trustee may apply to the court for directions on any matter arising in the bankruptcy.

15.3.5 Should the trustee enter into any transaction with a person who is an associate[1] of his, the court may set the transaction aside and order the trustee to make restitution to the estate for any loss sustained on the application of any person interested.[2] The trustee may, however, obtain the prior consent of the court to any particular transaction.[3] Furthermore, no order may be made if the trustee satisfies the court that the transaction was for value and that when entering into it the trustee neither knew nor had reason to suppose that the other party to the transaction was an associate.[3] When the court is satisfied that the trustee has improperly solicited proxies or has improperly procured his appointment an order may be made precluding the trustee to be remunerated out of the estate, notwithstanding any resolution of the creditors.[4]

The Rules do not make express provision enabling the court to make orders where the trustee has made a secret profit or otherwise abused his position as trustee. However, the trustee is subject to the general provisions of law and equity with respect to a trustee when dealing with trust property and there is nothing in the Insolvency Act or Rules to restrict creditors making appropriate application where the estate suffers at the hands of a defaulting trustee.[5]

[1] See Insolvency Act 1986, s 435.
[2] Individual Insolvency Rules 1986, r 6.147(1).
[3] Ibid, r 6.147(2).
[4] Ibid, r 6.148.
[5] Ibid, r 6.147(3).

15.4 LIABILITY OF THE TRUSTEE

15.4.1 The Insolvency Act 1986, s 304 gives a wide power to the court to order restitution in the case of a defaulting trustee. This power is without prejudice to any other liability to which such a trustee may be subject. An application under s 304 may be made by the official receiver, the Secretary of State, a creditor or the bankrupt. Leave of the court is required if the application is made by the bankrupt or after the trustee has had his release (see para 15.5 below).

15.4.2 An order may be made on an application under this section where the court is satisfied either: (a) that the trustee has misapplied, retained or become accountable for money or other property comprised in the estate; or (b) that the estate has suffered loss in consequence of any misfeasance or breach of fiduciary or other duty by a trustee in the performance of his function.

If a case is made out the court may order the trustee to repay, restore or account for money or other property or make compensation, together with interest, for the benefit of the estate.

15.4.3 The trustee is given a statutory exemption from liability[1] where he seizes or disposes of any property not comprised in the bankrupt's estate but can show that at the time of seizure or disposal he believed, on reasonable grounds, that he was entitled so to act. The trustee will not be liable in these circumstances unless he caused loss or damage by being negligent.

Furthermore the trustee has a lien on any property seized, or the proceeds of sale after their disposal, for such expenses of the bankruptcy as were incurred in connection with the seizure or disposal.

It should be noted that the true owner of goods wrongly seized by a trustee in the administration of the estate has no standing to apply for an order under the Insolvency Act 1986, s 304. He will have to proceed under the Torts (Interference with Goods) Act 1971 or other suitable cause of action.

[1] Insolvency Act 1986, s 304(3).

15.5 REMOVAL AND RELEASE OF THE TRUSTEE

15.5.1 The trustee may be removed from office by the court or by a general meeting of the creditors summoned specifically for that purpose in accordance with the Rules.[1] In cases where the trustee is:

(a) the official receiver, having become trustee where no creditors' meeting was held, or following the failure of the creditors' meeting to make an appointment;
(b) appointed by the Secretary of State; or
(c) appointed by the court, (*other* than a supervisor of voluntary arrangements being appointed trustee),

then a general meeting of creditors may only be summoned where the trustee thinks fit, or the court directs, or not less than one-quarter in value of the creditors concur in a request for the meeting.[2]

There is express provision in the Rules[3] whereby the court on the application of any creditor may give directions as to the mode in which a meeting called to consider the removal of a trustee should be summoned, the sending out and return of forms of proxy, the conduct of the meeting or any other matter relating to the meeting. Notice of such meeting must be given to the official receiver.[4] If the official receiver does not chair the meeting he must be sent notice by the meeting's chairman, within three days, of any resolution passed for the removal of the trustee, the appointment of a new trustee, or that the removed trustee should not be given his release.[5] The meeting may elect any person to be chairman in place of the trustee or his nominee. If the trustee or his nominee is chairman he may not adjourn the meeting without the consent of at least one half of the creditors present in person or by proxy and entitled to vote.[6]

Where a resolution to remove the trustee is carried, the official receiver must file the certificate in court[7] though not before the Secretary of State certifies that the removed trustee has reconciled his account of the bankruptcy with that held by the Secretary of State.[8] The resolution is not effective until the official receiver files the certificate of removal in court,[9] and at the same time the official receiver should file the certificate of appointment of any new trustee appointed by the creditors.[10]

1 Insolvency Act 1986, s 298(1); Individual Insolvency Rules 1986, r 6.129(1), form 6.35.
2 Insolvency Act 1986, s 298(4).
3 Individual Insolvency Rules 1986, r 6.130.
4 Ibid, r 6.129(2).
5 Ibid, r 6.129(4).
6 Ibid, r 6.129(3).
7 Ibid, r 6.131(1).
8 Ibid, r 6.131(4).
9 Ibid, r 6.131(2).
10 Ibid, rr 6.120, 6.129(5).

15.5.2 Any creditor may apply to the court for the removal of the trustee, or for an order directing the trustee to summon a meeting of creditors for the purpose of removing him.[1] The trustee and the official receiver must be given at least 14 days' notice of the hearing. This power in the court to remove a trustee on any creditor's application is particularly important where minority creditors allege that the trustee is acting improperly with the connivance of the majority in value of creditors.

1 Individual Insolvency Rules 1986, r 6.132. Nb the court may dismiss the application if no sufficient cause is shown, but must give applicant the opportunity to attend on seven days notice, ex parte, to support his application.

15.5.3 A general meeting of creditors is precluded from removing a trustee (a) where the official receiver is trustee in a criminal bankruptcy and (b) at any time when a certificate for summary administration is in force.[1]

[1] Insolvency Act 1986, s 298(2) and (3).

15.5.4 The Secretary of State may, by direction, remove a trustee appointed by him.[1] Any creditor, with the concurrence of not less than one-quarter in value of the creditors, may apply to the Secretary of State to remove a trustee who he has appointed.[2]

[1] Insolvency Act 1986, s 298(5).
[2] Individual Insolvency Rules 1986, r 6.133.

15.5.5 The trustee may resign in the prescribed circumstances by giving notice to the court.[1] He must, before resigning, call a meeting of creditors and give notice to the official receiver.[2] The trustee may only resign in the following circumstances:[3]

(a) ill health;
(b) he intends to cease practising as an insolvency practitioner;
(c) there is some conflict of interest which precludes him from acting further as trustee; or
(d) he is one of two or more trustees and in the opinion of himself and the other trustee or trustees, it is no longer expedient to have joint trustees.

At that meeting of creditors, the creditors may determine whether or not to give the trustee his release and they may appoint another trustee.[4] If the meeting accepts the trustee's resignation notice must be given to him forthwith and he must send a copy of the notice to the official receiver. The trustee's resignation is effective from such time as the official receiver files the notice in court.[5] If the meeting resolves not to accept the trustee's resignation he may apply to the court for an order giving him leave to resign.[6]

The trustee must, of course, vacate office if he ceases to qualify as an insolvency practitioner or the bankruptcy order is annulled. Once the final meeting has been held (Insolvency Act 1986, s 331, see below) the trustee must give notice to the court of that fact and of any decision taken by the meeting. The trustee vacates his office only on giving such notice.

[1] Insolvency Act 1986, s 298(7).
[2] Individual Insolvency Rules 1986, r 6.126(1).
[3] Ibid, r 6.126(3)(4).
[4] Ibid, r 6.127; where a new trustee is appointed he must state in the advertisement of his appointment that the former trustee has resigned or been removed and whether he has been given his release; ibid, r 6.134.
[5] Ibid, r 6.127(5)–(7).
[6] Ibid, r 6.128.

15.5.6 *Release of official receiver.* On completion of his administration the official receiver obtains his release from such time as the Secretary of State shall determine after he gives notice to the Secretary of State that the administration of the bankrupt's estate is 'for practical purposes' complete. Where the official receiver is replaced by an insolvency practitioner appointed by general meeting of the creditors or by the Secretary of State he is released on giving notice to the court. Where the court replaces the official receiver, the court determines the date of release.[1] Before applying for his release, the official receiver must notify the bankrupt and all the creditors, giving them a summary of his receipts and payments.[2]

[1] Insolvency Act 1986, s 299(1) and (2).
[2] Individual Insolvency Rules 1986, r 6.136.

15.5.7 *Release of practitioner-trustee.* An insolvency practitioner is released with effect from the following time, namely:[1]

(a) where removed by a general meeting which has not resolved against his release, the time at which notice is given to the court under the Rules;
(b) where removed; (i) by a general meeting which has resolved against his release; or (ii) by the court; or (iii) by the Secretary of State; or (iv) because he has ceased to qualify as an insolvency practitioner, at such time as the Secretary of State shall determine, on the application of the insolvency practitioner;
(c) where he resigns, at the time at which his notice of resignation takes effect under the Rules;
(d) where he has vacated office on giving notice to the court that a final meeting has been held, at the date of vacation of office unless the final meeting has resolved against the practitioner's release in which case at such time as the Secretary of State shall determine upon application by the practitioner; or
(e) where the bankruptcy order is annulled at such time as the court may determine.

[1] Insolvency Act 1986, s 299(3) and (4); Individual Insolvency Rules 1986, r 6.135.

15.5.8 *Final meeting to release trustee.* When the trustee has completed the administration of the estate, he calls a final meeting, giving at least 28 days' notice to the bankrupt and all creditors who have proved their debts.[1] The trustee must prepare a final report of his administration and lay it before the meeting. The creditors are entitled to question the trustee on any matter contained in his final report.[2] If there is no quorum at the final meeting, a quorum being at least three creditors or their proxies or all the creditors if their number does not exceed three,[3] the trustee shall report the fact to the court and it shall be deemed that the final meeting was held and that the trustee obtained his release.[4] Where there is a quorum, the trustee will obtain his release unless the creditors positively vote against it. Where the creditors do so resolve the trustee may only obtain his release from the Secretary of State.[5] After the conclusion of the meeting, the trustee must give notice to the court and the official receiver that the meeting has taken place and state whether or not he obtained his release.[6] Should the trustee consider that his remuneration has proved insufficient, he may apply to the final meeting for an increase.[7]

[1] Individual Insolvency Rules 1986, r 6.137(1).
[2] Ibid, r 6.137(2) and (3).
[3] Ibid, r 6.92 nb one person himself entitled to vote and holding two proxies may constitute a quorum.

[4] Ibid, r 6.137(5).
[5] Ibid, rr 6.135 and 137(6).
[6] Ibid, r 6.137(4).
[7] Ibid, r 6.140.

15.5.9 *Effect of release.* Upon release the trustee is discharged from any liability arising out of his administration of the estate or conduct as trustee, subject to the court's powers under s 304, under which an application for restitution or compensation may be brought with leave of the court.[1] This applies equally to the official receiver and a trustee who is an insolvency practitioner. Where the trustee is followed by another trustee of the estate, he is under an obligation to account to his successor for the whole of the assets of the estate and to deliver up all the cash and record books relating to his administration.[2]

[1] Insolvency Act 1986, s 299(5).
[2] Individual Insolvency Rules 1986, r 6.146.

15.5.10 *Death of trustee.* Where a trustee dies, his personal representatives are under a duty to notify the official receiver.[1] Notice may, however, be accepted by the official receiver from any partner of the deceased trustee if the latter was a partner in a firm of insolvency practitioners.[2] The official receiver must give notice to the court for the purpose of fixing the time of the release of the deceased trustee.[3]

[1] Individual Insolvency Rules 1986, r 6.143(1).
[2] Ibid, r 6.143(2).
[3] Insolvency Act 1986, s 299(3)(a); Individual Insolvency Rules 1986, r 6.143(4).

15.6 INFORMATION TO CREDITORS AND CREDITORS' MEETINGS

15.6.1 Creditors' involvement in the conduct of the bankruptcies under the Bankruptcy Act 1914 was minimal and that situation will remain. The principal purpose of statutory meetings of creditors is to appoint a trustee in bankruptcy and a creditors' committee. To ensure that the general body of creditors is informed as to the state of the bankruptcy, the Individual Insolvency Rules require that information is sent to them at least once after the making of the bankruptcy order. This will usually comprise a report on the statement of affairs submitted by the bankrupt and the Rules invite, but do not require, the official receiver to make observations on the bankrupt's position as disclosed by the statement of affairs. The Rules also provide a straightforward procedure for the calling and conduct of meetings after the statutory or 'first' meeting of creditors.

Information to creditors

15.6.2 The official receiver is required by the Rules[1] to send a report to the creditors concerning the bankruptcy proceedings and the state of the bankrupt's affairs at least once after the making of the bankruptcy order.

The creditors to whom the report must be sent are those identified in the statement of affairs or, where no statement has been submitted, those creditors who are known to the official receiver.[2]

[1] Individual Insolvency Rules 1986, r 6.73.
[2] Ibid, r 6.74.

15.6.2.1 *(a) Report where statement of affairs lodged.* After the bankrupt has submitted a statement of affairs, the official receiver must send a report to all creditors containing a summary of the statement together with any observations he considers fit to make.[1] This report need not be sent, however, where the official receiver has previously reported to the creditors and he is of the opinion that there are no additional matters to be brought to their attention.[2]

[1] Individual Insolvency Rules 1986, r 6.75(1).
[2] Ibid, r 6.75(2).

15.6.2.2 *(b) Report where statement of affairs dispensed with.* In this event the official receiver 'as soon as may be' after the bankrupt has been released from submitting a statement, must send a report to the creditors, summarising the bankrupt's affairs so far as is within his knowledge.[1] He need not do so if he has reported previously and is of the opinion that there are no additional matters to report.

[1] Individual Insolvency Rules 1986, r 6.76.

15.6.2.3 *(c) Annulment of bankruptcy order.* The official receiver's duty to send reports ceases on the bankruptcy order being annulled.[1] If the official receiver thinks fit, however, he may send a report to all or any of the creditors explaining the circumstances in which the bankruptcy was terminated.

The official receiver may apply to the court to relieve him of his duty to send reports or authorise him to carry out his duty in an alternative manner. In considering whether to accede to the application, the court is to have regard to the cost of sending reports, the amount of funds available and to the extent of the interest of the creditors or any class of them.[2]

[1] Individual Insolvency Rules 1986, r 6.78.
[2] Ibid, r 6.77.

First meeting of creditors

15.6.3 The holding of this meeting is at the discretion of the official receiver,[1] subject to the power of not less than one-quarter in value of the creditors to require the summoning of such a meeting.[2] Where the official receiver decides to hold a meeting he must fix a time and place for the meeting to take place not more than four months from the date of the bankruptcy order.[3] Where the official receiver holds a meeting at the request of the creditors, he must fix a time and place for the meeting within three months of his receipt of the creditors' request.[4]

When the time and place for the meeting have been fixed, the official receiver must:[5]

(i) notify the court forthwith;
(ii) notify the creditors at least 21 days before the date fixed for the meeting;
(iii) specify a date, which must be notified to the creditors, by which creditors must lodge proofs and proxies. Such date must be not more than four days before the meeting; and
(iv) publicly advertise the meeting.

The official receiver takes the chair at the first meeting of creditors.[6] The business which may be conducted at the first meeting is closely prescribed by the Rules.[7] In essence, the meeting may do no more than appoint one or more named insolvency practitioners as trustee, specify the remuneration of the trustee, apportion the trustee's functions if more than one practitioner is appointed, and establish a creditors' committee. The meeting may be adjourned for not more than three weeks. The chairman may allow other business on special reasons.[8] No resolution may be proposed to appoint the official receiver as trustee.[9]

1 Insolvency Act 1986, s 293 and see para 15.2.2 above.
2 Insolvency Act 1986, s 294(2). NB Any creditor may request a meeting, but the request need only be acceded to if made with the concurrence of 25% in value of the creditors.
3 Individual Insolvency Rules 1986, r 6.79(1).
4 Ibid, r 6.79(6).
5 Ibid, r 6.79(2)–(5).
6 Ibid, r 6.82(1), unless he is not the convenor of the meeting in which event the convenor or his nominee is chairman, r 6.82(2).
7 Ibid, r 6.80.
8 Ibid, r 6.80(1)(g).
9 Ibid, r 6.80(2).

Subsequent meetings of creditors

15.6.4 There is a general power in the official receiver or trustee in bankruptcy to summon meetings on 21 days' notice to the creditors.[1] The chairman at meetings will be the person summoning the meeting, ie the official receiver or trustee, or any person nominated by him to act in his place.[2] Should a resolution be proposed to remove the trustee, the meeting may elect another chairman and the trustee may not adjourn the meeting without the consent of at least one-half of the creditors present in person or by proxy and entitled to vote.[3] If a resolution to remove the trustee is carried, the person acting as chairman must notify the official receiver within three days.[4]

Any request by creditors for a meeting to be summoned must be accompanied by a list of creditors concurring with the request, their respective claims in the bankruptcy and a statement of the purpose of the proposed meeting.[5] Following a request under the Insolvency Act 1986, s 314(7) which enables one-tenth in value of the creditors to require a meeting to be held, the trustee must fix a time and place for the meeting to take place not more than 35 days from the receipt of the request, and give 21 days' notice to every creditor.[6]

1 Individual Insolvency Rules 1986, r 6.81.
2 Ibid, r 6.82.

[3] Ibid, r 6.129(3).
[4] Ibid, r 6.129(4).
[5] Ibid, r 6.83(1).
[6] Ibid, r 6.83(2).

Procedure at meetings

15.6.5 The procedure to be followed at meetings is determined by the meeting acting through the chairman. The Individual Insolvency Rules contain provisions governing the following matters:

(a) Advertisement. The court may order that notice of the meeting be given by advertisement rather than individual notice to the persons concerned.[1]
(b) Place and time. The trustee or official receiver summoning the meeting is required to have regard to the convenience of the creditors. Except with a court direction to the contrary, meetings must commence between 10.00 am and 4.00 pm on a business day.[2]
(c) Attendance of bankrupt. The bankrupt must be given 21 days' notice of any meeting and may take part in the meeting at the discretion of the chairman. The bankrupt may be required to attend and answer questions, subject to a discretion in the chairman as to questions which may be put to him.[3]
(d) Non-receipt of notice. The proceedings and resolutions at a meeting are valid even though not all the creditors received notice of the meeting.[4]
(e) Quorum. At least three creditors (or all the creditors if there are no more than three) in person or by proxy are required to attend for a creditors' meeting to be competent to act except for the following business:
(i) election of a chairman;
(ii) the admission of creditors' proofs; and
(iii) adjourning the meeting.[5]
(f) Entitlement to vote. A creditor is only entitled to vote if he has duly lodged a proof of debt and his proof has been admitted. A creditor for an unliquidated or unascertained debt may only vote where the chairman agrees to put a minimum value on the debt for the purposes of voting. A secured creditor may only vote in respect of the balance of his debt after deducting the value of his security. The court may, in exceptional circumstances allow a creditor or class of creditors to vote without proof of debt.[6]
(g) Admission or rejection of proof. The chairman has power to admit or reject any part or all of a creditor's proof of debt for the purposes of voting. If in doubt, the chairman may allow the creditors to vote subject to the vote being subsequently declared invalid. Any decision by the chairman is subject to appeal to the court by any creditor or the bankrupt. If necessary the court may order another meeting to take place.[7]
(h) Resolutions. A resolution is carried by a majority in value of the creditors present, personally or by proxy and voting on the resolution.[8]
(i) Suspension and adjournment. The chairman may suspend a meeting for any period up to one hour.[9] The chairman may, in his discretion, adjourn any meeting for up to 21 days and must do so if a quorum is not present within 30 minutes of the time appointed for the meeting to commence. If no

person is present to act as chairman a chairman may be agreed from among those present. Failing agreement, the meeting is adjourned to the same time and place the following week.[10]

(j) Record. The chairman is responsible for minutes to be taken recording all resolutions passed and listing all creditors attending. Certified minutes must be filed at court not more than 21 days after the date of the meeting.[11]

(k) Expenses. Where one or more creditors summon a meeting, they are responsible for the expenses of so doing and must deposit with the official receiver or trustee such sum as he shall determine as security. The meeting may, however, vote that the expenses of summoning it shall be payable out of the estate.[12]

1 Individual Insolvency Rules 1986, r 6.85.
2 Ibid, r 6.86.
3 Ibid, r 6.84.
4 Ibid, r 12.16.
5 Ibid, r 6.92. Nb with sufficient proxies one person may constitute a quorum.
6 Ibid, r 6.93.
7 Ibid, r 6.94.
8 Ibid, r 6.88.
9 Ibid, r 6.90.
10 Ibid, r 6.91.
11 Ibid, r 6.95.
12 Ibid, r 6.87.

Proxies

15.6.6 Any creditor (a 'principal') may give authority to a proxy-holder to attend a creditors' meeting and speak and vote as his representative as directed. Only one person may act as a proxy for any one creditor but alternative proxy holders may be specified.[1] Proxies may be given to the official receiver or trustee even as chairman.[2] A chairman holding a proxy requiring him to vote for a particular resolution must himself propose it if no other person does or notify his principal of the reason why not forthwith after the meeting.[3]

Every notice summoning a meeting must be accompanied with a form of proxy.[4] The form must not have inserted in it the name or description of any person as proxy holder. A proxy given for a particular meeting may be used at any adjournment of that meeting.[5] Proxies used for voting at any meeting may be inspected by any creditor and after the meeting must be delivered to and retained by the responsible insolvency practitioner.[6] A proxy-holder may not vote in favour of any resolution which might financially benefit him or any associate of his unless the principal specifically directs him to vote that way.[7]

1 Individual Insolvency Rules 1986, r 8.1(1) and (3).
2 Ibid, r 8.1(4).
3 Ibid, r 6.89.
4 Ibid, r 8.2, forms 8.1 to 8.5.
5 Ibid, r 8.3.
6 Ibid, rr 8.4, 8.5.
7 Ibid, r 8.6.

15.7 CREDITORS' COMMITTEE

15.7.1 The Review Committee[1] voiced concern that creditors were generally apathetic and indifferent to the conduct of bankruptcies. That this is so is hardly surprising where the average creditor must accept that he is likely to receive a small, if any, dividend from the bankruptcy. The hope was expressed by the Review Committee that creditors might in the future be encouraged to participate more actively in bankruptcies by the implementation of two changes in the law. First, the reduction in the classes of preferential debts aimed at increasing the size of the dividend received by ordinary creditors. Second, a move away from the concept of creditor-control towards creditor-participation ie reducing the powers and responsibilities of the creditors and their committee, the name of which is changed from committee of inspection to creditors' committee. Both these changes have found their way into the New Law on Bankruptcy, with the result that the creditors' committee under the Individual Insolvency Rules is formed as a body participating with and not controlling, the trustee in bankruptcy.

1 See the Report of the Review Committee on Insolvency Law and Practice, chaired by Sir Kenneth Cork (Cmnd 8558) ch 19.

15.7.2 *Membership and establishment.* The committee shall consist of at least three and not more than five members.[1] All the members must be creditors and any creditor may be a member so long as he has lodged a proof of debt which has not been disallowed.[2] It is established by the creditors' vote at general meeting[3] but does not come into being until the chairman at the general meeting voting for the committee issues a certificate of due constitution[4] for which at least three members must first be duly elected.[5]

1 Individual Insolvency Rules 1986, r 6.150(1).
2 Ibid, r 6.150(2). Nb a corporate body may be a member of the committee acting by a member's representative: r 6.150(3).
3 Insolvency Act 1986, s 301(1).
4 Individual Insolvency Rules 1986, r 6.151(1), form 6.52.
5 Ibid, r 151(3).

15.7.3 *Meetings of the creditors' committee.* The meetings are determined by the trustee, who must call the first meeting within three months of his appointment or the commitee's establishment (whichever is the later) and subsequent meetings within 21 days of a request by any member.[1] The trustee, or person appointed by him in writing as his deputy, chairs the meeting,[2] which is duly constituted if at least two members are present or represented.[3] Any member of the committee may (and a corporate member must) appoint a representative by signed letter of authority, to act on his behalf.[4]

The committee acts by a majority of its members present or represented, one vote per member or representative[5] and every resolution passed must be recorded in writing and placed in the record book.[6] The trustee may, however, obtain the agreement of committee members by post.[7] The reasonable expenses of committee members in attending meetings may be defrayed by the trustee out of the estate.[8]

1 Individual Insolvency Rules 1986, r 6.153. Seven days' notice in writing of meeting is to be given to every member of the committee: r 6.153(3).
2 Ibid, r 6.154.
3 Ibid, r 6.155.
4 Ibid, r 6.156.
5 Ibid, r 6.161(1).
6 Ibid, r 6.161(2).
7 Ibid, r 6.162. The procedure laid down by this useful rule enables any member to require the trustee to summon a meeting to consider the matters raised by the resolution.
8 Ibid, r 6.164.

15.7.4 *Obligations of trustee to committee and committee's functions.* The trustee is under a duty[1] to report to the committee on all matters which appear to him to be, or which they have indicated to him as being, of concern with respect to the bankruptcy. Where the committee is established more than 28 days after the trustee's appointment he must provide a report in summary form of the actions taken by him since his appointment and answer any questions put to him regarding his conduct of the bankruptcy.[2] Additionally, the trustee must send a written report to every member of the committee explaining the position generally on the progress of the bankruptcy, drawing the committee's attention to any important matters, as and when directed by the committee and in the absence of such direction at least every six months.[3] The members of the committee have access to the trustee's cash book and record book.[4]

A number of the trustee's powers may only be exercised with the consent of the committee.[5] It is also incumbent on the committee to consider the circumstances of any disposition of property to an associate of the bankrupt or the employment of a solicitor, either of which matters, the trustee is obliged to notify to the committee.[6] The committee is, however, unable to exercise any direct control over the trustee and should a dispute arise, the committee can do no more than refer the matter to the court.[7]

1 Individual Insolvency Rules 1986, r 6.152(1).
2 Ibid, r 6.152(3).
3 Ibid, r 6.163.
4 Ibid, r 6.152(5).
5 See Insolvency Act 1986, s 314(1)(a), Sch 5, Part I.
6 Ibid, s 303(1).
7 Ibid, s 303(1).

15.7.5 *Resignation and removal.* A member of the creditors committee may resign by notice in writing delivered to the trustee.[1] The general meeting of creditors may remove a member of the creditors' committee by resolution provided 14 days' notice has been given of the intention to move that resolution.[2] An individual's membership of the creditors' committee is automatically terminated if:[3]

(a) he becomes bankrupt or compounds with his creditors, though his trustee in bankruptcy may replace him on the committee;
(b) he is neither present or represented at three consecutive meetings of the committee, unless it is resolved at the third of these meetings that the rule should not apply; or

(c) he ceases to be, or is found never to have been, a creditor.

Vacancies in the committee may be filled by the trustee with the consent of the remaining members of the committee,[4] or by the general meeting of creditors with 14 days' notice first given of the intention to move the appropriate resolution.[5] Changes in the membership must be notified to the trustee by the chairman of the meeting if the trustee is not present.[6]

[1] Individual Insolvency Rules 1986, r 6.157.
[2] Ibid, r 6.159.
[3] Ibid, r 6.158.
[4] Ibid, r 6.160(3).
[5] Ibid, r 6.160(4).
[6] Ibid, r 6.160(5).

15.7.6 *Restrictions on committee members.* Neither members of the creditors' committee nor their representatives may directly or indirectly purchase any asset forming part of the bankrupt's estate without the leave of the court.[1] On the application of any person interested, the court may set aside a purchase of assets for which leave was not obtained or validate it on such terms (if any) as it thinks fit.[2] Members of the committee or their representatives may not, either directly or indirectly, obtain any profit from a transaction arising out of the bankruptcy or receive from the estate any payment for services rendered or goods supplied in connection with the administration of the estate without the leave of the court.[3] Such leave may be obtained retrospectively in cases of urgency provided an application is made without undue delay after the date of the services being rendered or the goods delivered as the case may be.[4]

[1] Individual Insolvency Rules 1986, r 6.165(1)–(3).
[2] Ibid, r 6.165(5).
[3] Ibid, r 6.165(1)–(3).
[4] Ibid, r 6.165(3).

CHAPTER 16

Administration of the Estate: Proofs of Debt and Distribution to Creditors

16.1 INTRODUCTION

16.1.1 It is the trustee's duty to get in, realise and distribute the bankrupt's estate, and in doing so the trustee is expressly allowed to use his own discretion, subject to the provisions of the Insolvency Act 1986, Pt IX, chap IV.[1] The intention behind these provisions is to simplify the statutory requirements of the Bankruptcy Act 1914 and lessen the burden of administration on the trustee. Under the New Law 'after acquired' property does not automatically vest in the trustee and, theoretically, this should relieve the trustee of some investigative and administrative work. However, this makes the statutory duty on the bankrupt to give full information to his trustee,[2] including any receipt of income and the acquisition of property the more important. The reputed ownership provisions of the 1914 Act have been repealed and not replaced.

[1] Insolvency Act 1986, s 305(2). A bankrupt has no right to challenge a bona fide exercise by the trustee of this discretion: *Re a debtor, ex p debtor v Dodwell* [1949] Ch 236.
[2] Insolvency Act 1986, s 333.

16.1.2 Where the trustee is not the official receiver the trustee is under a duty to give the official receiver such assistance as he may reasonably require to enable him to perform his functions in the bankruptcy.[1] Assistance includes furnishing information and producing for inspection books papers and other records. This duty is of particular importance where a bankrupt who does not qualify for automatic discharge applies to the court for discharge. The official receiver is then required to make a report to the court to assist in determining when a discharge should be ordered: see chs 10 above and 18 below.

[1] Insolvency Act 1986, s 305(3). This duty may be enforced by the court on the application of the official receiver, Individual Insolvency Rules 1986, r 6.149.

16.1.3 The official name of the trustee is 'the trustee of the estate of [A.N. Other] a bankrupt'[1] and it is in this name that the trustee should serve notices, hold property, make contracts, execute documents, sue and be sued, etc.[2] The trustee may be referred to as 'the trustee in bankruptcy' of the particular bankrupt.

[1] Insolvency Act 1986, s 305(4).
[2] Ibid, s 314(5).

16.2 VESTING OF PROPERTY IN TRUSTEE

16.2.1 Immediately upon a trustee's appointment taking effect or on the official receiver becoming trustee the whole of the bankrupt's estate vests in the trustee without any formal document or procedure.[1] The estate comprises all the bankrupt's property at the commencement of the bankruptcy and that which is subsequently acquired by or is treated as being part of the estate, but excluding equipment necessary for the bankrupt's livelihood and household goods and provisions necessary for domestic needs: see para 16.1 above.

[1] Insolvency Act 1986, s 306. In the case of a chose in action it is deemed to have been assigned to the trustee. Notice of assignment is not necessary, except for the purpose of protecting the trustee's priority: s 311(4). See Individual Insolvency Rules 1986, r 6.125. The trustee must first discharge any balance due to the official receiver on account of fees, expenses, etc or give a written undertaking to do so out of the first realisation of assets.

16.2.2 The exemption from the bankrupt's estate for tools, books, vehicles and other items of equipment used for earning his living and household goods and provisions for satisfying the 'basic domestic needs' of the bankrupt and his family, are subject to the trustee's rights to replace such equipment and goods with less extravagant alternatives. Within 42 days of learning of the equipment or goods in question which the trustee believes can be replaced at less than the realisable value of the goods, the trustee may serve a written notice on the bankrupt which has the effect of vesting title in the property in the trustee as from the commencement of the bankruptcy.[1] The 42-day period for the trustee's notice may be extended by leave of the court.[2] Bona fide purchasers for value without notice of the bankruptcy are protected and retain their rights in any property purchased from the bankrupt.[3] The trustee must furnish the bankrupt with 'reasonably adequate' alternative property out of the estate, this obligation being a priority over distribution.[4] The trustee may accept money in lieu of sale if this is offered by a third party.[5]

[1] Insolvency Act 1986, s 308(1).
[2] Ibid, s 309(1)(b).
[3] Ibid, s 308(2).

[4] Ibid, s 308(3) and (4) and see Individual Insolvency Rules 1986, r 6.187. The trustee may replace the property either before or after realising the bankrupt's property but need not do so until he has sufficient funds in the estate.
[5] Individual Insolvency Rules 1986, r 6.188.

16.2.3 *After acquired property.* After acquired property, i e any property which is acquired by or has devolved upon the bankrupt after the commencement of the bankruptcy only vests in the trustee if he serves a notice in writing claiming it.[1] Except with the leave of the court a trustee may only serve a notice within 42 days of his learning of the property being acquired by or devolving upon the bankrupt. The property vests in the trustee immediately upon service of the notice on the bankrupt.[2] The trustee's title then relates back to the date upon which the bankrupt acquired the property, save as against:
(a) a purchaser in good faith for value without notice of the bankruptcy;
(b) a banker who enters into a transaction in good faith and without notice of the bankruptcy; or
(c) any person who derives title to any property through a purchaser or banker qualifying under (a) or (b) above.

Against these categories of person a trustee has no remedy in respect of any estate property which they have acquired.

For the purpose of the 42-day time limit a successor trustee is fixed with the knowledge of his predecessor, but knowledge of a person acquired before his appointment as trustee is deemed to come to his notice on the date that his appointment takes effect. In the case of the official receiver this is the date on which he becomes trustee.

A trustee may not serve an after acquired property notice in respect of necessary equipment or household provisions, property excluded by other statutes, or property acquired by the bankrupt after his discharge, except where it is a condition of his discharge that he transfers his interest in such property as the court may direct.[3]

[1] Insolvency Act 1986, s 307.
[2] As to the service of notices, see Individual Insolvency Rules 1986, r 6.200
[3] Insolvency Act 1986, s 280(2)(c).

16.2.4 *Income payments order.* Income, of whatever nature, earned by the bankrupt after the commencement of the bankruptcy may be made the subject of 'an income payments order',[1] and sums received in pursuance of such an order will form part of the bankrupt's estate. Income is widely defined as comprising every payment in the nature of income which is from time to time made to the bankrupt or to which he from time to time becomes entitled. It includes any payment in respect of the carrying on of a business or in respect of any office or employment.

The bankrupt is under a duty to notify the trustee of any property acquired by or devolving on him, or of any increase in his income within 21 days of his becoming aware of the relevant facts.[2] Failure to do so is punishable as a contempt of court.[3] After the bankrupt has served notice on the trustee informing him of his acquisition of property he may not dispose of the property during the period of 42 days from the date of the notice without the trustee's consent in writing.[4] If he does so, the bankrupt is obliged to provide any information necessary to enable the trustee to trace the property and recover it for the estate.[5] The trustee has 28 days from becoming aware of the identity of the recipient disponee of the property to serve a notice on him claiming the property for the estate.[6] Any costs of recovering the property fall on the estate.[7]

Where a bankrupt continues to carry on a business after the commencement of his bankruptcy he is not obliged to notify the trustee of property acquired by him in the ordinary course of that business. Instead, he is required[8] to provide his trustee with accounts of the business at least every six months showing the goods bought and sold and the profit and loss of the business.

On the trustee's application the court may order either the bankrupt or the employer or other person making the payments to pay a specified amount to the trustee during the period of the order. In so doing the court may discharge or vary any existing attachment of earnings order in force against the bankrupt's earnings. In making the order the court is prohibited from reducing the bankrupt's income to below that necessary for meeting the 'reasonable domestic needs' of himself and his family. The order automatically ceases on discharge, although it may be continued or replaced by an order for making payments as a condition of discharge.[9] The bankrupt is under a duty to inform the trustee of any increase in his income. Failure to do so is punishable as a contempt of court.[10]

The Rules[11] provide for the bankrupt to be given 28 days' notice of the hearing and to be served with a short statement of the grounds on which it is made. Should the bankrupt fail to comply with an order, the trustee may apply ex parte to vary the order so as to be an order to the payer of the relevant income.[12] An income payments order may be reviewed by the court on the application of trustee or bankrupt on the ground of material change in circumstances since the order was made.[13]

1 Insolvency Act 1986, s 310.
2 Ibid, s 333(2); Individual Insolvency Rules 1986, r 6.200(1).
3 Insolvency Act 1986, s 333(4).
4 Individual Insolvency Rules 1986, r 6.200(2).
5 Ibid, r 6.200(3).
6 Ibid, r 6.201.
7 Ibid, r 6.202.
8 Ibid, r 6.200(4) and (5).
9 Insolvency Act 1986, s 310(6).
10 Ibid, s 333(2)(4).
11 Individual Insolvency Rules 1986, r 6.189.
12 Ibid, r 6.191. For administering the order on the payer see r 6.192.
13 Ibid, r 6.193.

16.3 PROPERTY AVAILABLE TO THE TRUSTEE

16.3.1 The law's intention is that the totality of the bankrupt's valuable property held by him at the commencement of the bankruptcy should pass to the trustee for realisation and distribution to the creditors. 'Property' is defined in the Act as 'including money, goods, things in action, land and every description of property wherever situated and also obligations and every description of interest, whether present or future or vested or contingent, arising out of, or incidental to, property.'[1]

It will be noted that there is no geographical restriction on property vesting in or becoming available to the trustee. Save in cases where the trustee can set aside charges and incumbrances made by the bankrupt as preferences or under valued transactions under the Insolvency Act 1986 (see ch 17 below) or otherwise as fraudulent dispositions[2] the trustee has no better title to property than the bankrupt himself had immediately before the bankruptcy. The property vesting in him is subject to all the equities and liabilities which existed when in the bankrupt's ownership.

[1] Insolvency Act 1986, s 436.
[2] See, e g avoiding dispositions made with intent to defraud creditors under the Insolvency Act 1986, s 423–425.

16.3.2 It is possible therefore for a great variety of property to become available or be potentially available to the trustee as part of the bankrupt's estate. It is not possible to discuss every conceivable class or type of property which may form part of a bankrupt's estate, or give rise to uncertainty as to whether or not it does form part of such estate. The following observations are made, however, in respect of certain types of property:

16.3.2.1 *(i) Contracts.* Bankruptcy does not, as a general rule, determine a contract. Except where the bankrupt's personal skill or conduct is an essential part of the consideration, the trustee has the right to enforce unexecuted or uncompleted contracts to which the bankrupt was a party. Bankruptcy may, however, affect the respective rights of the parties to a contract in that a trustee may be in a different position to that the bankrupt would have been in had he not become insolvent. Common examples will be the sale of goods on credit or by instalments. Where property and possession have passed to the trustee the unpaid seller in possession of the goods may exercise his statutory lien, and may retain possession against the trustee until he is paid in full. In order to guard against the effects of bankruptcy where possession in goods passes before payment 'Romalpa' (retention of title) clauses, whereby the seller retains title in the goods in question until payment is made, are increasingly common. The intricacies of such clauses are outside the scope of the present work but it is noted that in the context of individual insolvency there is no general requirement for equitable charges to be registered nor is there any provision whereby they are void against the trustee in bankruptcy if not registered. This particular area of difficulty in relation to retention of title clauses does not arise therefore in bankruptcy.

16.3.2.2 *(ii) Determinable interests.* It is perfectly valid for an interest in property to be determinable on the holder's bankruptcy in which event it passes to another person, provided, however, that the person creating the interest is not the bankrupt himself.[1] The instrument creating the interest must be carefully drafted to ensure that the property passes away from the bankrupt in the event of his bankruptcy without any remaining interest, even a future interest, in the bankrupt and that it passes to another holder. Under the Old Bankruptcy Law the interest determines when the act of bankruptcy was committed. With the New Law it is the making of the bankruptcy order which has that effect.

1 *Re Ashby, ex p Wreford* [1892] 1 QB 872.

16.3.2.3 *(iii) Expectancies.* An expectancy, or the possibility that a bankrupt may have or receive an interest in property is not property which vests in the trustee. Should an actual interest arise during the bankruptcy the trustee may claim it as after acquired property on serving the requisite notice. A possibility coupled with an interest does, however, comprise property which vests in the trustee.[1]

1 See *Higden v Williamson* (1732) 3 P Wms 132 and the cases in 5 The Digest (Re-Issue), Part xx, Section 4(2)(B).

16.3.2.4 *(iv) Gifts.* Subject to compliance with the rule that an effective gift inter vivos may only be made by deed or delivery,[1] gifts to the bankrupt pass to the trustee and gifts by the bankrupt do not. The latter may be set aside as an undervalue transaction if made within two years of the commencement of the bankruptcy or within five years if the bankrupt was insolvent when making the gift or became insolvent as a result of making the gift.[2]

1 *Re Cole, ex p Trustee of Property of Bankrupt v Cole* [1963] Ch 175, where it was held that a husband who told his wife that all the furniture in the house where they both continued to live was a gift to her had not perfected the gift by adequate delivery.
2 Insolvency Act 1986, s 339.

16.3.2.5 *(v) Goodwill.* The goodwill of any business carried on by the bankrupt is property and passes to the trustee, subject to any equities that the bankrupt may have created. Accordingly the bankrupt must cooperate with the trustee if necessary in order to realise the goodwill, for example disclosing secret formulae used in manufacture or providing customer lists.[1] When the trustee sells the bankrupt's business, however, he cannot require the bankrupt to enter into restrictive covenants to protect the purchaser, however usual or reasonable such covenants might be. Accordingly, while the bankrupt must not pass himself off in a new business as a proprietor of the old, he cannot be restrained from carrying on a similar business or even soliciting his former customers.[2] It is doubtful whether the goodwill of a bankrupt professional man, being personal to him, would pass to the trustee. In any event it is unlikely that there would be any realisable value in such goodwill.

1 *Re Keene* [1922] 2 Ch 475.
2 *Trego v Hunt* [1896] AC 7; *Green & Sons (Northampton) Ltd v Morris* [1914] 1 Ch 562; *Walker v Mottram* (1881) 19 Ch D 355. A bankrupt will be bound, however, by an agreement entered into by him with the purchaser at the time of sale *Buxton and High Peak Publishing v Mitchell* [1885] Cab & El 527.

16.3.2.6 *(vi) Land and leaseholds.* Interests in land which are not expectancies, will pass to the trustee: see generally ch 29.2 below. For the special considerations which relate to the matrimonial home see ch 22 below. The trustee may enforce a contract entered into by the bankruptcy for the purchase of land[1] but such a contract will not normally be enforced against him.[2] Where the bankrupt has agreed to sell or mortgage property before his bankruptcy the property vests in the trustee subject to an obligation to perform the contract.[3]

1 *Crosbie v Tooke* (1833) 1 My & K 431.
2 *Holloway v York* (1877) 25 WR 627; *Re Oldham, ex p Lucas* (1833) 3 Deac & Ch 144.
3 *Pearce v Bastable's Trustee in Bankruptcy* [1901] 2 Ch 122; *Re Pooley, ex p Rabbidge* (1878) 8 Ch D 367.

16.3.2.7 *(vii) Mortgages and charges.* The interest of a bankrupt mortgagor or mortgagee passes on bankruptcy. In the case of a bankrupt mortgagor the property vesting in the trustee is subject to the mortgagee's interest including his right to take possession and exercise all the other rights of a mortgagee notwithstanding the bankruptcy. Agricultural charges are subject to the provisions of the Agricultural Credits Act 1928. Where a farmer becomes bankrupt within three months of executing an agricultural charge, whether fixed or floating, the charge does not secure the amount owing to the chargee immediately before the making of the charge unless it can be shown that the farmer was solvent when, and immediately after, making the charge.[1] Agricultural charges which have not been registered will be void against the trustee.[2]

Any legal or equitable mortgagee of land or any interest in land belonging to the bankrupt may apply to the court in the bankruptcy for an order directing that the land be sold.[3] The court may direct accounts to be taken and enquiries made as to the sums due under the mortgage and rents or profits received by the mortgagee if in occupation in like manner as in the Chancery Division of the High Court.[4] The order for sale may contain directions as to the conduct of the sale and the application of the proceeds.[5]

1 Agricultural Credits Act 1928, s 8(5).
2 Ibid, s 9.
3 Individual Insolvency Rules 1986, r 6.197(1).
4 Ibid, r 6.197(2)–(4).
5 Ibid, rr 6.198 and 6.199.

16.3.2.8 *(viii) Partnership property.* The trustee is entitled to the bankrupt's due share in the partnership and is not bound by any agreement between the partners which purports to allow the other partners to acquire a bankrupt partner's share for no, or inadequate, consideration: see para 24.6.4 below.

16.3.2.9 *(ix) Patents, copyright and royalties.* Such interests pass to the trustee, though where a patent is sold by the patentee's trustee in bankruptcy, the patentee cannot be prevented from denying the validity of the patent or otherwise impugning it.[1] A trustee in bankruptcy may register title to a patent.[2] The trustee may assign a registered trade mark with or without an assignment of the goodwill of the business, provided the mark does not become deceptive in consequence.[3]

1 *Smith v Cropper* [1885] 10 App Cas 249.

[2] Patents Act 1977, s 33(3)(a); Patent Rules 1982, rr 4, 46, Sch 2.
[3] Trade Marks Act 1938, s 22(1); *R J Reuter Co Ltd v Ferd Mulheus* [1954] Ch 50.

16.3.2.10 *(x) Pensions, annuities and life insurances.* The bankrupt's interest in any pensions, annuities and life insurances pass to the trustee who may realise them by assignment or surrender so far as may be possible under their terms. It is, however, most unlikely that the trustee may realise anything of value from pension policies. Pension benefits payable under the Social Security Act 1975 may not pass to the trustee. As for private pensions qualifying under the Income and Corporation Taxes Act 1970, s 226 it is an essential condition of such policies that no pension or other payments are made until at least the age of 60 or on death. It may therefore be difficult or impossible for a trustee in bankruptcy to realise the assets of the bankrupt which have been paid into a pension fund. Such payments would not appear to be transactions at an undervalue for the purposes of the Insolvency Act 1986, s 339, nor would they constitute preferences for the bankrupt himself is not a person to whom a preference can be given: see the Insolvency Act 1986, s 340(3) and ch 17 below. The trustee may, however:

(a) apply for relief under the Insolvency Act 1986, ss 423–425 where he can show that the bankrupt made pension contributions in order to put assets beyond the reach of his creditors: see ch 20 below; or
(b) where the bankrupt does not qualify for automatic discharge, seek to persuade the court to make any order of discharge conditional upon payment of all or part of the bankrupt's entitlement from the pension fund when it falls due.

Plainly, the age of the bankrupt will be an important consideration when an order for conditional discharge is considered by the court. And of course it is only where the bankrupt does not qualify for automatic discharge that such an order may be made at all. It is perhaps a serious lacuna in the Act that a person who qualifies for automatic discharge (and who complies with his administrative obligations to his trustee) cannot be made the subject of such a conditional order. It could well follow that a bankrupt who obtains his automatic discharge shortly before retirement will be able to keep the full benefits of his retirement policies even though some of the premiums have been paid at the expense of his creditors.

Where a bankrupt has effected life assurance on his own life expressed to be for the benefit of a third party, the policy money, in the absence of a declaration of trust, belongs to his estate. But where such life assurance is for the benefit of the bankrupt's spouse and/or children, a trust is created in their favour and so long as the spouse or any of the children remain alive, the money paid under the policy does not form part of the bankrupt's estate or become subject to his debts.[1] Where the trustee is able to prove that the policy was effected and the premiums paid with the intent to defraud creditors, he may seek an order for restitution.[2] In the absence of such proof, the trustee will normally be able to impeach the contract of insurance as an undervalue transaction within the two- or five-year period allowed for in the Insolvency Act 1986[3] and obtain a return of the premiums paid together, possibly, with a further sum in respect of any accured benefits where the premiums were paid to an endownment fund.[4]

[1] Married Women's Property Act 1882, s 11.

[2] Either under Married Women's Property Act 1882, s 11 (a sum equal to premiums paid only) or Insolvency Act 1986, s 423 (any order the court thinks fit).
[3] S 339.
[4] See Insolvency Act 1986, s 342(1).

16.3.2.11 *(xi) Rights of action.* The trustee may exercise the rights of action of the bankrupt, though where they arise after the commencement of the bankruptcy the requisite notice in respect of after acquired property must be served. If the action has commenced before the bankruptcy the trustee may apply ex parte to replace or join the bankrupt as plaintiff.[1] The trustee does not, however, acquire the right to any cause of action arising from the bodily or mental injury to, or the personal inconvenience of, the bankrupt.[2] Damages awarded to the bankrupt for personal injury (pain, suffering and loss of amenity) do not pass to the trustee, though should the bankrupt invest the damages or acquire property with the money paid as damages it then seems that such investment or property passes to the trustee if surplus to the bankrupt's requirements for maintenance.[3]

[1] RSC Ord 15, r 7.
[2] *Beckham v Drake* (1849) 2 HL Cas 579 and see the cases at 5 The Digest (Re-Issue) Part XXI Section I.
[3] *Re Wilson, ex p Vine* (1878) 8 Ch D 364; *Re Job, ex p Graham* (1870) 21 LT 802.

16.3.2.12 *(xii) Shares and securities.* Shares and other securities pass to the trustee, including shares in a private company with provisions restricting ownership. The trustee is not bound by any provision in the articles or otherwise requiring the shares to be sold for less than their full value on a bankruptcy of the shareholder.[1] The trustee will be liable to pay any calls on partly paid shares, or unpaid instalments on the purchase price.

[1] *Borland's Trustee v Steel Bros & Co Ltd* [1901] 1 Ch 279.

Exempt property

16.3.3 (a) Social security payments, pensions, supplementary benefits, family allowances and similar benefits are expressly exempted from the bankrupts' estate vesting in the trustee: see Social Security Act 1975, s 87; Supplementary Benefit Act 1976, s 16; Family Allowances Act 1965, s 510; Naval and Marine Pay and Pensions Act 1865, s 4; Army Act 1955, s 203; Air Force Act 1955; Police Pensions Act 1976, ss 9, 11 and other statutes.

(b) Trust property, where the bankrupt is trustee, is also exempted from the estate which vests in the trustee in bankruptcy: see para 29.5.1 below.

(c) The causes of action referred to in para 16.3.2.11 above.

16.4 THE TRUSTEE'S POWERS

16.4.1 Generally, the trustee is in precisely the same position as that which the bankrupt enjoyed in relation to all the bankrupt's property. The trustee has all the powers and duties of a receiver of property appointed by the High Court, and he may apply to the Court for any necessary order to enable him to retain or acquire property of or due to the estate.[1] The trustee is deemed to be an officer of the court and is subject to the 'rule in *Ex p James*'[2] which requires the trustee to do what is just and right and not to take advantage of mistakes. The 'rule' is, however, no more than a discretionary power of the court and only appears to have been exercised in cases where there has been some form of enrichment of the assets of a bankrupt or insolvent company at the expense of the person seeking recompense.[3]

1 Insolvency Act 1986, s 311(2).
2 *Re Condon, ex p James* (1874) 9 Ch App 609; and see *Re Stokes, ex p Mellish* [1919] 2 K B 256.
3 *Re Government of India Ministry of Finance v Taylor* [1955] AC 491.

16.4.2 The trustee is empowered and required to take possession of all books, papers and other records which relate to the bankrupt's estate or affairs, including papers not only in his possession but also within his control.[1] Expressly included within this power to obtain papers are documents which would be privileged from disclosure in legal proceedings.[2] Corresponding obligations to surrender control of property and documents of whatever description are placed on[3]:

(a) the bankrupt, who has a general duty to do anything reasonably required by the trustee to assist him to administer the estate, even after his discharge;
(b) the official receiver, a former trustee of the bankrupt's estate, or a person who has been the supervisor of an approved composition or scheme;
(c) a banker of the bankrupt; and
(d) any agent of the bankrupt or any other person who holds property to the account of or for the bankrupt.

A banker or agent of the bankrupt may, however, retain as against the trustee any property or documents of title which he is entitled to retain by law. This statutory obligation to surrender does not therefore operate to defeat liens on documents which constitute title to property and are held for that purpose. Liens on other documents, books, papers and records are unenforceable against the official receiver or trustee.[4]

Failure to surrender documents and in the case of the bankrupt failure to do anything reasonably required by the trustee without reasonable excuse, is punishable as a contempt of court.[5]

1 Insolvency Act 1986, s 311(1).
2 See ch 26 'Solicitors acting in bankruptcy matters'.
3 Insolvency Act 1986, s 312.
4 Ibid, s 349.
5 Ibid, s 333(1).

16.4.3 The trustee may apply to the court for directions in relation to any particular matter arising under the bankruptcy.[1] The court is not bound to give him directions, however.[2] Should directions be given with which the trustee is dissatisfied, he should not as a general rule appeal, and on an unsuccessful appeal he is likely to be made personally liable for the costs.[3]

1 Insolvency Act 1986, s 303(2).

2 *Re Webb & Sons, ex p Webb & Sons* (1887) 4 Morr 52; *Re Pilling, ex p Salaman* [1906] 2 KB 644.
3 *Re Malden, Gibson & Co* (1886) 3 Morr 185.

16.4.4 Under the Old Bankruptcy Law[1] the trustee's general discretion in the administration of the estate had to be exercised with regard to any directions given by the committee of inspection or resolution of creditors in general meeting, with the creditors in general meeting prevailing in cases of conflict. The Insolvency Act 1986 does not repeat this general supervisory role towards the trustee in the creditors of the committee. The creditors' committee has a more limited function.[2]

1 Bankruptcy Act 1914, s 79(1).
2 See para 15.7 above.

General powers of trustee

16.4.5 The general powers of the trustee expressly conferred by the Act[1] are divided into two classes; those which he may exercise on his own accord and those for which he requires the permission of the committee of creditors or the Court.

1 Insolvency Act 1986, s 314, Sch 5.

Powers exerciseable on trustee's own accord

16.4.6 *(i) Power of sale.*[1] The trustee may sell any part of the property comprised for the time being in the bankrupt's estate, including the goodwill and book debts of any business. He must sell on an immediate cash basis unless he obtains the consent of the committee: see para 16.4.17 below. The Court may set aside[2] any transaction in which the trustee sells estate property to an associate of his without the prior consent of the Court unless the trustee did not know that he was dealing with an associate and value was given, see para 15.3.5 above. If he sells to an associate of the bankrupt he must give notice to the committee.[3]

This provision recognises the fact that trustees have been thought guilty in the past of disposing of assets at a low price to associates of the bankrupt in collusion with them. The creditors' committee must be put on notice that assets are being disposed of to associates of the bankrupt and they have the opportunity to scrutinise the transaction. If appropriate, the creditors' committee may challenge the transaction under the Insolvency Act 1986, s 303 and seek a summary order for restitution under the Insolvency Act 1986, s 304.

The trustee may use an agent or auctioneer to effect a sale and when selling assets on behalf of a secured creditor the trustee may deduct from the proceeds of sale a sum equivalent to the remuneration chargeable by the official receiver under general regulations.[4]

1 Insolvency Act 1986, s 314(1)(b), Sch 5, para 9.
2 Individual Insolvency Rules 1986, r 6.147.
3 Insolvency Act 1986, s 314(6).
4 Individual Insolvency Rules 1986, r 6.139; Insolvency Regulations 1986, SI 1986/1994.

16.4.7 *(ii) Power to give receipts.*[1] The trustee may give receipts for any money received by him, being receipts which effectively discharge the person paying the money from all responsibility in respect of its application.

[1] Insolvency Act 1986, s 314(1)(b), Sch 5, para 10.

16.4.8 *(iii) Power to prove for bankrupt's debt.*[1] The trustee may prove, rank, claim and draw a dividend in respect of such debts due to the bankrupt as are comprised in the bankrupt's estate.

[1] Insolvency Act 1986, s 314(1)(b), Sch 5, para 11.

16.4.9 *(iv) General powers in relation to property.*[1] The trustee may exercise in relation to any property comprised in the bankrupt's estate any powers, the capacity to exercise which are vested in the trustee under the Act. Such powers include making contracts, employing agents, executing powers of attorney, deeds or other instruments or other acts which are 'necessary or expedient'.

[1] Insolvency Act 1986, s 314(1)(b), (5), Sch 5, para 14.

16.4.10 *(v) Power over entailed property.*[1] The trustee may deal with any property to which a bankrupt is beneficially entitled as tenant in tail in the same manner as the bankrupt may have dealt with it.

[1] Insolvency Act 1986, s 314(1)(b), Sch 5, para 13.

16.4.11 *(vi) Power to transfer on other's books.*[1] In respect of property of the bankrupt comprising stock or shares in a company shares in a ship or any other property transferable in the books of a company, office or person the trustee may exercise such right to transfer the property as was exerciseable by the bankrupt before his bankruptcy.

[1] Insolvency Act 1986, s 311(3).

16.4.12 *(vii) Power in respect of goods held by way of pledge pawn or other security.*[1] Initially the official receiver will have power to inspect and redeem such goods if he thinks fit before the appointment of the trustee[2]. If the official receiver has not done so, the trustee may serve a notice in writing on the person holding the goods of the bankrupt as security of his intention to inspect the goods. That person must give the trustee reasonable opportunity of inspecting the goods and if the trustee thinks fit he may exercise the bankrupt's right of redemption in the goods concerned.

[1] Insolvency Act 1986, s 311(5).
[2] Ibid, s 285(5).

16.4.13 *(viii) Power to charge dwelling house.*[1] Where the bankrupt's estate includes an interest in a dwelling house occupied by the bankrupt his spouse or former spouse, and the trustee is unable to realise that interest for whatever reason, the trustee may apply to the court for a charging order for the benefit of the estate. Any charge imposed is enforceable for any amounts due in the bankruptcy and interest other than payments made to the bankrupt out of his estate. The order must provide that the property charged is to cease to be comprised in the bankrupt's estate and shall vest in the bankrupt subject to the charge made by the court and any prior charge.[2] A charging order made under this provision will be subject to the Charging Orders Act 1979, s 3(1), (2), (4), (5) and (6). Accordingly the court may impose conditions as to when the charge is to become enforceable or as to other matters, and may discharge or vary the order on the application of any person interested. The Land Charges Act 1972 and the Land Registration Act 1925 apply to the charging order.

1 Insolvency Act 1986, s 313.
2 Ibid, s 313(3); Individual Insolvency Rules 1986, r 6.237 and see para 22.11 below.

16.4.14 *(ix) Power to disclaim onerous property.* See para 16.4.28 below.

Powers exerciseable with consent of committee or court[1]

16.4.15 *(i) Power to carry on business.* The trustee may carry on any business of the bankrupt so far as may be necessary for winding it up beneficially and so far as he is able to do so without contravening any requirement imposed by or under any enactment. If he carries it on the trustee should keep detailed accounts and should take care not to become personally responsible for the contracts of any employees.[2] The trustee may use the services of the bankrupt: see para 6.4.22 below.

1 Insolvency Act 1986, s 314(1)(a), Sch 5, paras 1–8, s 314(2).
2 See ch 27, 'Employment' below.

16.4.16 *(ii) Power to litigate.* The trustee may bring, institute or defend any action or legal proceedings relating to the property comprised in the bankrupt's estate. In appropriate circumstances he may assign his rights in litigation.[1]

1 *Guy v Churchill* (1888) 40 Ch D 481; *Seear v Lawson* (1880) 15 Ch D 426.

16.4.17 *(iii) Power to sell on credit.* The trustee may accept as consideration for the sale of any property comprised in the bankrupt's estate a sum of money payable at a future time subject to such stipulations as to security or otherwise as the committee or court thinks fit.

16.4.18 *(iv) Power to raise money on mortgage.* The trustee may mortgage or pledge any part of the property comprised in the bankrupt's estate for the purpose of raising money for the payment of his debts.

16.4.19 *(v) Power to exercise option or power.* Where any right, option or other power forms part of the bankrupt's estate the trustee may make payments or incur liabilities with a view to distraining for the benefit of creditors, any property which is the subject of the right, option or power.

16.4.20 *(vi) Power to compromise with debtors.* The trustee may refer to arbitration or compromise on such terms as may be agreed on, any debts, claims or liabilities subsisting or supposed to subsist between the bankrupt and any person who may have incurred any liability to the bankrupt. Under the Old Bankruptcy Law, the court would only rarely interfere with the refusal of the creditors to approve a compromise even where the committee is in favour of the proposed terms.[1]

[1] *Re Ridgeway, ex p Hurlbatt* [1889] 61 LT 647.

16.4.21 *(vii) Power to compromise with creditors.* The trustee may make such compromise or other arrangement as may be thought expedient with creditors, or persons claiming to be creditors, in respect of bankruptcy debts.

16.4.22 *(viii) Power to make other compromise.* The trustee may make such compromise or other arrangement as may be thought expedient with respect to any claim arising out of or incidental to the bankrupt's estate made or capable of being made on the trustee by any person or by the trustee of any person.

16.4.23 *(ix) Power to appoint bankrupt to assist.* The trustee may appoint the bankrupt (a) to superintend the management of the estate or any part of it, (b) to carry on any business for the benefit of his creditors, or (c) to assist in any other respect in administrating the estate in such manner and on such terms as the trustee may direct.

16.4.24 *(x) Power to divide property.* The trustee may divide in its existing form amongst the bankrupt's creditors according to its estimated value any property which from its peculiar nature or other special circumstances cannot be readily or advantageously sold.[1]

[1] Insolvency Act 1986, s 326(1).

16.4.25 Consent given by the committee or the court is to extend only to a particular transction; the Insolvency Act 1986 does not allow general permission to be given.[1] In cases of urgency the trustee may seek the ratification of the committee or the court in respect of acts requiring permission which was not obtained. The committee must be satisfied as to the urgency facing the trustee and that he then sought their ratification without delay. Without such ratification the trustee will not be able to meet his expenses out of the bankrupt's estate.[2]

[1] Insolvency Act 1986, s 314(3).
[2] Ibid, s 314(4).

16.4.26 A third party who deals with the trustee in respect of any transaction or matter where the trustee requires the permission of the committee or the court need not be concerned to enquire whether the permission was given. Provided that he acts in good faith and for value the third party may assume that all necessary permissions have been duly granted.[1]

[1] Insolvency Act 1986, s 314(3).

16.4.27 Where a trustee disposes of property comprised in the estate to an associate of the bankrupt or employs a solicitor he must give notice to the committee that he has done so.[1] The trustee may summon a general meeting of the bankrupt's creditors at any time, and must do so when requested by a creditor with the concurrence of not less than one-tenth in value of the bankrupt's creditors.[2]

[1] Insolvency Act 1986, s 314(6).
[2] Ibid, s 314(7).

16.4.28 *Disclaimer of onerous property.* In the main the property which will be disclaimed by trustees is leasehold interest in land. The disclaimer of leases is discussed in paras 29.5 to 29.8 below. The trustee's power of disclaimer does, however, extend to any onerous property which is defined in the Act[1] as '(a) any unprofitable contract; and (b) any other property comprised in the bankrupt's estate which is unsaleable or not readily saleable or is such that it may give rise to a liability to pay money or perform any other onerous act.' There is no doctrine of affirmation applicable to disclaimer and the trustee is not precluded from disclaiming property by the fact that he has exercised rights of ownership in relation to it by taking possession of it, attempting to sell it or otherwise.

[1] Insolvency Act 1986, s 315(2).

16.4.29 The trustee disclaims by giving the prescribed notice.[1] Where the property is leasehold the disclaimer does not take effect unless a copy has been served on every person claiming under the bankrupt as sub-lessee or mortgagee.[2] Leave of the court is required before a notice of disclaimer is served in respect of property which has been claimed for the estate by the trustee under the provisions relating to after-acquired property.[3] Any person interested in any property which might be disclaimed may force the issue by applying in writing to the trustee requiring him to decide whether to disclaim or not.[4] On the expiry of 28 days from the application without the trustee serving notice of disclaimer he is precluded from disclaiming the property subsequently and deemed to have adopted any contract which he is now precluded from disclaiming.[5]

If it appears to the trustee that there is some person who claims or may claim to have an interest in any property of which the trustee has a right to disclaim, he may give notice to that person requiring him to declare within 14 days whether he does claim an interest and if so the nature and extent of such interest. If the notice is not complied with the trustee may assume that the person concerned has no interest which will prevent or impede its disclaimer.[6] Any disclaimer of property by the trustee is presumed to be valid and effective, unless it is proved that the trustee was in breach of his duty to give notice of disclaimer or otherwise under the Insolvency Act 1986, ss 315–319 or the Individual Insolvency Rules, Part 6, Chapter 14.[7]

[1] Insolvency Act 1986, s 315(1); Individual Insolvency Rules 1986, r 6.178, form 6.61.
[2] Individual Insolvency Rules 1986, r 6.179.
[3] Insolvency Act 1986, s 315(4). Leave may be sought ex parte. Individual Insolvency Rules 1986, r 6.182.
[4] Individual Insolvency Rules 1986, r 6.183. The application must be in form 6.62 or in a 'substantially similar' form.

5 Insolvency Act 1986, s 316(1).
6 Individual Insolvency Rules 1986, r 6.184, form 6.63.
7 Ibid, r 6.185.

16.4.30 The effect of a disclaimer is to determine, as from the date of the disclaimer, all rights, interests and liabilities of the bankrupt and his estate in or in respect of the property disclaimed. A disclaimer also operates to discharge the trustee from all personal liability in respect of that property as from the commencement of his trusteeship.[1] Save as is necessary to relieve the bankrupt, the trustee and the estate from liability the disclaimer does not affect the rights and liabilities of any other person. In particular therefore a surety remains liable in respect of liabilities accruing before the date of disclaimer.

1 Insolvency Act 1986, s 315(3).

16.4.31 After property has been disclaimed any person interested in the disclaimed property may apply to the court for delivery up or a vesting order.[1] This is of particular importance to leasehold interests in land, see para 29.7 below. Any person who sustains loss or damage in consequence of a disclaimer is deemed to be a creditor of the bankrupt to the extent of the loss and damage and may prove for that loss or damage as a bankruptcy debt.[2]

1 Insolvency Act 1986, s 320, Individual Insolvency Rules, 1986, r 6.186. An applicant for a vesting order has three months from becoming aware of the disclaimer to make his application.
2 Insolvency Act 1986, s 315(5).

16.5 PROOF OF DEBTS

16.5.1 As a general rule all debts and liabilities, present or future, certain or contingent to which the debtor was actually or prospectively liable at the commencement of the bankruptcy or could have become liable subsequently are provable in the bankruptcy. The manner of proof by a secured or unsecured creditor and the admission or rejection of any proof is governed by the Rules.[1] Where a provable debt carries interest, any interest due in respect of a period prior to the commencement of the bankruptcy is provable. Interest arising after the bankruptcy cannot be proved. Where debts proved are contingent or unliquidated the trustee has to estimate their value, though he may apply to the court for an estimation, and that value is proved in respect of that debt. An aggrieved creditor may apply to the court to vary the trustee's estimate.[2]

1 Ibid, s 322. Individual Insolvency Rules 1986, Part 6, Chapter 8, and see Insolvency Act 1986, s 382(3) which provides that it is immaterial whether the debt is present or future, certain or contingent, fixed or liquidated or capable of being ascertained by fixed rules or as a matter of opinion.
2 Insolvency Act 1986, s 303, ie under the general power to apply to the court to control the trustee.

Rule against double proof

16.5.2 There cannot be two proofs in respect of one debt, a principle long established for the protection of other creditors. In the words of Mellish LJ 'The true principle is, that there is only to be one dividend in respect of what in substance is the same debt, although there may be two separate contracts.'[1] This principle is of important application in the case of guarantees, where a guarantor may not prove while the principal creditor is also proving, and in partnership.

[1] *Re Oriental Commercial Bank, ex p European Bank* (1871) 7 Ch App 99 at 103.

The hotchpotch rule

16.5.3 This rule arises when the bankrupt is subject to bankruptcy proceedings both in England and abroad. Where a creditor proves in both proceedings he may not receive a dividend in England without any dividend that he has received abroad being taken into account. Until all the English creditors have received a dividend at the same rate as the foreign dividend the creditor is not entitled to dividends in the English proceedings.[1]

[1] *Re Douglas, ex p Wilson* (1872) 7 Ch App 490; *Re Hooper, Banco de Portugal v Waddell* (1880) 5 App Cas 161.

Mutual credit and set off

16.5.4 Where before the commencement of the bankruptcy there have been mutual credits, mutual debts or other mutual dealings between the bankrupt and any creditor of the bankrupt pursuing or claiming to prove for a bankruptcy debt, an account must be taken of what is due from each party to the other in respect of the mutual dealings and the amounts set off. It is only for the balance that the creditor may prove in the bankruptcy or the trustee may claim from the creditor, as appropriate.[1] These statutory provisions are mandatory and cannot be excluded by agreement of the parties.[2] All cases where a mutual credit, debt or dealing exists are subject to set off, not merely cases arising in contract.[3] The debt of dealing must be mutual and therefore a joint debt cannot be set off against separate debts, unless there is express agreement that they should be set off by all parties concerned. An equitable debt may be set off against a legal debt, as the Bankruptcy Court proceeds on equitable principles.[4] A right to set off is restricted to money liabilities and cannot apply to a claim for return of goods.[5] A set off is not prevented by one of the debts being a future debt, nor uncertain in amount such as an unliquidated claim in damages.[6] A debt is not to be set off, however, where at the time it became due the other party had notice that a bankruptcy petition relating to the bankrupt was pending against him.[7]

[1] Insolvency Act 1986, s 323.
[2] *National Westminster Bank Ltd v Halesowen Presswork and Assemblies Ltd* [1972] AC 785.
[3] *Re D H Curtis (Builders) Ltd* [1978] Ch 162 where the Crown set off an input tax repayment due to the company against company debts to the Inland Revenue and DHSS.
[4] *Mathieson's Trustee v Burrup, Matthieson & Co* [1927] 1 Ch 562.

[5] See, eg *Ellis & Co's Trustee v Dixon-Johnson* [1925] AC 489 though where property is held subject to directions to convert it into money a set off is possible: *Rolls Razor Ltd v Cox* [1967] 1 QB 552.
[6] *Tilley v Bowman Ltd* [1910] 1 KB 745; *Rolls Razor Ltd v Cox* [1967] 1 QB 552.
[7] Insolvency Act 1986, s 323(3).

Particular classes of debts

16.5.5 The trustee may have to deal with proofs of debt of all descriptions. No comprehensive survey is here attempted, but the following observations are offered:

16.5.5.1 *(i) Calls on shares.* A company or its liquidator may prove against the estate for calls made and for the value of the bankrupt's liability to future calls, subject to the trustee's right of disclaimer.[1] The trustee may also have rights in the company's liquidation, though not as a fully paid shareholder if the bankrupt estate's dividend is less than 100p in the pound.[2]

[1] *Re McMahon, Fuller v McMahon* [1900] 1 Ch 173.
[2] *Re West Coast Gold Fields Ltd, Rowe's Trustee's Claim* [1906] 1 Ch 1.

16.5.5.2 *(ii) Contingent debts.* The value of such debts are estimated by the trustee, subject to an application to the court by either trustee or creditor as discussed above. All contingent liabilities which might give rise to the payment of money are provable, except where they cannot be reasonably estimated. Examples are:

(a) the lessee or assignor of a lease may prove in the assignee's bankruptcy in respect of rent and amounts payable by a further assignee which the original lessee and assignor might become liable to pay should the further assignee default and which the bankrupt assignee would then have become liable to pay under his covenant to the original lessee and assignor;[1]
(b) proof of supplier for breach of covenant to purchase goods in the future;[2]
(c) proof of annuitant for the value of annuity;[3] and
(d) proof in respect of a covenant to pay a sum of money out of the covenant's estate within six months of his death.[4]

[1] *Hardy v Fothergill* (1888) 13 App Cas 351.
[2] *Re Allen & Co, ex p Strong and Hanbury* (1893) 10 Morr 84; *Re Moore and Thomas, ex p Beer* (1868) 18 LT 418.
[3] *Re Gieve, ex p Shaw* (1899) 80 LT 737.
[4] *Barnett v King* [1891] 1 Ch 4.

16.5.5.3 *(iii) Costs of legal proceedings.* Costs will follow the subject matter of the action in respect of which they were incurred. Therefore if the action is for a provable claim and the plaintiff has either obtained judgment before the commencement of the bankruptcy, or was in a position to do so for default or on the defendant's admission, the costs are also provable.[1] But where the claim is one which does not give rise to a provable debt (eg unliquidated damages in tort) costs are not provable unless judgment and an order for costs was obtained before the commencement of the bankruptcy.[2]

[1] *Re Duffield, ex p Peacock* (1873) 8 Ch App 682; *Re British Gold Fields of West Africa Ltd* [1899] 2 Ch 7.
[2] *Re Newman, ex p Brooke* (1876) 3 Ch D 494.

16.5.5.4 *(iv) Foreign creditors and Revenue claims.* A foreign creditor may prove, but he must bring into account any sum he has received in the bankrupt's bankruptcy abroad, and may not receive dividends until the English creditors have received similar proportion of their debts: see para 16.5.3 above. However, claims to prove in England for debts due to a foreign state, or an agency of the state, of a Revenue nature are not admissible.[1]

[1] *Brokaw v Seatrain UK Ltd* [1971] 2 QB 476.

16.5.5.5. *(v) Gaming debts.* Such debts are not provable, even though judgment has been obtained on the debt.[1] Equally an account stated which is comprised of betting transactions, or security given for losses or such transactions is unenforceable.[2]

[1] *Re Lopes, ex p Hardway and Topping* (1889) 5 TLR 685. The judgment was, however, obtained under RSC Ord 14 where the debtor failed to comply with the terms on which he obtained conditional leave to defend.
[2] *William Hill (Park Lane) Ltd v Hofman* [1950] 1 All ER 1013.

16.5.5.6 *(vi) Guarantees.* See ch 28 below.

16.5.5.7 *(vii) Moneylending liabilities.* These may be impeached as extortionate credit transactions: see para 17.2.2 below. A proof of debt in respect of a moneylending transaction made before 27 January 1980, where the creditor was at the time of the transaction a licensed moneylender, must have endorsed on or annexed to it a statement setting out in detail the particulars referred to in the Moneylenders Act 1927, s 9(2).[1]

[1] Individual Insolvency Rules 1986, r 6.102.

16.5.5.8 *(viii) Negotiable instruments.* See ch 29.4 below. The holder of a bill of exchange or promissory note may proceed against all parties liable on it until he has 100p in the pound. He can prove in the estate of any person liable, and need not take into account sums received from other parties after proof (he must do so in respect of sums received before proof) until he is paid in full. A proof in respect of money owed on any negotiable instrument or security may not be admitted unless the instrument or security is produced, or the court orders otherwise.[1]

[1] Individual Insolvency Rules 1986, r 6.108.

16.5.5.9 *(ix) Partnership liabilities.* See ch 24 below.

16.5.5.10 *(x) Rent.* The lessor has a limited right of distress after which he may prove for the balance, or if he prefers not to levy distress the lessor may prove for all rent due. A lessor may suffer loss as a result of the lease being disclaimed in which event he may prove for the difference between the rent reserved under the lease and the estimated rents he can obtain during the remainder of the term: see ch 29.2.22 below.

16.5.5.11 *(xi) Royalties and copyrights.* A trustee may not exploit any copyright comprised in the bankrupt's estate under which a royalty is payable to the author on exploitation, whether by fee or share of profits, without paying that royalty in full.

16.5.5.12 *(xii) Secured debts.* A secured creditor may prove for the balance of his debt if there is an unsecured balance, but only after realising his security.[1] He may, however, voluntarily surrender his security for the general benefit of creditors and then prove for his whole debt as if it were unsecured.[2] As for valuation and redemption of security, and the loss of the security where it is not disclosed in the proof of debt, see para 16.6.5 below.

[1] Individual Insolvency Rules 1986, r 6.109(1).
[2] Ibid, r 6.109(2).

16.5.5.13 *(xiii) Statute barred debts.* A creditor may not prove a debt barred by the Limitation Act.[1] The fact that the debt is time barred does not, however, destroy the creditor's rights to enforce a lien.[2]

[1] *Ex p Dewdney, ex p Seaman* (1809) 15 Ves 479.
[2] *Re Hepburn, ex p Smith* (1884) 14 QBD 394 at 400.

16.5.5.14 *(xiv) Unliquidated damages.* Under the Old Bankruptcy Law such damages were provable only if they arose in claims founded on contract, promise or breach of trust. Accordingly claims for damages for assault and battery, conversion, misrepresentation on a prospectus and misfeasance by a director have not been admitted.[1] Such damages were provable if they had become liquidated by judgment or agreement before the commencement of the bankruptcy. The Insolvency Act 1986, s 382(2) provides that in determining whether any liability in tort is a bankruptcy debt, the bankrupt is deemed to become subject to their liability by reason of an obligation incurred at the time when the cause of action accrued. Therefore provided the cause of action has accrued before the commencement of the bankruptcy, any person to whom the bankrupt is liable in tort may prove in the bankruptcy even if the amount of damages has not been ascertained.

[1] See *Re Rickett, ex p Insecticide Activated Products Ltd v Official Receiver* [1949] 1 All ER 737 and the cases at 4 The Digest (Re-Issue) Part VIII Section 4(2).

16.6 PROCEDURE ON PROVING DEBTS

Forms of proof

16.6.1 Any person claiming to be a creditor of the bankrupt and who wishes to prove in the bankruptcy must submit his claim in writing to the official receiver or, if one has been appointed, the trustee in bankruptcy. The prescribed form, known as the 'proof of debt' form must be used.[1] The form must be signed by the creditor or his authorised agent. Proof of debt forms must be sent out by the official receiver or the trustee to all known creditors and should accompany the notice calling a meeting of creditors, or the notice under the Insolvency Act 1986, s 293(2) informing creditors that no meeting is proposed to be called or the notice given by the trustee under the Insolvency Act 1986, s 297(7) of his appointment by the court, whichever is sent.[2] When the trustee advertises his appointment with leave of the court, proof of debt forms must be sent to all known creditors within four months of the bankruptcy order, unless the court orders otherwise.[3]

1 Individual Insolvency Rules 1986, r 6.96, from 6.37.
2 Ibid, r 6.97(1) and (2).
3 Ibid, r 6.97(3) and (4), for advertising appointment see Insolvency Act 1986, s 297(7).

Contents of proof

16.6.2 The proof of debt must contain the eight matters specified in the Rules[1] and should specify any documents which substantiate the debt proved.[2] Such documents need not be submitted with the proof. They may, however, be called for by the official receiver or trustee,[3] who may at any time require a claim to be verified by affidavit for which purpose the 'affidavit of debt' form is used.[4] This affidavit may be sworn before an official receiver, an assistant official receiver or a duly authorised officer of the Department or the court.[5]

The cost of proving his own debt falls on the creditor, while the costs of the trustee in estimating the value of bankruptcy debts falls on the estate.[6] The trustee must allow any creditor to inspect the proofs while the proofs remain in his hands.[7]

1 As to which see Individual Insolvency Rules 1986, r 6.98(1).
2 Individual Insolvency Rules 1986, r 6.98(2).
3 Ibid, r 6.98(3).
4 Ibid, r 6.99, form 6.39.
5 Ibid, r 6.99(3).
6 Ibid, r 6.100.
7 Ibid, r 6.101.

Admission and rejection of proofs

16.6.3 The official receiver or the trustee if appointed, to whom the official receiver must send all proofs of debt immediately on his appointment,[1] considers the proofs of debt and admits or rejects any proof or part of it.[2] Where the trustee rejects the whole or any part of a proof, he must send a written statement of his reasons to the creditor concerned.[3] The creditor then has 21 days in which to apply to the court to reverse or vary the trustee's decision.[4] The bankrupt or any other creditor may apply to the court to reverse or vary any decision by the trustee on a proof of debt, such application to be made within 21 days of becoming aware of the trustee's decision.[5] On any application to the court notice must be given to the trustee and, where appropriate, to the creditor whose proof it is.[6] The trustee must file the proof and any statement of his reasons rejecting the proof at court.[7] The official receiver cannot be held liable for any applicant's costs incurred in challenging a decision on a proof, neither will a privately appointed trustee unless the court determines that an order for costs should be made against him.[8] The court has complete power to expunge a proof, reduce or increase the amount claimed and may do so on the trustee's application where the trustee considers that any proof has been improperly admitted.[9] Consequent upon the court's order a creditor may have to repay to the estate any amount overpaid, but a creditor whose proof is increased may not disturb distributions already made.[10]

1 Individual Insolvency Rules, r 6.103.
2 Ibid, r 6.104(1).
3 Ibid, r 6.104(2).
4 Ibid, r 6.105(1).
5 Ibid, r 6.105(2).
6 Ibid, rr 6.105(3).
7 Ibid, r 6.105(4).
8 Ibid, r 6.105(6).
9 Ibid, r 6.107(1).
10 Ibid, r 11.8(1).

Quantification of claim

16.6.4 The trustee is responsible for quantifying all the proofs of debt, placing a value on any future, contingent or unascertained debts. He may apply to the court for an estimation of the value under his general power to apply for directions.[1] The Individual Insolvency Rules do not provide guidelines for quantifying debts generally, but do contain the following specific provisions:

(i) Discounts.[2] All trade and other discounts which would have been available to the bankrupt should be deducted in making the claim, except discounts for immediate, early or cash settlement.
(ii) Foreign currency.[3] Debts in foreign currency should be converted into sterling on the date of the bankruptcy order. The exchange rate to be used is the middle market rate at the Bank of England as published for the date in question.
(iii) Periodical payments including rent.[4] The creditor may prove for any amounts due and unpaid at the date of the bankruptcy order including any amount which would have been due on that date if the periodical payment had been accruing from day to day.
(iv) Interest.[5] A creditor may claim interest if expressly agreed with the bankrupt. Where interest was not expressly agreed or reserved the creditor may include a claim for interest for the period up to the date of the bankruptcy order provided either:
(a) the debt is due under a written instrument and is payable at a certain time; or
(b) before the presentation of the petition a demand for payment was made in writing by or on behalf of the debtor and notice given that interest would be payable from the date of demand to the date of payment.
Interest would then be payable from the time certain for payment or date of demand, as appropriate, at the Bank of England middle market rate published on the day the bankruptcy order was made or the rate referred to in the written demand, if lower.
(v) Future debt. A creditor may prove for a debt payment of which was not due at the date of the bankruptcy order, but dividends' payable on such a debt must be adjusted in accordance with the formula specified in, r 11.13.[6]

(vi) Withdrawal or variation. A creditor's proof may at any time be withdrawn or varied in amount by agreement between the creditor and the trustee.[7]

[1] Insolvency Act 1986, s 303(2).
[2] Individual Insolvency Rules, 1986, r 6.110.
[3] Ibid, r 6.111, in the absence of a published rate the court may fix a rate.
[4] Ibid, r 6.112.
[5] Ibid, r. 6.113.
[6] Ibid, r. 6.114.
[7] Ibid, r. 6.106.

Secured creditors

16.6.5 A creditor who holds any security for his debt must give particulars of that security in his proof of debt, the date on which it was given and the value which he puts on his security.[1] He may subsequently alter the value placed on the security in his proof of debt, at any time, with the agreement of the trustee or the leave of the court.[2] The leave of the court must be obtained, however, if the secured creditor is the petitioner and has put a value on his security in the petition or has voted in respect of the unsecured balance of his debt.[3]

Should a secured creditor omit to disclose his security in his proof of debt, he must surrender it to the general benefit of creditors, unless the court on the creditor's application relieves him on the ground that the omission was inadvertent or the result of honest mistake. In granting relief, the court may require amendment of the proof of debt on such terms as may be just.[4]

The trustee may at any time redeem a creditor's security by serving notice that he intends to do so after 28 days from the date of the notice at the value put on it in the creditor's proof of debt. The creditor then has 21 days to revalue his security should he wish to do so, and where the security be revalued the trustee may only redeem it at the new value.[5] If the security is redeemed, any costs involved in transferring it are borne by the estate.[6] Should the trustee be dissatisfied with the value put on his security by the creditor, he may require the security to be offered for sale on such terms as he thinks fit after consultation with the creditor.[7] If the sale is by auction, the trustee, on behalf of the court or the creditor, on his own behalf, may appear and bid.[8]

A secured creditor may, by written notice, at any time call on the trustee to elect whether he will or will not exercise his power to redeem the security. The trustee then has six months in which to make his election.[9]

[1] Individual Insolvency Rules 1986, r 6.98(1)(g).
[2] Ibid, r 6.115(1). If a creditor subsequently realises his security the net amount realised shall be substituted for the value previously assessed by the creditor; ibid, r 6.119.
[3] Ibid, r 6.115(2).
[4] Ibid, r 6.116.
[5] Ibid, r 6.117(1) and (2) nb the trustee may allow the creditor a longer period than 21 days.
[6] Ibid, r 6.117(3).
[7] Ibid, r 6.118(1).
[8] Ibid, r 6.118(2).
[9] Ibid, r 6.117(4).

16.7 MANNER OF DISTRIBUTION

16.7.1 Whenever the trustee has sufficient funds, he is required,[1] subject to a proper retention or provision for the expenses of the bankruptcy, debts not proved or determined and disputed proofs and claims, to calculate and declare a dividend. The trustee must first give notice of his intention to declare a dividend to all creditors who have not proved their debts.[2] This notice must specify a date, termed 'the last date for proving' up to which proofs may be lodged. This date must be not less than 21 days from the date of the notice and must be the same for all creditors. The notice must also state the trustee's intention to declare a dividend, whether interim or final, within the period of four months from the last date for proving.[3] This period may, however, be postponed or the dividend cancelled by the trustee in the event that a creditor makes an application to the court to reverse or vary any decision taken by the trustee in respect of a proof,[4] and, except with the leave of the court no dividend may be declared while an application to reverse or vary a decision of the trustee or to expunge or reduce a proof is pending.[5] The trustee must deal with every proof within seven days from the last date of proving by admitting or rejecting it in whole or in part, or making such provision as he thinks fit in respect of it.[6] The trustee has a complete discretion as to whether he deals with proofs lodged after the last date for proving.[7]

1 Insolvency Act 1986, s 324.
2 Individual Insolvency Rules 1986, r 11.2; where the proposed distribution is to preferential creditors notice need only be given to such creditors, ibid, r 11.12.
3 Ibid, r 11.2(3).
4 Ibid, r 11.4.
5 Ibid, r 11.5. Nb the court may give leave to declare a dividend on terms that the trustee makes provision for the proof in question.
6 Ibid, r 11.3(1).
7 Ibid, r 11.3(2).

16.7.2 The trustee must give notice of the dividend containing the particulars prescribed by the Rules[1] to all creditors who have proved their debts. The dividend may be distributed with the notice. A creditor who has not proved his debt by the time a dividend is declared, or whose proof is increased after payment of a dividend, may not disturb the dividend because he did not participate in it. But he is entitled to payment of any dividend he missed from any monies in the hands of the trustee before any further dividends are declared.[2] An action does not lie against the trustee for a dividend either before or after it is declared. Where the trustee refuses to pay a dividend the creditor's remedy is to apply to the court[3] for an order that the dividend be paid, and on such application the court may order the trustee to pay not only the dividend but also interest at judgment rate from the date it was withheld, and the costs of the application proceedings.

1 Individual Insolvency Rules 1986, r 11.6.
2 Ibid, r 11.8; similarly a secured creditor who revalues his security so as to result in an increase in the value of his unsecured claim may not disturb declared dividends, but where the security is revalued upwards the creditor must forthwith repay any excess dividend already received, ibid, r 11.9.
3 An application may be made under the Insolvency Act 1986, s 303.

16.7.3 *Final distribution.* When the trustee is aware that the dividend of which he is giving notice is the final dividend he should specify this to be the case in his notice of intended dividend.[1] It may be, however, that the trustee is unable to declare a dividend at all or no further dividend to those already declared. In this event he must notify all creditors that no funds have been realised or, as the case may be, that the funds realised have already been distributed or used or allocated for defraying the expenses of administration.[2] Where a dividend is payable in respect of a debt payable at a future time the Rules[3] make provision for the calculation of a reduction of the amount of the creditor's proof. A dividend may be assigned by the creditor giving notice to the trustee.[4] Where a secured creditor contravenes any provision of the Insolvency Act 1986 or the Rules relating to the valuation of securities, the trustee may apply to the Court for an order that the creditor be wholly or partly disqualified from participation in any dividend.[5]

1 Individual Insolvency Rules 1986, r 11.2(3).
2 Ibid, r 11.7.
3 Ibid, r 11.13.
4 Ibid, r 11.11.
5 Ibid, r 11.10.

Final meeting

16.7.4 A trustee who is not the official receiver must summon a final general meeting of the bankrupt's creditors to receive his report of his administration of the estate.[1] This meeting determines whether he should have his release: see para 15.5 above. The final meeting may not be held until the trustee is able to report that the administration of the bankrupt's estate is, for practical purposes, complete. This includes a determination as to what should happen with the bankrupt's dwelling house or any home occupied by the bankrupt's spouse or former spouse if not by then realised. The Act provides[2] that the trustee may not summon a final meeting unless either:

(a) the court has made a charging order on the property for the benefit of the bankrupt's estate; or
(b) the court has declined to make an order on such an application; or
(c) the Secretary of State has issued a certificate to the trustee stating that it would be inappropriate or inexpedient for such an application to be made in the case in question.

1 Insolvency Act 1986, s 331, Individual Insolvency Rules 1986, r 6.137, form 6.35.
2 Ibid, s 332.

16.8 DISTRIBUTION TO CREDITORS

16.8.1 In comparison with the Bankruptcy Act 1914, the Insolvency Act 1986 removes the preferential category of debts, restricts the extent and amount of preferential claims and, in allowing a reasonable rate of interest to be paid on all debts, makes this a separate category of debt payable after the ordinary debts. The aim is to make more money available for ordinary creditors.

Order for payment

16.8.2 Repeating the unlikely assumption made in para 9.5 above that the trustee is able to realise enough to achieve a surplus in the estate for return to the bankrupt, the order of priority for payment is:[1]

(i) those entitled to payment of bankruptcy costs and expenses;
(ii) preferential creditors (debts but not interest);
(iii) ordinary creditors (debts but not interest);
(iv) interest on both preferential and ordinary creditors debts;
(v) bankrupt's spouse (debt and interest);
(vi) the bankrupt.

The debts of each class rank equally between themselves.

1 Insolvency Act 1986, ss 328, 329.

Bankruptcy costs and expenses

16.8.3 These are governed by the Rules.[1] They include as a first charge on the estate any expenses properly incurred in an abortive composition or scheme under the Act.[2]

1 Individual Insolvency Rules 1986, r 6.224 which lists the expenses of the bankruptcy in order of priority.
2 Insolvency Act 1986, s 276(2).

Preferential claims

16.8.4 These claims,[1] in contrast to the position under the Bankruptcy Act 1914, see para 9.5 above, are:

(a) deductions from emoluments made in respect of PAYE payments during the 12 months preceding the bankruptcy order, or appointment of interim receiver if any;
(b) VAT referable to and due within the period of six months preceding the bankruptcy;
(c) car tax, general betting duty, bingo duty, duty under Betting and Gaming Duties Act 1981, s 12(1), gaming licence duty referable to and due within the period of 12 months preceding the bankruptcy;
(d) Social Security Act 1975, Class 1, Class 2 or assessed Class 4 contributions for one year preceding the bankruptcy;
(e) contributions owed to occupational pension schemes (without limit in time);
(f) remuneration of employees payable in respect of the period of four months preceding the bankruptcy subject to a prescribed limit;
(g) accrued holiday remuneration owed to an employee (without limit in time); and
(h) money advanced for and applied to the payment of any debt which would have been a debt under (f) or (g) above. This is particularly important for banks which may be asked to pay wages when a business is going through a rough patch. Without the encouragement of preferential status for sums advanced for wages, banks may prefer to allow the business to go under.

It is to be noted that rates and the bankrupt's own income tax and other tax liabilities are no longer preferential claims but will rank with the ordinary debts.

1 See Insolvency Act 1986, Sch 6.

Ordinary claims

16.8.5 All debts not falling within any other category.

Interest

16.8.6 Interest is payable on both preferential and ordinary debts at the judgment rate[1] at the commencement of the bankruptcy or any contractual or other applicable rate (eg under the Bills of Exchange Act 1882) whichever is the greater.[2] All interest claims rank equally.

1 Ie the rate specified under the Judgments Act 1838, s 17.
2 Insolvency Act 1986, s 328(5).

Bankrupt's spouse

16.8.7 Debts owed in respect of credit provided by a person who was the bankrupt's spouse at the commencement of the bankruptcy, whether or not the individual concerned was a spouse at the time the credit was provided are deferred behind other creditors and claims for interest. Interest on spouse's debts is payable and ranks with the debt.

16.9 SECOND BANKRUPTCY

16.9.1 It is no bar to further bankruptcy proceedings that the debtor is an undischarged bankrupt. A court may therefore make a further adjudication. Under the Old Law there was a discretion when considering the petition, and the court could refuse to make a further bankruptcy order if satisfied that there were no assets available to comprise an estate to be administered under the second or subsequent bankruptcy.[1] It is arguable that such a discretion remains under the New Law.

1 *Re Betts* [1897] 1 QB 50.

16.9.2 Where a second or subsequent bankruptcy order is made, the provisions of the Insolvency Act 1986, ss 334, 335 are applicable. Where the existing trustee has been given the prescribed notice of the presentation of the petition for the later bankruptcy, any distribution or other disposition by him of anything in the specified categories of property shall be void unless made with the consent of or subsequently ratified by the court. The specified categories are:

(a) after acquired property of the bankrupt which vested in the existing trustee after the service of written notice;
(b) any money paid to the existing trustee under an income payment order; and

(c) any money in the hands of the existing trustee representating the proceeds of sale of property from category (a) or the application of money falling within category (a) or (b).

All such property as is comprised in the above three categories is to be treated as being comprised in the second bankruptcy estate,and until there is a trustee of the second estate, the existing trustee must deal with it in accordance with the Rules.[1] As may be necessary, the court may give consequential directions to modify an income payment order obtained on behalf of the existing or first estate to be transferred to the second estate. The existing trustee retains however a first charge over all such property for any bankruptcy expenses incurred by him in respect of its acquisition and administration.[2]

[1] Individual Insolvency Rules 1986, rr 6.226, 6.227.
[2] Ibid, r 6.228

16.9.3 The creditors in any earlier bankruptcy may not prove in any later bankruptcy in respect of the same debts. The existing trustee may, however, prove in the later bankruptcy for:

(a) the unsatisfied balance of debts provable against the bankrupt's estate in the earlier bankruptcy;
(b) any interest payable on that balance; and
(c) any unpaid expenses of the earlier bankruptcy.[1]

[1] Insolvency Act 1986, s 335(5).

CHAPTER 17

Effect of Bankruptcy on Other Transactions

17.1 PREFERENCES AND UNDERVALUED TRANSACTIONS

17.1.1 The Insolvency Act 1986[1] avoids the use of the term 'fraudulent' by which preferential transactions had come to be known under the 1914 Act and dispenses with the settlement and fraudulent conveyance provisions of that Act. For these provisions and the Old Law generally see para 8.4 above. In place of these provisions the Act renders liable to impeachment both transactions at an undervalue and 'preferences'. With the former the trustee can apply to the court for an order to restore the position to what it would have been had the bankrupt not entered into the transaction without reference to the bankrupt's state of mind when engaged in the transaction. With preferences the trustee must show that the bankrupt was 'influenced' in giving the preference by a desire to improve the creditor's position in the bankruptcy. In theory therefore the trustee has a lower hurdle to overcome in setting aside preferences than under the 1914 Act where the payment had to be made 'with a view' to give the creditor a preference in the bankruptcy. In either case where an individual is adjudged bankrupt and he has entered into a transaction with any person at an undervalue or given any person a preference within the relevant time period before the commencement of the bankruptcy, the trustee may seek an order under the Insolvency Act 1986, s 339 to restore the position to what it would have been had the bankrupt not entered into the undervalued transaction or given the preference.

[1] Insolvency Act 1986, ss 339-341.

17.1.2 *Undervalue transactions.* A transaction is at an undervalue if the individual concerned enters into a transaction with another person in which he:
(a) makes a gift or otherwise receives no consideration under the terms of that transaction;
(b) enters into the transaction in consideration of marriage; or
(c) enters into a transaction in which he provides a consideration which in money or money's worth is significantly less than the value of the consideration he receives.

Such a transaction may be impeached by the trustee if it took place within five years of the presentation of the petition provided that the individual was insolvent at the time of the transaction or became insolvent in consequence of that transaction. Where the transaction was with an associate of the individual[1] it is presumed that the individual was insolvent at the time of the transaction, unless the contrary is shown. Transactions entered into within two years of the presentation of the petition may be the subject of a s 339 order irrespective of the solvency of the individual at the time they were made.[2]

[1] 'Associate' is widely defined in the Insolvency Act 1986, s 435 and includes spouse, relative or spouse's relative and that relative's spouse, partner or partner's spouse, employer or beneficiary of a trust of which the bankrupt is trustee. For the purposes of s 339 an employee who does not come within any other class of associate is deemed not to be an associate of the individual: Insolvency Act 1986, ss 340(5), 341(1)(b).

[2] Insolvency Act 1986, s 341(2).

17.1.3 An individual is insolvent either (a) if he is unable to pay his debts as they fall due, or (b) where the value of his assets is less than the amount of his liabilities, taking into account his contingent and prospective liabilities.[1] The Insolvency Act 1986 does not define 'assets' but does define 'property' of which assets must be comprised. By s 436 of the Act:

> '"Property" includes money, goods, things in action, land and every description of property wherever situated and also obligations and every description of interest, whether present or future or vested or contingent, arising out of, or incidental to, property.'

Accordingly where it cannot be shown that the individual was not meeting his debts as they fell due, the determination of whether he was insolvent could well prove a complex balancing of assets and liabilities requiring consideration of all the prospective or contingent property and liabilities to which the individual was respectively entitled or subject. The value of the individual's future and contingent property is a matter for assessment by the court. Under the Old Law when considering the value of the individual's assets when determining his solvency for the purposes of avoiding a voluntary settlement, the value of any asset was the sum which could be raised on that asset at the date of the settlement, if necessary by forced sale.[2] But it should be noted that the test under the Bankruptcy Act 1914[3] was whether the individual making the settlement was able to pay all his debts *at the time of making the settlement* without the aid of the property comprised in the settlement. Under the New Law a comparison of assets and liabilities is required, and a valuation of assets on an 'immediate realisation' basis would not appear to be appropriate.

[1] Insolvency Act 1986, s 341(3).

[2] See, e g *Freeman v Pope* (1870) 5 Ch App 538 and *Re Butterworth, ex p Russell* (1882) 19 Ch D 588.

[3] Bankruptcy Act 1914, s 42(1).

17.1.4 *Preferences.* A preference is widely defined and includes anything which the individual does or allows to be done, which puts a creditor or guarantor into a better position than he would have been in had the thing not been done, in the event of the individual's bankruptcy. It is essential that the individual was influenced by a desire to give the creditor or guarantor a preference in any possible subsequent bankruptcy. Where the creditor or guarantor is an associate[1] of the individual it is presumed that the individual was so influenced unless the contrary is shown. It is to be noted that a preference is not prevented from being such by the fact only that it was done in pursuance of a court order.[2] The court is entitled to look behind the order and consider the circumstances in which it came to be made.

[1] See n 1 to para 17.1.2 above.
[2] Insolvency Act 1986, s 340(6).

17.1.5 A preference may only be impeached by the trustee where:[1]
(a) the bankrupt making it was insolvent at the time he made it or became insolvent in consequence of the preference; and
(b) the preference was made within six months of the presentation of the bankruptcy petition.

This period of six months is extended to two years in the case of associates of the bankrupt. Where, however, a transaction is both a preference and a transaction at an undervalue, it is to be treated as a transaction at an undervalue for the purposes of time limits and so the longer time periods applicable to undervalue transactions will apply.

[1] Insolvency Act 1986, s 341(1).

17.1.6 It will be noted that a preference for the purposes of a s 339 order may be given not only to a creditor of the individual but also to a guarantor or surety for any of the individual's debts or liabilities. Any act which has the effect of putting a guarantor into a better position is a preference. Accordingly an act which is done by the individual with a view to benefitting himself, which has the effect of putting his guarantor into a better position, will be a preference which may be the subject of a s 339 order. This is in contrast with the position on fraudulent preferences under the Old Law.[1] Payments made to any person in trust for or as agent for a creditor or guarantor will also have the effect of putting the creditor or guarantor into a better position in the event of the bankruptcy of the individual making the payments and may qualify as preferences.

[1] See eg *Tomkins v Saffery* (1877) 3 App Cas 213.

17.1.7 The act or thing constituting a preference for the purpose of a s 339 order must have been influenced by a desire to produce a better position for the creditor or guarantor in any subsequent bankruptcy. This is a different test than that required for fraudulent preferences under the Old Law which had to be made 'with a view', ie a principal or dominant view of giving the preference. For the trustee to have to show only that the individual was 'influenced' by a desire to prefer is a lesser burden than having to prove that the making of the preference was the principal or dominant view. There may in future be some cases where the lesser test produces a different result. In the main, however, the considerations under the New Law are likely to be much the same as under the Old Law, and the principal investigation remain whether the act was done voluntarily or under bona fide pressure from the creditor or guarantor.[1] Thus where a payment is made or other act done because of real pressure by the creditor or guarantor, in particular the threat of legal proceedings, it is unlikely that the creditor or guarantor has been preferred. Whether the creditor or guarantor applied pressure is not the only consideration. There may be circumstances which are sufficient to show that the individual was not in any way motivated by an intention to prefer.[2] But where the individual pays one or more debts while leaving others unpaid as they fall due there must be a strong inference that in the absence of bona fide pressure he is influenced in preferring those creditors whom he does pay. The ultimate question, however, is the individual's state of mind at the date on which he made the payment or did the act in question.

1 For cases on 'pressure' by a creditor or guarantor under the Old Law see e g *Sharp v Jackson* [1899] AC 419; *Re Cooper, ex p Hall* [1882] 19 Ch D 580; *Re Cutts, ex p Bognor Mutual Building Society v Trustee in Bankruptcy* [1956] 2 All ER 537; *Re Allen Fairhead & Sons Ltd* (1971) 115 Sol Jo 244.
2 For examples under the Old Law see 5 The Digest (Re-Issue) Part XX, Section 12(4) C-G, pp 944–962.

17.1.8 *Criminal bankruptcy.* The time period in which undervalue transactions and preferences in criminal bankruptcies may be impeached will commence on the date specified for the purpose in the criminal bankruptcy order.[1] The time periods stated above for other bankruptcies do not apply. No order under s 339 may be made pending any appeal against the conviction on which the criminal bankruptcy order was made.

1 Insolvency Act 1986, s 341(4).

17.1.9 *Orders under s 339.* In making an order under s 339 to restore the position to that which it would have been had the bankrupt not made the undervalue transaction or preference the court has a complete discretion. Without prejudice to this discretion the Act[1] sets out seven heads of possible orders that the court may make to which the reader is referred.

An order under s 339 may impose an obligation on a person or affect his property whether or not he was a party to the transaction or preference, provided always that:

(a) the interests of any bona fide purchaser of property for value without notice of the relevant circumstances[2] or person deriving title through such a purchaser are not prejudiced; and
(b) no requirement to pay a sum to the trustee may be imposed upon a person who received a benefit from the transaction or preference in good faith for value without notice of the relevant circumstances[2] except where he was a party to the transaction or received the preference as a creditor of the bankrupt.[3] Any sum paid to the trustee in accordance with an order under s 339 is to form part of the bankrupt's estate.[4]

1 Insolvency Act 1986, s 342. See Appendix 1.
2 As defined in the Insolvency Act 1986, s 342(4) namely the circumstances by virtue of which an order under s 339 would be made if the individual concerned were adjudged bankrupt within the appropriate period *and* if the period has expired, the fact that the individual was adjudged bankrupt.
3 Insolvency Act 1986, s 339(3).
4 Ibid, s 340(3).

17.1.10 Generally, it should be noted that the provisions in bankruptcy relating to preferences and undervalue transactions are almost precisely the same as those affecting company liquidations,[1] the drafting suitably modified for the law of bankruptcy. Accordingly, decisions of the court with respect to company preferences and undervalue transactions are likely to be of direct relevance to such cases in bankruptcy.

[1] Insolvency Act 1986, ss 238–241.

17.2 OTHER TRANSACTIONS WHICH MAY BE AVOIDED

17.2.1 The Act also provides for the avoiding of any of the following:
(1) extortionate credit transactions;
(2) general assignment of book debts not registered under the Bills of Sale Act 1878;
(3) execution against goods or land, or the attachment of debts not completed before the commencement of the bankruptcy;
(4) distress for rent save for six months' rent accrued due before the commencement of the bankruptcy;
(5) a lien or other right to possession of books papers or other records of the bankrupt to the extent that the official receiver or trustee could be denied possession; and
(6) transactions to defraud creditors.

1 Extortionate credit transactions

17.2.2 Extortionate credit transactions entered into within three years of the commencement of the bankruptcy may be reopened by the court on the application of the trustee.[1] Any transaction for, or involving the provision of credit to the bankrupt may be the subject of an order. The transaction is extortionate if, having regard to the risk accepted by the person providing credit:
(a) the terms of it require grossly exorbitant payments to be made for the provision of credit, whether unconditionally or on any contingency; and
(b) it otherwise grossly contravenes ordinary principles of fair dealing.
It is immaterial that the transaction was completed before the commencement of the bankruptcy, provided that it was entered into by the bankrupt within three years of his bankruptcy.

[1] Insolvency Act 1986, s 343.

17.2.3 The onus of proof is on the creditor seeking to uphold the transaction to prove that it was not extortionate.[1] Where the court does reopen a transaction there is a wide discretion as to the order which may be made. There is express power in the Act[2] to:
(a) set aside in whole or in part any obligation arising under the transaction;
(b) vary either the terms of the transaction or the terms on which any security is held;
(c) require any party to the transaction to repay to the trustee any sums paid by the bankrupt;

(d) require any person to surrender any property held as security to the trustee; and
(e) direct accounts to be taken.
Any sums recovered by the trustee under an order are comprised in the bankrupt's estate.

[1] Insolvency Act 1986, s 343(3).
[2] Ibid, s 343(4).

17.2.4 The power of the trustee to apply for an order to reopen an extortionate credit transaction under the Act is in place of the general power to reopen extortionate credit bargains under the Consumer Credit Act 1974.[1] Neither a trustee nor an undischarged bankrupt may make an application under the Consumer Credit Act. While the provisions of the relevant sections of each Act are broadly similar it may be noted that the Insolvency Act 1986 grants the court a complete discretion in making orders in respect of extortionate transactions whereas the Consumer Credit Act provides that the court may make an order 'for the purpose of relieving the debtor from payment of any sum in excess of that fairly due and reasonable'. Nevertheless it is envisaged that in making orders the court will not penalise the creditor but so adjust the transaction as to make it accord with the ordinary views of fair credit terms at the date on which the transaction was entered into. A similar provision applies in the case of company liquidation.[2]

[1] S 139. Compare generally Consumer Credit Act 1974, ss 137–139, and in particular s 138 which goes into greater detail than does the Insolvency Act as to the considerations applicable to the determination whether a credit bargain is 'extortionate', and see para 29.1.4ff below.
[2] Insolvency Act 1986, s 244.

2 General assignment of book debts

17.2.5 Where the bankrupt was engaged in any business and has made a general assignment to another person of his existing or future book debts, or any class of them, the assignment is void against the trustee unless the assignment has been registered under the Bills of Sale Act 1878.[1] This provision only applies to book debts which were not paid before presentation of the petition; those that were paid remain valid in the hands of the assignee. This provision repeats the position in respect of book debts under the Bankruptcy Act 1914.[2] 'Assignment' is defined to include any assignment by way of security or charge. Specific assignments are not caught by this provision, and therefore the following assignments are not void, namely of book debts:
(a) due at the date of assignment from specified debtors;
(b) becoming due under specified contracts;
(c) included in a transfer of a business made in good faith and for value; and
(d) included in an assignment of assets for the benefit of creditors generally.
For the purposes of registration under the Bills of Sale Act an assignment of book debts is treated as if it were a bill of sale given otherwise then by way of security for the payment of a sum of money.

[1] Insolvency Act 1986, s 344.
[2] Bankruptcy Act 1914, s 43.

3 Enforcement procedures

17.2.6 A creditor who has issued execution against a debtor's land or goods or attached a debt due to the debtor is not entitled to retain the benefit of the execution or attachment of any sums paid to avoid it unless the execution or attachment was completed or the sums paid before the commencement of the bankruptcy.[1] For the purposes of this provision the execution or attachment is complete in the following circumstances:

(a) in the case of an execution of goods by seizure or sale or by the making of a charging order under the Charging Orders Act 1979, s 1;
(b) in the case of an execution against land by seizure or the appointment of a receiver or by the making of a charging order; or
(c) where there is an attachment of a debt by the receipt of that debt.

[1] Insolvency Act 1986, s 346. These provisions restate in an expanded form the provisions of the Bankruptcy Act 1914, ss 40 and 41 as amended by the Charging Orders Act 1979, s 4.

17.2.6.1 *Sheriff's duties.* Where goods have been taken in execution and before the completion of the execution, notice is given to the sheriff (or any other officer levying execution) that the debtor has been adjudged bankrupt, then at the request of the official receiver or trustee the sheriff must deliver up the goods and any money received or recovered in part satisfaction of the execution. The costs of the execution then become a first charge on the goods or money delivered up.

Where the sheriff is levying execution in respect of a sum exceeding the prescribed sum[1] and sells any goods or accepts money to avoid a sale the sheriff must keep the balance of the proceeds of sale or money received after deducting the costs of execution for a period of 14 days. For if before the end of the 14-day period he is given notice that a bankruptcy petition has been presented against the debtor the sheriff must not dispose of this balance until the petition is heard and if a bankruptcy order is made he must pay the balance to the official receiver or trustee.[2]

There is, however, a general power in the court to set aside the right of the official receiver or trustee in favour of the creditor who has issued execution or attachment on such terms as may be thought fit. Further, the interest of any person who has acquired goods under a sheriff's sale in good faith is unassailable by the trustee. These restrictions on the sheriff's duties of execution do not apply to after acquired property unless before the execution is complete the trustee has claimed the property for the bankrupt's estate and has served a copy of his s 307 notice claiming the property on the sheriff.

[1] Prescribed sum, is £500; Insolvency Proceedings (Monetary Limits) Order 1986, SI 1986/1996.
[2] Insolvency Act 1986, s 346(3) and (4).

4 Distress for rent

17.2.7 See para 29.2.8 below.

5 Liens

17.2.8 Liens or other rights to retain possession of any of the books, papers or other records of the bankrupt are enforceable to the extent that possession would be denied to the official reciever or trustee.[1] This power of the official receiver or trustee to override liens does not apply to a lien on any document which gives title to property and is held for the purpose of proving title.

[1] Insolvency Act 1986, s 349.

6 Transactions to defraud creditors

17.2.9 The Act provides for a general power in the court to make an appropriate order where a person has entered into a transaction with another person at an undervalue for the purpose of putting his assets beyond the reach of any person who is making or may at some time make a claim against that person and thereby prejudicing satisfaction of the claim if successful.[1] An application for such an order is not restricted to cases where the person concerned has become bankrupt, and is covered in more detail in ch 20 below. In the case of a bankrupt, the official receiver or trustee may apply for an order restoring the bankrupt's position to what it would have been had the transaction not been entered into by the bankrupt. Any individual prejudiced by the transaction in question may also apply for an order, but only with the leave of the court where the relevant person has been adjudged bankrupt.[2]

[1] Insolvency Act 1986, ss 423–425.
[2] Ibid, s 424(1)(a).

17.3 UNEXECUTED CONTRACTS AND APPRENTICESHIPS

17.3.1 *Unexecuted contracts.* Where a contract to which a person who subsequently becomes bankrupt is not fully executed before the commencement of the bankruptcy, another party to that contract may apply to the court for an order discharging obligations under that contract on such terms as to payment of damages for non-performance or otherwise as appears equitable.[1] Any damages payable by the bankrupt are provable as a bankruptcy debt. This helpful provision obviates the necessity for contracting parties who have claims against the bankrupt from issuing or continuing with proceedings against the trustee. Their rights, if any, may be adjudicated by the court in the bankruptcy. And, by way of exception to the general rule, where an undischarged bankrupt is a joint contractor with another person, that person may sue on the contract without joining the bankrupt to the proceedings.[2]

[1] Insolvency Act 1986, s 345.
[2] Ibid, s 345(4), and see RSC Ord 15, r 4.

17.3.2 *Apprenticeships and articled clerks.* The indenture of apprenticeship or articles of agreement of an apprentice or articled clerk are discharged from the commencement of the bankruptcy where the bankrupt or his apprentice or clerk gives notice of termination.[1] The apprentice or articled clerk then has two alternative courses open to him:
(a) where he has paid money to the bankrupt as a fee he may apply to the

trustee for a payment. The trustee is then empowered to pay such sum as he considers reasonable having regard to the amount of the fee the proportion of the period in respect of which the fee was paid which has been served by the apprentice or clerk and all other circumstances of the case. This power of the trustee to make a payment has priority over the obligations of the trustee to distribute the estate; or

(b) he may apply to the trustee to transfer his indenture or articles to some other person. In this even the apprentice or clerk forgoes his right to a payment from the estate.

[1] Insolvency Act 1986, s 348.

17.4 TRANSITIONAL PROVISIONS

17.4.1 The Insolvency Act 1986, Sch 11, para 17, provides that a preference given, assignment made or other transaction entered into before 29 December 1986 shall not be set aside under any of the provisions of ss 339–344 of the Act except to the extent that it could have been set aside under the law in force immediately before that date. The provisions of this law, the Old Bankruptcy Law under the Bankruptcy Act 1914, are dealt with in ch 8 above.

17.4.2 The setting aside of a preference, assignment or other transaction for the purposes of the transitional provisions includes the making of any order which varies or reverses any effect of a preference, assignment or other transaction.[1]

[1] Insolvency Act 1986, Sch 11, para 17(2).

CHAPTER 18

Discharge and Annulment

18.1 DISCHARGE

18.1.1 The bankruptcy of any individual against whom a bankruptcy order has been made commences with the day on which the order is made and continues until that individual is discharged.[1] The Insolvency Act 1986 continues the move towards automatic discharge begun with the Insolvency Act 1976. For some years to come, there will be a number of different categories of bankruptcy from the viewpoint of discharge from bankruptcy. These categories are listed and discussed in ch 10 above.

[1] Insolvency Act 1986, s 278.

18.1.2 The Insolvency Act 1986 draws the distinction between the individual who has been adjudicated bankrupt on a criminal bankruptcy petition or who has been an undischarged bankrupt at the time during the period of 15 years preceding the making of the bankruptcy order and any other cases. Automatic discharge applies to the latter cases.[1] It operates after three years from the commencement of the bankruptcy unless a certificate for the summary administration of the bankrupt's estate has been issued and not revoked. In this event, the bankrupt is automatically discharged after a period of two years from the commencement of the bankruptcy.[2] When the bankrupt is discharged he may require the Secretary of State to give notice in the *Gazette* or in any newspaper in which the bankruptcy was advertised.[3] Should the bankrupt wish to do so he may apply to the court for a certificate of his discharge showing the date from which it is effective.[4]

[1] Insolvency Act 1986, s 279(1).
[2] Ibid, s 279(2).
[3] Individual Insolvency Rules 1986, r 6.220(2).
[4] Ibid, r 6.220(1).

18.1.3 The relevant period for automatic discharge, whether two years or three, may be suspended by order of the court if satisfied, on the application of the official receiver, that an undischarged bankrupt has failed or is failing to comply with any of his obligations under the bankruptcy.[1] On making such an application, the official receiver must file a report setting out the reasons in support of his application and serve a copy on the bankrupt and his trustee at least 21 days before the hearing. The bankrupt should, not later than seven days before the hearing, file in court and serve on the official receiver, a notice specifying which statement in the official receiver's report he intends to deny or dispute[2] a procedure similar to that on an application by the bankrupt for his discharge when the automatic discharge provisions do not apply. An order of the court on such an application may provide that the relevant period shall cease to run for a specified period of time or shall cease to run at all until the bankrupt fulfils specified conditions. The court may leave the official receiver to determine whether conditions are satisfied or may require the bankrupt to satisfy the court that he has complied with whatever conditions have been specified in the order. After a period of suspension has expired or conditions fulfilled, the bankrupt may apply to the court for the order of suspension to be discharged and a certificate issued stating that the suspension has been lifted.[3]

1 Application is made by the official receiver under the Insolvency Act 1986, s 279(3).
2 Individual Insolvency Rules 1986, r 6.215.
3 Ibid, r 6.216.

18.1.4 The criminal bankrupt, or the bankrupt who has been bankrupt before within 15 years of his present bankruptcy, may only be discharged by an order of the court.[1] He must wait at least five years from the commencement of the bankruptcy before applying for discharge which is obtained by the order of the court under the Insolvency Act 1986.[2] Applications under the Insolvency Act 1986, s 280 are likely to follow the practice which has developed for equivalent applications under the Bankruptcy Act 1914, s 26, see para 10.3 above. The official receiver is obliged to make a report to the court on the prescribed matters relating to the bankrupt's conduct and affairs.[3] On the hearing of the application for discharge, the court may make or refuse the order, or make a conditional order of discharge.[4] An order of discharge may be suspended for any period the court considers fit or pending the fulfillment of any conditions laid down by the court. The suspended order of discharge may be contrasted with a conditional order of discharge. The latter is an order of discharge (which may be suspended) which is subject to conditions requiring the bankrupt to pay over either income or property which he acquires after his discharge to the general benefit of his creditors. The court is given a complete discretion under the Insolvency Act 1986, s 280 to impose any such conditions as it thinks fit.[5] It should be noted, however, that the provisions for income payments orders under the Insolvency Act 1986, s 310 expressly allow the court on an application under the Insolvency Act 1986, s 280 to make an income payments order which continues or takes effect after the bankrupt's discharge.

1 Insolvency Act 1986, s 279(1).
2 Ibid, s 280(1) and Individual Insolvency Rules 1986, r 6.217.
3 Insolvency Act 1986, s 289(2); prescribed matters, see Individual Insolvency Rules 1986, r 6.218.

[4] Insolvency Act 1986, s 280(2). The order takes effect from the date on which it is made: Individual Insolvency Rules 1986, r 6.219, but it is not issued or gazetted until the time allowed for appealing has expired or any appeal determined: r 6.221.

[5] These provisions are markedly simpler than the equivalent law under the Bankruptcy Act 1914, s 26 as amended by the Bankruptcy (Amendment) Act 1926, s 1. Some assistance may yet be had from decisions under the Old Law, see 4 Digest (Re-Issue) Part XVIII, Section 3 and *Re Badcock, ex p Badcock* (1886) 3 Morr 138; *Re Barker, ex p Constable* (1890) 25 QBD 285; *Re Freeman ex p Freeman* (1890) 7 Morr 38; *Re Tobias & Co, ex p Tobias* [1891] 1 QB 463; *Re Swabey, ex p Swabey* (1897) 76 LT 534; *Re Gaskell* [1904] 2 KB 478; and *Re Smith* [1947] 1 All ER 769.

18.2 EFFECT OF DISCHARGE

18.2.1 The discharge, whether automatic or by order, releases the bankrupt from all the bankruptcy debts.[1] The bankruptcy debts comprise:[2]

(a) any debt or liability to which the bankrupt is subject at the date on which the bankruptcy order is made, including contingent and unliquidated debts or liabilities;
(b) any debt or liability to which the bankrupt becomes subject after the commencement of his bankruptcy (including after his discharge from bankruptcy) by reason of any obligation incurred before the commencement of the bankruptcy;
(c) any amount specified in any criminal bankruptcy order; and
(d) any interest due on provable debts or liabilities.

Liabilities of the bankrupt in tort may be bankruptcy debts. For the purposes of proving in the bankruptcy and therefore release or discharge, the bankrupt is deemed to become subject to the liability in tort by reason of an obligation incurred at the time when the cause of action accrued.[3]

[1] Insolvency Act 1986, s 281(1).
[2] Ibid, s 382(1).
[3] Ibid, s 382(2).

18.2.2 Discharge does not release the bankrupt from, or affect the interests of the creditor in, the following categories of debt:

(i) Secured debts. The creditor remains entitled to enforce his security after the bankrupt's discharge though the bankrupt will be released from the debt itself.[1]
(ii) Fraud or fraudulent breach of trust. The bankrupt remains liable after discharge in respect of any bankruptcy debt which was either incurred by, or forbearance in respect of which was secured by the fraud or fraudulent breach of trust of the bankrupt.[2]
(iii) Fines or recognisances. The bankrupt remains liable to pay fines imposed for criminal offences or any liability due under a recognisance. In the case of a public revenue penalty or recognisance, the Treasury may consent to a release.[3]
(iv) Personal injury damages or maintenance orders. Save to such extent and to such conditions as the court may direct, discharge does not release a bankrupt from any bankruptcy debt which comprises damages for personal injury, whatever the cause of action, or arises under any order made in family or domestic proceedings.[4]

(v) Prescribed debts. Discharge does not release the bankrupt for such debts as are not provable in the bankruptcy which are prescribed by the Rules.[5]

[1] Insolvency Act 1986, s 281(2).
[2] Insolvency Act 1986, s 281(3).
[3] Insolvency Act 1986, s 281(4) and (8). 'Fine' (see Magistrates Courts Act 1980, s 150(1) includes any pecuniary penalty or pecuniary forfeiture or pecuniary compensation payable under a conviction.
[4] Insolvency Act 1986, s 281(5) and (8). 'Personal injuries' includes death and any disease or other impairment of a person's physical or mental condition. 'Family proceedings' are defined by reference to the Matrimonial and Family Proceedings Act 1984, Part V. Section 32 of that Act defines 'family business' as business of any description which in the High Court is for the time being assigned to the Family Division and to no other Division by or under the Supreme Court Act 1981, s 61, Sch 1. 'Family proceedings' are proceedings which are family business. 'Domestic proceedings' are proceedings so defined in the Magistrates' Courts Act 1980, s 65 meaning proceedings under the following enactments: Maintenance Orders (Facilities for Enforcement) Act 1920, National Assistance Act 1948, ss 43 and 44, Marriage Act 1949, s 3, Affiliation Proceedings Act 1957, Guardianship of Minors Acts 1971 and 1973, Maintenance Orders (Reciprocal Enforcement) Act 1972, Part I, Children Act 1975, Part II, Adoption Act 1976 (except s 34: proceedings to remove a child from unsuitable surroundings), Supplementary Benefits Act 1976, ss 18 and 19, Domestic Proceedings and Magistrates' Courts Act 1978, Part I, Child Care Act 1980, ss 47, 49 and 50, Magistrates' Court Act 1980, s 60.
[5] Insolvency Act 1986, s 281(6), and see Individual Insolvency Rules 1986, r 6.223, confiscation order under Drug Trafficking Offences Act 1986, s 1.

18.2.3 The discharge of the bankrupt has no effect on the administration of the bankruptcy should that not be complete at the date of discharge.[1] The trustee continues to carry out his function and the discharged bankrupt continues to owe his duty to the trustee to provide information, attend on the trustee and do all such things as the trustee may reasonably require of him.[2] The rights of creditors in the bankruptcy are not affected by discharge and a creditor may even prove in the bankruptcy after discharge. The trustee, of course, retains his responsibility to the creditors for the proper administration of the estate.

[1] Insolvency Act 1986, s 281(1).
[2] Ibid, s 333(3).

18.2.4 No other person's rights are affected or improved by the bankrupt's discharge. Thus a partner or co-trustee of the bankrupt or any other person who is jointly liable with the bankrupt remains liable in respect of the relevant liability even though the bankrupt has been released from such liability. Equally a guarantor or any person who stands in the position of surety to the guarantor remains liable to the creditor even though the bankrupt is released by his discharge from any future liability on the principal debt.[1]

[1] Insolvency Act 1986, s 281(7).

18.3 DISQUALIFICIATIONS

18.3.1 The undischarged bankrupt is disqualified from holding a number of offices and most notably, he is disqualified from:

(a) sitting or voting in the House of Lords;
(b) being elected to or sitting or voting in the House of Commons; and
(c) sitting or voting in a committee of either House.[1]

A member of the House of Commons who continues to be disqualified by reason of bankruptcy for a period of six months after adjudication, must vacate his seat.[2] This disqualification is removed immediately on discharge.[3]

[1] Insolvency Act 1986, s 427(1).
[2] Ibid, s 427(4).
[3] Ibid, s 427(4).

18.3.2 Other offices or positions from which an undischarged bankrupt is disqualified include:
(a) membership of local valuation panel;[1]
(b) membership of local authority;[2]
(c) the holding of a solicitors' practising certificate;[3]
(d) membership of land drainage committee[4]
(e) practising on his own behalf as an estate agent;[5] and
(f) appointment as superintendent registrar or registrar of births and deaths or registrar of marriages.[6]

Under the New Law such disqualifications cease on discharge. Previously, disqualification could continue for up to five years after discharge.

[1] General Rate Act 1967, s 90(2) as amended by Insolvency Act 1985, Sch 8, para 14.
[2] Local Government Act 1972, s 81(1) as amended by Insolvency Act 1985, sch 8, para 22.
[3] Solicitors Act 1974, ss 12 and 15.
[4] Land Drainage Act 1976, Sch 1 para 8 as amended by the Insolvency Act 1985, Sch 8, para 29.
[5] Estate Agents Act 1979, s 23(2).
[6] Registration of Births, Deaths and Marriages Regulations 1968, SI 1968/2049, reg 5.

18.3.3 The Company Directors Disqualification Act 1986 prohibits an undischarged bankrupt from acting directly or indirectly as a director of a company[1] save with leave of the court by which he was made bankrupt.[2] Securing his discharge releases the bankrupt from this inhibition. An application for leave to act as a director of a company or to take part in, or be concerned in the promotion, formation or management of a company is governed by the Individual Insolvency Rules.[3] The application must be supported by affidavit specifying the prescribed matters[4] and notice of the application must be given to the official receiver and the trustee.[5] The official receiver may serve a report not less than 14 days before the hearing date and the bankrupt should specify not less than seven days before the hearing date which statements in the official receiver's report he intends to dispute.[6] The official receiver and the trustee may appear on the hearing of the application and question the bankrupt.[7] If the court grants the bankrupt's application for leave under the Company Directors Disqualification Act 1986, s 11, the order must specify what it is that the bankrupt has leave to do.[8]

[1] As defined in the Company Directors Disqualification Act, s 22.
[2] Ibid, s 11(1) and (3).
[3] Individual Insolvency Rules 1986, Part 6, Chap 20.
[4] Ibid, r 6.203(1), (2), (3) and (4).
[5] Ibid, r 6.204(1).

[6] Ibid, r 6.204(2) and (3).
[7] Ibid, r 6.204(4).
[8] Ibid, r 6.205.

18.4 ANNULMENT

18.4.1 An order of annulment restores the bankrupt to his pre-bankruptcy status and he remains fully liable for all bankruptcy debts. It is to be contrasted with an order for discharge which releases the bankrupt from those debts. The fact that a bankrupt has become discharged from his bankruptcy does not prevent him applying for and obtaining an order of annulment.[1] Quite apart from any personal considerations a bankrupt may have for seeking an annulment of a bankruptcy order against him, whether relating to disqualification or otherwise, a bankruptcy which has been annulled is to be disregarded on any subsequent bankruptcy when determining whether or not the bankrupt is entitled to automatic discharge in that subsequent bankruptcy.[2]

[1] Insolvency Act 1986, ss 279(4), 282(3).
[2] Ibid, s 282(5), and see para 18.1.3 above.

18.4.2 There are five grounds on which a bankruptcy order may be annulled:
(a) the order ought not to have been made on any grounds existing at the date of the order;[1]
(b) the bankruptcy debts and expenses have all been paid or secured to the satisfaction of the court;[2]
(c) a composition or scheme in respect of the bankruptcy debts has been approved by the creditors' meeting called to consider it;[3]
(d) the petition on which the order was made was pending at a time when a criminal bankruptcy order was made;[4] and
(e) a criminal bankruptcy must be annulled where the relevant criminal bankruptcy order is rescinded on appeal.[4]

The first two ground are grounds for annulment under the Old Bankruptcy Law and in their application to the Old Bankruptcy Law are considered in paras 11.3 and 11.4 above. The court's power to order annulment is discretionary and where the merits of the case or the behaviour of the bankrupt justifies it, the court may refuse to annul an order for technical reasons or where the debts have been paid in full. Where a composition or scheme has been approved, no order of annulment may be made within 28 days of the date on which the chairman of the meeting's report to the court is made, or an application to the court challenging the meeting's decision to approve the scheme is pending.[5] Again, the jurisdiction of the court to order annulment is discretionary.

[1] Insolvency Act 1986, s 282(1)(a).
[2] Ibid, s 282(1)(b).
[3] Ibid, s 261(1).
[4] Ibid, s 282(2).
[5] Ibid, s 261(2) and see para 12.3 above.

18.4.3. *Criminal bankruptcy.* The fourth ground listed above enables a criminal bankruptcy consequent upon a criminal bankruptcy order to take precedence over a bankruptcy ordered on a petition presented by a creditor, the debtor or supervisor of voluntary arrangements which was presented after the date of the criminal bankruptcy order. The official petitioner may apply to the court for an order annulling such other petition where:

(a) that petition was pending at a time when a criminal bankruptcy order was made or was presented after the criminal bankruptcy order was made; or
(b) no appeal is pending against the conviction on which the criminal bankruptcy order was made.[1]

The power of the court is described in discretionary terms but presumably the annulment will invariably be made where the official petitioner has or is about to present a petition for a criminal bankruptcy under the Insolvency Act 1986, s 302(1) (d).

[1] Insolvency Act 1986, s 282(2).

18.4.4 *Acts of administration prior to annulment.* Whenever an order of annulment is made, any sale or other disposition of property, any payment made or any other action duly done by the official receiver, trustee in bankruptcy or person acting on their behalf, or by the court, is, and remains, valid.[1]

[1] Insolvency Act 1986, s 282(4)(a).

18.4.5 *Revesting of estate.* On making an order of annulment, the court makes any necessary consequential directions.[1] Should any part of the bankrupt's estate be vested in the official receiver or trustee, the court may vest it in such person as may be appointed or revest it in the bankrupt.

[1] Insolvency Act 1986, s 282(4)(b); Individual Insolvency Rules 1986 r 6.213.

18.4.6 *Criminal offences.* An individual, the bankruptcy order against whom is annulled, may neverthless be prosecuted for a bankruptcy offence but proceedings for an offence may not be instituted after the annulment.[1]

[1] Insolvency Act 1986, s 350(2).

18.4.7 *Procedure.* Where an application is made by the bankrupt under grounds (a) or (b) of those listed at para 18.4.2 above, the applicant should state in his notice of application[1] on which of these grounds he relies.[2] The application must be supported by an affidavit, and in the case of an application on ground (b), namely that the debts and expenses have all been paid or secured, it must set out the matters required by the rules[3] namely that:

(a) all bankruptcy debts which have been proved have been paid in full, subject to debts falling under the following head,
(b) where a debt is disputed or a creditor who has proved his debt cannot be traced the bankrupt has given adequate security either by a payment into court or by a bond entered into with approved sureties.

The affidavit need not deal expressly with the payment of bankruptcy expenses. The applicant must give not less than 28 days' notice of the hearing, together with copies of the application and supporting affidavit to the trustee or official receiver.[4] He is required to prepare a report not less than 21 days before the date fixed for the hearing dealing with the following matters:[5]

1 the circumstances leading to the bankruptcy;
2 a summary of the bankrupt's assets and liabilities both at the commencement of the bankruptcy and the date of the application;
3 details of any creditors who he knows have claims but have not proved;
4 any other relevant information for the court; and
5 the extent and the manner in which the debts and expenses of the bankruptcy have been paid or secured.

This report is to be sent to the applicant at least 14 days from the hearing date and the applicant may file further evidence.[6] Where a trustee has been appointed he must send a copy of the report of the official receiver.[7]

[1] See form 7.2.
[2] Individual Insolvency Rules 1986, r 6.206.
[3] Ibid, r 6.211.
[4] Ibid, r 6.206(4).
[5] Ibid, r 6.207(2) and (3).
[6] Ibid, r 6.207(4).
[7] Ibid, r 6.207(5).

18.4.8 The trustee must attend the hearing of the application. At or before the hearing the court may stay the proceedings[1] on the ex parte application of any person interested, or in the case of an application on the ground that all debts have been paid or secured, adjourn the application so as to enable creditors who have not proved their debts to have a further 21 days in which to do so.[2] If the court makes an order of annulment it should be in form 6.71,[3] and where the official receiver has notified creditors of the bankruptcy he must notify them of the annulment.[4] The court notifies the Secretary of State of the annulment order, and the former bankrupt may require the Secretary of State to give notice of the order in the *Gazette* and in any newspaper in which the bankruptcy order was advertised.[5] The former bankrupt must apply in writing and may be required to pay the costs of the advertisement before it takes place.

[1] Individual Insolvency Rules 1986, r 6.208.
[2] Ibid, r 6.209.
[3] Ibid, r 6.210(3) and the order must include provision for the vacation of the registration of the bankruptcy petition as a pending action and of the bankruptcy order in the register of writs and orders affecting land, r 6.213(1).
[4] Ibid, r 6.212, the expense of giving notification falls on the former bankrupt.
[5] Ibid, r 6.213(2) and (3).

18.4.9 *Trustee's final account.* The annulment order where made under the Insolvency Act 1986, s 282 does not release the trustee from any duty or obligation imposed on him to account for all his transactions in connection with the former bankrupt's estate.[1] The trustee must prepare a final account and submit it to the Secretary of State as soon as practicable after the making of the order.[2] This final account is filed in court and must be reconciled with the account held by the Secretary of State.[3] The trustee obtains his release from such time as the court may determine.[4] An annulment order releases the official receiver from his duties to send reports to the creditors.[5]

1 Individual Insolvency Rules 1986, r 6.214(1).
2 Ibid, r 6.214(2).
3 Ibid, r 6.214(3).
4 Ibid, r 6.214(4).
5 Ibid, r 6.78.

CHAPTER 19

Bankruptcy Offences

19.1 OFFENCES COMMITTED BY BANKRUPT

19.1.1 The Insolvency Act 1986, Second Group of Parts, Chap VI specifies a number of offences which may be committed by the bankrupt either (a) after an order has been made on a bankruptcy petition presented against him or (b) by acts done prior to the commencement of the bankruptcy which may become offences after a bankruptcy order has been made. Proceedings for any of these offences may only be instituted by the Secretary of State or by, or with the consent of, the Director of Public Prosecutions.[1]

[1] Insolvency Act 1986, s 350(5).

19.1.2 The bankrupt is potentially liable in respect of any act or omission arising during the relevant period whether before or from the date of the bankruptcy order and ending at the date of the bankrupt's discharge or the annulment of the order. He may, however, be prosecuted for an offence committed during this period after his discharge or the annulment of the order provided, in the case of annulment only, that the proceedings were instituted before the annulment.[1] It is no defence to any proceedings under this Chapter of the 1986 Act that the whole or any part of any act relied on as constituting the whole or part of any offence was committed outside England and Wales.[2]

[1] Insolvency Act 1986, s 350(2) and (3).
[2] Ibid, s 350(4).

19.1.3 In respect of every offence, except those listed below, the bankrupt has a defence if he is able to prove that, at the time of the conduct constituting the offence, he had not intended to defraud or to conceal the state of his affairs, the 'defence of innocent intention'.[1]

The burden of proof of the dishonesty aspect of the mens rea of these offences is thus transferred to the bankrupt. The offences excepted from this defence are all offences which incorporate a specific mens rea element and are the following (figures refer to offences listed in section 19.2 below):

(8) failure to account for or explain loss of property;
(12) failure to inform of false proof;
(13) advancing fictitious losses;
(14) fraudulently obtaining creditors' consent;
(19) obtaining credit without disclosing status as undisharged bankrupt;
(20) use of business name other than name in which adjudicated bankrupt;
(21) failure to keep and preserve proper accounts; and
(22) gambling or engaging in rash and hazardous speculations.

[1] Insolvency Act 1986, s 352.

19.2 SPECIFIED OFFENCES

19.2.1 *Failure to disclose property.* The bankrupt commits an offence if he does not disclose all the property comprised in his estate to the best of his knowledge and belief to the official receiver or trustee.[1] Although after acquired property no longer comprises property of the bankrupt's estate, it may become part of the estate if the trustee serves a notice claiming it under the Insolvency Act 1986, s 307. The trustee may also claim property which the bankrupt is using for his business or household needs under the Insolvency Act 1986, s 310. The Act[2] provides that any property which the trustee may claim under either of these sections is included as property comprised in the bankrupt's estate for the purposes of this offence. The disclosure must be to the official receiver or trustee, so disclosure to creditors will not suffice though it may well be strong evidence in support of a defence of innocent intention. The primary place for disclosure is the statement of affairs which the bankrupt must submit to the official receiver within 21 days of the commencement of the bankruptcy.[3] The statement of affairs and any other statement made by the bankrupt when required to do so, may be used in evidence against the bankrupt in any proceedings against him.[4]

[1] Insolvency Act 1986, s 353(1)(a).
[2] Ibid, s 351(a).
[3] Ibid, s 288.
[4] Ibid, s 433.

19.2.2 *Failure to disclose disposal of property.* The bankrupt commits an offence if he does not inform the official receiver or trustee of any disposal of property which, but for that disposal, would be comprised in his estate.[1] Full details of the disposal must be given showing how, when, to whom and for what consideration the property was disposed. The offence does not cover the disclosure of any disposal in the ordinary course of the bankrupt's business, or any payment of the ordinary expenses of the bankrupt or his family. The Act does not specify how far back the disclosure should go. It will be noted that the court has jurisdiction to set aside any transaction which was entered into for the purpose of putting assets beyond the reach of creditors and this jurisdiction is not limited in time.[2] Plainly, disclosure of any such transaction may be required of the bankrupt irrespective of its age.

[1] Insolvency Act 1986, s 353(1)(b) and see para 14.3 above.
[2] Ibid, s 423.

19.2.3 *Failure to deliver up property.* The bankrupt commits an offence if he fails to deliver up any property to the official receiver or trustee which he is required by law to deliver up and which is in his possession or under his control.[1] The official receiver or trustee may direct the bankrupt to give possession of only part of his property in which case only that part is relevant for the purposes of this offence.

[1] Insolvency Act 1986, s 354(2)(a).

19.2.4 *Concealment of debts or property.* The bankrupt commits an offence if he conceals any debt due to or from him or conceals any property which he is required to deliver up to the official receiver or trustee, the value of which is not less than the prescribed amount.[1]

[1] Insolvency Act 1986, s 354(1); prescribed amount is £500; see Insolvency Proceedings (Monetary Limits) Order 1986.

19.2.5 *Concealment prior to bankruptcy.* The bankrupt commits an offence if he conceals debts or property valued at not less than the prescribed amount during the twelve months preceding the presentation of the petition or between the presentation of the petition and the commencement of the bankruptcy.[1] In the case of accounting records for the bankrupt's business, the period during which the offence may be committed is extended from 12 months to two years.[2]

[1] Insolvency Act 1986, s 354(1)(c); prescribed amount is £500.
[2] Ibid, s 361(4).

19.2.6 *Removal of property.* The bankrupt commits an offence if he removes any property the value of which is not less than the prescribed amount and which he is required to deliver up to the official receiver or trustee at any time after the presentation of the petition against him.[1]

[1] Insolvency Act 1986, s 354(2).

19.2.7 *Failure to account for or explain loss of property.* The bankrupt commits an offence if, on being required to do so by the official receiver, or by the court, he fails without reasonable excuse to account for the loss of any substantial part of his property incurred during the twelve months prior to the presentation of the petition or between the presentation of the petition and the commencement of the bankruptcy, or to give a reasonable explanation of the manner in which such a loss was incurred.[1]

[1] Insolvency Act 1986, s 354(3).

19.2.8 *Concealment of records.* The bankrupt commits an offence if he does not deliver up to the official receiver or trustee all the books, papers and other records of which he has possession or control and which relate to his estate or affairs or such books, papers, etc which the official receiver or trustee direct him to deliver up.[1]

[1] Insolvency Act 1986, s 355(1).

19.2.9 *Destruction, mutilation, falsification, etc of records.* The bankrupt commits an offence if he:[1]

(a) prevents the production of any books, papers or records relating to his estate and affairs at any time after the presentation of the petition;
(b) conceals, destroys, mutilates or falsifies any such books, papers or other records or causes or permits such concealment, destruction, mutilation or falsification at any time after the date 12 months prior to the presentation of the petition; or
(c) makes any false entries in any book, document or record relating to his estate or affairs or causes or permits the making of any such false entry at any time after the date 12 months prior to the presentation of the petition.[2]

[1] Insolvency Act 1986, s 355(2).
[2] Ibid, s 355(3).

19.2.10 *Disposal or alteration of records.* The bankrupt commits an offence if he disposes of, alters or makes any omission in any book, document or record relating to his estate or affairs or causes or permits such disposal, alteration or making any omission at any time after the date 12 months prior to the presentation of the petition.[1]

[1] Insolvency Act 1986, s 355(3).

19.2.11 *False statements.* The bankrupt commits an offence if he makes any material omission in his statement of affairs or any other statement relating to his affairs required of him under the Insolvency Act 1986[1].

[1] Insolvency Act 1986, s 356(1).

19.2.12 *Failure to inform of false proof.* The bankrupt commits an offence if knowing or believing that a false debt has been proved by any person under the bankruptcy, he fails to inform the trustee as soon as practicable.[1]

[1] Insolvency Act 1986, s 356(2)(a).

19.2.13 *Advancing fictitious losses.* The bankrupt commits an offence it he attempts to account for any part of his property by fictitious losses or expenses. This offence may be committed by the bankrupt at any meeting of his creditors at any time after the date 12 months prior to the presentation of the petition or by a fictitious account in any circumstances after the presentation of the petition.[1]

[1] Insolvency Act 1986, s 356(2)(b) and (c).

19.2.14 *Fraudulently obtaining creditors' consent.* The bankrupt commits an offence if he makes any false representation or perpetrates any other fraud designed to obtain the consent of his creditors or any of them to an agreement relating to his affairs or his bankruptcy.[1]

[1] Insolvency Act 1986, s 356(2)(d).

19.2.15 *Fraudulent disposal of property.* The bankrupt commits an offence if he makes or causes to be made at any time after the date five years prior to the commencement of the bankruptcy any gift or transfer of or any charge on his property.[1] The statutory defence of innocent intention[2] will be the critical consideration for this offence. Making a transfer of or charge on property includes causing or conniving at the levying of execution against that property.[3]

[1] Insolvency Act 1986, s 357(1).
[2] Ibid, s 352.
[3] Ibid, s 357(2).

19.2.16 *Concealment or removal of property to defeat a judgment.* The bankrupt commits an offence if he conceals or removes any part of his property after or within two months before the date on which a judgment or order for the payment of money has been obtained against him where that judgment or order is not satisfied before the commencement of the bankruptcy.[1]

[1] Insolvency Act 1986, s 357(3).

19.2.17 *Absconding with property.* The bankrupt commits an offence if he leaves or makes preparations to leave England and Wales with any property the value of which is not less than the prescribed amount and possession of which he is required to deliver to the official receiver or trustee at any time after the date six months prior to the presentation of the petition.[1]

[1] Insolvency Act 1986, s 358; prescribed amount is £500.

19.2.18 *Dealing with property on credit.* The bankrupt is guilty of an offence if he disposes of any property which he had obtained on credit at a time when he has not paid for it, at any time after the date 12 months prior to the presentation of the petition.[1] The offence is not committed where the acquisition and disposal of the property was in the ordinary course of business of the bankrupt. In determining whether the acquisition or disposal is in the ordinary course of business, regard may be had in particular to the price paid for the property.[2] The 'disposal' of property includes pawning or pledging the property.[3]

[1] Insolvency Act 1986, s 359(1).
[2] Ibid, s 359(3) and (4).
[3] Ibid, s 359(5).

19.2.19 *Obtaining credit without disclosure of status.* The bankrupt commits an offence if either alone, or jointly with another person, he obtains credit at or above the prescribed amount without disclosing to the person

extending credit that he is an undischarged bankrupt (or that his estate has been sequestrated in Scotland and that he has not been discharged).[1] Obtaining credit includes both:
(a) obtaining goods on hire purchase or conditional sale terms; and
(b) being paid in advance for the supply of goods or services.[2]

[1] Insolvency Act 1986, s 360(1)(a) and (4); prescribed amount is £250.
[2] Ibid, s 360(2).

19.2.20 *Use of business name.* A bankrupt commits an offence if he engages either directly or indirectly in any business under a name other than that in which he was adjudged bankrupt without disclosing to all persons with whom he enters into any business transaction the name in which he was so adjudged.[1]

[1] Insolvency Act 1986, s 360(1)(b).

19.2.21 *Failure to keep and present proper accounts.* Where the bankrupt has engaged in any business at any time during the period of two years prior to the presentation of the petition, he commits an offence if he has not kept proper accounting records throughout that period and any further period during which he carried on business after presentation of the petition and before the commencment of the bankruptcy or has not preserved all the accounting records which he has kept.[1] The bankrupt is not guilty of an offence where:
(a) his unsecured liabilities at the commencment of the bankruptcy did not exceed the prescribed amount;[2] or
(b) he proves that in the circumstances in which he carried on business the omission was honest and excusable.[3]

For the purposes of this offence, a person is to be deemed not to have kept proper accounting records if he has not kept such records as are necessary to show or explain his transactions and financial position in his business, including:
(a) records containing entries from day to day, in sufficient detail, of all cash received and paid;
(b) where the business involved dealings in goods, statements of annual stock-takings; and
(c) except in the case of goods sold by way of retail trade to the actual customer, records of all goods sold and purchased showing the buyers and sellers in sufficient detail to enable the goods and the buyers and sellers to be identified.

[1] Insolvency Act 1986, s 361(1).
[2] Ibid, s 361(2)(a): prescribed amount is £20,000; see Insolvency Proceedings (Monetary Limits) Order 1986.
[3] Ibid, s 361(2)(b).

19.2.22 *Gambling.* A bankrupt commits an offence if he has materially contributed to or increased the extent of his insolvency by gambling or rash and hazardous speculations at any time after the date two years prior to the presentation of the petition.[1] In determining for the purposes of this offence whether any speculations were rash or hazardous, the financial position of the bankrupt at the time when he entered into them must be taken into consideration.[2]

[1] Insolvency Act 1986, s 362(1).
[2] Ibid, s 362(2).

19.3 PENALTIES

For convictions under offences (1), (2), (3), (4), (5), (6), (8), (9), (10), (11), (12), (13), (14), and (18) above the penalty on summary conviction is up to six months' imprisonment or a fine not exceeding the statutory maximum or both, and on conviction on indictment imprisonment for up to seven years or a fine or both. For conviction under offences (7), (15), (16), (17), (19), (20), (21), and (22) above the penalty on summary conviction is up to six months' imprisonment or a fine not exceeding the statutory maximum or both and on conviction on indictment, imprisonment for a term not exceeding two years or a fine or both.[1]

[1] Insolvency Act 1986, s 430, Sch 10.

19.4 OFFENCES COMMITTED BY OTHER PERSONS

There are no specific bankruptcy offences relating to false claims in the bankruptcy or fraudulent behaviour generally in respect of another's bankruptcy. Such offences are likely to be covered by the general criminal law, in particular the Theft Act 1968, ss 15–17, obtaining property or pecuniary advantage by deception, the Theft Act 1978, ss 1 and 2 obtaining services or evading liabilities by deception, and the law regarding aiding and abetting criminal offences.

The Insolvency Act 1986 does, however, provide for a specific offence when another person obtains property from the bankrupt which the bankrupt had obtained on credit. The offence is committed where the person concerned acquires or receives property from the bankrupt knowing or believing that the bankrupt:

(a) owed money in respect of that property; and
(b) did not intend or was unlikely to be able to pay the money he owed on the property.

The offence may be committed at any time during the period commencing 12 months before the presentation of the petition and ending on the commencement of the bankruptcy.[1] The offence is not committed where the bankrupt dealt with the property in the ordinary course of his business.[2] In determining whether his dealing was in the ordinary course of business, particular regard may be had to the price paid for the property.[3]

[1] Insolvency Act 1986, s 359(2).
[2] Ibid, s 359(3).
[3] Ibid, s 359(4).

19.5 TRANSITIONAL PROVISIONS

In contrast with other procedures in bankruptcy, the commission of bankruptcy offences does not fall to be considered either under the Old Bankruptcy Law or the New Law, depending upon the date on which the petition is presented, but cuts across the Old and New Law. This preserves the principle that the citizen should know beforehand that any act of omission of his may involve him in criminal liability. The commencement date of the Insolvency Act 1986[1] is the determining factor for offences committed in the context of New Law bankruptcies. Although a bankrupt is adjudicated under the Insolvency Act 1986 he may be prosecuted in respect of anything done by him before the commencement date under the Bankruptcy Act 1914, provided that the facts disclose an offence under the 1914 Bankruptcy Act.[2] For this purpose, the repeal of the Bankruptcy Act 1914, consequent upon the commencement of the Insolvency Act 1986, is saved. Acts or omissions arising after the commencement date fall to be prosecuted under the New Law, set out above.

Offences committed in bankruptcy which is proceeding under the Old Bankruptcy Law, remain liable to prosecution under the Old Bankruptcy Law, irrespective of the date on which the acts or omissions alleged to constitute the offence were committed or omitted. There is, however, one change to the Old Bankruptcy Law procedure for bankruptcy offences. In place of the provisions that allowed offences to be prosecuted with the leave of the court[3] is substituted the New Law provision[4] that prosecution may only be instituted by the Secretary of State or by or with the consent of the Director of Public Prosecutions.[5]

1 Commencement date 29 December 1986.
2 Insolvency Act 1986, Sch 11, para 18(1). For Old Law offences see ch 7.6 above.
3 See Bankruptcy Act 1914, ss 157(2), 158(2), 161 and 165.
4 Insolvency Act 1986, s 350(5).
5 Insolvency Act 1986, Sch 11, para 18(2).

CHAPTER 20

Bankruptcy Courts, Frauds, Summary Administrations and Miscellaneous

20.1 TRANSACTIONS DEFRAUDING CREDITORS

20.1.1 Strictly within the context of bankruptcy law there are statutory provisions enabling the court to set aside transactions entered into by the bankrupt before his bankruptcy. The relevant provisions of the Bankruptcy Act 1914 for use in the continuing Old Bankruptcy Law cases are referred to in ch 8 above. The relevant provisions of the Insolvency Act 1986, covering preferences and undervalue transactions are discussed in ch 17 above. But quite apart from these provisions there has, since the statute 13 Eliz c 5 (1571), been a statutory power in the court to set aside transactions made with intent to defraud creditors. This power may be exercised irrespective of the bankruptcy of the person making the relevant transaction.

20.1.2 Prior to the commencement of the Insolvency Act 1986 this general power of the court was exerciseable under the Law of Property Act 1925, s 172. The Cork Committee in their Review of Insolvency Law and Practice[1] made a number of criticisms of this section of the 1925 Act and proposed its replacement in a more clear and certain form. This proposal has largely found its way into the Insolvency Act 1986, ss 423–425 which gives the court a wide power to make orders where it is satisfied that a transaction has been entered into for the purpose of putting assets beyond the reach of creditors. The power of the court under the Insolvency Act 1986, ss 423–425 can be exercised alongside the bankruptcy provisions relating to transactions at an undervalue and preferences.[2] While this power comes into force on the commencement date of the Insolvency Act 1986,[3] on which date the Law of Property Act 1925, s 172 is repealed, transactions entered into before that date may only be set aside under the law in force before the repeal of the Law of Property Act 1925, s 172.[4] This law therefore remains relevant to all pre-Insolvency Act 1986 conveyances, even where the grantor is made bankrupt under the provisions of the Insolvency Act 1986.

[1] (Cmnd 8558) paras 1210–1220.

[2] Insolvency Act 1986, s 339.
[3] 29 December 1986.
[4] Insolvency Act 1986, Sch 11, para 20.

20.1.3 By the Law of Property Act 1925, s 172(1) 'every conveyance of property made . . . with intent to defraud creditors, shall be voidable, at the instance of any person thereby prejudiced'. To safeguard innocent purchasers the Law of Property Act 1925, s 172(3) provided that sub-s (1) should not extend 'to any estate or interest in property conveyed for valuable consideration and in good faith to any person not having, at the time of the conveyance, notice of intent to defraud creditors'.

20.1.4 *Conveyance of property.* As will be noted the section refers expressly only to 'conveyances'. It has therefore been questioned whether this section applies only to written conveyances of real or personal property or whether it extends to any disposition of property. The original statutory provision of 13 Eliz c 5 was 'for the avoiding and abolishing of feigned, covinous and fraudulent feoffments, gifts, grants, alienations, conveyances, bonds, suits, judgments, and executions, as well of lands and tenements as of goods and chattels . . .'. It is well arguable in the context of the 1925 legislation that the Law of Property Act 1925, s 172 was intended to be as wide as the statute it replaced, and that in the light of the wording of the earlier statute any transfer of property, whether by written conveyance or otherwise, would be caught by the section. This view appears to have been accepted by Harman J in *Re Eichholz Eichholz's Trustee v Eichholz*[1] but in that case he found that there had been a written conveyance. The point must still be open to doubt. Subject to this question, the conveyance of any type of property conveyed by a grantor may be avoided. The section has been applied to equitable reversionary interests in personal property[2] and the proceeds recoverable in a pending action.[3] It would appear unlikely, however, that the section could be applied to the payment of money.

[1] [1959] Ch 708.
[2] *Ideal Bedding Co Ltd v Holland* [1907] 2 Ch 157.
[3] *Glegg v Bromley* [1912] 3 KB 474.

20.1.5 *Intent to defraud.* It is necessary for the creditor seeking to set aside the conveyance to prove intent to defraud. That intent may, however, be presumed from the circumstances of the transaction.[1] The intention to defraud may be inferred from the fact that the conveyance was made with an eye to the future, as when the conveyance is made by an individual who is about to engage in a hazardous endeavour.[2] While a fraudulent intent may readily be presumed when the individual making the conveyance cannot pay his debts without the property conveyed[3] that is not sufficient by itself to obtain an order. Even where the grantor is unable to pay his debts the conveyance will not be avoided where it appears that he had no intention to defraud.[4] In *Lloyds Bank Ltd v Marcan*[5] the Court of Appeal was divided as to whether an intent to deprive creditors of assets was sufficient without actual deceit or dishonesty.[6] There is no need to show an intent to defraud any particular creditor. A fraudulent intention to prefer one creditor over others is not sufficient under the Law of Property Act 1925, s 172 to avoid a conveyance which is not caught by the law of bankruptcy, except perhaps where the individual debtor concerned is himself in some way benefitted by the conveyance.[7]

[1] *Godfrey v Poole* (1888) 13 App Cas 497, 503 PC.
[2] *Mackay v Douglas* (1872) LR 14 Eq 106; and see *Re Butterworth, ex p Russell* (1882) 19 Ch D 588 at 598 (Jessel MR).
[3] *Freeman v Pope* (1870) 5 Ch App 538.
[4] *Re Wise, ex p Mercer* (1886) 17 QBD 290; *Maskelyne and Cooke v Smith* [1902] 2 KB 158; affd [1903] 1 KB 671.
[5] [1973] 3 All ER 754.
[6] Russell LJ followed Pennycuick VC at first instance in stating that it was not necessary to show actual deceit or dishonesty. Cairns LJ disagreed. Goulding J, the third member of the Court of Appeal, expressed no opinion.
[7] See *Re Lloyds Furniture Palace Ltd, Evans v Lloyds Furniture Palace* [1925] Ch 853.

20.1.6 *Avoidance.* An application to avoid the conveyance can be made by any person prejudiced by it. A creditor will be and remain prejudiced as long as his debt remains enforceable by action and is not statute-barred. He is not precluded from applying for relief because he has known about the conveyance for nearly ten years without taking proceedings[1] or because the grantor has died.[2] A creditor whose debt subsisted at the time of the conveyance has an undoubted right to apply, and provided any debt which existed at the date of the conveyance remains unpaid subsequent creditors may apply to avoid the conveyance.[3] Where only subsequent debts remain unpaid it may be necessary for the relevant creditors to show an intention to defraud them.[4] A subsequent creditor who can show that the grantor was able to pay existing debts by incurring the subsequent debt will be subrogated to the rights of existing creditors and may apply himself to avoid the conveyance.[5]

[1] *Re Maddever, Three Towns Banking Co v Maddever* (1884) 27 Ch D 523.
[2] See *Re Gould, ex p Official Receiver* (1887) 19 QBD 92.
[3] *Freeman v Pope* (1870) 5 Ch App 538.
[4] *Cadogan v Cadogan* [1977] 1 All ER 200; *Re Butterworth, ex p Russell* (1882) 19 Ch D 588.
[5] *Spirett v Willows* (1864) 3 De G J & S 293.

20.1.7 *Effect on transferee.* An innocent transferee who takes an estate or interest in the property in good faith for valuable consideration and without notice of the intent to defraud is protected by the Act.[1] Similarly a bona fide purchaser from the transferee without notice of the fraudulent intent is protected.[2] Where a transferee takes for value knowing of the fraud he is not protected.[3] The avoidance of the settlement does not, however, extend any further than is necessary to pay the creditors. Any property remaining after paying the creditors still vests in the transferee.[4] The proper form of order in such circumstances is to direct the transferee to join and concur in all acts and things necessary for making the property available for satisfying the claims of the creditors.[4] A transferee who is aware that the conveyance to him prejudices the grantor's creditors may be presumed to have notice of an intent to defraud on the part of the grantor.[5]

[1] Law of Property Act 1925, s 172(3). By s 205(1) (xxi) valuable consideration includes marriage.

[2] Ibid, s 172(3) and see *Harrods Ltd v Stanton* [1923] 1 KB 516.
[3] *Kevan v Crawford* (1877) 6 Ch D 29; *Re Holland, Gregg v Holland* [1902] 2 Ch 360.
[4] *Ideal Bedding Co Ltd v Holland* [1907] 2 Ch 157.
[5] *Cornish v Clarke* (1872) LR 14 Eq 184.

20.1.8 The Law of Property Act 1925, s 172(2) provides that the section does not affect the operation of a disentailing assurance, or the law of the bankruptcy. The right to bar an entail either absolutely or so as to create an interest equivalent to a base fee applies not only to interests in real property but also to interests in personal property.[1]

[1] Law of Property Act 1925, s 130(1).

20.1.9 *Insolvency Act 1986, ss 423–425.* The Cork Committee's recommendations were that the Law of Property Act 1925, s 172 should be re-enacted so amended as to make clear:

(a) that the section applies to the mere payment of money, as well as to any disposition of property whether effected by an instrument in writing or not;
(b) that the necessary intent is an intent on the part of the debtor to defeat, hinder, delay or defraud creditors, or to put assets belonging to the debtor beyond their reach, and that such intent may be inferred whenever this is the natural and probable consequence of the debtor's actions, in the light of the financial circumstances of the debtor at the time, as known, or taken to have been known to him;
(c) that the section applies to any disposition made with the necessary intent, even if supported by valuable consideration, where that does not consist of full consideration in money or money's worth received by the debtor; but
(d) that no disposition may be set aside if made in favour of a bona fide purchaser for money or money's worth without notice, at the time of the disposition of the debtor's fraudulent intent.

These recommendations are met in the provisions of the Insolvency Act 1986, ss 423–425. It should be noted that these sections apply not only to bankruptcies but also to corporate insolvencies and cases generally irrespective of insolvency.

20.1.10 The Insolvency Act 1986, s 423(1)(2) and (3) provide that where a person (and this includes a corporate body) described as the 'debtor' (a) has entered into a transaction with any other person at an undervalue, and (b) the court is satisfied that it was entered into for the purpose of putting assets beyond the reach of someone entitled or to become entitled to make a claim against the debtor or of otherwise prejudicing that person's interests in relation to his claim, then the court may make 'such order as it thinks fit for restoring the position to what it would have been if the transaction had not been entered into and of protecting the interests of the persons on whose behalf the application is treated as made, described as the 'victims'.

20.1.11 A person enters into a transaction with another person at an under value if[1]

(a) he makes a gift to that other person, or the terms of the transaction provide for him to receive no consideration;

(b) he enters into a transaction with that other person in consideration of marriage; or
(c) he enters into a transaction with that other person for a consideration, the value of which, in money or money's worth, is significantly less than the value, in money or money's worth, of the consideration provided by the debtor.

[1] Insolvency Act 1986, s 423(1).

20.1.12 *Applications for orders.* The following persons are entitled to make an application for an order under the Insolvency Act 1986, s 423(2).[1] Where the debtor is:
(a) an individual who is bankrupt: the official receiver or his trustee in bankruptcy;
(b) a company which is being wound up: the liquidator;
(c) a company in relation to which an administration order is in force: the administrator;
(d) in any of the above three cases: any victim, ie a person who is or is capable of being prejudiced by the transaction, but only with the leave of the court;
(e) an individual or company which has entered into voluntary arrangements: by the supervisor of the composition or scheme or by any person, whether or not he is bound by the arrangements who is or might be prejudiced by the transaction; and
(f) in any other case: by any person who is or is capable of being prejudiced by the transaction (a 'victim').

Once an application is made by any person entitled as above to bring it before the court it is treated as made on behalf of every victim of the transaction. The application is made to the High Court or any other court having a bankruptcy jurisdiction over the debtor where he is an individual or a winding up jurisdiction over the debtor where a corporate body.[2]

[1] Insolvency Act 1986, s 421(1)(2).
[2] Ibid, s 423(4).

20.1.13 *Orders under s 423.* As quoted above the Insolvency Act 1986, s 423 gives the court a complete discretion as to the type of order it makes. The aims of any order made should be twofold. First to restore the position to what it would have been had the transaction not been entered into. Second to protect the interests of every person who is or is capable of being prejudiced by the transaction. The court is thus required to look beyond the immediate interests of the applicant seeking the order and take into consideration the interests of all potential victims of the transaction which is being impugned. Without prejudice to this general discretion the Insolvency Act 1986, s 425(1) provides that orders under s 423 may:
(a) require property which has been transferred to be vested in a particular person either absolutely or for the benefit of others;
(b) require property acquired from the proceeds of transferred property to be so vested;
(c) release or discharge any security given by the relevant person, in whole or in part;

(d) require a transferee or beneficiary of property transferred to pay money to a particular person;
(e) revive the obligations of any surety or guarantor released through the transfer by the debtor; and
(f) provide for security to be provided for the discharge of any obligation imposed or arising under the order. Such security may be charged on particular property such charge to have the same priority as any security or charge released or discharged under the transaction.

20.1.14 *Effect on transferee and third parties.* An order under s 423 may affect the property of or impose any obligation on the transferee or any third party even though he was not the person with whom the debtor entered into the transaction. Innocent third parties are given protection, however,[1] and orders may not be made by the court which:
(a) prejudice any interest in property which was acquired from a person other than the debtor and was acquired in good faith, for value and without notice of the relevant circumstances;
(b) prejudice any interest deriving from such an interest; or
(c) require a person who received a benefit from a transaction in good faith, for value and without notice of the relevant circumstances to pay any sum unless he was a party to the transaction.
The 'relevant circumstances' are those circumstances which give rise to the making of an order under s 423[2] (i e those circumstances which enable the court to find that the transaction impugned was at an undervalue and was entered into for the purpose of putting assets beyond the reach of creditors or other persons with claims against the debtor).

1 Insolvency Act 1986, s 425(2).
2 Ibid, s 425(3).

20.2 SUMMARY ADMINISTRATIONS

20.2.1 The Insolvency Act 1986 provides for the 'summary administration' of the bankrupt's estate where on the debtor's own petition it appears to the court that if a bankruptcy order were made the aggregate amount of the unsecured bankruptcy debts would be less than the bankruptcy level[1] and the debtor has not been adjudged bankrupt nor made a composition or scheme of arrangement with his creditors within the preceding five years.[2] The court may issue a certificate for summary administration in the bankruptcy order itself.[3]

1 Under Insolvency Act 1986, s 267(4). This level is £750 but may be varied by order by statutory instrument.
2 Insolvency Act 1986, s 275.
3 Individual Insolvency Rules 1986, r 6.48.

20.2.2 A bankrupt whose bankruptcy proceeds under the summary administration procedure secures his discharge[1] automatically on the expiry of two years beginning with the commencement of the bankruptcy.[2]

1 See chs 10 and 18 above.
2 Insolvency Act 1986, s 279(2)(a).

20.2.3 In summary administrations the creditors in general meeting do not appoint a trustee in bankruptcy[1] neither may a general meeting of creditors be held to remove the trustee.[2] The official receiver acts as trustee unless the court appoints some other person.[3]

[1] Insolvency Act 1986, s 292.
[2] Ibid, s 298.
[3] Ibid, s 297.

20.2.4 The court may, under the Insolvency Act 1986, s 275(3) revoke a certificate for summary administration either of its own motion or on the application of the official receiver.[1]

[1] Individual Insolvency Rules 1986, r 6.50.

20.3 THE OFFICIAL RECEIVER AND THE OFFICIAL PETITIONER

20.3.1 The duties, powers and responsibilities of the official receiver in Old Law bankruptcies are dealt with in ch 4 above. His statutory position was covered by the Bankruptcy Act 1914, ss 70–75 in Old Law cases.

The Insolvency Act 1986 ss 399 and 400 cover his position under New Law. Those sections are contained in Part XIV of the Act and are not confined in any sense to individual insolvency, or bankruptcy, alone.

20.3.2 An official receiver is attached either to the High Court or to a county court having bankruptcy jurisdiction and once appointed he has authority to act both in bankruptcy and in corporate winding up cases within the jurisdiction of the court in which he is appointed. The Secretary of State is required to ensure that there is at least one official receiver attached to each bankruptcy court, though the same person may act as official receiver to more than one court, and the official receiver so attached is authorised to act as such in every bankruptcy or winding up falling within the jurisdiction of that court.[1]

[1] Insolvency Act 1986, s 399(4).

20.3.3 In exercising the functions of the office the official receiver is under the general direction of the Secretary of State who may also authorise an officer to act on behalf of the official receiver in the official receiver's absence for certain examinations and applications[1]. He is also an officer of the court in relation to which he acts as official receiver.[2]

[1] Individual Insolvency Rules 1986, r 10.2.
[2] Insolvency Act 1986, s 400(2).

20.3.4 The office of official petitioner for the purposes of proceedings following the making of a criminal bankruptcy order (see ch 23 below) is continued by s 402 by virtue of which the Director of Public Prosecutions continues to be, ex officio petitioner.

20.4 INCAPACITATED PERSONS IN BANKRUPTCY

20.4.1 In Old Bankruptcy Law cases there are provisions in the Bankruptcy Rules 1952[1] for the court to appoint a person to represent the interests of a debtor creditor or other person whom the court finds 'by inquisition' to be of unsound mind.

Provisions in the New Law are more wide ranging in that they provide for any debtor or other person affected by the bankruptcy proceedings to be represented by some other person if that person has become incapable of managing or administering his property and affairs by reason either of a 'mental disorder' within the meaning of the Mental Health Act 1983 or due to physical affliction or disability.[2]

1 R 297.
2 Individual Insolvency Rules 1986, Part 7, Chap 7, r 7.43.

20.4.2 Application is made ex parte and, unless it is made by the official receiver, is to be supported by an affidavit from a registered medical practitioner.[1] The order may be made by (a) the court on its own motion, or (b) on the application of a person appointed by a court to manage the affairs of, or to represent, the bankrupt (eg the official solicitor or a receiver appointed by the Court of Protection), or (c) by any relative or friend of the incapacitated person who appears to the court to be a proper person to make the application, (d) by the official receiver, or (e) by the responsible insolvency practitioner.[2]

1 Individual Insolvency Rules 1986, r 7.45.
2 Ibid, r 7.44.

20.5 BANKRUPTCY COURTS

20.5.1 The appropriate court in bankruptcy in relation to any individual is discussed in para 13.7 above. The High Court has jurisdiction over the London Insolvency District, and the bankruptcy county court over its specified insolvency district. In exercising its bankruptcy jurisdiction the bankruptcy county court has all the powers and jurisdiction of the High Court, and the orders of the court may be enforced accordingly.[1] Proceedings may be transferred between bankruptcy courts and no proceedings should be invalidated on the grounds that they were initiated or continued in the wrong bankruptcy court.[2]

1 Insolvency Act 1986, s 373.
2 Ibid, s 373(4).

20.5.2 *Powers of the bankruptcy court.* The Insolvency Act 1986, ss 363–371 gives the bankruptcy court general control over the bankruptcy[1]. The court has 'full' power to determine to decide all questions of priorities, issues of law and questions of fact arising in the bankruptcy. There are also specific provisions designed to promote the efficacy of bankruptcy proceedings. These powers extend to the bankrupt, third parties, property and documents.

1 Insolvency Act 1986, s 363(1).

20.5.3 *Powers relating to the bankrupt.* The court has extensive powers over the person of the bankrupt, and these powers continue after discharge so long as the bankrupt's estate is still being administered.[1] Thus the bankrupt is required to comply with any directions of the court given for the purposes of his bankruptcy or the administration of his estate.[2] Failure to do so without reasonable excuse will render him liable to punishment for contempt of court.[3] The court may in specified circumstances order the arrest and detention of a bankrupt or a debtor to whom a bankruptcy petition relates[4] and the seizure and retention of any books, papers, records, money or goods in his possession.[5] The specified circumstances are where:

(a) there are reasonable grounds for believing that the bankrupt or debtor has absconded or is about to abscond with intent to avoid or delay debts or frustrate bankruptcy proceedings;[6]
(b) he is about to remove his goods with a view to preventing or delaying the taking of possession by the official receiver or trustee;[7]
(c) there are reasonable grounds for believing that he has concealed or destroyed any of his goods, papers or records which might be of use to his creditors in the course of the bankruptcy, or is about to do so;[8]
(d) without leave of the official receiver or his trustee he has removed goods exceeding in value such sum as is prescribed;[9] or
(e) he has failed without reasonable excuse to attend any examination ordered by the court.[10]

1 See Insolvency Act 1986, ss 363(2), (3), 364 and 369.
2 Ibid, s 363(2).
3 Ibid, s 363(4).
4 Ibid, s 364(1)(a).
5 Ibid, s 364(1)(b).
6 Ibid, s 364(2)(a).
7 Ibid, s 364(2)(b).
8 Ibid, s 364(2)(c).
9 Ibid, s 364(2)(d). Prescribed sum is £500: Insolvency Proceedings (Monetary Limits) Order 1986, SI 1986/1996.
10 Insolvency Act 1986, s 364(2)(e).

20.5.4 *Powers relating to third parties.* The court's powers of coercion are extended by the Insolvency Act 1986, to include third parties.[1] These are the spouse or former spouse of the bankrupt,[2] any person indebted to the bankrupt or believed to have in his possession property comprised in the bankrupt's estate[3] and any person appearing to the court to be able to give information concerning the bankrupt, his affairs or property.[4] The court may require any such person to appear before it. Any debtor or person in possession of estate property or relevant information may be required to submit an affidavit reciting their dealings with the bankrupt or produce documents in their possession or control relating to the bankrupt or his dealings, affairs or property. The Act confers powers of arrest and seizure of property when a person fails without reasonable excuse to appear before the court when summoned or when it is reasonably believed that he has absconded or is about to do so intending to avoid such appearance.[5] The other provisions empower the court to order a person appearing before it to be examined on oath, either orally or by interrogatories,[6] to order the delivery up,[7] or payment,[8] to the official receiver or trustee, of any property comprised in the bankrupt's estate, or debt owed to the bankrupt, respectively by any person who possesses such property or owes such debt; to order the examination in any part of the UK or in any place abroad of any person liable to be summoned to appear before the court under this section.[9] The section applies with appropriate amendment where an interim receiver has been appointed under s 286.[10]

1 S 366.
2 Insolvency Act 1986, s 366(1)(a).
3 Ibid, s 366(1)(b).
4 Ibid, s 366(1)(c).
5 Ibid, s 366(3).
6 Ibid, s 367(4).
7 Ibid, s 367(1).
8 Ibid, s 367(2).
9 Ibid, s 367(3).
10 Ibid, s 365.

20.5.5 *Powers in respect of property and documents.* In addition to the powers to seize documents at the time of arrest referred to above[1] the court may, at any time after bankruptcy order has been made, issue a warrant for the seizure of any property comprised in the bankrupt's estate and any books, papers or records relating to that estate which are in the possession or control of the bankrupt or any other person who is required to deliver them to the official receiver or trustee.[1] The person executing the warrant may break open any premises where the bankrupt or anything directed to be seized is or is believed to be. The court is specifically empowered to issue a warrant for the search of premises not belonging to the bankrupt if it is satisfied that any property comprised in the bankrupt's estate is concealed there.[2] For the specific purposes of a public examination[3] or any inquiry under s 366 the court may order an Inland Revenue official to produce to the court returns and accounts submitted by the bankrupt at any time,[4] any assessments or determination made by an Inland Revenue official,[5] or any correspondence between the bankrupt and any Inland Revenue official.[6] Such documents are not automatically disclosed to the official receiver or trustee but after production the court may order disclosure to the official receiver or trustee and also the creditors.[7] After a bankruptcy order has been made the court may from time to time order the Post Office to redirect the bankrupt's mail to the official receiver or trustee for a period not exceeding three months.[8]

1 Insolvency Act 1986, s 365(1).
2 Ibid, s 365(3).
3 See Insolvency Act 1986, s 290 and para 14.3.6 above.
4 Insolvency Act 1986, s 369(1)(a).
5 Ibid, s 369(1)(b).
6 Ibid, s 369(1)(c).
7 Ibid, s 369(2).
8 Ibid, s 371.

20.5.6 *Special manager.* Where it appears to the official receiver or trustee that the nature of the estate or the interests of the creditors generally require it[1] the court may appoint any person to be special manager of the bankrupt's estate, of the business of an undischarged bankrupt or the property or business of a debtor of which an interim receiver has been appointed under s 286.[2] There would seem to be no reason why the bankrupt himself may not, in special circumstances, be appointed special manager in his own estate.[3] The powers of the special manager must be prescribed by the court[4] which may direct than any provisions of the bankruptcy part of the Act which have effect in relation to the official receiver, interim receivership or trustee shall have the like effect in relation to the special manager.[5] The special manager must give such security and keep and produce such accounts as are prescribed by the rules.[6] The application is made by the official receiver or trustee under s 370 and is supported by a request setting out the reasons for the application. Rule 6.167 sets out the information to be contained in such an application. The application may be for a fixed period, or until the occurence of a specific event or be subject to further order of the court.

1 Insolvency Act 1986, s 370.
2 Ibid, s 370(1).
3 See s 314(3) which authorises the trustee, with the permission of the committee of creditors, to appoint the bankrupt for example to carry on his business, and assist in the administration of the estate along with s 286 which refers to 'any person' being appointed.
4 Insolvency Act 1986, s 370(3).
5 Ibid, s 370(4).
6 Ibid, s 370(5).

20.5.7 *Co-operation between United Kingdom and other courts exercising bankruptcy jurisdiction.* The Insolvency Act 1986, s 426 contains provisions which expand upon the old provisions of the Bankruptcy Act 1914, ss 121–123. It provides for inter-jurisdictional co-operation and enforcement of orders in insolvency matters. Previously such co-operation between jurisdictions was restricted to bankruptcy matters, but it is now to extend both to bankruptcy and corporate insolvency.

(a) *United Kingdom courts*
Section 426(1) provides that an order made by a court in any part of the United Kingdom in the exercise of jurisdiction in relation to insolvency law shall be enforced in any part of the United Kingdom as if it were made by a court exercising the corresponding jurisdiction in that other part. This power of enforcement is subject to the proviso that the enforcing court is not required to enforce an order insofar as it relates to property situated within the enforcing court's jurisdiction. However, s 426(3) empowers the Secretary of State (with the concurrence of the Lord Chancellor) to make orders[1] which will enable the trustee or assignee of a bankrupt's property in any part of the United Kingdom to have the same rights in respect of property situated in any other part of the United Kingdom as he would as trustee or assignee under the law of that other part. Under the provisions of the Bankruptcy Act 1914 there existed a large measure of co-operation between the jurisdictions of the United Kingdom courts.[2] To the provisions under the Insolvency Act 1986 referred to above is added the injunction in s 426(4) that 'The courts having jurisdiction in relation to insolvency law in

any part of the United Kingdom shall assist the courts having the corresponding jurisdiction in any other part of the United Kingdom . . .' The co-operation between the United Kingdom jurisdictions should therefore not only continue but be enhanced.

(b) *Non-United Kingdom courts*
The injunction on the insolvency courts in s 426(4) quoted above continues '. . . or any relevant country or territory.' The aim here is to ensure 'due recognition and respect abroad' for English insolvency proceedings by offering reciprocal enforcement powers, as advocated by the Cork Committee.[3] A 'relevant country or territory' is defined in s 426(11) as meaning '(a) any of the Channel Islands or the Isle of Man; or (b) any country or territory designated for the purposes of this section by the Secretary of State by order made by statutory instrument.' The countries of whose courts assistance is to be afforded will thus be certain and the arguments as to what constituted a 'British Court elsewhere' for the purposes of the Bankruptcy Act 1914, s 122[4] will be avoided.

(c) *Provision of assistance*
In cases where assistance is sought from the jurisdiction of a relevant country or territory the United Kingdom court acts only upon a request from the court of that jurisdiction.[5] Where assistance is sought from within the United Kingdom, the court may also act upon the application of the trustee or assignee of the bankrupt's estate.[6] In either event the potentially assisting court has a discretion whether to act or not expressly stated by s 426.[4] The discretion is 'to apply, in relation to any matters specified in the request, the insolvency law which is applicable by either Court in relation to comparable matters falling within its jurisdiction'. For the purposes of s 426, 'insolvency law' is defined by s 426(10) by reference to the relevant statutory enactments in England and Wales, Scotland and Northern Ireland. In relation to any relevant country or territory, insolvency law is defined as 'so much of the law of that country or territory as corresponds to provisions falling within any of' [the relevant UK statutes]. It is left to the Courts to determine what foreign law 'corresponds' to the relevant United Kingdom law. Where the foreign law is codified the corresponding provisions of insolvency law will usually be sufficiently clear. In considering what law is comparable in the rare cases where foreign law is not codified assistance may be gained from the observations of Goulding J in *Re a Debtor, ex p Viscount of the Royal Court of Jersey*[7] on what form of procedure may be described as 'bankruptcy', where Goulding J held that a wide construction should be adopted.

In exercising its discretion whether or not to lend assistance to the requesting court or trustee/assignee, the United Kingdom court is required to 'have regard in particular to the rules of private international law'. No detailed analysis is here attempted of these rules but the following observations are made:

(1) *Immoveable property.* English courts will not recognise an adjudication in bankruptcy in a foreign court as vesting title to immoveable property situated in England in the foreign trustee.[8] The court may avoid this general rule however by appointing the foreign trustee (or curator) receiver of the bankrupt's immoveable property with a power of sale,[9] subject to all prior charges and incumbrances.[10]

(2) *Moveable property*. The general principle is the doctrine of universality, by which all moveable property passes to and vests in the foreign trustee.[11] The foreign trustee's title extends to all moveables including choses in action and is superior to the right of a creditor who attaches property by due process in England after the commencement of the bankruptcy.

(3) *Competing procedures*. In cases where the debtor has been made bankrupt both in England and abroad, all issues arising in the administration of property which under English law vests in the English trustee are determined by English law, even though the foreign bankruptcy may have commenced earlier.[12]

(4) *Public policy*. The English courts will not assist where it can be shown that the relevant judgment or adjudication has been obtained by fraud[13] or in proceedings which were contrary to natural justice[14] or where the enforcement of foreign bankruptcy proceedings will be to the benefit of foreign revenue authorities.[15] This last prohibition is part of the rule that English courts will not aid the enforcement of a foreign revenue law. As the overwhelming majority of insolvencies involve revenue authorities a strict application of this rule will make a nonsense of international co-operation and will be particularly harsh to the other creditors. It is perhaps time this rule was relaxed, at least in cases where the foreign revenue authorities are not the sole creditors.

(d) *Form of assistance*

This is left to the discretion of the court within the general provision that the Court is to apply either its own or the comparable foreign law. Provided that secured creditors are protected and the hotchpotch rule is observed[16] an English court would appear to be free to make any practical order to ensure that the bankrupt's assets are realised for the benefit of the general body of creditors.

1 No orders have as yet been made.
2 See generally Cheshire and North, *Private International Law*, 10th edn, p 557.
3 Report of the Review Committee, Cmnd 8558, para 1902–1914.
4 See e g *Re Osborn, ex p Trustee* [1931–32] B & C R 189 (Manx law); *Re A Debtor, ex p Viscount* [1981] Ch 384, (Jersey law).
5 Insolvency Act 1986, s 426(5).
6 Insolvency Act 1986, s 426(6).
7 [1981] Ch 384 at 400.
8 *Waite v Bingley* (1882) 21 Ch D 674 at 681, 682; *Re Levy's Trusts* (1885) 30 Ch D 119.
9 *Re Kooperman* [1928] B & CR 49, *Re Osborn* (supra).
10 *Galbraith v Grimshaw* [1910] AC 508.
11 *Solomons v Ross* (1764) 1 Hy B1 131, *Alivon v Furnival* (1834) 1 Cr M & R 277.
12 *Re Melbourn, ex p Melbourn* (1870) 6 Ch App 64, *Re Morton, ex p Robertson* (1875) LR 20 Eq 733.
13 *Aboulof v Oppenheimer* (1882) 10 QBD 295.
14 *Jacobson v Frachone* (1927) 138 LT 386.
15 *Government of India Ministry of Finance (Revenue Division) v Taylor* [1955] AC 491, *Brokaw v Seatrain UK Ltd* [1971] 2 QB 476.
16 See para 16.5.3 above.

20.6 SUPPLIES BY UTILITIES

Special provision is made by the Insolvency Act 1986, s 372 for the protection of utilities, supplying gas, electricity, water and telecomunication services[1] at the request of the official receiver, trustee, interim receiver or supervisor of a scheme or composition ('the office holders') for the purpose of continuing the business of the debtor or bankrupt which he has previously carried on alone or in partnership.[2] After the 'relevant day' the supplier of any of these services may make it a condition of further supply that the 'office holder' personally guarantees payment.[3] No condition may, however, be imposed in respect of supplies provided before the relevant day.[4] The 'relevant day'[5] is the day on which:

(a) a bankruptcy order is made against the individual or an interim receiver of his property is appointed;
(b) a composition or scheme proposed by an individual is approved by his creditors; or
(c) a deed of arrangement is made for the benefit of all individual creditors.

1 Insolvency Act 1986, s 372(4). Cable services are not telecommunication services: s 372(5).
2 Insolvency Act 1986, s 372.
3 Ibid, s 372(2)(a).
4 Ibid, s 372(2)(b).
5 Ibid, s 372(1).

PART 3

Provisions Applicable to Old and New Law Cases

CHAPTER 21

Stays, Reviews and Appeals

21.1 STAYS

21.1.1 The stay which becomes available to a bankrupt on litigation being brought against him on his bankruptcy, and the effect of bankruptcy upon litigation or arbitration to which the bankrupt is a party, is dealt with in ch 30 below.

This section deals with stays of the bankruptcy proceedings themselves.

A stay of the bankruptcy proceedings or a part of them (e g advertisement) can in itself be of considerable significance in the organisation of a debtor's affairs.

21.1.2 There is specific provision for a stay of proceedings on a petition under the Old Bankruptcy Law where a petition is based on a bankruptcy notice and the judgment on which the notice was issued is the subject of an appeal.[1] This provision becomes redundant as all the petitions under the Old Bankruptcy Law are disposed of. Even in such cases, it is clear that the registrar has an absolute discretion as to whether or not a stay of the bankruptcy proceedings is appropriate in all the circumstances. Generally a stay is ordered if the appeal in question appears bona fide.[2]

[1] Bankruptcy Act 1914, s 5(4).
[2] See *Re French, ex p French* (1889) 24 QBD 63.

21.1.3 Apart from the specific provisions of the Bankruptcy Act 1914, s 4, the Act contains a general provision to the effect that the court may at any time, for sufficient reason, make an order staying the bankruptcy proceedings, generally for a limited period, on such terms and conditions as it thinks fit.[1]

A common example of the use of this power has been in the stay of advertisement. The making of a receiving order under the Old Bankruptcy Law must be gazetted and advertised in a local paper in the prescribed manner.[2] However, where the debtor has a genuine appeal or may be able to raise sufficient funds to pay all his creditors, he may, on appropriate terms, for example as to the filing of a statement of affairs, be granted a stay of advertisement pending that appeal or the payment off of his creditors.

[1] Bankruptcy Act 1914, s 113.
[2] Ibid, s 11.

21.1.4 The power of the court to stay proceedings under s 113 is plainly wide and flexible. It can be used at any time, for example after receiving order but in order to prevent an order of adjudication if there are circumstances peculiar to the particular case which render a stay appropriate in all the circumstances.

21.1.5 The ability of the bankruptcy court to stay Old Bankruptcy Law proceedings is different from its specific discretionary ability to adjourn such proceedings before it, on such terms as it thinks fit, pursuant to the provisions of the Bankruptcy Act 1914, s 109.

21.1.6 While the Insolvency Act 1986 does not contain a general power to stay the bankruptcy proceedings of the type found in the Bankruptcy Act 1914, s 113, the Insolvency Act 1986 does contain the same provisions concerning the court's power to review, rescind or vary its own orders[1] so that it seems clear that the court retains an inherent power to order a stay of proceedings before it.

[1] Cf Bankruptcy Act 1914, s 108 and Insolvency Act 1986, s 375; see also 21.2 below.

21.1.7 *The procedure for a stay.* An application for a stay is made in the same way as any other general application in bankruptcy.[1]

At the hearing of a petition under the Old Bankruptcy Law, and when a receiving order has been made application may be made to the court for a general stay pending appeal, or for a stay of advertisement alone. Whilst the court is plainly empowered to order such a stay, it may adjourn the application for a short time in order to ensure that the official receiver is made a party to the application and so that he may make such submissions on the application as he thinks are appropriate.

If the application for a stay in an Old Law case proceeds on a notice of motion the court fixes a date for the hearing of the motion and seals and issues the applicant with copies of the notice of motion for service on the respondents to the application.

[1] In New Law cases application is made in accordance with the procedure in the 1986 Rules, rr 7.3, 7.4, i e in writing setting out the grounds and made to the Registrar who files the date and place of hearing.

21.2 REVIEWS AND REHEARINGS

21.2.1 A bankruptcy court's unique power to rehear and rescind or vary an order it has already made 'is, in a proper case, almost without limit'.[1]

Cases under the Old Bankruptcy Law and under the New Law enjoy the same opportunities for review[2] and there is no reason to suppose that the court's approach under the New Law will be any different than under the Old.

For a comparison between the power of the court to rescind one of its orders and the power to reverse a decision on appeal see *Re Cohen, ex p Bankrupt v IRC* [1950] 2 All ER 36 at 40, per Evershed MR.[3]

[1] The statement to this effect in *Williams & Muir Hunter* (19th edn) p 457 (ie the Old Bankruptcy law) was approved by Dillon LJ in *Re Thomas, ex p IRC v Falconer* [1984] 1 WLR 232 at 235.
[2] Bankruptcy Act 1914, s 108(1) and Insolvency Act 1986, s 375(1).
[3] And see para 21.12 below.

21.2.2 *Procedure on reviews.* It must be appreciated that the review procedure is not an appeal. It must proceed before the court whose decision is being reviewed. Thus, a judge of the county court cannot *review* its registrar's order,[1] and the fact that an appeal is proceeding against the order being reviewed is no bar to that review taking place.[2]

The application to rehear should not, as a general rule, be made ex parte, but should be made on notice of motion or on common application[3] in the ordinary way, as for an application for a stay (see para 21.1.7 above).

[1] *Re Maugham, ex p Maugham* (1888) 21 QBD 21, DC.
[2] *Re Wike, ex p Keighley* (1874) 9 Ch App 667.
[3] In New Law cases under the procedure in the Individual Insolvency Rules 1986, rr 7.1–7.4.

21.3 APPEALS

21.3.1 The system for hearing appeals from orders in bankruptcy is substantially different for cases proceeding under the New Law as opposed to the Old. Subject to the qualification that the leave of the court is required to appeal as consent order or an order as to costs only,[1] all orders in bankruptcy are subject to appeal. The Bankruptcy Act 1914, s 108(2) specifically provides that appeals be available to 'any person aggrieved'.[2] However, the corresponding provision in New Law cases, the Insolvency Act 1986, s 375(2) contains no reference to 'persons aggreived'. The Individual Insolvency Rules provide[3] that the Secretary of State may appeal an order for recission or anulment of a bankruptcy order or for a bankrupt's discharge but the Rules give no other guidance in New Law cases. Thus if, as appears to be the case, 'persons aggrieved', rather than only the parties, are now excluded from appealing bankruptcy court orders, there is a substantial difference in the appeal processes which operate in New Law cases as opposed to Old Bankruptcy Law cases. See para 21.3.10 below.

[1] See Bankruptcy Rules 1952, rr 127 and 128.
[2] See *A–G of Gambia v N'Jie* [1961] AC 617.
[3] Individual Insolvency Rules 1986, r 7.48.

1 Old Bankruptcy Law cases

21.3.2 *From the county court.* Appeal lies to the Divisional Court of the High Court of Justice.[1] The Bankruptcy Act 1914 provides that at least one bankruptcy judge of the Chancery Division should sit in this Divisional Court.[2] In practice the Court is usually of two judges, both of them bankruptcy judges.

[1] This is so, even though the order or judgment in question is made by a registrar of the court rather than a judge.
[2] Bankruptcy Act 1914, s 108(2)(a).

21.3.3 *Appeals from the Divisional Court.* These appeals are to the Court of Appeal but only if the Divisional Court of the Court of Appeal itself gives special leave. If such leave is given the decision of the Court of Appeal is final and no appeal lies therefrom to the House of Lords.[1]

[1] Bankruptcy Act 1914, s 108(2)(a).

21.3.4 *Appeals from the High Court (in bankruptcy).* Appeals from the registrars in bankruptcy in the High Court lie directly to the Court of Appeal.

21.3.5 *Appeals from the Court of Appeal.* As indicated above, there is no appeal from a decision of the Court of Appeal in its determination of appeals from the county court. However, in appeals from the High Court an appeal does lie from a decision of the Court of Appeal. This appeal is to the House of Lords but only with leave of the Court of Appeal[1] which will only be given when an important question of law arises.[2]

[1] Bankruptcy Act 1914, s 108(2)(b).
[2] Bankruptcy (Amendment No 3) Rules 1982, SI 1982/1437.

2 New Law cases

21.3.6 The system of appeals outlined above is changed by the Insolvency Act 1986 so that under that Act it is as follows:

21.3.7 *From county court and from the High Court registrar.* Appeal is to a single judge of the High Court[1] (rather than a Divisional Court in Old Bankruptcy Law cases).

[1] Insolvency Act 1986, s 375(2), Individual Insolvency Rules 1986, r 7.48(2).

21.3.8 *From the single appellate judge.* Appeal is to the Court of Appeal,[1] but only with the leave of the judge or of the Court of Appeal.

[1] Insolvency Act 1986, s 375(2), Individual Insolvency Rules 1986, r 7.48(2).

21.3.9 *Appeals from the Department of Trade and Industry.* An appeal lies to the High Court from decisions of the Department of Trade and Industry relating to the release of the trustee[1] and to the trustee's removal from office where creditors disapprove of the removal.[1]

[1] See chs 4 and 15 above.

21.3.10 A person is 'aggrieved' for the purposes of deciding if he is able to appeal an order of a bankruptcy court in an Old Bankruptcy Law case (see para 21.3.1 above), if he is a person 'against whom a decision has been pronounced which has wrongfully deprived him of something, or wrongfully affected his title to something'[1] or if he is 'a person who has a genuine grievance because an order has been made which prejudicially affects his interests.'[2]

The official receiver is a necessary party to an appeal in any case where a receiving order has been made. Unless there are special circumstances the official receiver does not appear on the hearing of an appeal against the making of a receiving order although he is the only respondent in case of an appeal against an order of adjudication.[3]

[1] *Re Sidebotham, ex p Sidebotham* (1880) 14 Ch D 458
[2] *A–G of the Gambia, v N'Jie* [1961] AC 617.
[3] *Re Baron, ex p Debtor v Official Receiver* [1943] Ch 177.

21.3.11 Because of the ability of a bankruptcy court to review its own decisions (see para 21.2.1 above), there are really two different methods whereby an order in bankruptcy may be challenged, ie by review or on appeal. As to which method is used much depends on the status of the person applying and upon whether the applicant is seeking to rely on an exercise of discretion or upon a claim that the original order was wrong in law.

In *Re Noble, ex p Bankrupt v Official Receiver*[1] Russell LJ distinguished the statutory power to review from the appellate jurisdiction, by indicating that review was a matter for the discretion of the court originally making the order to which objection is taken, whereas if an appeal is brought against such an order the court has no discretion but must allow the appeal if the objection is valid in law, or dismiss it if the objection is without legal foundation.[2]

Nevertheless, an appeal to the Divisional Court in an Old Bankruptcy Law case is by way of rehearing. Thus the court may not only review findings of fact but hear evidence in chief, or allow cross-examination on affidavits.[3]

[1] [1965] Ch 129 at 146.
[2] And see *Re Cohen, ex p Bankrupt v IRC* [1950] 2 All ER 36.
[3] See *Re Clarke, ex p Debtor v S Aston & Son Ltd* [1967] Ch 1121.

21.3.12 Appeals must be brought within four weeks, in the case of the Divisional Court from the perfection of the order,[1] or in the case of an appeal from the county court from the date of the making of the order appealed against.[2]

Whilst the court has power[3] to extend the time for appeal on such terms as it thinks just, the power has been restrictively exercised in bankruptcy[4] and it has been found that even the Court of Appeal cannot extend the time for appealing from the Divisional Court, nor entertain an appeal against the refusal of the Divisional Court to grant such an extension.[5]

If a party seeks to appeal against the refusal by the court to review and rescind one of its earlier decisions, that party may, in effect be seeking to appeal out of time against the original decision and he should more properly apply for leave to appeal out of time. This position was discussed in *Re Patel, ex p Debtor v Dullomo*[6] where Browne-Wilkinson V–C, restated the principles, set out in an unreported case,[7] which should be applied by the court when considering whether an extension of time should be granted.

There are five matters to which regard should be paid, namely:

(i) whether there is reasonable excuse for the delay;
(ii) whether there is substance in the proposed appeal;

(iii) whether the applicant will obtain any real benefit if the appeal succeeds;
(iv) whether it would be a hardship or an injustice to other parties if the application were granted; and
(v) whether the applicant's conduct has been such as to forfeit any claim to favourable consideration in the exercise of the court's discretion.

The Bankruptcy Act 1914 did not contain the provision now in the Insolvency Act 1986, at s 376 expressly giving the Court power to extend the time for doing anything limited by a specified time limit but it is not thought that s 376 will alter the Court's approval to time limits on appeals as set out above.

[1] RSC Ord 59, r 4(1).
[2] Ibid, r 4(1)(b).
[3] RSC Ord 3, r 5(1), Insolvency Act 1986, s 376.
[4] See *Macadam (No 2), ex p Guillaume v Trustee* [1950] 1 All ER 659; *Re Vanbergen, ex p Trustee of Property of Bankrupt, ex p Vanbergen* [1955] 1 All ER 40; *Re Noble, ex p Bankrupt v Official Receiver* [1965] Ch 129.
[5] *Podbery v Peak* [1981] Ch 344.
[6] [1986] 1 WLR 221 at 224.
[7] *Re Benson* (8 March 1971, Civil Division, Transcript 94).

21.3.13 The procedural table below sets out provisions for the lodgment of security for the costs of appeal. If necessary the court may increase or diminish the amount of security required. Applications relating to security for costs should be made on notice of motion, served on any person affected, supported by an affidavit setting out the circumstances relied on by the applicant.[1]

[1] Under the Old Bankruptcy Law, application is made under the Bankruptcy Rules 1952, r 129.

21.3.14 The procedural table below sets out the established practice and procedure for appeals under the Old Bankruptcy Law.

All appeals are subject to the Rules of the Supreme Court,[1] and in particular Ord 59, although the functions of the Registrar of Civil Appeals are exercisable by the Chief Bankruptcy Registrar.[2]

The Insolvency Rules provide that in New Law cases the procedure and practice of the Supreme Court relating to appeals to the Court of Appeal apply to appeals in bankruptcy.[3]

[1] Bankruptcy Rules 1952, r 132.
[2] Bankruptcy (Amendment No 3) Rules 1982, SI 1982/1437.
[3] Individual Insolvency Rules 1986, r 7.49.

21.4 PROCEDURAL TABLE FOR APPEALS

21.4.1 Appeals under the 'Old Bankruptcy Law'

Summary of table
Appeal from official receiver or Department of Trade and Industry to High Court (Steps 1, 2)
Appeal from county court to Divisional Court (Steps 3–11)
Appeal to Court of Appeal (Steps 12–16)

Steps to be Taken	RSC Ord 59	Bankruptcy Act 1914	Bankruptcy Rules 1952
Appeal from official receiver or Department of Trade and Industry to High Court			
1. Appellant files notice of motion as notice of appeal supported by affidavit.			
TIME: Within 4 weeks from time when decision appealed against was pronounced or made, unless time is extended.		s 108(3)	
This procedure applies to all appeals from decisions of the official receiver or Department of Trade and Industry, e g:		s 108(3)	
(1) Granting or withholding release of trustee;		s 93	
(2) removing trustee;		s 95(2)	
(3) relating to claims for money paid into the Insolvency Services Account; and		s 153(4)	
(4) admission or rejection by chairman of creditors' meeting of proof for purpose of voting.		Sch 1, para 14	
2. Judge hears appeal in open court and may allow or dismiss appeal.			
Appeal from county court to Divisional Court			
3. Appellant:			
(1) Lodges in High Court £75 as security for costs.			r 129
(2) Files notice of appeal with supporting affidavit, if any.	r 3(1)		
TIME: Within 4 weeks from date of judgment or order of county court unless extended by Chief Bankruptcy Registrar.	rr 4(1)(b), 19(3)(a); r 5(1)		
FEE ON ENTERING APPEAL: £15.			
Appeals from the county court lie to the Divisional Court except for appeals against committal, which lie direct to the Court of Appeal.		s 108(2)(a)	

Steps to be Taken	RSC Ord 59	Bankruptcy Act 1914	Bankruptcy Rules 1952
If a question of law is involved the county court judge may state a case for the opinion of the High Court.		s 100(3)	
Lodgement of the security is effected by taking the request for lodgment to the Supreme Court Pay Office for examination of the title. It is then presented at the Law Courts branch of the Bank of England, together with the notice of appeal and £20 in cash. The receipt for the money is indorsed on the notice of appeal, which is taken, together with the order appealed from, to the High Court of Justice in Bankruptcy, Thomas Moore Building, Royal Courts of Justice, Strand, London WC2, and entered.			
The Divisional Court may order a greater or lesser sum to be lodged as security for costs, or may dispense with it.			r 129
The fact that the appellant is legally-aided does not necessarily mean that the deposit will be reduced or dispensed with. In order to secure reduction of or dispensation with the security the appellant must show by evidence that an arguable appeal would otherwise go unheard through lack of funds.			
The grounds of appeal should be stated in the notice of appeal.	r 3(2)–(4)		
Failure to state the grounds does not necessarily lead to dismissal of the appeal. An appellant may rely on a point not taken in the court below if the court gives leave to raise the new point.			
Application for leave to appeal out of time should be made by separate notice of motion to the Divisional Court before the appeal is set down.			
4. Appellant serves notice of appeal on: (1) respondent; (2) all parties to proceedings in county court directly affected by appeal;	r 3(5)		
(3) Registrar of county court.	r 19(2).		
The supporting affidavit is not served.			

Steps to be Taken	RSC Ord 59	Bankruptcy Act 1914	Bankruptcy Rules 1952
5. If respondent wishes to contend that the decision of the county court should be varied or affirmed on other grounds, respondent files and serves respondent's notice on Appellant and all parties to proceedings in county court directly affected by appeal.	r 6 r 6(4)		
TIME: Within 4 weeks of service of notice of appeal.	r 6(4)(b)		
6. County Court Registrar: (1) enters date of service on the notice of appeal and files it with the proceedings.			r 131(a)
TIME: On being served with notice of appeal.			r 131(a)
(2) transmits file of proceedings to Chief Bankruptcy Registrar.			r 131(b)
TIME: Upon the application of the Chief Bankruptcy Registrar.			r 131(b)
7. Appellant applies to county court for: (1) copy of transcript of shorthand notes of judgment under appeal, if any; and (2) copy of judge's or registrar's notes.	r 19(4)		
8. Appellant sets down appeal by leaving with Chief Bankruptcy Registrar: (1) copy of judgment or order;	r 5(1)(a)		
(2) 2 copies of notice of appeal, one indorsed with amount of fee paid and the other indorsed with a certificate of date of service.	r 5(1)(b)		
(3) office copy of list of exhibits, if any.	r 5(1)(c)		
TIME: Within 7 days after service of notice of appeal, unless extended.	r 5(1)		
9. Appellant gives notice that appeal has been set down to all parties on whom notice of appeal was served, specifying list in which appeal is set down and any extension of the time allowed for setting down.	r 5(4)		
TIME: Within 2 days after appeal is set down.	r 5(4)		
10. Appellant leaves 2 sets of papers, for use of Divisional Court Judges, at Chief Bankruptcy Registrar's Department, Thomas Moore Building, Royal Courts of Justice, Strand, London WC2.			

Steps to be Taken	RSC Ord 59	Bankruptcy Act 1914	Bankruptcy Rules 1952
TIME: Not less than 7 days before the appeal is likely to be listed for hearing.	r 9(1)		
Each set of papers should contain copies of:			
(1) notice of appeal	r 9(1)(a)		
(2) order appealed from;	r 9(1)(d)		
(3) respondent's notice (if any), any pleadings and any supplementary notices of appeal;	r 9(1)(b), (c), (e)		
(4) all relevant affidavits filed;	r 9(1)(i)		
(5) all documents, including correspondence, required for the hearing;			
(6) transcripts of shorthand notes of judgment, if any, or copy notes of judgment as agreed between the parties and approved by registrar or judge who made order;	r 9(1)(f)		
(7) judge's or registrar's notes.	r 9(1)(f), (g)		
The documents in each set should be numbered; each set should have an index referring to such numbers left with the documents.			
11. Parties attend on appointed day for hearing of appeal. Appeals from county courts in bankruptcy are heard in the second fortnight of every term. At the end of the periods term the chief clerk settles the list of appeals to be heard in the following term.			
Appeal to Court of Appeal			
12. Appellant:			
(1) lodges in High Court £20 as security for costs;			r 129
(2) files notice of appeal.	r 3(1)		
TIME: Within 21 days from date on which judgment or order of court below was signed, entered or otherwise perfected, unless time is extended by Chief Bankruptcy Registrar.	r 4(1)(b) r 5(1)		
FEE ON ENTERING APPEAL: £15.			
Appeals from the High Court and the Divsional Court, and appeals against committal lie to the Court of Appeal. Special leave of the			

Steps to be Taken	RSC Ord 59	Bankruptcy Act 1914	Bankruptcy Rules 1952
Divisional Court of Appeal is required to appeal from the Divisional Court to the Court of Appeal.		s 108(2)(a)	
Applications for leave to appeal out of time should be made by separate notice of motion to the Court of Appeal before setting down the appeal.			
The grounds of appeal should be stated in the notice of appeal.	r 3(2)–(4)		
The Court of Appeal may order a greater or lesser sum than £75 to be paid as security for costs, or may dispense with it.			r 129 proviso
13. Appellant: (1) serves notice of appeal on respondent and all parties to proceedings in court below directly affected by appeal;	r 3(5)		
(2) applies for notes of judge or registrar.	r 19(4)		
14. Appellant sets down appeal as in Steps 8, 9.			
15. If respondent wishes to contend that the decision appealed against should be varied or affirmed on other grounds or was wrong, respondent files and serves respondent's notice as in Step 5.	r 6		
16. Appellant leaves 3 sets of papers, for use of Court of Appeal, at Room 136, Royal Courts of Justice, Strand, London WC2.	r 9(1), (2)		
TIME: Not less than 7 days after appeal is set down.		r 9(1)	
The sets of papers contain copies of the same documents as in Step 10; copies of the judge's or registrar's notes are, however, only required where no shorthand note was taken or mechanical recording made. Application for the notes is made as in Step 7 so that they are ready in time for the hearing of the appeal.			
17. Parties attend on appointed day for hearing of appeal.			

CHAPTER 22

The Matrimonial Home

22.1 INTRODUCTION

In many bankruptcies the house which provides the bankrupt and his family with their home will be the principal asset in the estate available for realisation and distribution among the creditors. As selling his home is likely to render not only the bankrupt but also his wife and children homeless a conflict of interest arises between the creditors, on the one hand, and the bankrupt's family, on the other, which has difficult social as well as financial implications.

The provisions of the Housing Act 1985 will usually ensure that the family, if evicted, will find shelter. But these provisions place the burden of housing the evicted family on the local community which already faces difficulty in meeting its various statutory obligations from stretched resources.

Not surprisingly, the rights of occupation of the bankrupt and his family were the subject of some controversy during the passage of the Insolvency Act 1985.[1] The Cork Committee Report[2] made recommendations which, had they been implemented, were likely to have resulted in a significant shift in the favour of the bankrupt's family when the court considered its competing claims with those of the creditors. These proposals met with considerable opposition, and the government took the view that they were too heavily weighted against the interests of creditors. An attempt in the

House of Lords to amend the Insolvency Bill along similar lines to the Cork Committee's proposals was defeated but the government agreed to hold further consultations and to consider the matter in the light of the debate in the House of Lords. In the event the Insolvency Act 1986 contains provisions[3] which effect some improvement in the position of the bankrupt and his or her spouse.

In the case of the spouse or former spouse who is a joint owner of the home, this improvement in her position is rather limited. The spouse who has no legal interest in the matrimonial property before the bankruptcy will benefit more. Effectively she had no rights under the Old Bankruptcy Law, because the Matrimonial Homes Act charge protecting her rights of occupation under that Act was void against the trustee in bankruptcy.[4] Under the New Law the bankrupt's spouse has continued rights of occupation which are a charge on the bankrupt's estate equivalent to the rights under the Matrimonial Homes Act 1983. The trustee will not be able to obtain a possession order against her except by application under that Act. However, as will be seen below, the interests of creditors will prevail in all but exceptional circumstances where the trustee seeks possession of the home after a delay of one year from the date on which the estate vests in him.

For convenience, throughout this chapter it is assumed that where one party only to the marriage becomes bankrupt it is the husband. The law applies equally, in theory at least, where the bankrupt spouse is the wife.

[1] For Insolvency Act 1985 see para 1.5.9 above.
[2] The Report of the Insolvency Law Review Committee, ch 24.
[3] Ss 336–338.
[4] Matrimonial Homes Act 1983, s 2(7), now repealed by the Insolvency Act 1986.

22.2 TITLE AND RIGHTS OF OCCUPATION

It should be stressed that the provisions of the Insolvency Act 1986 are directed only to the rights of the bankrupt and his spouse to *occupy* the matrimonial home. Nothing in the Insolvency Act affects the respective interests of the parties in the matrimonial home and which are vested in the bankrupt or his spouse. The trustee in bankruptcy can, of course, take no better title on adjudication than that already held by the bankrupt. All the bankrupt's property, including the matrimonial home, vests in the trustee subject to all such equities as affected it in the bankrupt's own hands. These equities include an equitable claim by a wife to an interest in the matrimonial home of which the legal estate is vested solely in the husband's name. The wife's equitable interest in the property itself must be distinguished from the wife's rights of occupation which are personal, and not proprietorial, rights. The equities also include an irrevocable licence given by the bankrupt to a relative who assisted in the purchase of the matrimonial home and thereafter lived in the premises.[1]

[1] *Re Sharpe, Trustee of Bankrupt v Sharpe* [1980] 1 All ER 198.

22.3 THE BANKRUPT'S BENEFICIAL INTEREST

Before considering what rights of occupation the bankrupt or his spouse may have in the matrimonial home, the trustee in bankruptcy or bankrupt spouse's legal advisor will have to ascertain the respective beneficial interests of the bankrupt and his spouse in the matrimonial home. As a preliminary matter, the trustee will be concerned to see whether an interest in the matrimonial home has been transferred to or acquired by the bankrupt's spouse in circumstances where the relevant transaction may be set aside as a voluntary disposition or avoidable settlement under the Old Bankruptcy Law or a transaction at an undervalue or to defraud creditors under the New Law.[1] Such circumstances may be a straightforward transfer of a property out of the husband's name and into joint names or the name of the wife, or an acquisition in joint names or the wife's sole name from funds supplied by the husband.

Cases will also arise where a property adjustment order is made in matrimonial proceedings which has the effect of reducing or even eliminating the bankrupt's beneficial interest in the matrimonial home. The fact that a settlement or transfer of property has to be made in order to comply with a property adjustment order does not prevent that settlement or transfer from being a settlement of property which can be avoided under the Bankruptcy Act 1914, s 42 or transactions at an under value or preference which can be set aside or varied under the Insolvency Act 1986, ss 339, 340.[2] The trustee may therefore seek to impeach the settlement or transfer without fetter from the matrimonial order. The existence of the wife's rights to financial relief against her husband may, however, provide the necessary consideration to support a settlement for the purposes of the Bankruptcy Act 1914 or give sufficient value to prevent the transaction being at an undervalue within the context of the Insolvency Act 1986. In *Re Abbott, ex p Trustee of Property of the Bankrupt v Abbott*[3] a wife compromised her claim for a property adjustment order in return for part of her husband's share of the proceeds of sale of the matrimonial home which they had owned jointly. The wife had no knowledge of her husband's insolvency. The husband became bankrupt within two years of the consent order in the matrimonial proceedings and his trustee applied to avoid the settlement under the Bankruptcy Act 1914, s 42. The Divisional Court held that the wife was a purchaser for valuable consideration and rejected the trustee's application. Where the matrimonial order is made after an available act of bankruptcy on the part of the husband, it will be set aside if the wife had notice of that act of bankruptcy before the order was made.[4] The fact that a matrimonial order might subsequently be set aside in the bankruptcy should not discourage the court from making the order.[5]

1 Old Law: ch 8 above; Bankruptcy Act 1914, s 42; Law of Property Act 1925, s 172; New Law: ch 17 above; Insolvency Act 1986, ss 339, 340 and s 423.
2 Matrimonial Causes Act 1973, s 39 as amended by Insolvency Act 1985, Sch 8, para 23, and Insolvency Act 1986, Sch 14.
3 [1983] Ch 45.
4 Bankruptcy Act 1914, s 45.
5 *Mullard v Mullard* (1981) 3 FLR 330.

22.4 GENERAL LAW RELATING TO PROPERTY

The respective beneficial interests of the bankrupt and his spouse will depend upon the general law relating to property and no attempt is made here to provide a comprehensive summary of those principles.

The following points, however, are noted:

22.4.1 Where legal title to the matrimonial home is vested in joint names and, as is not infrequently the case, the parties' beneficial interests are declared in the conveyance, or in a trust deed executed at the same time, that declaration is conclusive in the absence of fraud or mistake.[1] Usually such a declaration will be to the effect that the husband and wife are joint tenants in equal shares. In such a case neither the trustee nor the bankrupt's spouse may argue that the beneficial interests of the spouses should be adjusted to take into account a greater financial contribution by one party, even if that party has provided the whole of the money which has financed the acquisition of the property. The doctrine of implied or constructive trusts cannot apply to a transaction where an express declaration of trust has been made.[2] And a declaration that the parties are joint tenants in equal shares remains a conclusive declaration of the parties' respective interests after the severance of the joint tenancy.[3]

[1] *Wilson v Wilson* [1963] 2 All ER 447; *Leake v Bruzzi* [1974] 2 All ER 1196. NB *Bedson v Bedson* [1965] 2 QB 666 is not to be treated as good law.

[2] *Pettitt v Pettitt* [1970] AC 777; *Pink v Lawrence* (1977) 36 P & CR 98 CA. Whether trusts that are not express are resulting or constructive is outside the scope of this work. Besides, Lord Denning in *Hussey v Palmer* [1972] 1 WLR 1286 at 1289 suggested that it was 'more a matter of words than anything else . . . By whatever name it is described, it is a trust imposed by law whenever justice and good conscience require it'. This view is not generally shared, but it is a feature of this area of the law that the formulation of trusts in the reported cases is not amenable to rigorous consistent analysis.

[3] *Goodman v Gallant* [1986] 1 All ER 311.

22.4.2 Where the parties have separated, and one party remains in the home making all the mortgage repayments, that party is entitled to credit for one-half the capital element of those repayments before the division of the proceeds of sale. The interest repayments are properly regarded as equivalent to rent or payment for use and occupation and do not of course reduce the sum owing on the mortgage with a corresponding increase in the value of the equity of redemption. Accordingly the party in occupation must bear this element of the mortgage repayments in full.[1]

[1] *Leake v Bruzzi* [1974] 2 All ER 1196; *Suttil v Graham* [1977] 3 All ER 1117.

22.4.3 Where there is no express declaration of the parties' beneficial interests, either where the legal title is in joint names, or more usually in the husband's name alone, then normal trust principles apply. The principal authorities remain the House of Lords' decisions in *Pettitt v Pettitt*[1] and *Gissing v Gissing*.[2] For reference to the guiding principles applicable for the purposes of the Law of Property Act 1925, s 30, and equivalent applications, see para 22.14 below.

[1] [1970] AC 777.

[2] [1971] AC 886.

22.4.4 Where a spouse has made a substantial contribution in money or money's worth to the improvement of the matrimonial home, the spouse concerned may be treated as having acquired a share or enlarged share in the property by virtue of that contribution subject to any agreement between the spouses, express or implied; Matrimonial Proceedings and Property Act 1970, s 37. The exact size of any increased interest may be determined by the court if not agreed between the parties. In either event the trustee in bankruptcy of the spouse of the improver is bound by the increased interest.

22.4.5 Where an agreement to marry is terminated, the law relating to the rights of husband and wife including the provision as to improvements, see para 22.4.4 above, applies to any property in which either or both the previously engaged couple has or have a beneficial interest; Law Reform (Miscellaneous Provisions) Act 1970, s 2.

22.5 REALISING THE BANKRUPT'S INTEREST: OLD BANKRUPTCY LAW

22.5.1 Having determined the bankrupt's interest in the matrimonial home the trustee must seek to realise that interest by sale, either to the bankrupt's spouse or to a third party. In the latter case it will be necessary to obtain an order for possession against the bankrupt's spouse and family and, of course, against the bankrupt. The bankrupt has no right to remain in the home under the Old Bankruptcy Law. Not only has the whole of his interest passed to the trustee in bankruptcy, but he is obliged to do whatever is necessary to assist in the realisation of his property.[1] The bankrupt must therefore leave the house when called on to do so by the trustee and he has no defence to possession proceedings brought by the trustee.

[1] Bankruptcy Act 1914, s 22(3).

22.5.2 The wife with a beneficial interest in the home may not be prepared to leave at the request of the trustee. Faced with a wife maintaining a claim to occupy the home and with whom the trustee cannot negotiate a satisfactory sale of the bankrupt's interest, the trustee must seek an order for sale from the court under the Law of Property Act 1925, s 30 in order to comply with his obligation to realise the bankrupt's assets.

The application, by notice of motion in the High Court and by originating application in the county court, in either case supported by affidavit[1] will normally be for:

(a) declaratory relief as to beneficial interests of the parties if there is any dispute as to the extent of the wife's beneficial interest;
(b) an order that the wife as trustee for sale of the property do join with the trustee in selling the property with vacant possession;
(c) an order that the conduct of the sale of the property be given to the trustee;
(d) an order that the proceeds of sale, after the deduction of all necessary expenses of sale and of such sums as are required to redeem any charges

on the property, be distributed between the trustee and the wife in accordance with the beneficial interests; or

(e) consequential directions, further or other relief and costs.

[1] RSC Ord 8 rr 1–5, 14; CCR Ord 3, r 4.

22.5.3 Under the Law of Property Act 1925, s 30 the court on an application for an order for sale 'may make such order as it thinks fit'. The court accordingly has a discretion whether or not to order an immediate sale. The trustee makes his application in his own right as a 'person interested in the trusts for sale'. He is not therefore standing in the shoes of the bankrupt and will not fail in his application merely because the bankrupt, as a husband, would have failed.[1] By the same token he is not entitled, automatically, to an order for sale simply because of his duty to realise the bankrupt's assets.[2]

In *Re Turner*[3]: Goff J stated that 'the guiding principle in the exercise of the court's discretion is not whether the trustee or the wife is being reasonable but, in all the circumstances of the case, whose voice in equity ought to prevail'. Goff J then went on to hold that 'based on his statutory duty' the trustee had the stronger claim and required the court 'to treat his voice as the one which ought to prevail in equity'.

[1] *Re Holliday, ex p Trustee of Bankrupt v Bankrupt* [1981] Ch 405, CA. The trustee is not therefore concerned with the 'underlying purpose' of the trust nor its 'primary object' as between the husband and wife which are relevant considerations in the matrimonial law context: *Williams v Williams* [1976] Ch 278; *Re Evers Trust, Papps v Evers* [1980] 3 All ER 399.

[2] *Re Turner, ex p Trustee of Bankrupt v Turner* [1975] 1 All ER 5.

[3] Ibid, at p 1558.

22.5.4 The considerations behind the respective applications of the trustee for a quick sale and the wife for a postponed sale are very different and will usually be hard to compare. The cases show that the approach of Goff J stated above is the correct starting point and accordingly it is only in exceptional circumstances that the wife's voice will prevail.

The fact that the wife and family of the bankrupt will be rendered homeless is not an exceptional circumstance. As Walton J stated in *Re Lowrie, ex p Trustee of the Bankrupt v the Bankrupt*:[1]

> '. . . I think it is desirable to step back for a moment and look at the situation which must in these cases inevitably occur, or at any rate must occur so frequently as to be almost inevitable. The first one of course is that the whole family are going to be rendered homeless. That is not an exceptional circumstance. It is a normal circumstance and is the result, the all too obvious result, of a husband having conducted the financial affairs of the family in a way which has led to bankruptcy. The second result almost invariably is that it is going to be incredibly hard and incredibly hard luck on the co-owner, the wife, who is in most cases a totally innocent person who has done nothing to bring about the bankruptcy. Of course, as against that, one has to realise that she has been enjoying, over whatever period it may be, the fruits of the debts which the bankrupt has contracted and which debts are not at the moment being paid. So that, although it may be very bad luck on her, she has had some enjoyment of the fruits which led to the bankruptcy.'

[1] [1981] 3 All ER 353 at 356.

22.5.5 With these comments in mind, it seems likely that exceptional circumstances will be made out only where children of the family or serious illness come into the consideration.

Matters which may be relied on by the wife such as, for example, creditors' money not having been used to purchase or improve the home, or the bankrupt having deserted the home long before the bankruptcy (even perhaps when he was solvent and before he started the business by which he became bankrupt), or the creditors all being institutions or government agencies who will not suffer in any meaningful sense by a postponement of part of their dividends in the bankruptcy, or the non-availability of alternative accommodation, or the prospect that the wife's employment may be disrupted, may all be relevant considerations but appear unlikely, by themselves, to give rise to exceptional circumstances.

22.5.6 As will be seen below, an 'exceptional circumstances' test has now been enacted in the New Law. Accordingly, as the cases decided under the Old Bankruptcy Law proceeded, in general terms, along this basis and will therefore be relevant when considering the parties' rights to occupy the matrimonial home under the New Law as well as the Old Bankruptcy Law, summaries of the main cases reported in the last 20 years are set out below. It will be noted that only in *Re Holliday* was a postponement of any length ordered, and that case was indeed exceptional. Where she cannot make out a case of exceptional circumstances, and there is no convenient date to which to delay possession, e g the end of a school term, the wife is likely to be given about three months to arrange her affairs before the order for sale is enforced. Should there be a possibility that the wife may buy out her husband's interests the court will usually allow her sufficient time to ascertain what sum is required and to seek financial assistance to enable her to make an appropriate offer.[1]

When considering these cases under the New Law, the possibility that the imposition of a charging order under the Insolvency Act 1986, s 313 might affect the exercise of the court's discretion should be borne in mind: see para 22.11 below.

[1] See e g, *Re Pittertou, ex p Trustee of Property of Bankrupt v Bankrupt* [1985] 1 All ER 285.

Case summaries

22.5.7 *Re Solomon, ex p Trustee of Property of Bankrupt v Solomon* [1967] Ch 573

Hearing: June 1966.
H and W purchased property as joint tenants in 1949.
H deserted 1954.
H adjudicated bankrupt 1964.

When H's trustee in bankruptcy applied for an order for sale W relied not only on the fact that she was a deserted wife and part-owner of the property but also upon an undertaking H had given in matrimonial proceedings on a consent order for maintenance to the effect that he would allow the wife to occupy the property rent free for life and would not dispose of or otherwise deal with the property without providing for the wife's rights of occupation therein.

Goff J held that the undertaking was a personal right of the wife which did not create an interest in the land and thus did not bind the trustee in bankruptcy. An order for sale was made and stayed for a reasonable time (not reported) to allow the wife 'to find other accommodation and to arrange her affairs.'

22.5.8 *Re Turner, ex p Trustee of Bankruptcy v Turner* [1975] 1 All ER 5

Although the statement of principles which this decision contains are frequently quoted the facts of the case are not well reported.

Hearing: July 1974.
H and W owned matrimonial home as joint tenants in equity and law.
The matrimonial home was the only realisable asset in the bankruptcy.
No figures are given in the report of the case concerning the extent of the bankrupt's liabilities or the value of his equity in the matrimonial home.

This case propounds the principle referred to in the text of this chapter that it is not reasonableness but 'whose voice in equity should prevail in all the circumstances' that governs the exercise of the court's discretion and that in deciding whose voice should prevail the trustee in bankruptcy's statutory duty to realise the husband's interest gives him the stronger claim. An order for sale was made. Having given judgment the court suspended the order for sale for two months to give W an opportunity to negotiate a purchase with the trustee in bankruptcy.

22.5.9 *Re McCarthy, ex p Trustee of Bankruptcy v McCarthy* [1975] 2 All ER 857

H and W joint tenants at law and in equity.
W did not actively contest an order for sale.

This case is reported as it resolved doubts whether the court could order one joint tenant to give up possession to the trustee in bankruptcy of the other joint tenant. Goff J held that such an order for possession could be made, although he did not do so in this case, and indicated that a possession order would be made if any party in possession obstructed the sale, e g making it difficult for prospective purchasers to view the property.

22.5.10 *Re Densham, ex p Trustee of Bankruptcy v Densham* [1975] 3 All ER 726

Hearing: March 1975.

Considerable debts. House only substantial asset.
H and W married 1970, purchased house October 1970 for £5,650. W contributed to deposit. Not joint owner at law but name had been deleted from contract due to some misunderstanding. Agreement by H to give W half held void as voluntary settlement. W's beneficial interest assessed to be one-ninth.

On question of postponement of sale W relied on her nervous illness brought on by H's imprisonment for theft from employers, bankruptcy and associated difficulties, together with possible harmful effects on children in moving. Goff J made an order for sale but with a 'generous' time for possession, six months.

22.5.11 *Re Bailey, Bailey v Trustee of Property of Bankrupt* [1977] 2 All ER 26

Hearing: 11 October 1976.
H left W in 1971.
One child aged 16 in custody of W.
Decree Absolute 1974.

W and son in occupation of matrimonial home.
H adjudicated bankrupt June 1975.
Matrimonial home vested in joint names.
Equity in house after sale; £12,000.00.
Debts and expenses: £4,000.

The county court judge in July 1976 ordered a sale of the property but postponed its effect for ten months, conditional upon W paying £3,000 to trustee in bankruptcy in two months.

The son's full-time education would not be completed until two years after the county court hearing. On appeal the Divisional Court (Megarry V–C, Walton J) found that in the circumstances of the case, and the house being the only real asset in the bankruptcy and since a move of house would not necessarily mean a change of school for the son, an immediate sale should take place, W being unable to comply with the county court judge's condition. The Divisional Court ordered possession to be given on 7 January 1977.

22.5.12 *Re Holliday, ex p Trustee of Bankrupt v Bankrupt* [1981] Ch 405

Hearing: October 1979.
H & W married 1962.
Three children, aged 14, 11 and 6.
H left matrimonial home May 1974.
W obtained decree nisi 1974 and custody of the children.
Matrimonial home: purchased November 1970 in joint names. On W's application for ancillary relief in the divorce proceedings H filed his own petition and was adjudicated the same day. He was insolvent.

When H served notice under the Law of Property Act 1925, s 30 W applied, as a person interested, to annul H's adjudication in bankruptcy as an abuse of the process of the court. This aspect of the decision is referred to in ch 6 above. For these purposes, even accepting that H's actions were motivated by a desire to frustrate W's ancillary applications in the matrimonial proceedings, the court had to consider how to exercise its discretion under the Law of Property Act 1925, s 30 to order a sale. In deciding whether to exercise its discretion to order a sale the test is whether in equity, the voice of the trustee in favour of sale of the matrimonial home for the benefit of the creditors or that of the wife in favour of retention for herself and the children should prevail. In applying that test the existence of young children does not prolong the secondary or collateral purpose of the trust for sale but it is a factor to be taken into account so far as it affects the equities as between the persons entitled to the beneficial interests.

In this case, Foster J ordered immediate sale. However, on fresh evidence being adduced six months later, showing W's inability to purchase a house for herself and the children out of her resources and a half-share of the equity of redemption, linked with the possible upsetting of the children's education and the fact that, in this case, as the court held, no great hardship would be caused to the creditors by a deferment of the sale, the Court of Appeal ordered that the sale be postponed for five years.

22.5.13 *Re Lowrie, ex p Trustee of Bankrupt v Bankrupt* [1981] 3 All ER 353

Hearing: 11 May 1981.
H and W married 1974.
Two children aged 3 and 1.
H insolvent from August 1975.
H adjudicated bankrupt August 1979.
Matrimonial home in H's sole name with current value £30,000.00 and equity of redemption £20,000. A total of £9,600 was needed to discharge the debts and expenses of the bankruptcy.

The county court judge determined that the wife was entitled to half beneficial interest in house. Made an order for sale on 24 February 1981 but suspended the order for 30 months partly because children were young and partly to allow time for wife to try and pay off the bankrupt husband's debts. On appeal to Divisional Court in bankruptcy, the court ordered suspension of order for sale for only three months, the existence of the young children not being exceptional and the idea of allowing the wife time to pay the debts being misguided. The creditors being entitled to only 4% interest, and the value of money being diminished year by year by inflation, it was held that the creditors were suffering unnecessary hardship if they were kept out of their money for any appreciable length of time.

22.6 REALISING THE BANKRUPT'S INTEREST: NEW LAW

The rights of occupation of bankrupt's spouse[1]

22.6.1 These rights apply equally to a spouse or former spouse but do not extend to a co-habitee or any dependent relative who may be living with the bankrupt at the date of his bankruptcy. For these purposes there are two categories of spouse to consider. The spouse who does have a beneficial interest in the property comprising the matrimonial home, whether or not she also has a legal interest, and the spouse who does not. For the spouse who does have a legal or beneficial interest in the property, and who will face an application by the trustee under the Law of Property Act 1925, s 30 for an order for possession and sale, the Act specifies the considerations to which the court must have regard when exercising its discretion on such an application. See para 22.7 below.

For the spouse who has no interest in the property either legal or equitable, the scheme of the Act is to extend the spouse's rights of occupation under the Matrimonial Homes Act 1983 beyond the commencement of the bankruptcy and make such rights binding on the trustee in bankruptcy.[2] Accordingly if the trustee wishes to obtain possession of the property he must make an application under the Matrimonial Homes Act 1983. On the determination of such an application the court must have regard to the same considerations as those specified for the purposes of applications under the Law of Property Act 1925, s 30.

1 Insolvency Act 1986, s 336.
2 Accordingly Matrimonial Homes Act 1983, s 2(7), which provides that the charge on the bankrupt's estate which comprises the rights of occupation of the spouse is void against the trustee in bankruptcy, is repealed: Insolvency Act 1985, s 235, Sch 10.

22.6.2 The rights of occupation under the Matrimonial Homes Act 1983 arise where one spouse (for present purposes the debtor who becomes bankrupt) 'is entitled to occupy a dwelling house by virtue of a beneficial estate or interest or contract or by virtue of any enactment giving him the right to remain in occupation', and the other spouse has no such entitlement. The rights of occupation given to the spouse not so entitled are:[1]

> '(a) if in occupation, a right not to be evicted or excluded from the dwelling house or any part thereof by the other spouse except with the leave of the court given by an order under Section 1 of the Matrimonial Homes Act 1983;
> (b) if not in occupation, a right with the leave of the court so given to enter into and occupy the dwelling house'.

The spouse has her rights of occupation over all the property which the debtor spouse was entitled to occupy before the bankruptcy. Thus, where the debtor was entitled to occupy two or more properties his spouse has rights of ocupation over all of them and is not restricted to any one property which may have been treated as the primary family home. The scope of the debtor spouse's entitlement covers not only freehold and leasehold interests in land, which are not themselves leased (beneficial estates or interests), but also licences or contracts to purchase a freehold or leasehold title (contracts) and also statutory tenancies (enactments giving rights to remain in occupation).

However, only dwelling houses which have actually been occupied as a matrimonial home of the spouses concerned may be the subject of Matrimonial Homes Act rights. Where, for example, a husband occupied a flat belonging to his wife but never shared occupation with her, he acquired no rights of occupation in that flat.[2] These rights are of course personal to the spouse enjoying them and cannot be assigned.

1 Matrimonial Homes Act 1983, s 1(1).
2 Matrimonial Homes Act 1983, s 1(10); *Collins v Collins* (1973) 4 Fam Law 133.

22.6.3 The wife's rights under the Matrimonial Homes Act, if any, are determined as at the date on which the petition is presented against the debtor and on which he is subsequently adjudicated bankrupt. Nothing which the bankrupt does between the date of the petition and the date on which his property vests in the trustee, may give rise to any rights of occupation under the 1983 Act.[1] The Insolvency Act 1986 does not preclude the possibility that the bankrupt may cause matrimonial homes rights to be lost after the presentation of the petition, but this supposes divorce proceedings in which the wife will be entitled to seek property and financial relief.

The rights of occupation of a spouse under the 1983 Act constitute a charge on the relevant estate or interest.[2] The charge takes priority as an equitable interest created at whichever is the later date of the following:

(a) the date on which the debtor spouse acquired his estate or interest;
(b) the date of the marriage; or
(c) 1 January 1968 (the date on which the Matrimonial Homes Act 1967 came into force).

The charge can be registered as a land charge and should be registered to protect the spouse's priority and bind subsequent purchasers. Only one charge may, however, be registered even where the wife has rights of occupation over several properties.[3] The charge continues to subsist after the bankruptcy, and until an order is made terminating it, the charge binds both the trustee in bankruptcy and any persons deriving title under the trustee, provided of course that it has been registered.

1 Insolvency Act 1986, ss 336(1) and 284.
2 Matrimonial Homes Act 1983, s 2.
3 Matrimonial Homes Act 1983, s 3.

22.7 APPLICATION BY THE TRUSTEE FOR POSSESSION AND SALE

22.7.1 Whether the trustee has to bring his application under the Law of Property Act 1925, s 30 or under the Matrimonial Homes Act 1983, s 1, he must proceed in the court having jurisdiction in relation to the bankruptcy.[1] As stated above, the court has a discretion whether to make an order on the trustee's application and if so on what terms, under either statutory provision, and the Insolvency Act 1986[2] specifies the considerations to which the court shall have regard. These are the same for either application. The Insolvency Act provides that the court shall make such order under the Matrimonial Homes Act 1983, s 1 or the Law of Property Act 1925, s 30 as it thinks just and reasonable having regard to:

(a) the interests of the bankrupt's creditors;
(b) the conduct of the spouse or former spouse so far as contributing to the bankruptcy;
(c) the needs and financial resources of the spouse or former spouse;
(d) the needs of any children; and
(e) all the circumstances of the case other than the needs of the bankrupt.

A wife facing an application by the trustee for possession or sale may therefore initiate an extensive review of the relevant facts and circumstances of the bankruptcy. The 'interests of the bankrupt's creditors' may, on the one hand, be pressing, where small businesses are owed debts which form a significant proportion of their total income and failure to receive an early dividend may spell great hardship. On the other hand, the creditor's interests may be of no immediate concern where the likely dividend in the bankruptcy will be a tiny proportion of the creditor's income.

The 'conduct of the spouse so far as contributing to the bankruptcy' is likely to give rise to widespread issues from assisting in the bankrupt's business to leading a lavish lifestyle unrelated to her husband's real income. The 'needs and financial resources of the spouse' and 'the needs of the children' will encompass not only the financial aspects of accommodation and household expenses but also the educational or training needs of the children.

1 Insolvency Act 1986, s 336(2)(6) for matrimonial homes applications. Insolvency Act 1986, s 336(3) for Law of Property Act 1925, s 30 applications. For the court having jurisdiction in relation to the bankruptcy see generally, ch 13.7 above. It may be noted that while the Matrimonial Homes Act provides that either spouse may apply to the court for an order, the Insolvency Act 1986 does not expressly extend to the trustee in bankruptcy the right to apply for an order under the 1983 Act. Parliament was presumably satisfied that the trustee could rely on his general powers to bring legal proceedings relating to the property comprised in the bankrupt's estate, and his general role standing in the shoes of the bankrupt.
2 Insolvency Act 1986, s 336(5).

22.7.2 Such a wide ranging review of the relevant facts and circumstances could well lead the trustee into lengthy, time-consuming and expensive litigation, probably against a legally-aided wife. By waiting for one year after the property vests in him, however, the trustee can cut through much of the potential complexity of his application and circumvent most, if not all, of the matters which may be raised by the wife to defeat or postpone an order for sale. The Act provides[1] that where the trustee makes his application after this one-year period 'the Court shall assume, unless the circumstances of the case are exceptional, that the interests of the bankrupt's creditors outweigh all other considerations'. The trustee will then be in much the same position as he was with applications under the Law of Property Act 1925, s 30 before the Insolvency Act 1986. For applications under the Old Law, see paras 22.5.3 to 22.5.13 above which suggests that it is only in very rare cases that he will encounter exceptional circumstances. For the purposes of applications under the New Law, the wife's legal advisers should consider whether the imposition of a charging order under the Insolvency Act 1986, s 313 might affect the exercise of the court's discretion, see para 22.11 below.

1 Insolvency Act 1986, s 336(5).

22.8 OTHER ORDERS FROM THE COURT

The fact that the trustee either has to wait a year or more because of a refusal by the court to make an order for possession or sale against the wife, or feels that he has to wait a year in order to have good prospects of obtaining an order for possession at all may lead him to consider seeking other orders against the wife in respect of her continuing occupation of the matrimonial home. The Matrimonial Homes Act 1983, s 1(3) enables the court to make any order it thinks just and reasonable, including:

(i) an order that a spouse occupying the dwelling house or any part of it shall make periodical payments in respect of the occupation; and

(ii) an order imposing obligations as to the repair and maintenance of the dwelling house or the discharge of any liabilities in respect of the dwelling house.

The prospects of the trustee obtaining such an order will depend substantially on the length of time he is likely to be kept out of occupation and any particular circumstances of the case. For example, a wife who has no beneficial interest in the property (yet having income or assets of her own) ought in principle to contribute to the outgoings on the property, especially where she is not in occupation at the date of the bankruptcy but seeks to exercise her right to enter into and occupy the matrimonial home. Where the wife does have a beneficial interest in the property, and the trustee is proceeding by way of application under the Law of Property Act 1925, s 30, he cannot obtain an occupation rent against the wife as co-owner. The trustees for sale do, however, have all the powers of a tenant for life and the trustees of a settlement under the Settled Land Act 1925[1] and these powers include powers of management of the property.

The court has a wide discretion under the Law of Property Act 1925, s 30 to make orders in respect of a failure to exercise any of the powers conferred on the trustees for sale, and the trustee is in a position to seek appropriate orders against the wife as co-owner relating to the management of the property and the discharge of obligations arising on it.

[1] Law of Property Act 1925, s 28.

22.9 THE BANKRUPT'S RIGHTS OF OCCUPATION[1]

22.9.1 In order to safeguard the interests of children, the Act provides for rights of occupation to be extended to a bankrupt where children have their home with the bankrupt both at the time that the bankruptcy petitition was presented and at the commencement of the bankruptcy. The Act operates by vesting in the bankrupt rights equivalent to the rights of occupation arising under the Matrimonial Homes Act 1983. These rights of occupation are extended to a bankrupt with a beneficial estate or interest in a dwelling house with whom

> 'any persons under the age of eighteen with whom (the bankrupt) had at some time occupied that dwelling house had their home with (the bankrupt) at the time when the bankruptcy petition was presented and at the commencement of the bankruptcy.'

It is not necessary that the infants are children of the bankrupt or of his family in the matrimonial law sense. The law requires only that they should have occupied the house before or at the presentation of the petition and that they had their home there at the date of the presentation of the petition and the date of the bankruptcy order.

[1] Insolvency Act 1986, s 337.

22.9.2 Where the bankrupt qualifies for rights of occupation by reason of having children with their home in his house, he has as against the trustee of his estate, and irrespective of whether any spouse of his has Matrimonial Homes Act rights, the following rights:[1]

> '(i) if in occupation, a right not to be evicted or excluded from the dwelling house or any part thereof, except with the leave of the Court,
> (ii) if not in occupation, a right with the leave of the Court to enter into and occupy the dwelling house.'

It will thus be seen that these rights follow the definition of the rights of occupation under the Matrimonial Homes Act 1983, and as with matrimonial homes rights, the bankrupt's rights are a charge on the estate or interest which vests in the trustee.[2] This charge has the same priority as an equitable interest created immediately before the commencement of the bankruptcy. As the bankrupt's rights vest irrespective of any rights which his spouse may have, the fact that his wife is living in the dwelling house at the commencement of the bankruptcy does not prevent him obtaining his rights of occupation. Accordingly these provisions apply equally to the bankrupt who is living in the matrimonial home with his wife and family as to the bankrupt deserted by or without a spouse who is looking after children.

1 Insolvency Act 1986, s 337(2).
2 Ibid, s 337(2)(b).

22.9.3 These rights of occupation vested in the bankrupt take effect as rights under the Matrimonial Homes Act 1983.[1] Thus if the trustee wishes to obtain an order for possession against the bankrupt he must bring an application under the Matrimonial Homes Act 1983, s 1. This application must be made to the court having jurisdiction in relation to the bankruptcy. As in the case of the bankrupt's spouse, the Act specifies the considerations to which the court must have regard when making such order as it thinks just and reasonable. These considerations are:[2]

(a) the interests of the creditors;
(b) the bankrupt's financial resources;
(c) the needs of the children; and
(d) all the circumstances of the case other than the needs of the bankrupt.

Again, as with applications by the trustee against the bankrupt's spouse, where the trustee brings his application after the end of one year from the date on which the property first vests in him, the court is required to assume, unless the circumstances of the case are exceptional, that the interests of the creditors outweigh all other considerations.

1 Insolvency Act 1986, s 337(3).
2 Ibid, s 338.

22.10 OTHER ORDERS UNDER THE MATRIMONIAL HOMES ACT 1983

As noted in para 22.8 above it is possible for the court to make an order under the Matrimonial Homes Act 1983, s 1 that a spouse makes periodical payments in respect of occupation, or imposing obligations as to repair or the discharging of liabilities. In relation to the bankrupt living with children such an order may be made on the separate application of the trustee or by the court when considering an application by the bankrupt to enter into and occupy the dwelling house. Should the bankrupt occupy any premises comprised in the estate on condition that he makes payments towards satisfying any mortgage or other liabilities arising in respect of the premises, whether by virtue of a Matrimonial Homes Act order or otherwise, the Insolvency Act 1986[1] is careful to provide that the bankrupt does not acquire any interest in the premises by virtue of those payments.

[1] Insolvency Act 1986, s 338.

22.11 CHARGE ON DWELLING HOUSE

22.11.1 The trustee has power to apply to the court for a charging order on any property consisting of an interest in a dwelling house occupied by the bankrupt, his spouse or his former spouse, for the benefit of the bankrupt's estate.[1] If made, such a charging order will be subject to the Charging Orders Act 1979, s 3 and accordingly the court has a general power to impose conditions inter alia as to when the charge is to become enforceable. The charge will be enforceable for any amounts due in the bankruptcy together with interest, other than payments made to the bankrupt out of his estate. The power to impose a charge for the benefit of the estate on property which already forms part of that estate becomes meaningful when it is appreciated that should the property cease to be part of the estate and revest in the bankrupt on his discharge, it nevertheless remains charged for the benefit of the creditors. The charging order must so provide.[2]

The purpose of introducing this power into the Act was to enable a trustee, in circumstances where he was not able to dispose of a bankrupt's interest in a dwelling house by the time he had completed the remainder of the administration of the estate, to obtain his release without leaving the property vested in the official receiver, possibly for many years. The possibility that the trustee may impose a charge on the property which carries a reasonable rate of interest[3] may be a matter which will influence the exercise of a court's discretion when considering whether to order an immediate or postponed sale of the dwelling house on the application of the trustee against the bankrupt or his spouse. On such applications the interests of the creditors must always be a prime consideration, and as noted above, on applications made more than one year after the property has vested in the trustee, the interests of the creditors outweigh all other considerations.

It will be recalled that in *Re Lowrie*, para 22.5.13 above, the court held that the creditors were prejudiced by the value of their money being diminished by inflation, the interest rate on debts proved in the bankruptcy being fixed at 4% per annum under the Old Bankruptcy Law. With the more realistic interest rates accruing under the New Law that prejudice at least is removed, although the creditors are also prejudiced simply by being kept out of their money. In appropriate cases it may be possible for the bankrupt or his spouse to succeed in achieving a postponed or conditional sale of the dwelling house where a charging order is imposed to safeguard the interests of the creditors. Only the trustee may formally apply for a charging order but, it is suggested, the court ought not to allow a trustee who fails to make an application for a charging order to prejudice otherwise satisfactory arrangements which both protect the interests of the creditors and allow the bankrupt and his family to continue living in the matrimonial home.

1 Insolvency Act 1986, s 313, and see para 16.4.6 above.
2 Insolvency Act 1986, s 313(3).
3 The rate will be prescribed but will usually be the rate applicable to judgment debts.

22.11.2 *Procedure.* The Rules[1] provide that a trustee applying for a charging order on property consisting of an interest in a dwelling house must join the bankrupt's spouse or former spouse as respondents to the application, together with any other persons interested in the property who the court may direct should also be joined as respondents. The trustee is required[2] to make a report to the court particularizing both (a) the extent of the bankrupt's interest in the subject property and (b) the amount remaining owing to unsecured creditors of the bankrupt at the date of the application. The terms of any charge to be imposed are to be settled by the court only if agreement cannot be reached between the trustee and the bankrupt.[3] The Rules prescribe seven matters which must be included in the court's order imposing a charge.[4] These include the specifying of the date on which the property charged should revest in the bankrupt. Ordinarily this will be the date of registration of the charge.[5]

1 Individual Insolvency Rules 1986, r 6.237(2).
2 Ibid, r 6.237(3).
3 Ibid, r 6.237(4).
4 Ibid, r 6.237(5)(6).
5 Ibid, r 6.237(7).

22.12 THE SPOUSE'S EQUITY OF EXONERATION

22.12.1 In the course of running his business the husband will not infrequently need to borrow money. Banks and other financial institutions will rarely lend money without security and in many instances this will involve a charge on the matrimonial home. In the light of recent decisions[1] institutional lenders will be careful to ensure that any charge on the home is executed by the wife as well as the husband. Where the loan is purely for the business purposes of the husband, the wife will not derive any direct benefit from it, although her interest in the house will have been charged. In these circumstances, it may be possible for the wife to invoke her equitable right of exoneration and throw the burden of the debt secured by the charge on to his share of the matrimonial home. Then, when the trustee obtains an order for sale the whole of the relevant charge or charges will be deducted from the husband's share of the proceeds of sale and the wife's share will be correspondingly greater.

1 See in particular *Williams & Glyns Bank Ltd v Boland* [1981] AC 487 where the House of Lords held that a wife who had a beneficial though no legal interest in the property and who was in actual occupation had an overriding interest for the purpose of the Land Registration

Act 1925, s 70 to which the bank's charge on the legal title created solely by the husband was subject. Accordingly the bank was unable to obtain possession of the property as against the wife. Nb *Bristol & West Building Society v Henning* [1985] 2 All ER 606, CA on the priority of equitable interests as between mortgagee and cohabitee who knew that the property was purchased with the aid of a mortgage.

22.12.2 The equity is indeed wider in scope than is implied above and extends to a right of indemnity where the wife's property is charged for the benefit of the husband. The statement of principle expressed in 22 Halsbury's Laws (4th edn) para 1071 has recently been approved by the court[1] namely:

> 'If the property of a married woman is mortgaged or charged in order to raise money for the payment of her husband's debts, or otherwise for his benefit, it is presumed, in the absence of evidence showing an intention to the contrary, that she meant to charge her property merely by way of security, and in such case she is in the position of surety, and is entitled to be indemnified by the husband, and to throw the debt primarily on his estate to the exoneration of her own.'

This equity is not limited to cases in bankruptcy but is of general application and will apply for example in the administration of estates. In the context of bankruptcy it will be appreciated that the wife's right of indemnity against the husband's estate will be of very little value. The husband being bankrupt is unlikely to be in a position to satisfy the indemnity, and the wife's priority in the distribution of assets is, as set out in para 16.8, very low. It should be pointed out, however, that where a wife as surety meets the claim of her husband's creditor she may prove in her husband's bankruptcy with the same priority as that creditor would have had. But while the wife's right of indemnity may be of little practical use, as has been indicated above, her right to throw the burden of any charge onto the husband's share of the matrimonial home, or any other property jointly owned and charged, may well be of real financial significance.[2]

1 See Scott J in *Re Pittortou, ex p Trustee of Property of Bankrupt* [1985] 1 WLR 58 at 61.
2 Any doubt as to whether the wife surety is able to claim an enhanced proprietary interest against the trustee by exercising her right of exoneration 'against' the bankrupt's share of the equity in the property was dispelled by the Bankruptcy Divisional Court in *Re Debtor (No 24 of 1971), ex p Marley v Trustee* [1976] 2 All ER 1010.

22.12.3 It must be noted, however, that the equity of exoneration is only a presumptive right. It depends upon the intention of the parties being that the wife should be standing in the position of surety for her husband. No intention need be expressed; it is to be ascertained from all the relevant circumstances in any individual case.[1] And while the cases describe the right as presumptive, there is no evidential burden on the husband or trustee to disprove it. In the words of Lindley MR:[2]

> 'To say that in all such cases there is a presumption in favour of the wife, and that it is for the husband to rebut it, is, in our opinion, to go too far and to use language calculated to mislead. The circumstances of each case must all be weighed in order to see what inference ought to be drawn; and until an

inference in favour of the wife arises there is no presumption for the husband to rebut. If this is forgotten, error may creep in.'

1 *Paget v Paget* [1898] 1 Ch 470, 474, per Lindley MR; *Clinton v Hooper* (1791) 1 Ves 173; and see, e g *Pocock v Lee* (1707) 2 Vern 604; *Aguilar v Aguilar Lousada* (1820) 5 Madd 414; *Gee v Smart* (1857) 8 E and B 313 and generally the cases cited at 27(1). The Digest (Re-issue) pp 168–173.
2 *Paget v Paget* n 1 above, at 475.

22.12.4 No inference has been drawn in favour of the wife in circumstances where:
(a) the evidence showed that the wife intended to make a gift to the husband;[1]
(b) the money was raised to pay debts of the husband incurred to maintain an extravagent life style on the part of both husband and wife;[2]
(c) the money was raised in part to discharge the wife's debts and the husband had the benefit of the surplus. The court here inferred that as there was only one transaction there was a uniform intention that the wife's interest should be primarily liable.[3] This case must be compared with the position where the wife's interest is charged partly for the husband's benefit and partly for hers for the discharge of their respective obligations or to raise money for their individual purposes. In this event the wife may be entitled to exoneration to the extent of her husband's interest;[4] and
(d) the money was borrowed for the wife's benefit either wholly or jointly with her husband. Into this latter category will fall money which is used in general household and family living expenses.[5]

There is authority which suggests that a presumption does arise that the money was for the husband's benefit and that the wife was simply a surety for it where the husband covenants to repay the money raised on the wife's property or where the mortgage deed states that the money was paid only to the husband.[6] Perhaps today the better approach is to treat such matters as strong indications of the intention of the parties without dealing in presumptions. The money raised may after all go to a number of different purposes, particularly where the charge on the matrimonial home secures overdraft or other bank facilities. It is not necessary to treat the whole of the money secured as being either subject to the equity or not. The court may order an enquiry[7] as to which sums forming part of the money raised under the charge went solely to the benefit of the husband and in respect of which the wife's interest in the property may be exonerated and which went for the benefit of the wife, either solely or jointly with her husband, children or third parties. In respect of these latter sums the wife has no right of exoneration.

1 *Clinton v Hooper* (1791) 3 Bro C C 201.
2 *Paget v Paget* [1898] 1 Ch 470.
3 *Lewis v Nangle* (1752) 1 Cox Eq Cas 240.
4 *Gee v Smart* (1857) 8 E & B 313.
5 *Hudson v Carmichael* (1854) Kay 613; *Gray v Dowman* (1858) 27 LJ Ch 702; *Re Pittortou* [1985] 1 All ER 285.
6 *Hudson v Carmichael* (1854) Kay 613; *Hall v Hall* [1911] 1 Ch 487.
7 Such an enquiry was ordered by Scott J in *Re Pittortou* n 5 above.

Wife as surety or lender

22.12.5 A careful distinction must be drawn between the case where the wife creates a charge over her interest as surety for her husband, and where she does so in order to lend money to him. Bankruptcy debts which are loans made by the bankrupt's spouse are expressly postponed in the distribution of the assets by the trustee when paying dividends both under the Old Bankruptcy Law and the New Law.[1] It would plainly be wrong for the wife to exercise a right of exoneration in respect of the security by which she raised the loan, for then she would in effect be repaid in priority to the other creditors instead of being postponed to them.

[1] Old Law: Bankruptcy Act 1914, s 36(2); New Law: Insolvency Act 1986, s 329.

Mutuality

22.12.6 Although this section has proceeded upon the basis that the wife is seeking the equity of exoneration, the principle applies equally to a husband who has charged his property as surety for the benefit of his wife.[1]

[1] *Bagot v Oughton* (1717) 1 P Wms 347; *Gray v Dowman* (1858) 27 LJ Ch 702.

Modern day application of equity

22.12.7 The possibility that a joint charge on jointly-owned property for the husband's business purposes might be treated as a loan had led to doubts as to the applicability of the equity in modern day conditions.[1] However, the decision, *Re Pittertou, ex p Trustee of Property of Bankrupt v Bankrupt*[2] is an illustrative example of the equity in current practice. There the bankrupt husband ran a restaurant business on his own account. The matrimonial home was in joint names and the husband and wife executed a second charge in favour of a bank to secure borrowings on the husband's bank account. The husband used the money borrowed for various purposes which Scott J divided into three broad categories:

(i) payments made 'for the joint benefit of the household' e g mortgage instalments and other payments made for the purposes of the occupation of the property by the husband, the wife and their daughter together with their living expenses;
(ii) the debts of the restaurant business; and
(iii) debts incurred by the husband when he left his family and set up a separate home with another woman.

It was held that money paid from the secured bank account to pay debts falling within categories (ii) and (iii) should fall on the bankrupt's share of the matrimonial home, while debts within category (i) should be shared. An inquiry was directed as to which payments fell within the respective categories, and while a sale was ordered it may be noted that the court postponed sale until the wife was in a position, following the inquiry, to make a fully informed offer to the trustee to purchase his interest in the property.

[1] See *Re Woodstock* [1980] CLY 148 (not otherwise reported).
[2] [1985] 1 All ER 285.

22.13 THE SPOUSE AND MORTGAGEES

22.13.1 Within the context of bankruptcy and the matrimonial home, instances arise where a wife who has an interest in the property wishes to have a mortgage or charge which affects her interest set aside on the ground of fraud, duress or undue influence. Fraud, whether by fraudulent misrepresentation, forgery or other means will vitiate the transaction giving rise to the charge wherever it can be proved. The fact that the bankrupt himself may be responsible in no way alters the position. A forged signature purporting to be that of the wife is no more the wife's signature because her husband, rather than a third party, forged it. Furthermore the fraud of the husband on his wife may vitiate the transaction between the creditor and the wife to which the fraud was directed if the creditor has allowed the husband to interpose in the transaction. In *Kings North Trust v Bell*[1] the husband wanted to raise money for his business and raised a loan from the plaintiffs secured by a second mortgage on the matrimonial home. The plaintiff's solicitors sent the mortgage documents to the husband's solicitors who in turn asked the husband to obtain his wife's signature. The husband fraudulently misrepresented the purpose of the loan to his wife, who signed the documents relying on her husband and without independent advice. The husband defaulted and the plaintiffs sought possession. The Court of Appeal held that the husband's creditors could not be in a better position against the wife than her husband through whom the signature had been obtained. Where the husband obtains his wife's signature through fraud or undue influence the wife is not bound to the document signed unless she received independent advice.

1 [1986] 1 All ER 423.

Duress and undue influence

22.13.2 A transaction giving rise to a charge may be set aside on the grounds of duress in law, or undue influence in equity. Duress at common law is a doctrine of limited scope. Actual violence or threats of violence calculated to cause the person threatened to fear loss of life or bodily harm is required.[1] Provided such violence or threats deflect the will of the contracting party so that the agreement is unwillingly entered into, that agreement is voidable at the instance of the party threatened.[2] In the last ten years the English courts have recognised the possibility that duress may be imposed by economic means.[3] It is, however, only in the most exceptional circumstances that threats of an economic nature will constitute a sufficient coercion of the contracting party that consent to transactions will be held to have been vitiated.

1 *Friedberg Seely v Klass* (1957) 101 Sol Jo 275; *Barton v Armstrong* [1976] AC 104.
2 *DPP for Northern Ireland v Lynch* [1975] AC 653.
3 *Occidental Worldwide Investment Corpn v Skibs A/S Avanti* [1976] 1 Lloyd's Rep 293; *North Ocean Shipping Co Ltd v Hyundai Construction Co Ltd* [1979] QB 705; *Pao On v Lau Yiu Long* [1980] AC 614; *Universe Tankships Inc of Monrovia v International Transport Workers Federation* [1981] ICR 129.

22.13.3 The equitable doctrine of undue influence is of wider application and following the Court of Appeal decision in *Lloyd's Bank Ltd v Bundy*[1] was often relied on by wives seeking to avoid the consequences of charges they had entered into on the matrimonial home. No precise definition can be given of the doctrine for, in the words of Lord Chelmsford LC[2] 'the courts have always been careful not to fetter this useful jurisdiction by defining the exact limits of its exercise'. The cases in which relief has been granted, and the relevant transaction set aside, fall into two broad categories, namely cases where a relationship exists between the parties which give rise to a presumption of undue influence and cases where no such relationship exists.

This distinction is important for present purposes. It is always open for the party seeking relief to prove that a relationship existed between him and the other party to a transaction the nature of which gave rise to a presumption of undue influence.[3] In a limited class of cases the courts will, however, presume that the relationship existed. These cases include parents over child,[4] son over elderly parents,[5] solicitor over client,[6] doctor over patient,[7] trustee over beneficiary[8] and spiritual advisers over adherent.[9] The cases do not, however, include bank manager and customer.[10]

1 [1975] QB 326.
2 *Tate v Williamson* (1866) 2 Ch App 55 at 61.
3 See e g *Re Craig Meneces v Middleton* [1971] Ch 95 (elderly man and his secretary companion); *Hodgson v Marks* [1971] Ch 892 (elderly landlady and her lodger).
4 *Bainbrigge v Browne* (1881) 18 Ch D 188; *Re Paulings Settlement Trusts Younghusband v Coutts & Co* [1964] Ch 303.
5 *Avon Finance Company Ltd v Bridger* [1985] 2 All ER 281.
6 *Wright v Carter* [1903] 1 Ch 27.
7 *Mitchell v Homfray* (1881) 8 QBD 587.
8 *Ellis v Barker* (1871) 7 Ch App 104; *Plowright v Lambert* (1885) 52 LT 646.
9 *Allcard v Skinner* (1887) 36 Ch D 145.
10 *National Westminster Bank Plc v Morgan* [1985] AC 686; see Lord Scarman at 707.

22.13.4 Where the courts do not presume undue influence from the nature of the relationship between the parties, the burden of proof is on the party seeking relief to show the presence of influence in respect of the transaction.[1] It will be a very rare case where a bank manager or other representative of a lending institution has such a relationship with the wife of the subsequent bankrupt. The wife may understand little of what is happening and will be in a very unequal position vis à vis the bank in terms of bargaining power. But the House of Lords has stated that this does not by itself affect the validity of any transaction into which she enters.[2] Where the relationship giving rise to a presumption of undue influence does exist, either because it is proved or presumed, then the transaction complained of will be set aside unless it is shown that the party who may have been influenced had independent advice or for some other reason did not enter into the transaction under the influence of the other party to it. However, as the law now stands a charge on the matrimonial home entered into by the wife will seldom be set aside on the grounds of undue influence.

1 *Lancashire Loans Ltd v Black* [1934] 1 KB 380.
2 *National Westminster Bank Plc v Morgan* [1985] AC 686 where Lord Scarman, at 708, questioned whether the law need erect a general principle of relief against inequality of bargaining power. This was a legislative task for parliament.

22.14 THE POSITION OF CO-HABITEES

22.14.1 Neither the Insolvency Act 1986 nor the Matrimonial Homes Act 1983 grant any rights or afford any protection to the co-habitee of the bankrupt in their joint home. Where the co-habitee has no interest in the property comprising the home she cannot in her own right resist an application for possession by the trustee in bankruptcy. The co-habitee may, however, have a beneficial interest in the property under an implied or resulting trust whether or not she has a legal interest. In this event she may assert her beneficial interest against the trustee who will need to seek an order under the Law of Property Act 1925, s 30 if he is to obtain possession of the property and be able to effect a sale. The principles applicable on such an application are discussed above. The co-habitee will not be able to claim the advantage available under the New Law to the spouse that the creditors' interests should not be presumed to prevail during the first year in which the property vests in the bankrupt's trustee. She will be in a similar position to the spouse under the Old Bankruptcy Law.

Ascertaining the co-habitee's interest in the property

22.14.2 The trustee stepping into the shoes of the bankrupt will need to ascertain the respective interests of the bankrupt and co-habitee, often in circumstances where the parties' co-habitation began in a very informal manner. Where no express arrangement was entered into by the couple when they began co-habiting in the property the court may infer an agreement from the circumstances at the time of acquisition and from the parties conduct then and subsequently. The following guiding principles may be applicable:

1 Where an express agreement is made the terms of that agreement are conclusive.[1] A general agreement to share without any specification as to proportions will give rise to a resulting trust in equal shares.
2 If the property is purchased outright in unequal shares the purchasers are presumed to acquire beneficial interests in the same proportion as the sums paid.[2] This is only a presumption and may be rebutted by evidence of a contrary agreement.
3 Where a property is purchased with the assistance of a mortgage, the intention as to the respective interests may be inferred from the source of the deposit and arrangements made for repaying the mortgage instalments. It is not only direct payments towards the mortgage instalments that are taken into account, but also financial contributions to the household expenses. The fact that the co-habitee has contributed to the joint expenditure to an extent which has assisted the subsequent bankrupt to maintain the mortgage repayments will be taken into account.[3]
4 Substantial contributions in terms of labour towards the reparation of a house may give rise to a beneficial interest, particularly where the co-habitee understood that she would have a financial interest in the property as a result.[4]
5 Contributions which do not substantially affect the acquisition of or value

of the property, whether financial or in terms of labour, are not taken into account.[5] Buying the odd piece of furniture or kitchen equipment, spending weekends decorating, laying a patio, improving the lawn, cleaning the house, doing the cooking, bringing up children are all examples of contribution to the joint life of the parties which do not affect the respective beneficial interests of the parties.

6 There is no particular time at which the court must determine the respective interests. The court is entitled to look at the period of co-habitation as a whole and assess the respective contributions in a broad sense.[6]

[1] Eg *Gissing v Gissing* [1971] AC 886 per Lord Diplock at 905. The fact that the agreement may not be in writing does not prevent a resulting or implied trust.
[2] *Bull v Bull* [1955] 1 QB 234; *Bernard v Josephs* [1982] Ch 391; *Burns v Burns* [1984] Ch 317.
[3] *Bernard v Josephs* [1982] Ch 391; *Young v Young* [1984] Fam Law 271; *Gordon v Douce* [1983] 2 All ER 228.
[4] *Eves v Eves* [1975] 3 All ER 768; *Cooke v Head* [1972] 2 All ER 38.
[5] *Pettit v Pettit* [1970] AC 777; *Gissing v Gissing* [1971] AC 886; *Richards v Dove* [1974] 1 All ER 888; *Burns v Burns* [1984] Ch 317.
[6] *Walker v Hall* [1984] Fam Law 21; *Burns v Burns* n 5 above.

22.15 OTHER INTERESTS IN THE MATRIMONIAL HOME

The trustee in bankruptcy of an owner or co-owner of the matrimonial home may find that the bankrupt's estate is bound by a variety of other interests created by the bankrupt before his bankruptcy. Where appropriate, and this in the nature of such interests will be seldom, the trustee may seek to avoid such interests as avoidable settlements under the Old Law or undervalue transactions under the Insolvency Act 1986. Such interests may include:
(a) the application of the doctrine of proprietary estoppel;[1]
(b) an equitable lien over property;[2]
(c) an irrevocable contractual licence to occupy property;[3] and
(d) an irrevocable equitable licence to occupy property.[4]

Save in the case of contractual licence, where an agreement between the parties, express or implied, is necessary, the above interests are species of equitable interests which the court may employ to safeguard the interests of a person who is a stranger to the ownership of the property, but who has so contributed or acted towards the owners that it would be inequitable to exclude that party from any benefit whatsoever.

[1] *Inwards v Baker* [1965] 2 QB 29; *Pasco v Turner* [1979] 2 All ER 945; *Greasley v Cooke* [1980] 3 All ER 710.
[2] *Unity Joint Stock Mutual Banking Association v King* (1858) 25 Beav 72; *Hussey v Palmer* [1972] 3 All ER 744.
[3] *Re Sharpe, Trustee of Bankrupt v Sharpe* [1980] 1 All ER 198; *Chandler v Kerly* [1978] 2 All ER 942.
[4] *Williams v Staite* [1979] Ch 291.

CHAPTER 23

Criminal Bankruptcy

23.1 INTRODUCTION

23.1.1 The basic purpose of the criminal bankruptcy is to give assistance to the financial victims of criminals who are convicted of offences in circumstances in which the loss or damage amounts, in aggregate, to a certain specified minimum, (currently £15,000). Financial damage which is attributable to personal injury[1] is not included.

The legislation, which was originally introduced by the Criminal Justice Act 1972, and then embodied in the Powers of Criminal Courts Act 1973, and is now amended by the Insolvency Act 1986, is designed to smooth the way for the presentation of a petition. It places the ability to present a petition with a public servant, named the Official Petitioner (who is, and has been since the legislation came into force, the Director of Public Prosecutions[2]) and gives that public servant rights to act as a proving creditor in the bankruptcy generally.

Thus, persons who, perhaps financially or because of fear of reprisal or a simple lack of knowledge about what may be complex facts may not take bankruptcy proceedings, can in effect be represented by the Director of Public Prosecutions and his department in the realisation of the estate of the convicted criminal who has caused loss to his unfortunate creditors.

1 For which loss he may have recourse to the Criminal Injuries Compensation Board.
2 The DPP now holds the office of Official Petitioner by virtue of the Insolvency Act 1986, s 402.

23.1.2 Where the death of a convicted person follows the making of a criminal bankruptcy order against him, the criminal bankruptcy proceeds with his estate as with an ordinary insolvent estate. In this case, a criminal bankruptcy administration order may be applied for, by a creditor or by the Official Petitioner.[1]

1 Powers of Criminal Courts Act 1973, Sch 2, paras 11 and 16.1.

23.2 THE CRIMINAL BANKRUPTCY ORDER

23.2.1 The power to make criminal bankruptcy orders is contained in the Powers of Criminal Courts Act 1973, s 39. The Crown Court has power to make a criminal bankruptcy order against a person whom it convicts of an offence in addition to dealing with him in any other way.[1] Such an order may be made if it appears to the court that, as a result of that offence and any other offences of which the person is convicted in the same proceedings or which are taken into consideration[2] in determining sentence, known persons have suffered loss or damage, not attributable to personal injury, in excess of £15,000.[3]

A criminal bankruptcy order must specify the amount of the loss or damage, and if there was more than one offence, the amount attributable to each offence.[4] It must specify the person or persons who have suffered loss or damage[5] and the amount of the loss which each has suffered.[6] It must also state the date on which the offence, or the earliest offence, was committed.[7] The order may be made against two or more offenders in respect of the same loss or damage.[8]

Schedule 2 to the Act contains the effects of the making of a criminal bankruptcy order on any bankruptcy which flows from the making of such an order.

1 Powers of Criminal Courts Act 1973, s 39(1).
2 These offences are restricted to offences which the defendant admits and agrees to be taken into consideration in determining sentence: *DPP v Anderson* [1978] 2 All ER 512.
3 Powers of Criminal Courts Act 1973, s 39(1); but the Secretary of State may by order substitute another minimum amount: s 39(6).
4 Powers of Criminal Courts Act 1973, s 39(3)(a).
5 Ibid, s 39(3)(b).
6 Ibid, s 39(3)(c).
7 Ibid, s 39(3)(d).
8 Ibid, s 39(4).

23.2.2 Under the Old Bankruptcy Law the making of a criminal bankruptcy order against a debtor had the effect of the debtor being treated as if he had committed an act of bankruptcy on the date of the making of the criminal bankruptcy order.[1]

1 Powers of Criminal Courts Act 1973, s 39(5).

23.2.3 Thus, the Official Petitioner, that is to say, the Director of Public Prosecutions, or any creditor named in the criminal bankruptcy order could present a bankruptcy petition relying on the criminal bankruptcy order as the available act of bankruptcy.

Under the New Law the making of a criminal bankruptcy order is a ground for presenting a petition for a bankruptcy order under the Insolvency Act 1986[1] although the fact that a debt is specified in a criminal bankruptcy order is not enough, in itself, to make the debt a liquidated debt for purposes of any petition presented as a result of the criminal bankruptcy order (see para 13.2.1(b) above).

1 S 264(1)(a).

23.2.4 In deciding whether or not to petition for a bankruptcy order the Official Petitioner has certain functions to discharge.[1] He must consider whether it is in the public interest that he should himself present a petition[2] and if it is, he must present a petition. He is also empowered to assist financially, creditors who have taken bankrupt proceedings based upon a criminal bankruptcy order.[3]

The Official Petitioner may delegate his duties to any person acting with his authority[4] and he enjoys effective immunity, along with those acting under his authority, from liability in respect of the discharge of his duties and functions as Official Petitioner.[5]

1 Powers of Criminal Courts Act 1973, s 41(1).
2 Insolvency Act 1986, s 402(2)(b).
3 Ibid, s 402(2)(c).
4 Ibid, s 402(3).
5 Ibid, s 402(4).

23.2.5 The criminal bankruptcy order must specify:[1]

(a) the amount of the loss or damage appearing to the court to have resulted from the offence or, if more than one, each of the offences;
(b) the person or persons appearing to the court to have suffered that loss or damage;
(c) the amount of that loss or damage which it appears to the court that that person, or each of those persons has suffered;[2] and
(d) a date which is to be the relevant date for the purposes of the court examining and taking steps in relation to the giving of preference, or other offences by the debtor. This date will be the earliest date on which any apparent bankruptcy offence was committed.[3]

1 Powers of Criminal Courts Act 1973, s 39(3).
2 The fixing of this amount is sufficient evidence for the purpose of that creditor lodging a proof of debt in the subsequent bankruptcy: Powers of Criminal Courts Act 1973, Sch 2, para 9(1).
3 See para 23.3.3 below.

23.3 CRIMINAL BANKRUPTCY PROCEEDINGS

23.3.1 If a petition for a bankruptcy order is presented on a criminal bankruptcy order then the production of a copy of the criminal bankruptcy order itself obliges the court[1] to make a bankruptcy order unless the criminal bankruptcy order itself has been rescinded in consequence of a successful appeal against conviction by the debtor.[2]

1 Subject to the court's general power to dismiss if there has been a 'contravention of the rules or for other reason': Insolvency Act 1986, s 266(3).
2 Insolvency Act 1986, s 277. Powers of Criminal Courts Act 1973, Sch 2, para 17.

23.3.2 The easing of the path to a receiving order under the Old Bankruptcy Law and to a bankruptcy order under the New Law is not the only assistance given to creditors in a criminal bankruptcy. The Official Petitioner becomes, in effect, a representative creditor for all purposes.

In Old Bankruptcy Law cases, the Official Petitioner can:

(i) participate in meetings of creditors and be entitled to receive any notice or document to which a creditor has a right;
(ii) become a member of the committee of inspection; and
(iii) appear as a creditor at the debtor's public examination.

Additionally he has the rights of a creditor or, where appropriate, a creditor who has proved or tendered a proof, in relation to the appointment of a special manager in the debtor's affairs, a composition or scheme of arrangement, discharge of the bankrupt, the relation back of the trustee's title, reports to the creditors of the debtor's proposals, appeal to the court against the trustee's act or decision and the administration in bankruptcy of the deceased debtor's estate.

Similarly, in New Law cases the Official Petitioner is, by virtue of r 6.230 of the 1986 Rules, regarded for all purposes of the Insolvency Act 1986 and the Rules as a creditor of the bankrupt. He may therefore appear at the debtor's public examination[1] if there is one. The provisions of the Insolvency Act 1986 concerning the committee of creditors,[2] as opposed to the committee of inspection in Old Bankruptcy Law cases, mean that his real influence in New Law cases, will be at a public examination, if he attends in order to use whatever information he might have which is of benefit in questioning the bankrupt concerning his estate.

The official receiver is always the trustee in a criminal bankruptcy.[3] In New Law cases he cannot be removed as trustee[4] nor can he apply to the Secretary of State for the appointment of some other person to act as trustee under the Insolvency Act 1986, s 296(1) nor be removed by the creditors under s 298.[5] There is no committee of creditors in a case where the official receiver is trustee.[6]

1 Insolvency Act 1986, s 298(4)(a).
2 Under Ibid, s 301.
3 Power of Criminal Courts Act 1973, Sch 2, para 8 in Old Bankruptcy Law cases and Insolvency Act 1986, s 297(1) in New Law cases.
4 Insolvency Act 1986, s 298(1).
5 Ibid, s 298(2).
6 Ibid, s 301(2).

23.3.3 When making the criminal bankruptcy order the Crown Court is obliged to specify a date for the purposes of certain bankruptcy offences.[1]

In Old Bankruptcy Law cases the official receiver, in his capacity as trustee, can apply to the High Court for an order requiring the recipient under any disposition of property or interest in property, made by the bankrupt, on or after the date nominated in the criminal bankruptcy order as provided for by the Powers of Criminal Courts Act 1973, s 39(3)(d) by way of gift, or for an undervalue, or any other person who acquired such property, to transfer the whole or part of that property to the trustee.[2]

No order can be made if the recipient appears to have given full value for something taken by him under a relevant disposition or to claim, directly or indirectly, through a person who gave full value.[3]

The recipient of such a disposition may be ordered to make such payments to the trustee as the court thinks just. Thus he is not only susceptible to an order for the restitution of the amount wrongfully taken out of the estate but he may be ordered to make a payment which takes account of any increase in value since the disposition was made and the order itself may contain such consequential directions as the court thinks fit.[4]

Thus the court's powers in an old law criminal bankruptcy case are greater than those contained in the Bankruptcy Act 1914, s 42 (ch 8 above).

No order may be made under these provisions so long as the debtor has an appeal pending against the conviction which led to the making of the criminal bankruptcy order.[5]

In New Law cases a transaction entered into or a preference given by a debtor against whom a bankruptcy order is made as a result of a criminal bankruptcy order is treated as having been entered into, or given, at a 'relevant time' for the purposes of the Insolvency Act 1986, ss 339–341[6] if it was entered into, or given, at any time on or after the date specified for that purpose in the criminal bankruptcy order itself under the provisions for that purpose in the Powers of Criminal Courts Act 1973, s 39(3)(d).[7]

1 See chs 19 and para 23.2.5 above.
2 Powers of Criminal Courts Act 1973, Sch 2, para 10(2).
3 Ibid, Sch 2, para 10.
4 Ibid, Sch 2, para 10(4).
5 Ibid, Sch 2, para 13(2).
6 See ch 17 above.
7 Insolvency Act 1986, s 341(4).

23.3.4 A person who has a bankruptcy order made against him on a petition based on a criminal bankruptcy order has to apply for his discharge under the provisions of the Insolvency Act 1986, s 280 (see ch 18 above).[1]

1 Insolvency Act 1986, s 279(1).

23.4 APPEALS

23.4.1 In principle no appeal lies against the making of a criminal bankruptcy order[1] although this prohibition does not apply to orders which are wrong in law.[2]

Moreover, the fact that an appeal is pending against any conviction by virtue of which a criminal bankruptcy order was made does not preclude the taking of the criminal bankruptcy proceedings nor their progress through the usual bankruptcy process.[3]

However, no distribution may be made out of the debtor's estate while such an appeal is pending.[4]

1 Powers of Criminal Courts Act 1973, s 40(1).
2 See *R v Cain* [1985] AC 46. A criminal bankruptcy order is not a nullity because the court failed to allow counsel for the defence to address the court before it was made: *R v Prefas*, (1986) Times, 12 November.
3 Old Bankruptcy Law cases: see Powers of Criminal Courts Act 1973, Sch 2, para 13(1); New Law cases: see Insolvency Act 1986, s 277.
4 Old Bankruptcy Law cases: see Powers of Criminal Courts Act 1973, Sch 2, para 13(2); New Law cases: see Insolvency Act 1986, s 327.

23.4.2 For the purposes of criminal bankruptcy an appeal is pending against conviction in any case, until the expiry of 28 days from the conviction and, thereafter, if notice of appeal to the Court of Appeal is given (and the official receiver given notice thereof) until the final determination of the appeal, or any appeal therefrom to the House of Lords.[1]

[1] Old Bankruptcy law cases; see Powers of Criminal Courts Act 1973, Sch 2, para 13(3); New Bankruptcy Law cases: see Insolvency Act 1986, s 277.

23.4.3 If, as a result of a successful appeal against conviction a criminal bankruptcy order is rescinded[1] then, the bankruptcy petition lapses and any receiving order, adjudication order, or bankruptcy order made consequently upon the petition ceases to have effect, but without prejudice to anything done under such orders.[2]

In such an event the property of the debtor reverts to him and the relevant bankruptcy court is empowered to make such consequential orders to assist in that reversion of property as it thinks necessary or desirable.[3]

[1] As it must be, by virtue of the Powers of Criminal Courts Act 1973, s 40(2).
[2] Powers of Criminal Courts Act 1973, Sch 2, para 13(4).
[3] Ibid, Sch 2, para 13(a), (b) and (c).

23.5 PROOF OF DEBT

23.5.1 The making of a bankruptcy order on a criminal bankruptcy petition does not affect the right of creditors to prove for their debts arising otherwise than in consequence of the criminal proceedings.[1]

[1] Individual Insolvency Rules 1986, r 6.232(1).

23.5.2 A person specified in a criminal bankruptcy order as having suffered loss or damage shall be treated as a creditor of the bankrupt and a copy of the criminal bankruptcy order is sufficient evidence of his claim, subject to its being shown by any party to the bankruptcy proceedings that the loss or damage actually suffered was more or less then the amount specified in the order.[1]

[1] Individual Insolvency Rules 1986, r 6.232(2).

CHAPTER 24

Partnership and Agency

24.1 PROCEEDINGS IN THE NAME OF A FIRM

24.1.1 Any two or more partners or any person carrying on business under a partnership name, may take proceedings or be proceeded against in bankruptcy in the name of that firm. Under the Old Bankruptcy Law this is expressly provided for by the Bankruptcy Act 1914, s 119 which further provides that any person interested may apply to the court for an order that the names of all the partners should be disclosed in such manner as the court may direct, if appropriate to be verified on oath.

The Insolvency Act 1986 contains no provisions expressly relating to partnerships. Instead, the Insolvency Act 1986, s 420 empowers the Lord Chancellor to order by statutory instrument that the Insolvency Act 1986 including the provisions which relate to the winding up of registered and unregistered companies should apply to insolvent partnerships with any appropriate modifications.[1]

Where two or more persons practise or trade together as a firm, they may collectively become bankrupt and in this event, a petitioning creditor may proceed against the firm as a whole without concerning himself with the identification of the various individuals comprising the partnership. This was perhaps more important under the Old Bankruptcy Law, with its more complex procedures, than it will be under the New Law. As there will remain cases to be dealt with under the Old Bankruptcy Law, its application to partnerships is briefly considered below.

[1] Insolvent Partnerships Order 1986 SI 1986/2142.

24.2 PROCEEDINGS TO ADJUDICATION OF THE PARTNERSHIP UNDER THE OLD BANKRUPTCY LAW

24.2.1 *Acts of bankruptcy.* The basic underlying principle of partnership that one partner has power to act for and bind the firm as a whole, is expressly extended to proceedings in bankruptcy.[1] However, an act of bankruptcy was a personal act or default and a principal was not liable for an act which might have constituted an act of bankruptcy committed by his agent unless he authorised it or was aware of it and took no steps to prevent or nullify it.[2]

The various statutory acts of bankruptcy as enacted by the Bankruptcy Act 1914 (ss 1 and 107(4)) and the Insolvency Act 1976, s 11, are referred to in chs 1 and 2 above. Few of these acts of bankruptcy were used regularly and for the most part, a petition would rely on the firm's failure to comply with a bankruptcy notice. Firms in financial difficulties might seek to transfer property, which if with the intent to cheat creditors, would be 'fraudulent' for the purposes of the Bankruptcy Act 1914, s 1 and therefore an act of bankruptcy, or assign their business to a limited company. In the latter event, even where the company agreed to pay the assignor firm's creditors,[3] the assignment could be treated as an act of bankruptcy (provided that a petition was presented within three months of the assignment) or be set aside under the Law of Property Act 1925, s 172 if the company also had knowledge of the fraudulent intent.[4]

[1] Bankruptcy Act 1914, s 149.
[2] *Mills v Bennett* (1814) 2 M & S 556; *Re Sawers, ex p Blain* (1879) 12 Ch D 522. But an agent might cause his principal unknowingly to commit a fraudulent preference *Re Drabble Bros* [1930] 2 ch 211.
[3] *Re Fasey, ex p Trustees* [1923] 2 Ch 1 and see *Re Sarflax Ltd* [1979] Ch 592.
[4] See also ch 8 above.

24.2.2 *Petitions.* Where the firm had failed to comply with a bankruptcy notice or committed some other act of bankruptcy, a petition could be duly served on all members of the partnership, if served on one partner at the principal place of business of the firm in England, or on any person having, at the time of service, control or management of the partnership business at the firm's principal place of business.[1] Where an individual carried on business in a firm's name, a petition could be properly served by service on any person having the control or management of that business in England.[2] Where acts of bankruptcy committed by individual partners were relied on, a joint petition could be presented against two or more persons provided each had committed an act of bankruptcy. It was not necessary that this should have been a joint act of bankruptcy or even an act of the same kind. A debtor's petition filed by a firm had to contain the full names of all the partners but could be signed in the firm's name by one partner if accompanied by an affidavit showing that all the partners concurred in the filing of the petition.[3] Where two or more petitions have been presented against the same debtor or joint debtors, the court may consolidate the proceedings, or any of them, on such terms as are thought fit.[4]

[1] Bankruptcy Rules 1952, r 280.
[2] See ch 6 above for the nature and effects of adjudication generally.
[3] Bankruptcy Rules 1952, r 281.
[4] Bankruptcy Act 1914, s 110.

24.2.3 *Defences to a petition.* See ch 2 above. The important aspect of the law, particularly from the debtor firm's point of view, was that the Bankruptcy Court was entitled to enquire into the validity of the debt and even go behind a judgment. The Bankruptcy Court could, for example, question the validity of a contract on which a judgment debt was obtained or consider the merits of any dispute where interlocutory judgment had been obtained.[1] A receiving order could then be refused if the reality of the debt was doubted. A refusal to make a receiving order does not, however, prevent the creditor relying on the same debt in the future and serving another bankruptcy notice in respect of it, or, particularly, petitioning under the New Law on the same debt.[2]

[1] Bankruptcy Act 1914, s 5(3) and see *Re Beauchamp, ex p Beauchamp* [1904] 1 KB 572; *Boaler v Power* [1910] 2 KB 229; and *Re A Debtor* (No. 229 of 1927), [1927] 2 Ch 367.
[2] *Re Vitoria, ex p Vitoria* [1894] 2 QB 387.

24.2.4 *Receiving order.* A receiving order made against a firm operates as if it were a receiving order made against each of the persons who, at the date of the order, is a partner in that firm.[1] The official receiver becomes the receiver of the estates of each of the partners, and the joint and separate creditors are summoned collectively to the first meeting of creditors.[2] Where a receiving order has been made on a bankruptcy petition against one member of a partnership, any other bankruptcy petition against a member of the same partnership must be filed in or transferred to the court in which the existing petition is presented and, unless the court directs otherwise, the same trustee or receiver should be appointed.[3]

It is plainly advisable for practical reasons for the same trustee to be appointed where more than one partner in the same firm is bankrupt. This applies equally where a partner dies insolvent and his estate is being administered in bankruptcy[4].

[1] Bankruptcy Rules 1952, r 285.
[2] Ibid, r 291.
[3] Bankruptcy Act 1914, s 116.
[4] *Re Greaves, ex p Official Receiver* [1904] 2 KB 493.

24.2.5 *Adjudication.*[1] Even where the petition and the receiving order are against the firm, the partners of the firm may not be adjudicated bankrupt in the firm's name. An order of adjudication must be made against each of the partner's individually.[2] Where there are partners who are dormant or merely nominal, they may be adjudicated bankrupt but may also be excluded from the orders of adjudication.[3]

Once the various orders of adjudication have been made, the same trustee is appointed to administer the estates of the various partners. In the bankruptcy of a partnership, the trustee may be appointed by the joint creditors with the Department of Trade acting as trustee in default of appointment.[4] The joint creditors may have their own committees of inspection.

In addition to the joint creditors, there may well be other creditors who are owed debts by individual partners in the course of transactions outside the partnership business. Each 'set' of separate creditors, while they have no power over, or say in, the appointment of the trustee, may appoint their own committee of inspection to oversee the trustee and safeguard their interests. Should any set of separate creditors not appoint their own committee of inspection, they are deemed to have appointed the committee, if any, appointed by the joint creditors.[5]

While the separate creditors are excluded from the choice of a trustee under the bankruptcy of a partnership the reverse is not the case in the bankruptcy of a sole partner. For the Bankruptcy Act 1914[6] provides that where a receiving order is made against one partner of a firm, any creditor to whom that partner is indebted jointly with the other partners of the firm, or any of them, may prove his debt for the purpose of voting at any meeting of creditors and shall be entitled to vote at the meeting.

1 See ch 6 above and the nature and effects of adjudication generally.
2 Bankruptcy Rules 1952, r 288.
3 *Ex p Hamper* (1811) 17 Ves 403 (included); *Ex p Benfield* (1800) 5 Ves 424 (omitted).
4 Bankruptcy Rules 1952, r 294(1).
5 Ibid, r 294(2).
6 Sch 1, para 13.

24.2.6 *Annulling or reviewing an adjudication.* The adjudication may be annulled if the court is of the opinion that the debtor ought not to have been adjudged bankrupt or his debts have been paid in full.[1] In any other case where the partnership or any individual debtor wishes to challenge any order in the bankruptcy, an application may be made under the Bankruptcy Act 1914, s 108 under which the court has a general discretion to review, rescind or vary any order made in its bankruptcy jurisdiction; see ch 21 above.

1 Bankruptcy Act 1914, s 29.

24.3 PROCEEDINGS TO ADJUDICATION OF INDIVIDUAL PARTNERS UNDER THE OLD BANKRUPTCY LAW

24.3.1 In general, the proceedings in bankruptcy against a person who is a partner in one or more firms follow the usual course as dealt with in Part I of this work. In addition to the usual provisions of bankruptcy law, the following points may be noted:

24.3.1.1 A creditor may, if he chooses, proceed against one partner alone. Whilst a debt owing by one partner solely cannot support a joint petition against him and his co-partners, a debt owed by the partnership is sufficient to support a petition against any one of them.[1] A partner who finds himself singled out by a creditor for service of a bankruptcy notice, may seek to defend the petition on the grounds that the partnership could as a whole meet the debt. The inevitable uncertainty is likely, at the least, to result in lengthy adjournment if not dismissal of the petition and a creditor is ill advised not to serve his bankruptcy notice on the firm as a whole, which he may do at the principal place of business of the firm in England and on any one partner or on any person having at the time of service control or management of the partnership business there.[2] Such a bankruptcy notice will preclude a defence simply involving the other partners. The single partner facing a petition based on the firm's debt cannot involve his partners on the petition, but may serve bankruptcy notices on his partners and, if necessary, petition against them; see below.

1 Bankruptcy Act 1914, s 114.
2 Bankruptcy Rules 1952, r 280.

24.3.1.2 A partner who is a creditor of his co-partner may petition for a receiving order against his co-partner.[1] Any debt on which an action might be founded may support a petition whether it arises within the context of the partnership or outside it. An action for an account cannot support a bankruptcy petition until judgment is obtained for an ascertained amount. A partner who wishes to petition against his co-partner must take care not to allow the debt to become intermingled with the partnership accounts, as this will prevent his presenting a petition on that debt.[2]

1 *Re Notley, ex p Notley* (1833) 1 Mont & A 46; *Re Palmer, ex p Richardson & Son* (1833) Deac & Ch 244.
2 *Ex p Gray* (1835) 2 Mont & A 283.

24.3.1.3 A petition presented against one partner for the primary purpose of effecting a dissolution of the partnership, whether by a co-partner or a creditor acting at the instigation of a co-partner, may be liable to dismissal as an abuse of the process of the court[1] or stayed pending the resolution of any partnership dispute.[2] Even where the proceedings proceed to an adjudication, an annullment might be obtained if the debtor is able to satisfy the court that the adjudication had been obtained solely to dissolve a partnership to which the co-partner would otherwise remain committed.[3]

1 *Re Barrow, ex p Christie* (1832) Mont & B 352; *Re Johnson, ex p Johnson* (1842) 2 Mont D & De G 6 78; *Re Coulson and Phipps, ex p Phipps* (1844) 3 Mont D & De G 505.
2 Bankruptcy Act 1914, s 113.
3 See cases under n 1 above.

24.3.1.4 Should the joint adjudication in bankruptcy of a firm be followed by a separate adjudication of one of the partners, the trustee in bankruptcy of the firm (who will also become the trustee in bankruptcy of the partner under the provisions of the Bankruptcy Act 1914, s 116 unless the court directs otherwise) should prove in the bankruptcy of the partner for any unsatisfied balance of joint liabilities of the firm.[1]

1 *Re Moss, ex p Everitt* (1923) 93 LJ Ch 98.

24.3.1.5 A joint adjudication of a firm may follow a separate adjudication of a partner. In this event, it may well be appropriate for the court to exercise the power given in the Bankruptcy Act 1914, s 116 to consolidate the two proceedings and give directions for the appointment of one trustee satisfactory to the creditors as a whole.[1]

[1] See, for example, *R Helliwell, ex p Mackenzie* (1875) LR 20 Eq 758 or *Re Abbott, ex p Official Receiver* [1894] 1 QB 442.

24.4 PROCEEDINGS TO PARTNERSHIP BANKRUPTCY UNDER THE NEW LAW

24.4.1 The New Law is governed by Statutory Instrument[1] and deals with three aspects not covered by the Old Law. Firstly the Bankruptcy Act 1914 did not deal with corporate partners. Secondly it did not cover the European Economic Interest Grouping ie a partnership between parties in different EEC member states. Thirdly it was difficult for the trustee of one insolvent partner to secure control of partnership assets where other partners were not insolvent.

There are now two separate methods for winding up partnerships. First, any partnership with two or more members, whether individual or corporate, irrespective of nationality, may be wound up as an unregistered company.[2] Such an insolvency may proceed without the bankruptcy or liquidation of any individual partner, who is here treated as if an officer of the unregistered company. Second, petitions may be presented both against the partnership and any or all of the partners, individual or corporate. This brings formal insolvency on the partners and ensures that their private assets are available to meet partnership debts as well as the partnership assets. A series of petitions against the members of a partnership are 'connected petitions' and follow the service of written demands on the partnership and all partners against whom the petitioner seeks a bankruptcy or winding up order. The demands must relate to a presently due debt of at least £750 owed by the partnership. The various petitions must indicate that they are connected with each other. Only one deposit is required, on the petition against the partnership. Service of the petitions will be in the usual manner except that petitions based on a judgment debt may be served at the partnership's place of business on a person with responsibility for that business. The making of bankruptcy or winding up orders depends on the partnership petition. Each partner may appear on the partnership petition and if an order is made on this petition, individual orders against the partners follow automatically.

In cases where an individual partner has been adjudicated bankrupt on a petition not based on a partnership debt, his trustee is entitled to petition for the winding up of the partnership. If the court is satisfied that the partnership cannot pay its debts, or it is otherwise just and equitable to wind it up, it may make a winding up order and appoint the trustee as liquidator in the partnership winding up.

[1] Insolvent Partnerships Order 1986, SI 1986/2142.
[2] See Insolvency Act 1986, s 221.

24.5 RECOVERY OF ASSETS BY TRUSTEE IN BANKRUPTCY

24.5.1 Subject to the statutory exceptions (see chs 8 and 14 above) all property of whatever nature to which the bankrupt is beneficially entitled at the commencment of the bankruptcy vests in the trustee. In general terms, the trustee's duty and powers to gather in all the available assets which might be distributed to creditors are the same under the Old Bankruptcy Law and the New Law. There are, however, two important differences between the Old and the New Law relating to the vesting of property in the trustee.

24.5.2 First, the doctrine of relation back under the Old Bankruptcy Law[1] provides that the bankruptcy is deemed to commence at the earliest time[2] at which the bankrupt committed an act of bankruptcy with three months before the petition on which the receiving order was made.

The New Law[3] provides that the bankruptcy shall commence with the day on which the bankruptcy order is made.

1 Bankruptcy Act 1914, s 37.
2 *Re Bamptus, ex p White* [1908] 2 KB 330, the very hour of the day on which the act of bankruptcy was committed.
3 Insolvency Act 1986, s 278.

24.5.3 Second, under the Old Bankruptcy Law[1] all property acquired by the bankrupt after the commencement of his bankruptcy and before his discharge, 'after acquired property' automatically vests in the trustee. The New Law[2] provides that title in after acquired property should remain in the bankrupt unless the trustee serves a notice in writing claiming it for the bankrupt's estate, in which event, the trustee's title relates back to the time at which the property was acquired by the bankrupt.

The joint property of a bankrupt firm, or the joint property of two or more partners made bankrupt together, vests in the trustee as well as the separate property of each bankrupt partner.[3] The trustee holds the joint property as such and need not determine the various bankrupt partner's respective shares in the property.[4]

1 Bankruptcy Act 1914, s 38.
2 Insolvency Act 1986, s 307.
3 *Re Waddell's Contract* (1876) 2 Ch D 172.
4 *Re Payton, ex p Hunter* (1816) 2 Rose 382.

24.6 POSITION OF TRUSTEE OF BANKRUPT PARTNER

24.6.1 Where one of several partners becomes bankrupt, his trustee becomes entitled to the bankrupt's separate property and his interest as partner in the joint property of the partnership. The trustee does not, however, become a partner of the solvent partners and, indeed, unless the partners agree otherwise, the bankruptcy of one of their number will automatically dissolve the partnership.[1] The trustee can be in no better position than the partner was when solvent and the co-partners' rights in the property, including liens, may be enforced against the trustee.[2]

1 Partnership Act 1890, s 33.
2 *West v Skip* (1749) 1 Ves Sen 239.

24.6.2 The trustee is entitled to require an account to be taken with a sale and distribution so as to realise the bankrupt partner's share in the partnership.[1] Until the account has been duly taken and all the joint creditors have been paid, the trustee has no enforceable claim.[2]

1 *Wilson v Greenwood* (1818) 1 Swan 471; *Whitmore v Mason* (1861) 2 John & H 204.
2 *Taylor v Fields* (1799) 4 Ves 396; *Holderness v Shackels* (1828) 8 B & C 612; *West v Skip* (1749) 1 Ves Sen 239.

24.6.3 To assist the trustee in the realisation of the bankrupt partner's share of the partnership business, the trustee, with the leave of the court, may commence and prosecute any action in the names of himself and the solvent co-partner or co-partners.[1] Any release by the latter of the debt or demand to which the action relates, is void. When applying to the court for authority to commence proceedings, the trustee must give notice to the co-partners. They may apply for a direction that they should receive their proper share of the proceeds of the action; alternatively, if they do not claim any benefit from the action, the court may direct that they should be indemnified against any costs arising. If he prefers, the trustee may avoid becoming involved in partnership litigation. For where a bankrupt is a contractor in respect of any contract jointly with another person or persons, the solvent joint contractor or contractors may sue or be sued in respect of the contract without the joinder of the bankrupt or his trustee.[2]

1 Bankruptcy Act 1914, s 117; Insolvency Act 1986, s 420; Insolvent Partnerships Order 1986.
2 Bankruptcy Act 1914, s 118; Insolvency Act 1986, s 420; Insolvent Partnerships Order 1986.

24.6.4 The trustee of a bankrupt partner will not be bound by any agreement between the partners, even if contained in the partnership deed, that in the event of the bankruptcy of one of their number, his share should become vested in his co-partners or may be acquired by them for less than its full value whether directly or under a formula which has that effect.[1] In cases where the partnership deed provides that the partnership should continue notwithstanding the bankruptcy of one of the partners, the co-partners will presumably be concerned to keep the partnership business going and to make provision in the partnership agreement that they may buy the bankrupt's share at a proper valuation. The probability is that the trustee will be fully prepared to accede to such a scheme provided he is content with the method of valuation. But whether the solvent partners can in law prevent a trustee requiring an account and sale is doubtful. The case of *Wilson v Greenwood*[2] appears to be authority to the contrary, but the supplemental deed relied on by the solvent partners in that case was executed only a few months before the relevant partner's bankruptcy and enabled the solvent partners to pay by instalments. It is to be hoped that the decision would be different where a purchase at true valuation was provided for in a deed not made in apparent knowledge of an impending bankruptcy.

1 *Whitmore v Mason* (1861) 2 John & H 204; *Re Williams, ex p Warden* (1872) 21 WR 51.
2 (1818) 1 Swan 471: and see *Borland's Trustee v Steel Bros & Co Ltd* [1901] 1 Ch 279.

24.6.5 The trustee will also be entitled to a share of any profits made by the partnership after the commencement of the bankruptcy so long as the bankrupt's capital is being utilised. Should the solvent partners contribute further capital between the bankruptcy and winding up of the partnership, they do not thereby lessen the trustee's share of the profits and capital, which remains as originally agreed between the partners.[1]

[1] *Crawshay v Collins* (1826) 2 Russ 325.

24.6.6 Under the Old Bankruptcy Law, where the bankrupt partner continues to work in the business and earn more than sufficient to maintain himself and his family, the 'trustee may direct that part of such earnings must be set aside for the benefit of the creditors'.[1] The distinction must be made between the profits of the business which vest in the trustee and the personal earnings of the bankrupt, dependent upon the skill and knowledge of his own hands and brain, which do not so vest.

In the case of a professional partnership, this distinction may be hard to draw. In *Re Rogers*[2] the bankrupt was a dental surgeon who continued to practise under the terms of the partnership deed. Prior to his bankruptcy, he had mortgaged his share in the partnership business. The court held that the trustee's claim defeated the interests of the mortgagees as his earnings from the dental practice, albeit highly dependent on his personal skill, were profits of the partnership business.

It is probable, however, that a bankrupt may mortgage or assign his future earnings beyond a claim by his trustee provided that such earnings are the fruit of his own skill and knowledge and not in fact the earnings of a business which has vested in the trustee.[3]

[1] *Re Rogers, ex p Collins* [1894] 1 QB 425; *Re Dowling, ex p Banks* (1877) 4 Ch D 689.
[2] See n 1 above.
[3] *Re Green, ex p Official Receiver v Cutting* [1979] 1 All ER 832.

24.6.7 The position is different under the New Law. Here the whole of any income received by the bankrupt after the commencment of the bankruptcy remains his, subject to any income payment order made by the court on the application of the trustee.[1] In making such an order, the income with which the court is concerned:

> 'comprises every payment in the nature of income which is from time to time made to the bankrupt or to which he from time to time becomes entitled, including any payment in respect of the carrying on of any business or in respect of any office or employment.'[2]

The court is given express power to discharge or vary any attachment of earnings order which is in force.[3] While there is no provision in the statute dealing directly with a mortgage or assignment of future earnings by the bankrupt, the size of the income payments order is discretionary (provided it does not reduce the bankrupt's income to below that necessary for meeting the reasonable domestic needs of himself and his family) and any such dealing by the bankrupt, and the circumstances surrounding the transaction, may be taken into consideration by the court when making an order.

[1] Insolvency Act 1986, s 310.
[2] Ibid, s 310(7).
[3] Ibid, s 310(4).

24.7 CONTROL AND REALISATION OF THE ESTATE

In the control and realisation of the estates of bankrupt partners, the trustee administers the joint or separate estates in accordance with the general rules dealt with in chs 9 and 16 above.

From the viewpoint of a bankruptcy in the context of a partnership, the following points are to be noted:

24.7.1 *Mutual credit and set-off.* Both under the Old Bankruptcy Law and the New Law[1] the basic principle is that in all mutual dealings between a bankrupt and a creditor, the sums due from one party must be set off against the sums due from the other, leaving the creditor to prove in the bankruptcy for any balance left due to him. The cross-demands between the parties must be strictly mutual and, accordingly, joint debts cannot be set off against separate debts.

In partnership therefore, a demand by one or more partners cannot be set off against a cross-demand against the firm of which they are partners, neither may a demand against the firm be set off against a cross-demand of one or some of its partners.[2] This rule is strictly observed and, accordingly, three part-owners of a ship could not set off their proportions of a debt due to a bankrupt against the debts due from the bankrupt to all of the part-owners but severally.[3]

Mutuality may be affected, either way, by specific agreement between the parties. Should, therefore, parties agree that a demand be kept distinct for a specific purpose then, in a subsequent bankruptcy, that demand may not be set off against a cross-demand outside the specific purpose even where, but for the agreement, a mutual set off would apply.[4] Conversely, where all parties agree that a joint demand may be set off against a separate cross-demand, such an agreement will be binding in a subsequent bankruptcy.[5]

It will be recalled that demands arising after the other party's notice of an act of bankruptcy by the bankrupt (Old Bankruptcy Law) or the presentation of a bankruptcy petition against the bankrupt (New Bankruptcy Law) cannot be the subject of a mutual set off.

1 Bankruptcy Act 1914, s 31; Insolvency Act 1986, s 323.
2 *Re Pennington and Owen Ltd* [1925] Ch 825.
3 *Ex p Christie* (1804) 10 Ves 105.
4 *Young v Bank of Bengal* (1836) 1 Deac 622.
5 *Kinnerley v Hossack* (1809) 2 Taunt 170.

24.7.2 *The Old Bankruptcy Law doctrine of relation back.* By virtue of the Bankruptcy Act 1914, s 37, the title of the trustee to the bankrupt's property relates back to the date and time of the act of bankruptcy on which the receiving order was made against him.[1] When a partner becomes bankrupt, he may no longer bind the firm[2] and his loss of authority dates back to the relevant act of bankruptcy.[3] This has two distinct consequences. First, the estate of the bankrupt partner is not liable for partnership debts contracted after the relevant act of bankruptcy.[4] Second, creditors of the firm who receive partnership assets from the partner who subsequently becomes bankrupt, may have to return them, and debtors of the firm who made payments to this partner with notice that an available act of bankruptcy has been committed, or after the receiving order is made, will have to repay their debt.[5]

The solvent partners may continue to bind the firm and carry on the partnership business, though if, as in the usual case, the bankruptcy dissolves the partnership, this authority is limited to those acts necessary to wind up the affairs of the partnership.

[1] See ch 8 above.
[2] Partnership Act 1890, s 38.
[3] *Thomason v Frere* (1809) 10 East 418.
[4] Partnership Act 1890, s 36(3).
[5] Creditor: *Burt v Moult* (1833) 1 Cr & M 525; debtor: Bankruptcy Act 1914, s 45.

24.7.3 *The Old Bankruptcy Law doctrine of reputed ownership.* By virtue of the Bankruptcy Act 1914, s 38(c), all goods in the possession or control of the bankrupt, in his trade or business, with the consent of the true owner, under circumstances in which the bankrupt is the apparent owner of the goods, form part of the bankrupt's estate.[1] Where one of several partners is bankrupt, the joint estate of the firm might be in the bankrupt's reputed ownership by being in his separate possession or control. However, the joint estate is necessarily in the joint possession or control of all of the partners and therefore the bankrupt's separate property cannot be in the reputed ownership of the firm as it would then still be in the possession or control of the bankrupt.

The doctrine of reputed ownership could cause difficulties to the partners where there is a change in membership of the firm, and for any remaining problems in this area, reference should be made to the cases cited in 5 Digest (Re-Issue), Part XX, sub-sections 3(A)(b), 3(B)(d) and 6(B).

[1] See ch 6.3.3 above.

24.8 DISTRIBUTION OF BANKRUPT PARTNER'S ASSETS

General principles

24.8.1 Whether under the Old Bankruptcy Law or the New Law, distribution follows the order of priority discussed in chs 9 and 16 above. The trustee must, however, be careful to distinguish, on the one hand, the partners' joint and separate estates and, on the other, joint and separate debts of the partnership and partners.

24.8.2 In administering the various estates, the trustee must first pay the joint creditors out of the separate estates of which they are creditors. Any set of creditors may be paid in full out of the appropriate estate even where other creditors fall far short of full payment. Only if there is a surplus in any one estate will assets from that estate be applied to supply any deficiency there may be in the other estate or estates.[1] This rule was strongly criticised in the Cork Report[2] and its abolition recommended.

It is essential therefore that the trustee maintains distinct accounts of the joint estate and the separate estate or estates.[3] The Bankruptcy Rules 1952 further provide that the trustee may not transfer a surplus from a separate estate to the joint estate until notice of his intention has been given in the *Gazette*.[4] With distinct accounts being kept of the various estates and each set of creditors being entitled to appoint their own committees of inspection, it is possible for the trustee's costs to be paid from the estates to which they relate and his remuneration for administering each estate to be fixed by the creditors of that estate and paid from the assets of the estate. The rules so provide.

[1] Bankruptcy Act 1914, ss 33(6), 63; Insolvency Act 1986, s 420 and Insolvent Partnerships Order 1986.
[2] Cork Report, ch 39.
[3] Bankruptcy Rules 1952, r 371; Insolvency Regulations 1986, SI 1986/1994.
[4] Bankruptcy Rules 1952, r 296.

24.8.3 Before the appointment of a trustee, the incidence of costs and expenses may not be so clearly defined or definable. Under the Old Bankruptcy Law, the Rules provided that costs payable out of the estate incurred up to and inclusive of the receiving order, shall be apportioned between the joint and separate estates of the partners in such proportions as the official receiver may determine.[1]

[1] Bankruptcy Rules 1952, r 118.

24.8.4 From receiving order to appointment of trustee under the New Law, the costs and charges fall to the appropriate estate. If that estate cannot meet the expenses, the separate estates may be called on to pay expenses of the joint estate or the joint estate to pay the separate estates by the official receiver in such proportions as he thinks fit. No payment may be made, however, without the consent of the committee of inspection of the estate called on to make it, and, if the committee refuse consent, without an order of the court.[1]

[1] Bankruptcy Rules 1952, r 119.

Joint and separate estates

24.8.5 Subject to questions of reputed ownership under the Old Bankruptcy Law, (see above), the trustee must determine:

(a) whether any particular property belongs jointly to all the partners in whatever shares or exclusively to one or some of them; and
(b) whether in the case of property belonging to one or some of the partners exclusively one or more of the other partners have liens or other rights over such property.

This will be a question of fact in each case. The trustee will be bound by any bona fide agreement concluded between the partners before the commencement of the bankruptcy. The partners are free to agree that property of the bankrupt should become the property of an individual partner or vice versa. The most likely situation for such an agreement to arise is on the retirement of partners from the business. Where retiring partners agree that the firm's property should become the property of a sole remaining partner who is continuing the business, on a subsequent bankruptcy of the firm, the former partnership property must be distributed as the separate estate of the remaining partner.[1] Without a specific agreement that the partnership assets should vest entirely in the remaining partner, however, he continues the business of the firm with those assets subject to the rights of the retiring partners to have them applied in discharge of joint debts. For the purpose of distribution they are joint estates.[2]

1 *Ex p Ruffin* (1801) 6 Ves 119; *Ex p Williams* (1805) 11 Ves 3; *Re Simpson* (1874) 9 Ch App 572.
2 *Re White, ex p Dear* (1876) 1 Ch D 514; *Re Mellor, ex p Butcher* (1880) 13 Ch D 465.

Joint and several creditors

24.8.6 There are three categories of creditors with whose debts the trustee may be concerned:
(1) joint creditors to whom all the partners in the firm are jointly liable;
(2) several creditors, i e the separate creditors of any particular partner to whom no other partner is liable; and
(3) joint and several creditors to whom all the partners are liable jointly and each partner is also liable individually.

24.8.7 The classification of the various creditors will follow general legal principles. For present purposes, the following points are noted:
1 The debts of the firm are joint debts and are not several unless a partner has expressly made himself individually liable in addition to his joint liability.[1]
2 The liability of all the partners of a firm for frauds or breaches of trust committed by any one or more partners of the firm, is both joint and several.[2]
3 Where a partner who is also a trustee uses trust property in the firm's business in breach of trust, no other partner is liable to the beneficiaries. Such liability is separate to the defaulting trustee partner.[3]
4 Dormant or nominal partners are jointly liable with the active partner or partners but the creditor has the option of treating his debt as joint or as the several debt of the active partner. Once the creditor has made his election, he may not change his position.[4]
5 A separate bond may be given to secure a joint debt, and extinguishes the joint debt, leaving only a several debt.[5] To have this effect, however, the bond must be taken in satisfaction of the original demand. A creditor is entitled to take additional security for an existing debt, be it a separate security for a joint debt or vice versa, without losing his right to pursue the original debt in its original classification.
6 A judgment recovered against any one joint debtor does not bar an action, or the continuance of an action against any other joint debtor.[6]
7 A creditor cannot be bound without his consent to any alteration in the position of his debtor made by the debtor with other parties, for example, incoming and outgoing partners. And a partner who retires from the firm remains jointly liable with his former partners for partnership debts and obligations incurred before his retirement.[7]

1 Partnership Act 1890, s 9.

[2] Ibid, s 12.
[3] Ibid, s 13.
[4] *Re Bazley and Chapman, ex p Law* (1839) 3 Deac 541; *Scarf v Jardine* (1882) 7 App Cas 345.
[5] *Re Ewens, ex p Hernaman* (1848) 17 L J Bcy 17.
[6] Civil Liability (Contribution) Act 1978, s 3.
[7] Partnership Act 1890, s 17.

Proofs of debt

24.8.8 As mentioned above, the joint creditors in proving against the joint estate, are entitled to be paid in full before separate creditors of individual partners may prove in the joint estate. A partner who is also a creditor of the firm may not prove in competition with the joint creditors of the firm and his individual creditors are similarly precluded from proof until the joint creditors have been paid in full.[1] A partner who has been discharged from the joint debts by a compromise or discharge in bankruptcy and subsequently becomes a creditor of the firm, is no longer in competition with the joint creditors and may prove against the joint estate.[2]

[1] *Re Goodchilds & Co ex p Sillitoe* (1824) 1 Gl & J 374.
[2] *Re Hepburn, p Smith* (1884) 14 QBD 394; *Re Douglas, ex p Douglas Executors* [1930] 1 Ch 342.

24.8.9 There are two exceptions to the rule that a creditor partner and his creditors may not prove in the joint estate for his debt:
(i) where the partner's individual property has been fraudulently converted by one or more co-partners to the use of the firm;[1] and
(ii) where there are two distinct firms carrying on separate trades with the same or overlapping partners. In this event, where one firm becomes the creditor of the other bona fide in the ordinary course of business, the creditor firm may prove in the joint estate of the debtor firm even though there are partners in common between the firms.[2]

[1] *Re Goodchilds & Co, ex p Sillitoe* (1824) 1 GI & J 374.
[2] *Re Petherbridge, ex p Cook* (1831) Mont 228. Here one member of a partnership also carried on business on his own account. He supplied goods to the firm in the ordinary course of trading and also advanced money. He was able to prove for the debt due on the goods but not for the money advanced to the partnership.

24.8.10 When administering the separate estate of a partner, the trustee must pay the proofs of the separate creditors in full before joint creditors may prove, subject to four exceptions. The first two exceptions are the converse of the exceptions referred to above where separate creditors may prove against the joint estate. Thus:
(i) where an individual partner fraudulently converts a partnership property to his own use such property must form part of the joint estate and the joint estate may prove against the individual's estate in respect of it;[1]
(ii) where one of a firm's partners has carried on his own separate and distinct trade and has become indebted to the firm bona fide in the ordinary course of trading, the firm may prove in the individual's bankruptcy;[2]

(iii) a further exception exists where there is no joint estate. Here the joint creditors are entitled to prove as separate creditors against the several estates of the various partners.[3] This rule allows creditors of the firm to prove in the bankruptcy of one partner where the co-partners are not bankrupt if there is no joint estate;[3] and

(iv) finally, it appears that the petitioning creditor himself is excepted, somewhat extraordinarily, and a joint petitioning creditor may prove and receive dividends from the separate estates.[4]

1 *Read v Bailey* (1877) 3 App Cas 94.
2 *Ex p St Barbe* (1805) 11 Ves 413.
3 *Re Lomax, ex p Bauerman and Christie* (1838) 3 Deac 476.
4 See *Ex p Hall* (1804) 9 Ves 349 and the other cases cited at 4 Digest (Re-Issue) p 484.

24.8.11 A co-partner creditor of an individual partner, and his creditors, may not prove in the individual partner's estate until both the separate creditors and the joint creditors of the firm have been paid in full. This follows from the principle of non-competition by a bankrupt with his own creditors. As the separate estate of the individual partner may become available to meet the claims of the joint creditors of the firm should the separate creditors be paid in full, to allow a co-partner to prove in the individual partner's estate would be to allow the co-partner to compete with his own creditors and indeed ahead of them.

24.8.12 Joint and several creditors have, as a basic rule, to elect whether they wish to prove and receive dividends against the joint estate or the several estate or any of them against which they have rights.[1]

This prevents their infringing the rule against double proof. Plainly, before electing, the creditor will wish to know which estate will pay the better dividend, for once an election is made, it is final.[2] Before committing himself, the creditor is allowed to wait until the trustee has declared a dividend or is in a position to do so, and where a creditor has proved against the joint estate in ignorance of his right to prove against the separate estate of the partners, he was allowed to refund a dividend and prove in the separate estates.[3] There are a number of cases which suggest that a creditor is not conclusively bound by an election until he has knowledge of the true position with respect to the various estates in which he may prove.[4] The prudent course would be to prove against all estates and elect from which he will receive when the dividends are declared.

Although the basic rule is that the joint and several creditor must elect against which estate he will receive dividends, he may make a double proof against both joint and separate estates where the debtor was liable in two distinct capacities on two or more separate contracts.[5] The debtor may be a member of two partnerships or a partner and a sole contractor. Where in different capacities he incurs debts to the same creditor on separate contracts, the creditor may prove against both the joint and the separate estates.

1 *Ex p Hay* (1808) 15 Ves 4.
2 *Re Robinson, ex p Dixon* (1841) 2 Mont D & De G 312.
3 *Re Mackenzie, ex p Bolton* (1816) Buck 7.

[4] See 4 Digest (Re-Issue) p 491.
[5] Bankruptcy Act 1914, Sch 2, para 19.

24.9 DISCHARGE[1]

Bankrupt partners will obtain their discharge under the Old Bankruptcy Law or New Law as appropriate, and in the usual case, discharge will now be automatic after three years from the commencement of the bankruptcy under the Insolvency Act 1986.[2]

The discharge operates to discharge the bankrupt from all debts which could have been proved in his bankruptcy including any demand which may have been made by co-partners. The discharge of one of a number of joint debtors does not discharge the co-debtors[3] and, accordingly, solvent partners continue to be liable for debts of the firm which cannot be pursued against the discharged bankrupt partner, unless the creditor has compromised his debt in the partner's bankruptcy.

[1] Insolvency Act 1986, s 278.
[2] Bankruptcy Act 1914, s 28(4); Insolvency Act 1986, s 281(7).
[3] See chs 10 and 18 above.

24.10 VOLUNTARY ARRANGEMENTS

Whether by a composition or scheme of arrangement under the Bankruptcy Act 1914 or by voluntary arrangements under the Insolvency Act 1986, a partnership as well as an individual debtor may make arrangements with their creditors. The provisions of the Bankruptcy Act 1914 relating to such arrangements are now of little relevance; the position as to voluntary arrangements under the Insolvency Act 1986 is discussed in ch 12 above.

24.11 BANKRUPTCY OF PRINCIPAL TO AGENCY AGREEMENT

Effect on express authority of agent

24.11.1 *Old Law.* Under the Old Law it is well established that the express authority of every agent however conferred is revoked by the bankruptcy of the principal,[1] except where the authority is irrevocable, see below. The legal principle rests upon the fact that agency is a personal relationship. As upon the principal's adjudication his rights and liabilities are vested in his trustee, the agency relationship cannot continue, without the agent's express agreement,[2] with a new principal, the trustee in bankruptcy. Accordingly it follows that the agency relationship is not terminated in respect of any powers or transactions relating to property which does not pass to the trustee in bankruptcy.[3] The prime example of such property which remains vested in the bankrupt is property of which he is trustee.

The agency is revoked by the first act of bankruptcy committed by the principal during the three months immediately preceding the date of the presentation of the petition on which the adjudication of the principal is made.[4] The act of bankruptcy may indeed be committed by the act of the agent.[5]

In cases where the agent's authority is given in order to protect the agent's position in relation to transactions with the principal, which will often be in the course of mutual dealings between parties, the agent's authority is not revoked until the agent has actual notice of an available act of bankruptcy[6] by the principal, or a receiving order is made against the principal.[7]

1 *Dawson v Sexton* (1823) 1 LJOS Ch 185; *Markwick v Hardingham* (1880) 15 ChD 339, nb mere formal acts to complete a transaction already binding may be performed by the agent.

2 And then only with the consent of the committee of inspection: see Bankruptcy Act 1914, s 56(3).

3 Bankruptcy Act 1914, s 38 defines the property which comprises the bankrupt's estate.

4 Bankruptcy Act 1914, s 37 and see e g *Pearson v Graham* (1837) 6 Ad & El 899; *Re Lamb, ex p Gibson and Bolland* (1886) 55 LT 817; affd (1887) 3 TLR 303; *Re Pollitt, ex p minor* [1893] 1 QB 455; *Re British Folding Bed Co, ex p Trustee v NA Woodiwiss* [1948] Ch 635, [1948] 2 All ER 216.

5 Eg *Re Lamb, ex p Gibson and Bolland* (above), agent giving notice of suspension of payments; *Re Lewis, ex p Helder* (1883) 24 Ch D 339, payment of money, principal insolvent; and *Re White, ex p Ward and Afford* (1898) 78 LT 25, accountant sending out accounts.

6 'available act of bankruptcy', is any act of bankruptcy on which a petition could have been based (whether or not it was so used) at the date on which the petition was presented on which the receiving order was made. Petitions may only be presented on acts of bankruptcy committed within three months of the date of presentation, and hence acts of bankruptcy cannot be 'available' before such period: Bankruptcy Act 1914, ss 1, 4(1) and 167.

7 Bankruptcy Act 1914, s 31.

24.11.2 *New Law.* Where the bankruptcy occurs under the Insolvency Act 1986 the property of the bankrupt principal at the date of the commencement of the bankruptcy vests in the principal's trustee in bankruptcy. The agent's authority in respect of this property will be revoked. The date of revocation of the agent's authority will effectively be the date of presentation of the petition on which the bankruptcy order was made. For the Insolvency Act 1986[1] provides that any disposition of property of the bankrupt made between the date of presentation of the petition and the date of vesting of the bankrupt's estate in the trustee[2] shall be void unless it was made with the consent of the court or is subsequently ratified by the court.

The Insolvency Act 1986 does not, however, vest in the trustee in bankruptcy property acquired by the bankrupt principal after the commencement of the bankruptcy. Such property remains the bankrupt's subject to the trustee's rights to claim such property for the estate.[3] A question therefore arises as to whether the agent who is appointed by a principal on terms which do not expressly determine the agency relationship upon the principal's bankruptcy continues to have authority to conduct transactions after the commencement of the bankruptcy in respect of property acquired after that date by the principal. In principle the agent's authority is not revoked by the bankruptcy in respect of powers over property not comprised in the estate. The agent will continue therefore to be empowered, depending upon the terms of his appointment, to deal with any after-acquired property within the ambit of his authority, subject to the service of written notice by the trustee claiming it for the estate. In practice it may be anticipated that the trustee will claim all valuable after-acquired property for the estate. But it may take some time for the trustee to learn of the property and serve the required notice.[4] Although on serving notice claiming the property the trustee's title relates back to the time at which the bankrupt acquired the property,[5] the Insolvency Act 1986 provides that any person who acquires after-acquired property in good faith for value and without notice of the bankruptcy, together with persons deriving title through such a person, is protected from any remedy the trustee would otherwise have against them.[6] An agent whose authority does not expressly determine upon the principal's bankruptcy might therefore give good title to after-acquired property to third parties, and the trustee would be restricted to recovering the proceeds of sale or other disposition from the agent, less any commission properly due to the agent.

1 S 284(1)(3), nb such a disposition is void whether or not the property which would be comprised in the bankrupt's estate, with the exception of a disposition of property held on trust: s 284(6).
2 The bankrupt's property vests in the trustee immediately his appointment takes effect: Insolvency Act 1986, s 306, Individual Insolvency Rules, 1986, r 6.125.
3 S 307 and see para 16.2.3 above.
4 S 307(5): the trustee has 42 days from learning of the property to serve his notice; see para 24.11.6 below.
5 Insolvency Act 1986, s 307(3).
6 Ibid, s 307(4).

Protection of agent and third parties

24.11.3 As stated above the agent's authority is revoked by the first available act of bankruptcy under the Old Law. Where the agent, or the third party with whom he deals, is not aware of the revocation of authority there is a measure of statutory protection for transactions completed before the receiving order or commencement of the bankruptcy, and even beyond. Under the Bankruptcy Act 1914 every act of whatever nature (including the making and receiving of payments) with which the agent is concerned in the course of his agency is valid if committed or made after the act of bankruptcy from which the bankruptcy commences but before the date of the receiving order (a) as respects the agent provided that he had no notice of any available act of bankruptcy at the time the act of agency was performed,[1] and (b) as respects any third party dealing with the agent for valuable consideration and without notice of any available act of bankruptcy by the principal.[2] The Bankruptcy (Amendment) Act 1926[3] extends protection to an agent who is in possession of money or property of a principal and pays or transfers it to a third party between the date of the receiving order and the date on which the order is gazetted.[4] Claims by the trustee against such an agent are not enforceable save and in so far as the court is satisfied that it is not reasonably practicable for the trustee to recover in respect of the money or property or part thereof from the person to whom it was paid or transferred. The agent must prove that when he made the payment or transfer he had not had notice of the receiving order. This provision was designed to give some protection to bankers who honour cheques drawn by the bankrupt and which are presented after the receiving order.

1 Bankruptcy Act 1914, s 45; see e g *Re Lewis, ex p Helder* (1883) 24 Ch D 339; *Re Beyts & Craig, ex p Trustee* (1894) 70 LT 561; *Re Pollock, Official Receiver v Haslip* [1936] 3 All ER 157.

[2] Bankruptcy Act 1914, s 45.
[3] S 4.
[4] The time taken to gazette a receiving order is usually in the order of 7 days.

24.11.4 Under the Insolvency Act 1986[1] the interests of both agent and third party are protected in respect of any property or payment received before the commencement of the bankruptcy[2] in good faith, for value and without notice that the petition has been presented. The trustee has no remedy against the agent or third party so protected nor against persons deriving any interest in property, which includes money,[3] from them.[4] In place of the Bankruptcy (Amendment) Act 1926, s 4, the Insolvency Act 1986[5] provides that where a bankrupt incurs a debt to a banker or other person after the commencement of his bankruptcy by reason of making a payment which is void because made after presentation of the petition and without the consent or ratification of the court, that debt shall be deemed to have been incurred before the commencement of the bankruptcy unless (a) the banker or other person had notice of the bankruptcy before the debt was incurred, or (b) it is reasonably practicable for the amount of the payment to be recovered from the person to whom it was made. Bankers therefore who after the commencement of the bankruptcy honour a cheque drawn by the bankrupt in making a void payment before the bankruptcy commenced (and who had no notice of the bankruptcy and cannot recover from the payee) will be able to prove in the bankruptcy as their debt is deemed to have been incurred before the commencement of the bankruptcy.

[1] S 284(4)(a).
[2] Ie the date on which the bankruptcy order is made: Insolvency Act 1986, s 278(a).
[3] See disposition of 'property': Insolvency Act 1986, s 436.'
[4] Insolvency Act 1986, s 284(4)(b).
[5] S 284(5).

Effect on apparent authority of agent

24.11.5 Apparent or ostensible authority arises where a principal by words or conduct holds out a person as being an agent authorised to act on his behalf. The principal will then be bound by the acts of the agent.[1] Apparent authority may arise both where there is some specific holding out of a person not otherwise the principal's agent, or where the agent is appointed to or allowed to assume a position carrying with it a usual or implied authority and the principal does not draw to the attention of the third party any limitation of that usual or implied authority which he has placed upon the agent or, indeed, that the agent has no authority to assume that position at all. It has been generally accepted for the purposes of the law under the Bankruptcy Act 1914 that there could be no apparent authority after the bankruptcy of the principal. The bankrupt's property is all vested in the trustee in bankruptcy and the principal is accordingly incapable of vesting apparent authority in an agent. In any event the Bankruptcy Act 1914[2] protects third parties and agents who have no notice of the act of bankruptcy in respect of dealings with a bankrupt's agent before the date of the receiving order.

[1] See generally Fridman *Law of Agency* (5th edn) pp 105–115.
[2] S.45.

24.11.6 Under the Insolvency Act 1986, however, a bankrupt may own property which has been acquired by him after the commencement of the bankruptcy. The bankrupt would be under no incapacity in dealing with after-acquired property, and therefore would be able to vest an agent with apparent authority in relation to dealings with such property. A third party who has notice of the bankruptcy of the principal would presumably be put on enquiry as to the principal's right to deal with valuable after-acquired property irrespective of questions of authority on the part of the agent. In any case he would not have title against the trustee in bankruptcy. A trustee has 42 days to serve a notice claiming after-acquired property for the estate.[1] This time period begins to run when the trustee first obtains knowledge of the property and the period may be extended by leave of the court. The trustee is then entitled to the property against all the world except a person who acquired the property in good faith for value and without notice of the bankruptcy or any person deriving title through such a bona fide purchaser.[2] There is no reason to suppose that under the New Law the bona fide purchaser for value without notice may not acquire title through an agent acting with apparent authority.

1 Insolvency Act 1986, s 309(1)(a).
2 Ibid, s 307(4), nb bankers are also protected where they enter into transactions in good faith without notice of the bankruptcy even though they have not given value.

Irrevocable authority

24.11.7 The principal may, however, vest his agent with irrevocable authority. Such authority may be given as a means of providing security for the agent or for protecting an interest of the agent. Provided irrevocable authority is given expressly for the purpose of effecting such security, and is given by deed or for valuable consideration, then it is irrevocable for as long as is necessary to maintain the agent's security or interest.[1] The mere fact that an agent's power is declared to be irrevocable does not vest the power with irrevocability. Neither is an agent's power irrecovable just because he has an interest in its exercise.[2] Irrevocability only attaches to authority that is expressly given to effect security for an interest of the agent or advances made by him to the principal.[3] It is not essential that the authority creating the security is expressed to be irrevocable. Irrevocable authority in an agent is not determined by the bankruptcy of the principal.[4] As such authority constitutes the agent's security he is entitled to that security as against the principal's trustee in bankruptcy as is any other secured creditor.

1 *Re Hannan's Empress Gold Mining and Development Co, Carmichael's Case* [1896] 2 Ch 643; *Re Olympic Fire and General Reinsurance Co Ltd, Pole's Case* [1920] 2 Ch 341.
2 *Smart v Sanders* (1848) 5 CB 895; *Frith v Frith* [1906] AC 254.
3 *Spooner v Sandilands* (1842) 1 Y & C Ch Cas 390; *Clerk v Laurie* (1857) 2 H & N 199; *Frith v Frith* [1906] AC 254.
4 *Alley v Hotson* (1815) 4 Camp 325.

Powers of attorney

24.11.8 In general powers of attorney follow the rules relating to any other type of agency. Powers of attorney may be irrevocable, provided that the statutory requirements are met. The Powers of Attorney Act 1971[1] provides that a power of attorney shall be irrevocable:

(a) where it is expressed to be irrevocable, and
(b) it is given to secure either (i) a proprietary interest of the donee of the power or (ii) the performance of an obligation owed to the donee.

The power of attorney will then remain irrevocable for so long as the donor has the interest or the obligation remains undischarged. An example of proprietary interest thus secured would be an equitable mortgage containing an irrevocable power of attorney to convey the legal estate where the power of sale is exercised. The irrevocable power of attorney may not be revoked by the death, incapacity or bankruptcy of the donor.[2]

1 Powers of Attorney Act 1971, s 4(1).
2 Ibid, s 4(1)(i)(ii).

24.11.9 The Powers of Attorney Act 1971 provides a measure of protection for the donee agent and third parties where a power of attorney is revoked.

1 A donee who acts in pursuance of the power at a time when it has been revoked shall not incur any liability to the donor or third party by reason of the revocation if at the time he acted he was unaware that the power had been revoked.[1]
2 Where a third party without knowledge of a revocation deals with the donee of the power the transaction between them shall be valid in favour of the third party, as if the power had not been revoked.[2]
3 Where the instrument creating the power of attorney expresses it to be irrevocable and to be given by way of security, a third party dealing with the donee without knowledge that the power is not in fact irrevocable is entitled to assume that it is irrevocable except by the donor acting with the consent of the donee.[3]
4 Where the interest of a purchaser depends upon whether the third party was aware or not of the revocation of the donee's power (under 2 above) it is to be conclusively presumed in favour of the purchaser that the third party did not know of the revocation of the power if:
   (a) the transaction between donee and third party was completed within 12 months of the power coming into operation; or
   (b) the third party makes a statutory declaration before or within three months of the purchase that he did not at the material time know that the power of attorney had been revoked.[4]
5 Where a donee as transferor executes an instrument transferring registered securities within the meaning of the Stock Transfer Act 1963 and that instrument is executed for the purposes of a Stock Exchange transaction it is to be conclusively presumed in favour of the transferee that the power had not been revoked at the date of the instrument if a statutory declaration to that effect is made by the donee of the power on or within three months after that date.[5]

An enduring power of attorney, where the donor appoints an attorney to act for him notwithstanding any subsequent mental incapacity of his, is revoked by the attorney's bankruptcy, whatever its circumstances.[6]

1 Powers of Attorney Act 1971, s 4(1).

[2] Ibid, s 5(2).
[3] Ibid, s 5(3).
[4] Ibid, s 5(4).
[5] Ibid, s 6(1).
[6] Enduring Powers of Attorney Act 1985, s 2(10).

Position of agent and principal's trustee

24.11.10 Where the agent is not covered by statutory protection, see above, or irrevocable authority he continues to act after notice of an act of bankruptcy or presentation of the petition at his peril. If adjudication or bankruptcy follows the agent may be held personally liable for any loss to the estate.[1] He may still be liable where he sells goods belonging to his principal and pays the proceeds to his principal.[2] Under the Old Law, where the agent's act constitutes the act of bankruptcy the act is not avoided by the bankruptcy, and the agent is not liable upon it, because the bankruptcy relates back to and commences on the completion of the act of bankruptcy.[3]

The agent will be able to prove in the bankruptcy for all sums due to him as any other creditor. If there have been mutual dealings the agent is entitled to a right of set off against all monies of the principal received before the date of the receiving order if he has had no notice of the act of bankruptcy.[4] Under the New Law an account of mutual credits and set offs is taken at the commencement of the bankruptcy unless the agent had notice that a petition was being presented or that a petition was pending. The agent is not entitled to include in the account any sums due from the bankrupt principal after the date of such notice.[5]

The agent may be required by the trustee to deliver up any property or books of account belonging to his principal, but the agent may exercise against the trustee any lien which is enforceable against his principal.[6]

Insofar as the agent's authority is not revoked by the principal's bankruptcy the agent may apply to the court for an order discharging his remaining obligations under the contract of agency[7]

[1] Bankruptcy Act 1914, s 37; Insolvency Act 1986, s 284(2) and the general principles of law applicable to persons who interfere with another's property.
[2] *King v Leith* (1787) 2 Term Rep 141.
[3] *Re Lewis, ex p Helder* (1883) 24 Ch D 339.
[4] Bankruptcy Act 1914, s 31.
[5] Insolvency Act 1986, s 323(1), (3).
[6] *Drinkwater v Goodwin* (1775) 1 Cowp 251; Insolvency Act 1986, s 312(3).
[7] Insolvency Act 1986, s 345.

24.12 BANKRUPTCY OF AGENT

24.12.1 *Effect on authority of agent.* As a matter of law the authority of an agent is not terminated by his bankruptcy.[1] Whether the agent's bankruptcy does determine the agreement of agency and enable the principal to withdraw the agent's authority without due notice under the agreement is a question of fact which depends upon the proper interpretation of the agreement. The mere fact that the bankrupt agent receives money on account for his principal under the agency agreement is not of itself a defence to an action against the principal by the agent for wrongful dismissal.[2] Where the bankruptcy and its circumstances cannot be shown to make the agent any the less fit or competent to carry out his duties,[3] or where the acts he is authorised to do are merely formal in nature[4] the bankruptcy of the agent will not determine the agreement or terminate his authority. Where the agent continues to have express authority while he is bankrupt, there is no rule of law to prevent him binding his principal under the doctrine of apparent or ostensible authority. Where the agreement for the agent's services contained a provision for liquidated damages to be paid on default the court held that the agreement was determined by the agent's bankruptcy.[5] In the case of many professional men it will be noted that they are precluded from acting for clients after bankruptcy under the rules of their profession.[6] Where an attorney is appointed under the Enduring Powers of Attorney Act 1985 to act as attorney for a donor notwithstanding any subsequent mental incapacity of the donor, the power of attorney is revoked by the attorney's bankruptcy whatever the circumstances of the bankruptcy.[7]

1 *Hudson v Granger* (1821) 5 B & Ald 27; *Phelps v Lyle* (1839) 8 LJ QB 236; *Bailey v Thurston & Co Ltd* [1903] 1 KB 137, CA; and see *Tharsis Sulphur & Copper Co v Société Industrielle Commerciale des Metaux* (1889) 60 LT 924.
2 *McCall v Australian Meat Co Ltd* (1870) 19 WR 188.
3 Ibid; *Bailey v Thurston & Co Ltd* [1903] 1 KB 137, CA.
4 *Dixon v Ewart* (1817) Buck 94.
5 *Beckham v Drake* (1849) 2 HL Cas 579.
6 E g *Chartered Accountants*. Institute of Chartered Accountants in England and Wales, by-law 33(b); membership ceases on bankruptcy, by-law 76(e): member liable to disciplinary action if fails to satisfy judgment debt or makes arrangement with creditors.
Certified Accountants. Chartered Association of Certified Accountants, by-law 25: membership ceases 2 months after bankruptcy, subject to extension.
Solicitors. Solicitors Act 1974, s 15: bankruptcy suspends practising certificate.
Surveyors. Royal Institution of Chartered Surveyors, by-law 25(2): member liable to suspension or expulsion on bankruptcy as a disciplinary matter.
Valuers and Auctioneers. Incorporated Society of Valuers and Auctioneers Articles of Association, art 23: membership ceases unless Council decrees otherwise.
7 Enduring Powers of Attorney Act, 1985, s 2(10).

24.12.2 *Rights of agent against principal.* The general principle is that an agent is entitled to reimbursement and indemnity from his principal in respect of losses liabilities and expenses incurred in the proper performance of his duties, and this is so by implication where there is no express provision in the agency agreement.[1] But where the agent incurs losses liabilities or expenses as a result of his own insolvency or bankruptcy the principal has no obligation to indemnify him or his trustee in bankruptcy in respect of any such loss the agent may sustain.[2]

Every agent has a lien on the property of his principal in respect of all claims of the agent arising out of the agency subject to any express provision to the contrary in the agency agreement.[3] The lien does not arise in respect of goods entrusted to the agent for a specific purpose inconsistent with his having a lien.[4] The lien may be relied on in respect of claims for remuneration or for expenses and liabilities incurred even though the agent's claim may be statute barred.[5] The lien will generally be a particular lien confined to such claims as relate to the property held by the agent[6] though a general lien extending to all claims relating to the agency may exist by express agreement or by usage.[7] An agent loses his lien on parting with possession of the property concerned, subject to an express reservation by the agent or fraud on the part of the principal, but the vesting of the agent's estate in his trustee in bankruptcy and any loss of possession connected therewith does not destroy the lien.[8] The agent's trustee may therefore enforce the lien against the principal. If there are mutual credits and set off to be accounted between principal and agent the trustee is obliged to bring the agent's claim in respect of which the lien is claimed into the account and so release the principal's property.[9]

1 *Bayliffe v Butterworth* (1847) 1 Exch 425; *Thacker v Hardy* (1878) 4 QBD 685; *Adams v Morgan & Co* [1924] 1 KB 751.
2 *Duncan v Hill* (1873) LR 8 Exch 242.
3 *Fisher v Smith* (1878) 4 App Cas 1; *Re Bowes, Earl Strathmore v Vane* (1886) 33 Ch D 586; *Rolls Razor Ltd v Cox* [1967] 1 QB 552, nb the mutual set off provisions in bankruptcy cannot be ousted by express agreement.
4 *Brandao v Barnett* (1846) 12 Cl & Fin 787; *Skinner v Reed's Trustee* [1967] Ch 1194.
5 *Spears v Hartly* (1800) 3 Esp 81.
6 *Bock v Gorrissen* (1861) 30 LJ Ch 39.
7 General liens are by usage vested, inter alia, in bankers: *London Chartered Bank of Australia v White* (1879) 4 App Cas 413; factors: *Baring v Corrie* (1818) 2 B & Ald 137; insurance brokers: *Mann & Forrester* (1814) 4 Camp 60; solicitors: *Re Broomhead* (1847) 5 Dow & L 52; and see Solicitors Act 1974, s 73; and stockbrokers: *Re London and Globe Finance Corpn* [1902] 2 Ch 416.
8 *Giles v Perkins* (1807) 9 East 12.
9 Bankruptcy Act 1914, s 31; Insolvency Act 1986, s 323.

24.12.3 *Principal's rights against agent's trustee.* On the bankruptcy of the agent the principal is entitled to follow and recover any property of his in the possession of the bankrupt agent[1] together with any outstanding debts due to the bankrupt in his capacity as agent for the principal.[2] This right of the principal is good against both the trustee and the bankrupt agent's creditors. It may be subject, however, to any of the following considerations:

(a) the bankrupt agent may have a lien on some or all of the principal's property at the commencement of the bankruptcy and this lien remains enforceable in the hands of the trustee;[3]
(b) under the Bankruptcy Act 1914,[4] though not under the Insolvency Act 1986 which does not re-enact these provisions, the principal may not recover goods or debts which at the commencement of the bankruptcy were in the order or disposition of the agent under such circumstances as to make the agent the reputed owner of such goods or debts. The principal is then left to prove in the bankruptcy for the value of the goods or debts concerned;[5] or
(c) where there have been mutual dealings, it is necessary for an account to be taken of the mutual credits and debts with sums due from one party set off against sums due from the other.[6]

The principal's right to follow or trace his money or property is not precluded by the agent mixing his principal's money or property with his own. The principal has a first charge on the mixed fund or property or the proceeds of sale of mixed property.[7] This charge is effective against the agent's trustee and creditors for so long as the principal's property or the proceeds can be clearly identified.[8] When, however, the principal's property can no longer be traced he becomes an ordinary creditor.[9]

[1] *Ex p Sayers* (1800) 5 Ves 169; *Re Thickbroom, ex p Greenwood* (1862) 6 LT 558.
[2] *Re Smith, ex p Bright* (1879) 10 Ch D 566.
[3] *Giles v Perkins* (1807) 9 East 12.
[4] Bankruptcy Act 1914, s 38.
[5] *Re Sutton, ex p Haviside* [1907] 2 KB 180.
[6] Bankruptcy Act 1914, s 31; Insolvency Act 1986, s 323.
[7] *Hancock v Smith* (1889) 41 Ch D 4 56; *Re Hallett & Co, ex p Blane* [1894] 2 QB 237; *Re Hallett's Estate, Knatchbull v Hallett* (1880) 13 Ch D 696.
[8] *Harris v Truman* (1882) 9 QBD 264; and note that the principal is entitled to any profits earned by the agent on his property or money; *Re Hammond, ex p Brooke* (1869) 20 LT 547.
[9] The general equitable rules of tracing will apply. For example where money belonging to several principals has been paid into one account, the principals have priority over the fund in the account in reverse order to the date of payment of their respective moneys into the account. The money first paid in is deemed to have been paid out first; see the rule in *Clayton's Case* (1816) 1 Mer 572; and *Re Diplock* [1948] Ch 465.

24.12.4 Where the agent is in possession of property belonging to, and with the consent of, his principal such property is, as a general rule, liable to be taken by way of distress for rent due from the agent in respect of the premises where he keeps the property.[1] An exception to the general rule, however, arises where an agent carries on a 'public trade' in the course of which his principal's property is entrusted to him and kept on his property.[2] A public trade is one where an agent performs acts on or with respect to his principal's goods such as carriage, repair, improvement, or management including sale.[3] Examples will be cars sent for repair to a garage or furniture sent for re-upholstery. The essential feature of the exemption from the levying of distress is that if property is delivered to the agent's premises to remain there it is distrainable: if it is sent for a particular purpose and is due to remain there only for as long as that purpose requires the property may not be the subject of distress.[4] Thus, for example, horses and carriages on the agent's premises because standing at livery may be distrained[5] but a horse sent to be shod or a carriage sent to a coachmaker for repair or sale may not.[6] Goods which are warehoused for a specific period of time may not be distrained;[7] goods left on an agent's premises for convenience may be.[8] It should also be noted that the exemption applies only to public trade and will not cover purely private arrangements.[9]

[1] *Gilman v Elton* (1821) 3 Brod & Bing 75.
[2] *Simpson v Hartopp* (1744) Willes 512.
[3] *Lyons v Elliott* (1876) 1 QBD 210.
[4] *Parsons v Gingell* (1847) 4 CB 545.
[5] *Francis v Wyatt* (1764) 1 WmBl 483.
[6] *Kersey v Dixon* (1843) 1 LT(OS) 76; *Findon v M'Laren* (1845) 6 QB 891.
[7] *Thompson v Mashiter* (1823) 1 Bing 283; *Miles v Furber* (1873) LR 8 QB 77.
[8] *Clarke v Millwall Dock Co* (1886) 17 QBD 494.
[9] *Tapling & Co v Weston* (1883) Cab & El 99; and see *Challoner v Robinson* [1908] 1 Ch 49.

24.12.5 *Attachment of agent.* An agent who has received money on behalf of his principal in a fiduciary capacity becomes liable to attachment if he fails to comply with an order of the court to pay over the money. This liability is not avoided where the agent has parted with the money and has become bankrupt.[1]

[1] Debtors Act 1869 s 4; *Crowther v Elgood* (1887) 34 Ch D 691; *Litchfield v Jones* (1887) 36 Ch D 530.

CHAPTER 25

Rights Against Bankrupt's Insurers

25.1 SUBROGATION UNDER STATUTE

At common law an injured third party had no rights against the insurers of an insured person even where the risk insured was damage or loss to a class of persons of which the third party was one. He was not a party to the contract of insurance and could not therefore rely on it, nor even attach or garnishee money payable by the insurers to the insured under the policy of insurance.

Even where a claim by the insured in respect of the third party injuries was met by insurers, the third party had no recourse to that fund either in law or equity. Therefore, when the insured becomes insolvent, the insurance monies went into the bankrupt's general fund of assets to which the third party ranked only as an ordinary creditor.[1]

Under the Workmen's Compensation Act 1897 a statutory right of subrogation had been given to a workman against his employer's insurers in the event of the employer's bankruptcy or liquidation. This right was limited to the workman's statutory compensation rights under the Act. Following judicial criticism of the hardship caused to injured third parties,[2] statutory rights of subrogation were enacted, the Third Parties (Rights against

Insurers) Act 1930, which has general application, and the Road Traffic Act 1930, which modified those rights in respect of road traffic cases.

1 *Re Law Guarantee Trust and Accident Society Ltd* [1914] 2 Ch 617, CA.
2 *Re Harrington Motor Co, ex p Chaplin* [1928] Ch 105, CA; *Hoods' Trustees v Southern Union General Insurance of Australasia* [1928] Ch 793, CA.

25.2 THIRD PARTIES (RIGHTS AGAINST INSURERS) ACT 1930

The Act applies where under any contract of insurance, a person who is insured against particular liabilities to third parties incurs such liabilities and, in the case of an individual, the insured becomes bankrupt or makes a composition or arrangement with his creditors. (In the case of an insured company, the Act applies if a winding up order is made, or a resolution for a voluntary winding up is passed or a receiver or manager is appointed.) In any of these events, the Act operates to transfer to and vest in the third party the insured's rights against his insurers in respect of his liability to the third party. It is immaterial whether the liability to the third party was incurred before or after the insured became bankrupt or made a composition or arrangement with creditors. The Act operates in either case.

25.3 DECEASED DEBTOR

Where an order is made under the Bankruptcy Act 1914, s 130 for the administration of the estate of a deceased debtor or an insolvent estate is administered under the Insolvency Act 1986, s 421, s 1(2) of the 1930 Act provides that where the deceased debtor has rights against insurers under a contract of insurance in respect of any debt payable in bankruptcy, those rights shall be transferred to and vest in the third party to whom the debt is owing.

25.4 NO CONTRACTING OUT

The 1930 Act, by s 1(3), makes of no effect any provision in a contract of insurance which seeks directly or indirectly to avoid the consequences of the Act or alter the rights of the parties of the contract in the event that the Act becomes operable. It has been pointed out[1] that this provision may not operate as a comprehensive safeguard to third parties. The effect of the Act might be circumvented were the contract of insurance to provide that no liability arises on the part of the insurers before the insured has paid the third party. However, as a matter of practice, such a provision is not generally found in policies of insurance.

1 *MacGillivray on Insurance* (7th edn) para 1990.

25.5 EXCEPTIONS

The 'liabilities to third parties' of the insured under a contract of insurance to which the Act relates do not include any liability of the insured under some other contract of insurance.[1] Thus the Act does not apply to contracts of reinsurance: the third party's rights are solely against the principal insurer.

The Act expressly does not apply to companies wound up voluntarily merely for purposes of reconstruction or amalgamation nor to the Workmen's Compensation Act 1925, s 7, which consolidated the 1897 Act provision referred to above. The Workmen's Compensation Acts have of course long since been repealed, and there are now no separate or special provisions for injured employees. Subject to these exceptions, all liabilities to third parties are covered by the Act not only in tort but also in contract.

[1] Third Parties (Rights Against Insurers) Act 1930, s 1(5).

25.6 OPERATION OF THE ACT

The Act transfers to the third party not the claim against the insurers but the contracted rights of the insured, and only those contracted rights directly relating to the liability to the third party are transferred. Before the Act operates to transfer those rights, it is necessary either for the claim to be admitted by the insurers or for the liability of the insured to the third party to be established by Court judgment or arbitration award.

The third party may not, therefore, bring proceedings against the insurance company before liability has been established. Thus the Court of Appeal in *Post Office v Norwich Union Fire Insurance Society Ltd*[1] held that the action was premature where the Post Office, which had a disputed claim against contractors for damaging its cables, took proceedings against the contractors' public liability insurers when the contractors went into liquidation and before the claim against them had been heard. Lord Denning MR at 373E, said:

> 'Under that section the injured person steps into the shoes of the wrongdoer. There are transferred to him the wrongdoer's "rights against the insurers under the contract". What are those rights? When do they arise? So far as the "liability" of the insured is concerned, there is no doubt that his liability to the injured person arises at the time of the accident, when negligence and damage coincide. But the "rights" of the insured person against the insurer do not arise at that time. The policy says that "the company will indemnify the insured against all sums which the insured shall be legally liable to pay as compensation in respect of loss of or damage to property". It seems to me that the insured only acquires a right to sue for the money when his liability to the injured person has been established so as to give rise to a right of indemnity. His liability to the injured person must be ascertained and determined to exist either by judgment of the court or by an award in arbitration or by agreement.'

[1] [1967] 2 QB 363; see also *Socony Mobil Oil Inc, Mobil Oil Co Ltd and Mobil Oil v West of England Ship Owners Mutual Insurance Association (London) Ltd* [1984] 2 Lloyds Rep 408.

25.7 POSITION OF THIRD PARTY IS NO BETTER THAN INSURED'S

25.7.1 As indicated above, the Act operates by transferring to the third party the rights of the insured under the contract of insurance. The third party cannot therefore place himself in a better position vis-à-vis the insurers than that of the insured before his insolvency. The point was graphically made by Harman LJ in the *Post Office v Norwich Union Fire Insurance Society Ltd*[1] case where, it should be noted from the quotation from Lord Denning's judgment above, the policy provided that the insurers' liability to indemnify the contractors only arose in respect of sums which the contractors were 'legally liable to pay as compensation in respect of loss of or damage to property'. Thus, at 376D, Harman LJ stated:

> '. . . the contract contains not only rights, but limitations of those rights. You cannot, I think, assign to somebody part of the rights under the contract without assigning to him the condition subject to which those rights exist. Consequently, I think the Post Office is saddled with the inability of Potters to sue direct themselves before the liability is ascertained, because that would amount to a breach of condition 3 of the policy which would in itself be a defence to the insurance company.
>
> Therefore, I would decide this case on the narrow ground that the right assigned to the Post Office by the statute must be coupled with the rest of the particular rights and obligations which make up the contract of insurance. You cannot pick out one bit – pick out the plums and leave the duff behind. Therefore I think that, as Potters could not sue, so their statutory assignees, the Post Office, cannot sue until the amount has been ascertained and quantified.'

1 [1967] 2 QB 363.

25.7.2 Before the third party may recover against insurers therefore it is essential not only that the insured's liability to the third party be established but also the insurers' liability under the policy to the insured. Accordingly, if the policy of insurance contains an arbitration clause, the third party may be required to go to arbitration.[1] If, as in the *Post Office v Norwich Union* case (para 25.7.1 above) the insurer has the right to require the assured's liability to the third party to be ascertained, the third party cannot enforce the policy until that liability has been determined. The third party may find that the assured has in some way repudiated the policy or given the insurer ground to avoid it, by material non-disclosure, fraud or misrepresentation. Should the insurer accept the repudiation or avoid the policy, the third party will lose his rights.[2] In the absence of fraud, the third party will not be able to recover against an insurer who has compromised with or has been released by the assured,[3] provided the compromise or release has been made before the bankruptcy of the assured. Any such agreement made after the assured's bankruptcy and the incurring of liability to the third party is void by reason of the provisions of s 3 of the 1930 Act.

1 *Freshwater v Western Australian Assurance Co Ltd* [1933] 1 KB 515; *Dennehy v Bellamy* [1938] 2 All ER 262; *Smith v Pearl Assurance Co* [1939] All ER 95 where the Court of Appeal stated that where there may be a discretion in the court as to whether or not to order a stay, the court should look at the matter as between the assured and the insurer without taking account of any considerations personal to the third party.

2 *McCormick v National Motor and Accident Insurance Union Ltd* (1934) 50 TLR 528; *Cleland v London General Insurance Co Ltd* (1935) 51 Ll L Rep 156.

3 *Farrell v Federated Employers' Insurance Association Ltd* [1970] 3 All ER 632, CA; *Hassett v Legal & General Assurance Society Ltd* (1939) 63 Ll L Rep 278.

25.8 THIRD PARTY BOUND BY PROCEDURAL OR ADMINISTRATIVE REQUIREMENTS OF POLICY

The third party is also bound by any procedural or administrative requirement of the policy. This can be a serious matter for the third party. It is common for policies of insurance to require the assured to notify the insurer of any circumstances which might give rise to a claim within a relatively short time period and to require the assured to forward immediately a copy of any writ or other proceedings served on them in respect of which they will seek indemnity.

If these requirements are conditions precedent to liability the assured, and in turn the third party, may lose the cover provided under the policy if they are not complied with.[1] The third party is of course unlikely to be in any position to ensure that the policy requirements are adhered to, and even if he is aware of the assured's insurers, he may be unable to satisfy the requirements of the policy by giving notice of his own claim to the insurers. In *The Vainqueur Jose*[2] the court held that the notice of claim required by the assured's P & I Club had to be given by the assured or his duly authorised agent. Notice by another interested party, in that case a firm of New York attorneys who had previously acted for the assured but had not been expressly instructed for this particular matter, was insufficient for the purposes of the insurance.

In the case of employer's liability insurance, however, the effect of this rule on the third party employee seeking to recover damages for injuries sustained at work against a bankrupt employer are mitigated by the Employers' Liability (Company Insurance) General Regulations 1971.[3] Regulation 2(1) prohibits any condition in an employer's liability policy which provides, in whatever terms, that no liability shall arise under the policy '. . . in the event of some specified thing being done or omitted to be done after the happening of the event giving rise to a claim under the policy'. This wording should be wide enough to nullify any procedural requirement likely to defeat a third party employee's claim.

1 *Farrell v Federated Employers' Insurance Association Ltd* [1970] 3 All ER 632, CA; *Hassett v Legal & General Assurance Society Ltd* (1939) 63 Ll L Rep 278.
2 [1979] 1 Lloyd's Rep 557.
3 SI 1971/1117.

25.9 LIQUIDATION OF THE INSURER

Decisions of the courts under the subrogation provisions of the Workman's Compensation Acts suggest that a third party's rights against the insurers are not affected by the insurers going into liquidation or becoming bankrupt, whether this is before or after the bankruptcy of the assured.[1] The liability of the insurers is determined at the date of their liquidation and the third party can then prove in the liquidation or bankruptcy.[2] Unless the policy of insurance expressly provides that unpaid premiums may be set off against claims, the insurer facing a third party claim may not counter-claim for premiums left unpaid by the bankrupt assured.[3]

1 *Re Renishaw Iron Co Ltd* [1917] 1 Ch 199 and *Re Pethick, Dix & Co, Burrow's Claim* [1915] 1 Ch 26.

[2] *Re Law Car and General Insurance Corpn Ltd* (1913) 110 LT 27.
[3] *Murray v Legal and General Assurance Society Ltd* [1970] 2 QB 495.

25.10 DUTY TO GIVE INFORMATION[1]

The duty arises in the event of bankruptcy or a person making a composition or arrangement with his creditors, which will include the voluntary arrangements and interim orders under the New Law. The duty is owed by the bankrupt, or the debtor making an arrangement, his personal representations and the trustee in bankruptcy or any person in possession of the bankrupt/debtor's property, including an interim receiver. At the request of any third person claiming that the bankrupt or debtor is under a liability to him, the duty requires the provision of such information as may reasonably be required by the third person for the purpose of ascertaining whether any rights against an insurer have been transferred to and vested in the third person by the Act. The third person is also entitled to information reasonably required to enable him to enforce his statutory rights against the relevant insurer. Any provision in the contract of insurance which seeks to prohibit the giving of such information or to alter the rights of the parties to the contract on giving such information, is void.

Should the information obtained by the third person disclose reasonable ground for supposing that third party rights have been transferred to him under the Act, the duty extends to the insurers concerned and they can be required to give reasonable information. The duty extends to disclosure of documents including 'all contracts of insurance, receipts for premiums, and other relevant documents in the possession or power of the person on whom the duty is so imposed'. Documents may be inspected and copies taken.

[1] Third Parties (Rights Against Insurers) Act 1930, s 2.

25.11 SETTLEMENT BETWEEN INSURER AND ASSURED

Where the assured has become bankrupt, no agreement made between the insurer and the assured after liability has been incurred to a third party and after the commencement of the bankruptcy, nor any waiver, assignment or other disposition made by, or payment made to, the assured after the commencement of the bankruptcy, shall be effective to defeat or affect the rights transferred to the third party under the 1930 Act. These rights shall be the same as if no such agreement, waiver, assignment, disposition or payment had been made.[1]

These provisions do not apply to agreements made before the commencement of the bankruptcy, even where the assured has entered into a scheme of arrangement or composition. Under the Insolvency Act 1986 an agreement benefitting the insurers made before the presentation of the petition may be liable to be avoided by the trustee in bankruptcy as a fraudulent preference (see ch 17 above).

[1] Third Parties (Rights Against Insurers) Act 1930, s 3.

25.12 EXTENT AND PROSECUTION OF CLAIMS

The rights vested by the Act in the third party against the insurer do not affect the third party's rights against the assured where the insurer's liability is less than the total of the third party's claim on the assured. The third party will be entitled to prove in the bankruptcy for the balance and interest as an ordinary creditor. Conversely, should there be a liability on the part of the insurers to the bankrupt assured greater than the assured's liability to the third party, the trustee in bankruptcy may recover any balance on his behalf for the benefit of the estate.[1]

Once the third party has overcome any conditions precedent in the insurance policy, (see para 25.7 above), he may sue the insurers to recover his loss. The insurers may have declined to become involved in initial proceedings in which event they will be unable to contest the quantum of any judgment or bona fide settlement. On the other hand, the insurers may have become involved in the defence of the third party's proceedings, at least initially, until some fact emerged which allowed them to avoid liability under the policy. In circumstances where the insurers exercise their right to conduct the assured's defence, it is improbable, in the light of the decision in *Soole v Royal Insurance Co*[2] that, as between the assured and the insurer, the insurer will have compromised his rights to avoid the policy and be stopped from denying liability to indemnify the assured. As between the insurer and the third party, however, it is possible that in the conduct of the defence, the insurer or his solicitor may have represented that the assured would be indemnified and thereby encouraged the third party to continue an action against a defendant whom he knew or suspected would be unable to meet a judgment personally. Should the insurer disclaim liability to the assured during the course of the proceedings, he would be well advised to inform the third party.

[1] Third Parties (Rights Against Insurers) Act 1930.
[2] [1971] 2 Lloyd's Rep 332.

25.13 ROAD TRAFFIC CASES AND MOTOR VEHICLE INSURANCE

In passing the Road Traffic Act 1930, Parliament was aware that provisions no wider than those in the Third Parties (Rights Against Insurers) Act 1930 would often leave an injured third party without a remedy, for example because of breaches of condition in motor policies. More extensive rights of subrogation were therefore provided for road traffic cases and these rights have been extended in subsequent legislation, the relevant statutory provisions now being found in the Road Traffic Act 1972, ss 143–151. The position of the third party in road traffic cases is improved in two ways.

First, there are extensive statutory restrictions on conditions in motor policies which may have the effect of limiting or excluding the rights of a third party proving a claim against insurers under the Third Parties (Rights Against Insurers) Act 1930 where the assured is bankrupt.

Second, where a judgment has been obtained against an assured, it may, if certain conditions are met, be enforced directly against the insurers to the extent that it relates to injuries in respect of which there is compulsory insurance under the 1972 Act. In the latter case, there is no need for the assured to be bankrupt before the judgment can be enforced.

25.14 COMPULSORY REQUIREMENTS

Under the Road Traffic Act 1972, it is an offence to use or permit the use of a motor vehicle on the road without a policy of insurance which complies with the requirement of the Act. These requirements[1] are that the policy must be issued by an authorised insurer and must insure against any liability which may be incurred in respect of the death of, or bodily injury to, any person caused by or arising out of the use of the vehicle on the road and in respect of the statutory liability for payment for emergency treatment. A policy need not cover any employer's liability to the assured nor any contractual liability. A certificate of insurance must be delivered by the insurer to the assured, otherwise the policy of insurance is not valid for the purposes of the 1972 Act.[2]

[1] Road Traffic Act 1972, s 145.
[2] Road Traffic Act 1972, s 147. For the form of the certificate see Motor Vehicles (Third Party Risks) Regulations 1972, SI 1972/1217.

25.15 STATUTORY RESTRICTIONS ON POLICY CONDITIONS

25.15.1 Where a certificate of insurance has been delivered to the assured any condition of the policy which seeks to restrict the liability of the insurers with respect to the following matters are of no effect against third parties:[1]
(a) the age or physical or mental condition of persons driving the vehicle; or
(b) the condition of the vehicle; or
(c) the number of persons that the vehicle carries; or
(d) the weight or physical characteristics of the goods that the vehicle carries; or
(e) the times at which or the areas within which the vehicle is used; or
(f) the horse power or cylinder capacity or value of the vehicle; or
(g) the carrying on the vehicle of any particular apparatus; or
(h) the carrying on the vehicle of any particular means of identification other than any means of identification required to be carried by or under the Vehicles (Excise) Act 1971.

[1] Road Traffic Act 1972, s 148(1).

25.15.2 Procedural or administrative conditions are also restricted.[1] Any policy condition which provides that no liability shall arise, or that any liability so arising shall cease, in the event of some specified thing being done or omitted to be done after the happening of the event giving rise to a claim under the policy, shall have no effect in connection with such liabilities as are compulsorily required to be covered by insurance under the Act.[1] The effect of this provision, in the words of Branson J,[2] is that:

> 'if all was in order between the assured and the underwriter when the accident happened, the position cannot be altered by subsequent breaches or by acts or omissions on the part of the assured so as to make him (through his insurers) less able to compensate the person who has been injured.'

The insurer remains entitled to recover from the assured sums paid to a third party in respect of claims against the assured should the policy of insurance enable the insurer to do so.

1 Road Traffic Act 1972, s 148(2).
2 *Gray v Blackmore* [1934] 1 KB 95 at 107.

25.16 LIABILITY OF INSURER TO SATISFY JUDGMENT

After delivery of a certificate of insurance to the assured, the insurer is liable to satisfy any judgment obtained by a third party in respect of any liability which is the subject of compulsory insurance, notwithstanding that the insurer may be entitled to avoid or cancel or may have already avoided or cancelled, the policy of insurance.[1] The insurer is also liable to pay any interest or costs awarded. This liability does not arise:

(a) unless the insurer had notice of the bringing of proceedings before or within seven days of their commencement;
(b) so long as execution is stayed pending appeal; or
(c) where the policy has been cancelled before the relevant accident and the certificate of insurance was surrendered to the insurer (or the assured has made a statutory declaration stating that the certificate has been lost or destroyed) either before the accident or within 14 days of the cancellation of the policy (even if after the accident) or where the insurer commences proceedings within 14 days of the cancellation of the policy in respect of the failure to surrender the certificate following the cancellation.

The right of the third party to enforce judgments under s 149 of the 1972 Act does not affect any right the third party may have under the Third Parties (Rights Against Insurers) Act 1930 if the assured becomes bankrupt or enters into a scheme or arrangement with his creditors. And in this event, the assured remains liable in respect of any liability as is required to be covered by a policy of insurance under s 145 of the 1972 Act.[2]

1 Road Traffic Act 1972, s 149.
2 Ibid, s 150.

25.17 ASSIGNMENT OF POLICIES OF INSURANCE

25.17.1 A contract of insurance is a personal contract. It will not ordinarily run with title to the subject matter of the insurance. By operation of law, however, both the subject matter and the policy of insurance will pass to the trustee in bankruptcy.[1] No formal assignment of the policy is required, although some policies contain a condition that the policy be endorsed with the trustee's interest.

1 Bankruptcy Act 1914, ss 48(5), 53; Insolvency Act 1986, s 306.

25.17.2 Where a loss occurs before the commencement of the bankruptcy or where the subject matter of the policy is in the hands of the trustee, the trustee may enforce it for the benefit of the bankrupt's estate. Being in the position of an assignee, the trustee is bound by all the terms of the policy, and the insurer's liability to the trustee can be no greater than that to the bankrupt assured. Any non-disclosure, fraud, misrepresentation of the assured before the commencement of the bankruptcy may defeat the trustee's claim.[1] After assignment to the trustee in bankruptcy, the bankrupt has no standing in respect of the policy. If, therefore, the insurer pays a claim direct to the bankrupt or enters into a compromise with him, the trustee's rights are unaffected and the insurer can find himself having to pay twice.[2]

1 *Re Carr and Sun Fire Insurance Co* (1897) 13 TLR 186 and note also *Jackson v Forster* (1860) 1 E & E 470, Ex Ch when the assured committed suicide after the commencement of the bankruptcy and this vitiated the policy. Ordinarily of course, no act or omission of the bankrupt after the commencement of the bankruptcy could affect the validity of the policy: *Bruton v Gore District Mutual Insurance Co* (1865) 12 Gr 156 (Can).

2 *McEntire v Potter & Co* (1889) 22 QBD 438; *Hood's Trustees v Southern Union General Insurance Co of Australasia* [1928] Ch 793.

25.17.3 During the course of administering the estate the trustee will have to dispose of the subject matter of the insurance and the question may arise whether he may assign the policy without obtaining the consent of the insurers. In *Re Birkbeck Permanent Building Society, Official Receiver v Licences Insurance Corpn*[1] Neville J held that the consent of the insurer was not required. In that case, the building society lent money upon mortgage and insured repayment of the loan. The policy stipulated that the insurance would cease if the whole or any part of the Society's interest in the mortgage debt or mortgaged property should pass from the Society otherwise than by will or operation of law. Under the policy, 'the insured' was expressed to include a successor in interest. The Building Society was wound up by the court, and the official receiver gave notice to the insurers of his intention to assign the mortgage together with the policy. The insurers refused consent to the assignment. In addition to findings on construction of the policy, it was held that the official receiver as liquidator was under an obligation to assign, and therefore the policy would pass to the assignee by operation of law, the consent of the insurers being unnecessary. Whether this is a correct construction of 'operation of law' is, however, open to doubt. Many policies today do extend the indemnity offered to the named assured and all persons to whom his interest in the subject matter of the insurance may pass by will or by operation of law.

1 [1913] 2 Ch 34.

CHAPTER 26

Solicitors Acting in Bankruptcy Matters

26.1 ACTING FOR THE PETITIONING CREDITOR

26.1.1 On the coming into effect of the Insolvency Act 1986, there will be very many outstanding bankruptcy petitions. On all these cases the Old Bankruptcy Law continues to apply.[1]

[1] See para 1.4 above for transitional provisions.

26.1.2 One critical application of the doctrine of relation back, relevant in all Old Bankruptcy Law cases is that it enables a trustee[1] of the property of a bankrupt to recover payments made by the debtor to his petitioning creditor, or the petitioning creditor's solicitors, at any time after the first act of bankruptcy committed by the debtor within three months immediately preceding the presentation of the petition. There will be many petitions which are adjourned from time to time whilst a debtor makes payments on account and/or seeks to persuade the court not to make a receiving order, and which were pending when the Insolvency Act came into force.

In the first place petitioning creditors and their advisers must remember that if payments on account are made which bring the debt down to a figure below the statutory minimum for founding a petition then the right to proceed with the petition and ask for a receiving order is lost.[2]

Perhaps more importantly, however, the petitioning creditor's solicitor must decide whether to press for a receiving order, in the knowledge that a competent trustee will justifiably be bound to ask for repayment (because of the doctrine of relation back) or agree to a dismissal of the petition[3] and perhaps take fresh proceedings under the Insolvency Act 1986. In such a case, the bankruptcy will only commence at the date of the making of the bankruptcy order (but see para 26.1.3 below).

[1] Explained in para 8.2 above.

[2] *Re Patel, ex p Debtor v Dallomo* [1986] 1 All ER 522 (and see para 2.3(i) above).
[3] See, however, *Re Thomas, ex p IRC v Falconer* [1984] 1 WLR 232 and para 8.2.4 above.

26.1.3 Whilst the doctrine of relation back is not carried into the Insolvency Act 1986 there are provisions which will cause problems with respect to dispositions by the debtor made after the presentation of a petition against him.[1] In practical effect, when examining the problem which arises when a debtor pays a petitioning creditor on account, the position under the New Law, although technically different, is very similar to that under the Old Bankruptcy Law.

[1] Bankruptcy Act 1914, s 48.

26.1.4 The Insolvency Act 1986, s 284 contains a provision for subsequent ratification of dispositions by a bankrupt between the presentation of the petition and the vesting of his property in a trustee, but, by analogy with the similar provision applicable to companies by the Insolvency Act 1986, s 127[1], it is unlikely that ratification will be given for payments on account to a petitioning creditor after the bankruptcy process had begun.

[1] S 127 reenacts the Companies Act 1985, s 522, formerly Companies Act 1948, s 227.

26.2 ACTING FOR THE TRUSTEE

26.2.1 Under the Old Bankruptcy Law a trustee, save in cases of extreme urgency, had to obtain the permission of his committee of inspection, the Department of Trade or the court to employ a solicitor.[1]

However, there are transitional provisions in the Insolvency Act 1986[2] to the effect that a trustee in bankruptcy may employ a solicitor to assist him in the carrying out of his duties without the permission of the committee of inspection.[3]

If he does so employ a solicitor he must inform the committee of inspection that he has done so.[3]

[1] Bankruptcy Act 1914, s 56.
[2] In Sch 11.
[3] Ibid, para 14(6).

26.2.2 In the New Law cases where, or course, the trustee must be an insolvency practitioner,[1] the trustee's general powers are set out in the Insolvency Act 1986, s 314.

Where the trustee, in the exercise of the powers conferred on him, employs a solicitor and there is at that time a creditors' committee[2] he must give notice to the committee of the employment of a solicitor.[3]

[1] Insolvency Act 1986, s 388 and see ch 15 above.
[2] As to which see Individual Insolvency Rules, 1986, rr 6.150–6.166.
[3] Insolvency Act 1986, Sch 11, para 14(6).

Taxation of costs

26.2.3 The Old Bankruptcy Law expressly provided for the taxation, on a common fund basis,[1] of all costs (in excess of £100) incurred by solicitors acting for a trustee in bankruptcy.[2]

The Insolvency Act 1986 itself does not so provide, but even so, a trustee will presumably impose a limit on the expense which his solicitor should incur. If the creditors' committee resolves that a solicitor's costs or expenses be taxed then the Trustee must require a taxation. Before such costs can be taxed the taxing officer will require a certificate of employment endorsed on the bill and signed by the trustee. Rule 7.35(2) sets out the information to be contained in the certificate.

Rules 7.35(3), (4) and (5) contain provisions which result in a solicitor forfeiting his right to costs against a trustee personally if he fails to deliver his bill for taxation or obtain an extension of time for doing so, within 14 days of it being required to do so.

1 See *Re Lavey, ex p Cohen and Cohen* [1921] 1 KB 344.
2 Bankruptcy Act 1914, s 83.

Compromises

26.2.4 In Old Bankruptcy Law cases, the trustee will, from time to time, have to refer to his committee of inspection (see para 6.5 above) whilst in New Law cases, he will, or may have, a committee of creditors. These committees are considered in the texts of ch 6 and 16 above and their powers and responsibilities are not repeated here.

One relatively small point is worthy of mention, however, since it is not covered in the texts previously referred to: namely that in litigation the single most overlooked requirement by solicitors is for the need, on the withdrawal or compromise of an action by a trustee in bankruptcy both in the High Court and in a county court to produce a certified copy of the resolution of the committee of inspection whereby the trustee is authorised to withdraw or compromise the suit in question. Alternatively, if there is no committee of inspection, or because of a lack of quorum or for whatever reason, such a resolution cannot be obtained then the consent of the Department of Trade or an order of the court in which the bankruptcy is pending must be secured.

26.2.5 Hopefully, in those cases proceeding under the Old Bankruptcy Law, solicitors are acting under properly obtained sanctions. The limit on a sanction for costs may be increased before or within three months after it has been reached.

It had been thought[1] that a sanction could not be obtained retrospectively but Scott J in *Re a Debtor (No 26a of 1975)*[2] restated the principle[3] that the sanction was to protect the bankrupt's estate and not to afford any sort of defence to third parties (who sought in that case to avoid liability for costs where the trustee's solicitors did not have a proper sanction) and he retrospectively sanctioned the work done by solicitors in that case.

1 See *Williams & Muir Hunter* (19th edn) p 429.
2 [1984] 3 All ER 995.
3 *Re Branson, ex p Trustee* [1914] 2 KB 701.

26.3 ACTING FOR THE DEBTOR

26.3.1 Questions concerning a debtor's or bankrupt's right to legal aid are dealt with in para 26.7 below.

26.3.2 In Old Bankruptcy Law cases, based on the concept of the act of bankruptcy,[1] a solicitor frequently had to be very careful in respect of any dealing in his client's property after he had notice of his client's act of bankruptcy.[2]

[1] See ch 1 above.
[2] See *Re Dalton, ex p Herrington and Carmichael v Trustee* [1963] Ch 336.

26.3.3 A frequent problem arising out of a solicitor's often inevitable knowledge of his client's act of bankruptcy[1] was, and will until 29 December 1986 continue to be, whether or not he can accept funds on account of costs from his client.

[1] For the consequences of which see paras 8.2 and 8.3 above.

26.3.4 A safe course, if it is possible, is for the solicitor to insist upon funds for his costs being provided by a third party. This course really has to be insisted upon for the costs incurred by a solicitor other than for the purposes of opposing a bankruptcy petition against his client.

A solicitor is entitled to receive money from his debtor client for the purposes of funding the costs of opposing the petition itself[1] but this exception to the doctrine of relation back[2] does not extend to the use of money already held by a solicitor for the account of his client[3] nor does it extend to the conduct of an appeal against a receiving order.[4]

[1] *Re Sinclair, ex p Payne* (1885) 15 QBD 616; *Re Pollitt, ex p Minor* [1893] 1 QB 455.
[2] Ch 8 above.
[3] *Re Spackman, ex p Foley* (1890) 24 QBD 728; *Re Pollitt, ex p Minor* [1893] 1 QB 455.
[4] *Re Debtor (No. 490 of 1935)* [1937] Ch 92.

26.3.5 The cases referred to above were all decided before the Legal Aid and Advice Act 1949 and it may be argued that, where legal aid would have been available to the debtor (which despite the circumstances is certainly not necessarily the case) a court might find that modern circumstances do not justify the exception to the doctrine of relation back referred to above, which, incidentally, has been described as having been 'engrafted on to the (Old) Bankruptcy Law by the dictates of humanity'.[1]

[1] See 3 Halsbury's Laws (4th edn) para 684 and the cases cited therein.

26.3.6 The whole concept of the available act of bankruptcy will have gone, however, after the 29th December 1986 when many such problems theoretically disappear because of the fact that the bankruptcy order under the Insolvency Act 1986 results in the bankruptcy commencing on the day on which the order is made.[1]

[1] Insolvency Act 1986, s 278.

26.3.7 However, if a debtor seeks to defend a creditor's petition for a bankruptcy order under the Insolvency Act 1986 a new inhibition upon a solicitor accepting funds on account from his client for that purpose appears to have arisen.

The Insolvency Act 1986, s 284 contains provisions to the effect that any disposition of property by a debtor in the period between the presentation of the petition for the bankruptcy order and the vesting of property in the bankrupt's trustee is void unless subsequently ratified by the court.[1]

Since this provision provides for *subsequent* ratification it does not seem possible for solicitors to apply to the court for leave to receive funds from a debtor to assist him to defend himself.

Receipt of such funds will cause no problem if the defence is successful[2] but solicitors may be wary of receiving funds from a debtor (the payment necessary being a disposition by the debtor) in the hope that such disposition will subsequently be ratified.

[1] See, para 26.1.4.
[2] Since s 284 only applies if a person is adjudged bankrupt.

26.3.8 Thus, unless the courts soon develop a humanitarian gloss for the New Law, as they did in the Old Bankruptcy Law provisions described above, solicitors are well advised to act only on legal aid or receipt of third party funds.

26.4 PRIVILEGE

26.4.1 For Old Bankruptcy Law cases the Bankruptcy Act 1914[1] provides that the trustee shall take possession of the bankrupt's deeds, books and documents. In practice this has been taken to mean all such documentation relating to the bankrupt's property and estate, including communications between him and his solicitors.

However, the position is made clear in the New Law cases, since the Insolvency Act 1986 specifically provides for the delivery to the official receiver on a bankruptcy order being made[2] and to the trustee (on acquisition of control by the trustee)[3] of all books, papers and other records which relate to the bankrupt's estate or affairs, 'including any which would be privileged from disclosure in any proceedings'.

[1] S 48.
[2] S 291(1)(b).
[3] S 306.

26.4.2 The Insolvency Act 1986, s 291 also refers to documents 'under the control' of the bankrupt.

If the bankrupt's solicitors' costs have been paid so that no question of lien (as against the bankrupt) arises[1] the solicitors' files, other than, arguably, attendance notes and the solicitors' own records are under the theoretical control of the bankrupt.

It remains to be seen whether official receivers will, under s 291, invariably demand delivery up of solicitors papers.

[1] See Lien at para 26.6 below.

26.4.3 Quite apart from the questions which might be raised because of the provision in New Law cases, there have, of course, been innumerable privilege problems in the past.

Solicitors who have acted for a person who subsequently becomes bankrupt are frequently approached by the official receiver or the trustee in bankruptcy for information or documents relating to the bankrupt's affairs. In the first place it should be recognised that the only obligation to supply information or documents[1] arises under the Bankruptcy Act 1914, s 25 in Old Bankruptcy Law cases and under the Insolvency Act 1986, s 366 in New Law cases, that is to say, if necessary, by formal examination under one or other of those provisions.

[1] Other than documents of title to property which has become vested in the trustee.

26.4.4 On the question of whether or not the solicitor should claim legal privilege some difficult problems often arise. The ordinary law of legal privilege still, of course, applies. Matters which have been communicated to a solicitor for the purposes of obtaining professional advice and assistance are privileged. Thus:

> 'questions relating to the client's personal life and his personal affairs, including his defence to the bankruptcy proceedings . . . to criminal proceedings and divorce proceedings *except so far as they relate directly to the client's property*, should be answered only with the client's authority.'[1]

[1] *Guide to Professional Conduct of Solicitors* (Law Society, 1974) chapter 2 para 11:2(e). The 1986 *Guide* offers no guidance on the subject.

26.4.5 The words in italics above are important. It must be appreciated that, under the Old Bankruptcy Law, the law applying to the majority of bankruptcies until the 1990s, the property of the client does not vest in the trustee in bankruptcy until adjudication.[1] However, upon adjudication, if the advice in respect of which questions of privilege arise related to property which has become vested in the trustee then the privilege relating to that item of property also passes to the trustee and privilege may not be claimed as against the trustee.

[1] See ch 6 above.

26.4.6 If, despite para 26.4.3 above, a solicitor is obliged to claim privilege in respect of advice given to a bankrupt client then it is thought that the court has power to order the bankrupt client to release that privilege in order to ensure that information required by the trustee is released.[1]

[1] See para 7.6.3 above.

26.4.7 If a solicitor is approached by an official receiver or trustee for information, he is entitled to a reasonably detailed enquiry, in writing, so that he has an opportunity of considering whether any questions of privilege apply.

26.5 THE COSTS OF ASSISTING A TRUSTEE

26.5.1 If a solicitor is subjected to a s 25 examination under the Old Bankruptcy Law[1] he is entitled to reasonable conduct money.[2]

The Insolvency Act 1985 contains similar provisions[3] to the Bankruptcy Act 1914, s 25 but the Act itself does not refer to conduct money. It refers only to the consequences of a person failing to attend an examination under the Act 'without reasonable excuse'.

1 See para 8.10 above.
2 Bankruptcy Act 1914, s 25(2) and Bankruptcy Rules 1952, r 64.
3 At s 366.

26.5.2 Since a solicitor is a professional witness he is entitled to witness fees upon the basis allowed to such witnesses. This has been found to be the case in Old Bankruptcy Law cases[1] and will presumably apply to New Law cases.

1 *Chamberlain v Stoneham* (1889) 24 QBD 113.

26.5.3 Although, as explained,[1] no solicitor can be made to assist a trustee save under the formal statutory provisions, the fact is that official receivers and trustees in bankruptcy very often ask the solicitor of bankrupt clients for informal assistance on questions in respect of which no privilege problems arise, either for the reasons explained above or because the client simply waives it.

The official receiver or trustee will very often ask for information upon the basis that it shall be provided without charge. Some trustees will rely on the Bankruptcy Act 1914 (in Old Bankruptcy Law cases) to suggest that, without a retainer authorised by the committee of inspection he *cannot* agree to pay the solicitor for his time in providing information.

1 See para 26.4.1 above.

26.5.4 Under the Old Bankruptcy law (and there is no reason to suppose that there is any difference in New Law cases) the Law Society took the advice of leading counsel and, as a result the following advice was given to solicitors faced with this problem:

'(a) Except under s 25 of the Bankruptcy Act 1914, the solicitor is under no obligation to supply information or documents (other than documents of title to property which has vested in the trustee) to the trustee. Accordingly, if the trustee asks for information or documents (other than as aforesaid) it would be proper for the solicitor, before complying, to ask the trustee to pay his reasonable costs of complying with the trustee's request, and it would be proper for the solicitor to refuse to comply with the trustee's request if the trustee has refused to pay the solicitor's reasonable costs of complying.

(b) It is, in practice, not uncommon for a trustee to agree to pay a modest fee, where the matters on which information is requested are of some considerable age and the work of looking out files and searching through them is involved, and for the solicitor to be reimbursed the costs of any copying work he is asked to carry out. Should the solicitor refuse to co-operate with the official receiver or trustee, except at a fee greater than that which the trustee is able or willing to pay, he may well be faced with an application to the court for his examination under s 25.

(c) If an examination under s 25 is ordered, the solicitor who attends is entitled not merely to conduct money tendered with the summons, but also to be paid his witness allowance under r 64(3). This allowance is on the High Court scale, even if the proceedings are in the county court. A solicitor is entitled to expenses as a professional witness.

(d) In cases of examination under s 25, there is no general right to be reimbursed the costs of appearing by counsel or another solicitor. It would seem in any event that a solicitor would only need representation in the exceptional circumstances that he was being examined by the trustee in a potentially adverse capacity. Awards of costs in favour of witnesses are rare, although they have been known to be made.'[1]

[1] *Guide to Professional Conduct of Solicitors* (Law Society, 1974). The 1986 Guide offers no advice on the point.

26.6 LIEN

26.6.1 A solicitor's lien attaches, of course, to documents. It is no answer to a s 25 (Old Bankruptcy Law) nor a s 366 (New Law) examination, that to answer a question would result in the effective defeat of the lien.

26.6.2 There is no lien in respect of documents coming into the possession of the solicitor after the making of a receiving order or, under the New Law, a bankruptcy order.

26.6.3 The court has power to order the production of documents in the possession or under the control of any person. If those documents relate to the bankrupt, his dealings, affairs or property[1] the existence of a lien for costs is not sufficient to entitle the solicitor to refuse to produce them nor to challenge an order for their production to the court.[2]

[1] Bankruptcy Act 1914, s 25(1); Insolvency Act 1985, s 366(1).
[2] *Re Toleman and England, ex p Bramble* (1880) 13 Ch D 885, and Bankruptcy Rules 1952, r 386.

26.7 LEGAL AID

For the debtor

26.7.1 Legal aid is theoretically available to a person wishing to defend a petition under Old Bankruptcy Law or the New Law. In the ordinary way he has to show that he has a case and, as in any other legal aid application, demonstrate that it is reasonable in all the circumstances that he should have legal aid.[1]

[1] Legal Aid (General) Regulations 1980, reg 29.

26.7.2 It has been seen[1] that a debtor remains entitled to certain causes of action essentially those personal to him, such as damages (other than loss of earnings) for wrongful imprisonment. The debtor's bankruptcy is no bar to his obtaining legal aid to pursue such claims. Similarly it has been seen that a receiving order under the Old Bankruptcy Law and the making of a bankruptcy order under the New Law effect an immediate stay on all legal proceedings against the debtor.[2]

The debtor is entitled to an order of the court to protect him from any attempt to press proceedings against him after the receiving order[3] or if New Law bankruptcy proceedings are pending against him[4] and legal aid should be available to him to apply for such an order.

[1] See paras 6.3.4 above (Old Bankruptcy Law) and 16.2.11 (New Law).
[2] Bankruptcy Act 1914, s 7(1) (Old Bankruptcy Law); Insolvency Act 1986, s 285(1) (New Law).
[3] Bankruptcy Act 1914, s 9(1).
[4] See Insolvency Act 1986, s 285(1).

For the trustee in bankruptcy

26.7.3 In theory a trustee in bankruptcy, or even the official receiver, can obtain legal aid for the purposes of conducting litigation for the benefit of the estate in bankruptcy. In practice, however, the circumstances of the case in question would have to be more than a little unusual for him to obtain it.

In the first place he must pass the ordinary 'reasonableness' test applied in all legal aid applications.[1]

[1] See para 26.7.1 above, and Legal Aid (General) Regulations 1980, reg 29.

26.7.4 Applications by a trustee are made under the Legal Aid (General) Regulations 1980, reg 34 which provide that in such applications the Legal Aid General Committee:

> '(a) shall take into account the value of any property or estate, or the amount of any fund out of which the applicant is entitled to be indemnified, and the disposable income and disposable capital and maximum contributions of any persons (including the applicant if appropriate) who might benefit from the proceedings';

and, having done so,

> '(b) may . . . either
> (i) approve the application subject to the payment from the property specified in sub paragraph (a) of any contribution which it may in its discretion determine, or,
> (ii) refuse the application, if it concludes that to do so would not cause hardship.'

26.7.5 Thus, if the trustee can recover his costs from the bankrupt's estate he will not qualify and, if whatever the other considerations, the relevant legal aid area concludes that 'hardship' would not be caused then it may refuse the trustee's application.

26.7.6 If these, and the reasonableness, hurdles can be overcome the biggest problem will be the provision in reg 34 concerning 'the disposable income and disposable capital and maximum contributions of any persons who might benefit from the proceedings'.

Making the polite assumption that no reference was intended to the solicitor or counsel whom the trustee proposes to instruct, the obvious persons who will benefit are the creditors of the bankrupt. The regulation (which was not, of course, designed for bankruptcies but for all trustee/fiduciary applicants) is plainly designed to benefit the financially weak beneficiary.

Many creditors of bankrupts might well qualify for legal aid but, equally many will not, obvious examples are any limited companies, the Inland Revenue.

26.7.7 In a case on earlier, rather different, legal aid regulations Lord Goddard said: 'the use of public funds to enable trustees in bankruptcy to bring actions for the benefit of creditors, who may be very wealthy concerns, seems quite foreign to its intention . . .'[1]

If current thinking is as Lord Goddard's was in 1952, and the Legal Aid Regulations 1980 suggest it might be, a trustee will thus only obtain legal aid in that rare case where the debtor's statement of affairs does not list the Inland Revenue, a local authority, Her Majesty's Commissioners of Customs and Excise (VAT) nor any limited liability company as a creditor.

[1] *R v Manchester Legal Aid Committee, ex p Brand & Co Ltd* [1952] 2 QB 413.

26.7.8 If all the above is not enough to sink an application, one other point could be taken on which it has to be conceded that arguments could be entertained. Most trustees, a fortiori with those under the New Law being approved insolvency practitioners, will not qualify on financial grounds personally. However, they are remunerated by a percentage of the realised estate of the bankrupt. By that remuneration it could be argued that a trustee 'might have benefit from the proceedings' and thus be susceptible to assessment of means. Thus, the theory of a trustee in bankruptcy obtaining legal aid is likely to be a long way from the practice. The theory, however, remains attainable until any judicial decision otherwise.

26.8 UNDERTAKINGS

26.8.1 An innumerable quantity of business, conveyancing and other financial transactions proceed, these days, upon the basis of solicitors' undertakings. Similarly when a debtor's financial position is bleak, a solicitor's undertaking, perhaps to preserve a fund, or dispose of a fund in a particular way, may be the only thing which will stop a creditor from pressing on to the bankruptcy of his debtor.

26.8.2 In many cases, the bankruptcy of a client supervening an undertaking given by a solicitor will not affect the undertaking or the solicitor's legal or professional obligation to comply with it. If, for example, a solicitor has undertaken to hold his client's deeds or documents to the order of a third party, the bankruptcy of the client does not affect the solicitor who remains bound by his undertaking, legally and professionally.

26.8.3 Problems do arise, however, where a solicitor undertakes to make a payment to a third party or various third parties out of an identified fund or out of client's funds generally.

If the identified fund is supplied by a third party and held by the solicitor on trust for that third party, no problem arises. A trustee in bankruptcy does not become entitled to property held on trust[1] and the trustee in bankruptcy will have no claim on the fund out of which the solicitor will be making payment.

[1] Bankruptcy Act 1914, s 38(1); Insolvency Act 1986, s 283(3)(a).

26.8.4 On the other hand, if the indicated fund is the property of the bankrupt then the bankruptcy of the client causes great difficulty because, by operation of law, the fund passes to the client's trustee.[1] The problem can be solved, however, if the solicitor, whose undertaking is required, succeeds in creating a charge over the fund in question. Unlike in company liquidation cases where unregistered charges of particular assets are void against a liquidator if not registered,[2] there are no bankruptcy requirements to the effect that a legal or equitable charge over the assets of a person who subsequently becomes bankrupt, should be registered in any way.

There are of course various provisions in both the Old Bankruptcy Law and the New Law which affect, for example, assignments of book debts and fraudulent preference,[3] which have to be avoided but reference to the relevant fund being charged with payment to be creditor should offer protection.

[1] Bankruptcy Act 1914, ss 37 and 38 (Old Bankruptcy Law); Insolvency Act 1986, s 287 (New Law).
[2] Companies Act 1985, ss 395–398 inclusive.
[3] See Chs 8 (Old Bankruptcy law) and 17 (New Law).

26.8.5 Alternatively, if a solicitor is aware of potential problems he should limit any undertaking to his having legal control of the fund in question. The obvious problem with this is that it may be unacceptable to the astute creditor.

CHAPTER 27

Employment

27.1 INTRODUCTION

27.1.1 The bankruptcy of the employer does not automatically determine his employee's contract of employment, unless there is also an appointment by the court of a receiver.

The employee continues to be employed by the estate (and not the trustee) even where the trustee carries on the bankrupt's business. The trustee in bankruptcy will, however, be personally liable in respect of a contract of employment he creates where he enters into one or adopts an existing one. A material alteration in the terms of an existing contract of employment may amount to an adoption and it is advisable therefore for a trustee who continues the bankrupt's business to take particular care, if he alters the scope of an employee's duties or makes any potentially material amendment to the terms and conditions of an employee's employment, not to become personally liable on the contract.

27.1.2 The trustee is empowered to carry on the bankrupt's business, subject to the limitation that he may do so 'so far as may be necessary for the beneficial winding up of the estate'.[1] The trustee requires the permission of the committee of inspection or creditors' committee (as the case may be) or the court before continuing the business and where he does so he must keep a distinct account of the trading, verified by affidavit in the form required by the Bankruptcy Rules.[2] Employees are paid from this account.

The trustee also has express authority to employ the bankrupt to superintend the management of the business or any part of it, or otherwise assist the trustee[3] if he thinks it appropriate.

[1] Bankruptcy Act 1914, s 56(1); Insolvency Act 1986, s 314(1)(a), Sch 5, Pt 1.
[2] Bankruptcy Rules 1952, r 364 and generally see r 350; Individual Insolvency Rules 1986, r 12.1.
[3] Bankruptcy Act 1914, s 57; Insolvency Act 1986, s 314(2) and see ch 16 above.

27.1.3 The bankruptcy of the employee does not automatically determine the contract of employment. It is not uncommon, however, for contracts to provide that the employer may terminate the employment when the employee becomes bankrupt.

27.2 PRIORITIES VESTED IN THE EMPLOYEE

27.2.1 Any outstanding remuneration or other financial benefits due to the employee at the commencement of the bankruptcy are debts in the bankruptcy for which the employee must prove as any other creditor. The status of these debts is not affected by a continuation of the employee's employment by the trustee in bankruptcy and the employee may, and indeed should, prove for his outstanding remuneration due prior to the bankruptcy while continuing to work for the business controlled by the trustee.

27.2.2 The employee has priority, albeit to a rather limited extent, as a preferential creditor on the distribution of assets.[1] Under both the Old Bankruptcy Law and the New Law, an employee of the bankrupt who is owed remuneration in respect of the whole or any part of the four-month period immediately prior to the commencment of the bankruptcy, has priority up to £800 or, for the future, such sum as may be prescribed by the Secretary of State.[2] It is immaterial that the employee may have been discharged by the bankruptcy during that period of four months or spent the whole or any part of the time absent, sick or for other good cause. The priority extends to accrued holiday remuneration in respect of any period of employment before the commencement of the bankruptcy,[3] and also to any other creditor who advances money expressly for the purpose of paying wages or salary.[4]

[1] For distribution generally see chs 9 (Old Bankruptcy Law) and 16 (New Law) above.
[2] Bankruptcy Act 1914, s 33(1) and see Bankruptcy (Amendment) Act 1926, s 2 which expressly extends the priority to commission payments; Insolvency Act 1986, Sch 6, para 9.
[3] Insolvency Act 1986, Sch 6, para 10.
[4] Ibid, para 11.

27.2.3 In practice, since the establishment of the Redundancy Fund, employees usually claim for redundancy and unpaid remuneration on the Fund and the Secretary of State for Employment makes payment and is then subrogated to the rights of the employee in the employers bankruptcy[1] (and see paras 27.3 and 27.6 below).

[1] Employment Protection (Consolidation) Act 1978, s 106.

27.3 EMPLOYMENT PROTECTION (CONSOLIDATION) ACT 1978 ('EP(C)A')

27.3.1 This statute, in Part VII, extends the scope of debts which attracted priority on distribution under the Old Bankruptcy Law and affords the employee the right to recover certain debts owing to him by an insolvent employer from the Redundancy Fund. EP(C)A, s 121 provided for four categories of payment to be treated as remuneration for the purposes of priority on distribution, and has now been replaced by the Insolvency Act 1985, s 218(4) which adds a fifth category, statutory sick pay. Accordingly all the following payments have preferential status in the bankruptcy, up to the prescribed limit:

(a) a guaranteed payment for a 'workless day';
(b) remuneration on suspension on medical grounds;
(c) a payment for time off, e g for trade union or public duties or for training or looking for work;
(d) remuneration under a protective award made under the Employment Protection Act 1975, s 101 and
(e) statutory sick pay, payable under the Social Security and Housing Benefits Act 1982, Part I.

27.3.2 The Redundancy Fund operates as a safeguard to ensure that a basic level of claim by an employee is met notwithstanding the bankrupt employer's inability to pay. There are six categories of claim which the fund will meet:[1]

(i) any arrears of pay in respect of one or more but not more than eight weeks;
(ii) any amount which the employer is liable to pay to the employee for failing to give the minimum statutory period of notice for terminating the employee's contract of employment;
(iii) holiday pay in respect of one or more periods of holiday not exceeding six weeks in all to which the employee became entitled during the 12 months before the employer's bankruptcy or the termination of the employee's employment, whichever is the later;
(iv) the basic award of compensation for unfair dismissal;[2]
(v) any reasonable sum by way of reimbursement of the whole or any part of any fee or premium paid by an apprentice or articled clerk;[3] and
(vi) any unpaid contributions to an occupational pension scheme. A claim under this head is made by the persons competent to act in respect of the occupational pension scheme.

[1] EP(C)A, ss 122, as amended by Insolvency Act 1985, s 218, and 123 (occupational pension scheme).
[2] EP(C)A, ss 72 and 73, in general taking the years of continuous employment by the employee. One and a half weeks' pay for each year when the employee was aged 41 and over, 1 week's pay for each year between 22 and 41 and half a week's pay for each year between 18 and 22, subject to a limit of 20 years.
[3] Under Bankruptcy Act 1914, s 34 or Insolvency Act 1986, s 348, there is a preferential claim for an apprentice or articled clerks to recover money paid or a reasonable part of it where the indenture or articles of agreement are terminated.

27.3.3 The total amount payable to an employee in respect of any category of claim which is calculated by reference to a period of time is not to exceed the statutory weekly limit for awards under EP(C)A.[1] This statutory weekly limit represents the gross amount of the employee's claim, from which tax and national insurance contributions must be deducted when arrears of pay and holiday pay are claimed against the fund.[2] Any unemployment or supplementary benefit received in respect of the period to which the claim relates must also be deducted from the claim.[3]

[1] EP(C)A, s 122(5) and the Employment Protection (Variation of Limits) Orders by which the statutory weekly limit for awards under EP(C)A is increased from time to time.
[2] *Morris v Secretary of State for Employment* [1985] ICR 522.
[3] *Westwood v Secretary of State for Employment* [1985] AC 20.

27.3.4 There is no express link between these claims and the employee's preferred rights in the bankruptcy of the employer. Accordingly, the employee is not bound by the £800 or prescribed preferential limit when proving a claim under EP(C)A against the Redundancy Fund. Furthermore, it could well be that the claim under EP(C)A overlaps the preferential claim. There is nothing in EP(C)A to prevent the employee proving in the bankruptcy for his preferential arrears of remuneration during the last four months before the bankruptcy and then choosing another eight weeks for his claim for arrears of pay under EP(C)A. Whether an employee is prepared to remain in unpaid employment for a sufficient length of time to make such considerations a practical proposition is perhaps unlikely, but as both types of claim are limited in amount to well below the levels of remuneration that many employees enjoy, careful specification of period when making these claims could prove financially advantageous.

The procedure for payment from the redundancy fund

27.3.5 The employee seeks a payment from the Redundancy Fund by making an application in writing to the Secretary of State.[1] No form is prescribed and there is no limitation period for applications. Before authorising a payment, the Secretary of State must be satisfied that (a) the employer is insolvent (b) the employment of the employee has been terminated and (c) that on the 'relevant date' the employee was entitled to be paid the whole or any part of the debt in respect of which the claim is made. The determination of the relevant date has been amended by the Insolvency Act 1985, s 218(3). The 'relevant date' now depends upon the debt in respect of which a claim is made:

(i) where the debt is arrears of pay or holiday pay (but not including remuneration due under a protective award) the relevant date is the date on which the employer became insolvent;
(ii) where the debt is a basic award and a compensatory award for unfair dismissal the relevant date is the later of (a) the date the employer became insolvent (b) the date of termination of the employee's employment and (c) the date on which the award was made; and
(iii) where the debt does not fall into either category (i) or (ii) above, the relevant date is the latest of (a) the date the employer became insolvent and (b) the date of termination of the employee's employment.

Accordingly employees who continue to be employed by the trustee in bankruptcy will not now have their applications delayed. The 'insolvency of the employer' includes the making of a bankruptcy order, the making of a composition or arrangement with creditors or, where the employer dies, the making of an order under the Insolvency Act, 1986, s 421. In practical terms, the Secretary of State will need to consult with the person responsible for the insolvent employer's affairs before he can be satisfied that the Redundancy Fund should make a payment. EP(C)A provides that the relevant officer (be he the trustee in bankruptcy, receiver, supervisor of voluntary arrangements or trustee under a composition or arrangement) is to provide the Secretary of State as soon as reasonably practicable after request, with a statement of the amount of the debt due to the employee.[3]

1 EP(C)A, s 122(1).
2 Insolvency Act 1985, Sch 8, para 31(5) amending EP(C)A, s 127(1).
3 EP(C)A, s 122(10), 123(7).

27.3.6 The Secretary of State also has powers[1] exercisable by notice in writing to require:

(a) the employer to provide him with such information as he may reasonably require; and
(b) any person having custody or control of any relevant records or documents to produce such documents as are specified for examination.

1 EP(C)A, s 126.

27.3.7 The Secretary of State 'shall not' make a payment from the Redundancy Fund in respect of any claim until he has received the statement required from the relevant officers. However, where six months have elapsed following the employee's application, the Secretary of State, if satisfied that a payment should be made and that to await the statement from the relevant officer is likely to occasion further delay, may make a payment without receiving a statement either on his own instigation or at the request of the employee.[1]

1 EP(C)A, ss 122(11), 123(8).

27.3.8 Should a claimant be dissatisfied with a decision of the Secretary of State, he may present a complaint to an industrial tribunal that no payment was made or the payment was less than it should have been. The complaint must be presented within three months of the communication of the decision or if not reasonably practicable, within such further period as is reasonable.[1] Where the industrial tribunal finds that a payment should have been made, it is to make a declaration to that effect and state the sum which should have been paid.[2]

1 EP(C)A, s 124(1). For 'not reasonably practicable' see EP(C)A, s 67(2) and the many decisions thereunder.
2 EP(C)A, s 124(3).

Occupational pension contributions[1]

27.3.9 To qualify for a claim against the Redundancy Fund, the contribution must be payable in accordance with an occupational pension scheme either on the employer's account or on behalf of the employee. An employee's contribution will only qualify where an equivalent sum has been deducted from his pay. There are restrictions on the size of the claim in respect of both the employer's and the employee's contributions.

1 EP(C)A, s 123.

27.3.10 On the employer's contributions, the sum payable from the Redundancy Fund is the least of the following:
(a) the balance of contribution unpaid in respect of the 12 months immediately preceding the date of insolvency, (as to which date see para 27.4 above);
(b) the amount certified by an actuary to be necessary for the purpose of meeting the liability of the scheme, on dissolution, to pay the benefits provided by the scheme; or
(c) an amount equal to 10% of the total remuneration due to the employee in respect of the 12 months immediately preceeding the date of insolvency.

27.3.11 On claims for employee's contributions, the limit is the amount deducted from the employee's pay in respect of pension contributions during the 12 months immediately preceding the date of the employer's insolvency.

27.3.12 A complaint to an industrial tribunal that no payment or a payment of insufficient amount has been made into the resources of the scheme, may be made by the persons competent to act in respect of the occupational pension scheme.[1]

[1] EP(C)A, s 124(2).

Transfer of rights and remedies to Secretary of State

27.3.13 Where the Secretary of State makes any payment out of the Redundancy Fund in respect of any claim listed under para 27.3 above, any rights and remedies held by the claimant vest in the Secretary of State.[1] The Secretary of State will thus acquire the priority of the employee in proving in the employee's bankruptcy under the Old Bankruptcy Law or New Law as appropriate.[2] Any sum recovered by the Secretary of State in proving any remedy he has acquired, is to be paid to the Redundancy Fund.

[1] EP(C)A, s 125.
[2] Ie Bankruptcy Act 1914, s 33; Insolvency Act 1986, ss 328 and 348 (apprentices/articled clerks) and Sch 6.

27.4 TRANSFER OF THE BANKRUPT'S BUSINESS

27.4.1 Under the common law, the contracts of employment of the workforce of a business automatically determined where the business was transferred to another proprietor. This principle was in some small degree moderated by EP(C)A, s 94 which provides that where an employer transfers his business as a going concern and the new proprietor of the business offers re-employment to an employee before the transfer takes place, the employee maintains his continuity of employment notwithstanding the transfer. The provisions of EP(C)A governing renewals or re-engagements[1] apply to this offer or re-employment and accordingly the employee has a trial period of four weeks during which he can make up his mind to accept the re-employment without prejudice to his entitlement to a redundancy payment (which he loses on acceptance of the re-employment).

[1] EP(C)A, s 84. For the four-week trial period see s 84(4).

27.4.2 More detailed provisions governing the rights of employees on the transfer of the business for which they work are contained in the Transfer of Undertakings (Protection of Employment) Regulations 1981.[1] These regulations were consequent upon EEC Directive 1977/187 on Acquired Rights of Employees with respect to their contracts of employment, which directive aimed to harmonise the laws of member states relating to the safeguarding of undertakings, businesses and parts of businesses. This area of law impinges on the conflict of interests which arise on the insolvency of a business between the creditors, the employees and all those who are concerned to rescue all or part of the insolvent business for future viability.

[1] SI 1981/1794.

27.4.3 The 1981 Regulations were late in being formulated (for the 1977 directive allowed only two years for implementation) and do not go as far as the Directive envisaged on the protection of employees' rights. They do, however, leave a measure of assistance to receivers and others concerned in rescue operations, given the imposed need to have regulations at all.

The transfer of employment

27.4.4 The basic purpose of the Regulations is to introduce the principle of automatic transfer of individual contracts of employment, collective agreements and trade union recognition on the takeover of a business.

27.4.5 The dismissal of any employee, other than for an economic, technical or organisational reason of either the transferor or the transferee of the business, is automatically unfair. The Regulations apply to a 'relevant transfer' of a business in the UK. Regulation 3(1) defines relevant transfer as 'a transfer from one person to another of an undertaking'.[1] It follows that the Regulations do not apply where there is the sale of the share capital of a business even where the shares are wholly (save one) owned by a single proprietor who becomes insolvent along with his business. In contractual terms this is logical, for there is no alteration in the identity of the contracting parties. This definition has the effect, however, of making it unnecessary for there to be consultation with any recognised trade union under reg 10 where the transfer of the business is to be by share takeover.

[1] By reg 3(4) a transfer may involve a series of two or more transactions.

27.4.6 In addition to share takeovers, there are two important categories of transfer which fall outside the Regulations:

(i) where the transfer involves the physical assets of the business only and the business is not transferred as a going concern. Regulation 2(2) requires that the transfer of parts of the undertaking are not relevant transfers unless 'transferred as a business'. There must be some transfer of goodwill for a relevant transfer;[1] and

(ii) where the transfer involves undertakings which are not commercial ventures. Regulation 2(1) excludes from the definition of 'undertaking' any undertaking which is not 'in the nature of a commercial venture'. Thus employees of charitable bodies, local authorities or health authorities or other employees within the National Health Service are not covered by the Regulations even where there is a transfer to the private sector of public functions.

1 See, eg *Atkin v Ward and Haines Watts* [1983] IRLR 285 and other cases on EP(C)A, s 94(1)(a) and change in ownership of business.

27.4.7 At the heart of the conflict of interests referred to above, is the transfer of viable parts of the business commonly called 'hiving down'. Frequently practised by receivers in corporate insolvency, it is less important in personal insolvency where the transfer of parts of the bankrupt's business prior to sale to a third party to another person or company, formed for the purpose, would appear to be outside the scope of the general powers of the trustee in bankruptcy. For completeness, it is noted here that reg 4 of the 1981 Regulations provides that employees working for the insolvent business immediately before the transfer of the viable 'hived down' part of the undertaking, are automatically transferred to the new owner of the business.

The effects of a relevant transfer

27.4.8 There are three effects of a relevant transfer provided for in the Regulations:

(i) Transfer of individual contracts of employment. Individual contracts of employment are automatically transferred to the new owner of the business. This involves a complete transfer of rights and remedies not only of future benefits and obligations but also of past actions.[1] Thus anything done before the transfer which concerned the relationship of transferor and employee is deemed to have been done as between the transferee and employee. The only exceptions to this complete transfer of rights are criminal matters[2] and the occupational pension schemes.[3] The transfer affects only employees and apprentices under contracts of employment and not workers 'employed' under a contract for services.[4] In order to benefit from the Regulations, the employee must be employed 'immediately before' the transfer of the undertaking, or immediately before any one of a series of transactions if the transfer is effected in various stages.[5] The employee is not to be prejudiced should the practical effects of the transfer result in a 'substantial change in his working conditions to his detriment'. In this event the employee may terminate the contract and, where appropriate, claim that he has been constructively dismissed. The employee may also rely upon the identity of his new employer to terminate his contract provided he can show that the change of employer is in the circumstances a significant change and to his detriment.[6] This would cover the position where there was individual animosity between

the employee and the transferee of the business.

[1] Reg 5(1) and (2).
[2] Reg 5(4), eg offences under the Health and Safety at Work etc. Act 1974.
[3] Reg 7.
[4] See definition of 'employee' in reg 2(1).
[5] Reg 5(3). In *Apex Leisure Hire v Barrett* [1984] IRLR 224 the EAT held that an employee dismissed on Friday evening and told to report for work on Monday for the new company was employed 'immediately before' the transfer on Monday afternoon.
[6] Reg 6.

(ii) Transfer of collective agreements. The transferor's collective agreements with a recognised trade union automatically pass to the transferee.[1] Such transfer is, however, expressly without prejudice to the legal unenforceability of such agreements should this be the case, which it almost invariably is, and is accordingly of little legal significance.

[1] Reg 6.

(iii) Transfer of agreement for trade union recognition. Subject to the important proviso that after the transfer, the transferred undertaking maintains an identity distinct from the remainder of the transferee's business, trade union recognition agreements are continued over the transfer.[1]

[1] Reg 9.

Unfair dismissal and duty to inform

27.4.9 If an employee is dismissed either before or after a relevant transfer, the dismissal is automatically unfair if the transfer is the reason or principal reason behind it.[1] The usefulness of this right for the employee is, however, almost entirely taken away by the fact that it does not apply where the reason for the dismissal is 'an economic, technical or organisational reason entailing changes before or after a relevant transfer'.[2] This provision would appear to be broad enough to cover any practical situation unless the courts apply a severely restrictive interpretation of this Regulation through the words 'entailing changes in the work force'.

Under reg 10, the employer of employees likely to be affected by the transfer (whether or not employed in the undertaking to be transferred) and who have a recognised trade union, has a duty to consult the trade union and provide information concerning the nature, extent, reasons and timing of the transfer. Failure to consult or give information renders the employer liable on a successful complaint to an industrial tribunal, to pay an award of up to two weeks' pay to each employee affected.[3]

Any provision of an agreement designed to contract out of regs 5, 8, 10 or 11 of the 1981 Regulations is void.[4]

[1] Reg 8(1).
[2] Reg 8(2).
[3] Reg 11.
[4] Reg 12.

27.5 REDUNDANCY

27.5.1 Following the introduction of the redundancy payment in the Redundancy Payments Act 1965, the dismissed employee was anxious to show that his dismissal was by reason of redundancy so as to qualify for a payment. With the advent of the concept of unfair dismissal, bringing with it the prospect of an award of compensation much greater than the amount of a redundancy payment, the position was reversed and the employee's interest was to show that he was not made redundant and so qualified only for the lower redundancy payment. With the insolvency of the proprietor of the business, dismissals of employees are almost certain to be by reason of redundancy and the employees will qualify for their redundancy payment.[1] This payment is, in effect, guaranteed by the Redundancy Fund which meets any payment due from an employer who is insolvent and unable to pay.[2] The law relating to redundancy payments is now contained in EP(C)A, Part VI. In connection with employees becoming redundant as a result of their employer's bankruptcy, the following points are made:

(i) A 'redundancy' for the purposes of a redundancy payment arises when an employee who has at least two years' continuous employment, is either dismissed by reason of redundancy or is laid off or put onto short-time working to the extent specified by EP(C)A.[3]

(ii) An employee is excluded from entitlement to a redundancy payment if, as a man, he has attained the age of 65, or, as a woman, has attained the age of 60.[4]

(iii) An employee is not redundant if his contract of employment is renewed or he is re-engaged within four weeks of the ending of his previous employment.[5]

(iv) An employee is not entitled to a redundancy payment where the employer is entitled to determine the employee's contract of employment summarily and either: (a) does so; or (b) gives shorter notice than is required under the contract; or (c) gives full notice accompanied by a statement in writing that the employer is by reason of the employee's conduct entitled to terminate the contract without notice.[6]

(v) Limitation period. An employee is not entitled to a redundancy payment unless within six months of the relevant date[7]: (a) the payment has been agreed and paid; or (b) the employee has made a claim in writing on the employer; or (c) a question as to the employee's entitlement has been referred to an industrial tribunal; or (d) the employee has presented a complaint relating to his dismissal.[8]

[1] The payment is calculated by reference to periods of continuous employment reckoning backwards from the date of redundancy and allowing:
(a) one and a half weeks' pay for each year of employment consisting wholly of weeks in which the employee was not below the age of 41 years;
(b) one week's pay for each year in which the employee was between the ages of 22 and 41;
(c) half a week's pay for each year in which the employee was between the ages of 18 and 22.
There is, however, a maximum of 20 years which may be taken into account: EP(C)A, s 81, Sch 4, paras 13 and 14.

[2] EP(C)A, s 106.

[3] EP(C)A, ss 81(1), 87 and 88. Under s 87 'Lay off' involves a week without work in circumstances where the employee is not entitled to remuneration under his contract as a result of not having work to do. If the employee's work is limited so that he receives less than half a week's pay, he is on 'short time'. The employee must give notice of his intention to claim a redundancy payment and must show that he has been laid off or on short time for four or more consecutive weeks or for a total of six weeks within a period of 13 weeks before seeking the notice: s 88.

[4] EP(C)A, s 82(1).

[5] EP(C)A, s 84.

[6] EP(C)A, s 82(2).

[7] EP(C)A, s 90.

[8] Ibid, s 101.

CHAPTER 28

Guarantees and Suretyship

28.1 CONTRACT OF GUARANTEE

28.1.1 A guarantee is an agreement by one person (the 'guarantor' or 'surety') to meet the present or future debt of another person ('the principal' or 'principal debtor') due to a party who is an actual or prospective creditor of the principal debtor, in the event and to the extent that the principal debtor fails to make payment.

A guarantee is only enforceable by action if it is evidenced by a memorandum in writing signed by the guarantor or by some other person duly authorised by him.[1] Consideration is required to support a guarantee, unless it is under seal, but it is not necessary to specify the consideration in the document of guarantee or memorandum in writing.[2] A contract of guarantee is to be contrasted with a contract of indemnity. In the latter the promisor agrees to render the promisee harmless from a liability which may arise in a particular transaction. The promisor becomes primarily liable on the contract. With a contract of guarantee the principal debtor retains primary liability and only through that primary liability will the guarantor become liable.

1 Statute of Frauds (1677), s 4.
2 Mercantile Law Amendment Act 1856, s 3.

28.2 BANKRUPTCY OF THE PRINCIPAL DEBTOR

The rights of the creditor

28.2.1 The creditor is entitled to prove in the bankruptcy of the principal debtor irrespective of his ability to recover against the guarantor. He must, though, give credit for all value received from the guarantor before proof, including payments, and for the realisation of securities or securities as yet unrealised.[1] Should the guarantor also be bankrupt the creditor must give credit for any dividend declared out of the guarantor's estate even where it has yet to be paid.[2]

[1] *Re Oriental Commercial Bank, ex p Maxoudoff* (1868) LR 6 Eq 582; *Re Daunt, ex p Joint Stock Discount Co* (1871) 6 Ch App 455; *Re Bedell, ex p Gilbey* (1878) 8 Ch D 248.
[2] *Ex p Leers* (1802) 6 Ves 644.

28.2.2 The creditor does not, however, have to give credit for moneys from the guarantor until they are actually received and applied by him. In *Re Walker & Co, ex p Watson*[1] the creditor realised a security deposited by the guarantor on both his own and the principal debtor's account and after satisfying the guarantor's account placed the balance on a suspense account. It was held that this was not a receipt of the balance by the creditor who did not, therefore, need to give credit in his proof in the bankruptcy of the principal debtor. This principle has been much used by the English clearing banks. It is common procedure for the banks to place the proceeds of realised securities and guarantor's payments on a suspense or securities realised account. Such sums are appropriated by the bank when it thinks fit, and until appropriation need not be deducted from the bank's proof against the principal debtor's estate.

[1] (1880) 42 LT 516; and see *Re Sass, ex p National Provincial Bank of England Ltd* [1896] 2 QB 12.

28.2.3 A creditor cannot be obliged to exercise his rights against a guarantor by the trustee in bankruptcy or the other creditors either in law or in equity.[1] A creditor holding a guarantee is not a 'secured creditor' for the purposes of the Bankruptcy Act 1914, Sch 2 or the Individual Insolvency Rules under the Insolvency Act 1986. He cannot therefore be made to value or surrender the guarantee or charge on the guarantor[2] even where the guarantor has a security on the estate of the principal debtor.[3]

[1] *Ex p Kendal* (1811) 17 Ves 514.
[2] As for valuing and surrending securities see ch 9 above and the Individual Insolvency Rules 1986, ch 9, rr 6.115–6.119.
[3] *Midland Banking Co v Chambers* (1869) 4 Ch App 398. And generally see *Re Melton, Milk v Towers* [1918] 1 Ch 37 and in particular the judgment of Scrutton LJ in its approach to problems of this nature.

The rights of the guarantor

28.2.4 When the guarantor pays anything under the guarantee he has a right of action against the principal debtor in the same amount. If the principal debtor is bankrupt, the guarantor may prove in the bankruptcy.

But such proof is subject to the creditor's proof in respect of the principal debt. There must be no double proof.[1] Thus, the creditor's proof prevails and while the creditor is proving for the debt the guarantor may not do so even where he has paid sums to the creditor. Once, however, the creditor has been paid in full from all sources the guarantor is entitled to the benefit of the creditor's proof for any remaining dividends.[2] The guarantor may prove against any claim which may arise under his guarantee whether present or future, certain or contingent. Whether or not he does so the bankrupt is protected in respect of any such claim on his discharge.[3]

1 *Hardy v Fothergill* (1888) 13 App Cas 351; *Re Fitzgeorge, ex p Robson* [1905] 1 KB 462; *Re Lennard, Lennard's Trustee v Lennard* [1934] Ch 235.
2 *Re Pyke Davis v Jeffreys* (1910) 55 Sol Jo 109; *Re Fothergill, ex p Turquand* (1876) 3 Ch D 445; *Re Melton, Milk v Towers* [1918] 1 Ch 37.
3 Bankruptcy Act 1914, s 30(3) (proof), s 28(2) (protection of principal debtor on discharge) Insolvency Act 1986, Sch 9, para 17 and Individual Insolvency Rules 1986, ch 8, rr 6.96–6.114.

28.2.5 Where the guarantor holds a security upon the principal debtor's estate, he is limited in his rights to benefit from the creditor's proof to the amount by which the guarantee liability exceeds the value of the security. Should the creditor take dividends from the estate and call on the guarantee to enable him to recover the debt in full, the guarantor will be entitled to realise any security he has on the principal debtor's estate. Should the realisation of this security result in the estate paying more than the amount of the debt the guarantor must account for the balance to the estate.[1] It is common form today for bank guarantees to provide that the bank may take all dividends from the principal debtor's estate and still hold the guarantor liable to the full extent of the guarantee. In this event proof by the bank (or other creditor holding a similar guarantee) does not affect any security held by the guarantor over the principal's estate.[2]

1 *Baines v Wright* (1885) 16 QBD 330.
2 *Midland Banking Co v Chambers* (1869) 4 Ch App 398; *Re Lennard, Lennard's Trustee v Lennard* [1934] 1 Ch 235.

28.2.6 A guarantor who has made payment under the guarantee may set off such payments against debts due by him to the principal debtor[1] but the set off extends only to the extent of payments made and not to prospective liabilities under the guarantee. This is because until the creditor has finally exercised his rights of proof in the estate the guarantor's contingent set off might become effectively a double proof.[2] Neither is a set off allowed in respect of payments made after the commencement of the bankruptcy.[3]

1 Bankruptcy Act 1914, s 31; Insolvency Act 1986, s 323.
2 *Re Fenton, ex p Fenton Textile Association Ltd* [1931] 1 Ch 85.
3 *Re Debtor (No 66 of 1955), ex p Debtor v Trustee of Property of Waite* [1956] 3 All ER 225.

The guarantor's equity of exoneration

28.2.7 Where the principal debtor and the guarantor both charge their properties for the principal debt, the guarantor's equity of exoneration is to have the debt paid out of the principal debtor's property before the guarantor's property is appropriated for the debt. This principle is effective against the principal debtor's trustee in bankruptcy.

An example of the application of this principle is to be found in the decision of the Bankruptcy Divisional Court in *Re Debtor (No 24 of 1971), ex p Marley v Trustee of Property of Debtor*.[1] There a father conveyed his freehold house into the joint names of himself and his son so that his son could obtain a bank loan. A charge was then executed on the house by both father and son in the bank's favour. The son's business failed and he became bankrupt. It was accepted that the father was in the position of a guarantor. The Court held that an intention should be implied that the son's beneficial interest should bear the burden of the debt and that the father could be regarded as having an actual charge on the bankrupt son's interest in the house.[2] On the sale of the property the father was entitled to insist as against the son's trustee in bankruptcy that the son's share was used to meet the outstanding bank loan in priority to the father's share.

1 [1979] 2 All ER 1010, Foster and Fox JJ.

2 Following the principle discussed in *Gee v Liddell* [1913] 2 Ch 62 at 72. For spouse's equity of exoneration see ch 22 above, and see *Re Pittortou, ex p Trustee of Property of Bankrupt v Bankrupt* [1985] 1 All ER 285.

28.3 THE BANKRUPTCY OF THE GUARANTOR

The rights of the creditor

28.3.1 There is old authority that the bankruptcy of the guarantor does not by itself revoke the guarantee.[1] It is perhaps arguable under the Bankruptcy Act 1914, s 30 that once the creditor has received notice of an act of bankruptcy by the guarantor no further sums becoming due from the principal debtor will be caught by the guarantee. A similar argument could be advanced in respect of sums arising after notice to the creditor of the presentation of a petition against the guarantor under the Insolvency Act 1986. In either case, however, the circumstances in which the further sums became due would be important, and in particular whether the creditor was in a position to prevent further debts due to him being incurred by the principal debtor. The bankruptcy of one guarantor does not affect the rights of the creditor against remaining guarantors jointly liable with the bankrupt guarantor. Under both the Old Bankruptcy Law and the New Law the guarantee is not discharged by the discharge of a bankrupt guarantor.[2]

The creditor may prove for any amount due and payable by the guarantor at the commencement of the bankruptcy, subject to deductions for any payments or the value of any securities or dividends received from the principal debtor or that debtor's estate. Where there are a number of co-guarantors jointly and severally liable for the principal debt the creditor may prove in the bankruptcy of one guarantor for the whole amount then due under the principal debt. He need not give credit for money or value received from the other co-guarantors after the commencement of the bankruptcy provided he does not recover more than the total debt due.[3] Neither need the creditor who has a security from another co-guarantor apply it to reduce the proof in the co-guarantor's bankruptcy. This includes money in a suspense account.[4]

Where a creditor has waived his remedy against another guarantor he is not precluded from proof in the co-guarantor's bankruptcy, but an allowance must be made for the contribution which may have been had from the released co-guarantor.[5]

A guarantor may become bankrupt before the principal debt is due. The creditor's debt would then be contingent and in amount highly speculative and extremely difficult, if not impossible, to determine. The creditor may nevertheless prove in the guarantor's bankruptcy.[6]

[1] *Boyd v Robins and Langlands* (1859) 5 CBNS 597.
[2] Bankruptcy Act 1914, s 28(4); Insolvency Act 1986, s 281(7).
[3] *Re Houlder* [1929] 1 Ch 205.
[4] *Commercial Bank of Australia v John Wilson & Co's Estate Official Assignee* [1893] AC 181.
[5] *Ex p Gifford* (1802) 6 Ves 805.
[6] Bankruptcy Act 1914, s 30(3); Insolvency Act 1986, Sch 9, para 17 and Individual Insolvency Rules, 1986, r 12.3. See also cases cited at para 28.2.4 n (1) above.

Guarantor as mortgagor

28.3.2 When the creditor is secured by a legal charge executed by the guarantor he may enforce that security, subject to the provisions of the charge, in the event of the guarantor's bankruptcy. Where the guarantor has given an equitable mortgage or charge by way of security for the guarantee any deed creating the charge may contain an irrevocable power of attorney clause enabling the creditor to make title when the guarantor mortgagor becomes bankrupt. Such a clause cannot be revoked by the guarantor's bankruptcy and the creditor mortgagee is able to make title without the co-operation of the guarantor's trustee in bankruptcy.[1] Other equitable charges without such a clause have to be enforced against the trustee.

[1] Powers of Attorney Act 1971, s 4.

28.4 BANKRUPTCY OF BOTH PRINCIPAL DEBTOR AND GUARANTOR

28.4.1 *The rights of the creditor.* The creditor is entitled to prove against both the principal debtor and the guarantor for the full amount due at the date of proof. He can take dividends from either or both estates until he is repaid in full.[1] When the principal debtor has given security to the guarantor in respect of the debt that security is to be applied to discharge the principal debt to the creditor.[2] The creditor having had the benefit of the money realised by the security, may then prove in the guarantor's bankruptcy for the balance of the debt.

[1] *Ex p Rushforth* (1805) 10 Ves 409, and see cases in 26 The Digest pp 125–129.
[2] *Ex p Waring* (1815) 19 Ves 345.

28.4.2 *The rights of the guarantor's estate.* No proof can be made on behalf of the guarantor's estate in the principal debtor's bankruptcy in respect of dividends declared out of the guarantor's estate once the creditor has proved in the principal debtor's estate.[1] However, when the creditor has been paid in full from all sources, the guarantor's estate is entitled to the benefit of the creditor's proof in the principal debtor's estate in respect of any further dividends paid.[2]

[1] *Re Oriental Commercial Bank, ex p European Bank* (1871) 7 Ch App 99.
[2] *Re Whitehouse, Whitehouse v Edwards* (1887) 37 Ch D 683.

28.5 BANKRUPTCY OF CO-GUARANTOR

28.5.1 *The rights of the co-guarantor.* One of several co-guarantors who pays the principal debt, or more than his proportionate share, is entitled to contribution in respect of the excess from the other guarantors. In taking proceedings for that excess the co-guarantor should make the principal debtor a party to the action unless the principal debtor is insolvent.

28.5.2 The co-guarantor may prove in another guarantor's bankruptcy when liability under the guarantee has arisen. He also has a right to prove in respect of his contingent claim against the other guarantor when no liability has yet arisen on behalf of that or any guarantor.[1] However, the rule against double proof prevents a co-guarantor proving in respect of any sum for which the creditors may prove so this right is not one which in practice is likely to be exercisable. The co-guarantor is left with his right to take over the creditor's proof should the creditor be paid in full. Then the co-guarantor may take dividends up to the amount of his liability to contribute. If the creditor does not prove in the other guarantor's estate the co-guarantor may then, having paid the creditor, exercise his right to prove. Whatever he has paid to the creditor the co-guarantor may only prove in the sum which could be recovered from the other guarantor as contribution.[2]

[1] *Wolmerhausen v Gullick* [1893] 2 Ch 514.
[2] *Re Parker, Morgan v Hill* [1894] 3 Ch 400.

28.6 POSITIONS ANALOGOUS TO SURETYSHIP

There are cases outside a formal guarantee where a person is liable to meet a liability primarily owed by another person should the person with primary liability default in his obligations. The principles relating to bankruptcy and proof will also apply in such cases, which include a drawer or indorser of a bill of exchange[1] a partner paying the whole of a partnership debt[2] and an executor facing the default of a co-executor.[3] A lessee who is called upon to honour the covenants in the lease which he has assigned to an assignee has a primary liability and is not in an equivalent position to a guarantor.[4]

[1] *Haigh v Jackson* (1838) 3 M & W 598; *Duncan Fox & Co v North and South Wales Bank* (1880) 6 App Cas 1 at 19.
[2] *Aflalo v Fourdinier* (1829) 6 Bing 306.
[3] *Lincoln v Wright* (1841) 4 Beav 166.
[4] *Hardy v Fothergill* (1888) 13 App Cas 351.

28.7 COMPOSITION BY PRINCIPAL DEBTOR

A voluntary composition outside the law of bankruptcy in which the creditor allows the principal debtor time to pay or a reduction in his liability discharges the guarantor,[1] subject to the provisions of the guarantee or deed of composition. A creditor may reserve his remedies against the guarantor.[2] But within the context of bankruptcy law, a release or indulgence to the principal debtor does not discharge the guarantor, whether as part of an Old Bankruptcy Law composition or scheme or a New Law voluntary arrangement. Such a release or indulgence is an act of law.[3] The principal debtor will be protected from the suit of the guarantor, either by the arrangement or discharge, but the guarantor remains liable to the creditor. The guarantor's rights are limited to paying off the creditor and taking his place in the arrangement or bankruptcy proceedings.[4]

Where the principal debtor enters into a composition guaranteed by guarantors, other than a voluntary arrangement under the New Law, and then defaults, the creditor may prove for the full amount of the debt giving credit for sums actually received.[5] The creditor is not limited to outstanding sums in the composition, save in exceptional circumstances where there has been accord and satisfaction of the debt or a part of the debt.[6]

1 *Re Lewis, ex p Smith* (1739) 3 Bro CC 1.
1 *Re Renton, ex p Glendinning* (1819) Buck 517; *Bateson v Gosling* (1871) LR 7 CP 9.
3 *Re Jacobs, ex p Jacobs* (1875) 10 Ch App 211.
4 *Browne v Carr* (1831) 7 Bing 508; *Ellis v Wilmot* (1874) LR10 Exch 10.
5 *Re Bedell, ex p Gilbey* (1878) 8 Ch D 248.
6 See eg *Perry v National Provincial Bank of England* [1910] 1 Ch 464.

28.8 DISCLAIMER OF LEASES

A trustee in bankruptcy's disclaimer of a lease releases the guarantor from the date of the disclaimer.[1] Liabilities which have accrued before that date, both in respect of rent and covenants, including repairing covenants, remain enforceable against the guarantor by the landlord. Should the guarantor consider that the lease may be of value he may apply to the court for an order vesting the lease in him.[2]

1 *Stacey v Hill* [1901] 1KB 660 and see *Re Katherine et Cie Ltd* [1932] 1 Ch 70 and *Warnford Investments Ltd v Duckworth* [1979] Ch 127.
2 Bankruptcy Act 1914, s 54(6); Insolvency Act 1986, s 320(2); and see para 29.2.24 below.

28.9 PAYMENT OF DIVIDENDS

Any dividends paid to the creditor in the principal debtor's bankruptcy are treated as made rateably in respect of every part of the debt. And where the principal debt is due in instalments a dividend paid in respect of the whole debt must, for the purpose of the guarantor's continuing liability be distributed over all the instalments.[1] Subject to express agreement to the contrary, the dividends received by the creditor release co-guarantors rateably. Where the guarantee is for a limited amount less than the total debt, the general rule is that the guarantor's liability to the creditor will be reduced on payment of dividends to the creditor in rateable proportion as the guarantee limit bears to the total debt. Bank guarantees are usually careful to avoid this rule and provide that the bank may prove for its own benefit above the guarantee limit before dividends operate to reduce the guarantor's liability.[2] Where a number of co-guarantors split up the guarantee liability in definite proportions it appears that dividends received by the creditor must be applied rateably in reducing the liability of each guarantor.[3] Where the proportions of each co-guarantor's liability have not been specified in advance the creditor is not bound to apportion payments from the principal debtor between them.[4]

1 *Martin v Breknell* (1813) 2 M & S 39.
2 See *Re Rees, ex p National Provincial Bank of England* (1881) 17 Ch D 98 and *Re Sass, ex p National Provincial Bank of England* [1896] 2 QB 12.
3 *Pendlebury v Walker* (1841) 10 LJ Ex Eq 27.
4 *Ellis v Emmanuel* (1876) 1 Ex D 157.

28.10 DISCHARGE OF BANKRUPT PRINCIPAL DEBTOR

On his discharge the principal debtor is released from all debts which were or might have been proved in his bankruptcy. This discharge does not, however, affect the liability of the guarantor who continues to be responsible to the creditor for the principal debt.[1] The principle does not, however, apply to guarantors of obligations under leases which have been disclaimed by the trustee in bankruptcy, see above, and is subject to any actions taken by the creditor during the bankruptcy which may affect the guarantee.

An example is to be found in *Re Moss, ex p Hallet.*[2] In that case the principal debtor assigned a life insurance policy on his own life to the creditor as security for his debt and the guarantor agreed to guarantee the payment of the premiums under the policy. The principal debtor became bankrupt without repaying the debt, and the creditor proved in the bankruptcy for the principal money less the value of the life policy. The guarantor sought to prove for his future liability to the creditor but it was held that in placing a value on the policy in his proof the creditor had effectively disposed of his security and thereby discharged the guarantor.

1 Bankruptcy Act 1914, s 28(4); Insolvency Act 1986, s 281(7).
2 [1905] 2 KB 397.

28.11 THE RIGHT OF THE GUARANTOR TO SET OFF PRINCIPAL DEBTOR'S CLAIMS AGAINST CREDITOR

28.11.1 A question arises not infrequently as to how far a guarantor is entitled to rely on a set-off or cross-claim available to the principal debtor against the creditor to reduce or extinguish his liability under the guarantee when the guarantor is called on to pay by the creditor. A common example is the case of the director of a small company who has had to give a personal guarantee to a supplier in order that his company may obtain goods on credit terms. When the supplier proceeds against the director on his guarantee how far may the director rely on any set-off or cross-claim his company may have against the supplier.

28.11.2 A distinction should be drawn between claims which arise out of the same transaction as gave rise to the guaranteed debt, and claims which do not. In the former case no difficulty arises. A guarantor is entitled to the benefit of any set-off which arises out of the same transaction as that in which the guarantee was given. For example, a guarantor of the payment of the price under a contract for the sale of land may plead in reduction of his liability an arbitration award of compensation to the principal debtor by way of abatement in price in respect of a deficiency in acreage.[1]

[1] *Murphy v Glass* (1869) LR 2 PC 408; *Bechervaise v Lewis* (1872) LR 7 PC 372.

28.11.3 In cases where the guarantee was given in a transaction separate to that in which the set off or cross-claim arises the right of the guarantor to rely on the remedies available to the principal debtor is at best uncertain. The Court of Appeal in *Hyundai Shipbuilding and Heavy Industries Co Ltd v Pournaras*[1] appear to have given approval to the passage in Halsbury's Laws of England[2] which reads:

> 'On being sued by the creditor for payment of the debt guaranteed, a surety may avail himself of any right to set off or counterclaim which the principal debtor possesses against the creditor, and any division of the High Court can give effect to it or to any equitable defence raised.'

[1] [1978] 2 Lloyd's Rep 502. This case came before a two-man court under RSC Ord 14.
[2] Halsbury's Laws (4th edn) para 190.

28.11.4 However, the point was not argued before the court and neither in the event, perhaps because of the commercial policy reasons involved, did the court allow the set-off relied on by the guarantor. Additionally the court did not quote the sentence in Halsbury following that quoted above, namely:

> 'Whenever the set-off or counterclaim relied on does not operate directly to reduce the debt guaranteed, the principal debtor should be made a party, so as to bind him and prevent him afterwards claiming payment from the creditor.'

28.11.5 It may be considered wrong in principle that a creditor may obtain payment in full on a guarantee from the guarantor where his claim against the principal debtor, e g for the price, could be met by a set-off, e g for breach of warranty. But as against this there are a number of objections which might be taken against giving the guarantor an unfettered right to make use of the principal debtor's claims against the creditor. Thus:

(a) the cross-claim which is not a mere failure of consideration but an independent claim is vested in the principal debtor who should be entitled to elect whether his damages are to be claimed by set-off/counter-claim or reserved for a separate action;
(b) if the guarantor successfully sets off the cross-claim of the principal debtor, the latter may not be bound by the judgment and may

subsequently recover on the same claim against the creditor; alternatively if the principal debtor is bound by the judgment he will lose the benefit of any part of his cross-claim which may exceed the amount due under the guarantee; or

(c) where there are a number of guarantors with separate liabilities no one should be able to assume a more advantageous position than the others.

28.11.6 In *Wilson v Mitchell.*[1] one co-guarantor who had submitted to judgment against the creditor sought a contribution from his fellow guarantor who had raised a cross-claim of the principal debtor by way of set-off. Finlay LJ sitting at first instance stated that a guarantor could not rely on a counter-claim for breach of warranty open to the principal debtor. But he went on to say that if he were wrong in that view, the counter-claim would not avail the guarantor unless the principal debtor was before the court. In the Australian case *Cellulose Products Ltd v Truda*[2] Isaacs J, in a lengthy judgment reviewing the authorities, held that a guarantor cannot set-off a claim for unliquidated damages available to the principal debtor arising from any breach of contract.

1 [1939] 2 KB 869.
2 (1970) 92 WN (NSW) 561.

28.11.7 A guarantor facing a claim on his guarantee from the creditor and who is aware that the principal debtor has a claim against the creditor ought therefore to ensure that the principal debtor is before the court as third party or in a separate action heard together with the original proceedings. The guarantor may of course join the principal debtor as third party and claim an indemnity from him, and once joined the debtor may join the creditor as fourth party.

CHAPTER 29

Hire Purchase and Consumer Credit; Landlord and Tenant; Licensing; Negotiable Instruments; Administration of Estates

29.1 CONSUMER CREDIT AND HIRE PURCHASE

Bankruptcy of creditor or owner

29.1.1 The interest of the creditor or owner of goods under a consumer credit or hire-purchase transaction forms part of the property of the bankrupt. It will vest in the official receiver or any trustee in bankruptcy when the bankrupt is adjudicated bankrupt under the Old Law or when the bankruptcy order is made under the New Law.[1] The trustee will own any goods which have been bailed to a hirer subject to the terms of the hire agreement. The continuance of the hire agreement will not be affected by the owner's bankruptcy unless there is an express provision to the contrary in the agreement. The trustee may exercise any of the powers over the goods which are specified in the agreement or which would in any event be consistent with the interest of the bailor of goods. An exception, however, may be powers which are held to be personal rights not capable of assignment. In *Re Davis & Co, ex p Rawlings*[2] an owner of furniture let on hire-purchase agreement assigned the agreements, due notice being given to the hirers. The agreements provided that if the hirer defaulted in punctual payment of the hire instalments, the owner might enter upon the hirer's dwelling house and take possession of, remove and sell the furniture. The Court of Appeal held that the licence to enter and take possession of the furniture was a personal right not capable of assignment. The trustee in bankruptcy of the owner may rely on his rights of ownership to recover possession of the goods should the lender be in default, but may not exercise such personal licences as may be granted under the agreement.[3]

1 Bankruptcy Act 1914, ss 38(a) and 167; Insolvency Act 1986, ss 306, 283 and 436.
2 (1888) 22 QBD 193 applied in *Chatterton v Maclean* [1951] 1 All ER 761 (hire purchase of a motor car).
3 *Lucas v Moncrieff* (1905) 21 TLR 683.

Bankruptcy of debtor or hirer

29.1.2 Subject to any express terms of the agreement, the rights of the debtor under the consumer credit or hire-purchase agreement both to exercise powers over the goods and to acquire ownership on the fulfilment of any specified condition pass to the debtor's trustee in bankruptcy. Under the Old Law the doctrine of reputed ownership might apply to vest full property in the goods in the debtor's trustee in bankruptcy. For the doctrine to apply the goods must be in the sole possession order or disposition of the bankrupt at the commencement of the bankruptcy in connection with his trade or business.[1] The bankrupt must be in possession of the goods in circumstances in which he is the reputed owner of them. Such reputation may not arise where it is frequently the case that goods of the particular description are in the possession of hirers for business purposes. For example the courts have taken judicial notice of the fact that hotel-keepers have furniture on hire purchase.[2] With the growth of consumer credit the doctrine is infrequently applied today, and it is not re-enacted in the Insolvency Act 1986.

[1] Bankruptcy Act 1914, s 38; see para 6.3 above.
[2] *Re Parker, ex p Turquand* (1885) 14 QBD 636.

29.1.3 In practice hire-purchase and consumer credit agreements almost invariably give the creditor/owner the right to terminate the agreement where the debtor/hirer commits an act of bankruptcy or has a receiving order made against him. Agreements drafted for use after 29 December 1986 will presumably refer to failure to comply with a demand under the Insolvency Act 1986, s 267 or the making of a bankruptcy order. Where, however, a debtor/hirer becomes bankrupt under a petition presented after 29 December 1986 and his hire-purchase or consumer credit agreement refers to act of bankruptcy or receiving order the creditor/owner faces the fact that neither of these concepts have legal significance. The Insolvency Act's transitional provisions[1] provide that 'acts of bankruptcy' are deemed to include failure to comply with a demand served under the Insolvency Act 1986, s 268(1). There is no equivalent provision, however, in respect of receiving orders.[2]

Where the creditor/owner exercises his right to terminate the agreement on the debtor/hirer's bankruptcy the trustee in bankruptcy's interest in the agreement will be restricted to the rights of the debtor/hirer on termination. Where the agreement is regulated under the Consumer Credit Act 1974 the relevant provisions of Part VII of that Act will be applicable including the restriction on the hirer repossessing the hired goods without an order of the court where at least one-third of the total price for the goods has been paid.[3]

[1] Insolvency Act 1986, Sch 11, para 12.
[2] The provisions of the Insolvency Act 1986, Sch 11, para 11.
[3] Consumer Credit Act 1974, s 90.

Extortionate credit transactions

29.1.4 Under the new law the trustee in bankruptcy may apply to the court to re-open any credit transaction which the debtor entered into within three years of the commencement of the bankruptcy. Any transaction either for or involving credit may be impugned by the trustee where he can show that it was or is extortionate.[1] The transaction is extortionate if, having regard to the risk accepted by the person providing the credit:

(a) the terms of it are or were such as to require grossly exhorbitant payments to be made for the provision of credit whether unconditionally or in specified contingencies; or
(b) it otherwise grossly contravened ordinary principles of fair dealing.[2]

On the making of any application by the trustee it is to be presumed that the transaction concerned is or was extortionate, unless the creditor proves to the contrary.[2] The Court has a wide discretion to make an order when reopening extortionate credit transactions. All or any part of the obligation arising under the transaction may be set aside or varied, orders may be made to return property, release security or repay sums paid under the transaction or a direction made for accounts to be taken.[3]

1 Insolvency Act 1986, s 343.
2 Ibid, s 343(3).
3 Ibid, s 343(4).

29.1.5 The power of the trustee to seek an order reopening an extortionate credit transaction is expressly in place of the power to apply under the Consumer Credit Act 1974.[1] Neither the trustee in bankruptcy nor an undischarged bankrupt may make an application under the 1974 Act. The powers of the court in reopening exorbitant transactions are wider under the Insolvency Act 1986 than under those enacted by the Consumer Credit Act. In contrast to the wide discretion under the Insolvency Act mentioned above, a court order on an application under the Consumer Credit Act is directed to relieving the debtor (or a surety) from payment of any sum in excess of that fairly due and reasonable. Whether in the event the bankruptcy court will use its powers to penalise creditors and leave them less than they would have with an order under the 1974 Act remains to be seen.

1 See Consumer Credit Act 1974, ss 137–139.

29.1.6 It should also be noted that while the Insolvency Act 1986 follows the terms of the Consumer Credit Act 1974[1] in defining an extortionate credit transaction, it does not follow the 1974 Act in specifying various factors to which the court should have regard when determining whether or not the particular transaction is extortionate.[2] It seems improbable, however, that any difference in practice will result for the factors specified in the 1974 Act to which the court shall have regard are matters which no court would ignore when considering whether the credit transaction is extortionate. These factors are:

(a) the interest rates prevailing at the time the credit transaction was made;
(b) the debtor's age, experience, business capacity and state of health;
(c) the degree to which the debtor was under financial pressure when he entered into the credit transaction, and the nature of such pressure;
(d) the degree of risk accepted by the creditor, having regard to the value of the security provided;
(e) the creditor's relationship with the debtor;

(f) whether or not the creditor quoted a colourable cash price for any goods or services included in the credit transaction;
(g) where the credit transaction is linked to a regulated agreement under the Consumer Credit Act 1974, how far the credit transaction was reasonably required for the protection of the debtor or creditor or was in the interest of the debtor; and
(h) any other relevant consideration.

1 Consumer Credit Act 1974, s 138(1).
2 Ibid, s 138(2), (3), (4) and (5).

29.1.7 The provisions governing the content of extortionate credit bargains under the Consumer Credit Act 1974 have been in force since 16 May 1977 but as yet there have been few reported decisions and no judicial guidelines have emerged. Some guidance may be had from decisions under the Moneylenders Acts.[1] Four cases arising under the Consumer Credit Act 1974 are noted. In *Ketley Ltd v Scott*[2] the court held that an interest rate of 48% pa was not extortionate. The debtor there had borrowed £20,800 at very short notice in order to buy a house in which he was a protected tenant. The debtor was unable to raise a mortgage and was at risk of losing his deposit. The creditor, however, accepted a substantial risk, having no time to investigate the debtor's financial position, and lending over 80% of the value of the property. The court found that the debtor knew what he was doing and in the circumstances a loan over three months at 12% interest was not extortionate. In *Wills v Wood*[3] the Court of Appeal drew a distinction between 'extortionate' and 'unwise', stating that the jurisdiction to reopen credit transactions seemed to contemplate at least a substantial imbalance in bargaining power of which one party had taken advantage. The Court of Appeal in *Coldunell Ltd v Gallon*,[4] a case concerned with a son exercising undue influence over his father to secure a loan for the son's business, stated that a lender could not be expected to do more than properly and fairly point out to the guarantor the desirability of obtaining independent advice and to require the documents to be executed in the presence of a solicitor. A lender could not be expected to take steps to ensure that the guarantor did obtain legal advice or to guard against interception of documents. The transaction was a proper commercial bargain, the interest charged being 20% pa, and the lenders acted in an ordinary commercial manner. It could not therefore be an extortionate bargain because undue influence was exerted and improper behaviour took place without the knowledge or connivance of the lenders. In *Davies v Directloans Ltd*[5] a rate of 21.6% (APR)[6] who held not to be extortionate. The borrower had been warned that the cost of credit would be high and there was a significant risk to the lender in advancing the money.

1 See *Meston on Moneylenders* (5th edn) pp 172–190.
2 [1981] ICR 241, Foster J.
3 (1984) 128 Sol Jo 222, CA.
4 [1986] 1 All ER 429.
5 [1986] 2 All ER 783.
6 See the Consumer Credit (Total Charge for Credit) Regulations, SI 1980/51.

Consumer credit licences

29.1.8 A licence is required to carry on a consumer credit business, a consumer hire business or an ancillary credit business.[1] The licence is issued by the Director General of Fair Trading and will be either a standard licence or a group licence.[2] A person who engages in a business requiring a licence when he does not have a valid licence commits an offence[3] and cannot enforce any agreement entered into by him without the requisite order made by the Director General of Fair Trading.[4] A standard licence held by an individual terminates if he is adjudged bankrupt[5] or if he enters into a scheme of arrangement under the Bankruptcy Act 1914 or voluntary arrangement under the Insolvency Act 1986.[6] Where a licence is vested in a partnership it terminates only when all the partners are adjudicated bankrupt or enter into a scheme of or voluntary arrangement.[7] On discharge from bankruptcy a fresh application for a licence will need to be made before a consumer credit or hire business may be resumed.

1 Consumer Credit Act 1974, ss 21(1) and 147(1).
2 Ibid, s 22. Group licences are primarily issued for ancillary credit businesses. Very few have been issued but the group licences in force include:
- (i) a group licence to cover the activities of liquidators, trustees in bankruptcy, receivers and administrators in the course of such work. The licence licenses all credit, hire or ancillary credit transactions. The individual trustee in bankruptcy must, however, already be covered by a standard or group licence (either individual or partnership) to come within the licence;
- (ii) all chartered and certified accountants to carry on consumer credit, credit brokerage, debt-counselling and debt-adjusting business in the course of their accountancy practice;
- (iii) all solicitors holding a practising certificate to carry on consumer credit, credit brokerage, debt-adjusting, debt-counselling and debt-collecting business in the course of their practice as solicitors.

3 Consumer Credit Act 1974, s 39(1).
4 Ibid, s 40, which enables the person concerned to make representations to the Director General in writing or orally: see s 34(1)(b).
5 Ibid, s 37(1)(b).
6 Consumer Credit (Termination of Licences) Regulations 1976. SI 1976/1002, Sch, para 4.
7 Ibid, Sch, paras 8 and 10.

29.2 LANDLORD AND TENANT

29.2.1 Generally, upon the making of a receiving order (under the Old Bankruptcy Law) or a bankruptcy order (New Law) the official receiver acts as receiver and manager of the bankrupt's estate, and may while acting as receiver or manager take any steps considered appropriate or necessary with regard to any leases in the bankrupt's estate. In this connection the official receiver has the same powers as if he were a receiver or manager appointed by the High Court.[1] On the appointment of the trustee in bankruptcy the bankrupt's interest in any lease vests in the trustee. Thereafter, subject to his right of disclaimer, or the operation of a forfeiture clause in case of bankruptcy, the trustee is personally liable under the lease though with a right to be indemnified out of the assets in the estate.[2] He acquires the bankrupt's rights and obligations in full and may therefore, for example, exercise the bankrupt's option to claim a lease,[3] enforce or assign the bankrupt's contract for a lease,[4] or claim against the landlord or tenant, as appropriate, at the end of the lease all the bankrupt tenant or bankrupt landlord could have claimed arising out of the lease.[5] On the other hand, the trustee will also be liable on all tenant's covenants which run with the land, and is a 'successor in title' with regard to any covenant binding the lessor and his successors in title.[6]

The trustee's title is complete upon his appointment without the need for any action on his part. Where the bankrupt is interested in settled land, the legal estate does not vest in the trustee of an estate owner unless and until the estate owner becomes absolutely and beneficially entitled to the settled land, free from all limitations, powers, and charges taking effect under the settlement.[7] Although the bankrupt's life interest in settled land passes to his trustee the Settled Land Act powers do not, but remain exercisable by the tenant for life.[8] The court may, however, make an order authorising the trustee of the settlement to exercise the powers of the tenant for life if satisfied that the tenant has unreasonably refused to exercise his powers having lost his interest by reason of bankruptcy.[9]

The trustee of a freehold property in the estate of the bankrupt may create leases, and the trustee of a tenant bankrupt may grant sub-leases to the extent permissible under the lease.

1 Insolvency Act 1986, s 287(2).
2 See *Titterton v Cooper* (1882) 9 QBD 473.
3 *Buckland v Papillon* (1866) 2 Ch App 67.
4 *Crosbie v Tooke* (1833) 1 My & K 431.
5 *Alloway v Steere* (1882) 10 QBD 22.
6 *Re Wright, ex p Landau v Trustee* [1949] Ch 729.
7 Settled Land Act 1925, s 103 as amended by the Insolvency Act 1985, Sch 8.
8 Settled Land Act 1925, s 104.
9 Ibid, s 24.

Bankruptcy of lessor

29.2.2 The reversion in the bankrupt's property held on lease vests in the trustee by operation of law.[1] The trustee holds the reversion subject to all such rights as were maintainable against the bankrupt. Where a trustee claimed arrears of rent from a tenant whose tenancy was subject to the Rent Acts, he could be met by the tenant's claim to deduct all payments of rent above the recoverable limit although those payments had been made to the bankrupt.[2] It is possible that a reversionary interest is subject to such onerous covenants or other burdens that the trustee wishes to exercise his right to disclaim the reversion, though the instances of this happening must be rare indeed.

1 Bankruptcy Act 1914, ss 53 and 167; Insolvency Act 1986, ss 306, 283 and 436.
2 *Hole v Cuzen* [1953] 1 All ER 87 and nb Rent Act 1977, s 57 as to recoverability of rent paid above registered limit.

Bankruptcy of lessee

29.2.3 The lessee becoming bankrupt will frequently activate a proviso for re-entry. The landlord will usually only be able to rely on the adjudication order (Old Bankrupty Law) or bankruptcy order (New Law) as forfeiting the lease. The presentation of his own petition by the debtor lessee is not a breach of a covenant not to assign.[1]

Although a proviso for re-entry by the lessor on the bankruptcy of the lessee has for many years been a standard proviso it is not a 'usual' covenant[2] and therefore will not be implied into a lease where an agreement for a lease does not specify the covenants to be contained in it.

The proviso for re-entry on bankruptcy will run with the land and although as usually drafted, is expressed to come into effect 'if the lessee, his executors, administrators or assigns' become bankrupt, it will only come into effect if the person holding the term becomes bankrupt.[3] The lessor cannot rely on the bankruptcy of the original lessee after he has assigned the residue of the term to the assignee.

The proviso for re-entry may be effected by peaceful entry, save where the property has been let as a dwelling[4] or by action for possession.

1 *Re Riggs, ex p Lovell* [1901] 2 KB 16.
2 *Hyde v Warden* (1877) 3 Ex D 72; *Chester v Buckingham Travel Ltd* [1981] 1 All ER 386.
3 *Smith v Gronow* [1891] 2 QB 394.
4 Protection from Eviction Act 1977, s 3.

29.2.4 Where court proceedings are required the landlord must comply with the Law of Property Act 1925, s 146, and serve a notice specifying the breach complained of. As the breach is not capable of remedy no requirement need be made for the lessee to remedy it. Relief may be sought from forfeiture but the circumstances in which relief may be granted are closely prescribed by the Law of Property Act 1925, s 146(9) and (10). If the applicant for relief cannot bring himself within these provisions there is no equitable jurisdiction in the court on which he may seek relief.[1]

Section 146(9) excludes: (and therefore excludes relief) (a) agricultural land, (b) mines or minerals, (c) a public house or licensed premises, (d) a house let as a dwelling house with the use of furniture, books, works of art or other moveable chattels, and (e) any property with respect to which the personal qualifications of the tenant are of importance for the preservation of the value or character of the property, or on the ground of neighbourhood to the lessor, or to any person holding under him.

In all other cases s 146(10) restricts the granting of relief to a period of one year from the date of bankruptcy and then only to cases where the lessee's interest is sold within that year. A 'sale' to qualify for relief against forfeiture, if not completed by conveyance, must be an absolute contract for sale concluded with the intending purchaser.[2]

Thus the trustee has one year in which to dispose of the bankrupt's leasehold interest before the landlord may enforce a right for re-entry.

1 *Official Custodian for Charities & Parway Estates Developments Ltd* [1985] Ch 151.
2 *Re Castle & Sons Ltd, Mitchell v Henry Castle & Sons Ltd* (1906) 94 LT 396.

29.2.5 Where a lease has been assigned and the assignee becomes bankrupt the lessor may proceed against the original lessee for obligations due under the lease, at least until such time as the lease is disclaimed. The lessee is not here in the position of a surety, but has a primary liability to the lessor. He will, however, have the benefit of a covenant of indemnity on the part of the assignee[1] and may prove in the bankruptcy of the assignee on that covenant not only where he has had to make payment to the lessor, but also in respect of contingent liabilities.[2]

Once the bankrupt assignee has his discharge he is released from all further liability on his covenant, including such contingent liabilities as may arise from covenants to repair and yield up in good condition.[3]

1 If not express this covenant is implied by Law of Property Act 1925, s 77, Sch 2, Part IX.
2 Insolvency Act 1986, s 322(3).
3 Ibid, s 281(1).

29.2.6 On the bankruptcy of an assignor, the right to indemnify under the assignee's covenant of indemnity is an asset which the trustee of the bankrupt assignor is able to assign. While it is seemingly unlikely that a purchaser might be found for such a chose, where there have been several assignments, the original lessee, when called upon to meet the obligations under the lease, might well prefer to proceed against a solvent assignee who took the lease from the bankrupt assignor, rather than prove in the bankruptcy of the party to whom he assigned.[1]

1 *Re Perkins, Poyser & Beyfus* [1898] 2 Ch 182.

29.2.7 A surety of the lessee will remain liable to the lessor in respect of the obligations owed by the lessee unless and until the lease is disclaimed by the trustee. This liability is not affected by the discharge of the lessee.[1]

1 Insolvency Act 1986, s 281(7).

Landlord's proof and distress for rent

29.2.8 The landlord's right to distrain for rent is, in the case of the bankruptcy of the tenant, restricted by statute to a maximum of six months' rent accrued before the commencement of the bankruptcy.[1] The actual period in respect of which the distress is levied is not limited and accordingly the six months' rent distrained need not necessarily have arisen immediately prior to the commencement of the bankruptcy.

The right to distrain is exercisable against the trustee after the bankrupt's goods have vested in him[2] but is lost on the bankrupt obtaining his discharge.[3]

The statutory limitation only applies to distress for rent. Where there is a right to distrain in respect of other obligations of the bankrupt besides rent, it is exercisable without restriction even though the right to distrain it is expressed to be exercisable as if distraint for rent.[4]

1 Bankruptcy Act 1914, s 35(1); Insolvency Act 1986, s 347(1).
2 Insolvency Act 1986, s 347(9).
3 Ibid, s 347(5).
4 Ibid, s 347(8).

29.2.9 Where a landlord levies distress on a tenant against whom a bankruptcy petition has already been presented and a bankruptcy order is subsequently made on that petition, then the landlord holds (a) any distress in excess of six months' rent and (b) any distress for rent arising after levy on behalf of the estate.

The trustee may set aside any distress levied in respect of a sham rent or an increase in rent designed to improve the landlord's position in the bankruptcy.[1] The right to distrain attaches only to the goods and chattels involved so that if the landlord acts too slowly and the goods have been sold by the trustee and removed from the premises, he has no right to follow the proceeds of sale.[2]

[1] *Re Knight, ex p Voisey* (1882) 21 Ch D 442.
[2] *Bradyll v Ball* (1785) 1 Bro CC 427.

29.2.10 Subject to the right to distrain the landlord must prove in the bankruptcy as any other creditor. In general terms the bankruptcy provisions relating to mutual credits and set off apply between landlord and tenant, but it appears that the landlord cannot set off arrears of rent against tenant-like compensation to which the trustee becomes entitled after the tenancy has vested in him.[1] The landlord, in proving for his rent is an ordinary creditor. Where, however, he has distrained upon goods of the bankrupt within three months of the commencement of the bankruptcy those goods, or the proceeds of their sale, are charged with the preferential debt of the bankrupt estate.[2] Should the landlord surrender any goods so charged to the trustee, or make a payment to the trustee in place of surrender, then to that extent, the landlord ranks as a preferential creditor except as against so much of the bankrupt's estate as has been made available by virtue of the surrender or payment.[3]

[1] *Alloway v Steere* (1882) 10 QBD 22. In this case the tenancy was of a farm and the trustee was entitled to the landlord's allowances for tillage and cultivation without set off for rent accrued before the bankruptcy. See, however, *Re Wilson, ex p Lord Hastings* (1893) 62 LJQB 628 where the court found a custom of the country allowing such a set off.
[2] Insolvency Act 1986, s 347(3).
[3] Ibid, s 347(4).

29.2.11 Where the trustee in bankruptcy remains in possession after the lease vests in him and does not disclaim, all rent accruing after the commencement of the bankruptcy may be distrained for and no leave of the court is required.[1]

[1] *Re Binns, ex p Hale* (1875) 1 Ch D 285.

Trustee's right of disclaimer

29.2.12 Under both the Old Bankruptcy Law[1] and the New Law,[2] the trustee of a bankrupt lessee has a right to disclaim leasehold property which is unsaleable or is not readily saleable notwithstanding any attempts made to dispose of it. Although in many cases there is unlikely to be any material practical difference between the operation of the Old Bankruptcy Law and the New Law, the Insolvency Act 1986 has brought about a number of changes.

[1] Bankruptcy Act 1914, s 54.
[2] Insolvency Act 1986, ss 315–321.

Disclaimer under the Old Law

29.2.13 The Bankruptcy Act 1914, s 54(1) imposes a time limit on disclaimer. The trustee has 12 months from his appointment, or where he does not become aware of the lease within one month of his appointment, 12 months from the date on which he does become aware of it. In either case however the court may extend the period of disclaimer.

29.2.14 A trustee may not disclaim a lease without the leave of the court, except in cases prescribed by the Rules. The Rules,[1] however, place the onus of taking a disclaimer before the court on the lessor or the person interested in the lease.

The cases prescribed by the Rules where a lease may be disclaimed without leave are:

1 where the bankrupt has not sublet the premises or part of them or created any mortgage or charge on the lease.
  (a) the estate is administered in a summary manner under Bankruptcy Act 1914, s 129.
  (b) the trustee serves the lessor with notice of his intention to disclaim, and the lessor does not within seven days after receipt of the notice give a cross notice to the trustee requiring the matter to be brought before the court;

2 where the bankrupt has created a sub-letting or a mortgage or charge upon the lease, and the trustee serves notice of his intention to disclaim on the lessor, sub-lessees, or mortgagees and none of them within 14 days after receipt of the notice require the matter to be brought before the court.

Should the question of a disclaimer go before the court, the court has power, before or on granting leave to disclaim, to require notices to be served and to impose such conditions as it may think fit and to make orders with respect to tenant's fixtures, improvements or any other matter arising out of the tenancy.[2]

1 Bankruptcy Rules 1952, r 278.
2 Bankruptcy Act 1914, s 54(3). As to the exercise of the court's discretion see *Re Clarke, ex p East & West India Dock Co* (1881) 17 Ch D 759, CA.

29.2.15 The lessor, sub-lessee or mortgagee requiring the matter to go before the court cannot claim his costs against the estate unless the court is satisfied that the application was necessary in order to do justice between the parties.[1] A disclaimer without leave when leave is required is void[2] and no disclaimer is operative until it is filed in court with particulars of the interest disclaimed and a statement of the persons to whom notice of the disclaimer has been given.[3]

1 Bankruptcy Rules 1952, r 278(4).
2 Ibid, r 278(2).
3 Ibid, r 278(3).

29.2.16 A trustee is not entitled to disclaim any lease or other property if he has received a written application from any person interested in that property requiring him to decide whether he will disclaim or not and the trustee has not disclaimed within 28 days or such extended period as the court may allow.[1]

[1] Bankruptcy Act 1914, s 54(4). For forms for application and disclaimer see 7 Court Forms (21st edn) forms 428–432.

29.2.17 On the application of any person claiming an interest in the property the court, on hearing such persons as it thinks fit, may make an order for the vesting of the lease in any person entitled to it on such terms as the court thinks just.

Once the vesting order is made the property vests accordingly in the person named in it without further conveyance or assignment.[1] The court may not vest the lease in an underlessee or mortgagee except on terms making the person in whom it is vested either (a) subject to the same liabilities and obligations as the bankrupt was under at the date the petition was filed or (b) subject to same liabilities and obligations as an assignee would have been made if the lease had been assigned on that date.[2] If no-one claiming under the bankrupt is willing to accept these terms the court has power to vest the bankrupt's estate in the property in any person liable either personally or in a representative character, and either alone or jointly with the bankrupt, to perform the lessee's covenants in the lease, freed and discharged from all estates, interests or incumbrances created by the bankrupt.[3]

[1] If the land concerned is registered the order must direct the attention of the registrar in favour of the person in whom the lease is vested. No right to indemnity arises by reason of the alteration: Land Registration Act 1925, s 42(2).
[2] Bankruptcy Act 1914, s 54(6).
[3] Ibid, s 54(6), proviso.

29.2.18 Any person injured by the operation of a disclaimer is deemed to be a creditor of the bankrupt to the extent of the injury and may accordingly prove for any loss sustained as a debt in the bankruptcy.[1] If, therefore, a lessor can only relet premises at a reduced rent he may prove for the difference over the remainder of the term.[2] Should the lease disclaimed be of partnership premises the lessor may prove against the separate estate of each partner.[3]

[1] Bankruptcy Act 1914, s 54(8).
[2] *Re McEwan, ex p Blake* (1879) 11 Ch D 572; *Re New Oriental Bank Corpn (No 2)* [1895] 1 Ch 753.
[3] *Re Shand, ex p Corbett* (1880) 14 Ch D 122.

Disclaimer under New Law

29.2.19 There is no time limit on disclaimer imposed by the Insolvency Act 1986, s 315. Neither is there an underlying requirement for the trustee to obtain the leave of the court.

29.2.20 A trustee may disclaim an onerous lease by giving the prescribed notice[1] and that notice is effective to disclaim the lease without more ado subject to the following four cases:

(i) should the lease be after acquired property, i e property which has been acquired by or devolved upon the bankrupt after the commencement of the bankruptcy, and the trustee has claimed it for the bankrupt's estate, he may not subsequently disclaim it without leave of the court;[2]

(ii) where a person interested in the property has applied in writing to the trustee, requiring the trustee to decide whether to disclaim or not and the trustee has not disclaimed within 28 days of the notice then the trustee loses his right to disclaim,[3]

(iii) where there is an underlessee or mortgagee claiming under the bankrupt, the disclaimer does not take effect unless a copy of it has been served (so far as the trustee is aware of their addresses) on every underlessee or mortgagee and either
  (a) no application is made under the Insolvency Act 1986, s 320 (see below) within 14 days of the date of service of the last notice to be served, or
  (b) where such an application has been made, the court directs that the disclaimer should take effect.

  When the court makes a direction that the disclaimer should take effect it may make any order it thinks fit with respect to fixtures, tenant's improvements and other matters arising out of the lease.[4]

(iv) where the property disclaimed is a dwelling house the disclaimer does not take effect unless a copy of the disclaimer has been served (so far as the trustee is aware of their addresses) on every person in occupation of or claiming a right to occupy the dwelling house and either
  (a) no application is made under the Insolvency Act 1986, s 320 (see below) within 14 days of the date of service of the last notice to be served, or
  (b) where such an application has been made, the court directs that the disclaimer should take effect.[5]

1 Insolvency Act 1986, s 315(1). The notice of disclaimer is governed by the Individual Insolvency Rules 1986, r 6.178, form 6.61. It must contain sufficient particulars of the property disclaimed as to enable it to be easily identified. Two copies must be delivered to the court to be endorsed with the date of delivery, and once endorsed one copy is returned to the trustee. Within seven days of receiving his copy back from the court the trustee must under r 6.179, send or give a copy of the notice to any person who claims under the bankrupt as underlessee or mortgagee or who is in occupation of or claims a right to occupy the property as a dwelling house. Should the trustee subsequently discover a person entitled to notice of disclaimer he should give him notice unless that person is already aware of the disclaimer or the court orders that notice need not be given: r 6.179(6). As and when a trustee gives notice to any person entitled to receive it he must file a report at court: r 6.181.

2 Insolvency Act 1986, s 315(4). The trustee may apply ex parte under Individual Insolvency Rules, r 6.182 which requires that the application be accompanied by a report which (a) identifies the property, (b) sets out the reasons for disclaiming despite claiming it for the estate, and (c) specifies the persons (if any) informed of the application. The court may give a hearing to any person entitled to apply for a vesting order under the Insolvency Act 1986, s 320.

3 Insolvency Act 1986, s 316(1), Individual Insolvency Rules 1986, r 6.183 applies in the case of an application by an interested party who should use Form 6.62 the 'notice to elect'.

4 Insolvency Act 1986, s 317(1) and (2).

5 Insolvency Act 1986, s 318, Individual Insolvency Rules 1986, r 6.186.

29.2.21 If it appears to the trustee in bankruptcy that there is a person who claims, or may claim, to have an interest in property which he may disclaim, the trustee may give notice to that person requiring him to declare within 14 days whether he does indeed claim any such interest and the nature and extent of it.[1] If the notice is not complied with the trustee is entitled to assume that the person concerned has no interest in the relevant property.[2]

[1] Individual Insolvency Rules 1986, r 6.184(1), notice should be in form 6.63.
[2] Ibid, r 6.184(2).

29.2.22 Any person sustaining loss or damage in consequence of the operation of a disclaimer is deemed to be a creditor of the bankrupt to the extent of the loss and damage and accordingly may prove for the loss or damage as a bankruptcy debt.[1] Any vesting order made under the Insolvency Act 1986, s 320 is to be taken into account in assessing the extent of any loss or damage sustained.[2]

[1] Insolvency Act 1986, s 315(5) and see nn 2 and 3 to para 29.2.18 above. It may also be noted that Individual Insolvency Rules 1986, r 6.180 provides that the trustee may at any time give notice of disclaimer to any person who in his opinion ought to be informed of the disclaimer, in the public interest or otherwise.
[2] Insolvency Act 1986, s 320(5).

29.2.23 Any disclaimer of property by the trustee in bankruptcy is presumed valid and effective, unless it is proved that he was in breach of his duties in respect of giving notice of disclaimer or otherwise in breach of the Insolvency Act 1986, s 315 or the Individual Insolvency Rules, Chap 14.[1]

[1] Individual Insolvency Rules 1986, r 6.185.

29.2.24 *Applications under the Insolvency Act 1986, s 320.* Where the trustee has disclaimed a lease an application may be made to the court for an order vesting the lease in the applicant or a person on his behalf by:
(a) any person deriving an interest in the lease;
(b) any person under any liability in respect of the lease which is not discharged by the disclaimer, e g a surety, but the court will only make an order to such an applicant where it appears just to do so for the purpose of compensating the applicant in respect of the disclaimer; or
(c) where the leasehold property is property in a dwelling house any person who, at the time when the bankruptcy petition was presented, was in occupation of or entitled to occupy the dwelling house.

An application to the court under the Insolvency Act 1986, s 320 by any person for the vesting of disclaimed property must be made within three months of the applicant becoming aware of the disclaimer, or of his receiving a copy of the notice of disclaimer, whichever is the earlier.[1]

If the court makes a vesting order it must be on terms that the person in whom the lease is vested is either (a) subject to the same liabilities and obligations to which the bankrupt was subject under the lease, on the day the bankruptcy petition was presented, or (b) if the court thinks fit, subject to the same liabilities and obligations as an assignee would be subject to if taking an assignment on that day. An order may be made vesting part only of the property in the applicant.[2]

[1] Individual Insolvency Rules 1986, r 6.186.
[2] Insolvency Act 1986, s 321(2).

29.2.25 If an applicant declines to accept an order vesting the leasehold property in him on the terms specified by the court, that person is thereafter excluded from all interest in the property.[1] Where no person is willing to accept a vesting order the court may vest the estate or interest of the bankrupt in the property in any person who is liable, in whatever capacity, to perform the lessee's covenants in the lease. In vesting the estate or interest in such a person the court may discharge him from all estates, incumbrances and interests created by the bankrupt.[2] A vesting order under s 320 of the 1986 Act does not need to be completed by any conveyance assignment or transfer.[3]

1 Insolvency Act 1986, s 321(4).
2 Ibid, s 321(3).
3 Ibid, s 320(6); Law of Property Act 1925, s 52(2) and (6) as amended by Insolvency Act 1985, Sch 8 and see n 1 to para 29.2.17 above regarding registered land.

Effect of disclaimer

29.2.26 Under both the Old Bankruptcy Law and the New Law the disclaimer:

(a) operates so as to determine, as from the date of the disclaimer, the rights, interests and liabilities of the bankrupt and his estate in or in respect of the property disclaimed;
(b) discharges the trustee from all personal liability in respect of that property as from the commencement of the trusteeship; but
(c) except so far as is necessary for the purpose of releasing the bankrupt and his estate and the trustee from liability does not affect the rights or liabilities of any other person.[1]

The bankrupt's interest in the lease is determined by the disclaimer and cannot be revived by the annulment of the bankruptcy.[2] The disclaimer does not however fully determine the lease when the bankrupt lessee has sub-let part of the property. In the absence of a vesting order the sub-lessee may be liable both to distress for the whole rent reserved by the lease or for forfeiture for non-payment of rent or breach of covenant on the part of the lessee.[3]

1 Bankruptcy Act 1914, s 54(2); Insolvency Act 1986, s 315(2).
2 *Re Hyams, ex p Lindsay v Hyams* (1923) 93 LJ Ch 184, CA.
3 *Re Thompson and Cottrell's Contract* [1943] Ch 97.

Disclaimer after assignment of lease

29.2.27 Where the bankrupt is the assignee of a lease, the disclaimer of his interest in it by his trustee in bankruptcy does not bring the lease to an end. The lease remains in existence although without an owner until a vesting order is made. Accordingly the original lessee remains liable to pay the reserved rent and on the covenants under the lease under his contract with the landlord.[1] The position of the original lessee is to be contrasted with the position of a guarantor of the obligations of the bankrupt assignee. The guarantor's liability to the landlord depends upon there being primary liability on the part of the assignee. Accordingly when the trustee disclaims the assignee's interest, the primary liability is at an end and the guarantor is no longer liable to the landlord.[2] Should the assignor become bankrupt following the bankruptcy of the assignee, his trustee may disclaim his obligations under the lease for even though the lease may not be vested in the assignor the definition of 'property' which may be disclaimed is sufficiently wide to cover such obligations to the landlord.[3]

[1] *Warnford Investments Ltd v Duckworth* [1979] Ch 127, where in a careful judgment Megarry V-C considered the respective positions of the various parties who may become involved at some length; *Hill v East and West India Dock Co* (1884) 9 App Cas 448.
[2] As in *Stacey v Hill* [1910] 1 KB 660, though this was a case where the original lessee became bankrupt without their having been an assignment.
[3] Insolvency Act 1986, s 315(2). 'Property' is defined in s 436 as including '. . . obligations and every description of interest, whether present or future or vested or contingent, arising out of, or incidental to property'.

Rent Act tenancies

29.2.28 Where the landlord of a Rent Act tenancy becomes bankrupt, the trustee and any assignees of the reversion will continue to be bound by the Rent Acts. The protection afforded by the Rent Acts is personal to the tenant who exercises his contractual rights to occupy the property.[1] Accordingly on the bankruptcy of a contractual tenant protected by the Rent Act, a disclaimer by the trustee destroys both contractual and statutory protection. The landlord can recover possession from the bankrupt because the bankrupt has lost his contractual rights and, with them, his right to statutory protection.[2] Should the trustee not disclaim, but allow the bankrupt to reside in the property, the bankrupt may continue his occupation so long as the lease continues. However, as soon as the lease comes to an end, which in the case of a periodic tenancy may soon be achieved by notice to quit, the bankrupt has no further rights of occupation. He cannot become a statutory tenant because having no contractual interest he was not a protected tenant immediately before the termination of the lease.

The position is to be contrasted with that of the statutory tenant who becomes bankrupt. His statutory tenancy does not vest in the trustee in bankruptcy and therefore he will continue to enjoy a personal right to occupy the dwelling house.[3]

[1] Rent Act 1977, s 2.
[2] *Reeves v Davies* [1921] 2 KB 486; *Smalley v Quarrier* [1975] 2 All ER 688.
[3] *Sutton v Dorf* [1932] 2 KB 304.

29.2.29 A contractual tenant who has committed an act of forfeiture effective at the time of bankruptcy has determined the lease before the commencement of the bankruptcy and therefore there is no lease for the trustee to disclaim. The tenant has therefore become a statutory tenant and may continue to reside in the dwelling house.[1] A landlord is, however, not obliged to accept an act of forfeiture as determining the lease. He is entitled to waive it, subject to the risk that it is a once and for all breach so that he cannot rely on it subsequently, and the astute landlord, wanting to obtain possession of the premises will be careful to waive any forfeiture and ensure that a contractual tenancy subsists at the commencement of the bankruptcy. The chances are that the trustee will disclaim and that the landlord will be able to obtain possession of the premises. The tenant's legal adviser in these circumstances should check whether any notices of increase in rent have been served during the tenancy. Such a notice operates to convert a protected tenancy into a statutory tenancy if a notice to quit could have been served by the landlord at the same time to bring the contractual tenancy to an end before the date specified in the notice of increase.[2]

This rather anomalous position under the Old Bankruptcy Law in which the statutory tenant is in a distinctly better position than the protected tenant is capable of remedy under the New Law. The contractual Rent Act protected tenant whose lease is disclaimed by his trustee in bankruptcy may apply to the court under the Insolvency Act 1986, s 320(2) for an order vesting the tenancy in him. The spouse of the bankrupt, having a right to occupy the dwelling house under the Matrimonial Homes Act 1983 may also apply for a vesting order in respect of the dwelling house.

[1] *Smith v Odder* (1949) 93 Sol Jo 433.
[2] Rent Act 1977, s 49(4).

29.2.30 After the protected tenancy has vested in him the trustee in bankruptcy is as bound by the provisions of the Rent Act as anyone else, so far as it applies to a tenant not in occupation. Therefore, a trustee who charges an illegal premium on the assignment of the tenancy must repay it in full irrespective of the amount of the estate still left in his hands at the time of the order.[1]

[1] *Adair v Murrell* (1981) 263 Estates Gazette 66.

29.3 LICENCES FOR INTOXICATING LIQUOR

Under the provisions of the Licensing Act 1964 a 'justices on-licence' is required for the sale or consumption of intoxicating liquor either on or off the premises for which the licence is granted, and a 'justices off-licence' for the sale of liquor for consumption off the premises only.

A licence is personal to the licensee and does not constitute property. It does not, therefore, pass to the bankrupt's trustee in bankruptcy on the commencement of the bankruptcy.[1] However, where the holder of a justices licence is adjudged bankrupt, or a trustee or supervisor is appointed in pursuance of a composition, scheme or voluntary arrangement to administer the relevant property or manage the licence-holder's business, the trustee is in the same position as if a protection order had been validly granted to him to carry on business under the licence on the date of the commencement of bankruptcy.[2] The protection order confers on its holder the same authority as that conferred by the licence which was previously in force for the premises. It continues in force until the conclusion of the second licensing session begun after the date of its coming into force, after which, if the trustee wishes to continue the business, he must apply for a transfer of the licence to him personally.

A trustee in bankruptcy or the supervisor of a scheme of voluntary arrangement together with a new tenant to whom the premises have been assigned in the management of the debtor's estate form one of the classes of persons to which the Licensing Act 1964 specifically empowers the licensing justices to grant a transfer of a justices' licence.[3]

[1] *Re Britnor, ex p Royle* (1877) 46 LJ Bcy 85.
[2] Licensing Act 1964, s 10(5) as amended by the Insolvency Act 1985, Sch 8, para 10.
[3] S 8(1)(c), as amended by the Insolvency Act 1985.

29.4 NEGOTIABLE INSTRUMENTS

Rights of holder

29.4.1 The Bills of Exchange Act 1882 expressly provides that the 'rules in bankruptcy relating to bills of exchange, promissory notes, and cheques, shall continue to apply' to such instruments notwithstanding anything in the Act. The 'Bankruptcy Rules' referred to are not simply the rules of procedure and practice that are so called, but the law of bankruptcy generally.[1]

[1] Bills of Exchange Act 1882, s 97(1); *Re Keever, ex p Trustee of Property of Bankrupt v Midland Bank Ltd* [1967] 1 Ch 182.

29.4.2 The holder of a bill of exchange or promissory note may proceed against the various parties liable on it until he has received payment in full. He must give credit for any payments received before making his proof, but, subject to this, the holder may prove in the bankruptcy of any party liable on the bill to the full amount of the sum due on the bill even though other parties to the bill are also liable on it.[1] Where the drawer or indorsee of the bill is bankrupt, the holder may give notice of dishonour either to the trustee or the bankrupt party himself.[2] The holder of a bill or note payable on demand or on notice may prove in the bankruptcy even though no demand was made or notice given before the commencement of the bankruptcy.[3] Bills and notes that are not due at the commencement of the bankruptcy may be proved, but subject to a deduction for early payment.[4]

[1] *Re Thompson and Mildred, ex p Prescott, Grote & Co* (1834) 4 Deac & Ch 23; *Re Corson, ex p De Tastet* (1810) 1 Rose 10; *Re Stein, ex p Royal Bank of Scotland* (1815) 2 Rose 197.
[2] Bills of Exchange Act 1882, s 49(10).
[3] *Ex p Beaufoy* (1787) Cooke's Bkpt Laws/8th ed. 180; *Re Mayor, ex p Whitworth* (1841) 2 Mont D & De G 158 (cases on demand), and *Re Mantle, ex p Elgar* (1826) 2 GL & J 1, *Re Dowman, ex p Dowman* (1827) 2 GL & J 241 and *Re Browne & Wingrove, ex p Ador* [1891] 2 QB 574 (cases on notice). On administering the estate the trustee will have to make any adjustment appropriate for early payment where a lengthy period of notice is specified in the note or bill.
[4] Bankruptcy Act 1914, Sch II, r 22, which provides for a rebate at 5% pa computed from the declaration of a dividend to the time when the bill or note would on its terms have become payable; Individual Insolvency Rules 1986, r 6.114.

29.4.3 Where the holder of a bill has received it from the bankrupt as security for a debt due to him which is smaller than the sum payable under the bill, the holder must restrict his proof to the actual amount of his debt due at the time of the bankruptcy.[1] Similarly where the creditor has received a bill from the bankrupt as guarantor for a third party debtor; the creditor/holder may only prove for the sum actually due to him.[2] However, a holder in due course who has received the bill from the drawer as security for a debt less in amount than the bill, may prove against the creditor's estate for the whole amount of the bill though he may not receive dividends beyond the amount of the debt.[3]

[1] *Ex p Bloxham* (1802) 6 Ves 600.
[2] *Re Willats, ex p Reader* (1819) Buck 381.
[3] *Re Bunyard, ex p Newton* (1880) 16 Ch D 330.

29.4.4 A holder who has purchased a bill in good faith for less than its face value may prove against the estate of any party to the bill for the whole amount.[1] Where the holder has bought a bill or promissory note of the bankrupt after the commencement of the bankruptcy he may prove against the estate provided that at the commencement of the bankruptcy it was held by a person entitled to prove.[2]

[1] *Jones v Gordon* (1877) 2 App Cas 616.
[2] *Re Bowles, ex p Rogers* (1820) Buck 490; *Re Hardcastle, ex p Botten* (1833) Mont & B 412.

29.4.5 A proof in respect of money owed on a bill of exchange, promissory note, cheque or other negotiable instrument cannot be admitted unless the instrument or a copy certified by the creditor or his authorised representative to be a true copy is produced.[1] The trustee may, however, allow proof without production of the instrument or certified copy in New Law cases only.

[1] Individual Insolvency Rules 1986, r 6.108; Bankruptcy Rules 1952, r 250.

Secured bills of exchange

29.4.6 Secured bills are bills accepted by a person who has received goods from the drawer by way of security, enabling the drawer to discount the bill and obtain cash. The drawer is entitled to redeem his goods by paying the amount due, and, where the goods are sold he is entitled to receive back any surplus above the amount due to the acceptor. The acceptor becomes a creditor of the drawer on paying the bill and can realise his security.[1]

On the bankruptcy of the drawer his trustee is in no better position than the drawer was and may only recover the goods by paying the amount due. The acceptor may prove against the drawer's estate but is ill advised to do so as, by exercising his right of proof, he must give up his security and return the goods.[2]

Where the acceptor becomes bankrupt his trustee is entitled to enforce the security if it is not redeemed by the drawer. Should the goods realise less than the amount due on the bills the trustee may recover the difference from the drawer; if the goods realise more the surplus must be paid over.

Where both drawer and acceptor are bankrupt, the goods pledged are applied in taking up the bills which were drawn against them. This follows the rule in *Ex p Waring*[3] that if both drawer and acceptor of a bill of exchange become bankrupt, the holder of the bill is entitled to have any securities given to the acceptor for accepting the bill applied in paying the amount due under the bill.

[1] *Re Suse, ex p Dever* (1884) 13 QBD 766; *Re Broad, ex p Neck* (1884) 13 QBD 740.
[2] Bankruptcy Act 1914, s 32, Sch 2 rr 10–18; Insolvency Act 1986, s 322; Individual Insolvency Rules 1986, r 6.109.
[3] (1815) 19 Ves 345 and see *City Bank v Luckie* (1870) 5 Ch App 773 and *Royal Bank of Scotland v Commercial Bank of Scotland* (1882) 7 App Cas 366.

Accommodation bills

29.4.7 An accommodation bill is one which is accepted or indorsed without consideration moving to the party making himself liable on the bill, for the purpose of lending his name to some other person. The party so making himself liable is in effect a guarantor and if he pays under the bill he may prove in the bankruptcy of the other person.[1] Where there is mutual accommodation by cross-acceptances and one party becomes bankrupt the other being solvent must take up his acceptance. Provided this is done the solvent party may prove in the bankruptcy of the bankrupt acceptor.[2] Where both parties become bankrupt, neither trustee can prove in the bankruptcy of the other party until the holders of the bills have been fully paid, irrespective of any inequality of the accommodation transactions.[3]

[1] *Re Fothergill, ex p Turquand* (1876) 3 Ch D 445.
[2] *Re Bowness and Padmore* (1789) 1 Cooke's Bkpt Laws 8th edn, 183.
[3] *Ex p Walker* (1798) 4 Ves 373.

29.5 TRUSTEE AND ADMINISTRATION OF ESTATES

Bankruptcy of trustee

29.5.1 Where a trustee of a trust himself becomes bankrupt, the trust property does not pass to the bankrupt trustee's trustee in bankruptcy. It remains vested in the trustee upon the trusts to which it is subject.[1] The court has a general power to appoint a new trustee whenever it is expedient to do so under the Trustee Act 1925.[2] This statute expressly provides that the bankruptcy of a trustee may be grounds for the exercise of this power. The interests of the beneficiaries are the court's paramount concern and where the nature of the trust requires the trustee to handle trust funds in circumstances in which he might misappropriate them a bankrupt trustee should be removed. Equally where there is no danger to the trust property a bankrupt trustee might not be removed.[3] A trustee who has defaulted is liable to make restitution to the trust, and where trust property or the proceeds of its disposition can be identified it may be traced in law or equity. Under the Old Law, where a defaulting trustee seeks to make restitution for his breach of trust shortly before his impending bankruptcy, the trustee in bankruptcy could not ordinarily expect to be able to set the restitution aside as a fraudulent preference,[4] but such acts may be more open to attack by the trustee in bankruptcy under the Insolvency Act 1986,[5] if indeed they warrant it.

After obtaining his discharge the defaulting trustee is protected from any further liability for his breach of trust, unless the breach was fraudulent and he was a party to the fraud.[6]

[1] Bankruptcy Act 1914, s 38(1); Insolvency Act 1986, s 283(3)(a).
[2] Trustee Act 1925, s 41. This power may be exercised either in the High Court or, within the jurisdictional limits, the county court.
[3] *Re Barker's Trust* (1875) 1 Ch D 43; *Re Adams Trusts* (1879) 12 Ch D 634.
[4] *Re Lake, ex p Dyer* [1901] 1 KB 710.
[5] Insolvency Act 1986, ss 339–341.
[6] Bankruptcy Act 1914, s 28(1); Insolvency Act 1986, s 281(3).

Bankruptcy of co-trustee

29.5.2 There is no particular legal effect on a trustee whose co-trustee becomes bankrupt, though he should take care to safeguard the trust property from any unintentional collection by the trustee in bankruptcy. He may find a replacement trustee appointed by the court, see above. Where two or more trustees are responsible for a breach of trust such liability is joint and several. Proceedings may be instituted and judgment executed against any one or all of the guilty trustees, and the judgment creditor may prove in the bankruptcy of the bankrupt trustee for the whole debt even where it is partly satisfied by another trustee.[1] Following the Civil (Liability) Contribution Act 1978[2] the defaulting trustees may seek contribution between themselves in respect of any restitution they may have made to the trust. In contribution proceedings the court has wide powers to direct the making of a contributing by a co-trustee from a full indemnity to a complete exemption. Where the aggrieved beneficiaries have proved in the bankruptcy of one co-trustee proofs from the other trustee will be prevented by the rule against double proof. Once the trust property has been restored in full, the co-trustee may pursue the beneficiaries' proof.

[1] *Edwards v Hood-Barrs* [1905] 1 Ch 20.
[2] See ss 1(1), s, 6(1), 7(3).

Bankruptcy of settlor

29.5.3 Voluntary settlements of property by the settlor creating a trust may be impeached by the settlor's trustee in bankruptcy under both the Old and the New Law.

The qualifying circumstances which enable the trustee in bankruptcy to set the settlement aside are discussed elsewhere in this book.[1] In summary, under the Old Bankruptcy Law[2] the trustee in bankruptcy can apply to the court to set aside any settlement made voluntarily within two years of the commencement of the bankruptcy and in respect of any settlement made within ten years of the commencement unless the settlor or beneficiaries can show that the settlor's interest in the trust property passed to the trustee on the execution of the settlement and, at that date, the settlor was able to pay all his debts without the aid of the trust property. Under the New Law[3] the trustee in bankruptcy can apply to the court to avoid any transaction at an undervalue made within two years of the presentation of the bankruptcy petition, or such a transaction within five years of the petition if at the time of entering into the transaction the settlor was insolvent or became insolvent as a result of that transaction. In any case the bona fide purchase of property for value without notice of the relevant circumstances is protected.

[1] Ch 8 above (Old Bankruptcy Law), ch 17 above (New Law).
[2] Bankruptcy Act 1914, s 42.
[3] Insolvency Act 1986, ss 339–341.

Bankruptcy of beneficiary

29.5.4 The trustee in bankruptcy acquires the bankrupt's interest in the trust property and, if the beneficiary is sui juris and his interest is not limited, the trustee has the right to require a transfer of the trust property.[1]

There are three ways, however, in which the settlor can protect the trust property against the trustee in bankruptcy and the creditors. These are discussed below:–

(i) Discretionary trust. The popularity of the discretionary trust has been due to the fiscal advantages that could be obtained. In addition it can serve to protect trust property against creditors. As the beneficiary has no right to any part of the income of the trust property, but merely a hope that the trustee will exercise their discretion in his favour, there is no interest which the trustee in bankruptcy can claim. This is so even when the settlor has settled money on himself.[2]

Where the trust is for the maintenance and benefit of a number of beneficiaries including the bankrupt there is conflicting authority as to whether the trustee in bankruptcy is entitled to the whole or any payments made to the beneficiary or only to any excess over and above that reasonably required for his maintenance.[3]

(ii) Interest determinable on bankruptcy. A limitation in the beneficiary's interest until he attempts to alienate it or becomes bankrupt is a valid limitation.[4] The interest ceases on the beneficiary's bankruptcy and the trustee has nothing to collect and realise. Such a limitation is to be contrasted with a condition against forfeiture on bankruptcy which is of no effect against the trustee in bankruptcy. A settlor cannot protect the trust in this way, however, if it is for his own benefit, and so defeat the interests of his creditors. Where settlor and beneficiary are the same person the trustee in bankruptcy acquires the beneficiary's interest free from the limitation.[5]

(iii) Protective trust. Under a protective trust the interest of the beneficiary is made determinable on, e g bankruptcy and, on that event occurring, a discretionary trust arises in favour of the beneficiary and other persons. By the Trustee Act 1925, s 33 it is implied that

(a) where the principal beneficiary does or attempts to do or suffers any act or thing whereby he would be deprived of the right to trust income, the trust determines; and
(b) for the remainder of the trust period the income is held upon trust for the maintenance and support of the principal beneficiary, spouse, children or more remote issue or, where the principal beneficiary has no spouse or issue, for the principal beneficiary and the persons who would be entitled to the trust property on the death of the principal beneficiary, on discretionary trusts.

[1] *Re Dugdale, Dugdale v Dugdale* (1888) 38 Ch D 176.
[2] *Twopeny v Peyton* (1840) 10 Sim 487; *Holmes v Penny* (1856) 3 K & J 90; and see *Re Gulbenkian's Settlements Trusts (No 2), Stevens v Maun* [1970] Ch 408.
[3] *Re Coleman, Henry v Strong* (1888) 39 Ch D 443; cf *Re Ashby, ex p Wreford* [1892] 1 QB 872.
[4] *Re Leach, Leach v Leach* [1912] 2 Ch 422.
[5] *Higginbotham v Holme* (1811) 19 Ves 88; *Mackintosh v Pogose* [1895] 1 Ch 505; *Re Burroughs-Fowler, Burroughs-Fowler's Trustee v Burroughs-Fowler* [1916] 2 Ch 251.

Bankruptcy of personal representative

29.5.5 *(i) Before grant.* The court has wide discretionary powers in granting administration under the Supreme Court Act 1981. Probate is not necessarily to be refused on the grounds of bankruptcy, and where the testator was aware of the insolvency of the executor it is unlikely that the court will interfere. The court may limit the administration or appoint a receiver should this be considered appropriate. While it is unlikely that letters of administration could be granted to a bankrupt such a grant would not be invalid. A trustee in bankruptcy of a named executor is not entitled under the Non-Contentious Probate Rules to be awarded a grant of probate, but he could apply for a grant under the discretionary powers of the Court.

29.5.6 *(ii) After grant.* Similarly an executor who becomes bankrupt is not thereby disqualified though he may possibly be removed, if there is reason to suppose that assets in his control as trustee could be at risk. The trustee in bankruptcy is not, of course, entitled to possession of any assets of the estate. The principle of reputed ownership in bankruptcy is abolished under the New Law. Under the Old Bankruptcy Law the principle had been applied in favour of creditors[1] but strong evidence would be necessary in the ordinary case that the beneficiaries had consented to the personal representative's possession.

Where the executor becomes a lessee of the testator's lease his bankruptcy will operate any proviso for re-entry on the bankruptcy of the lessee.[2] Where an executor who is indebted to the estate becomes bankrupt he may set off his costs prior to the commencement of the bankruptcy against the debt.[3] Costs incurred after the bankruptcy cannot be set off against the debt where the bankruptcy has the effect of discharging the debt.[4]

Should an executor who has been guilty of wasting the estate's assets become bankrupt, a proof for his 'devastavit' can be made in the bankruptcy. He may not prove in his own bankruptcy except with an order from the court, which will generally be given in the case of a sole executor.[5] Where the bankrupt is one of two or more executors, the other executors may prove in his bankruptcy for any assets received by him.[6]

[1] *Fox v Fisher* (1819) 3 B & Ald 135.
[2] *Doe d Bridgman v David* (1834) 1 Cr M & R 405.
[3] *Smith v Dale* (1881) 18 Ch D 516; *Re Basham Hannay v Basham* (1883) 23 Ch D 195.

4 *Lewis v Trask* (1882) 21 Ch D 862.
5 *Re Howard & Gibbs, ex p Shaw* (1822) 1 Gl & J 127; *Re Coleman, ex p Colman* (1833) 2 Deac & Ch 584.
6 *Ex p Brown* (1832) 1 Deac & Ch 118.

Bankruptcy of legatee

29.5.7 The legacy will form part of the bankrupt's property and will therefore vest in the trustee in bankruptcy who can give the personal representative a good receipt. Under the Bankruptcy Act 1914 should the personal representative pay an undischarged bankrupt with notice of the bankruptcy he will be liable for payment in full to the trustee in bankruptcy. Where he has no notice of the bankruptcy the personal representative was protected against proceedings by the trustee in bankruptcy before the 1914 Act.[1] Under the Bankruptcy Act 1914, s 47 the question was whether the personal representative's receipt for a legacy paid by him in good faith and in ignorance of the bankruptcy was 'value' within the meaning of s 47. On the analogy of *Re Pope, ex p Dicksee*[2] the release of a right constitutes value and no action would lie at the suit of the trustee in bankruptcy.

The Insolvency Act 1986 alters the law on property acquired after the commencement of the bankruptcy. It vests in the trustee in bankruptcy only after service of notice in writing by him. Before notice is served therefore the bankrupt can give a good receipt. After such notice has been served by the trustee in bankruptcy the personal representative pays the legacy to the bankrupt at his peril. He would not appear to come within the category of persons protected from the suit of the trustee in bankruptcy specified in the statute.[3]

1 *Herbert v Sayer* (1844) 5 QB 965; *Cohen v Mitchell* (1890) 25 QBD 262.
2 [1908] 2 KB 169.
3 Insolvency Act 1986, s 307(4).

Administration of an insolvent estate[1]

29.5.8 An estate is insolvent if there are insufficient assets to pay all funeral, testamentary and administration expenses as well as the debts of the deceased.[2] If necessary the court will direct an enquiry into the solvency of an estate. In administrating the insolvent estate the personal representative must follow the bankruptcy rules of priority under the Old or New Law as appropriate.[3]

In place of the bankruptcy costs and expenses the personal representative first pays funeral testamentary and administration expenses. 'Funeral expenses' are expenses reasonably incurred having regard to the position of the deceased.[4] 'Testamentary and administration expenses' include a wide variety of costs and payments which fall on the personal representative.[5]

Where proceedings have been commenced in any court for the administration of the estate, the court may transfer the proceedings to the bankruptcy court should it be known that the estate is insolvent. This power of transfer is discretionary and can be exercised after an order for general administration has been made.

1 See Bankruptcy Act 1914, s 130; Insolvency Act 1986, s 421 under which section the Lord Chancellor is empowered to order by statutory instrument that the provisions of the

Insolvency Act should apply to insolvent estates with such incidental, supplemental and transitional modifications as are necessary or expedient.

[2] *Re Leng, Tarn v Emmerson* [1895] 1 Ch 652; Insolvency Act 1986, s 421(4).

[3] See chs 9 and 16 above.

[4] *Re Walter, Slocock v Official Receiver* [1929] 1 Ch 647.

[5] See *Williams, Mortimer and Sunnecks on Executors etc* (16th edn) p 577.

29.5.9 Where a person dies before or after the presentation of a bankruptcy petition against him and his estate is insolvent, it is administered under the Administration of Insolvent Estates of Deceased Persons Order 1986.[1] Generally, this order applies to the administration of an insolvent deceased's estate the provisions of the Insolvency Act 1986 and the Individual Insolvency Rules 1986 appropriately modified. The 'insolvency administration petition' is served on the deceased's personal representative who has similar obligations towards the official receiver or trustee as the debtor would have had to submit a statement of affairs, surrender property, give information etc. Any acts done in good faith by the personal representative before the date of the insolvency administration order are protected from invalidation, and in exercising his functions the trustee must have due regard to any claim by the personal representative in respect of reasonable funeral, testamentary and administration expenses incurred by him. Where there is no personal representation the court may appoint a person on whom the petition or any notices may be served, and who shall prepare a statement of affairs.

[1] SI 1986/1999; Sch 3 to this order contains the forms to be used for petitions by a creditor or personal representative for an insolvency administration order, and the statement of affairs to be submitted on behalf of a deceased insolvent.

CHAPTER 30

Effect of Bankruptcy on Litigation and Arbitration

30.1 THE BANKRUPT'S ESTATE

Old Bankruptcy Law Cases

30.1.1 The estate of a bankrupt as defined in the Bankruptcy Act 1914, s 167 includes all real and personal property in which the bankrupt has a beneficial interest or over which he has a power of disposition at the commencement of the bankruptcy, with the following exceptions:
(a) the tools of his trade;
(b) clothing and bedding for himself and his immediate family;
(c) property held by him as trustee;
(d) property exempted by statute;[1]
(e) property which by its nature cannot pass;[2] and
(f) the right of nomination to a vacant ecclesiastical benefice.[3]

Under the doctrine of relation back, the bankruptcy commences at the time of the commission of the first available act of bankruptcy, as to which see para 6.3.2 above.

By s 38 of the 1914 Act, the trustee becomes entitled to all property vested in the bankrupt at the commencement of the bankruptcy, and which vests in him between commencement and discharge.

[1] Halsbury's Laws (4th edn) para 592.
[2] Ibid, para 590, n 9.
[3] Bankruptcy Act 1914, s 38(b).

The New Law

30.1.2 The estate of the bankrupt is defined in the Insolvency Act 1986, s 283; the types of property included within the scope of the estate are discussed in detail in para 16.3 above.

The estate of the bankrupt includes 'all property belonging to or vested in the bankrupt at the commencement of the bankruptcy'[1] with the exclusion of:

(a) the tools of his trade;
(b) clothing and basic household needs for himself and his family;
(c) property which he holds as trustee; and
(d) the right of nomination to a vacant ecclesiastical benefice.[2]

It should be noted that a power exercisable over or in respect of property is deemed by the Insolvency Act 1986 to vest in the person entitled to exercise it at the time of the transaction or event by virtue of which it is exercisable by that person, whether or not the power does indeed become exercisable at that time.[3]

Whereas property acquired by the bankrupt between the commission of an act of bankruptcy and discharge vests in the trustee automatically under the Old Law; under the New Law, property acquired by or devolving upon the bankrupt after the commencement of the bankruptcy remains vested in the bankrupt. The property may however be claimed by the trustee by service of the appropriate notice as to which see para 16.2.3 above.

1 Insolvency Act 1986, s 283(1).
2 Ibid, s 283(2), (3).
3 Ibid, s 283(4).

30.2 THE BANKRUPT AS PLAINTIFF

1 Old Bankruptcy Law Cases

30.2.1 The trustee upon his appointment becomes entitled to take proceedings in respect of such rights of action related to the bankrupt's estate as were vested in the bankrupt at the commencement of the bankruptcy, or which become vested in him between such time and discharge.

Rights of action not related to the estate are excluded. The rights of action which do not vest in the trustee include those of a purely personal nature, such as for example rights of action for the personal torts of assault or defamation.[1]

As to rights of action arising out of torts committed to the property of a bankrupt, such rights pass to the trustee where the only loss or damage is that suffered by the property itself. However, if the tortious act results in damage to property and personal injury or loss to the bankrupt, the position is otherwise.

If there are distinct and separate causes of action in respect of the different heads of loss, the trustee will be entitled to bring an action in respect of the damage to the property, while the bankrupt will retain the right to sue in respect of the loss or injury which he himself has suffered.[2]

If the causes of action cannot be severed, the bankrupt will lose his right of action, and the trustee alone will be entitled to institute proceedings.[3] The bankrupt will, however, be entitled to bring an action if the damage to his property is not appreciable or he claims aggravated damages.[4]

With regard to the earnings of the bankrupt, the distinction must be drawn between such earnings as are merely sufficient for the needs of himself and his family and any excess. Rights of action in respect of sums necessary to the maintenance of the bankrupt and his family will remain vested in the bankrupt;[5] the trustee alone is entitled to bring an action in respect of any excess.[6] Indeed, if an action is commenced by a bankrupt to recover personal earnings or wages, and if he is awarded a sum greater than that necessary, he will be required to account to the trustee for any excess.[7]

Where the bankrupt obtains damages for loss of earnings he or his employer may be required to pay to his trustee such sum, if any, as exceeds that which he reasonably requires for the maintenance of himself and his family.[8] Similarly, the trustee will become entitled on his appointment to bring an action founded on a contract for the personal services of the bankrupt where the cause of action had accrued to the bankrupt before his bankruptcy, either by virtue of his having become entitled to monies pursuant to the contract for services, or because a breach had been committed entitling him to claim damages.[9]

The cause of action will also vest in the trustee in respect of breaches which occur after the bankruptcy, but he must pass such income or wages as are necessary for the maintenance of the bankrupt and his family to him[10] and he may choose not to intervene in an action already started by the bankrupt.

The trustee of a bankrupt partner may also commence or continue proceedings in his name and that of the bankrupt's partners, insofar as the partnership property falls within the bankrupt's estate.

1 *Re Bourne, ex p Bourne* (1826) 2 Gl and J 137, LC; *White v Elliott* (1870) 30 UCR 253 (Can); *Beckham v Drake* (1849) 2 HL Cas 579 and see para 6.3(vi) above.
2 *Boddington v Castelli* (1853) 1 E & B 879; *Wilson v United Counties Bank Ltd* [1920] AC 102, HL.
3 *Stanton v Collier* (1854) 23 LJQB 116, CA; *Hodgson v Sidney* (1866) LR 1 Exch 313; *Wilson v United Counties Bank Ltd*, n 2 above.
4 *Rose v Buckett* [1901] 2 KB 449; *Brewer v Dew* (1843) 11 M & W 625.
5 *Re Roberts* [1900] 1 QB 122, CA.
6 *Mercer v Vans Colina* [1900] 1 QB 130.
7 *Re Roberts,* see n 5 above.
8 *Re Roberts* (above); *Bailey v Thurston & Co Ltd.* [1903] 1 KB 137.
9 Halsbury's Laws (4th edn) para 561.
10 *Beckham v Drake* (1849) 2 HL Cas 579.

2 Under the New Law

30.2.2 By virtue of the Insolvency Act 1986, s 314(1)(a) and Sch 5, Pt I the trustee may, subject to the permission of the committee, 'bring, institute or defend any action or legal proceedings relating to the property comprised in the bankrupt's estate'. Thus, prima facie, causes of action relating to any property forming part of the estate will vest in the trustee upon his appointment.

Although not specifically excluded by the Act, rights of action which would not pass in Old Bankruptcy Law cases would remain excluded, as not being related to property comprised in the estate.

The law in respect of the trustee's right to bring an action in respect of a tort to the bankrupt's property is now embodied in the Insolvency Act 1986, Sch 5, para 2, and the cases referred to above will continue to apply. In this context, rights of action which have been held to pass to the trustee under the Old Bankruptcy Law, and which now fall clearly within Sch 5, para 2 include actions for an indemnity,[1] for commission,[2] for wrongful dismissal[3] and for misrepresentation.[4]

1 *Re Perkins, Poyser v Beyfus* [1898] 2 Ch 182, CA.
2 *Re Byrne, ex p Henry* (1892) 9 Morr 213.
3 *Beckham v Drake* (1849) 2 HL Cas 579.
4 *Hodgson v Sidney* (1866) LR 1 Exch 313.

Bankruptcy before the commencement of proceedings

30.2.3 A creditor who is adjudged bankrupt may still sue in his own name unless and until his trustee chooses to intervene, provided that the cause of action accrues after the bankruptcy and that it is one which does not pass to the trustee.[1]

If the cause of action accrues before the commencement of the bankruptcy, it will pass to the trustee.[2] However, once a trustee is appointed, he may choose to intervene, and to start the action in his own name on behalf of the bankrupt's estate. The trustee cannot change his mind once he has intervened, unless his intervention was by mistake.[3] If the trustee chooses not to start proceedings, the bankrupt himself may do so, and may pursue the action, although the trustee in these circumstances may change his mind and intervene at a later stage.[4]

If the trustee has started proceedings and the bankrupt plaintiff also does so, the bankrupt's action will be dismissed as frivolous and vexatious, unless the trustee had no right to bring the action.[5]

1 *Affleck v Hammond* [1912] 3 KB 162; *Buchan v Hill* [1888] WN 233.
2 *Osman v Raphael* (1896) 12 TLR 376, CA.
3 *Hill v Settle* [1917] 1 Ch 319.
4 *Webb v Fox* (1797) 7 Term Rep 391.
5 *Metropolitan Bank Ltd v Pooley* (1885) 10 App Cas 210, HL.

Bankruptcy after the commencement of proceedings

30.2.4 *The sole plaintiff.* The trustee alone is entitled to continue proceedings commenced by a sole plaintiff bankrupt before his appointment, except in those cases where the cause of action does not by law vest in him.[1] In the latter case the plaintiff may continue the action subject to the question of security for costs (see below).

In order to continue the proceedings, the trustee must obtain an order of the court in which the proceedings are pending that his name be substituted for that of the plaintiff. Thereafter, the proceedings will continue with the trustee as plaintiff, or as co-plaintiff with the bankrupt.[2] The application is made by ex parte summons or notice of motion, either by the trustee himself or by any other party to the action.

A trustee appointed after the commencement of proceedings may, however, decline to continue the action, for example because to do so would be detrimental to the body of creditors. If he does so, the action may be stayed subject to notice being given by the defendant to the trustee[3] or the defendant may raise the adjudication (in an Old Bankruptcy Law case) or the bankruptcy order (under the New Law), but not the receiving order under the Old Law, as a defence.[4]

If the trustee continues the action, he will of course be in no better position on the pleadings than the bankrupt plaintiff. For this reason, if for no other, he may prefer not to become a party to the existing action, but rather to commence a fresh action in his own name founded on the same cause of action and claiming the same relief. He will not be debarred from doing so.[5]

1 See above.
2 RSC Ord 15, rr 6(2) and 7(2).
3 *Wright v Swindon, Marlborough and Andover Rly Co* (1876) 4 Ch D 164.
4 *Champion v Formby* (1878) 7 Ch D 373; *Foster v Gamgee* (1876) 1 QBD 666; cf *Re Berry, Duffield v Williams* [1896] 1 Ch 939.
5 *Bennett v Gamgee* (1877) 46 LJQB 204, CA.

30.2.5 *One of several plaintiffs.* Under the Old Bankruptcy Law, it is not necessary for a jointly contracting bankrupt or his trustee to be a party to proceedings arising out of the contract; under s 118 of the 1914 Act, the action may be pursued by his co-contractors without joining the bankrupt or his trustee. By virtue of the Insolvency Act 1986, s 345(4) this remains the position under the New Law.

Where the bankrupt is a co-plaintiff claiming in respect of joint and several liability, his trustee may apply to be made a party to the action in his place and pursue the action as co-plaintiff.[1]

It seems that if a plaintiff brings an action in respect of joint liability to himself and others the trustee must intervene or the action will abate[2] although this is probably not the case where liability is joint and several.

1 *Hoare & Co and Newton v Baker* (1887) 4 TLR 26, DC.
2 *Wolf v Van Boolen* (1906) 94 LT 502.

30.2.6 *Change in trustee.* If a new trustee is appointed during the course of proceedings commenced by the bankrupt plaintiff or his former trustee, he must apply to the court for an order that he be made a party to the action, in the same way as a trustee originally appointed. Once he has obtained such order, he must serve notice of it on the other parties to the action. This applies equally to a trustee who has been appointed in place of a former trustee who started the proceedings and to one who has continued an action commenced by the bankrupt plaintiff.[1]

1 *Pooley's Trustee v Whetham* (1886) 33 Ch D 76.

30.2.7 *Security for costs.*

(a) Action in name of bankrupt. The fact that a plaintiff is subsequently adjudged bankrupt is not a sufficient ground for an order for security to be made.[1] Thus, where a plaintiff is adjudicated bankrupt, or a bankruptcy order is made against him, during the course of proceedings commenced by him in an action in which the cause of action itself remains vested in the bankrupt he will be able to continue the action without giving security unless the defendant can establish another ground for obtaining an order for security.

It can be argued that, in actions where the cause of action vests in the trustee, then once the trustee is appointed the plaintiff is in effect a nominal plaintiff, and that security for costs should thus always be given. The bankrupt plaintiff will be treated as a nominal plaintiff and accordingly be required to give security for the defendant's costs in cases where he has by virtue of his bankruptcy no further interest in or entitlement to the subject matter of the proceedings. This will be the case, for example, where he has assigned the benefit of such proceedings to his creditors[2] or of course where his estate will be entitled to the proceeds by virtue of the cause of action having vested in his trustee.

Similarly, where a plaintiff charges or assigns the proceeds of the action to someone other than his general body of creditors he can be deemed a nominal plaintiff.[3] A creditor resident abroad and appealing against the rejection of his proof in an English bankruptcy will not be required to give security.[4]

(b) Action in name of trustee. A trustee in bankruptcy, being personally liable for the costs he incurs, will not be ordered to give security solely on the ground that he is a trustee.[5] It would appear that an insolvent trustee is in the same position with regard to the giving of security as an insolvent plaintiff[6] unless he is a trustee under a deed of assignment.[7] However, an insolvent plaintiff suing as trustee of a settlement will not normally be required to give security.[8]

1 *Cook v Whellock* (1890) 24 QBD 658.
2 *Lloyd v Hathern Station Brick Co. Ltd* (1901) 85 LT 158.
3 *Semler v Murphy* [1968] Ch 183.
4 *Re Semenza, ex p Paget* [1894] 1 QB 15.
5 *Pooley's Trustee v Whetham* (1886) 33 Ch D 76.
6 *Denston v Ashton* (1869) LR 4 QB 590.
7 *Greener v Kahn & Co Ltd* [1906] 2 KB 374.
8 *Cowell v Taylor* (1885) 31 Ch D 34.

Bankruptcy after judgment

30.2.8 An order that the name of the trustee in bankruptcy be substituted for that of the plaintiff may be made after judgment[1] unless the circumstances are such as to entitle the trustee to bring a fresh action.

Where the plaintiff bankrupt has sued successfully in his own name his trustee may obtain an order for leave to issue execution without the need first to apply for an order that he be made a party to the action.[2] The bankrupt judgment creditor is not entitled to issue execution once his trustee has been appointed.[3]

1 *Re Clements, ex p Clements* [1901] 1 KB 260.
2 *Re Bagley* [1911] 1 KB 317.
3 *Re Carter, ex p Carter* (1876) 2 Ch D 806, CA.

30.3 THE BANKRUPT AS DEFENDANT

Actions which may be maintained against bankrupt

30.3.1 *Old Bankruptcy Law cases.* As seen in ch 3 above, after the making of a receiving order, no action in respect of a provable debt may be commenced against the bankrupt except with the leave of the court and on such terms as the court may impose.[1] However, the right of a secured creditor to enforce his security prevails.[2]

Generally, provable debts include all liabilities and debts whether present or future, certain or contingent, to which the bankrupt is subject when the receiving order is made, and those incurred between that date and his discharge.[3] The following are expressly excluded (see ch 9 above):

(a) claims for unliquidated damages, other than those arising out of contract, promise or breach of trust;[4]
(b) claims arising out of a contract where the plaintiff had notice of an available act of bankruptcy by the defendant when the contract was made;[5] and
(c) debts and liabilities which the court considers cannot be fairly estimated.[6]

1 Bankruptcy Act 1914, s 7(1).
2 Ibid, s 7(2).
3 Ibid, s 30(3).
4 Ibid, s 30(1).
5 Ibid, s 30(2).
6 Ibid, s 30(6).

30.3.2 *Under the New Law.* By the Insolvency Act 1986, s 285(3):

> 'after the making of a bankruptcy order no person who is a creditor of the bankrupt in respect of a debt provable in the bankruptcy shall . . . (b) before the discharge of the bankrupt, commence any action . . . against the bankrupt except with the leave of the court and on such terms as the court may impose.'

For a discussion of debts provable see para 16.5 above.

Thus, a plaintiff may commence proceedings without leave only in respect of a debt for which he cannot prove in the bankruptcy.

A debt in respect of which proof can be submitted, a 'bankruptcy debt', is one to which the bankrupt is subject at the commencement of the bankruptcy or one arising from 'any obligation incurred before the commencement of the bankruptcy'.[1]

The Insolvency Act 1986 provides that it is 'immaterial whether the debt or liability is present or future, whether it is certain or contingent or whether its amount is fixed or liquidated, or is capable of being ascertained by fixed rules or as a matter of opinion . . .'[2] and 'liability' includes '. . . any liability in contract, tort or bailment . . .'.[3] Thus, the distinction between varieties of tort made under the Old Bankruptcy Law will no longer be relevant.

In order to ascertain whether liability in tort constitutes a bankruptcy debt, the cause of action is to be regarded as an obligation to the plaintiff, so that if the cause of action arose before the bankruptcy the plaintiff may submit a proof in respect of any tortious damage suffered even where unliquidated damages have not been ascertained by the date of the commencement of the bankruptcy.[4]

In the light of the above it would seem that in New Law cases a plaintiff can sue a bankrupt defendant notwithstanding the bankruptcy only in respect of torts committed by the bankrupt after the commencement of the bankruptcy.

1 Insolvency Act 1986, s 381(2).
2 Ibid, s 382(3).
3 Ibid, s 382(4).
4 Ibid, s 382(2).

Bankruptcy before commencement of proceedings

30.3.3 In Old Bankruptcy Law cases, in order to commence an action in respect of a provable debt against a debtor who is subject to a receiving order, pending his adjudication, the intending plaintiff must obtain the leave of the court with bankruptcy jurisdiction over the debtor.[1]

Under the New Law, however, leave must be obtained before any action is commenced.[2] It may be anticipated that such leave will not usually be given except in cases where the plaintiff would not otherwise be able to prove the debt in the bankruptcy; unless leave is obtained, the action may be stayed.[3]

1 Bankruptcy Act 1914, s 7(1).
2 Insolvency Act 1986, s 285(3)(b).
3 Ibid, s 285(1).

Bankruptcy after the commencement of proceedings

30.3.4 In Old Law cases the court has discretion whether to stay an action commenced against a defendant against whom a petition is subsequently presented, or to permit the action to continue upon terms[1] and it is usual for the proceedings to be stayed until the appointment of the trustee.[2] The receiving order may include a stay of all proceedings pending against the bankrupt.[3]

The court's discretion remains under the New Law[4] and it would seem unlikely that there will be any substantial change in its exercise. Where no application is made for a stay, the proceedings will continue with the bankrupt as a party.[5] The court may adjourn the proceedings pending the result of an adjudication application and if the defendant is subsequently adjudicated bankrupt the action may then be stayed or continued on such terms as the court deems fit. Generally, where the bankrupt is the sole defendant an action merely to recover a debt for which the plaintiff could prove in the bankruptcy will be stayed following presentation of the petition.[6] The plaintiff may then prove for the debt and any costs incurred before the receiving order in respect of which the court has made an order.[7]

However, an action involving issues which cannot be resolved on proof, or claims which will not be discharged on bankruptcy will not normally be stayed. For example, the plaintiff seeking an injunction,[8] maintenance[9] or an account[10] will be permitted to pursue proceedings commenced before the bankruptcy, but he must obtain an order that the trustee be added as a party. Where there are several defendants, the position will depend upon whether their liability is joint only or joint and several.

In the case of joint liability there is authority in Old Law cases to suggest that the trustee of the bankrupt defendant must be joined.[11] Under the New Law, the Insolvency Act 1986, s 345(4) provides that the joint contractors of a bankrupt may be sued without the joinder of the bankrupt. Under the Old Law, where liability is joint and several, it is established that the trustee need not (although he may) be joined;[12] the Insolvency Act does not alter this. If there is more than one trustee involved, and one refuses to continue in the proceedings, an order will be made on the application of a co-trustee that he be made a defendant.[13]

1 Bankruptcy Act 1914, s 7(1).
2 *Franco v Dutton* [1923] WN 40; *Hatton v Denison* [1926] WN 80.
3 Bankruptcy Rules 1952, r 180.
4 Insolvency Act 1986, s 285(2), Individual Insolvency Rules, r 6.33(3).
5 *Realisation Industrielles et Commerciales SA v Loescher & Partners* [1957] 3 All ER 241.
6 *Barter v Dubeux* (1881) 7 QBD 413.
7 *Re Pitchford* [1924] 2 Ch 260.
8 *Borneman v Wilson* (1884) 28 Ch D 53.
9 *Linton v Linton* (1885) 15 QBD 239.
10 *Watson v Holliday* (1882) 20 Ch D 780.
11 *Barter v Dubeux,* n 6 above.
12 *Lloyd v Dimmack* (1877) 7 Ch D 398.
13 *Jackson v North Eastern Rly Co* (1877) 5 Ch D 844.

30.3.5 *Payment into court.* It would appear that the Insolvency Act 1986 does not change or affect the law. Where a payment into court is made by a defendant who is subsequently adjudicated bankrupt, the effect is that the plaintiff creditor becomes a secured creditor to the extent of the payment in.[1] If the payment in is made after presentation of a petition by the plaintiff, but before adjudication or bankruptcy order, the plaintiff may choose either to accept the payment in or to proceed with the petition notwithstanding that the payment in is of the full amount claimed, even inclusive of costs.[2]

If payment in is made by a defendant who was required to make such payment as a condition of being granted leave to defend upon the plaintiff's application for summary judgment, the payment will not become part of the bankrupt's estate.[3]

If the plaintiff obtains judgment because of the defendant's failure to make a payment in the trustee of the defendant may apply for the judgment to be set aside.[4]

1 *Re Gordon, ex p Navalchand* [1897] 2 QB 516.
2 *Re Gentry* [1910] 1 KB 825.
3 *Re Ford, ex p Trustee* [1900] 2 QB 211.
4 *Re Lopes, ex p Hardway and Topping* (1889) 5 TLR 685.

Bankruptcy after judgment

30.3.6 The judgment creditor has no automatic right to commence execution proceedings against the bankrupt judgment debtor, unless the debt is not a provable or bankruptcy debt.[1]

1 Insolvency Act 1986, s 285(3)(a).

30.4 EXECUTION

General

30.4.1 In order to commence execution in respect of a debt for which judgment has been awarded in his favour, the execution creditor must serve notice of the judgment on the bankrupt defendant's trustee[1] and obtain leave to start execution. Such leave may be given at the discretion of the court and on such terms as the court thinks fit, or the action may be stayed.[2]

The court may similarly stay execution commenced before the presentation of the petition or impose terms upon the continuation of the execution proceedings.[3] Once execution has been completed, the trustee will have no claim against the proceeds.[4]

1 *Re Wicks, Wicks v Wicks* [1888] WN 9.
2 Insolvency Act 1986 s 285(1) and s 285(3)(b).
3 Ibid s 285(1) and (2), Individual Insolvency Rules, r 6.33(3): the bankruptcy order may include a stay of any other proceedings pending against the bankrupt. Subject to s 346 of the Act this applies to execution proceedings.
4 Ibid, s 346(1).

The completion of execution

30.4.2 *Old Bankruptcy Law cases.* Execution is completed:
(a) in the case of execution against goods by seizure and sale or by the making of a charging order under s 1 of the Charging Orders Act 1979.
(b) in the case of execution against land, by the appointment of a receiver or by seizure or by the making of a charging order;[1]
(c) in the case of a garnishee order, or attachment of a debt by receipt of the debt by the judgment creditor.[2]

In each case, to enable the judgment creditor to defeat the claim of the bankrupt's trustee, the execution must be completed before the date of the receiving order, and before notice of either the presentation of a petition or the commission of an available act of bankruptcy.[3] The onus of proof as to completion of the execution lies on the judgment creditor.[4]

Goods seized by the sheriff after commission of an available act of bankruptcy of which the judgment creditor does not have notice, although not the property of the bankrupt, but vested in his trustee[5] are available for execution.[6] Where the bankrupt has paid all or part of the debt to the sheriff before the making of a receiving order, the judgment creditor may be able to recover the sum paid in an action against the sheriff for money had and received[7] and such a claim if successful will defeat that of the trustee in a bankruptcy.

Payment in respect of sums claimed in a writ of fieri facias must be to the sheriff or his officer, not to the execution creditor.[8] In execution of a judgment for more than £20, the sheriff must retain the sum recovered after deduction of his costs for 14 days from the date of the sale[9] or receipt of payment from the debtor to avoid sale. If during that period a receiving order is made against the debtor either on a petition of which the sheriff already had notice or on one of which he receives notice during the 14 days he must pay the balance to the trustee in bankruptcy.[10] The claim of the trustee may be set aside in favour of the judgment creditor at the discretion of the court and on such terms as it thinks fit.[11] The 14 day period is not suspended by interpleader proceedings.

A purchaser of goods at a sheriff's sale without notice of creditors' claims acquires good title, and no claim can subsequently be made against the sheriff or his officers. As to the seizure of land, since the abolition of the writ of elegit, to which the 1914 Act refers, this may no longer be applicable. The writ of elegit has been replaced by charging orders, to which the 1914 Act does not refer, but an order under s 1 of the 1979 Act will complete execution.

With regard to the attachment of debts, payment must be made to the garnishor, and payment into court will not suffice.[12] If the debt has been validly assigned before service of the order nisi, irrespective of whether the garnishor has notice of the assignment, the assignee will take the benefit.[13]

1 Bankruptcy Act 1914, s 40(2) as amended by Administration of Justice Act 1956, s 36(4) (and note Supreme Court Act 1981, Sch 5) and as further amended by Charging Orders Act 1979, s 4.
2 Bankruptcy Act 1914, s 40(2).
3 Ibid, s 40(1).
4 *Pearson v Graham* (1837) 6 Ad & El 899.
5 Bankruptcy Act 1914, s 37(1).
6 *Re Love, ex p Official Receiver v Kingston-upon-Thames County Court Registrar* [1952] Ch 138, CA.
7 *Re a Debtor (No 2 of 1977) Debtor v Goacher* [1979] 1 All ER 870.
8 *Re Godding, ex p Trustee* [1914] 2 KB 70; *Re Pollock and Pendle, ex p Wilson and Mathieson Ltd* (1902) 87 LT 238.
9 *Re Cripps, Ross & Co, ex p Ross* (1888) 21 QBD 472.
10 Bankruptcy Act 1914, s 41(2).
11 Insolvency Act 1985, s 235(2), Sch 9, Pt III.
12 *Wild v Southwood* [1897] 1 QB 317; *Re Pollard, ex p Pollard* [1903] 2 KB 41, CA; *Re Hastings, ex p Brown* (1892) 61 LJQB 654.
13 *Wise v Birkenshaw* (1860) 29 LJ Ex 240.

30.4.3 *Under the New Law.* The completion of execution occurs:
(a) in the case of fieri facias by seizure and sale;[1]
(b) in the case of land, either:
   (i) by the making of a charging order under the Charging Orders Act 1979, s 1;[2] or
   (ii) by seizure;[3] or
   (iii) by the appointment of a receiver;[4] or
(c) in the case of attachment of a debt, by receipt of the debt.[5]

There is thus no difference between the Old and the New Law in this respect. However, in order to defeat the claim of the trustee, the execution creditor must show that the execution was completed before the commencement of the bankruptcy.[6] As under the Old Law, the sheriff who has seized goods but not completed the execution by sale must deliver any goods or money seized to the trustee if he receives notice of the adjudication before the sale[7] and his costs are a first charge on such goods or money in priority to claims of the body of creditors.[8] Such notice must be served by hand or posted by recorded delivery, to the office either of the under-sheriff or of the officer in charge of the execution.[9]

There is an exception to the basic rule that the trustee's claim is extinguished by the completion of execution before commencement of bankruptcy: as under the Old Law any sum in excess of such sum as is prescribed by the Rules passes to the estate[10] provided that the sheriff has notice[11] of presentation of the petition within 14 days of the sale.

There are similar provisions to those under the Old Law requiring the sheriff to retain the excess for 14 days after the sale or while the petition is pending, and to pay the excess to the trustee.[12] The court will remain empowered to set these provisions aside 'to such extent and on such terms as it thinks fit'.[13]

In the case of garnishee proceedings, the position is as under the Old Law, so that the garnishor is not assisted by payment into court by the garnishee[14] unless it is made in pursuance of an order of the court.[15]

The Act also protects third parties who acquire goods at a sheriff's sale in good faith.[16]

1 Insolvency Act 1986, s 346(5)(a).
2 Ibid, s 346(5)(a).
3 Ibid, s 346(5)(b).
4 Ibid, s 346(5)(b).
5 Ibid, s 346(5)(c).
6 Ibid, s 346(1)(b).
7 Ibid, s 346(2)(a).
8 Ibid, s 346(2)(b).
9 Individual Insolvency Rules, r 12.19.
10 Ibid, s 346(3). Prescribed sum is £500: Insolvency Proceedings (Monetary Limits) Order 1986, SI 1986/1996.
11 See note 9 above.
12 Ibid, s 346(4).
13 Ibid, s 346(6).
14 *Butler v Wearing* (1885) 17 QBD 182.
15 *Culverhouse v Wickens* (1868) LR 3 CP 295.
16 Insolvency Act 1986, s 346(7).

Interpleader proceedings

30.4.4 The execution debtor's trustee may be made a party in the interpleader trial if the bankruptcy occurs after the order.[1] The trustee may then apply for the order to be discharged if he so wishes.[2]

As stated above, the operation of the 14-day provisions applying to the sheriff in Old Law cases is not suspended by interpleader proceedings, and there is nothing in the Insolvency Act 1986 or the Rules to change this. It is, however, self evident that if the judgment debtor's title to the goods is defeated and the sheriff is therefore ordered to withdraw from possession the trustee can have no claim; conversely, if the third party claim fails, the execution may proceed; if he deposits or pays the value of the goods and the sheriff withdraws, the trustee can have no claim to the money paid.[3]

1 *Bird v Mathews* (1883) 52 LJ Ch 543.
2 *Watson v Holliday* (1882) 31 WR 536.
3 *Shuckburgh v Duthoit* (1892) 8 TLR 710, CA.

30.5 APPEALS IN ACTIONS TO WHICH THE BANKRUPT IS A PARTY

In the event of an appeal to the Court of Appeal, the appellant bankrupt will usually be required to give security for costs. If it is shown that any appellant's financial circumstances are such that he would not be able to pay the costs of the appeal, he will be ordered to give security, even before adjudication.[1] However, security may not be ordered where the appellant's bankruptcy has been caused by what is alleged to be wrongful conduct on the part of the respondent.[2]

1 *Harlock v Ashberry* (1881) 19 Ch D 84.
2 *Farrer v Lacey Hartland & Co* (1885) 28 Ch D 482.

30.6 TRANSFER OF PROCEEDINGS AFTER APPOINTMENT OF INTERIM RECEIVER

In addition to the discretion vested in the court to order that pending proceedings by or against the bankrupt be stayed, the Individual Insolvency Rules 1986[1] enable the transfer of proceedings to the High Court where an interim receiver has been appointed to the bankrupt's estate. Such a transfer may be on the court's own motion in any case where the bankruptcy order was made by the High Court or the bankruptcy proceedings have been transferred to the High Court.[2] Any proceedings which involve a claim against the bankrupt's estate,[3] including claims by mortgagees,[4] may be transferred to the High Court in bankruptcy including actions proceeding in another division of the High Court.

1 Individual Insolvency Rules 1986, r 7.15.
2 Ibid, r 7.15(1).
3 Ibid, r 7.15(2).
4 Ibid, r 7.15(3).

30.7 THE EFFECT OF INTERIM ORDERS

30.7.1 An interim order is made in connection with a debtor's voluntary arrangement see para 12.2 above. A debtor who wishes to put a proposal to his creditors for a composition or scheme of arrangement must apply to the court having jurisdiction in bankruptcy for an interim order. Where the order is made a creditors' meeting is held at which the debtor's proposals for voluntary arrangement may be approved, approved with modification, or rejected. Both the application for and the making of an interim order may affect proceedings against the debtor.

30.7.2 While an application for an interim order is pending there is a discretionary power in the court to stay any action, execution or other legal process against the debtor or his property.[1] This power is exercisable not only by the bankruptcy court in which the application for an interim order is pending, but also by the court in which the action against the debtor is proceeding.[2] This court may either stay the proceedings or allow them to continue on such terms as it thinks fit.[2]

1 Insolvency Act 1986, s 254(1).
2 Ibid, s 254(2).

30.7.3 Once an interim order has been made:
(a) no bankruptcy petition may be presented or proceeded with against the debtor; and
(b) no other proceedings and no execution or other legal process may be commenced or continued against the debtor or his property except with the leave of the court.[1]

The interim order has effect for an initial period of 14 days beginning with the day after the date on which it is made,[2] unless the nominee responsible for the scheme obtains further time from the court.[3] In cases where the court has made an interim order on a debtor's petition, (see para 13.6.3 above) the court is to specify the period during which the interim order is to have effect.[4]

1 Insolvency Act 1986, s 252(2).
2 Ibid, s 255(6).
3 Ibid, s 256(4).
4 Ibid, s 274(4).

30.7.4 During this initial period of the interim order the court considers the nominee's report on the proposed voluntary arrangements. If the court is satisfied after considering the nominee's report that a creditors' meeting should be summoned, the court may extend the period during which the interim order has effect for such further period as it may specify, in order to give time for the creditors' meeting to be held while the interim order is in force.[1] Thus the prohibition on bankruptcy petitions, and the prevention of other proceedings or execution of legal process against the debtor or his property without leave of the court remains in force while the creditors' meeting is held and the result of that meeting reported to the court by the chairman.[2]

1 Insolvency Act 1986, s 256(5).
2 Ibid, s 259(1).

30.7.5 Where the debtor's proposals for voluntary arrangements are approved by the creditors' meeting, the composition or scheme so approved comes into effect as if made by the debtor on the date of the meeting.[1] Every creditor who had notice of the meeting is bound whether he attended or not and irrespective of whether or how he cast his vote. No such creditor may then proceed with any action or execution against the debtor, save under the composition or scheme. The interim order in force immediately before the end of the period of 28 days beginning with the day on which the chairman of the creditors' meeting reported the result of the meeting to the court ceases to have effect at the end of that 28-day period.[2] The debtor is then liable to be proceeded against, subject to the effect of the approved composition or scheme.

1 Insolvency Act 1986, s 260(2).
2 Ibid, s 260(4).

30.7.6 Where the debtor's proposals for voluntary arrangements are not approved by the creditors' meeting, either with or without modifications, the court may discharge any interim order in force.[1] While the discharge of the interim order is not mandatory, it must necessarily follow if the debtor makes no further proposals for voluntary arrangements. After the discharge of the interim order proceedings may be instituted or continued against the debtor without leave or risk of stay. The court may however extend the force of the interim order where a challenge is made to the meeting's decision under the Insolvency Act 1986, s 262: see para 12.3.6 above.

1 Insolvency Act 1986, s 259(2).

30.8 THE EFFECT OF A COMPOSITION OR SCHEME ON PROCEEDINGS

30.8.1 *In Old Law cases.* Once a scheme or composition accepted by a majority in number and 75% in value of all creditors who have proved has been approved by the court it is generally binding on all creditors in respect of provable debts.[1] A creditor whose claim is for a debt or liability which an adjudication would not discharge is not bound unless he assents to the scheme or composition.[2] Such assent must be obtained genuinely, and not by fraud or misrepresentation.[3]

Where the debtor, having reached a valid and binding composition, is subsequently adjudicated bankrupt, if the scheme is one which provides that his property once again vests in him, the rights of those creditors who were not bound by the scheme are as though there had been no scheme or composition.[4]

A dissenting creditor will obtain leave to levy execution where the scheme is invalid as against him[5] unless he has been guilty of undue delay in opposing its validity.[6]

1 Bankruptcy Act 1914, Sch 1, r 14, ss 16(2), (3) and 151.
2 Ibid, s 17.
3 *Cooling v Noyes* (1795) 6 Term Rep 263; *Mallalieu v Hodgson* (1851) 16 QB 689; see generally 5 The Digest 9657 ff.
4 *Crew v Terry* (1877) 2 CPD 403.
5 *Re Cobb, ex p Fairfax and Bryson* (1866) 14 WR 289.
6 *Re Sullivan, ex p Sullivan* (1866) 15 LT 434.

30.8.2 *Under the New Law.* Once a composition has been finalised, the creditor who:

(a) had notice of, and
(b) was entitled to vote at

the meeting of creditors, irrespective of whether or not he chose to attend the meeting, is bound by the scheme, and any action brought by him will therefore be dismissed.[1] However, a creditor who had no notice of the meeting, or whose interests are unfairly prejudiced by the scheme, or who alleges that there has been a material irregularity at the meeting, may apply to the court within 28 days of the date on which the chairman of the meeting reports the result to the court. On such an application, the court may revoke the decision of the meeting and direct that the applicant creditor's proposals be considered at a fresh meeting, and give such further directions as it thinks fit.[2] The creditor whose claim is not for a bankruptcy debt, or is one which would not be discharged by the discharge of the bankrupt, will not be bound by a scheme or composition, and will therefore be able to pursue such claim in the courts. A judgment creditor is not entitled to issue a writ of fieri facias after a valid scheme or composition[3] nor is he permitted to execute a garnishee order;[4] it seems therefore that unless he has taken steps to oppose the validity of scheme generally or as against himself he will be debarred from execution and limited to his rights (if any) under the scheme.

1 Insolvency Act 1986, s 260(2).
2 Insolvency Act 1986, s 262.
3 *Stone v Jellicoe* (1864) 11 LT 140.
4 *Kent v Tomkinson* (1867) 17 LT 41.

30.9 THE TRUSTEE AS LITIGANT

Costs

30.9.1 *In Old Law cases.* If the trustee institutes proceedings on behalf of the estate, or becomes a party to proceedings either by virtue of an action being brought against him as trustee or because he is made plaintiff or defendant in that capacity, he is in the same position as the bankrupt himself would be.

Thus, he must initially fund the action or its defence out of his own pocket, and similarly pay any damages and costs which may be awarded against him.[1] If the action is one in which he has participated properly, he will be entitled to reimbursement from the estate.[2]

He will not be entitled to claim reimbursement from the estate if in the opinion of the court the litigation arose out of the trustee's reckless conduct or mismanagement of the dispute[3] or if he brings a frivolous[4] or unsuccessful[5] appeal. He may be ordered partly to fund the defence of an action himself where the action was in the first instance properly brought but where he should have applied to stay the action when its defence was no longer to the benefit of the estate.[6]

If the action was properly taken by the trustee, he may be able to claim a reimbursement notwithstanding the fact that he did not seek or obtain the approval of the committee of inspection;[7] conversely, he may be ordered to pay the costs in a proper case even though he has obtained such consent.[8]

1 *Pitts v La Fontaine* (1880) 6 App Cas 482.
2 Ibid.
3 *Re Bryant, ex p Gordon* (1889) 6 Morr 262.
4 *Re Vanderhaege, ex p Viney* [1888] WN 7, CA.
5 *Re Malden Gibson & Co, ex p James* (1886) 55 LT 708.
6 *Tanqueray v Bowles* (1872) LR 14 Eq 151.
7 *Re Branson, ex p Trustee* [1914] 2 KB 701.
8 *Re Attwater, ex p Watts* (1862) 3 De GJ & Sm 394.

30.9.2 *Under the New Law.* The trustee's power of participation in proceedings is subject to the permission of the creditors' committee[1] but he may obtain subsequent ratification either from the committee or from the court in order to recoup his expenses.[2] Such ratification may only be given if the trustee acted in an emergency and seeks it without undue delay. In other cases, he will be ordered to bear the cost of his actions himself.

1 Insolvency Act 1986, s 314(1)(a), Sch 5, para 2.
2 Ibid, s 314(4).

Forum

30.9.3 The trustee who brings an action should do so in the court having bankruptcy jurisdiction. In an existing action, the court making the receiving order may order that the action be transferred to it. In Old Law cases, such transfer is a discretionary matter[1] dependent upon the question of advantage to the estate;[2] under the New Law, the Rules provide for the transfer of proceedings, but the Insolvency Act 1986 expressly provides that the validity of proceedings is not to be affected by their being brought in the wrong court.[3]

1 *Re Somes, ex p Deller v Somes* (1895) 2 Mans 396.
2 *Re Ross, ex p Trustee* (1888) 5 Morr 281.
3 Insolvency Act 1986, s 373(4). Individual Insolvency Rules 1986, rr 7.11–7.15.

Title in litigation

30.9.4 *Under the Old Law.* An action against the trustee should be against 'The trustee of the property of AB, a bankrupt';[1] an action by the trustee should be in his own name as trustee.[2]

1 Bankruptcy Act 1914, s 76.
2 *Re Maberly, ex p National Bank of Scotland* (1834) 1 Mont & A 644.

30.9.5 *Under the New Law.* The trustee may sue or be sued in his official name 'the trustee of the estate of MN a bankrupt',[1] but the Act provides that he may be referred to as 'the trustee in bankruptcy' of the particular bankrupt.[2]

1 Insolvency Act 1986, ss 305(4) and 314(5) and Sch 5, para 14.
2 Ibid, s 305(4).

30.10 ARBITRATION

Arbitration agreement made before bankruptcy

30.10.1 By the Arbitration Act 1950 s 3(1) an arbitration clause is enforceable by or against the trustee of a bankrupt party provided that he adopts the contract in which the clause is a term.

If the contract is not adopted, the matter may still be referred to arbitration at the discretion of the court with bankruptcy jurisdiction, if it is one the determination of which is necessary in connection with the bankruptcy upon application to that court by another party to the contract or by the trustee with the consent of the committee.[1] An order that a matter be referred to arbitration following the bankruptcy of one of the parties to the arbitration agreement may only be made by such parties; the bankrupt himself has no locus standi.

An agreement to submit disputes to arbitration made between a person who subequently becomes bankrupt and another, or others, will remain valid notwithstanding the bankruptcy.[2] Nevertheless, if the trustee is appointed before an award is made, he may revoke the submission.[3] He loses his entitlement to do so if he adopts the contract which contains the arbitration agreement[4] or if the court has ordered that the matter in question be submitted to arbitration.[5]

1 Arbitration Act 1950, s 3(2).
2 Insolvency Act 1986, s 314(5), Sch 5, para 14; *Hemsworth v Brian* (1845) 1 CB 131.
3 *Marsh v Wood* (1829) 9 B & C 659.
4 Arbitration Act 1950, s 3(1) and see above.
5 Ibid, s 3(2); *Re Geddes, ex p Michie* (1840) 1 Mont D & De G 181.

Arbitration proceedings commenced before bankruptcy

30.10.2 Under the New Law such proceedings may be stayed following the bankruptcy of the respondent, or they may be stayed or allowed by the court to continue on such terms as it thinks fit.[1] There is no automatic revocation of the submission by virtue of the bankruptcy.[2]

1 Insolvency Act 1986, s 285(1) and (2).
2 *Hemsworth v Brian* (1845) 1 CB 131.

Proceedings commenced after bankruptcy

30.10.3 *The bankrupt claimant.* If the contract containing the arbitration clause has been adopted by the trustee he will be bound by the agreement to submit disputes to arbitration.[1] Thus, if he seeks to bring proceedings in connection with any dispute to which the agreement applies the respondent may obtain an order of the court to stay such proceedings.[2]

The court has a general discretion to order that an action be stayed where its subject matter comes within a valid arbitration clause.[3] The stay may be ordered pursuant to an application by any party to the court action if 'any party to an arbitration agreement, or any person claiming through or under him' commences such action; the application must be made before the applicant has taken any other step in the proceedings, and the court has jurisdiction to grant ancillary relief on such application.[4]

The Court of Appeal has held that an insolvent plaintiff, who alleged that his insolvency resulted from the actions of the defendant should be permitted to continue an action commenced in respect of a dispute to which a valid arbitration agreement applied, notwithstanding the agreement.[5] The reasons given for permitting the action to continue were that legal aid was available to the plaintiff in the court proceedings, as it would of course not be in an arbitration, and since the plaintiff would not be able to afford the cost of arbitration because of poverty caused by the actions of the defendant, to stay the court action would lead to a denial of justice.

However, a stay will not be granted merely because the applicant does not wish to incur the cost of arbitration, which is likely to be higher than that of court proceedings.[6]

The respondent will not automatically be entitled to stay proceedings commenced in court by the trustee of a bankrupt claimant, but in order to do so he must show:

(a) adoption of the contract containing the arbitration clause; and
(b) that the proceedings relate to a matter agreed to be referred to arbitration.[7]

Conversely, it would seem that if the trustee has disclaimed the contract, or has neither adopted it nor taken any steps in the arbitration proceedings, he may pursue other remedies, as he will not be bound by the arbitration agreement.

1 Arbitration Act 1950, s 3(1).
2 Ibid, s 4.
3 Ibid, s 4(1).
4 *Pini v Ronocoroni* [1892] 1 Ch 633.
5 *Fakes v Taylor Woodrow Construction Ltd* [1973] QB 436.
6 *Ford v Clarkson's Holidays* [1971] 3 All ER 454, CA.
7 Arbitration Act 1950, s 3(1).

30.10.4 *The bankrupt respondent.* The trustee will be placed in the position of the respondent by operation of law, and provided that he adopts the contract, the arbitration agreement will be prima facie enforceable against him.[1]

However, the prohibition against the commencement of a court action against a bankrupt after presentation of a petition and before adjudication extends to 'any other legal proceedings' and the court will therefore make an order on the application of the respondent that the arbitration proceedings be stayed unless such proceedings were commenced with the leave of the court having bankruptcy jurisdiction.[2]

As in the case of court proceedings, this applies only in respect of debts provable in the bankruptcy of the respondent. Moreover, if the claimant is a secured creditor and the arbitration clause is a term of his security, he may pursue the remedy of arbitration notwithstanding the bankruptcy.[3]

It has been held under the Old Law, a bankrupt can take part in a reference and an order for costs against him will be enforced, notwithstanding that the subject matter was in respect of a cause of action which passed to his trustee.[3]

1 Insolvency Act 1986, s 285(3).
2 Ibid, s 285(4).
3 *Re Milnes and Robertson* (1854) 15 CB 451.

The award

30.10.5 The trustee of a bankrupt party to a reference to arbitration will be bound by an award made pursuant to proceedings validly commenced or pursued in accordance with the criteria set out above, even if the bankrupt was not known by the other party to the reference to be so at the time of the making of the award.[1] However, it seems that if the bankruptcy commences before the making of the award and the trustee knows of the reference and, being in a position to object, chooses either not to do so, or not to appeal against the arbitrator's refusal to accept such objection, he is treated as having taken part in the arbitration and he will be bound by the award.[2]

The trustee who is bound by the award is in the position of the bankrupt party and must satisfy any conditions which the bankrupt would have had to fulful in order to be entitled to the benefit of the award such as, for example, the satisfaction of the bankrupt's solicitor's lien for costs.[3]

[1] *Whitacre v Pawlin* (1691) 2 Vern 229.
[2] *Dod v Herring* (1829) 3 Sim 143.
[3] Arbitration Act 1950, s 26.

Execution

30.10.6 The considerations in relation to an enforceable award are the same as those which apply to execution by a judgment creditor following proceedings in court.

The successful claimant in an arbitration must apply to the court for leave to enforce the award as if it were a judgment.[1] If the respondent is bankrupt, the court can theoretically only grant leave in respect of a debt or liability for which proof cannot be lodged in the bankruptcy.[2]

[1] Arbitration Act 1950, s 26.
[2] Ibid, s 26.

Appendices

Appendix 1

Insolvency Act 1986 (selected provisions)

THE SECOND GROUP OF PARTS: INSOLVENCY OF INDIVIDUALS; BANKRUPTCY

Part VIII: Individual Voluntary Arrangements

Moratorium for insolvent debtor

252 Interim order of court (1) In the circumstances specified below, the court may in the case of a debtor (being an individual) make an interim order under this section.
(2) An interim order has the effect that, during the period for which it is in force –
(a) no bankruptcy petition relating to the debtor may be presented or proceeded with, and
(b) no other proceedings, and no execution or other legal process may be commenced or continued against the debtor or his property except with the leave of the court.

253 Application for interim order (1) Application to the court for an interim order may be made where the debtor intends to make a proposal to his creditors for a composition in satisfaction of his debts or a scheme of arrangement of his affairs (from here on referred to, in either case, as a 'voluntary arrangement').
(2) The proposal must provide for some person ('the nominee') to act in relation to

the voluntary arrangement either as trustee or otherwise for the purpose of supervising its implementation.
(3) Subject as follows, the application may be made –
(a) if the debtor is an undischarged bankrupt, by the debtor, the trustee of his estate, or the official receiver, and
(b) in any other case, by the debtor.
(4) An application shall not be made under subsection (3)(a) unless the debtor has given notice of his proposal (that is, the proposal to his creditors for a voluntary arrangement) to the official receiver and, if there is one, the trustee of his estate.
(5) An application shall not be made while a bankruptcy petition presented by the debtor is pending, if the court has, under section 273 below, appointed an insolvency practitioner to inquire into the debtor's affairs and report.

254 Effect of application (1) At any time when an application under section 253 for an interim order is pending, the court may stay any action, execution or other legal process against the property or person of the debtor.
(2) Any court in which proceedings are pending against an individual may, on proof that an application under that section has been made in respect of that individual, either stay the proceedings or allow them to continue on such terms as it thinks fit.

255 Cases in which interim order can be made (1) The court shall not make an interim order on an application under section 253 unless it is satisfied –
(a) that the debtor intends to make such a proposal as is mentioned in that section;
(b) that on the day of the making of the application the debtor was an undischarged bankrupt or was able to petition for his own bankruptcy;
(c) that no previous application has been made by the debtor for an interim order in the period of 12 months ending with that day; and
(d) that the nominee under the debtor's proposal to his creditors is a person who is for the time being qualified to act as an insolvency practitioner in relation to the debtor, and is willing to act in relation to the proposal.
(2) The court may make an order if it thinks that it would be appropriate to do so for the purpose of facilitating the consideration and implementation of the debtor's proposal.
(3) Where the debtor is an undischarged bankrupt, the interim order may contain provision as to the conduct of the bankruptcy, and the administration of the bankrupt's estate, during the period for which the order is in force.
(4) Subject as follows, the provision contained in an interim order by virtue of subsection (3) may include provision staying proceedings in the bankruptcy or modifying any provision in this Group of Parts, and any provision of the rules in their application to the debtor's bankruptcy.
(5) An interim order shall not, in relation to a bankrupt, make provision relaxing or removing any of the requirements of provisions in this Group of Parts, or of the rules, unless the court is satisfied that that provision is unlikely to result in any significant diminution in, or in the value of, the debtor's estate for the purposes of the bankruptcy.
(6) Subject to the following provisions of this Part, an interim order made on an application under section 253 ceases to have effect at the end of the period of 14 days beginning with the day after the making of the order.

256 Nominee's report on debtor's proposal (1) Where an interim order has been made on an application under section 253, the nominee shall, before the order ceases to have effect, submit a report to the court stating –
(a) whether, in his opinion, a meeting of the debtor's creditors should be summoned to consider the debtor's proposal, and

(b) if in his opinion such a meeting should be summoned, the date on which, and time and place at which, he proposes the meeting should be held.

(2) For the purpose of enabling the nominee to prepare his report the debtor shall submit to the nominee –

(a) a document setting out the terms of the voluntary arrangement which the debtor is proposing, and

(b) a statement of his affairs containing –

(i) such particulars of his creditors and of his debts and other liabilities and of his assets as may be prescribed, and

(ii) such other information as may be prescribed.

(3) The court may, on an application made by the debtor in a case where the nominee has failed to submit the report required by this section, do one or both of the following, namely –

(a) direct that the nominee shall be replaced as such by another person qualified to act as an insolvency practitioner in relation to the debtor;

(b) direct that the interim order shall continue, or (if it has ceased to have effect) be renewed, for such further period as the court may specify in the direction.

(4) The court may, on the application of the nominee, extend the period for which the interim order has effect so as to enable the nominee to have more time to prepare his report.

(5) If the court is satisfied on receiving the nominee's report that a meeting of the debtor's creditors should be summoned to consider the debtor's proposal, the court shall direct that the period for which the interim order has effect shall be extended, for such further period as it may specify in the direction, for the purpose of enabling the debtor's proposal to be considered by his creditors in accordance with the following provisions of this Part.

(6) The court may discharge the interim order if it is satisfied, on the application of the nominee –

(a) that the debtor has failed to comply with his obligations under subsection (2), or

(b) that for any other reason it would be inappropriate for a meeting of the debtor's creditors to be summoned to consider the debtor's proposal.

257 Summoning of creditors' meeting (1) Where it has been reported to the court under section 256 that a meeting of the debtor's creditors should be summoned, the nominee (or his replacement under section 256(3)(a) shall, unless the court otherwise directs, summon that meeting for the time, date and place proposed in his report.

(2) The persons to be summoned to the meeting are every creditor of the debtor of whose claim and address the person summoning the meeting is aware.

(3) For this purpose the creditors of a debtor who is an undischarged bankrupt include –

(a) every person who is a creditor of the bankrupt in respect of a bankruptcy debt, and

(b) every person who would be such a creditor if the bankruptcy had commenced on the day on which notice of the meeting is given.

Consideration and implementation of debtor's proposal

258 Decisions of creditors' meeting (1) A creditors' meeting summoned under section 257 shall decide whether to approve the proposed voluntary arrangement.

(2) The meeting may approve the proposed voluntary arrangement with modifications, but shall not do so unless the debtor consents to each modification.

(3) The modifications subject to which the proposed voluntary arrangement may be approved may include one conferring the functions proposed to be conferred on the nominee on another person qualified to act as an insolvency practitioner in relation to the debtor.

But they shall not include any modification by virtue of which the proposal ceases to be a proposal such as is mentioned in section 253.

(4) The meeting shall not approve any proposal or modification which affects the right of a secured creditor of the debtor to enforce his security, except with the concurrence of the creditor concerned.

(5) Subject as follows, the meeting shall not approve any proposal or modification under which –

(a) any preferential debt of the debtor is to be paid otherwise than in priority to such of his debts as are not preferential debts, or

(b) a preferential creditor of the debtor is to be paid an amount in respect of a preferential debt that bears to that debt a smaller proportion than is borne to another preferential debt by the amount that is to be paid in respect of that other debt.

However, the meeting may approve such a proposal or modification with the concurrence of the preferential creditor concerned.

(6) Subject as above, the meeting shall be conducted in accordance with the rules.

(7) In this section 'preferential debt' has the meaning given by section 386 in Part XII; and 'preferential creditor' is to be construed accordingly.

259 Report of decisions to court (1) After the conclusion in accordance with the rules of the meeting summoned under section 257, the chairman of the meeting shall report the result of it to the court and, immediately after so reporting, shall give notice of the result of the meeting to such persons as may be prescribed.

(2) If the report is that the meeting has declined (with or without modifications) to approve the debtor's proposal, the court may discharge any interim order which is in force in relation to the debtor.

260 Effect of approval (1) This section has effect where the meeting summoned under section 257 approves the proposed voluntary arrangement (with or without modifications).

(2) The approved arrangement –

(a) takes effect as if made by the debtor at the meeting, and

(b) binds every person who in accordance with the rules had notice of, and was entitled to vote at, the meeting (whether or not he was present or represented at it) as if he were a party to the arrangement.

(3) The Deeds of Arrangement Act 1914 does not apply to the approved voluntary arrangement.

(4) Any interim order in force in relation to the debtor immediately before the end of the period of 28 days beginning with the day on which the report with respect to the creditors' meeting was made to the court under section 259 ceases to have effect at the end of that period.

This subsection applies except to such extent as the court may direct for the purposes of any application under section 262 below.

(5) Where proceedings on a bankruptcy petition have been stayed by an interim order which ceases to have effect under subsection (4), that petition is deemed, unless the court otherwise orders, to have been dismissed.

261 Effect where debtor an undischarged bankrupt (1) Subject as follows, where the creditors' meeting summoned under section 257 approves the proposed voluntary arrangement (with or without modifications) and the debtor is an

undischarged bankrupt, the court may do one or both of the following, namely –
(a) annul the bankruptcy order by which he was adjudged bankrupt;
(b) give such directions with respect to the conduct of the bankruptcy and the administration of the bankrupt's estate as it thinks appropriate for facilitating the implementation of the approved voluntary arrangement.
(2) The court shall not annul a bankruptcy order under subsection (1) –
(a) at any time before the end of the period of 28 days beginning with the day on which the report of the creditors' meeting was made to the court under section 259, or
(b) at any time when an application under section 262 below, or an appeal in respect of such an application, is pending or at any time in the period within which such an appeal may be brought.

262 Challenge of meeting's decision (1) Subject to this section, an application to the court may be made, by any of the persons specified below, on one or both of the following grounds, namely –
(a) that a voluntary arrangement approved by a creditors' meeting summoned under section 257 unfairly prejudices the interests of a creditor of the debtor;
(b) that there has been some material irregularity at or in relation to such a meeting.
(2) The persons who may apply under this section are –
(a) the debtor;
(b) a person entitled, in accordance with the rules, to vote at the creditors' meeting;
(c) the nominee (or his replacement under section 256(3)(a) or 258(3)); and
(d) if the debtor is an undischarged bankrupt, the trustee of his estate or the official receiver.
(3) An application under this section shall not be made after the end of the period of 28 days beginning with the day on which the report of the creditors' meeting was made to the court under section 259.
(4) Where on an application under this section the court is satisfied as to either of the grounds mentioned in subsection (1), it may do one or both of the following, namely –
(a) revoke or suspend any approval given by the meeting;
(b) give a direction to any person for the summoning of a further meeting of the debtor's creditors to consider any revised proposal he may make or, in a case falling within subsection (1)(b), to reconsider his original proposal.
(5) Where at any time after giving a direction under subsection (4)(b) for the summoning of a meeting to consider a revised proposal the court is satisfied that the debtor does not intend to submit such a proposal, the court shall revoke the direction and revoke or suspend any approval given at the previous meeting.
(6) Where the court gives a direction under subsection (4)(b), it may also give a direction continuing or, as the case may require, renewing, for such period as may be specified in the direction, the effect in relation to the debtor of any interim order.
(7) In any case where the court, on an application made under this section with respect to a creditors' meeting, gives a direction under subsection (4)(b) or revokes or suspends an approval under subsection (4)(a) or (5), the court may give such supplemental directions as it thinks fit and, in particular, directions with respect to –
(a) things done since the meeting under any voluntary arrangement approved by the meeting, and
(b) such things done since the meeting as could not have been done if an interim order had been in force in relation to the debtor when they were done.
(8) Except in pursuance of the preceding provisions of this section, an approval given at a creditors' meeting summoned under section 257 is not invalidated by any irregularity at or in relation to the meeting.

263 Implementation and supervision of approved voluntary arrangement (1) This section applies where a voluntary arrangement approved by a creditors' meeting summoned under section 257 has taken effect.
(2) The person who is for the time being carrying out, in relation to the voluntary arrangement, the functions conferred by virtue of the approval on the nominee (or his replacement under section 256(3)(a) or 258(3)) shall be known as the supervisor of the voluntary arrangement.
(3) If the debtor, any of his creditors or any other person is dissatisfied by any act, omission or decision of the supervisor, he may apply to the court; and on such an application the court may –
(a) confirm, reverse or modify any act or decision of the supervisor,
(b) give him directions, or
(c) make such other order as it thinks fit.
(4) The supervisor may apply to the court for directions in relation to any particular matter arising under the voluntary arrangement.
(5) The court may, whenever –
(a) it is expedient to appoint a person to carry out the functions of the supervisor, and
(b) it is inexpedient, difficult or impracticable for an appointment to be made without the assistance of the court,
make an order appointing a person who is qualified to act as an insolvency practitioner in relation to the debtor, either in substitution for the existing supervisor or to fill a vacancy.
This is without prejudice to section 41(2) of the Trustee Act 1925 (power of court to appoint trustees of deeds of arrangement).
(6) The power conferred by subsection (5) is exercisable so as to increase the number of persons exercising the functions of the supervisor or, where there is more than one person exercising those functions, so as to replace one or more of those persons.

Part IX: Bankruptcy

BANKRUPTCY PETITIONS; BANKRUPTCY ORDERS

Preliminary

264 Who may present a bankruptcy petition (1) A petition for a bankruptcy order to be made against an individual may be presented to the court in accordance with the following provisions of this Part –
(a) by one of the individual's creditors or jointly by more than one of them,
(b) by the individual himself,
(c) by the supervisor of, or any person (other than the individual) who is for the time being bound by, a voluntary arrangement proposed by the individual and approved under Part VIII, or
(d) where a criminal bankruptcy order has been made against the individual, by the Official Petitioner or by any person specified in the order in pursuance of section 39(3)(b) of the Powers of Criminal Courts Act 1973.
(2) Subject to those provisions, the court may make a bankruptcy order on any such petition.

265 Conditions to be satisfied in respect of debtor (1) A bankruptcy petition shall not be presented to the court under section 264(1)(a) or (b) unless the debtor –
(a) is domiciled in England and Wales,
(b) is personally present in England and Wales on the day on which the petition is presented, or
(c) at any time in the period of 3 years ending with that day –

(i) has been ordinarily resident, or has had a place of residence, in England and Wales, or
(ii) has carried on business in England and Wales.

(2) The reference in subsection (1)(c) to an individual carrying on business includes –
(a) the carrying on of business by a firm or partnership of which the individual is a member, and
(b) the carrying on of business by an agent or manager for the individual or for such a firm or partnership.

266 Other preliminary conditions (1) Where a bankruptcy petition relating to an individual is presented by a person who is entitled to present a petition under two or more paragraphs of section 264(1), the petition is to be treated for the purposes of this Part as a petition under such one of those paragraphs as may be specified in the petition.
(2) A bankruptcy petition shall not be withdrawn without the leave of the court.
(3) The court has a general power, if it appears to it appropriate to do so on the grounds that there has been a contravention of the rules or for any other reason, to dismiss a bankruptcy petition or to stay proceedings on such a petition; and, where it stays proceedings on a petition, it may do so on such terms and conditions as it thinks fit.
(4) Without prejudice to subsection (3), where a petition under section 264(1)(a), (b) or (c) in respect of an individual is pending at a time when a criminal bankruptcy order is made against him, or is presented after such an order has been so made, the court may on the application of the Official Petitioner dismiss the petition if it appears to it appropriate to do so.

Creditor's petition

267 Grounds of creditor's petition (1) A creditor's petition must be in respect of one or more debts owed by the debtor, and the petitioning creditor or each of the petitioning creditors must be a person to whom the debt or (as the case may be) at least one of the debts is owed.
(2) Subject to the next three sections, a creditor's petition may be presented to the court in respect of a debt or debts only if, at the time the petition is presented –
(a) the amount of the debt, or the aggregate amount of the debts, is equal to or exceeds the bankruptcy level,
(b) the debt, or each of the debts, is for a liquidated sum payable to the petitioning creditor, or one or more of the petitioning creditors, either immediately or at some certain, future time, and is unsecured,
(c) the debt, or each of the debts, is a debt which the debtor appears either to be unable to pay or to have no reasonable prospect of being able to pay, and
(d) there is no outstanding application to set aside a statutory demand served (under section 268 below) in respect of the debt or any of the debts.

(3) A debt is not to be regarded for the purposes of subsection (2) as a debt for a liquidated sum by reason only that the amount of the debt is specified in a criminal bankruptcy order.
(4) 'The bankruptcy level' is £750; but the Secretary of State may by order in a statutory instrument substitute any amount specified in the order for that amount or (as the case may be) for the amount which by virtue of such an order is for the time being the amount of the bankruptcy level.
(5) An order shall not be made under subsection (4) unless a draft of it has been laid before, and approved by a resolution of, each House of Parliament.

268 Definition of 'inability to pay', etc; the statutory demand (1) For the purposes of section 267(2)(c), the debtor appears to be unable to pay a debt if, but only if, the debt is payable immediately and either –

(a) the petitioning creditor to whom the debt is owed has served on the debtor a demand (known as 'the statutory demand') in the prescribed form requiring him to pay the debt or to secure or compound for it to the satisfaction of the creditor, at least 3 weeks have elapsed since the demand was served and the demand has been neither complied with nor set aside in accordance with the rules, or
(b) execution or other process issued in respect of the debt on a judgment or order of any court in favour of the petitioning creditor, or one or more of the petitioning creditors to whom the debt is owed, has been returned unsatisfied in whole or in part.

(2) For the purposes of section 267(2)(c) the debtor appears to have no reasonable prospect of being able to pay a debt if, but only if, the debt is not immediately payable and –
(a) the petitioning creditor to whom it is owed has served on the debtor a demand (also known as 'the statutory demand') in the prescribed form requiring him to establish to the satisfaction of the creditor that there is a reasonable prospect that the debtor will be able to pay the debt when it falls due,
(b) at least 3 weeks have elapsed since the demand was served, and
(c) the demand has been neither complied with nor set aside in accordance with the rules.

269 Creditor with security (1) A debt which is the debt, or one of the debts, in respect of which a creditor's petition is presented need not be unsecured if either –
(a) the petition contains a statement by the person having the right to enforce the security that he is willing, in the event of a bankruptcy order being made, to give up his security for the benefit of all the bankrupt's creditors, or
(b) the petition is expressed not to be made in respect of the secured part of the debt and contains a statement by that person of the estimated value at the date of the petition of the security for the secured part of the debt.

(2) In a case falling within subsection (1)(b) the secured and unsecured parts of the debt are to be treated for the purposes of sections 267 and 270 as separate debts.

270 Expedited petition In the case of a creditor's petition presented wholly or partly in respect of a debt which is the subject of a statutory demand under section 268, the petition may be presented before the end of the 3-week period there mentioned if there is a serious possibility that the debtor's property or the value of any of his property will be significantly diminished during that period and the petition contains a statement to that effect.

271 Proceedings on creditor's petition (1) The court shall not make a bankruptcy order on a creditor's petition unless it is satisfied that the debt, or one of the debts, in respect of which the petition was presented is either –
(a) a debt which, having been payable at the date of the petition or having since become payable, has been neither paid nor secured or compounded for, or
(b) a debt which the debtor has no reasonable prospect of being able to pay when it falls due.

(2) In a case in which the petition contains such a statement as is required by section 270, the court shall not make a bankruptcy order until at least 3 weeks have elapsed since the service of any statutory demand under section 268.

(3) The court may dismiss the petition if it is satisfied that the debtor is able to pay all his debts or is satisfied –
(a) that the debtor has made an offer to secure or compound for a debt in respect of which the petition is presented,
(b) that the acceptance of that offer would have required the dismissal of the petition, and

(c) that the offer has been unreasonably refused;

and, in determining for the purposes of this subsection whether the debtor is able to pay all his debts, the court shall take into account his contingent and prospective liabilities.

(4) In determining for the purposes of this section what constitutes a reasonable prospect that a debtor will be able to pay a debt when it falls due, it is to be assumed that the prospect given by the facts and other matters known to the creditor at the time he entered into the transaction resulting in the debt was a reasonable prospect.

(5) Nothing in sections 267 to 271 prejudices the power of the court, in accordance with the rules, to authorise a creditor's petition to be amended by the omission of any creditor or debt and to be proceeded with as if things done for the purposes of those sections had been done only by or in relation to the remaining creditors or debts.

Debtor's petition

272 Grounds of debtor's petition (1) A debtor's petition may be presented to the court only on the grounds that the debtor is unable to pay his debts.

(2) The petition shall be accompanied by a statement of the debtor's affairs containing –

(a) such particulars of the debtor's creditors and of his debts and other liabilities and of his assets as may be prescribed, and

(b) such other information as may be prescribed.

273 Appointment of insolvency practitioner by the court (1) Subject to the next section, on the hearing of a debtor's petition the court shall not make a bankruptcy order if it appears to the court –

(a) that if a bankruptcy order were made the aggregate amount of the bankruptcy debts, so far as unsecured, would be less than the small bankruptcies level,

(b) that if a bankruptcy order were made, the value of the bankrupt's estate would be equal to or more than the minimum amount,

(c) that within the period of 5 years ending with the presentation of the petition the debtor has neither been adjudged bankrupt nor made a composition with his creditors in satisfaction of his debts or a scheme of arrangement of his affairs, and

(d) that it would be appropriate to appoint a person to prepare a report under section 274.

'The minimum amount' and 'the small bankruptcies level' mean such amounts as may for the time being be prescribed for the purposes of this section.

(2) Where on the hearing of the petition, it appears to the court as mentioned in subsection (1), the court shall appoint a person who is qualified to act as an insolvency practitioner in relation to the debtor –

(a) to prepare a report under the next section, and

(b) subject to section 258(3) in Part VIII, to act in relation to any voluntary arrangement to which the report relates either as trustee or otherwise for the purpose of supervising its implementation.

274 Action on report of insolvency practitioner (1) A person appointed under section 273 shall inquire into the debtor's affairs, and, within such period as the court may direct, shall submit a report to the court stating whether the debtor is willing, for the purposes of Part VIII, to make a proposal for a voluntary arrangement.

(2) A report which states that the debtor is willing as above mentioned shall also state –

(a) whether, in the opinion of the person making the report, a meeting of the debtor's creditors should be summoned to consider the proposal, and

(b) if in that person's opinion such a meeting should be summoned, the date on which, and time and place at which, he proposes the meeting should be held.

(3) On considering a report under this section the court may –

(a) without any application, make an interim order under section 252, if it thinks that it is appropriate to do so for the purpose of facilitating the consideration and implementation of the debtor's proposal, or

(b) if it thinks it would be inappropriate to make such an order, make a bankruptcy order.

(4) An interim order made by virtue of this section ceases to have effect at the end of such period as the court may specify for the purpose of enabling the debtor's proposal to be considered by his creditors in accordance with the applicable provisions of Part VIII.

(5) Where it has been reported to the court under this section that a meeting of the debtor's creditors should be summoned, the person making the report shall, unless the court otherwise directs, summon that meeting for the time, date and place proposed in his report.

The meeting is then deemed to have been summoned under section 257 in Part VIII, and subsections (2) and (3) of that section, and sections 258 to 263 apply accordingly.

275 Summary administration (1) Where on the hearing of a debtor's petition the court makes a bankruptcy order and the case is as specified in the next subsection, the court shall, if it appears to it appropriate to do so, issue a certificate for the summary administration of the bankrupt's estate.

(2) That case is where it appears to the court –

(a) that if a bankruptcy order were made the aggregate amount of the bankruptcy debts so far as unsecured would be less than the small bankruptcies level (within the meaning given by section 273), and

(b) that within the period of 5 years ending with the presentation of the petition the debtor has neither been adjudged bankrupt nor made a composition with his creditors in satisfaction of his debts or a scheme of arrangement of his affairs,

whether the bankruptcy order is made because it does not appear to the court as mentioned in section 273(1)(b) or (d), or it is made because the court thinks it would be inappropriate to make an interim order under section 252.

(3) The court may at any time revoke a certificate issued under this section if it appears to it that, on any grounds existing at the time the certificate was issued, the certificate ought not to have been issued.

Other cases for special consideration

276 Default in connection with voluntary arrangement (1) The court shall not make a bankruptcy order on a petition under section 264(1)(c) (supervisor of, or person bound by, voluntary arrangement proposed and approved) unless it is satisfied –

(a) that the debtor has failed to comply with his obligations under the voluntary arrangement, or

(b) that information which was false or misleading in any material particular or which contained material omissions –

   (i) was contained in any statement of affairs or other document supplied by the debtor under Part VIII to any person, or

   (ii) was otherwise made available by the debtor to his creditors at or in connection with a meeting summoned under that Part, or

(c) that the debtor has failed to do all such things as may for the purposes of the voluntary arrangement have been reasonably required of him by the supervisor of the arrangement.

(2) Where a bankruptcy order is made on a petition under section 264(1)(c), any expenses properly incurred as expenses of the administration of the voluntary arrangement in question shall be a first charge on the bankrupt's estate.

277 Petition based on criminal bankruptcy order (1) Subject to section 266(3), the court shall make a bankruptcy order on a petition under section 264(1)(d) on production of a copy of the criminal bankruptcy order on which the petition is based.

This does not apply if it appears to the court that the criminal bankruptcy order has been rescinded on appeal.

(2) Subject to the provisions of this Part, the fact that an appeal is pending against any conviction by virtue of which a criminal bankruptcy order was made does not affect any proceedings on a petition under section 264(1)(d) based on that order.

(3) For the purposes of this section, an appeal against a conviction is pending –

(a) in any case, until the expiration of the period of 28 days beginning with the date of conviction;

(b) if notice of appeal to the Court of Appeal is given during that period and during that period the appellant notifies the official receiver of it, until the determination of the appeal and thereafter for so long as an appeal to the House of Lords is pending within the meaning of section 40(5) of the Powers of Criminal Courts Act 1973.

Commencement and duration of bankruptcy; discharge

278 Commencement and continuance The bankruptcy of an individual against whom a bankruptcy order has been made –

(a) commences with the day on which the order is made, and

(b) continues until the individual is discharged under the following provisions of this Chapter.

279 Duration (1) Subject as follows, a bankrupt is discharged from bankruptcy –

(a) in the case of an individual who was adjudged bankrupt on a petition under section 264(1)(d) or who had been an undischarged bankrupt at any time in the period of 15 years ending with the commencement of the bankruptcy, by an order of the court under the section next following, and

(b) in any other case, by the expiration of the relevant period under this section.

(2) That period is as follows –

(a) where a certificate for the summary administration of the bankrupt's estate has been issued and is not revoked before the bankrupt's discharge, the period of 2 years beginning with the commencement of the bankruptcy, and

(b) in any other case, the period of 3 years beginning with the commencement of the bankruptcy.

(3) Where the court is satisfied on the application of the official receiver that an undischarged bankrupt in relation to whom subsection (1)(b) applies has failed or is failing to comply with any of his obligations under this Part, the court may order that the relevant period under this section shall cease to run for such period, or until the fulfilment of such conditions (including a condition requiring the court to be satisfied as to any matter), as may be specified in the order.

(4) This section is without prejudice to any power of the court to annul a bankruptcy order.

280 Discharge by order of the court (1) An application for an order of the court discharging an individual from bankruptcy in a case falling within section 279(1)(a) may be made by the bankrupt at any time after the end of the period of 5 years beginning with the commencement of the bankruptcy.

(2) On an application under this section the court may –

(a) refuse to discharge the bankrupt from bankruptcy.

(b) make an order discharging him absolutely, or

(c) make an order discharging him subject to such conditions with respect to any income which may subsequently become due to him, or with respect to property devolving upon him, or acquired by him, after his discharge, as may be specified in the order.

(3) The court may provide for an order falling within sub-section (2)(b) or (c) to have immediate effect or to have its effect suspended for such period, or until the fulfilment of such conditions (including a condition requiring the court to be satisfied as to any matter), as may be specified in the order.

281 Effect of discharge (1) Subject as follows, where a bankrupt is dicharged, the discharge releases him from all the bankruptcy debts, but has no effect –

(a) on the functions (so far as they remain to be carried out) of the trustee of his estate, or

(b) on the operation, for the purposes of the carrying out of those functions, of the provisions of this Part;

and, in particular, discharge does not affect the right of any creditor of the bankrupt to prove in the bankruptcy for any debt from which the bankrupt is released.

(2) Discharge does not affect the right of any secured creditor of the bankrupt to enforce his security for the payment of a debt from which the bankrupt is released.

(3) Discharge does not release the bankrupt from any bankruptcy debt which he incurred in respect of, or forbearance in respect of which was secured by means of, any fraud or fraudulent breach of trust to which he was a party.

(4) Discharge does not release the bankrupt from any liability in respect of a fine imposed for an offence or from any liability under a recognisance except, in the case of a penalty imposed for an offence under an enactment relating to the public revenue or of a recognisance, with the consent of the Treasury.

(5) Discharge does not, except to such extent and on such conditions as the court may direct, release the bankrupt from any bankruptcy debt which –

(a) consists in a liability to pay damages for negligence, nuisance or breach of a statutory, contractual or other duty, being damages in respect of personal injuries to any person, or

(b) arises under any order made in family proceedings or in domestic proceedings.

(6) Discharge does not release the bankruptcy from such other bankruptcy debts, not being debts provable in his bankruptcy, as are prescribed.

(7) Discharge does not release any person other than the bankrupt from any liability (whether as partner or co-trustee of the bankrupt or otherwise) from which the bankrupt is released by the discharge, or from any liability as surety for the bankrupt or as a person in the nature of such a surety.

(8) In this section –

'domestic proceedings' means domestic proceedings within the meaning of the Magistrates' Courts Act 1980 and any proceedings which would be such proceedings but for section 65(1)(ii) of that Act (proceedings for variation of order for periodical payments);

'family proceedings' means the same as in Part V of the Matrimonial and Family Proceedings Act 1984;

'fine' means the same as in the Magistrates' Courts Act 1980; and

'personal injuries' includes death and any disease or other impairment of a person's physical or mental condition.

282 Court's power to annul bankruptcy order (1) The court may annul a bankruptcy order if it at any time appears to the court –

(a) that, on any grounds existing at the time the order was made, the order ought not to have been made, or

(b) that, to the extent required by the rules, the bankruptcy debts and the expenses of the bankruptcy have all, since the making of the order, been either paid or secured for to the satisfaction of the court.

(2) The court may annul a bankruptcy order made against an individual on a petition under paragraph (a), (b) or (c) of section 264(1) if it at any time appears to the court, on an application by the Official Petitioner –
(a) that the petition was pending at a time when a criminal bankruptcy order was made against the individual or was presented after such an order was so made, and
(b) no appeal is pending (within the meaning of section 277) against the individual's conviction of any offence by virtue of which the criminal bankruptcy order was made;
and the court shall annul a bankruptcy order made on a petition under section 264(1)(d) if it at any time appears to the court that the criminal bankruptcy order on which the petition was based has been rescinded in consequence of an appeal.
(3) The court may annul a bankruptcy order whether or not the bankrupt has been discharged from the bankruptcy.
(4) Where the court annuls a bankruptcy order (whether under this section or under section 261 in Part VIII) –
(a) any sale or other disposition of property, payment made or other thing duly done, under any provision in this Group of Parts, by or under the authority of the official receiver or a trustee of the bankrupt's estate or by the court is valid, but
(b) if any of the bankrupt's estate is then vested, under any such provision, in such a trustee, it shall vest in such person as the court may appoint or, in default of any such appointment, revert to the bankrupt on such terms (if any) as the court may direct;
and the court may include in its order such supplemental provisions as may be authorised by the rules.
(5) In determining for the purposes of section 279 whether a person was an undischarged bankrupt at any time, any time when he was a bankrupt by virtue of an order that was subsequently annulled is to be disregarded.

Chapter II: Protection of Bankrupt's Estate and Investigation of His Affairs

283 Definition of bankrupt's estate (1) Subject as follows, a bankrupt's estate for the purposes of any of this Group of Parts comprises –
(a) all property belonging to or vested in the bankrupt at the commencement of the bankruptcy, and
(b) any property which by virtue of any of the following provisions of this Part is comprised in that estate or is treated as falling within the preceding paragraph.
(2) Subsection (1) does not apply to –
(a) such tools, books, vehicles and other items of equipment as are necessary to the bankrupt for use personally by him in his employment, business or vocation;
(b) such clothing, bedding, furniture, household equipment and provisions as are necessary for satisfying the basic domestic needs of the bankrupt and his family.
This subsection is subject to section 308 in Chapter IV (certain excluded property reclaimable by trustee).
(3) Subsection (1) does not apply to –
(a) property held by the bankrupt on trust for any other person, or
(b) the right of nomination to a vacant ecclesiastical benefice.
(4) References in any of this Group of Parts to property, in relation to a bankrupt, include references to any power exercisable by him over or in respect of property except in so far as the power is exercisable over or in respect of property not for the time being comprised in the bankrupt's estate and –
(a) is so exercisable at a time after either the official receiver has had his release in respect of that estate under section 299(2) in Chapter III or a meeting summoned by the trustee of that estate under section 331 in Chapter IV has been held, or
(b) cannot be so exercised for the benefit of the bankrupt;

and a power exercisable over or in respect of property is deemed for the purposes of any of this Group of Parts to vest in the person entitled to exercise it at the time of the transaction or event by virtue of which it is exercisable by that person (whether or not it becomes so exercisable at that time).
(5) For the purposes of any such provision in this Group of Parts, property comprised in a bankrupt's estate is so comprised subject to the rights of any person other than the bankrupt (whether as a secured creditor of the bankrupt or otherwise) in relation thereto, but disregarding –
(a) any rights in relation to which a statement such as is required by section 269(1)(a) was made in the petition on which the bankrupt was adjudged bankrupt, and
(b) any rights which have been otherwise given up in accordance with the rules.
(6) This section has effect subject to the provisions of any enactment not contained in this Act under which any property is to be excluded from a bankrupt's estate.

284 Restrictions on dispositions of property (1) Where a person is adjudged bankrupt, any disposition of property made by that person in the period to which this section applies is void except to the extent that it is or was made with the consent of the court, or is or was subsequently ratified by the court.
(2) Subsection (1) applies to a payment (whether in cash or otherwise) as it applies to a disposition of property and, accordingly, where any payment is void by virtue of that subsection, the person paid shall hold the sum paid for the bankrupt as part of his estate.
(3) This section applies to the period beginning with the day of the presentation of the petition for the bankruptcy order and ending with the vesting, under Chapter IV of this Part, of the bankrupt's estate in a trustee.
(4) The preceding provisions of this section do not give a remedy against any person –
(a) in respect of any property or payment which he received before the commencement of the bankruptcy in good faith, for value and without notice that the petition had been presented, or
(b) in respect of any interest in property which derives from an interest in respect of which there is, by virtue of this subsection, no remedy.
(5) Where after the commencement of his bankruptcy the bankrupt has incurred a debt to a banker or other person by reason of the making of a payment which is void under this section, that debt is deemed for the purposes of any of this Group of Parts to have been incurred before the commencement of the bankruptcy unless –
(a) that banker or person had notice of the bankruptcy before the debt was incurred, or
(b) it is not reasonably practicable for the amount of the payment to be recovered from the person to whom it was made.
(6) A disposition of property is void under this section notwithstanding that the property is not or, as the case may be, would not be comprised in the bankrupt's estate; but nothing in this section affects any disposition made by a person of property held by him on trust for any other person.

285 Restriction on proceedings and remedies (1) At any time when proceedings on a bankruptcy petition are pending or an individual has been adjudged bankrupt the court may stay any action, execution or other legal process against the property or person of the debtor or, as the case may be, of the bankrupt.
(2) Any court in which proceedings are pending against any individual may, on proof that a bankruptcy petition has been presented in respect of that individual or that he is an undischarged bankrupt, either stay the proceedings or allow them to continue on such terms as it thinks fit.
(3) After the making of a bankruptcy order no person who is a creditor of the bankrupt in respect of a debt provable in the bankruptcy shall –

(a) have any remedy against the property or person of the bankrupt in respect of that debt, or

(b) before the discharge of the bankrupt, commence any action or other legal proceedings against the bankrupt except with the leave of the court and on such terms as the court may impose.

This is subject to sections 346 (enforcement procedures) and 347 (limited right to distress).

(4) Subject as follows, subsection (3) does not affect the right of a secured creditor of the bankrupt to enforce his security.

(5) Where any goods of an undischarged bankrupt are held by any person by way of pledge, pawn or other security, the official receiver may, after giving notice in writing of his intention to do so, inspect the goods.

Where such a notice has been given to any person, that person is not entitled, without leave of the court, to realise his security unless he has given the trustee of the bankrupt's estate a reasonable opportunity of inspecting the goods and of exercising the bankrupt's right of redemption.

(6) References in this section to the property or goods of the bankrupt are to any of his property or goods, whether or not comprised in his estate.

286 Power to appoint interim receiver (1) The court may, if it is shown to be necessary for the protection of the debtor's property, at any time after the presentation of a bankruptcy petition and before making a bankruptcy order, appoint the official receiver to be interim receiver of the debtor's property.

(2) Where the court has, on a debtor's petition, appointed an insolvency practitioner under section 273 and it is shown to the court as mentioned in subsection (1) of this section, the court may, without making a bankruptcy order, appoint that practitioner, instead of the official receiver, to be interim receiver of the debtor's property.

(3) The court may by an order appointing any person to be an interim receiver direct that his powers shall be limited or restricted in any respect; but, save as so directed, an interim receiver has, in relation to the debtor's property, all the rights, powers, duties and immunities of a receiver and manager under the next section.

(4) An order of the court appointing any person to be an interim receiver shall require that person to take immediate possession of the debtor's property or, as the case may be, the part of it to which his powers as interim receiver are limited.

(5) Where an interim receiver has been appointed, the debtor shall give him such inventory of his property and such other information, and shall attend on the interim receiver at such times, as the latter may for the purpose of carrying out his functions under this section reasonably require.

(6) Where an interim receiver is appointed, section 285(3) applies for the period between the appointment and the making of a bankruptcy order on the petition, or the dismissal of the petition, as if the appointment were the making of such an order.

(7) A person ceases to be interim receiver of a debtor's property if the bankruptcy petition relating to the debtor is dismissed, if a bankruptcy order is made on the petition or if the court by order otherwise terminates the appointment.

(8) References in this section to the debtor's property are to all his property, whether or not it would be comprised in his estate if he were adjudged bankrupt.

287 Receivership pending appointment of trustee (1) Between the making of a bankruptcy order and the time at which the bankrupt's estate vests in a trustee under Chapter IV of this Part, the official receiver is the receiver and (subject to section 370 (special manager)) the manager of the bankrupt's estate and is under a duty to act as such.

(2) The function of the official receiver while acting as receiver or manager of the bankrupt's estate under this section is to protect the estate; and for this purpose –

(a) he has the same powers as if he were a receiver or manager appointed by the High Court, and
(b) he is entitled to sell or otherwise dispose of any perishable goods comprised in the estate and any other goods so comprised the value of which is likely to diminish if they are not disposed of.
(3) The official receiver while acting as receiver or manager of the estate under this section –
(a) shall take all such steps as he thinks fit for protecting any property which may be claimed for the estate by the trustee of that estate,
(b) is not, except in pursuance of directions given by the Secretary of State, required to do anything that involves his incurring expenditure,
(c) may, if he thinks fit (and shall, if so directed by the court) at any time summon a general meeting of the bankrupt's creditors.
(4) Where –
(a) the official receiver acting as receiver or manager of the estate under this section seizes or disposes of any property which is not comprised in the estate, and
(b) at the time of the seizure or disposal the official receiver believes, and has reasonable grounds for believing, that he is entitled (whether in pursuance of an order of the court or otherwise) to seize or dispose of that property,
the official receiver is not to be liable to any person in respect of any loss or damage resulting from the seizure or disposal except in so far as that loss or damage is caused by his negligence; and he has a lien on the property, or the proceeds of its sale, for such of the expenses of the bankrupcy as were incurred in connection with the seizure or disposal.
(5) This section does not apply where by virtue of section 297 (appointment of trustee; special cases) the bankrupt's estate vests in a trustee immediately on the making of the bankruptcy order.

288 Statement of affairs (1) Where a bankruptcy order has been made otherwise than on a debtor's petition, the bankrupt shall submit a statement of his affairs to the official receiver before the end of the period of 21 days beginnning with the commencement of the bankruptcy.
(2) The statement of affairs shall contain –
(a) such particulars of the bankrupt's creditors and of his debts and other liablities and of his assets as may be prescribed, and
(b) such other information as may be prescribed.
(3) The official receiver may, if he thinks fit –
(a) release the bankrupt from his duty under subsection (1), or
(b) extend the period specified in that subsection;
and where the official receiver has refused to exercise a power conferred by this section, the court, if it thinks fit, may exercise it.
(4) A bankrupt who –
(a) without reasonable excuse fails to comply with the obligation imposed by this section, or
(b) without reasonable excuse submits a statement of affairs that does not comply with the prescribed requirements,
is guilty of a contempt of court and liable to be punished accordingly (in addition to any other punishment to which he may be subject).

289 Investigatory duties of official receiver (1) Subject to subsection (5) below, it is the duty of the official receiver to investigate the conduct and affairs of every bankrupt and to make such report (if any) to the court as he thinks fit.
(2) Where an application is made by the bankrupt under section 280 for his discharge from bankruptcy, it is the duty of the official receiver to make a report to the court

with respect to the prescribed matters; and the court shall consider that report before determining what order (if any) to make under that section.
(3) A report by the official receiver under this section shall, in any proceedings, be prima facie evidence of the facts stated in it.
(4) In subsection (1) the reference to the conduct and affairs of a bankrupt includes his conduct and affairs before the making of the order by which he was adjudged bankrupt.
(5) Where a certificate for the summary administration of the bankrupt's estate is for the time being in force, the official receiver shall carry out an investigation under subsection (1) only if he thinks fit.

290 Public examination of bankrupt (1) Where a bankruptcy order has been made, the official receiver may at any time before the discharge of the bankrupt apply to the court for the public examination of the bankrupt.
(2) Unless the court otherwise orders, the official receiver shall make an application under subsection (1) if notice requiring him to do so is given to him, in accordance with the rules, by one of the bankrupt's creditors with the concurrence of not less than one-half, in value, of those creditors (including the creditor giving notice).
(3) On an application under subsection (1), the court shall direct that a public examination of the bankrupt shall be held on a day appointed by the court; and the bankrupt shall attend on that day and be publicly examined as to his affairs, dealings and property.
(4) The following may take part in the public examination of the bankrupt and may question him concerning his affairs, dealings and property and the causes of his failure, namely –
(a) the official receiver and, in the case of an individual adjudged bankrupt on a petition under section 264(1)(d), the Official Petitioner,
(b) the trustee of the bankrupt's estate, if his appointment has taken effect,
(c) any person who has been appointed as special manager of the bankrupt's estate or business,
(d) any creditor of the bankrupt who has tendered a proof in the bankruptcy.
(5) If a bankrupt without reasonable excuse fails at any time to attend his public examination under this section he is guilty of a contempt of court and liable to be punished accordingly (in addition to any other punishment to which he may be subject).

291 Duties of bankrupt in relation to official receiver (1) Where a bankruptcy order has been made, the bankrupt is under a duty –
(a) to deliver possession of his estate to the official receiver, and
(b) to deliver up to the official receiver all books, papers and other records of which he has possession or control and which relate to his estate and affairs (including any which would be privileged from disclosure in any proceedings).
(2) In the case of any part of the bankrupt's estate which consists of things possession of which cannot be delivered to the official receiver, and in the case of any property that may be claimed for the bankrupt's estate by the trustee, it is the bankrupt's duty to do all such things as may reasonably be required by the official receiver for the protection of those things or that property.
(3) Subsections (1) and (2) do not apply where by virtue of section 297 below the bankrupt's estate vests in a trustee immediately on the making of the bankruptcy order.
(4) The bankrupt shall give the official receiver such inventory of his estate and such other information, and shall attend on the official receiver at such times, as the official receiver may for any of the purposes of this Chapter reasonably require.
(5) Subsection (4) applies to a bankrupt after his discharge.

(6) If the bankrupt without reasonable excuse fails to comply with any obligation imposed by this section, he is guilty of a contempt of court and liable to be punished accordingly (in addition to any other punishment to which he may be subject).

Chapter III: Trustees in Bankruptcy

Tenure of office as trustee

292 Power to make appointments (1) The power to appoint a person as trustee of a bankrupt's estate (whether the first such trustee or a trustee appointed to fill any vacancy) is exercisable –
(a) except at a time when a certificate for the summary administration of the bankrupt's estate is in force, by a general meeting of the bankrupt's creditors;
(b) under section 295(2), 296(2) or 300(6) below in this Chapter, by the Secretary of State; or
(c) under section 297, by the court.
(2) No person may be appointed as trustee of a bankrupt's estate unless he is, at the time of the appointment, qualified to act as an insolvency practitioner in relation to the bankrupt.
(3) Any power to appoint a person as trustee of a bankrupt's estate includes power to appoint two or more persons as joint trustees; but such an appointment must make provision as to the circumstances in which the trustees must act together and the circumstances in which one or more of them may act for the others.
(4) The appointment of any person as trustee takes effect only if that person accepts the appointment in accordance with the rules. Subject to this, the appointment of any person as trustee takes effect at the time specified in his certificate of appointment.
(5) This section is without prejudice to the provisions of this Chapter under which the official receiver is, in certain circumstances, to be trustee of the estate.

293 Summoning of meeting to appoint first trustee (1) Where a bankruptcy order has been made and no certificate for the summary administration of the bankrupt's estate has been issued, it is the duty of the official receiver, as soon as practicable in the period of 12 weeks beginning with the day on which the order was made, to decide whether to summon a general meeting of the bankrupt's creditors for the purpose of appointing a trustee of the bankrupt's estate.
This section does not apply where the bankruptcy order was made on a petition under section 264(1)(d) (criminal bankruptcy); and it is subject to the provision made in sections 294(3) and 297(6) below.
(2) Subject to the next section, if the official receiver decides not to summon such a meeting, he shall, before the end of the period of 12 weeks above mentioned, give notice of his decision to the court and to every creditor of the bankrupt who is known to the official receiver or is identified in the bankrupt's statement of affairs.
(3) As from the giving to the court of a notice under subsection (2), the official receiver is the trustee of the bankrupt's estate.

294 Power of creditors to requisition meeting (1) Where in the case of any bankruptcy –
(a) the official receiver has not yet summoned, or has decided not to summon, a general meeting of the bankrupt's creditors for the purpose of appointing the trustee, and
(b) a certificate for the summary administration of the estate is not for the time being in force,
any creditor of the bankrupt may request the official receiver to summon such a meeting for that purpose.
(2) If such a request appears to the official receiver to be made with the concurrence

of not less than one-quarter, in value, of the bankrupt's creditors (including the creditor making the request), it is the duty of the official receiver to summon the requested meeting.
(3) Accordingly, where the duty imposed by subsection (2) has arisen, the official receiver is required neither to reach a decision for the purposes of section 293(1) nor (if he has reached one) to serve any notice under section 293(2).

295 Failure of meeting to appoint trustee (1) If a meeting summoned under section 293 or 294 is held but no appointment of a person as trustee is made, it is the duty of the official receiver to decide whether to refer the need for an appointment to the Secretary of State.
(2) On a reference made in pursuance of that decision, the Secretary of State shall either make an appointment or decline to make one.
(3) If –
(a) the official receiver decides not to refer the need for an appointment to the Secretary of State, or
(b) on such a reference the Secretary of State declines to make an appointment,
the official receiver shall give notice of his decision or, as the case may be, of the Secretary of State's decision to the court.
(4) As from the giving of notice under subsection (3) in a case in which no notice has been given under section 293(2), the official receiver shall be trustee of the bankrupt's estate.

296 Appointment of trustee by Secretary of State (1) At any time when the official receiver is the trustee of a bankrupt's estate by virtue of any provision of this Chapter (other than section 297(1) below) he may apply to the Secretary of State for the appointment of a person as trustee instead of the official receiver.
(2) On an application under subsection (1) the Secretary of State shall either make an appointment or decline to make one.
(3) Such an application may be made notwithstanding that the Secretary of State has declined to make an appointment either on a previous application under subsection (1) or on a reference under section 295 or under section 300(4) below.
(4) Where the trustee of a bankrupt's estate has been appointed by the Secretary of State (whether under this section or otherwise), the trustee shall give notice to the bankrupt's creditors of his appointment or, if the court so allows, shall advertise his appointment in accordance with the court's directions.
(5) In that notice or advertisement the trustee shall –
(a) state whether he proposes to summon a general meeting of the bankrupt's creditors for the purpose of establishing a creditors' committee under section 301, and
(b) if he does not propose to summon such a meeting, set out the power of the creditors under this Part to require him to summon one.

297 Special cases (1) Where a bankruptcy order is made on a petition under section 264(1)(d) (criminal bankruptcy), the official receiver shall be trustee of the bankrupt's estate.
(2) Subject to the next subsection, where the court issues a certificate for the summary administration of a bankrupt's estate, the official receiver shall, as from the issue of that certificate, be the trustee.
(3) Where such a certificate is issued or is in force, the court may, if it thinks fit, appoint a person other than the official receiver as trustee.
(4) Where a bankruptcy order is made in a case in which an insolvency practitioner's report has been submitted to the court under section 274 but no certificate for the summary administration of the estate is issued, the court, if it thinks fit, may on making the order appoint the person who made the report as trustee.

(5) Where a bankruptcy order is made (whether or not on a petition under section 264(1)(c) at a time when there is a supervisor of a voluntary arrangement approved in relation to the bankrupt under Part VIII, the court, if it thinks fit, may on making the order appoint the supervisor of the arrangement as trustee.
(6) Where an appointment is made under subsection (4) or (5) of this section, the official receiver is not under the duty imposed by section 293(1) (to decide whether or not to summon a meeting of creditors).
(7) Where the trustee of a bankrupt's estate has been appointed by the court, the trustee shall give notice to the bankrupt's creditors of his appointment or, if the court so allows, shall advertise his appointment in accordance with the directions of the court.
(8) In that notice or advertisement he shall –
(a) state whether he proposes to summon a general meeting of the bankrupt's creditors for the purpose of establishing a creditors' committee under section 301 below, and
(b) if he does not propose to summon such a meeting, set out the power of the creditors under this Part to require him to summon one.

298 Removal of trustee; vacation of office (1) Subject as follows, the trustee of a bankrupt's estate may be removed from office only by an order of the court or by a general meeting of the bankrupt's creditors summoned specially for that purpose in accordance with the rules.
(2) Where the official receiver is trustee by virtue of section 297(1), he shall not be removed from office under this section.
(3) A general meeting of the bankrupt's creditors shall not be held for the purpose of removing the trustee at any time when a certificate for the summary administration of the estate is in force.
(4) Where the official receiver is trustee by virtue of section 293(3) or 295(4) or a trustee is appointed by the Secretary of State or (otherwise than under section 297(5)) by the court, a general meeting of the bankrupt's creditors shall be summoned for the purpose of replacing the trustee only if –
(a) the trustee thinks fit, or
(b) the court so directs, or
(c) the meeting is requested by one of the bankrupt's creditors with the concurrence of not less than one-quarter, in value, of the creditors (including the creditor making the request).
(5) If the trustee was appointed by the Secretary of State, he may be removed by a direction of the Secretary of State.
(6) The trustee (not being the official receiver) shall vacate office if he ceases to be a person who is for the time being qualified to act as an insolvency practitioner in relation to the bankrupt.
(7) The trustee may, in the prescribed circumstances, resign his office by giving notice of his resignation to the court.
(8) The trustee shall vacate office on giving notice to the court that a final meeting has been held under section 331 in Chapter IV and of the decision (if any) of that meeting.
(9) The trustee shall vacate office if the bankruptcy order is annulled.

299 Release of trustee (1) Where the official receiver has ceased to be the trustee of a bankrupt's estate and a person is appointed in his stead, the official receiver shall have his release with effect from the following time, that is to say –
(a) where that person is appointed by a general meeting of the bankrupt's creditors or by the Secretary of State, the time at which the official receiver gives notice to the court that he has been replaced, and

(b) where that person is appointed by the court, such time as the court may determine.

(2) If the official receiver while he is the trustee gives notice to the Secretary of State that the administration of the bankrupt's estate in accordance with Chapter IV of this Part is for practical purposes complete, he shall have his release with effect from such time as the Secretary of State may determine.

(3) A person other than the official receiver who has ceased to be the trustee shall have his release with effect from the following time, that is to say –

(a) in the case of a person who has been removed from office by a general meeting of the bankrupt's creditors that has not resolved against his release or who has died, the time at which notice is given to the court in accordance with the rules that that person has ceased to hold office;

(b) in the case of a person who has been removed from office by a general meeting of the bankrupt's creditors that has resolved against his release, or by the court, or by the Secretary of State, or who has vacated office under section 298(6), such time as the Secretary of State may, on an application by that person, determine;

(c) in the case of a person who has resigned, such time as may be prescribed;

(d) in the case of a person who has vacated office under section 298(8) –

(i) if the final meeting referred to in that sub-section has resolved against that person's release, such time as the Secretary of State may, on an application by that person, determine; and

(ii) if that meeting has not so resolved, the time at which the person vacated office.

(4) Where a bankruptcy order is annulled, the trustee at the time of the annulment has his release with effect from such time as the court may determine.

(5) Where the official receiver or the trustee has his release under this section, he shall, with effect from the time specified in the preceding provisions of this section, be discharged from all liability both in respect of acts or omissions of his in the administration of the estate and otherwise in relation to his conduct as trustee.

But nothing in this section prevents the exercise, in relation to a person who has had his release under this section, of the court's powers under section 304.

300 Vacancy in office of trustee (1) This section applies where the appointment of any person as trustee of a bankrupt's estate fails to take effect or, such an appointment having taken effect, there is otherwise a vacancy in the office of trustee.

(2) The official receiver shall be trustee until the vacancy is filled.

(3) The official receiver may summon a general meeting of the bankrupt's creditors for the purpose of filling the vacancy and shall summon such a meeting if required to do so in pursuance of section 314(7) (creditor's requisition).

(4) If at the end of the period of 28 days beginning with the day on which the vacancy first came to the official receiver's attention he has not summoned, and is not proposing to summon, a general meeting of creditors for the purpose of filling the vacancy, he shall refer the need for an appointment to the Secretary of State.

(5) Where a certificate for the summary administration of the estate is for the time being in force –

(a) the official receiver may refer the need to fill any vacancy to the court or, if the vacancy arises because a person appointed by the Secretary of State has ceased to hold office, to the court or the Secretary of State, and

(b) subsections (3) and (4) of this section do not apply.

(6) On a reference to the Secretary of State under subsection (4) or (5) the Secretary of State shall either make an appointment or decline to make one.

(7) If on a reference under subsection (4) or (5) no appointment is made, the official receiver shall continue to be trustee of the bankrupt's estate, but without prejudice to his power to make a further reference.

(8) References in this section to a vacancy include a case where it is necessary, in relation to any property which is or may be comprised in a bankrupt's estate, to revive the trusteeship of that estate after the holding of a final meeting summoned under section 331 or the giving by the official receiver of notice under section 299(2).

Control of trustee

301 Creditors' committee (1) Subject as follows, a general meeting of a bankrupt's creditors (whether summoned under the preceding provisions of this Chapter or otherwise) may, in accordance with the rules, established a committee (known as 'the creditors' committee') to exercise the functions conferred on it by or under this Act.
(2) A general meeting of the bankrupt's creditors shall not establish such a committee, or confer any functions on such a committee, at any time when the official receiver is the trustee of the bankrupt's estate, except in connection with an appointment made by that meeting of a person to be trustee instead of the official receiver.

302 Exercise by Secretary of State of functions of creditors' committee (1) The creditors' committee is not to be able or required to carry out its functions at any time when the official receiver is trustee of the bankrupt's estate; but at any such time the functions of the committee under this Act shall be vested in the Secretary of State, except to the extent that the rules otherwise provide.
(2) Where in the case of any bankruptcy there is for the time being no creditors' committee and the trustee of the bankrupt's estate is a person other than the official receiver, the functions of such a committee shall be vested in the Secretary of State, except to the extent that the rules otherwise provide.

303 General control of trustee by the court (1) If a bankrupt or any of his creditors or any other person is dissatisfied by any act, omission or decision of a trustee of the bankrupt's estate, he may apply to the court; and on such an application the court may confirm, reverse or modify any act or decision of the trustee, may give him directions or may make such other order as it thinks fit.
(2) The trustee of a bankrupt's estate may apply to the court for directions in relation to any particular matter arising under the bankruptcy.

304 Liability of trustee (1) Where on an application under this section the court is satisfied –
(a) that the trustee of a bankrupt's estate has misapplied or retained, or become accountable for, any money or other property comprised in the bankrupt's estate, or
(b) that a bankrupt's estate has suffered any loss in consequence of any misfeasance or breach of fiduciary or other duty by a trustee of the estate in the carrying out of his functions,

the court may order the trustee, for the benefit of the estate, to repay, restore or account for money or other property (together with interest at such rate as the court thinks just) or, as the case may require, to pay such sum by way of compensation in respect of the misfeasance or breach of fiduciary or other duty as the court thinks just.

This is without prejudice to any liability arising apart from this section.
(2) An application under this section may be made by the official receiver, the Secretary of State, a creditor of the bankrupt or (whether or not there is, or is likely to be, a surplus for the purposes of section 330(5) (final distribution)) the bankrupt himself.

But the leave of the court is required for the making of an application if it is to be made by the bankrupt or if it is to be made after the trustee has had his release under section 299.

(3) Where –

(a) the trustee seizes or disposes of any property which is not comprised in the bankrupt's estate, and

(b) at the time of the seizure of disposal the trustee believes, and has reasonable grounds for believing, that he is entitled (whether in pursuance of an order of the court or otherwise) to seize or dispose of that property,

the trustee is not liable to any person (whether under this section or otherwise) in respect of any loss or damage resulting from the seizure or disposal except in so far as that loss or damage is caused by the negligence of the trustee; and he has a lien on the property, or the proceeds of its sale, for such of the expenses of the bankruptcy as were incurred in connection with the seizure or disposal.

Chapter IV: Administration by Trustee

Preliminary

305 General functions of trustee (1) This Chapter applies in relation to any bankruptcy where either –

(a) the appointment of a person as trustee of a bankrupt's estate takes effect, or

(b) the official receiver becomes trustee of a bankrupt's estate.

(2) The function of the trustee is to get in, realise and distribute the bankrupt's estate in accordance with the following provisions of this Chapter; and in the carrying out of that function and in the management of the bankrupt's estate the trustee is entitled, subject to those provisions, to use his own discretion.

(3) It is the duty of the trustee, if he is not the official receiver –

(a) to furnish the official receiver with such information,

(b) to produce to the official receiver, and permit inspection by the official receiver of, such books, papers and other records, and

(c) to give the official receiver such other assistance,

as the official receiver may reasonably require for the purpose of enabling him to carry out his functions in relation to the bankruptcy.

(4) The official name of the trustee shall be 'the trustee of the estate of ...., a bankrupt' (inserting the name of the bankrupt); but he may be referred to as 'the trustee in bankruptcy' of the particular bankrupt.

Acquisition, control and realisation of bankrupt's estate

306 Vesting of bankrupt's estate in trustee (1) The bankrupt's estate shall vest in the trustee immediately on his appointment taking effect or, in the case of the official receiver, on his becoming trustee.

(2) Where any property which is, or is to be, comprised in the bankrupt's estate vests in the trustee (whether under this section or under any other provision of this Part), it shall so vest without any conveyance, assignment or transfer.

307 After-acquired property (1) Subject to this section and section 309, the trustee may by notice in writing claim for the bankrupt's estate any property which has been acquired by, or has devolved upon, the bankrupt since the commencement of the bankruptcy.

(2) A notice under this section shall not be served in respect of –

(a) any property falling within subsection (2) or (3) of section 283 in Chapter II,

(b) any property which by virtue of any other enactment is excluded from the bankrupt's estate, or

(c) without prejudice to section 280(2)(c) (order of court on application for discharge), any property which is acquired by, or devolves upon, the bankrupt after his discharge.

(3) Subject to the next subsection, upon the service on the bankrupt of a notice under this section the property to which the notice relates shall vest in the trustee as part of the bankrupt's estate; and the trustee's title to that property has relation back to the time at which the property was acquired by, or devolved upon, the bankrupt.

(4) Where, whether before or after service of a notice under this section –

(a) a person acquires property in good faith, for value and without notice of the bankruptcy, or

(b) a banker enters into a transaction in good faith and without such notice.

the trustee is not in respect of that property or transaction entitled by virtue of this section to any remedy against that person or banker, or any person whose title to any property derives from that person or banker.

(5) References in this section to property do not include any property which, as part of the bankrupt's income, may be the subject of an income payments order under section 310.

308 Vesting in trustee of certain items of excess value (1) Subject to the next section, where –

(a) property is excluded by virtue of section 283(2) (tools of trade, household effects, etc.) from the bankrupt's estate, and

(b) it appears to the trustee that the realisable value of the whole or any part of that property exceeds the cost of a reasonable replacement for that property or that part of it,

the trustee may by notice in writing claim that property or, as the case may be, that part of it for the bankrupt's estate.

(2) Upon the service on the bankrupt of a notice under this section, the property to which the notice relates vests in the trustee as part of the bankrupt's estate; and, except against a purchaser in good faith, for value and without notice of the bankruptcy, the trustee's title to that property has relation back to the commencement of the bankruptcy.

(3) The trustee shall apply funds comprised in the estate to the purchase by or on behalf of the bankrupt of a reasonable replacement for any property vested in the trustee under this section; and the duty imposed by this subsection has priority over the obligation of the trustee to distribute the estate.

(4) For the purposes of this section property is a reasonable replacement for other property if it is reasonably adequate for meeting the needs met by the other propoerty.

309 Time-limit for notice under s 307 or 308 (1) Except with the leave of the court, a notice shall not be served –

(a) under section 307, after the end of the period of 42 days beginning with the day on which it first came to the knowledge of the trustee that the property in question had been acquired by, or had devolved upon, the bankrupt;

(b) under section 308, after the end of the period of 42 days beginning with the day on which the property in question first came to the knowledge of the trustee.

(2) For the purposes of this section –

(a) anything which comes to the knowledge of the trustee is deemed in relation to any successor of his as trustee to have come to the knowledge of the successor at the same time; and

(b) anything which comes (otherwise than under paragraph (a)) to the knowledge of a person before he is the trustee is deemed to come to his knowledge on his appointment taking effect or, in the case of the official receiver, on his becoming trustee.

310 Income payments orders (1) The court may, on the application of the trustee, make an order ('an income payments order') claiming for the bankrupt's estate so much of the income of the bankrupt during the period for which the order is in force as may be specified in the order.
(2) The court shall not make an income payments order the effect of which would be to reduce the income of the bankrupt below what appears to the court to be necessary for meeting the reasonable domestic needs of the bankrupt and his family.
(3) An income payments order shall, in respect of any payment of income to which it is to apply, either –
(a) require the bankrupt to pay the trustee an amount equal to so much of that payment as is claimed by the order, or
(b) require the person making the payment to pay so much of it as is so claimed to the trustee, instead of the bankrupt.
(4) Where the court makes an income payments order it may, if it thinks fit, discharge or vary any attachment of earnings order that is for the time being in force to secure payments by the bankrupt.
(5) Sums received by the trustee under an income payments order form part of the bankrupt's estate.
(6) An income payments order shall not be made after the discharge of the bankrupt, and if made before, shall not have effect after his discharge except –
(a) in the case of a discharge under section 279(1)(a) (order of court), by virtue of a condition imposed by the court under section 280(2)(c) (income, etc after discharge), or
(b) in the case of a discharge under section 279(1)(b) (expiration of relevant period), by virtue of a provision of the order requiring it to continue in force for a period ending after the discharge but no later than 3 years after the making of the order.
(7) For the purposes of this section the income of the bankrupt comprises every payment in the nature of income which is from time to time made to him or to which he from time to time becomes entitled, including any payment in respect of the carrying on of any business or in respect of any office or employment.

311 Acquisition by trustee of control (1) The trustee shall take possession of all books, papers and other records which relate to the bankrupt's estate or affairs and which belong to him or are in his possession or under his control (including any which would be privileged from disclosure in any proceedings).
(2) In relation to, and for the purpose of acquiring or retaining possession of, the bankrupt's estate, the trustee is in the same position as if he were a receiver of property appointed by the High Court; and the court may, on his application, enforce such acquisition or retention accordingly.
(3) Where any part of the bankrupt's estate consists of stock or shares in a company, shares in a ship or any other property transferable in the books of a company, office or person, the trustee may exercise the right to transfer the property to the same extent as the bankrupt might have exercised it if he had not become bankrupt.
(4) Where any part of the estate consists of things in action, they are deemed to have been assigned to the trustee; but notice of the deemed assignment need not be given except in so far as it is necessary, in a case where the deemed assignment is from the bankrupt himself, for protecting the priority of the trustee.
(5) Where any goods comprised in the estate are held by any person by way of pledge, pawn or other security and no notice has been served in respect of those goods by the official receiver under subsection (5) of section 285 (restriction on realising security), the trustee may serve such a notice in respect of the goods; and whether or not a notice has been served under this subsection or that subsection, the trustee may, if he thinks fit, exercise the bankrupt's right of redemption in respect of any such goods.

(6) A notice served by the trustee under subsection (5) has the same effect as a notice served by the official receiver under section 285(5).

312 Obligation to surrender control to trustee (1) The bankrupt shall deliver up to the trustee possession of any property, books, papers or other records of which he has possession or control and of which the trustee is required to take possession.

This is without prejudice to the general duties of the bankrupt under section 333 in this Chapter.

(2) If any of the following is in possession of any property, books, papers or other records of which the trustee is required to take possession, namely –

(a) the official receiver.

(b) a person who has ceased to be trustee of the bankrupt's estate, or

(c) a person who has been the supervisor of a voluntary arrangement approved in relation to the bankrupt under Part VIII,

the official receiver or, as the case may be, that person shall deliver up possession of the property, books, papers or records to the trustee.

(3) Any banker or agent of the bankrupt or any other person who holds any property to the account of, or for, the bankrupt shall pay or deliver to the trustee all property in his possession or under his control which forms part of the bankrupt's estate and which he is not by law entitled to retain as against the bankrupt or trustee.

(4) If any person without reasonable excuse fails to comply with any obligation imposed by this section, he is guilty of a contempt of court and liable to be punished accordingly (in addition to any other punishment to which he may be subject).

313 Charge on bankrupt's home (1) Where any property consisting of an interest in a dwelling house which is occupied by the bankrupt or by his spouse or former spouse is comprised in the bankrupt's estate and the trustee is, for any reason, unable for the time being to realise that property, the trustee may apply to the court for an order imposing a charge on the property for the benefit of the bankrupt's estate.

(2) If on an application under this section the court imposes a charge on any property, the benefit of that charge shall be comprised in the bankrupt's estate and is enforceable, up to the value from time to time of the property secured, for the payment of any amount which is payable otherwise than to the bankrupt out of the estate and of interest on that amount at the prescribed rate.

(3) An order under this section made in respect of property vested in the trustee shall provide, in accordance with the rules, for the property to cease to be comprised in the bankrupt's estate and, subject to the charge (and any prior charge), to vest in the bankrupt.

(4) Subsections (1) and (2) and (4) to (6) of section 3 of the Charging Orders Act 1979 (supplemental provisions with respect to charging orders) have effect in relation to orders under this section as in relation to charging orders under that Act.

314 Powers of trustee (1) The trustee may –

(a) with the permission of the creditors' committee or the court, exercise any of the powers specified in Part I of Schedule 5 to this Act, and

(b) without that permission, exercise any of the general powers specified in Part II of that Schedule.

(2) With the permission of the creditors' committee or the court, the trustee may appoint the bankrupt –

(a) to superintend the management of his estate or any part of it,

(b) to carry on his business (if any) for the benefit of his creditors, or

(c) in any other respect to assist in administering the estate in such manner and on such terms as the trustee may direct.

(3) A permission given for the purposes of subsection (1)(a) or (2) shall not be a

general permission but shall relate to a particular proposed exercise of the power in question; and a person dealing with the trustee in good faith and for value is not to be concerned to enquire whether any permission required in either case has been given.
(4) Where the trustee has done anything without the permission required by subsection (1)(a) or (2), the court or the creditors' committee may, for the purpose of enabling him to meet his expenses out of the bankrupt's estate, ratify what the trustee had done.

But the committee shall not do so unless it is satisfied that the trustee has acted in a case of urgency and has sought its ratification without undue delay.
(5) Part III of Schedule 5 to this Act has effect with respect to the things which the trustee is able to do for the purposes of, or in connection with, the exercise of any of his powers under any of this Group of Parts.
(6) Where the trustee (not being the official receiver) in exercise of the powers conferred on him by any provision in this Group of Parts –
(a) disposes of any property comprised in the bankrupt's estate to an associate of the bankrupt, or
(b) employs a solicitor,
he shall, if there is for the time being a creditors' committee, give notice to the committee of that exercise of his powers.
(7) Without prejudice to the generality of subsection (5) and Part III of Schedule 5, the trustee may, if he thinks fit, at any time summon a general meeting of the bankrupt's creditors.

Subject to the preceding provisions in this Group of Parts, he shall summon such a meeting if he is requested to do so by a creditor of the bankrupt and the request is made with the concurrence of not less than one-tenth, in value, of the bankrupt's creditors (including the creditor making the request).
(8) Nothing in this Act is to be construed as restricting the capacity of the trustee to exercise any of his powers outside England and Wales.

Disclaimer of onerous property

315 Disclaimer (general power) (1) Subject as follows, the trustee may, by the giving of the prescribed notice, disclaim any onerous property and may do so notwithstanding that he has taken possession of it, endeavoured to sell it or otherwise exercised rights of ownership in relation to it.
(2) The following is onerous property for the purposes of this section, that is to say –
(a) any unprofitable contract, and
(b) any other property comprised in the bankrupt's estate which is unsaleable or not readily saleable, or is such that it may give rise to a liability to pay money or perform any other onerous act.
(3) A disclaimer under this section –
(a) operates so as to determine, as from the date of the disclaimer, the rights, interests and liabilities of the bankrupt and his estate in or in respect of the property disclaimed, and
(b) discharges the trustee from all personal liability in respect of that property as from the commencement of his trusteeship.
but does not, except so far as is necessary for the purpose of releasing the bankrupt, the bankrupt's estate and the trustee from any liability, affect the rights or liabilities of any other person.
(4) A notice of disclaimer shall not be given under this section in respect of any property that has been claimed for the estate under section 307 (after-acquired property) or 308 (personal property of bankrupt exceeding reasonable replacement value), except with the leave of the court.
(5) Any person sustaining loss or damage in consequence of the operation of a

disclaimer under this section is deemed to be a creditor of the bankrupt to the extent of the loss or damage and accordingly may prove for the loss or damage as a bankruptcy debt.

316 Notice requiring trustee's decision (1) Notice of disclaimer shall not be given under section 315 in respect of any property if –
(a) a person interested in the property has applied in writing to the trustee or one of his predecessors as trustee requiring the trustee or that predecessor to decide whether he will disclaim or not, and
(b) the period of 28 days beginning with the day on which that application was made has expired without a notice of disclaimer having been given under section 315 in respect of that property.
(2) The trustee is deemed to have adopted any contract which by virtue of this section he is not entitled to disclaim.

317 Disclaimer of leaseholds (1) The disclaimer of any property of a leasehold nature does not take effect unless a copy of the disclaimer has been served (so far as the trustee is aware of their addresses) on every person claiming under the bankrupt as underlessee or mortgagee and either –
(a) no application under section 320 is made with respect to the property before the end of the period of 14 days beginning with the day on which the last notice served under this subsection was served, or
(b) where such an application has been made, the court directs that the disclaimer is to take effect.
(2) Where the court gives a direction under subsection (1)(b) it may also, instead of or in addition to any order it makes under section 320, make such orders with respect to fixtures, tenant's improvements and other matters arising out of the lease as it thinks fit.

318 Disclaimer of dwelling house Without prejudice to section 317, the disclaimer of any property in a dwelling house does not take effect unless a copy of the disclaimer has been served (so far as the trustee is aware of their addresses) on every person in occupation of or claiming a right to occupy the dwelling house and either –
(a) no application under section 320 is made with respect to the property before the end of the period of 14 days beginning with the day on which the last notice served under this section was served, or
(b) where such an application has been made, the court directs that the disclaimer is to take effect.

319 Disclaimer of land subject to rentcharge (1) The following applies where, in consequence of the disclaimer under section 315 of any land subject to a rentcharge, that land vests by operation of law in the Crown or any other person (referred to in the next subsection as 'the proprietor').
(2) The proprietor, and the successors in title of the proprietor, are not subject to any personal liability in respect of any sums becoming due under the rentcharge, except sums becoming due after the proprietor, or some person claiming under or through the proprietor, has taken possession or control of the land or has entered into occupation of it.

320 Court order vesting disclaimed property (1) This section and the next apply where the trustee has disclaimed property under section 315.
(2) An application may be made to the court under this section by –
(a) any person who claims an interest in the disclaimed property,
(b) any person who is under any liability in respect of the disclaimed property, not being a liability discharged by the disclaimer, or

(c) where the disclaimed property is property in a dwelling house, any person who at the time when the bankruptcy petition was presented was in occupation of or entitled to occupy the dwelling house.

(3) Subject as follows in this section and the next, the court may, on an application under this section, make an order on such terms as it thinks fit for the vesting of the disclaimed property in, or for its delivery to –

(a) a person entitled to it or a trustee for such a person,

(b) a person subject to such a liability as is mentioned in subsection (2)(b) or a trustee for such a person, or

(c) where the disclaimed property is property in a dwelling house, any person who at the time when the bankruptcy petition was presented was in occupation of or entitled to occupy the dwelling house.

(4) The court shall not make an order by virtue of subsection (3)(b) except where it appears to the court that it would be just to do so for the purpose of compensating the person subject to the liability in respect of the disclaimer.

(5) The effect of any order under this section shall be taken into account in assessing for the purposes of section 315(5) the extent of any loss or damage sustained by any person in consequence of the disclaimer.

(6) An order under this section vesting property in any person need not be completed by any conveyance, assignment or transfer.

321 Order under s 320 in respect of leaseholds (1) The court shall not make an order under section 320 vesting property of a leasehold nature in any person, except on terms making that person –

(a) subject to the same liabilities and obligations as the bankrupt was subject to under the lease on the day the bankruptcy petition was presented, or

(b) if the court thinks fit, subject to the same liabilities and obligations as that person would be subject to if the lease had been assigned to him on that day.

(2) For the purposes of an order under section 320 relating to only part of any property comprised in a lease, the requirements of subsection (1) apply as if the lease comprised only the property to which the order relates.

(3) Where subsection (1) applies and no person is willing to accept an order under section 320 on the terms required by that subsection, the court may (by order under section 320) vest the estate or interest of the bankrupt in the property in any person who is liable (whether personally or in a representative capacity and whether alone or jointly with the bankrupt) to perform the lessee's covenants in the lease.

The court may by virtue of this subsection vest that estate and interest in such a person freed and discharged from all estates, incumbrances and interests created by the bankrupt.

(4) Where subsection (1) applies and a person declines to accept any order under section 320, that person shall be excluded from all interest in the property.

Distribution of bankrupt's estate

322 Proof of debt (1) Subject to this section and the next, the proof of any bankruptcy debt by a secured or unsecured creditor of the bankrupt and the admission or rejection of any proof shall take place in accordance with the rules.

(2) Where a bankruptcy debt bears interest, that interest is provable as part of the debt except in so far as it is payable in respect of any period after the commencement of the bankruptcy.

(3) The trustee shall estimate the value of any bankruptcy debt which, by reason of its being subject to any contingency or contingencies or for any other reason, does not bear a certain value.

(4) Where the value of a bankruptcy debt is estimated by the trustee under

subsection (3) or, by virtue of section 303 in Chapter III, by the court, the amount provable in the bankruptcy in respect of the debt is the amount of the estimate.

323 Mutual credit and set-off (1) This section applies where before the commencement of the bankruptcy there have been mutual credits, mutual debts or other mutual dealings between the bankrupt and any creditor of the bankrupt proving or claiming to prove for a bankruptcy debt.
(2) An account shall be taken of what is due from each party to the other in respect of the mutual dealings and the sums due from one party shall be set off against the sums due from the other.
(3) Sums due from the bankrupt to another party shall not be included in the account taken under subsection (2) if that other party had notice at the time they became due that a bankruptcy petition relating to the bankrupt was pending.
(4) Only the balance (if any) of the account taken under subsection (2) is provable as a bankruptcy debt or, as the case may be, to be paid to the trustee as part of the bankrupt's estate.

324 Distribution by means of dividend (1) Whenever the trustee has sufficient funds in hand for the purpose he shall, subject to the retention of such sums as may be necessary for the expenses of the bankruptcy, declare and distribute dividends among the creditors in respect of the bankruptcy debts which they have respectively proved.
(2) The trustee shall give notice of his intention to declare and distribute a dividend.
(3) Where the trustee has declared a dividend, he shall give notice of the dividend and of how it is proposed to distribute it; and a notice given under this subsection shall contain the prescribed particulars of the bankrupt's estate.
(4) In the calculation and distribution of a dividend the trustee shall make provision –
(a) for any bankruptcy debts which appear to him to be due to persons who, by reason of the distance of their place of residence, may not have had sufficient time to tender and establish their proofs,
(b) for any bankruptcy debts which are the subject of claims which have not yet been determined, and
(c) for disputed proofs and claims.

325 Claims by unsatisfied creditors (1) A creditor who has not proved his debt before the declaration of any dividend is not entitled to disturb, by reason that he has not participated in it, the distribution of that dividend or any other dividend declared before his debt was proved, but –
(a) when he has proved that debt he is entitled to be paid, out of any money for the time being available for the payment of any further dividend, any dividend or dividends which he has failed to receive; and
(b) any dividend or dividends payable under paragraph (a) shall be paid before that money is applied to the payment of any such further dividend.
(2) No action lies against the trustee for a dividend, but if the trustee refuses to pay a dividend the court may, if it thinks fit, order him to pay it and also to pay, out of his own money –
(a) interest on the dividend, at the rate for the time being specified in section 17 of the Judgments Act 1838, from the time it was withheld, and
(b) the costs of the proceedings in which the order to pay is made.

326 Distribution of property in specie (1) Without prejudice to sections 315 to 319 (disclaimer), the trustee may, with the permission of the creditors' committee, divide in its existing form amongst the bankrupt's creditors, according to its estimated

value, any property which from its peculiar nature or other special circumstances cannot be readily or advantageously sold.
(2) A permission given for the purposes of subsection (1) shall not be a general permission but shall relate to a particular proposed exercise of the power in question; and a person dealing with the trustee in good faith and for value is not to be concerned to enquire whether any permission required by subsection (1) has been given.
(3) Where the trustee had done anything without the permission required by subsection (1), the court or the creditors' committee may, for the purpose of enabling him to meet his expenses out of the bankrupt's estate, ratify what the trustee has done.

But the committee shall not do so unless it is satisfied that the trustee acted in a case of urgency and has sought its ratification without undue delay.

327 Distribution in criminal bankruptcy Where the bankruptcy order was made on a petition under section 264(1)(d) (criminal bankruptcy), no distribution shall be made under sections 324 to 326 so long as an appeal is pending (within the meaning of section 277) against the bankrupt's conviction of any offence by virtue of which the criminal bankruptcy order on which the petition was based was made.

328 Priority of debts (1) In the distribution of the bankrupt's estate, his preferential debts (within the meaning given by section 386 in Part XII) shall be paid in priority to other debts.
(2) Preferential debts rank equally between themselves after the expenses of the bankruptcy and shall be paid in full unless the bankrupt's estate is insufficient for meeting them, in which case they abate in equal proportions between themselves.
(3) Debts which are neither preferential debts nor debts to which the next section applies also rank equally between themselves and, after the preferential debts, shall be paid in full unless the bankrupt's estate is insufficient for meeting them, in which case they abate in equal proportions between themselves.
(4) Any surplus remaining after the payment of the debts that are preferential or rank equally under subsection (3) shall be applied in paying interest on those debts in respect of the periods during which they have been outstanding since the commencement of the bankruptcy; and interest on preferential debts ranks equally with interest on debts other than preferential debts.
(5) The rate of interest payable under subsection (4) in respect of any debt is whichever is the greater of the following –
(a) the rate specified in section 17 of the Judgments Act 1838 at the commencement of the bankruptcy, and
(b) the rate applicable to that debt apart from the bankruptcy.
(6) This section and the next are without prejudice to any provision of this Act or any other Act under which the payment of any debt or the making of any other payment is, in the event of bankruptcy, to have a particular priority or to be postponed.

329 Debts to spouse (1) This section applies to bankruptcy debts owed in respect of credit provided by a person who (whether or not the bankrupt's spouse at the time the credit was provided) was the bankrupt's spouse at the commencement of the bankruptcy.
(2) Such debts –
(a) rank in priority after the debts and interest required to be paid in pursuance of section 328(3) and (4), and
(b) are payable with interest at the rate specified in section 328(5) in respect of the period during which they have been outstanding since the commencement of the bankruptcy;

and the interest payable under paragraph (b) has the same priority as the debts on which it is payable.

330 Final distribution (1) When the trustee has realised all the bankrupt's estate or so much of it as can, in the trustee's opinion, be realised without needlessly protracting the trusteeship, he shall give notice in the prescribed manner either –
(a) of his intention to declare a final dividend, or
(b) that no dividend, or further dividend, will be declared.
(2) The notice under subsection (1) shall contain the prescribed particulars and shall require claims against the bankrupt's estate to be established by a date ('the final date') specified in the notice.
(3) The court may, on the application of any person, postpone the final date.
(4) After the final date, the trustee shall –
(a) defray any outstanding expenses of the bankruptcy out of the bankrupt's estate, and
(b) if he intends to declare a final dividend, declare and distribute that dividend without regard to the claim of any person in respect of a debt not already proved in the bankruptcy.
(5) If a surplus remains after payment in full and with interest of all the bankrupt's creditors and the payment of the expenses of the bankruptcy, the bankrupt is entitled to the surplus.

331 Final meeting (1) Subject as follows in this section and the next, this section applies where –
(a) it appears to the trustee that the administration of the bankrupt's estate in accordance with this Chapter is for practical purposes complete, and
(b) the trustee is not the official receiver.
(2) The trustee shall summon a final general meeting of the bankrupt's creditors which –
(a) shall receive the trustee's report of his administration of the bankrupt's estate, and
(b) shall determine whether the trustee should have his release under section 299 in Chapter III.
(3) The trustee may, if he thinks fit, give the notice summoning the final general meeting at the same time as giving notice under section 330(1); but, if summoned for an earlier date, that meeting shall be adjourned (and, if necessary, further adjourned) until a date on which the trustee is able to report to the meeting that the administration of the bankrupt's estate is for practical purposes complete.
(4) In the administration of the estate it is the trustee's duty to retain sufficient sums from the estate to cover the expenses of summoning and holding the meeting required by this section.

332 Saving for bankrupt's home (1) This section applies where –
(a) there is comprised in the bankrupt's estate property consisting of an interest in a dwelling house which is occupied by the bankrupt or by his spouse or former spouse, and
(b) the trustee has been unable for any reason to realise that property.
(2) The trustee shall not summon a meeting under section 331 unless either –
(a) the court has made an order under section 313 imposing a charge on that property for the benefit of the bankrupt's estate, or
(b) the court has declined, on an application under that section, to make such an order, or
(c) the Secretary of State has issued a certificate to the trustee stating that it would be inappropriate or inexpedient for such an application to be made in the case in question.

Supplemental

333 Duties of bankrupt in relation to trustee (1) The bankrupt shall –
(a) give to the trustee such information as to his affairs,
(b) attend on the trustee at such times, and
(c) do all such other things,
as the trustee may for the purposes of carrying out his functions under any of this Group of Parts reasonably require.
(2) Where at any time after the commencement of the bankruptcy any property is acquired by, or devolves upon, the bankrupt or there is an increase of the bankrupt's income, the bankrupt shall, within the prescribed period, give the trustee notice of the property or, as the case may be, of the increase.
(3) Subsection (1) applies to a bankrupt after his discharge.
(4) If the bankrupt without reasonable excuse fails to comply with any obligation imposed by this section, he is guilty of a contempt of court and liable to be punished accordingly (in addition to any other punishment to which he may be subject).

334 Stay of distribution in case of second bankruptcy (1) This section and the next apply where a bankruptcy order is made against an undischarged bankrupt; and in both sections –
(a) 'the later bankruptcy' means the bankruptcy arising from that order,
(b) 'the earlier bankruptcy' means the bankruptcy (or, as the case may be, most recent bankruptcy) from which the bankrupt has not been discharged at the commencement of the later bankruptcy, and
(c) 'the existing trustee' means the trustee (if any) of the bankrupt's estate for the purposes of the earlier bankruptcy.
(2) Where the existing trustee has been given the prescribed notice of the presentation of the petition for the later bankruptcy, any distribution or other disposition by him of anything to which the next subsection applies, if made after the giving of the notice, is void except to the extent that it was made with the consent of the court or is or was subsequently ratified by the court.

This is without prejudice to section 284 (restrictions on dispositions of property following bankruptcy order).
(3) This subsection applies to –
(a) any property which is vested in the existing trustee under section 307(3) (after-acquired property);
(b) any money paid to the existing trustee in pursuance of an income payments order under section 310; and
(c) any property or money which is, or in the hands of the existing trustee represents, the proceeds of sale or application of property or money falling within paragraph (a) or (b) of this subsection.

335 Adjustment between earlier and later bankruptcy estates (1) With effect from the commencement of the later bankruptcy anything to which section 334(3) applies which, immediately before the commencement of that bankruptcy, is comprised in the bankrupt's estate for the purposes of the earlier bankruptcy is to be treated as comprised in the bankrupt's estate for the purposes of the later bankruptcy and, until there is a trustee of that estate, is to be dealt with by the existing trustee in accordance with the rules.
(2) Any sums which in pursuance of an income payments order under section 310 are payable after the commencement of the later bankruptcy to the existing trustee shall form part of the bankrupt's estate for the purposes of the later bankruptcy; and the court may give such consequential directions for the modification of the order as it thinks fit.

(3) Anything comprised in a bankrupt's estate by virtue of subsection (1) or (2) is so comprised subject to a first charge in favour of the existing trustee for any bankruptcy expenses incurred by him in relation thereto.
(4) Except as provided above and in section 334, property which is, or by virtue of section 308 (personal property of bankrupt exceeding reasonable replacement value) is capable of being, comprised in the bankrupt's estate for the purposes of the earlier bankruptcy, or of any bankruptcy prior to it, shall not be comprised in his estate for the purposes of the later bankruptcy.
(5) The creditors of the bankrupt in the earlier bankruptcy and the creditors of the bankrupt in any bankruptcy prior to the earlier one, are not to be creditors of his in the later bankruptcy in respect of the same debts; but the existing trustee may prove in the later bankruptcy for –
(a) the unsatisfied balance of the debts (including any debt under his subsection) provable against the bankrupt's estate in the earlier bankruptcy;
(b) any interest payable on that balance; and
(c) any unpaid expenses of the earlier bankruptcy.
(6) Any amount provable under subsection (5) ranks in priority after all the other debts provable in the later bankruptcy and after interest on those debts and, accordingly, shall not be paid unless those debts and that interest have first been paid in full.

Chapter V: Effect of Bankruptcy on Certain Rights, Transactions, Etc

Rights of occupation

336 Rights of occupation etc of bankrupt's spouse (1) Nothing occurring in the initial period of the bankruptcy (that is to say, the period beginning with the day of the presentation of the petition for the bankruptcy order and ending with the vesting of the bankrupt's estate in a trustee) is to be taken as having given rise to any rights of occupation under the Matrimonal Homes Act 1983 in relation to a dwelling house comprised in the bankrupt's estate.
(2) Where a spouse's rights of occupation under the Act of 1983 are a charge on the estate or interest of the other spouse, or of trustees for the other spouse, and the other spouse is adjudged bankrupt –
(a) the charge continues to subsist notwithstanding the bankruptcy and, subject to the provisions of that Act, binds the trustee of the bankrupt's estate and persons deriving title under that trustee, and
(b) any application for an order under section 1 of that Act shall be made to the court having jurisdiction in relation to the bankruptcy.
(3) Where a person and his spouse or former spouse are trustees for sale of a dwelling house and that person is adjudged bankrupt, any application by the trustee of the bankrupt's estate for an order under section 30 of the Law of Property Act 1925 (powers of court where trustees for sale refuse to act) shall be made to the court having jurisdiction in relation to the bankruptcy.
(4) On such an application as is mentioned in subsection (2) or (3) the court shall make such order under section 1 of the Act of 1983 or section 30 of the Act of 1925 as it thinks just and reasonable having regard to –
(a) the interests of the bankrupt's creditors,
(b) the conduct of the spouse or former spouse, so far as contributing to the bankruptcy,
(c) the needs and financial resources of the spouse or former spouse,
(d) the needs of any children, and
(e) all the circumstances of the case other than the needs of the bankrupt.
(5) Where such an application is made after the end of the period of one year beginning with the first vesting under Chapter IV of this Part of the bankrupt's estate

in a trustee, the court shall assume, unless the circumstances of the case are exceptional, that the interests of the bankrupt's creditors outweigh all other considerations.

337 Rights of occupation of bankrupt (1) This section applies where –
(a) a person who is entitled to occupy a dwellinghouse by virtue of a beneficial estate or interest is adjudged bankrupt, and
(b) any persons under the age of 18 with whom that person had at some time occupied that dwelling house had their home with that person at the time when the bankruptcy petition was presented and at the commencement of the bankruptcy.
(2) Whether or not the bankrupt's spouse (if any) has rights of occupation under the Matrimonial Homes Act 1983 –
(a) the bankrupt has the following rights as against the trustee of his estate –
(i) if in occupation, a right not to be evicted or excluded from the dwelling house or any part of it, except with the leave of the court,
(ii) if not in occupation, a right with the leave of the court to enter into and occupy the dwelling house, and
(b) the bankrupt's rights are a charge, having the like priority as an equitable interest created immediately before the commencement of the bankruptcy, on so much of his estate or interest in the dwelling house as vests in the trustee.
(3) The Act of 1983 has effect, with the necessary modifications, as if –
(a) the rights conferred by paragraph (a) of subsection (2) were rights of occupation under that Act,
(b) any application for leave such as is mentioned in that paragraph were an application for an order under section 1 of that Act, and
(c) any charge under paragraph (b) of that subsection on the estate or interest of the trustee were a charge under that Act on the estate or interest of a spouse.
(4) Any application for leave such as is mentioned in subsection (2)(a) or otherwise by virtue of this section for an order under section 1 of the Act of 1983 shall be made to the court having jurisdiction in relation to the bankruptcy.
(5) On such an application the court shall make such order under section 1 of the Act of 1983 as it thinks just and reasonable having regard to the interests of the creditors, to the bankrupt's financial resources, to the needs of children and to all the circumstances of the case other than the needs of the bankrupt.
(6) Where such an application is made after the end of the period of one year beginning with the first vesting (under Chapter IV of this Part) of the bankrupt's estate in a trustee, the court shall assume, unless the circumstances of the case are exceptional, that the interests of the bankrupt's creditors outweigh all other considerations.

338 Payments in respect of premises occupied by bankrupt Where any premises comprised in a bankrupt's estate are occupied by him (whether by virtue of the preceding section or otherwise) on condition that he makes payments towards satisfying any liability arising under a mortgage of the premises or otherwise towards the outgoings of the premises, the bankrupt does not, by virtue of those payments, acquire any interest in the premises.

Adjustments of prior transactions, etc

339 Transactions at an undervalue (1) Subject as follows in this section and sections 341 and 342, where an individual is adjudged bankrupt and he has at a relevant time (defined in section 341) entered into a transaction with any person at an undervalue, the trustee of the bankrupt's estate may apply to the court for an order under this section.

(2) The court shall, on such an application, make such order as it thinks fit for restoring the position to what it would have been if that individual had not entered into that transaction.
(3) For the purposes of this section and sections 341 and 342, an individual enters into a transaction with a person at an undervalue if –
(a) he makes a gift to that person or he otherwise enters into a transaction with that person on terms that provide for him to receive no consideration,
(b) he enters into a transaction with that person in consideration of marriage, or
(c) he enters into a transaction with that person for a consideration the value of which, in money or money's worth, is significantly less than the value, in money or money's worth, of the consideration provided by the individual.

340 Preferences (1) Subject as follows in this and the next two sections, where an individual is adjudged bankrupt and he has at a relevant time (defined in section 341) given a preference to any person, the trustee of the bankrupt's estate may apply to the court for an order under this section.
(2) The court shall, on such an application, make such order as it thinks fit for restoring the position to what it would have been if that individual had not given that preference.
(3) For the purposes of this and the next two sections, an individual gives a preference to a person if –
(a) that person is one of the individual's creditors or a surety or guarantor for any of his debts or other liabilities, and
(b) the individual does anything or suffers anything to be done which (in either case) has the effect of putting that person into a position which, in the event of the individual's bankruptcy, will be better than the position he would have been in if that thing had not been done.
(4) The court shall not make an order under this section in respect of a preference given to any person unless the individual who gave the preference was influenced in deciding to give it by a desire to produce in relation to that person the effect mentioned in subsection (3)(b) above.
(5) An individual who has given a preference to a person who, at the time the preference was given, was an associate of his (otherwise than by reason only of being his employee) is presumed, unless the contrary is shown, to have been influenced in deciding to give it by such a desire as is mentioned in subsection (4).
(6) The fact that something has been done in pursuance of the order of a court does not, without more, prevent the doing or suffering of that thing from constituting the giving of a preference.

341 'Relevant time' under ss 339, 340 (1) Subject as follows, the time at which an individual enters into a transaction at an undervalue or gives a preference is a relevant time if the transaction is entered into or the preference given –
(a) in the case of a transaction at an undervalue, at a time in the period of 5 years ending with the day of the presentation of the bankruptcy petition on which the individual is adjudged bankrupt,
(b) in the case of a preference which is not a transaction at an undervalue and is given to a person who is an associate of the individual (otherwise than by reason only of being his employee), at a time in the period of 2 years ending with that day, and
(c) in any other case of a preference which is not a transaction at an undervalue, at a time in the period of 6 months ending with that day.
(2) Where an individual enters into a transaction at an undervalue or gives a preference at a time mentioned in paragraph (a), (b) or (c) of subsection (1) (not being, in the case of a transaction at an undervalue, a time less than 2 years before the end of the period mentioned in paragraph (a)), that time is not a relevant time for the purposes of sections 339 and 340 unless the individual –

(a) is insolvent at that time, or
(b) becomes insolvent in consequence of the transaction or preference;
but the requirements of this subsection are presumed to be satisfied, unless the contrary is shown, in relation to any transaction at an undervalue which is entered into by an individual with a person who is an associate of his (otherwise than by reason only of being his employee).
(3) For the purpose of subsection (2), an individual is insolvent if –
(a) he is unable to pay his debts as they fall due, or
(b) the value of his assets is less than the amount of his liabilities, taking into account his contingent and prospective liabilities.
(4) A transaction entered into or preference given by a person who is subsequently adjudged bankrupt on a petition under section 264(1)(d) (criminal bankruptcy) is to be treated as having been entered into or given at a relevant time for the purposes of sections 339 and 340 if it was entered into or given at any time on or after the date specified for the purposes of this subsection in the criminal bankruptcy order on which the petition is based.
(5) No order shall be made under section 339 or 340 by virtue of subsection (4) of this section where an appeal is pending (within the meaning of section 277) against the individual's conviction of any offence by virtue of which the criminal bankruptcy order was made.

342 Orders under ss 339, 340 (1) Without prejudice to the generality of section 339(2) or 340(2), an order under either of those sections with respect to a transaction or preference entered into or given by an individual who is subsequently adjudged bankrupt may (subject as follows) –
(a) require any property transferred as part of the transaction, or in connection with the giving of the preference, to be vested in the trustee of the bankrupt's estate as part of that estate;
(b) require any property to be so vested if it represents in any person's hands the application either of the proceeds of sale of property so transferred or of money so transferred;
(c) release or discharge (in whole or in part) any security given by the individual;
(d) require any person to pay, in respect of benefits received by him from the individual, such sums to the trustee of his estate as the court may direct;
(e) provide for any surety or guarantor whose obligations to any person were released or discharged (in whole or in part) under the transaction or by the giving of the preference to be under such new or revived obligations to that person as the court thinks appropriate:
(f) provide for security to be provided for the discharge of any obligation imposed by or arising under the order, for such an obligation to be charged on any property and for the security or charge to have the same priority as a security or charge released or discharged (in whole or in part) under the transaction or by the giving of the preference; and
(g) provide for the extent to which any person whose property is vested by the order in the trustee of the bankrupt's estate, or on whom obligations are imposed by the order, is to be able to prove in the bankruptcy for debts or other liabilities which arose from, or were released or discharged (in whole or in part) under or by, the transaction or the giving of the preference.
(2) An order under section 339 or 340 may affect the property of, or impose any obligation on, any person whether or not he is the person with whom the individual in question entered into the transaction or, as the case may be, the person to whom the preference was given; but such an order –
(a) shall not prejudice any interest in property which was acquired from a person other than that individual and was acquired in good faith, for value and without

notice of the relevant circumstances, or prejudice any interest deriving from such an interest, and

(b) shall not require a person who received a benefit from the transaction or preference in good faith, for value and without notice of the relevant circumstances to pay a sum to the trustee of the bankrupt's estate, except where he was a party to the transaction or the payment is to be in respect of a preference given to that person at a time when he was a creditor of that individual.

(3) Any sums required to be paid to the trustee in accordance with an order under section 339 or 340 shall be comprised in the bankrupt's estate.

(4) For the purposes of this section the relevant circumstances, in relation to a transaction or preference, are –

(a) the circumstances by virtue of which an order under section 339 or 340 could be made in respect of the transaction or preference if the individual in question were adjudged bankrupt within a particular period after the transaction is entered into or the preference given, and

(b) if that period has expired, the fact that that individual has been adjudged bankrupt within that period.

343 Extortionate credit transactions (1) This section applies where a person is adjudged bankrupt who is or has been a party to a transaction for, or involving, the provision to him of credit.

(2) The court may, on the application of the trustee of the bankrupt's estate, make an order with respect to the transaction if the transaction is or was extortionate and was not entered into more than 3 years before the commencement of the bankruptcy.

(3) For the purposes of this section a transaction is extortionate if, having regard to the risk accepted by the person providing the credit –

(a) the terms of it are or were such as to require grossly exorbitant payments to be made (whether unconditionally or in certain contingencies) in respect of the provision of the credit, or

(b) it otherwise grossly contravened ordinary principles of fair dealing;

and it shall be presumed, unless the contrary is proved, that a transaction with respect to which an application is made under this section is or, as the case may be, was extortionate.

(4) An order under this section with respect to any transaction may contain such one or more of the following as the court thinks fit, that is to say –

(a) provision setting aside the whole or part of any obligation created by the transaction;

(b) provision otherwise varying the terms of the transaction or varying the terms on which any security for the purposes of the transaction is held;

(c) provision requiring any person who is or was party to the transaction to pay to the trustee any sums paid to that person, by virtue of the transaction, by the bankrupt;

(d) provision requiring any person to surrender to the trustee any property held by him as security for the purposes of the transaction;

(e) provision directing accounts to be taken between any persons.

(5) Any sums or property required to be paid or surrendered to the trustee in accordance with an order under this section shall be comprised in the bankrupt's estate.

(6) Neither the trustee of a bankrupt's estate nor an undischarged bankrupt is entitled to make an application under section 139(1)(a) of the Consumer Credit Act 1974 (re-opening of extortionate credit agreements) for any agreement by which credit is or has been provided to the bankrupt to be re-opened.

But the powers conferred by this section are exercisable in relation to any transaction concurrently with any powers exercisable under this Act in relation to that transaction as a transaction at an undervalue.

344 Avoidance of general assignment of book debts (1) The following applies where a person engaged in any business makes a general assignment to another person of his existing or future book debts, or any class of them, and is subsequently adjudged bankrupt.
(2) The assignment is void against the trustee of the bankrupt's estate as regards book debts which were not paid before the presentation of the bankruptcy petition, unless the assignment has been registered under the Bills of Sale Act 1878.
(3) For the purposes of subsections (1) and (2) –
(a) 'assignment' includes an assignment by way of security or charge on book debts, and
(b) 'general assignment' does not include –
    (i) an assignment of book debts due at the date of the assignment from specified debtors or of debts becoming due under specified contracts, or
    (ii) an assignment of book debts included either in a transfer of a business made in good faith and for value or in an assignment of assets for the benefit of creditors generally.
(4) For the purposes of registration under the Act of 1878 an assignment of book debts is to be treated as if it were a bill of sale given otherwise than by way of security for the payment of a sum of money; and the provisions of that Act with respect to the registration of bills of sale apply accordingly with such necessary modifications as may be made by rules under that Act.

345 Contracts to which bankrupt is a party (1) The following applies where a contract has been made with a person who is subsequently adjudged bankrupt.
(2) The court may, on the application of any other party to the contract, make an order discharging obligations under the contract on such terms as to payment by the applicant or the bankrupt of damages for non-performance or otherwise as appear to the court to be equitable.
(3) Any damages payable by the bankrupt by virtue of an order of the court under this section are provable as a bankruptcy debt.
(4) Where an undischarged bankrupt is a contractor in respect of any contract jointly with any person, that person may sue or be sued in respect of the contract without the joinder of the bankrupt.

346 Enforcement procedures (1) Subject to section 285 in Chapter II (restrictions on proceedings and remedies) and to the following provisions of this section, where the creditor of any person who is adjudged bankrupt has, before the commencement of the bankruptcy –
(a) issued execution against the goods or land of that person, or
(b) attached a debt due to that person from another person,
that creditor is not entitled, as against the official receiver or trustee of the bankrupt's estate, to regain the benefit of the execution or attachment, or any sums paid to avoid it, unless the execution or attachment was completed, or the sums were paid, before the commencement of the bankruptcy.
(2) Subject as follows, where any goods of a person have been taken in execution, then, if before the completion of the execution notice is given to the sheriff or other officer charged with the execution that that person has been adjudged bankrupt –
(a) the sheriff or other officer shall on request deliver to the official receiver or trustee of the bankrupt's estate the goods and any money seized or recovered in part satisfaction of the execution, but
(b) the costs of the execution are a first charge on the goods or money so delivered and the official receiver or trustee may sell the goods or a sufficient part of them for the purpose of satisfying the charge.
(3) Subject to subsection (6) below, where –

(a) under an execution in respect of a judgment for a sum exceeding such sum as may be prescribed for the purposes of this subsection, the goods of any person are sold or money is paid in order to avoid a sale, and
(b) before the end of the period of 14 days beginning with the day of the sale or payment the sheriff or other officer charged with the execution is given notice that a bankruptcy petition has been presented in relation to that person, and
(c) a bankruptcy order is or has been made on that petition,
the balance of the proceeds of sale or money paid, after deducting the costs of execution, shall (in priority to the claim of the execution creditor) be comprised in the bankrupt's estate.
(4) Accordingly, in the case of an execution in respect of a judgment for a sum exceeding the sum prescribed for the purposes of subsection (3), the sheriff or other officer charged with the execution –
(a) shall not dispose of the balance mentioned in subsection (3) at any time within the period of 14 days so mentioned or while there is pending a bankruptcy petition of which he has been given notice under that subsection, and
(b) shall pay that balance, where by virtue of that subsection it is comprised in the bankrupt's estate, to the official receiver or (if there is one) to the trustee of that estate.
(5) For the purposes of this section –
(a) an execution against goods is completed by seizure and sale or by the making of a charging order under section 1 of the Charging Orders Act 1979;
(b) an execution against land is completed by seizure, by the appointment of a receiver or by the making of a charging order under that section;
(c) an attachment of a debt is completed by the receipt of the debt.
(6) The rights conferred by subsections (1) to (3) on the official receiver or the trustee may, to such extent and on such terms as it thinks fit, be set aside by the court in favour of the creditor who has issued the execution or attached the debt.
(7) Nothing in this section entitles the trustee of a bankrupt's estate to claim goods from a person who has acquired them in good faith under a sale by a sheriff or other officer charged with an execution.
(8) Neither subsection (2) nor subsection (3) applies in relation to any execution against property which has been acquired by or has devolved upon the bankrupt since the commencement of the bankruptcy, unless, at the time the execution is issued or before it is completed –
(a) the property has been or is claimed for the bankrupt's estate under section 307 (after-acquired property), and
(b) a copy of the notice given under that section has been or is served on the sheriff or other officer charged with the execution.

347 Distress, etc (1) The right of any landlord or other person to whom rent is payable to distrain upon the goods and effects of an undischarged bankrupt for rent due to him from the bankrupt is available (subject to subsection (5) below) against goods and effects comprised in the bankrupt's estate, but only for 6 months' rent accrued due before the commencement of the bankruptcy.
(2) Where a landlord or other person to whom rent is payable has distrained for rent upon the goods and effects of an individual to whom a bankruptcy petition relates and a bankruptcy order is subsequently made on that petition, any amount recovered by way of that distress which –
(a) is in excess of the amount which by virtue of subsection (1) would have been recoverable after the commencement of the bankruptcy, or
(b) is in respect of rent for a period or part of a period after the distress was levied,
shall be held for the bankrupt as part of his estate.

(3) Where any person (whether or not a landlord or person entitled to rent) has distrained upon the goods or effects of an individual who is adjudged bankrupt before the end of the period of 3 months beginning with the distraint, so much of those goods or effects, or of the proceeds of their sale, as is not held for the bankrupt under subsection (2) shall be charged for the benefit of the bankrupt's estate with the preferential debts of the bankrupt to the extent that the bankrupt's estate is for the time being insufficient for meeting those debts.
(4) Where by virtue of any charge under subsection (3) any person surrenders any goods or effects to the trustee of a bankrupt's estate or makes a payment to such a trustee, that person ranks, in respect of the amount of the proceeds of the sale of those goods or effects by the trustee or, as the case may be, the amount of the payment, as a preferential creditor of the bankrupt, except as against so much of the bankrupt's estate as is available for the payment of preferential creditors by virtue of the surrender or payment.
(5) A landlord or other person to whom rent is payable is not at any time after the discharge of a bankrupt entitled to distrain upon any goods or effects comprised in the bankrupt's estate.
(6) Where in the case of any execution –
(a) a landlord is (apart from this section) entitled under section 1 of the Landlord and Tenant Act 1709 or section 102 of the County Courts Act 1984 (claims for rent where goods seized in execution) to claim for an amount not exceeding one year's rent, and
(b) the person against whom the execution is levied is adjudged bankrupt before the notice of claim is served on the sheriff or other officer charged with the execution,

the right of the landlord to claim under that section is restricted to a right to claim for an amount not exceeding 6 months' rent and does not extend to any rent payable in respect of a period after the notice of claim is so served.
(7) Nothing in subsection (6) imposes any liability on a sheriff or other officer charged with an execution to account to the official receiver or the trustee of a bankrupt's estate for any sums paid by him to a landlord at any time before the sheriff or other officer was served with notice of the bankruptcy order in question.
But this subsection is without prejudice to the liability of the landlord.
(8) Nothing in this Group of Parts affects any right to distrain otherwise than for rent; and any such right is at any time exercisable without restriction against property comprised in a bankrupt's estate, even if that right is expressed by any enactment to be exercisable in like manner as a right to distrain for rent.
(9) Any right to distrain against property comprised in a bankrupt's estate is exercisable notwithstanding that the property has vested in the trustee.
(10) The provisions of this section are without prejudice to a landlord's right in a bankruptcy to prove for any bankruptcy debt in respect of rent.

348 Apprenticeships, etc (1) This section applies where –
(a) a bankruptcy order is made in respect of an individual to whom another individual was an apprentice or articled clerk at the time when the petition on which the order was made was presented, and
(b) the bankrupt or the apprentice or clerk gives notice to the trustee terminating the apprenticeship or articles.

(2) Subject to subsection (6) below, the indenture of apprenticeship or, as the case may be, the articles of agreement shall be discharged with effect from the commencement of the bankruptcy.
(3) If any money has been paid by or on behalf of the apprentice or clerk to the bankrupt as a fee, the trustee may, on an application made by or on behalf of the apprentice or clerk, pay such sum to the apprentice or clerk as the trustee thinks reasonable, having regard to –

(a) the amount of the fee,
(b) the proportion of the period in respect of which the fee was paid that has been served by the apprentice or clerk before the commencement of the bankruptcy, and
(c) the other circumstances of the case.

(4) The power of the trustee to make a payment under subsection (3) has priority over his obligation to distribute the bankrupt's estate.

(5) Instead of making a payment under subsection (3), the trustee may, if it appears to him expedient to do so on an application made by or on behalf of the apprentice or clerk, transfer the indenture or articles to a person other than the bankrupt.

(6) Where a transfer is made under subsection (5), subsection (2) has effect only as between the apprentice or clerk and the bankrupt.

349 Unenforceability of liens on books, etc (1) Subject as follows, a lien or other right to retain possession of any of the books, papers or other records of a bankrupt is unenforceable to the extent that its enforcement would deny possession of any books, papers or other records to the official receiver or the trustee of the bankrupt's estate.

(2) Subsection (1) does not apply to a lien on documents which give a title to property and are held as such.

Chapter VI: Bankruptcy Offences

Preliminary

350 Scheme of this Chapter (1) Subject to section 360(3) below, this Chapter applies where the court has made a bankruptcy order on a bankruptcy petition.

(2) This Chapter applies whether or not the bankruptcy order is annulled, but proceedings for an offence under this Chapter shall not be instituted after the annulment.

(3) Without prejudice to his liability in respect of a subsequent bankruptcy, the bankrupt is not guilty of an offence under this Chapter in respect of anything done after his discharge; but nothing in this Group of Parts prevents the institution of proceedings against a discharged bankrupt for an offence committed before his discharge.

(4) It is not a defence in proceedings for an offence under this Chapter that anything relied on, in whole or in part, as constituting that offence was done outside England and Wales.

(5) Proceedings for an offence under this Chapter or under the rules shall not be instituted except by the Secretary of State or by or with the consent of the Director of Public Prosecutions.

(6) A person guilty of any offence under this Chapter is liable to imprisonment or a fine, or both.

351 Definitions In the following provisions of this Chapter –
(a) references to property comprised in the bankrupt's estate or to property possession of which is required to be delivered up to the official receiver or the trustee of the bankrupt's estate include any property which would be such property if a notice in respect of it were given under section 307 (after-acquired property) or 308 (personal property and effects of bankrupt having more than replacement value);
(b) 'the initial period' means the period between the presentation of the bankruptcy petition and the commencement of the bankruptcy; and
(c) a reference to a number of months or years before petition is to that period ending with the presentation of the bankruptcy petition.

352 Defence of innocent intention Where in the case of an offence under any provision of this Chapter it is stated that this section applies, a person is not guilty of the offence if he proves that, at the time of the conduct constituting the offence, he had no intent to defraud or to conceal the state of his affairs.

Wrongdoing by the bankrupt before and after bankruptcy

353 Non-disclosure (1) The bankrupt is guilty of an offence if –
(a) he does not to the best of his knowledge and belief disclose all the property comprised in his estate to the official receiver or the trustee, or
(b) he does not inform the official receiver or the trustee of any disposal of any property which but for the disposal would be so comprised, stating how, when, to whom and for what consideration the property was disposed of.
(2) Subsection (1)(b) does not apply to any disposal in the ordinary course of a business carried on by the bankrupt or to any payment of the ordinary expenses of the bankrupt or his family.
(3) Section 352 applies to this offence.

354 Concealment of property (1) The bankrupt is guilty of an offence if –
(a) he does not deliver up possession to the official receiver or trustee, or as the official receiver or trustee may direct, of such part of the property comprised in his estate as is in his possession or under his control and possession of which he is required by law so to deliver up,
(b) he conceals any debt due to or from him or conceals any property the value of which is not less than the prescribed amount and possession of which he is required to deliver up to the official receiver or trustee, or
(c) in the 12 months before petition, or in the initial period, he did anything which would have been an offence under paragraph (b) above if the bankruptcy order has been made immediately before he did it.

Section 352 applies to this offence.
(2) The bankrupt is guilty of an offence if he removes, or in the initial period removed, any property the value of which was not less than the prescribed amount and possession of which he has or would have been required to deliver up to the official receiver or the trustee.

Section 352 applies to this offence.
(3) The bankrupt is guilty of an offence if he without reasonable excuse fails, on being required to do so by the official receiver or the court –
(a) to account for the loss of any substantial part of his property incurred in the 12 months before petition or in the initial period, or
(b) to give a satisfactory explanation of the manner in which such a loss was incurred.

355 Concealment of books and papers; falsification (1) The bankrupt is guilty of an offence if he does not deliver up possession to the official receiver or the trustee, or as the official receiver or trustee may direct, of all books, papers and other records of which he has possession or control and which relate to his estate or his affairs.

Section 352 applies to this offence.
(2) The bankrupt is guilty of an offence if –
(a) he prevents, or in the initial period prevented, the production of any books, papers or records relating to his estate or affairs;
(b) he conceals, destroys, mutilates or falsifies, or causes or permits the concealment, destruction, mutilation or falsification of, any books, papers or other records relating to his estate or affairs;

(c) he makes, or causes or permits the making of, any false entries in any book, document or record relating to his estate or affairs; or
(d) in the 12 months before petition, or in the initial period, he did anything which would have been an offence under paragraph (b) or (c) above if the bankruptcy order has been made before he did it.

Section 352 applies to this offence.

(3) The bankrupt is guilty of an offence if –
(a) he disposes of, or alters or makes any omission in, or causes or permits the disposal, altering or making of any omission in, any book, document or record relating to his estate or affairs, or
(b) in the 12 months before petition, or in the initial period, he did anything which would have been an offence under paragraph (a) if the bankruptcy order had been made before he did it.

Section 352 applies to this offence.

356 False statements (1) The bankrupt is guilty of an offence if he makes or has made any material omission in any statement made under any provision in this Group of Parts and relating to his affairs.

Section 352 applies to this offence.

(2) The bankrupt is guilty of an offence if –
(a) knowing or believing that a false debt has been proved by any person under the bankruptcy, he fails to inform the trustee as soon as practicable; or
(b) he attempts to account for any part of his property by fictitious losses or expenses; or
(c) at any meeting of his creditors in the 12 months before petition or (whether or not at such a meeting) at any time in the initial period, he did anything which would have been an offence under paragraph (b) if the bankruptcy order had been made before he did it; or
(d) he is, or at any time had been, guilty of any false representation or other fraud for the purpose of obtaining the consent of his creditors, or any of them, to an agreement with reference to his affairs or to his bankruptcy.

357 Fraudulent disposal of property (1) The bankrupt is guilty of an offence if he makes or causes to be made, or has in the period of 5 years ending with the commencement of the bankruptcy made or caused to be made any gift or transfer of, or any charge on, his property.

Section 352 applies to this offence.

(2) The reference to making a transfer of or charge on any property includes causing or conniving at the levying of any execution against that property.

(3) The bankrupt is guilty of an offence if he conceals or removes, or has at any time before the commencement of the bankruptcy concealed or removed, any part of his property after, or within 2 months before, the date on which a judgment or order for the payment of money has been obtained against him, being a judgment or order which was not satisfied before the commencement of the bankruptcy.

Section 352 applies to this offence.

358 Absconding The bankrupt is guilty of an offence if –
(a) he leaves, or attempts or makes preparations to leave, England and Wales with any property the value of which is not less than the prescribed amount and possession of which he is required to deliver up to the official receiver or the trustee, or
(b) in the 6 months before petition, or in the initial period, he did anything which would have been an offence under paragraph (a) if the bankruptcy order had been made immediately before he did it.

Section 352 applies to this offence.

359 Fradulent dealing with property obtained on credit (1) The bankrupt is guilty of an offence if, in the 12 months before petition, or in the initial period, he disposed of any property which he had obtained on credit and, at the time he disposed of it, had not paid for.

Section 352 applies to this offence.

(2) A person is guilty of an offence if, in the 12 months before petition or in the initial period, he acquired or received property from the bankrupt knowing or believing –

(a) that the bankrupt owed money in respect of the property, and

(b) that the bankrupt did not intend, or was unlikely to be able, to pay the money he so owed.

(3) A person is not guilty of an offence under subsection (1) or (2) if the disposal, acquisition or receipt of the property was in the ordinary course of a business carried on by the bankrupt at the time of the disposal, acquisition or receipt.

(4) In determining for the purposes of this section whether any property is disposed of, acquired or received in the ordinary course of a business carried on by the bankrupt, regard may be had, in particular, to the price paid for the property.

(5) In this section references to disposing of property include pawning or pledging it; and references to acquiring or receiving property shall be read accordingly.

360 Obtaining credit; engaging in business (1) The bankrupt is guilty of an offence if –

(a) either alone or jointly with any other person, he obtains credit to the extent of the prescribed amount or more without giving the person from whom he obtains it the relevant information about his status; or

(b) he engages (whether directly or indirectly) in any business under a name other than that in which he was adjudged bankrupt without disclosing to all persons with whom he enters into any business transaction the name in which he was so adjudged.

(2) The reference to the bankrupt obtaining credit includes the following cases –

(a) where goods are bailed to him under a hire-purchase agreement, or agreed to be sold to him under a conditional sale agreement, and

(b) where he is paid in advance (whether in money or otherwise) for the supply of goods or services.

(3) A person whose estate has been sequestrated in Scotland, or who has been adjudged bankrupt in Northern Ireland, is guilty of an offence if, before his discharge, he does anything in England and Wales which would be an offence under subsection (1) if he were an undischarged bankrupt and the sequestration of his estate or the adjudication in Northern Ireland were an adjudication under this Part.

(4) For the purposes of subsection (1)(a), the relevant information about the status of the person in question is the information that he is an undischarged bankrupt or, as the case may be, that his estate has been sequestrated in Scotland and that he has not been discharged.

361 Failure to keep proper accounts of business (1) Where the bankrupt has been engaged in any business for any of the period of 2 years before petition, he is guilty of an offence if he –

(a) has not kept proper accounting records throughout that period and throughout any part of the initial period in which he was so engaged, or

(b) has not preserved all the accounting records which he has kept.

(2) The bankrupt is not guilty of an offence under subsection (1) –

(a) if his unsecured liabilities at the commencement of the bankruptcy did not exceed the prescribed amount, or

(b) if he proves that in the circumstances in which he carried on business the omission was honest and excusable.

(3) For the purposes of this section a person is deemed not to have kept proper accounting records if he has not kept such records as are necessary to show or explain his transactions and financial position in his business, including –
(a) records containing entries from day to day, in sufficient detail, of all cash paid and received,
(b) where the business involved dealings in goods, statements of annual stock-takings, and
(c) except in the case of goods sold by way of retail trade to the actual customer, records of all goods sold and purchased showing the buyers and sellers in sufficient detail to enable the goods and the buyers and sellers to be identified.
(4) In relation to any such records as are mentioned in subsection (3), subsections (2)(d) and (3)(b) of section 355 apply with the substitution of 2 years for 12 months.

362 Gambling (1) The bankrupt is guilty of an offence if he has –
(a) in the 2 years before petition, materially contributed to, or increased the extent of, his insolvency by gambling or by rash and hazardous speculations, or
(b) in the initial period, lost any part of his property by gambling or by rash and hazardous speculations.
(2) In determining for the purposes of this section whether any speculations were rash and hazardous, the financial position of the bankrupt at the time when he entered into them shall be taken into consideration.

Chapter VII: Powers of Court In Bankruptcy

363 General control of court (1) Every bankruptcy is under the general control of the court and, subject to the provisions in this Group of Parts, the court has full power to decide all questions of priorities and all other questions, whether of law or fact, arising in any bankruptcy.
(2) Without prejudice to any other provision in this Group of Parts, an undischarged bankrupt or a discharged bankrupt whose estate is still being administered under Chapter IV of this Part shall do all such things as he may be directed to do by the court for the purposes of his bankruptcy or, as the case may be, the administration of that estate.
(3) The official receiver or the trustee of a bankrupt's estate may at any time apply to the court for a direction under subsection (2).
(4) If any person without reasonable excuse fails to comply with any obligation imposed on him by subsection (2), he is guilty of a contempt of court and liable to be punished accordingly (in addition to any other punishment to which he may be subject).

364 Power of arrest (1) In the cases specified in the next subsection the court may cause a warrant to be issued to a constable or prescribed officer of the court –
(a) for the arrest of a debtor to whom a bankruptcy petition relates or of an undischarged bankrupt, or of a discharged bankrupt whose estate is still being administered under Chapter IV of this Part, and
(b) for the seizure of any books, papers, records, money or goods in the possession of a person arrested under the warrant,

and may authorise a person arrested under such a warrant to be kept in custody, and anything seized under such a warrant to be held, in accordance with the rules, until such time as the court may order.
(2) The powers conferred by subsection (1) are exercisable in relation to a debtor or undischarged or discharged bankrupt if, at any time after the presentation of the bankruptcy petition relating to him or the making of the bankruptcy order against him, it appears to the court –

(a) that there are reasonable grounds for believing that he has absconded, or is about to abscond, with a view to avoiding or delaying the payment of any of his debts or his appearance to a bankruptcy petition or to avoiding, delaying or disrupting any proceedings in bankruptcy against him or any examination of his affairs, or
(b) that he is about to remove his goods with a view to preventing or delaying possession being taken of them by the official receiver or the trustee of his estate, or
(c) that there are reasonable grounds for believing that he has concealed or destroyed, or is about to conceal or destroy, any of his goods or any books, papers or records which might be of use to his creditors in the course of his bankruptcy or in connection with the administration of his estate, or
(d) that he has, without the leave of the official receiver or the trustee of his estate, removed any goods in his possession which exceed in value such sum as may be prescribed for the purposes of this paragraph, or
(e) that he has failed, without reasonable excuse, to attend any examination ordered by the court.

365 Seizure of bankrupt's property (1) At any time after a bankruptcy order has been made, the court may, on the application of the official receiver or the trustee of the bankrupt's estate, issue a warrant authorising the person to whom it is directed to seize any property comprised in the bankrupt's estate which is, or any books, papers or records relating to the bankrupt's estate or affairs which are, in the possession or under the control of the bankrupt or any other person who is required to deliver the property, books, papers or records to the official receiver or trustee.
(2) Any person executing a warrant under this section may, for the purpose of seizing any property comprised in the bankrupt's estate or any books, papers or records relating to the bankrupt's estate or affairs, break open any premises where the bankrupt or anything that may be seized under the warrant is or is believed to be and any receptacle of the bankrupt which contains or is believed to contain anything that may be so seized.
(3) If, after a bankruptcy order has been made, the court is satisfied that any property comprised in the bankrupt's estate is, or any books, papers or records relating to the bankrupt's estate or affairs are, concealed in any premises not belonging to him, it may issue a warrant authorising any constable or prescribed officer of the court to search those premises for the property, books, papers or records.
(4) A warrant under subsection (3) shall not be executed except in the prescribed manner and in accordance with its terms.

366 Inquiry into bankrupt's dealings and property (1) At any time after a bankruptcy order has been made the court may, on the application of the official receiver or the trustee of the bankrupt's estate, summon to appear before it –
(a) the bankrupt or the bankrupt's spouse or former spouse,
(b) any person known or believed to have any property comprised in the bankrupt's estate in his possession or to be indebted to the bankrupt,
(c) any person appearing to the court to be able to give information concerning the bankrupt or the bankrupt's dealings, affairs or property.

The court may require any such person as is mentioned in paragraph (b) or (c) to submit an affidavit to the court containing an account of his dealings with the bankrupt or to produce any documents in his possession or under his control relatiing to the bankrupt or the bankrupt's dealings, affairs or property.
(2) Without prejudice to section 364, the following applies in a case where –
(a) a person without reasonable excuse fails to appear before the court when he is summoned to do so under this section, or

(b) there are reasonable grounds for believing that a person has absconded, or is about to abscond, with a view to avoiding his appearance before the court under this section.

(3) The court may, for the purpose of bringing that person and anything in his possession before the court, cause a warrant to be issued to a constable or prescribed officer of the court –

(a) for the arrest of that person, and

(b) for the seizure of any books, papers, records, money or goods in that person's possession.

(4) The court may authorise a person arrested under such a warrant to be kept in custody, and anything seized under such a warrant to be held, in accordance with the rules, until that person is brought before the court under the warrant or until such other time as the court may order.

367 Court's enforcement powers under s 366 (1) If it appears to the court, on consideration of any evidence obtained under section 366 or this section, that any person has in his possession any property comprised in the bankrupt's estate, the court may, on the application of the official receiver or the trustee of the bankrupt's estate, order that person to deliver the whole or any part of the property to the official receiver or the trustee at such time, in such manner and on such terms as the court thinks fit.

(2) If it appears to the court, on consideration of any evidence obtained under section 366 or this section, that any person is indebted to the bankrupt, the court may, on the application of the official receiver or the trustee of the bankrupt's estate, order that person to pay to the official receiver or trustee, at such time and in such manner as the court may direct, the whole or part of the amount due, whether in full discharge of the debt or otherwise as the court thinks fit.

(3) The court may, if it thinks fit, order that any person who if within the jurisdiction of the court would be liable to be summoned to appear before it under section 366 shall be examined in any part of the United Kingdom where he may be for the time being, or in any place outside the United Kingdom.

(4) Any person who appears or is brought before the court under section 366 or this section may be examined on oath, either orally or by interrogatories, concerning the bankrupt or the bankrupt's dealings, affairs and property.

368 Provision corresponding to s 366, where interim receiver appointed Sections 366 and 367 apply where an interim receiver has been appointed under section 286 as they apply where a bankruptcy order has been made, as if –

(a) references to the official receiver or the trustee were to the interim receiver, and

(b) references to the bankrupt and to his estate were (respectively) to the debtor and his property.

369 Order for production of documents by inland revenue (1) For the purposes of an examination under section 290 (public examination of bankrupt) or proceedings under sections 366 to 368, the court may, on the application of the official receiver or the trustee of the bankrupt's estate, order an inland revenue official to produce to the court –

(a) any return, account or accounts submitted (whether before or after the commencement of the bankruptcy) by the bankrupt to any inland revenue official,

(b) any assessment or determination made (whether before or after the commencement of the bankruptcy) in relation to the bankrupt by any inland revenue official, or

(c) any correspondence (whether before or after the commencement of the bankruptcy) between the bankrupt and any inland revenue official.

(2) Where the court has made an order under subsection (1) for the purposes of any examination or proceedings, the court may, at any time after the document to which the order relates is produced to it, by order authorise the disclosure of the document, or of any part of its contents, to the official receiver, the trustee of the bankrupt's estate or the bankrupt's creditors.
(3) The court shall not address an order under subsection (1) to an inland revenue official unless it is satisfied that that official is dealing, or has dealt, with the affairs of the bankrupt.
(4) Where any document to which an order under subsection (1) relates is not in the possession of the official to whom the order is addressed, it is the duty of that official to take all reasonable steps to secure possession of it and, if he fails to do so, to report the reasons for his failure to the court.
(5) Where any document to which an order under subsection (1) relates is in the possession of an inland revenue official other than the one to whom the order is addressed, it is the duty of the official in possession of the document, at the request of the official to whom the order is addressed, to deliver it to the official making the request.
(6) In this section 'inland revenue official' means any inspector or collector of taxes appointed by the Commissioners of Inland Revenue or any person appointed by the Commissioners to serve in any other capacity.
(7) This section does not apply for the purposes of an examination under sections 366 and 367 which takes place by virtue of section 368 (interim receiver).

370 Power to appoint special manager (1) The court may, on an application under this section, appoint any person to be the special manager –
(a) of a bankrupt's estate, or
(b) of the business of an undischarged bankrupt, or
(c) of the property or business of a debtor in whose case the official receiver has been appointed interim receiver under section 286.
(2) An application under this section may be made by the official receiver or the trustee of the bankrupt's estate in any case where it appears to the official receiver or trustee that the nature of the estate, property or business, or the interests of the creditors generally, require the appointment of another person to manage the estate, property or business.
(3) A special manager appointed under this section has such powers as may be entrusted to him by the court.
(4) The power of the court under subsection (3) to entrust powers to a special manager includes power to direct that any provision in this Group of Parts that has effect in relation to the official receiver, interim receiver or trustee shall have the like effect in relation to the special manager for the purposes of the carrying out by the special manager of any of the functions of the official receiver, interim receiver or trustee.
(5) A special manager appointed under this section shall –
(a) give such security as may be prescribed,
(b) prepare and keep such accounts as may be prescribed, and
(c) produce those accounts in accordance with the rules to the Secretary of State or to such other persons as may be prescribed.

371 Re-direction of bankrupt's letters, etc (1) Where a bankruptcy order has been made, the court may from time to time, on the application of the official receiver or the trustee of the bankrupt's estate, order the Post Office to re-direct and send or deliver to the official receiver or trustee or otherwise any postal packet (within the meaning of the Post Office Act 1953) which would otherwise be sent or delivered by them to the bankrupt at such place or places as may be specified in the order.

(2) An order under this section has effect for such period, not exceeding 3 months, as may be specified in the order.

Part X: Individual Insolvency: General Provisions

372 Supplies of gas, water, electricity, etc (1) This section applies where on any day ('the relevant day') –
(a) a bankruptcy order is made against an individual or an interim receiver of an individual's property is appointed, or
(b) a voluntary arrangement proposed by an individual is approved under Part VIII, or
(c) a deed of arrangement is made for the benefit of an individual's creditors;
and in this section 'the office-holder' means the official receiver, the trustee in bankruptcy, the interim receiver, the supervisor of the voluntary arrangement or the trustee under the deed of arrangement, as the case may be.
(2) If a request falling within the next subsection is made for the giving after the relevant day of any of the supplies mentioned in subsection (4), the supplier –
(a) may make it a condition of the giving of the supply that the office-holder personally guarantees the payment of any charges in respect of the supply, but
(b) shall not make it a condition of the giving of the supply, or do anything which has the effect of making it a condition of the giving of the supply, that any outstanding charges in respect of a supply given to the individual before the relevant day are paid.
(3) A request falls within this subsection if it is made –
(a) by or with the concurrence of the office-holder, and
(b) for the purposes of any business which is or has been carried on by the individual, by a firm or partnership of which the individual is or was a member, or by an agent or manager for the individual or for such a firm or partnership.
(4) The supplies referred to in subsection (2) are –
(a) a public supply of gas,
(b) a supply of electricity by an Electricity Board,
(c) a supply of water by statutory water undertakers,
(d) a supply of telecommunication services by a public telecommunications operator.
(5) The following applies to expressions used in subsection (4) –
(a) 'public supply of gas' means a supply of gas by the British Gas Corporation or a public gas supplier within the meaning of Part I of the Gas Act 1986;
(b) 'Electricity Board' means the same as in the Energy Act 1983; and
(c) 'telecommunication services' and 'public telecommunications operator' mean the same as in the Telecommunications Act 1984, except that the former does not include services consisting in the conveyance of programmes included in cable programme services (within the meaning of the Cable and Broadcasting Act 1984).

373 Jurisdiction in relation to insolvent individuals (1) The High Court and the county courts have jurisdiction throughout England and Wales for the purposes of the Parts in this Group.
(2) For the purposes of those Parts, a county court has, in addition to its ordinary jurisdiction, all the powers and jurisdiction of the High Court; and the orders of the court may be enforced accordingly in the prescribed manner.
(3) Jurisdiction for the purposes of those Parts is exercised –
(a) by the High Court in relation to the proceedings which, in accordance with the rules, are allocated to the London insolvency district, and
(b) by each county court in relation to the proceedings which are so allocated to the insolvency district of that court.

(4) Subsection (3) is without prejudice to the transfer of proceedings from one court to another in the manner prescribed by the rules; and nothing in that subsection invalidates any proceedings on the grounds that they were initiated or continued in the wrong court.

374 Insolvency districts (1) The Lord Chancellor may by order designate the areas which are for the time being to be comprised, for the purposes of the Parts in this Group, in the London insolvency district and the insolvency district of each county court; and an order under this section may –
(a) exclude any county court from having jurisdiction for the purposes of those Parts, or
(b) confer jurisdiction for those purposes on any county court which has not previously had that jurisdiction.
(2) An order under this section may contain such incidental, supplemental and transitional provisions as may appear to the Lord Chancellor necessary or expedient.
(3) An order under this section shall be made by statutory instrument and, after being made, shall be laid before each House of Parliament.
(4) Subject to any order under this section –
(a) the district which, immediately before the appointed day, is the London bankruptcy district becomes, on that day, the London insolvency district;
(b) any district which immediately before that day is the bankruptcy district of a county court becomes, on that day, the insolvency district of that court, and
(c) any county court which immediately before that day is excluded from having jurisdiction in bankruptcy is excluded, on and after that day, from having jurisdiction for the purposes of the Parts in this Group.

375 Appeals etc from courts exercising insolvency jurisdiction (1) Every court having jurisdiction for the purposes of the Parts in this Group may review, rescind or vary any order made by it in the exercise of that jurisdiction.
(2) An appeal from a decision made in the exercise of jurisdiction for the purposes of those Parts by a county court or by a registrar in bankruptcy of the High Court lies to a single judge of the High Court; and an appeal from a decision of that judge on such an appeal lies, with the leave of the judge or of the Court of Appeal, to the Court of Appeal.
(3) A county court is not, in the exercise of its jurisdiction for the purposes of those Parts, to be subject to be restrained by the order of any other court, and no appeal lies from its decision in the exercise of that jurisdiction except as provided by this section.

376 Time-limits Where by any provision in this Group of Parts or by the rules the time for doing anything is limited, the court may extend the time, either before or after it has expired, on such terms, if any, as it thinks fit.

377 Formal defects The acts of a person as the trustee of a bankrupt's estate or as a special manager, and the acts of the creditors' committee established for any bankruptcy, are valid notwithstanding any defect in the appointment, election or qualifications of the trustee or manager or, as the case may be, of any member of the committee.

378 Exemption from stamp duty Stamp duty shall not be charged on –
(a) any document, being a deed, conveyance, assignment, surrender, admission or other assurance relating solely to property which is comprised in a bankrupt's estate and which, after the execution of that document, is or remains at law or in equity the property of the bankrupt or of the trustee of that estate,

(b) any writ, order, certificate or other instrument relating solely to the property of a bankrupt or to any bankruptcy proceedings.

379 Annual report As soon as practicable after the end of 1986 and each subsequent calendar year, the Secretary of State shall prepare and lay before each House of Parliament a report about the operation during that year of so much of this Act as is comprised in this Group of Parts, and about proceedings in the course of that year under the Deeds of Arrangement Act 1914.

Part XI: Interpretation for Second Group of Parts

380 Introductory The next five sections have effect for the interpretation of the provisions of this Act which are comprised in this Group of Parts; and where a definition is provided for a particular expression, it applies except so far as the context otherwise requires.

381 'Bankrupt' and associated terminology (1) 'Bankrupt' means an individual who has been adjudged bankrupt and, in relation to a bankruptcy order, it means the individual adjudged bankrupt by that order.
(2) 'Bankruptcy order' means an order adjudging an individual bankrupt.
(3) 'Bankruptcy petition' means a petition to the court for a bankruptcy order.

382 'Bankruptcy debt', etc (1) 'Bankruptcy debt', in relation to a bankrupt, means (subject to the next subsection) any of the following –
(a) any debt or liability to which he is subject at the commencement of the bankruptcy,
(b) any debt or liability to which he may become subject after the commencement of the bankruptcy (including after his discharge from bankruptcy) by reason of any obligation incurred before the commencement of the bankruptcy.
(c) any amount specified in pursuance of section 39(3)(c) of the Powers of Criminal Courts Act 1973 in any criminal bankruptcy order made against him before the commencement of the bankruptcy, and
(d) any interest provable as mentioned in section 322(2) in Chapter IV of Part IX.
(2) In determining for the purposes of any provision in this Group of Parts whether any liability in tort is a bankruptcy debt, the bankrupt is deemed to become subject to that liability by reason of an obligation incurred at the time when the cause of action accrued.
(3) For the purposes of references in this Group of Parts to a debt or liability, it is immaterial whether the debt or liability is present or future, whether it is certain or contingent or whether its amount is fixed or liquidated, or is capable of being ascertained by fixed rules or as a matter of opinion; and references in this Group of Parts to owing a debt are to be read accordingly.
(4) In this Group of Parts, except in so far as the context otherwise requires, 'liability' means (subject to subsection (3) above) a liability to pay money or money's worth, including any liability under an enactment, any liability for breach of trust, any liability in contract, tort or bailment and any liability arising out of an obligation to make restitution.

383 'Creditor', 'security', etc (1) 'Creditor' –
(a) in relation to a bankrupt, means a person to whom any of the bankruptcy debts is owed (being, in the case of an amount falling within paragraph (c) of the definition in section 382(1) of 'bankruptcy debt', the person in respect of whom that amount is specified in the criminal bankruptcy order in question), and
(b) in relation to an individual to whom a bankruptcy petition relates, means a

person who would be a creditor in the bankruptcy if a bankruptcy order were made on that petition.

(2) Subject to the next two subsections and any provision of the rules requiring a creditor to give up his security for the purposes of proving a debt, a debt is secured for the purposes of this Group of Parts to the extent that the person to whom the debt is owed holds any security for the debt (whether a mortgage, charge, lien or other security) over any property of the person by whom the debt is owed.

(3) Where a statement such as is mentioned in section 269(1)(a) in Chapter I of Part IX has been made by a secured creditor for the purposes of any bankruptcy petition and a bankruptcy order is subsequently made on that petition, the creditor is deemed for the purposes of the Parts in this Group to have given up the security specified in the statement.

(4) In subsection (2) the reference to a security does not include a lien on books, papers or other records, except to the extent that they consist of documents which give a title to property and are held as such.

384 'Prescribed' and 'the rules' (1) Subject to the next subsection, 'prescribed' means prescribed by the rules; and 'the rules' means rules made under section 412 in Part XV.

(2) References in this Group of Parts to the amount prescribed for the purposes of any of the following provisions –

section 273;
section 346(3);
section 354(1) and (2);
section 358;
section 360(1);
section 361(2); and
section 364(2)(d),

and references in those provisions to the prescribed amount are to be read in accordance with section 418 in Part XV and orders made under that section.

385 Miscellaneous definitions (1) The following definitions have effect –

'the court', in relation to any matter, means the court to which, in accordance with section 373 in Part X and the rules, proceedings with respect to that matter are allocated or transferred;

'creditor's petition' means a bankruptcy petition under section 264(1)(a);

'criminal bankruptcy order' means an order under section 39(1) of the Powers of Criminal Courts Act 1973;

'debt' is to be construed in accordance with section 382(3);

'the debtor' –

(a) in relation to a proposal for the purposes of Part VIII, means the individual making or intending to make that proposal, and
(b) in relation to a bankruptcy petition, means the individual to whom the petition relates;

'debtor's petition' means a bankruptcy petition presented by the debtor himself under section 264(1)(b);

'dwelling house' includes any building or part of a building which is occupied as a dwelling and any yard, garden, garage or outhouse belonging to the dwelling house and occupied with it;

'estate', in relation to a bankrupt is to be construed in accordance with section 283 in Chapter II of Part IX;

'family', in relation to a bankrupt, means the persons (if any) who are living with him and are dependent on him;

'secured' and related expressions are to be construed in accordance with section 383; and
'the trustee', in relation to a bankruptcy and the bankrupt, means the trustee of the bankrupt's estate.
(2) References in this Group of Parts to a person's affairs include his business, if any.

THE THIRD GROUP OF PARTS: MISCELLANEOUS MATTERS BEARING ON BOTH COMPANY AND INDIVIDUAL INSOLVENCY; GENERAL INTERPRETATION; FINAL PROVISIONS

Part XII: Preferential Debts in Company and Individual Insolvency

386 Categories of preferential debts (1) A reference in this Act to the preferential debts of a company or an individual is to the debts listed in Schedule 6 to this Act (money owed to the Inland Revenue for income tax deducted at source; VAT, car tax, betting and gaming duties; social security and pension scheme contributions; remuneration etc. of employees); and references to preferential creditors are to be read accordingly.
(2) In that Schedule 'the debtor' means the company or the individual concerned.
(3) Schedule 6 is to be read with Schedule 3 to the Social Security Pensions Act 1975 (occupational pension scheme contributions).

387 'The relevant date' (1) This section explains references in Schedule 6 to the relevant date (being the date which determines the existence and amount of a preferential debt).
(2) For the purposes of section 4 in Part I (meetings to consider company voluntary arrangement), the relevant date in relation to a company which is not being wound up is –
(a) where an administration order is in force in relation to the company, the date of the making of that order, and
(b) where no such order has been made, the date of the approval of the voluntary arrangement.
(3) In relation to a company which is being wound up, the following applies –
(a) if the winding up is by the court, and the winding-up order was made immediately upon the discharge of an administration order, the relevant date is the date of the making of the administration order;
(b) if the case does not fall within paragraph (a) and the company –
 (i) is being wound up by the court, and
 (ii) had not commenced to be wound up voluntarily before the date of the making of the winding-up order,
the relevant date is the date of the appointment (or first appointment) of a provisional liquidator or, if no such appointment has been made, the date of the winding-up order;
(c) if the case does not fall within either paragraph (a) or (b), the relevant date is the date of the passing of the resolution for the winding up of the company.
(4) In relation to a company in receivership (where section 40 or, as the case may be, section 59 applies), the relevant date is –
(a) in England and Wales, the date of the appointment of the receiver by debenture-holders, and
(b) in Scotland, the date of the appointment of the receiver under section 53(6) or (as the case may be) 54(5).
(5) For the purpose of section 258 in Part VIII (individual voluntary arrangements), the relevant date is, in relation to a debtor who is not an undischarged bankrupt, the date of the interim order made under section 252 with respect to his proposal.
(6) In relation to a bankrupt, the following applies –

(a) where at the time the bankruptcy order was made there was an interim receiver appointed under section 286, the relevant date is the date on which the interim receiver was first appointed after the presentation of the bankruptcy petition;
(b) otherwise, the relevant date is the date of the making of the bankruptcy order.

Part XIII: Insolvency Practitioners and their Qualification

RESTRICTIONS ON UNQUALIFIED PERSONS ACTING AS LIQUIDATOR, TRUSTEE IN BANKRUPTCY, ETC.

388 Meaning of 'act as insolvency practitioner' (1) A person acts as an insolvency practitioner in relation to a company by acting –
(a) as its liquidator, provisional liquidator, administrator or administrative receiver, or
(b) as supervisor of a voluntary arrangement approved by it under Part I.
(2) A person acts as an insolvency practitioner in relation to an individual by acting –
(a) as his trustee in bankruptcy or interim receiver of his property or as permanent or interim trustee in the sequestration of his estate; or
(b) as trustee under a deed which is a deed of arrangement made for the benefit of his creditors or, in Scotland, a trust deed for his creditors; or
(c) as supervisor of a voluntary arrangement proposed by him and approved under Part VIII; or
(d) in the case of a deceased individual to the administration of whose estate this section applies by virtue of an order under section 421 (application of provisions of this Act to insolvent estates of deceased persons), as administrator of that estate.
(3) References in this section to an individual include, except in so far as the context otherwise requires, references to a partnership and to any debtor within the meaning of the Bankruptcy (Scotland) Act 1985.
(4) In this section –
'administrative receiver' has the meaning given by section 251 in Part VII;
'company' means a company within the meaning given by section 735(1) of the Companies Act of a company which may be wound up under Part V of this Act (unregistered companies); and
'interim trustee' and 'permanent trustee' mean the same as in the Bankruptcy (Scotland) Act 1985.
(5) Nothing in this section applies to anything done by the official receiver.

389 Acting without qualification an offence (1) A person who acts as an insolvency practioner in relation to a company or an individual at a time when he is not qualified to do so is liable to imprisonment or a fine, or to both.
(2) This section does not apply to the official receiver.

The requisite qualification, and the means of obtaining it

390 Persons not qualified to act as insolvency practitioners (1) A person who is not an individual is not qualified to act as an insolvency practitioner.
(2) A person is not qualified to act as an insolvency practitioner at any time unless at that time –
(a) he is authorised so to act by virtue of membership of a professional body recognised under section 391 below, being permitted so to act by or under the rules of that body, or
(b) he holds an authorisation granted by a competent authority under section 393.
(3) A person is not qualified to act as an insolvency practitioner in relation to another person at any time unless –

(a) there is in force at that time security or, in Scotland, caution for the proper performance of his functions, and
(b) that security or caution meets the prescribed requirements with respect to his so acting in relation to that other person.
(4) A person is not qualified to act as an insolvency practitioner at any time if at that time –
(a) he has been adjudged bankrupt or sequestration of his estate has been awarded and (in either case) he has not been discharged,
(b) he is subject to a disqualification order made under the Company Directors Disqualification Act 1986, or
(c) he is a patient within the meaning of Part VII of the Mental Health Act 1983 or section 125(1) of the Mental Health (Scotland) Act 1984.

391 Recognised professional bodies (1) The Secretary of State may by order declare a body which appears to him to fall within subsection (2) below to be a recognised professional body for the purposes of this section.
(2) A body may be recognised if it regulates the practice of a profession and maintains and enforces rules for securing that such of its members as are permitted by or under the rules to act as insolvency practitioners –
(a) are fit and proper persons so to act, and
(b) meet acceptable requirements as to education and practical training and experience.
(3) References to members of a recognised professional body are to persons who, whether members of that body or not, are subject to its rules in the practice of the profession in question.
The reference in section 390(2) above to membership of a professional body recognised under this section is to be read accordingly.
(4) An order made under subsection (1) in relation to a professional body may be revoked by a further order if it appears to the Secretary of State that the body no longer falls within subsection (2).
(5) An order of the Secretary of State under this section has effect from such date as is specified in the order; and any such order revoking a previous order may make provision whereby members of the body in question continue to be treated as authorised to act as insolvency practitioners for a specified period after the revocation takes effect.

392 Authorisation by competent authority (1) Application may be made to a competent authority for authorisation to act as an insolvency practitioner.
(2) The competent authorities for this purpose are –
(a) in relation to a case of any description specified in directions given by the Secretary of State, the body or person so specified in relation to cases of that description, and
(b) in relation to a case not falling within paragraph (a), the Secretary of State.
(3) The application –
(a) shall be made in such manner as the competent authority may direct,
(b) shall contain or be accompanied by such information as that authority may reasonably require for the purpose of determining the application, and
(c) shall be accompanied by the prescribed fee;
and the authority may direct that notice of the making of the application shall be published in such manner as may be specified in the direction.
(4) At any time after receiving the application and before determining it the authority may require the applicant to furnish additional information.
(5) Directions and requirements given or imposed under subsection (3) or (4) may differ as between different applications.

(6) Any information to be furnished to the competent authority under this section shall, if it so requires, be in such form or verified in such manner as it may specify.
(7) An application may be withdrawn before it is granted or refused.
(8) Any sums received under this section by a competent authority other than the Secretary of State may be retained by the authority; and any sums so received by the Secretary of State shall be paid into the Consolidated Fund.

393 Grant, refusal and withdrawal of authorisation (1) The competent authority may, on an application duly made in accordance with section 392 and after being furnished with all such information as it may require under that section, grant or refuse the application.
(2) The authority shall grant the application if it appears to it from the information furnished by the applicant and having regard to such other information, if any, as it may have –
(a) that the applicant is a fit and proper person to act as an insolvency practitioner, and
(b) that the applicant meets the prescribed requirements with respect to education and practical training and experience.
(3) An authorisation granted under this section, if not previously withdrawn, continues in force for such period not exceeding the prescribed maximum as may be specified in the authorisation.
(4) An authorisation so granted may be withdrawn by the competent authority if it appears to it –
(a) that the holder of the authorisation is no longer a fit and proper person to act as an insolvency practitioner, or
(b) without prejudice to paragraph (a), that the holder –
  (i) has failed to comply with any provision of this Part or of any regulations made under this Part or Part XV, or
  (ii) in purported compliance with any such provision, has furnished the competent authority with false, inaccurate or misleading information.
(5) An authorisation granted under this section may be withdrawn by the competent authority at the request or with the consent of the holder of the authorisation.

394 Notices (1) Where a competent authority grants an authorisation under section 393, it shall give written notice of that fact to the applicant, specifying the date on which the authorisation takes effect.
(2) Where the authority proposes to refuse an application, or to withdraw an authorisation under section 393(4), it shall give the applicant or holder of the authorisation written notice of its intention to do so, setting out particulars of the grounds on which it proposes to act.
(3) In the case of a proposed withdrawal the notice shall state the date on which it is proposed that the withdrawal should take effect.
(4) A notice under subsection (2) shall give particulars of the rights exercisable under the next two sections by a person on whom the notice is served.

395 Right to make representations (1) A person on whom a notice is served under section 394(2) may within 14 days after the date of service make written representations to the competent authority.
(2) The competent authority shall have regard to any representations so made in determining whether to refuse the application or withdraw the authorisation, as the case may be.

396 Reference to Tribunal (1) The Insolvency Practitioners Tribunal ('the Tribunal') continues in being; and the provisions of Schedule 7 apply to it.
(2) Where a person is served with a notice under section 394(2), he may –
(a) at any time within 28 days after the date of service of the notice, or
(b) at any time after the making by him of representations under section 395 and before the end of the period of 28 days after the date of the service on him of a notice by the competent authority that the authority does not propose to alter its decision in consequence of the representations,
give written notice to the authority requiring the case to be referred to the Tribunal.
(3) Where a requirement is made under subsection (2), then, unless the competent authority –
(a) has decided or decides to grant the application or, as the case may be, not to withdraw the authorisation, and
(b) within 7 days after the date of the making of the requirement, gives written notice of that decision to the person by whom the requirement was made,
it shall refer the case to the Tribunal.

397 Action of Tribunal on reference (1) On a reference under section 396 the Tribunal shall –
(a) investigate the case, and
(b) make a report to the competent authority stating what would in their opinion be the appropriate decision in the matter and the reasons for that opinion,
and it is the duty of the competent authority to decide the matter accordingly.
(2) The Tribunal shall send a copy of the report to the applicant or, as the case may be, the holder of the authorisation; and the competent authority shall serve him with a written notice of the decision made by it in accordance with the report.
(3) The competent authority may, if he thinks fit, publish the report of the Tribunal.

398 Refusal or withdrawal without reference to Tribunal Where in the case of any proposed refusal or withdrawal of an authorisation either –
(a) the period mentioned in section 396(2)(a) has expired without the making of any requirement under that subsection or of any representations under section 395, or
(b) the competent authority has given a notice such as is mentioned in section 396(2)(b) and the period so mentioned has expired without the making of any such requirement,
the competent authority may give written notice of the refusal or withdrawal to the person concerned in accordance with the proposal in the notice given under section 394(2).

Part XIV: Public Administration (England and Wales)

Official Receivers

399 Appointment etc of official receivers (1) For the purposes of this Act the official receiver, in relation to any bankruptcy or winding up, is any person who by virtue of the following provisions of this section or section 401 below is authorised to act as the official receiver in relation to that bankruptcy or winding up.
(2) The Secretary of State may (subject to the approval of the Treasury as to numbers) appoint persons to the office of official receiver, and a person appointed to that office (whether under this section or section 70 of the Bankruptcy Act 1914) –
(a) shall be paid out of money provided by Parliament such salary as the Secretary of State may with the concurrence of the Treasury direct,
(b) shall hold office on such other terms and conditions as the Secretary of State may with the concurrence of the Treasury direct, and
(c) may be removed from office by a direction of the Secretary of State.

(3) Where a person holds the office of official receiver, the Secretary of State shall from time to time attach him either to the High Court or to a county court having jurisdiction for the purposes of the second Group of Parts of this Act.
(4) Subject to any directions under subsection (6) below, an official receiver attached to a particular court is the person authorised to act as the official receiver in relation to every bankruptcy or winding up falling within the jurisdiction of that court.
(5) The Secretary of State shall ensure that there is, at all times, at least one official receiver attached to the High Court and at least one attached to each county court having jurisdiction for the purposes of the second Group of Parts; but he may attach the same official receiver to two or more different courts.
(6) The Secretary of State may give directions with respect to the disposal of the business of official receivers, and such directions may in particular –
(a) authorise an official receiver attached to one court to act as the official receiver in relation to any case or description of cases falling within the jurisdiction of another court;
(b) provide, where there is more than one official receiver authorised to act as the official receiver in relation to cases falling within the jurisdiction of any court, for the distribution of their business between or among themselves.
(7) A person who at the coming into force of section 222 of the Insolvency Act 1985 (replaced by this section) is an official receiver attached to a court shall continue in office after the coming into force of that section as an official receiver attached to that court under this section.

400 Functions and status of official receivers (1) In addition to any functions conferred on him by this Act, a person holding the office of official receiver shall carry out such other functions as may from time to time be conferred on him by the Secretary of State.
(2) In the exercise of the functions of his office a person holding the office of official receiver shall act under the general directions of the Secretary of State and shall also be an officer of the court in relation to which he exercises those functions.
(3) Any property vested in his official capacity in a person holding the office of official receiver shall, on his dying, ceasing to hold office or being otherwise succeeded in relation to the bankruptcy or winding up in question by another official receiver, vest in his successor without any conveyance, assignment or transfer.

401 Deputy official receivers and staff (1) The Secretary of State may, if he thinks it expedient to do so in order to facilitate the disposal of the business of the official receiver attached to any court, appoint an officer of his department to act as deputy to that official receiver.
(2) Subject to any directions given by the Secretary of State under section 399 or 400, a person appointed to act as deputy to an official receiver has, on such conditions and for such period as may be specified in the terms of his appointment, the same status and functions as the official receiver to whom he is appointed deputy.

Accordingly, references in this Act (except section 399(1) to (5)) to an official receiver include a person appointed to act as his deputy.
(3) An appointment made under subsection (1) may be terminated at any time by the Secretary of State.
(4) The Secretary of State may, subject to the approval of the Treasury as to numbers and remuneration and as to the other terms and conditions of the appointments, appoint officers of his department to assist official receivers in the carrying out of their functions.

The Official Petitioner

402 Official Petitioner (1) There continues to be an officer known as the Official Petitioner for the purpose of discharging, in relation to cases in which a criminal bankruptcy order is made, the functions assigned to him by or under this Act; and the Director of Public Prosecutions continues, by virtue of his office, to be the Official Petitioner.

(2) The functions of the Official Petitioner include the following –

(a) to consider whether, in a case in which a criminal bankruptcy order is made, it is in the public interest that he should himself present a petition under section 264(1)(d) of this Act;

(b) to present such a petition in any case where he determines that it is in the public interest for him to do so;

(c) to make payments, in such cases as he may determine, towards expenses incurred by other persons in connection with proceedings in pursuance of such a petition; and

(b) to exercise so far as he considers it in the public interest to do so, any of the powers conferred on him by or under this Act.

(3) Any functions of the Official Petitioner may be discharged on his behalf by any person acting with his authority.

(4) Neither the Official Petitioner nor any person acting with his authority is liable to any action or proceeding in respect of anything done or omitted to be done in the discharge, or purported discharge, of the functions of the Official Petitioner.

(5) In this section 'criminal bankruptcy order' means an order under section 39(1) of the Powers of Criminal Courts Act 1973.

Insolvency Service finance, accounting and investment

403 Insolvency Services Account (1) All money received by the Secretary of State in respect of proceedings under this Act as it applies to England and Wales shall be paid into the Insolvency Services Account kept by the Secretary of State with the Bank of England; and all payments out of money standing to the credit of the Secretary of State in that account shall be made by the Bank of England in such manner as he may direct.

(2) Whenever the cash balance standing to the credit of the Insolvency Services Account is in excess of the amount which in the opinion of the Secretary of State is required for the time being to answer demands in respect of bankrupts' estates or companies' estates, the Secretary of State shall –

(a) notify the excess to the National Debt Commissioners, and

(b) pay into the Insolvency Services Investment Account ('the Investment Account') kept by the Commissioners with the Bank of England the whole or any part of the excess as the Commissioners may require for investment in accordance with the following provisions of this Part.

(3) Whenever any part of the money so invested is, in the opinion of the Secretary of State, required to answer any demand in respect of bankrupt's estates or companies' estates, he shall notify to the National Debt Commissioners the amount so required and the Commissioners –

(a) shall thereupon repay to the Secretary of State such sum as may be required to the credit of the Insolvency Services Account, and

(b) for that purpose may direct the sale of such part of the securities in which the money has been invested as may be necessary.

404 Investment Account Any money standing to the credit of the Investment Account (including any money received by the National Debt Commissioners by way of interest on or proceeds of any investment under this section) may be invested by the Commissioners, in accordance with such directions as may be given by the Treasury, in any manner for the time being specified in Part II of Schedule 1 to the Trustee Investments Act 1961.

405 Application of income in Investment Account; adjustment of balances (1) Where the annual account to be kept by the National Debt Commissioners under section 409 below shows that in the year for which it is made up the gross amount of the interest accrued from the securities standing to the credit of the Investment Account exceeded the aggregate of –
(a) a sum, to be determined by the Treasury, to provide against the depreciation in the value of the securities, and
(b) the sums paid into the Insolvency Services Account in pursuance of the next section together with the sums paid in pursuance of that section to the Commissioners of Inland Revenue,
the National Debt Commissioners shall, within 3 months after the account is laid before Parliament, cause the amount of the excess to be paid out of the Investment Account into the Consolidated Fund in such manner as may from time to time be agreed between the Treasury and the Commissioners.
(2) Where the said annual account shows that in the year for which it is made up the gross amount of interest accrued from the securities standing to the credit of the Investment Account was less than the aggregate mentioned in subsection (1), an amount equal to the deficiency shall, at such times as the Treasury direct, be paid out of the Consolidated Fund into the Investment Account.
(3) If the Investment Account is insufficient to meet its liabilities the Treasury may, on being informed of the insufficiency by the National Debt Commissioners, issue the amount of the deficiency out of the Consolidated Fund and the Treasury shall certify the deficiency to Parliament.

406 Interest on money received by liquidators and invested Where under rules made by virtue of paragraph 16 of Schedule 8 to this Act (investment of money received by company liquidators) a company has become entitled to any sum by way of interest, the Secretary of State shall certify that sum and the amount of tax payable on it to the National Debt Commissioners; and the Commissioners shall pay, out of the Investment Account –
(a) into the Insolvency Services Account, the sum so certified less the amount of tax so certified, and
(b) to the Commissioners of Inland Revenue, the amount of tax so certified.

407 Unclaimed dividends and undistributed balances (1) The Secretary of State shall from time to time pay into the Consolidated Fund out of the Insolvency Services Account so much of the sums standing to the credit of that Account as represents –
(a) dividends which were declared before such date as the Treasury may from time to time determine and have not been claimed, and
(b) balances ascertained before that date which are too small to be divided among the persons entitled to them.
(2) For the purposes of this section the sums standing to the credit of the Insolvency Services Account are deemed to include any sums paid out of that Account and represented by any sums or securities standing to the credit of the Investment Account.
(3) The Secretary of State may require the National Debt Commissioners to pay out of the Investment Account into the Insolvency Services Account the whole or part of any sum which he is required to pay out of that account under subsection (1); and the Commissioners may direct the sale of such securities standing to the credit of the Investment Account as may be necessary for that purpose.

408 Recourse to Consolidated Fund If, after any repayment due to it from the Investment Account, the Insolvency Services Account is insufficient to meet its liabilities, the Treasury may, on being informed of it by the Secretary of State, issue the amount of the deficiency out of the Consolidated Fund, and the Treasury shall certify the deficiency to Parliament.

409 Annual financial statement and audit (1) The National Debt Commissioners shall for each year ending on 31st March prepare a statement of the sums credited and debited to the Investment Account in such form and manner as the Treasury may direct and shall transmit it to the Comptroller and Auditor General before the end of November next following the year.
(2) The Secretary of State shall for each year ending 31st March prepare a statement of the sums received or paid by him under section 403 above in such form and manner as the Treasury may direct and shall transmit each statement to the Comptroller and Auditor General before the end of November next following the year.
(3) Every such statement shall include such additional information as the Treasury may direct.
(4) The Comptroller and Auditor General shall examine, certify and report on every such statement and shall lay copies of it, and of his report, before Parliament.

Supplementary

410 Extent of this Part This part of this Act extends to England and Wales only.

Part XV: Subordinate Legislation

General insolvency rules

411 Company insolvency rules (1) Rules may be made –
(a) in relation to England and Wales, by the Lord Chancellor with the concurrence of the Secretary of State, or
(b) in relation to Scotland, by the Secretary of State.
for the purpose of giving effect to Parts I and VII of this Act.
(2) Without prejudice to the generality of subsection (1), or to any provision of those Parts by virtue of which rules under this section may be made with respect to any matter, rules under this section may contain –
(a) any such provision as is specified in Schedule 8 to this Act or corresponds to provision contained immediately before the coming into force of section 106 of the Insolvency Act 1985 in rules made, or having effect as if made, under section 663(1) or (2) of the Companies Act (old winding-up rules), and
(b) such incidental, supplemental and transitional provisions as may appear to the Lord Chancellor or, as the case may be, the Secretary of State necessary or expedient.
(3) In Schedule 8 to this Act 'liquidator' includes a provisional liquidator; and references above in this section to Parts I to VII of this Act are to be read as including the Companies Act so far as relating to, and to matters connected with or arising out of, the insolvency or winding up of companies.
(4) Rules under this section shall be made by statutory instrument subject to annulment in pursuance of a resolution of either House of Parliament.
(5) Regulations made by the Secretary of State under a power conferred by rules under this section shall be made by statutory instrument and, after being made, shall be laid before each House of Parliament.
(6) Nothing in this section prejudices any power to make rules of court.

412 Individual insolvency rules (England and Wales) (1) The Lord Chancellor may, with the concurrence of the Secretary of State, make rules for the purpose of giving effect to Parts VIII to XI of this Act.
(2) Without prejudice to the generality of subsection (1), or to any provision of those

Parts by virtue of which rules under this section may be made with respect to any matter, rules under this section may contain –
(a) any such provision as is specified in Schedule 9 to this Act or corresponds to provision contained immediately before the appointed day in rules made under section 132 of the Bankruptcy Act 1914; and
(b) such incidental, supplemental and transitional provisions as may appear to the Lord Chancellor necessary or expedient.
(3) Rules under this section shall be made by statutory instrument subject to annulment in pursuance of a resolution of either House of Parliament.
(4) Regulations made by the Secretary of State under a power conferred by rules under this section shall be made by statutory instrument and, after being made, shall be laid before each House of Parliament.
(5) Nothing in this section prejudices any power to make rules of court.

413 Insolvency Rules Committee (1) The committee established under section 10 of the Insolvency Act 1976 (advisory committee on bankruptcy and winding-up rules) continues to exist for the purpose of being consulted under this section.
(2) The Lord Chancellor shall consult the committee before making any rules under section 411 or 412.
(3) Subject to the next subsection, the committee shall consist of –
(a) a judge of the High Court attached to the Chancery Division;
(b) a circuit judge;
(c) a registrar in bankruptcy of the High Court;
(d) the registrar of a county court;
(e) a practising barrister;
(f) a practising solicitor; and
(g) a practising accountant;
and the appointment of any person as a member of the committee shall be made by the Lord Chancellor.
(4) The Lord Chancellor may appoint as additional members of the committee any persons appearing to him to have qualifications or experience that would be of value to the committee in considering any matter with which it is concerned.

Fees orders

414 Fees orders (company insolvency proceedings) (1) There shall be paid in respect of –
(a) proceedings under any of Parts I to VIII of this Act, and
(b) the performance by the official receiver or the Secretary of State of functions under those Parts,
such fees as the competent authority may with the sanction of the Treasury by order direct.
(2) That authority is –
(a) in relation to England and Wales, the Lord Chancellor, and
(b) in relation to Scotland, the Secretary of State.
(3) The Treasury may by order direct by whom and in what manner the fees are to be collected and accounted for.
(4) The Lord Chancellor may, with the sanction of the Treasury, by order provide for sums to be deposited by such persons, in such manner and in such circumstances as may be specified in the order, by way of security for fees payable by virtue of this section.
(5) An order under this section may contain such incidental, supplemental and transitional provisions as may appear to the Lord Chancellor, the Secretary of State or (as the case may be) the Treasury necessary or expedient.

(6) An order under this section shall be made by statutory instrument and, after being made, shall be laid before each House of Parliament.
(7) Fees payable by virtue of this section shall be paid into the Consolidated Fund.
(8) References in subsection (1) to Parts I to VII of this Act are to be read as including the Companies Act so far as relating to, and to matters connected with or arising out of, the insolvency or winding up of companies.
(9) Nothing in this section prejudices any power to make rules of court; and the application of this section to Scotland is without prejudice to section 2 of the Courts of Law Fees (Scotland) Act 1895.

415 Fees orders (individual insolvency proceedings in England and Wales) (1) There shall be paid in respect of –
(a) proceedings under Parts VIII to XI of this Act, and
(b) the performance by the official receiver or the Secretary of State of functions under those Parts,
such fees as the Lord Chancellor may with the sanction of the Treasury by order direct.
(2) The Treasury may by order direct by whom and in what manner the fees are to be collected and accounted for.
(3) The Lord Chancellor may, with the sanction of the Treasury, by order provide for sums to be deposited, by such persons, in such manner and in such circumstances as may be specified in the order, by way of security for –
(a) fees payable by virtue of this section, and
(b) fees payable to any person who has prepared an insolvency practitioner's report under section 274 in Chapter I of Part IX.
(4) An order under this section may contain such incidental, supplemental and transitional provisions as may appear to the Lord Chancellor or, as the case may be, the Treasury, necessary or expedient.
(5) An order under this section shall be made by statutory instrument and, after being made, shall be laid before each House of Parliament.
(6) Fees payable by virtue of this section shall be paid into the Consolidated Fund.
(7) Nothing in this section prejudices any power to make rules of court.

Specification, increase and reduction of money sums relevant in the operation of this Act

416 Monetary limits (companies winding up) (1) The Secretary of State may by order in a statutory instrument increase or reduce any of the money sums for the time being specified in the following provisions in the first Group of Parts –
section 117(2) (amount of company's share capital determining whether county court has jurisdiction to wind it up);
section 120(3) (the equivalent as respects sheriff court jurisdiction in Scotland);
section 123(1)(a) (minimum debt for service of demand on company by unpaid creditor);
section 184(3) (minimum value of judgment, affecting sheriff's duties on levying execution);
section 206(1)(a) and (b) (minimum value of company property concealed or fraudulently removed, affecting criminal liability of company's officer).
(2) An order under this section may contain such transitional provisions as may appear to the Secretary of State necessary or expedient.
(3) No order under this section increasing or reducing any of the money sums for the time being specified in section 117(2), 120(3) or 123(1)(a) shall be made unless a draft of the order has been laid before and approved by a resolution of each House of Parliament.

(4) A statutory instrument containing an order under this section, other than an order to which subsection (3) applies, is subject to annulment in pursuance of a resolution of either House of Parliament.

417 Money sum in s 222 The Secretary of State may by regulations in a statutory instrument increase or reduce the money sum for the time being specified in section 222(1) (minimum debt for service of demand on unregistered company by unpaid creditor); but such regulations shall not be made unless a draft of the statutory instrument containing them has been approved by resolution of each House of Parliament.

418 Monetary limits (bankruptcy) (1) The Secretary of State may by order prescribe amounts for the purposes of the following provisions in the second Group of Parts –

section 273 (minimum value of debtor's estate determining whether immediate bankruptcy order should be made; small bankruptcies level);

section 346(3) (minimum amount of judgment, determining whether amount recovered on sale of debtor's goods is to be treated as part of his estate in bankruptcy);

section 354(1) and (2) (minimum amount of concealed debt, or value of property concealed or removed, determining criminal liability under the section);

section 358 (minimum value of property taken by a bankrupt out of England and Wales, determining his criminal liability);

section 360(1) (maximum amount of credit which bankrupt may obtain without disclosure of his status);

section 361(2) (exemption of bankrupt from criminal liability for failure to keep proper accounts, if unsecured debts not more than the prescribed minimum);

section 364(2)(d) (minimum value of goods removed by the bankrupt, determining his liability to arrest);

and references in the second Group of Parts to the amount prescribed for the purposes of any of those provisions, and references in those provisions to the prescribed amount, are to be construed accordingly.

(2) An order under this section may contain such transitional provisions as may appear to the Secretary of State necessary or expedient.

(3) An order under this section shall be made by statutory instrument subject to annulment in pursuance of a resolution of either House of Parliament.

Insolvency practice

419 Regulations for purposes of Part XIII (1) The Secretary of State may make regulations for the purpose of giving effect to Part XIII of this Act; and 'prescribed' in that Part means prescribed by regulations made by the Secretary of State.

(2) Without prejudice to the generality of subsection (1) or to any provision of that Part by virtue of which regulations may be made with respect to any matter, regulations under this section may contain –

(a) provision as to the matters to be taken into account in determining whether a person is a fit and proper person to act as an insolvency practitioner;
(b) provision prohibiting a person from so acting in prescribed cases, being cases in which a conflict of interest will or may arise;
(c) provision imposing requirements with respect to –
    (i) the preparation and keeping by a person who acts as an insolvency practitioner of prescribed books, accounts and other records, and
    (ii) the production of those books, accounts and records to prescribed persons;

(d) provision conferring power on prescribed persons –
 (i) to require any person who acts or has acted as an insolvency practitioner to answer any inquiry in relation to a case in which he is so acting or has so acted, and
 (ii) to apply to a court to examine such a person or any other person on oath concerning such a case;
(e) provision making non-compliance with any of the regulations a criminal offence; and
(f) such incidental, supplemental and transitional provisions as may appear to the Secretary of State necessary or expedient.

(3) Any power conferred by Part XIII or this Part to make regulations, rules or orders is exercisable by statutory instrument subject to annulment by resolution of either House of Parliament.
(4) Any rule or regulation under Part XIII or this Part may make different provision with respect to different cases or descriptions of cases, including different provision for different areas.

Other order-making powers

420 Insolvent partnerships (1) The Lord Chancellor may, by order made with the concurrence of the Secretary of State, provide that such provisions of this Act as may be specified in the order shall apply in relation to insolvent partnerships with such modifications as may be so specified.
(2) An order under this section may make different provision for different cases and may contain such incidental, supplemental and transitional provisions as may appear to the Lord Chancellor necessary or expedient.
(3) An order under this section shall be made by statutory instrument subject to annulment in pursuance of a resolution of either House of Parliament.

421 Insolvent estates of deceased persons (1) The Lord Chancellor may, by order made with the concurrence of the Secretary of State, provide that such provisions of this Act as may be specified in the order shall apply to the administration of the insolvent estates of deceased persons with such modifications as may be so specified.
(2) An order under this section may make different provision for different cases and may contain such incidental, supplemental and transitional provisions as may appear to the Lord Chancellor necessary or expedient.
(3) An order under this section shall be made by statutory instrument subject to annulment in pursuance of a resolution of either House of Parliament.
(4) For the purposes of this section the estate of a deceased person is insolvent if, when realised, it will be insufficient to meet in full all the debts and other liabilities to which it is subject.

422 Recognised banks, etc (1) The Secretary of State may, by order made with the concurrence of the Treasury and after consultation with the Bank of England, provide that such provisions in the first Group of Parts as may be specified in the order shall apply in relation to –
(a) recognised banks and licensed institutions within the meaning of the Banking Act 1979, and
(b) institutions to which sections 16 and 18 of that Act apply as if they were licensed institutions,

with such modifications as may be so specified.
(2) An order under this section may make different provision for different cases and may contain such incidental, supplemental and transitional provisions as may appear to the Secretary of State necessary or expedient.

(3) An order under this section shall be made by statutory instrument subject to annulment in pursuance of a resolution of either House of Parliament.

Part XVI: Provisions Against Debt Avoidance (England and Wales only)

423 Transactions defrauding creditors (1) This section relates to transactions entered into at an undervalue; and a person enters into such a transaction with another person if –

(a) he makes a gift to the other person or he otherwise enters into a transaction with the other on terms that provide for him to receive no consideration;
(b) he enters into a transaction with the other in consideration of marriage; or
(c) he enters into a transaction with the other for a consideration the value of which, in money or money's worth, is significantly less than the value, in money or money's worth, of the consideration provided by himself.

(2) Where a person has entered into such a transaction, the court may, if satisfied under the next subsection, make such order as it thinks fit for –

(a) restoring the position to what it would have been if the transaction has not been not entered into, and
(b) protecting the interests of persons who are victims of the transaction.

(3) In the case of a person entering into such a transaction, an order shall only be made if the court is satisfied that it was entered into by him for the purpose –

(a) of putting assets beyond the reach of a person who is making, or may at some time make, a claim against him, or
(b) of otherwise prejudicing the interests of such a person in relation to the claim which he is making or may make.

(4) In this section 'the court' means the High Court or –

(a) if the person entering into the transaction is an individual, any other court which would have jurisdiction in relation to a bankrutpcy petition relating to him;
(b) if that person is a body capable of being wound up under Part IV or V of this Act, any other court having jurisdiction to wind it up.

(5) In relation to a transaction at an undervalue, references here and below to a victim of the transaction are to a person who is, or is capable of being, prejudiced by it; and in the following two sections the person entering into the transaction is referred to as 'the debtor'.

424 Those who may apply for an order under s 423 (1) An application for an order under section 423 shall not be made in relation to a transaction except –

(a) in a case where the debtor has been adjudged bankrupt or is a body corporate which is being wound up or in relation to which an administration order is in force, by the official receiver, by the trustee of the bankrupt's estate or the liquidator or administrator of the body corporate or (with the leave of the court) by a victim of the transaction;
(b) in a case where a victim of the transaction is bound by a voluntary arrangement approved under Part I or Part VIII of this Act, by the supervisor of the voluntary arrangement or by any person who (whether or not so bound) is such a victim; or
(c) in any other case, by a victim of the transaction.

(2) An application made under any of the paragraphs of subsection (1) is to be treated as made on behalf of every victim of the transaction.

425 Provision which may be made by order under s 423 (1) Without prejudice to the generality of section 423, an order made under that section with respect to a transaction may (subject as follows) –

(a) require any property transferred as part of the transaction to be vested in any person, either absolutely or for the benefit of all the persons on whose behalf the application for the order is treated as made;

(b) require any property to be so vested if it represents, in any person's hands, the application either of the proceeds of sale of property so transferred or of money so transferred;
(c) release or discharge (in whole or in part) any security given by the debtor;
(d) require any person to pay to any other person in respect of benefits received from the debtor such sums as the court may direct;
(e) provide for any surety or guarantor whose obligations to any person were released or discharged (in whole or in part) under the transaction to be under such new or revived obligations as the court thinks appropriate;
(f) provide for security to be provided for the discharge of any obligation imposed by or arising under the order, for such an obligation to be charged on any property and for such security or charge to have the same priority as a security or charge released or discharged (in whole or in part) under the transaction.

(2) An order under section 423 may affect the property of, or impose any obligation on, any person whether or not he is the person with whom the debtor entered into the transaction; but such an order –
(a) shall not prejudice any interest in property which was acquired from a person other than the debtor and was acquired in good faith, for value and without notice of the relevant circumstances, or prejudice any interest deriving from such an interest, and
(b) shall not require a person who received a benefit from the transaction in good faith, for value and without notice of the relevant circumstances to pay any sum unless he was a party to the transaction.

(3) For the purposes of this section the relevant circumstances in relation to a transaction are the circumstances by virtue of which an order under section 423 may be made in respect of the transaction.
(4) In this section 'security' means any mortgage, charge, lien or other security.

Part XVII: Miscellaneous and General

426 Co-operation between courts exercising jurisdiction in relation to insolvency (1) An order made by a court in any part of the United Kingdom in the exercise of jurisdiction in relation to insolvency law shall be enforced in any other part of the United Kingdom as if it were made by a court exercising the corresponding jurisdiction in that other part.
(2) However, without prejudice to the following provisions of this section, nothing in subsection (1) requires a court in any part of the United Kingdom to enforce, in relation to property situated in that part, any order made by a court in any other part of the United Kingdom.
(3) The Secretary of State, with the concurrence in relation to property situated in England and Wales of the Lord Chancellor, may by order make provision for securing that a trustee or assignee under the insolvency law of any part of the United Kingdom has, with such modifications as may be specified in the order, the same rights in relation to any property situated in another part of the United Kingdom as he would have in the corresponding circumstances if he were a trustee or assignee under the insolvency law of that other part.
(4) The courts having jurisdiction in relation to insolvency law in any part of the United Kingdom shall assist the courts having the corresponding jurisdiction in any other part of the United Kingdom or any relevant country or territory.
(5) For the purposes of subsection (4) a request made to a court in any part of the United Kingdom by a court in any other part of the United Kingdom or in a relevant country or territory is authority for the court to which the request is made to apply, in relation to any matters specified in the request, the insolvency law which is applicable by either court in relation to comparable matters falling within its jurisdiction.

In exercising its discretion under this subsection, a court shall have regard in particular to the rules of private international law.

(6) Where a person who is a trustee or assignee under the insolvency law of any part of the United Kingdom claims property situated in any other part of the United Kingdom (whether by virtue of an order under subsection (3) or otherwise), the submission of that claim to the court exercising jurisdiction in relation to insolvency law in that other part shall be treated in the same manner as a request made by a court for the purpose of subsection (4).

(7) Section 38 of the Criminal Law Act 1977 (execution of warrant of arrest throughout the United Kingdom) applies to a warrant which, in exercise of any jurisdiction in relation to insolvency law, is issued in any part of the United Kingdom for the arrest of a person as it applies to a warrant issued in that part of the United Kingdom for the arrest of a person charged with an offence.

(8) Without prejudice to any power to make rules of court, any power to make provision by subordinate legislation for the purpose of giving effect in relation to companies or individuals to the insolvency law of any part of the United Kingdom includes power to make provision for the purpose of giving effect in that part to any provision made by or under the preceding provisions of this section.

(9) An order under subsection (3) shall be made by statutory instrument subject to annulment in pursuance of a resolution of either House of Parliament.

(10) In this section 'insolvency law' means –

(a) in relation to England and Wales, provision made by or under this Act or sections 6 to 10, 12, 15, 19(c) and 20 (with Schedule 1) of the Company Directors Disqualification Act 1986 and extending to England and Wales;

(b) in relation to Scotland, provision extending to Scotland and made by or under this Act, section 6 to 10, 12, 15, 19(c) and 20 (with Schedule 1) of the Company Directors Disqualification Act 1986, Part XVIII of the Companies Act or the Bankruptcy (Scotland) Act 1985;

(c) in relation to Northern Ireland, provision made by or under the Bankruptcy Acts (Northern Ireland) 1857 to 1980, Part V, VI or IX of the Companies Act (Northern Ireland) 1960 or Part IV of the Companies (Northern Ireland) Order 1978;

(d) in relation to any relevant country or territory, so much of the law of that country or territory as corresponds to provisions falling within any of the foregoing paragraphs;

and references in this subsection to any enactment include, in relation to any time before the coming into force of that enactment the corresponding enactment in force at the time.

(11) In this section 'relevant country or territory' means –

(a) any of the Channel Islands or the Isle of Man, or

(b) any country or territory designated for the purposes of this section by the Secretary of State by order made by statutory instrument.

427 Parliamentary disqualification (1) Where a court in England and Wales or Northern Ireland adjudges an individual bankrupt or a court in Scotland awards sequestration of an individual's estate, the individual is disqualified –

(a) for sitting or voting in the House of Lords,

(b) for being elected to, or sitting or voting in, the House of Commons, and

(c) for sitting or voting in a committee of either House.

(2) Where an individual is disqualified under this section, the disqualification ceases –

(a) except where the adjudication is annulled or the award recalled or reduced without the individual having been first discharged, on the discharge of the individual, and

(b) in the excepted case, on the annulment, recall or reduction, as the case may be.
(3) No writ of summons shall be issued to any lord of Parliament who is for the time being disqualified under this section for sitting and voting in the House of Lords.
(4) Where a member of the House of Commons who is disqualified under this section continues to be so disqualified until the end of the period of 6 months beginning with the day of the adjudication or award, his seat shall be vacated at the end of that period.
(5) A court which makes an adjudication or award such as is mentioned in subsection (1) in relation to any lord of Parliament or member of the House of Commons shall forthwith certify the adjudication or award to the Speaker of the House of Lords, or, as the case may be, to the Speaker of the House of Commons.
(6) Where a court has certified an adjudication or award to the Speaker of the House of Commons under subsection (5), then immediately after it becomes apparent which of the following certificates is applicable, the court shall certify to the Speaker of the House of Commons –
(a) that the period of 6 months beginning with the day of the adjudication or award has expired without the adjudication or award having been annulled, recalled or reduced, or
(b) that the adjudication or award has been annulled, recalled or reduced before the end of that period.
(7) Subject to the preceding provisions of this section, so much of this Act and any other enactment (whenever passed) and of any subordinate legislation (whenever made) as –
(a) makes provision for or in connection with bankruptcy in one or more parts of the United Kingdom, or
(b) makes provision conferring a power of arrest in connection with the winding up or insolvency of companies in one or more parts of the United Kingdom,
applies in relation to persons having privilege of Parliament or peerage as it applies in relation to persons not having such privlege.

428 Exemptions from Restrictive Trade Practices Act (1) No restriction in respect of any of the matters specified in the next subsection shall, on or after the appointed day, be regarded as a restriction by virtue of which the Restrictive Trade Practices Act 1976 applies to any agreement (whenever made).
(2) Those matters are –
(a) the charges to be made, quoted or paid for insolvency services supplied, offered or obtained;
(b) the terms or conditions on or subject to which insolvency services are to be supplied or obtained;
(c) the extent (if any) to which, or the scale (if any) on which, insolvency services are to be made available, supplied or obtained;
(d) the form or manner in which insolvency services are to be made available, supplied or obtained;
(e) the persons or classes of persons for whom or from whom, or the areas or places in or from which, insolvency services are to be made available or supplied or are to be obtained.
(3) In this section 'insolvency services' means the services of persons acting as insolvency practitioners or carrying out under the law of Northern Ireland functions corresponding to those mentioned in section 388(1) or (2) in Part XIII, in their capacity as such; and expressions which are also used in the Act of 1976 have the same meaning here as in that Act.

429 Disabilities on revocation of administration order against an individual (1) The following applies where a person fails to make any payment which he is required to make by virtue of an administration order under Part VI of the County Courts Act 1984.

(2) The court which is administering that person's estate under the order may, if it thinks fit –

(a) revoke the administration order, and

(b) make an order directing that this section and section 12 of the Company Directors Disqualification Act 1986 shall apply to the person for such period, not exceeding 2 years, as may be specified in the order.

(3) A person to whom this section so applies shall not –

(a) either alone or jointly with another person, obtain credit to the extent of the amount prescribed for the purposes of section 360(1)(a) or more, or

(b) enter into any transaction in the course of or for the purposes of any business in which he is directly or indirectly engaged,

without disclosing to the person from whom he obtains the credit, or (as the case may be) with whom the transaction is entered into, the fact that this section applies to him.

(4) The reference in subsection (3) to a person obtaining credit includes –

(a) a case where goods are bailed or hired to him under a hire-purchase agreement or agreed to be sold to him under a conditional sale agreement, and

(b) a case where he is paid in advance (whether in money or otherwise) for the supply of goods or services.

(5) A person who contravenes this section is guilty of an offence and liable to imprisonment or a fine, or both.

430 Provision introducing Schedule of punishments (1) Schedule 10 to this Act has effect with respect to the way in which offences under this Act are punishable on conviction.

(2) In relation to an offence under a provision of this Act specified in the first column of the Schedule (the general nature of the offence being described in the second column), the third column shows whether the offence is punishable on conviction on indictment, or on summary conviction, or either in the one way or the other.

(3) The fourth column of the Schedule shows, in relation to an offence, the maximum punishment by way of fine or imprisonment under this Act which may be imposed on a person convicted of the offence in the way specified in relation to it in the third column (that is to say, on indictment or summarily) a reference to a period of years or months being to a term of imprisonment of that duration.

(4) The fifth column shows (in relation to an offence for which there is an entry in that column) that a person convicted of the offence after continued contravention is liable to a daily default fine; that is to say, he is liable on a second or subsequent conviction of the offence to the fine specified in that column for each day on which the contravention is continued (instead of the penalty specified for the offence in the fourth column of the Schedule).

(5) For the purpose of any enactment in this Act whereby an officer of a company who is in default is liable to a fine or penalty, the expression 'officer who is in default' means any officer of the company who knowingly and wilfully authorises or permits the default, or contravention mentioned in the enactment.

431 Summary proceedings (1) Sumary proceedings for any offence under any of Parts I to VII of this Act may (without prejudice to any jurisdiction exercisable apart from this subsection) be taken against a body corporate at any place at which the body has a place of business, and against any other person at any place at which he is for the time being.

(2) Notwithstanding anything in section 127(1) of the Magistrates' Courts Act 1980, an information relating to such an offence which is triable by a magistrates' court in

England and Wales may be so tried if it is laid at any time within 3 years after the commission of the offence and within 12 months after the date on which evidence sufficient in the opinion of the Director of Public Prosecutions or the Secretary of State (as the case may be) to justify the proccedings comes to his knowledge.
(3) Summary proceedings in Scotland for such an offence shall not be commenced after the expiration of 3 years from the commission of the offence.

Subject to this (and notwithstanding anything in section 331 of the Criminal Procedure (Scotland) Act 1975), such proceedings may (in Scotland) be commenced at any time within 12 months after the date on which evidence sufficient in the Lord Advocate's opinion to justify the proceedings came to his knowledge or, where such evidence was reported to him by the Secretary of State, within 12 months after the date on which it came to the knowledge of the latter; and subsection (3) of that section applies for the purpose of this subsection as it applies for the purpose of that section.
(4) For purposes of this section, a certificate of the Director of Public Prosecutions, the Lord Advocate or the Secretary of State (as the case may be) as to the date on which such evidence as is referred to above came to his knowledge is conclusive evidence.

432 Offences by bodies corporate (1) This section applies to offences under this Act other than those excepted by subsection (4).
(2) Where a body corporate is guilty of an offence to which this section applies and the offence is proved to have been committed with the consent or connivance of, or to be attributable to any neglect on the part of, any director, manager, secretary or other similar officer of the body corporate or any person who was purporting to act in any such capacity he, as well as the body corporate, is guilty of the offence and liable to be proceeded against and punished accordingly.
(3) Where the affairs of a body corporate are managed by its members, subsection (2) applies in relation to the acts and defaults of a member in connection with his functions of management as if he were a director of the body corporate.

(4) The offences excepted from this section are those under sections 30, 39, 51, 53, 54, 62, 64, 66, 85, 89, 164, 188, 201, 206, 207, 208, 209, 210 and 211.

433 Admissibility in evidence of statements of affairs, etc In any proceedings (whether or not under this Act) –
(a) a statement of affairs prepared for the purposes of any provision of this Act which is derived from the Insolvency Act 1985, and
(b) any other statement made in pursuance of a requirement imposed by or under any such provision or by or under rules made under this Act,
may be used in evidence against any person making or concurring in making the statement.

434 Crown application For the avoidance of doubt it is hereby declared that provisions of this Act which derive from the Insolvency Act 1985 bind the Crown so far as affecting or relating to the following matters, namely –
(a) remedies against, or against the property of, companies or individuals;
(b) priorities of debts;
(c) transactions at an undervalue or preferences;
(d) voluntary arrangements approved under Part I or Part VIII, and
(e) discharge from bankruptcy.

Part XVIII: Interpretation

435 Meaning of 'associate' (1) For the purposes of this Act any question whether a person is an associate of another person is to be determined in accordance with the following provisions of this section (any provision that a person is an associate of another person being taken to mean that they are associates of each other).

(2) A person is an associate of an individual if that person is the individual's husband or wife, or is a relative, or the husband or wife of a relative, of the individual or of the individual's husband or wife.

(3) A person is an associate of any person with whom he is in partnership, and of the husband or wife or a relative of any individual with whom he is in partnership; and a Scottish firm is an associate of any person who is a member of the firm.

(4) A person is an associate of any person whom he employs or by whom he is employed.

(5) A person in his capacity as trustee of a trust other than –

(a) a trust arising under any of the second Group of Parts or the Bankruptcy (Scotland) Act 1985, or

(b) a pension scheme or an employees' share scheme (within the meaning of the Companies Act),

is an associate of another person if the beneficiaries of the trust include, or the terms of the trust confer a power that may be exercised for the benefit of, that other person or an associate of that other person.

(6) A company is an associate of another company –

(a) if the same person has control of both, or a person has control of one and persons who are his associates, or he and persons who are his associates, have control of the other, or

(b) if a group of two or more persons has control of each company, and the groups either consist of the same persons or could be regarded as consisting of the same persons by treating (in one or more cases) a member of either group as replaced by a person of whom he is an associate.

(7) A company is an associate of another person if that person has control of it or if that person and persons who are his associates together have control of it.

(8) For the purposes of this section a person is a relative of an individual if he is that individual's brother, sister, uncle, aunt, nephew, niece, lineal ancestor or lineal descendant, treating –

(a) any relationship of the half blood as a relationship of the whole blood and the stepchild or adopted child of any person as his child, and

(b) an illegitimate child as the legitimate child of his mother and reputed father;

and references in this section to a husband or wife include a former husband or wife and a reputed husband or wife.

(9) For the purposes of this section any director or other officer of a company is to be treated as employed by that company.

(10) For the purposes of this section a person is to be taken as having control of a company if –

(a) the directors of the company or of another company which has control of it (or any of them) are accustomed to act in accordance with his directions or instructions, or

(b) he is entitled to exercise, or control the exercise of, one third or more of the voting power at any general meeting of the company or of another company which has control of it;

and where two or more persons together satisfy either of the above conditions, they are to be taken as having control of the company.

(11) In this section 'company' includes any body corporate (whether incorporated in Great Britain or elsewhere); and references to directors and other officers of a company and to voting power at any general meeting of a company have effect with any necessary modifications.

436 Expressions used generally In this Act, except in so far as the context otherwise requires (and subject to Parts VII and XI) –

'the appointed day' means the day on which this Act comes into force under section 443;
'associate' has the meaning given by section 435;
'business' includes a trade or profession;
'the Companies Act' means the Companies Act 1985;
'conditional sale agreement' and 'hire-purchase agreement' have the same meanings as in the Consumer Credit Act 1974;
'modifications' includes additions, alterations and ommissions and cognate expressions shall be construed accordingly:
'property' includes money, goods, things in action, land and every description of property wherever situated and also obligations and every description of interest, whether present or future or vested or contingent, arising out of, or incidental to, property;
'records' includes computer records and other non-documentary records;
'subordinate legislation' has the same meaning as in the Interpretation Act 1978; and
'transaction' includes a gift, agreement or arrangement, and references to entering into a transaction shall be construed accordingly.

Part XIX: Final Provisions

437 Transitional provisions and savings The transitional provisions and savings set out in Schedule 11 of this Act shall have effect, the Schedule comprising the following Parts –

Part I: company insolvency and winding up (matters arising before appointed day, and continuance of proceedings in certain cases as before that day);
Part II: individual insolvency (matters so arising, and continuance of bankruptcy proceedings in certain cases as before that day);
Part III: transactions entered into before the appointed day and capable of being affected by orders of the court under Part XVI of this Act;
Part IV: insolvency practitioners acting as such before the appointed day; and
Part V: general transitional provisions and savings required consequentially on, and in connection with, the repeal and replacement by this Act and the Company Directors Disqualification Act 1986 of provisions of the Companies Act, the greater part of the Insolvency Act 1985 and other enactments.

438 Repeals The enactments specified in the second column of Schedule 12 to this Act are repealed to the extent specified in the third column of that Schedule.

439 Amendment of enactments (1) The Companies Act is amended as shown in Parts I and II of Schedule 13 to this Act, being amendments consequential on this Act and the Company Directors Disqualification Act 1986.
(2) The enactments specified in the first column of Schedule 14 to this Act (being enactments which refer, or otherwise relate, to those which are repealed and replaced by this Act or the Company Directors Disqualification Act 1986) are amended as shown in the second column of that Schedule.
(3) The Lord Chancellor may by order make such consequential modifications of any provision contained in any subordinate legislation made before the appointed day and such transitional provisions in connection with those modifications as appear to him necessary or expedient in respect of –
(a) any reference in that subordinate legislation to the Bankruptcy Act 1914;
(b) any reference in that subordinate legislation to any enactment repealed by Part III or IV of Schedule 10 to the Insolvency Act 1985; or
(c) any reference in that subordinate legislation to any matter provided for under

the Act of 1914 or under any enactment so repealed.
(4) An order under this section shall be made by statutory instrument subject to annulment in pursuance of a resolution of either House of Parliament.

440 Extent (Scotland) (1) Subject to the next subsection, provisions of this Act contained in the first Group of Parts extend to Scotland except where otherwise stated.
(2) The following provisions of this Act do not extend to Scotland –
(a) in the first Group of Parts –
sections 43;
sections 238 to 241; and
section 246;
(b) the second Group of Parts;
(c) in the third Group of Parts –
sections 399 to 402,
sections 412, 413, 415, 418, 420 and 421,
sections 423 to 425, and
sections 429(1) and (2); and
(d) in the Schedules –
Parts II and III of Schedule 11; and
Schedules 12 and 14 so far as they repeal or amend enactments which extend to England and Wales only.

441 Extent (Northern Ireland) (1) The following provisions of this Act extend to Northern Ireland –
(a) sections 197, 426, 427 and 428; and
(b) so much of section 439 and Schedule 14 as relates to enactments which extend to Northern Ireland.
(2) Subject as above, and to any provision expressly relating to companies incorporated elsewhere than in Great Britain, nothing in this Act extends to Northern Ireland or applies to or in relation to companies registered or incorporated in Northern Ireland.

442 Extent (other territories) Her Majesty may, by Order in Council, direct that such of the provisions of this Act as are specified in the Order, being provisions formerly contained in the Insolvency Act 1985, shall extend to any of the Channel Islands or any colony with such modifications as may be so specified.

443 Commencement This Act comes into force on the day appointed under section 236(2) of the Insolvency Act 1985 for the coming into force of Part III of that Act (individual insolvency and bankruptcy), immediately after that Part of that Act comes into force for England and Wales.

444 Citation This Act may be cited as the Insolvency Act 1986.

SCHEDULE 5: POWERS OF TRUSTEE IN BANKRUPTCY Section 314

Part I: Powers Exercisable with Sanction

1 Power to carry on any business of the bankrupt so far as may be necessary for winding it up beneficially and so far as the trustee is able to do so without contravening any requirement imposed by or under any enactment.

2 Power to bring, institute or defend any action or legal proceedings relating to the property comprised in the bankrupt's estate.

3 Power to accept as the consideration for the sale of any property comprised in the bankrupt's estate a sum of money payable at a future time subject to such stipulations as to security or otherwise as the creditors' committee or the court thinks fit.

4 Power to mortgage or pledge any part of the property comprised in the bankrupt's estate for the purpose of raising money for the payment of his debts.

5 Power, where any right, option or other power forms part of the bankrupt's estate, to make payments or incur liabilities with a view to obtaining, for the benefit of the creditors, any property which is the subject of the right, option or power.

6 Power to refer to arbitration, or compromise on such terms as may be agreed on, any debts, claims or liabilities subsisting or supposed to subsist between the bankrupt and any person who may have incurred any liability to the bankrupt.

7 Power to make such compromise or other arrangement as may be thought expedient with creditors, or persons claiming to be creditors, in respect of bankruptcy debts.

8 Power to make such compromise or other arrangement as may be thought expedient with respect to any claim arising out of or incidental to the bankrupt's estate made or capable of being made on the trustee by any person or by the trustee on any person.

Part II: General Powers

9 Power to sell any part of the property for the time being comprised in the bankrupt's estate, including the goodwill and book debts of any business.

10 Power to give receipts for any money received by him, being receipts which effectually discharge the person paying the money from all responsibility in respect of its application.

11 Power to prove, rank, claim and draw a dividend in respect of such debts due to the bankrupt as are comprised in his estate.

12 Power to exercise in relation to any property comprised in the bankrupt's estate any powers the capacity to exercise which is vested in him under Parts VIII to XI of this Act.

13 Power to deal with any property comprised in the estate to which the bankrupt is beneficially entitled as tenant in tail in the same manner as the bankrupt might have dealt with it.

Part III: Ancillary Powers

14 For the purposes of, or in connection with, the exercise of any of his powers under Parts VIII to XI of this Act, the trustee may, by his official name –
(a) hold property of every description,
(b) make contracts,
(c) sue and be sued,
(d) enter into engagements binding on himself and, in respect of the bankrupt's estate, on his successors in office,
(e) employ an agent,
(f) execute any power of attorney, deed or other instrument;

and he may do any other act which is necessary or expedient for the purposes of or in connection with the exercise of those powers.

SCHEDULE 6: THE CATEGORIES OF PREFERENTIAL DEBTS Section 386

Category 1: Debts due to Inland Revenue

1 Sums due at the relevant date from the debtor on account of deductions of income tax from emoluments paid during the period of 12 months next before that date.

The deductions here referred to are those which the debtor was liable to make under section 204 of the Income and Corporation Taxes Act 1970 (pay as you earn), less the amount of the repayments of income tax which the debtor was liable to make during that period.

2 Sums due at the relevant date from the debtor in respect of such deductions as are required to be made by the debtor for that period under section 69 of the Finance (No. 2) Act 1975 (sub-contractors in the construction industry).

Category 2: Debts due to Customs and Excise

3 Any value added tax which is referable to the period of 6 months next before the relevant date (which period is referred to below as 'the 6-month period').

For the purposes of this paragraph –

(a) where the whole of the prescribed accounting period to which any value added tax is attributable falls within the 6-month period, the whole amount of that tax is referable to that period; and

(b) in any other case the amount of any value added tax which is referable to the 6-month period is the proportion of the tax which is equal to such proportion (if any) of the accounting reference period in question as falls within the 6-month period;

and in sub-paragraph (a) 'prescribed' means prescribed by regulations under the Value Added Tax Act 1983.

4 The amount of any car tax which is due at the relevant date from the debtor and which became due within a period of 12 months next before that date.

5 Any amount which is due –

(a) by way of general betting duty or bingo duty, or

(b) under section 12(1) of the Betting and Gaming Duties Act 1981 (general betting duty and pool betting duty recoverable from agent collecting stakes), or

(c) under section 14 of, or Schedule 2 to, that Act (gaming licence duty),

from the debtor at the relevant date and which became due within the period of 12 months next before that date.

Category 3: Social security contributions

6 All sums which on the relevant date are due from the debtor on account of Class 1 or Class 2 contributions under the Social Security Act 1975 or the Social Security (Northern Ireland) Act 1975 and which became due from the debtor in the 12 months next before the relevant date.

7 All sums which on the relevant date have been assessed on and are due from the debtor on account of Class 4 contributions under either of those Acts of 1975, being sums which –

(a) are due to the Commissioners of Inland Revenue (rather than to the Secretary of State or a Northern Ireland department), and

(b) are assessed on the debtor up to 5th April next before the relevant date, but not exceeding, in the whole, any one year's assessment.

Category 4: Contributions to occupational pension schemes, etc

8 Any sum which is owed by the debtor and is a sum to which Schedule 3 to the Social Security Pensions Act 1975 applies (contributions to occupational pension schemes and state scheme premiums).

Category 5: Remuneration, etc of employees

9 So much of any amount which –
(a) is owed by the debtor to a person who is or has been an employee of the debtor, and
(b) is payable by way of remuneration in respect of the whole or any part of the period of 4 months next before the relevant date,
as does not exceed so much as may be prescribed by order made by the Secretary of State.

10 An amount owed by way of accrued holiday remuneration, in respect of any period of employment before the relevant date, to a person whose employment by the debtor has been terminated, whether before, on or after that date.

11 So much of any sum owed in respect of money advanced for the purpose as has been applied for the payment of a debt which, if it has not been paid, would have been a debt falling within paragraph 9 or 10.

12 So much of any amount which –
(a) is ordered (whether before or after the relevant date) to be paid by the debtor under the Reserve Forces (Safeguard of Employment) Act 1985, and
(b) is so ordered in respect of a default made by the debtor before that date in the discharge of his obligations under that Act,
as does not exceed such amount as may be prescribed by order made by the Secretary of State.

Interpretation for Category 5

13 (1) For the purpose of paragraphs 9 to 12, a sum is payable by the debtor to a person by way of remuneration in respect of any period if –
(a) it is paid as wages or salary (whether payable for time or for piece work or earned wholly or partly by way of commission) in respect of services rendered to the debtor in that period, or
(b) it is an amount falling within the following sub-paragraph and is payable by the debtor in respect of that period.
(2) An amount falls within this sub-paragraph if it is –
(a) a guarantee payment under section 12(1) of the Employment Protection (Consolidation) Act 1978 (employee without work to do for a day or part of a day);
(b) remuneration on suspension on medical grounds under section 19 of that Act;
(c) any payment for time off under section 27(3) (trade union duties), 31(3) (looking for work, etc) or 31A(4) (ante-natal care) of that Act; or
(d) remuneration under a protective award made by an industrial tribunal under section 101 of the Employment Protection Act 1975 (redundancy dismissal with compensation).

14 (1) This paragraph relates to a case in which a person's employment has been terminated by or in consequence of his employer going into liquidation or being adjudged bankrupt or (his employer being a company not in liquidation) by or in consequence of –

(a) a receiver being appointed as mentioned in section 40 of this Act (debenture-holders secured by floating charge), or

(b) the appointment of a receiver under section 53(6) or 54(5) of this Act (Scottish company with property subject to floating charge), or

(c) the taking of possession by debenture-holders (so secured), as mentioned in section 196 of the Companies Act.

(2) For the purposes of paragraphs 9 to 12, holiday remuneration is deemed to have accrued to that person in respect of any period of employment if, by virtue of his contract of employment or of any enactment that remuneration would have accrued in respect of that period if his employment had continued until he became entitled to be allowed the holiday.

(3) The reference in sub-paragraph (2) to any enactment includes an order or direction made under an enactment.

15 Without prejudice to paragraphs 13 and 14 –

(a) any remuneration payable by the debtor to a person in respect of a period of holiday or of absence from work through sickness or other good cause is deemed to be wages or (as the case may be) salary in respect of services rendered to the debtor in that period, and

(b) references here and in those paragraphs to remuneration in respect of a period of holiday include any sums which, if they had been paid, would have been treated for the purposes of the enactments relating to social security as earnings in respect of that period.

Orders

16 An order under paragraph 9 or 12 –

(a) may contain such transitional provisions as may appear to the Secretary of State necessary or expedient;

(b) shall be made by statutory instrument subject to annulment in pursuance of a resolution of either House of Parliament.

SCHEDULE 7: INSOLVENCY PRACTITIONERS TRIBUNAL — Section 396

Panels of members

1 (1) The Secretary of State shall draw up and from time to time revise –

(a) a panel of persons who are barristers, advocates or solicitors, in each case of not less than 7 years' standing, and are nominated for the purpose by the Lord Chancellor or the Lord President of the Court of Session, and

(b) a panel of persons who are experienced in insolvency matters;

and the members of the Tribunal shall be selected from those panels in accordance with this Schedule.

(2) The power to revise the panels includes power to terminate a person's membership of either of them, and is accordingly to that extent subject to section 8 of the Tribunals and Inquiries Act 1971 (which makes it necessary to obtain the concurrence of the Lord Chancellor and the Lord President of the Court of Session to dismissals in certain cases).

Remuneration of members

2 The Secretary of State may out of money provided by Parliament pay to members of the Tribunal such remuneration as he may with the approval of the Treasury determine; and such expenses of the Tribunal as the Secretary of State and the Treasury may approve shall be defrayed by the Secretary of State out of money so provided.

Sittings of Tribunal

3 (1) For the purposes of carrying out their functions in relation to any cases referred to them, the Tribunal may sit either as a single tribunal or in two or more divisions.

(2) The functions of the Tribunal in relation to any case referred to them shall be exercised by three members consiting of –

(a) a chairman selected by the Secretary of State from the panel drawn up under paragraph 1(1)(a) above, and

(b) two other members selected by the Secretary of State from the panel drawn up under paragraph 1(1)(b).

Procedure of Tribunal

4 (1) Any investigation by the Tribunal shall be so conducted as to afford a reasonable opportunity for representations to be made to the Tribunal by or on behalf of the person whose case is the subject of the investigation.

(2) For the purposes of any such investigation, the Tribunal –

(a) may by summons require any person to attend, at such time and place as is specified in the summons, to give evidence or to produce any books, papers and other records in his possession or under his control which the Tribunal consider it necessary for the purposes of the investigation to examine, and

(b) may take evidence on oath, and for the purpose administer oaths, or may, instead of administering an oath, require the person examined to make and subscribe a declaration of the truth of the matter respecting which he is examined;

but no person shall be required, in obedience to such a summons, to go more than ten miles from his place of residence, unless the necessary expenses of his attendance are paid or tendered to him.

(3) Every person who –

(a) without reasonable excuse fails to attend in obedience to a summons issued under this paragraph, or refuses to give evidence, or

(b) intentionally alters, suppresses, conceals or destroys or refuses to produce any document which he may be required to produce for the purpose of an investigation by the Tribunal,

is liable to a fine.

(4) Subject to the provisions of this paragraph, the Secretary of State may make rules for regulating the procedure on any investigation by the Tribunal.

(5) In their application to Scotland, sub-paragraphs (2) and (3) above have effect as if for any reference to a summons there were substituted a reference to a notice in writing.

SCHEDULE 11: TRANSITIONAL PROVISIONS AND SAVINGS

Part II: Individual Insolvency

Bankruptcy (general)

10 (1) Subject to the following provisions of this Part of this Schedule, so much of this Act as replaces Part III of the Insolvency Act 1985 does not apply in relation to any case in which a petition in bankruptcy was presented, or a receiving order or adjudication in bankruptcy was made, before the appointed day.

(2) In relation to any such case as is mentioned above, the enactments specified in

Schedule 8 to that Act, so far as they relate to bankruptcy, and those specified in Parts III and IV of Schedule 10 to that Act, so far as they so relate, have effect without the amendments and repeals specified in those Schedules.
(3) Where any subordinate legislation made under an enactment referred to in sub-paragraph (2) is in force immediately before the appointed day, that subordinate legislation continues to have effect on and after that day in relation to any such case as is mentioned in sub-paragraph (1).

11 (1) In relation to any such case as is mentioned in paragraph 10(1) the references in any enactment or subordinate legislation to a petition, order or other matter which is provided for under the Bankruptcy Act 1914 and corresponds to a petition, order or other matter provided for under provisions of this Act replacing Part III of the Insolvency Act 1985 continue on and after the appointed day to have effect as references to the petition, order or matter provided for by the Act of 1914; but otherwise those references have effect on and after that day as references to the petition, order or matter provided for by those provisions of this Act.
(2) Without prejudice to sub-paragraph (1), in determining for the purposes of section 279 of this Act (period of bankruptcy) or paragraph 13 below whether any person was an undischarged bankrupt at a time before the appointed day, an adjudication in bankruptcy and an annulment of a bankruptcy under the Act of 1914 are to be taken into account in the same way, respectively, as a bankruptcy order under the provisions of this Act replacing Part III of the Insolvency Act 1985 and the annulment under section 282 of this Act of such an order.

12 Transactions entered into before the appointed day have effect on and after that day as if references to acts of bankruptcy in the provisions for giving effect to those transactions continued to be references to acts of bankruptcy within the meaning of the Bankruptcy Act 1914, but as if such acts included failure to comply with a statutory demand served under section 268 of this Act.

Discharge from old bankruptcy

13 (1) Where a person –
(a) was adjudged bankrupt before the appointed day or is adjudged bankrupt on or after that day on a petition presented before that day, and
(b) that person was not an undischarged bankrupt at any time in the period of 15 years ending with the adjudication,

that person is deemed (if not previously discharged) to be discharged from his bankruptcy for the purposes of the Bankruptcy Act 1914 at the end of the discharge period.
(2) Subject to sub-paragraph (3) below, the discharge period for the purposes of this paragraph is –
(a) in the case of a person adjudged bankrupt before the appointed day, the period of 3 years beginning with that day, and
(b) in the case of a person who is adjudged bankrupt on or after that day on a petition presented before that day, the period of 3 years beginning with the date of the adjudication.

(3) Where the court exercising jurisdiction in relation to a bankruptcy to which this paragraph applies is satisfied, on the application of the official receiver, that the bankrupt has failed, or is failing, to comply with any of his obligations under the Bankruptcy Act 1914, any rules made under that Act or any such rules as are mentioned in paragraph 19(1) below, the court may order that the discharge period shall cease to run for such period, or until the fulfilment of such conditions (including a condition requiring the court to be satisfied as to any matter) as may be specified in the order.

Provisions relating to trustee

14 (1) This paragraph applies as regards the trustee in the case of a person adjudged bankrupt before the appointed day, or adjudged bankrupt on or after that day on a petition presented before that day.
(2) The official receiver may at any time when he is the trustee of the bankrupt's estate apply to the Secretary of State for the appointment of a person as trustee instead of the official receiver; and on any such application the Secretary of State shall either make an appointment or decline to make one.
(3) Where on the appointed day the trustee of a bankrupt's estate has not made an application under section 93 of the Bankruptcy Act 1914 (release of trustee), then –
(a) except where the Secretary of State otherwise directs, sections 298(8), 304 and 331(1) to (3) of this Act apply, and section 93 of the Act of 1914 does not apply, in relation to any trustee of the bankrupt's estate who holds office on or at any time after the appointed day and is not the official receiver;
(b) section 331(4) of this Act applies in relation to the carrying out at any time on or after the appointed day by the trustee of the bankrupt's estate of any of his functions; and
(c) a trustee in relation to whom section 298(8) of this Act has effect by virtue of this paragraph has his release with effect from the time specified in section 299(3)(d).
(4) Subsection (5) of section 299 has effect for the purposes of sub-paragraph (3)(c) as it has for the purposes of that section.
(5) In the application of subsection (3) of section 331 in relation to a case by virtue of this paragraph, the reference in that subsection to section 330(1) has effect as a reference to section 67 of the Bankruptcy Act 1914.
(6) The trustee of the bankrupt's estate may employ a solicitor to assist him in the carrying out of his functions without the permission of the committee of inspection; but if he does so employ a solicitor, he shall inform the committee of inspection that he has done so.

Copyright

15 Where a person who is adjudged bankrupt on a petition presented on or after the appointed day is liable, by virtue of a transaction entered into before that day, to pay royalties or a share of the profits to any person in respect of any copyright or interest in copyright comprised in the bankrupt's estate, section 60 of the Bankruptcy Act 1914 (limitation on trustee's powers in relation to copyright) applies in relation to the trustee of that estate as it applies in relation to a trustee in bankruptcy under the Act of 1914.

Second bankruptcy

16 (1) Sections 334 and 335 of this Act apply with the following modifications where the earlier bankruptcy (within the meaning of section 334) is a bankruptcy in relation to which the Act of 1914 applies instead of the second Group of Parts in this Act, that is to say –
(a) references to property vested in the existing trustee under section 307(3) of this Act have effect as references to such property vested in that trustee as was acquired by or devolved on the bankrupt after the commencement (within the meaning of the Act of 1914) of the earlier bankruptcy; and
(b) references to an order under section 310 of this Act have effect as references to an order under section 51 of the Act of 1914.
(2) Section 39 of the Act of 1914 (second bankruptcy) does not apply where a person who is an undischarged bankrupt under that Act is adjudged bankrupt under this Act.

Setting aside of preferences and other transactions

17 (1) A preference given, assignment made or other transaction entered into before the appointed day shall not be set aside under any of sections 339 to 344 of this Act except to the extent that it could have been set aside under the law in force immediately before that day.
(2) References in sub-paragraph (1) to setting aside a preference, assignment or other transaction include the making of any order which varies or reverses any effect of a preference, assignment or other transaction.

Bankruptcy offences

18 (1) Where a bankruptcy order is made under this Act on or after the appointed day, a person is not guilty of an offence under Chapter VI of Part IX in respect of anything done before that day; but, notwithstanding the repeal by the Insolvency Act 1985 of the Bankruptcy Act 1914, is guilty of an offence under the Act of 1914 in respect of anything done before the appointed day which would have been an offence under that Act if the making of the bankruptcy order had been the making of a receiving order under that Act.
(2) Subsection (5) of section 350 of this Act applies (instead of sections 157(2), 158(2), 161 and 165 of the Act of 1914) in relation to proceedings for an offence under that Act which are instituted (whether by virtue of sub-paragraph (1) or otherwise) after the appointed day.

Power to make rules

19 The preceding provisions of this Part of this Schedule are without prejudice to the power conferred by this Act under which rules under section 412 may make transitional provision in connection with the coming into force of those rules; and such provision may apply those rules in relation to a bankruptcy notwithstanding that it arose from a petition presented before either the coming into force of the rules or the appointed day.
(2) Rules under section 412 may provide for such notices served before the appointed day as may be prescribed to be treated for the purposes of this Act as statutory demands served under section 268.

Part III: Transitional Effect of Part XVI

20 (1) A transaction entered into before the appointed day shall not be set aside under Part XVI of this Act except to the extent that it could have been set aside under the law in force immediately before that day.
(2) References above to setting aside a transaction include the making of any order which varies or reverses any effect of a transaction.

Part IV: Insolvency Practitioners

21 Where an individual began to act as an insolvency practitioner in relation to any person before the appointed day, nothing in section 390(2) or (3) prevents that individual from being qualified to act as an insolvency practitioner in relation to that person.

Part V: General Transitional Provisions and Savings

Interpretation for this Part

22 In this Part of this Schedule, 'the former enactments' means so much of the Companies Act as is repealed and replaced by this Act, the Insolvency Act 1985 and the other enactments repealed by this Act.

General saving for past acts and events

23 So far as anything done or treated as done under or for the purposes of any provision of the former enactments could have been done under or for the purposes of the corresponding provision of this Act, it is not invalidated by the repeal of that provision but has effect as if done under or for the purposes of the corresponding provision; and any order, regulation, rule or other instrument made or having effect under any provision of the former enactments shall, insofar as its effect is preserved by this paragraph, be treated for all purposes as made and having effect under the corresponding provision.

Periods of time

24 Where any period of time specified in a provision of the former enactments is current immediately before the appointed day, this Act has effect as if the corresponding provision had been in force when the period began to run; and (without prejudice to the foregoing) any period of time so specified and current is deemed for the purposes of this Act –
(a) to run from the date or event from which it is running immediately before the appointed day, and
(b) to expire (subject to any provision of this Act for its extension) whenever it would have expired if this Act had not been passed;
and any rights, priorities, liabilities, reliefs, obligations, requirements, powers, duties or exemptions dependent on the beginning, duration or end of such a period as above mentioned shall be under this Act as they were or would have been under the former enactments.

Internal cross-references in this Act

25 Where in any provision of this Act there is a reference to another such provision, and the first-mentioned provision operates, or is capable of operating, in relation to things done or ommitted, or events occurring or not occurring, in the past (including in particular past acts of compliance with any enactment, failures of compliance, contraventions, offences and convictions of offences), the reference to the other provision is to be read as including a reference to the corresponding provision of the former enactments.

Punishment of offences

26 (1) Offences committed before the appointed day under any provision of the former enactments may, notwithstanding any repeal by this Act, be prosecuted and punished after that day as if this Act had not passed.
(2) A contravention of any provision of the former enactments committed before the appointed day shall not be visited with any severer punishment under or by virtue of this Act than would have been applicable under that provision at the time of the contravention; but where an offence for the continuance of which a penalty was provided has been committed under any provision of the former enactments, proceedings may be taken under this Act in respect of the continuance of the offence on and after the appointed day in the like manner as if the offence had been committed under the corresponding provision of this Act.

References elsewhere to the former enactments

27 (1) A reference in any enactment, instrument or document (whether express or implied, and in whatever phraseology) to a provision of the former enactments (including the corresponding provision of any yet earlier enactment) is to be read, where necessary to retain for the enactment, instrument or document the same force

and effect as it would have had but for the passing of this Act, as, or as including, a reference to the corresponding provision by which it is replaced in this Act.
(2) The generality of the preceding sub-paragraph is not affected by any specific conversion of references made by this Act, nor by the inclusion in any provision of this Act of a reference (whether express or implied, and in whatever phraseology) to the provision of the former enactments corresponding to that provision, or to a provision of the former enactments which is replaced by a corresponding provision of this Act.

Saving for power to repeal provisions in section 51

28 The Secretary of State may by order in a statutory instrument repeal subsections (3) to (5) of section 51 of this Act and the entries in Schedule 10 relating to subsections (4) and (5) of that section.

Saving for Interpretation Act 1978, ss 16, 17

29 Nothing in this Schedule is to be taken as prejudicing sections 16 and 17 of the Interpretation Act 1978 (savings from, and effect of, repeals); and for the purposes of section 17(2) of that Act (construction of references to enactments repealed and replaced, etc.), so much of section 18 of the Insolvency Act 1985 as is replaced by a provision of this Act is deemed to have been repealed by this Act and not by the Company Directors Disqualification Act 1986.

Appendix 2

Insolvency Rules 1986 (selected provisions)

THE SECOND GROUP OF PARTS: INDIVIDUAL INSOLVENCY; BANKRUPTCY

Part 5: Individual Voluntary Arrangements

5.1 Introductory (1) The Rules in this Part apply where a debtor, with a view to an application for an interim order under Part VIII of the Act, makes a proposal to his creditors for a voluntary arrangement, that is to say, a composition in satisfaction of his debts or a scheme of arrangement of his affairs.
(2) The Rules apply whether the debtor is an undischarged bankrupt ('Case 1'), or he is not ('Case 2').

SECTION A: THE DEBTOR'S PROPOSAL

5.2 Preparation of proposal The debtor shall prepare for the intended nominee a proposal on which (with or without amendments to be made under Rule 5.3(3) below) to make his report to the court under section 256.

5.3 Contents of proposal (1) The debtor's proposal shall provide a short explanation why, in his opinion, a voluntary arrangement under Part VIII is desirable, and give reasons why his creditors may be expected to concur with such an arrangement.
(2) The following matters shall be stated, or otherwise dealt with, in the proposal –
(a) the following matters, so far as within the debtor's immediate knowledge –
(i) his assets, with an estimate of their respective values,
(ii) the extent (if any) to which the assets are charged in favour of creditors,
(iii) the extent (if any) to which particular assets are to be exluded from the voluntary arrangement;

(b) particulars of any property, other than assets of the debtor himself, which is proposed to be included in the arrangement, the source of such property and the terms on which it is to be made available for inclusion;

(c) the nature and amount of the debtor's liabilities (so far as within his immediate knowledge), the manner in which they are proposed to be met, modified, postponed or otherwise dealt with by means of the arrangement and (in particular) –

(i) how it is proposed to deal with preferential creditors (defined in section 258(7)) and creditors who are, or claim to be, secured,

(ii) how associates of the debtor (being creditors of his) are proposed to be treated under the arrangement, and

(iii) (Case 2 only) whether there are, to the debtor's knowledge, any circumstances giving rise to the possibility, in the event that he should be adjudged bankrupt, of claims under –
section 339 (transactions at an undervalue),
section 340 (preferences), or
section 343 (extortionate credit transactions),

and, where any such circumstances are present, whether, and if so how, it is proposed under the voluntary arrangement to make provision for wholly or partly indemnifying the insolvent estate in respect of such claims;

(d) whether any, and if so what, guarantees have been given of the debtor's debts by other persons, specifying which (if any) of the guarantors are associates of his;

(e) the proposed duration of the voluntary arrangement;

(f) the proposed dates of distributions to creditors, with estimates of their amounts;

(g) the amount proposed to be paid to the nominee (as such) by way of remuneration and expenses;

(h) the manner in which it is proposed that the supervisor of the arrangement should be remunerated, and his expenses defrayed;

(j) whether, for the purposes of the arrangement, any guarantees are to be offered by any persons other than the debtor, and whether (if so) any security is to be given or sought;

(k) the manner in which funds held for the purposes of the arrangement are to be banked, invested or otherwise dealt with pending distribution to creditors;

(l) the manner in which funds held for the purpose of payment to creditors, and not so paid on the termination of the arrangement, are to be dealt with;

(m) if the debtor has any business, the manner in which it is proposed to be conducted during the course of the arrangement;

(n) details of any further credit facilities which it is intended to arrange for the debtor, and how the debts so arising are to be paid;

(o) the functions which are to be undertaken by the supervisor of the arrangement;

(p) the name, address and qualification of the person proposed as supervisor of the voluntary arrangement, and confirmation that he is (so far as the debtor is aware) qualified to act as an insolvency practitioner in relation to him.

(3) With the agreement in writing of the nominee, the debtor's proposal may be amended at any time up to the delivery of the former's report to the court under section 256.

5.4 Notice to intended nominee (1) The debtor shall give to the intended nominee written notice of his proposal.

(2) The notice, accompanied by a copy of the proposal, shall be delivered either to the nominee himself, or to a person authorised to take delivery of documents on his behalf.

(3) If the intended nominee agrees to act, he shall cause a copy of the notice to be endorsed to the effect that it has been received by him on a specified date.

(4) The copy of the notice so endorsed shall be returned by the nominee forthwith to the debtor at an address specified by him in the notice for that purpose.
(5) Where (in Case 1) the debtor gives notice of his proposal to the official receiver and (if any) the trustee, the notice must contain the name and address of the insolvency practitioner who has agreed to act as nominee.

5.5 Application for interim order (1) An application to the court of an interim order under Part VIII of the Act shall be accompanied by an affidavit of the following matters –
(a) the reasons for making the application;
(b) particulars of any execution or other legal process which, to the debtor's knowledge, has been commenced against him;
(c) that he is an undischarged bankrupt or (as the case may be) that he is able to petition for his own bankruptcy;
(d) that no previous application for an interim order has been made by or in respect of the debtor in the period of 12 months ending with the date of the affidavit; and
(e) that the nominee under the proposal (naming him) is a person who is qualified to act as an insolvency practitioner in relation to the debtor, and is willing to act in relation to the proposal.
(2) A copy of the notice to the intended nominee under Rule 5.4, endorsed to the effect that he agrees so to act, shall be exhibited to the affidavit.
(3) On receiving the application and affidavit, the court shall fix a venue for the hearing of the application.
(4) The applicant shall give at least 2 days' notice of the hearing –
(a) in Case 1, to the bankrupt, the official receiver and the trustee (whichever of those three is not himself the applicant),
(b) in Case 2, to any creditor who (to the debtor's knowledge) has presented a bankruptcy petition against him, and
(c) in either case, to the nominee who has agreed to act in relation to the debtor's proposal.

5.6 Hearing of the application (1) Any of the persons who have been given notice under Rule 5.5(4) may appear or be represented at the hearing of the application.
(2) The court, in deciding whether to make an interim order on the application, shall take into account any representations made by or on behalf of those persons (in particular, whether an order should be made containing such provision as is referred to in section 255(3) and (4)).
(3) If the court makes an interim order, it shall fix a venue for consideration of the nominee's report. Subject to the following paragraph, the date for that consideration shall be not later than that on which the interim order ceases to have effect under section 255(6).
(4) If under section 256(4) an extension of time is granted for filing the nominee's report, the court shall, unless there appear to be good reasons against it, correspondingly extend the period for which the interim order has effect.

5.7 Action to follow making of order (1) Where an interim order is made, at least 2 sealed copies of the order shall be sent by the court forthwith to the person who applied for it; and that person shall serve one of the copies on the nominee under the debtor's proposal.
(2) The applicant shall also forthwith give notice of the making of the order to any person who was given notice of the hearing pursuant to Rule 5.5(4) and was not present or represented at it.

5.8 Statement of affairs (1) In Case 1, if the debtor has already delivered a

statement of affairs under section 272 (debtor's petition) or 288 (creditor's petition), he need not deliver a further statement unless so required by the nominee, with a view to supplementing or amplifying the former one.
(2) In Case 2, the debtor shall, within 7 days after his proposal is delivered to the nominee, or within such longer time as the latter may allow, deliver to the nominee a statement of his (the debtor's) affairs.
(3) The statement shall comprise the following particulars (supplementing or amplifying, so far as is necessary for clarifying the state of the debtor's affairs, those already given in his proposal) –
(a) a list of his assets, divided into such categories as are appropriate for easy identification, with estimated values assigned to each category;
(b) in the case of any property on which a claim against the debtor is wholly or partly secured, particulars of the claim and its amount, and of how and when the security was created;
(c) the names and addresses of the debtor's preferential creditors (defined in section 258(7)), with the amounts of their respective claims;
(d) the names and addresses of the debtor's unsecured creditors, with the amounts of their respective claims;
(e) particulars of any debts owed by or to the debtor to or by persons who are associates of his;
(f) such other particulars (if any) as the nominee may in writing require to be furnished for the purposes of making his report to the court on the debtor's proposal.
(4) The statement of affairs shall be made up to a date not earlier than 2 weeks before the date of the notice to the nominee under Rule 5.4.

However, the nominee may allow an extension of that period to the nearest practicable date (not earlier than 2 months before the date of the notice under Rule 5.4) and if he does so, he shall give his reasons in his report to the court on the debtor's proposal.
(5) The statement shall be certified by the debtor as correct, to the best of his knowledge and belief.

5.9 Additional disclosure for assistance of nominee (1) If it appears to the nominee that he cannot properly prepare his report on the basis of information in the debtor's proposal and statement of affairs, he may call on the debtor to provide him with –
(a) further and better particulars as to the circumstances in which, and the reasons why, he is insolvent or (as the case may be) threatened with insolvency;
(b) particulars of any previous proposals which have been made by him under Part VIII of the Act;
(c) any further information with respect to his affairs which the nominee thinks necessary for the purposes of his report.
(2) The nominee may call on the debtor to inform him whether and in what circumstances he has at any time –
(a) been concerned in the affairs of any company (whether or not incorporated in England and Wales) which has become insolvent, or
(b) been adjudged bankrupt, or entered into an arrangement with his creditors.
(3) For the purpose of enabling the nominee to consider the debtor's proposal and prepare his report on it, the latter must give him access to his accounts and records.

5.10 Nominee's report on the proposal (1) The nominee's report shall be delivered by him to the court not less than 2 days before the interim order ceases to have effect.
(2) With his report the nominee shall deliver –
(a) a copy of the debtor's proposal (with amendments, if any, authorised under Rule 5.3(3)); and

(b) a copy or summary of any statement of affairs provided by the debtor.

(3) If the nominee makes known his opinion that a meeting of the debtor's creditors should be summoned under section 257, his report shall have annexed to it his comments on the debtor's proposal.

If his opinion is otherwise, he shall give his reasons for that opinion.

(4) The court shall cause the nominee's report to be endorsed with the date on which it is filed in court. Any creditor of the debtor is entitled, at all reasonable times on any business day, to inspect the file.

(5) In Case 1, the nominee shall send to the official receiver –

(a) a copy of the debtor's proposal,

(b) a copy of his (the nominee's) report and his comments accompanying it (if any), and

(c) a copy or summary of the debtor's statement of affairs.

In Case 2, the nominee shall send a copy of each of those documents to any person who has presented a bankruptcy petition against the debtor.

5.11 Replacement of nominee Where the debtor intends to apply to the court under section 256(3) for the nominee to be replaced, he shall give to the nominee at least 7 days' notice of his application.

SECTION B: ACTION ON THE PROPOSAL; CREDITORS' MEETING

5.12 Consideration of nominee's report (1) At the hearing by the court to consider the nominee's report, any of the persons who have been given notice under Rule 5.5(4) may appear or be represented.

(2) Rule 5.7 applies to any order made by the court at the hearing.

5.13 Summoning of creditors' meeting (1) If in his report the nominee states that in his opinion a meeting of creditors should be summoned to consider the debtor's proposal, the date on which the meeting is to be held shall be not less than 14, nor more than 28 days from that on which the nominee's report is filed in court under Rule 5.10.

(2) Notices calling the meeting shall be sent by the nominee, at least 14 days before the day fixed for it to be held, to all the creditors specified in the debtor's statement of affairs, and any other creditors of whom the nominee is otherwise aware.

(3) The notices shall specify the court to which the nominee's report on the debtor's proposal has been delivered; and with it there shall be sent –

(a) a copy of the proposal,

(b) a copy of the statement of affairs or, if the nominee thinks fit, a summary of it (the summary to include a list of the creditors and the amounts of their debts), and

(c) the nominee's comments on the proposal.

5.14 Creditors' meeting: supplementary (1) Subject as follows, in fixing the venue for the creditors' meeting, the nominee shall have regard to the convenience of creditors.

(2) The meeting shall be summoned for commencement between 10.00 and 16.00 hours on a business day.

(3) With every notice summoning the meeting there shall be sent out forms of proxy. [FORM 8.1]

5.15 The chairman at the meeting (1) Subject as follows, the nominee shall be chairman of the creditors' meeting.

(2) If for any reason the nominee is unable to attend, he may nominate another person to act as chairman in his place; but a person so nominated must be either –
(a) a person qualified to act as an insolvency practitioner in relation to the debtor, or
(b) an employee of the nominee or his firm who is experienced in insolvency matters.

5.16 The chairman as proxy holder The chairman shall not by virtue of any proxy held by him vote to increase or reduce the amount of the remuneration or expenses of the nominee or the supervisor of the proposed arrangement, unless the proxy specifically directs him to vote in that way.

5.17 Voting rights (1) Subject as follows, every creditor who was given notice of the creditor's meeting is entitled to vote at the meeting or any adjournment of it.
(2) In Case 1, votes are calculated according to the amount of the creditor's debt as at the date of the bankruptcy order, and in Case 2 according to the amount of the debt as at the date of the meeting.
(3) A creditor shall not vote in respect of a debt for an unliquidated amount, or any debt whose value is not ascertained, except where the chairman agrees to put upon the debt an estimated minimum value for the purposes of entitlement to vote.
(4) The chairman has power to admit or reject a creditor's claim for the purpose of his entitlement to vote, and the power is exercisable with respect to the whole or any part of the claim.
(5) The chairman's decision on entitlement to vote is subject to appeal to the court by any creditor, or by the debtor.
(6) If the chairman is in doubt whether a claim should be admitted or rejected, he shall mark it as objected to and allow the creditor to vote, subject to his vote being subsequently declared invalid if the objection to the claim is sustained.
(7) If on an appeal the chairman's decision is reversed or varied, or a creditor's vote is declared invalid, the court may order another meeting to be summoned, or make such other order as it thinks just.

The court's power to make an order under this paragraph is exercisable only if it considers that the matter is such as to give rise to unfair prejudice or a material irregularity.
(8) An application to the court by way of appeal under this Rule against the chairman's decision shall not be made after the end of the period of 28 days beginning with the day on which the chairman's report to the court is made under section 259.
(9) The chairman is not personally liable for any costs incurred by any person in respect of an appeal under this Rule.

5.18 Requisite majorities (1) Subject as follows, at the creditors' meeting for any resolution to pass approving or rejecting any proposal or modification there must be a majority in excess of three-quarters in value of the creditors present in person or by proxy and voting on the resolution.
(2) The same applies in respect of any other resolution proposed at the meeting, but substituting one-half for three-quarters.
(3) In the following cases there is to be left out of account a creditor's vote in respect of any claim or part of a claim –
(a) where written notice of the claim was not given, either at the meeting or before it, to the chairman or the nominee;
(b) where the claim or part is secured;
(c) where the claim is in respect of a debt wholly or partly on, or secured by, a current bill of exchange or promissory note, unless the creditor is willing –
   (i) to treat the liability to him on the bill or note of every person who is liable on it antecedently to the debtor, and against whom a bankruptcy order has not

been made (or, in the case of a company, which has not gone into liquidation), as a security in his hands, and

(ii) to estimate the value of the security and (for the purpose of entitlement to vote, but not of any distribution under the arrangement) to deduct it from his claim.

(4) Any resolution is invalid if those voting against it include more than half in value of the creditors, counting in these latter only those –

(a) to whom notice of the meeting was sent;

(b) whose votes are not to be left out of account under paragraph (3); and

(c) who are not, to the best of the chairman's belief, associates of the debtor.

(5) It is for the chairman of the meeting to decide whether under this Rule –

(a) a vote is to be left out of account in accordance with paragraph (3), or

(b) a person is an associate of the debtor for the purposes of paragraph (4)(c);

and in relation to the second of these two cases the chairman is entitled to rely on the information provided by the debtor's statement of affairs or otherwise in accordance with this Part of the Rules.

(6) If the chairman uses a proxy contrary to Rule 5.16, his vote with that proxy does not count towards any majority under this Rule.

(7) Paragraphs (5) to (9) of Rule 5.17 apply as regards an appeal against the decision of the chairman under this Rule.

5.19 Proceedings to obtain agreement on the proposal (1) On the day on which the creditors' meeting is held, it may from time to time be adjourned.

(2) If on that day the requisite majority for the approval of the voluntary arrangement (with or without modifications) has not been obtained, the chairman may, and shall if it is so resolved, adjourn the meeting for not more than 14 days.

(3) If there are subsequently further adjournments, the final adjournment shall not be to a day later than 14 days after that on which the meeting was originally held.

(4) If the meeting is adjourned under paragraph (2), notice of the fact shall be given by the chairman forthwith to the court.

(5) If following any final adjournment of the meeting the proposal (with or without modifications) is not agreed to, it is deemed rejected.

SECTION C: IMPLEMENTATION OF THE ARRANGEMENT

5.20 Resolutions to follow approval (1) If the voluntary arrangement is approved (with or without modifications), a resolution may be taken by the creditors, where two or more insolvency practitioners are appointed to act as supervisor, on the question whether acts to be done in connection with the arrangement may be done by any one of them, or must be done by both or all.

(2) If at the creditors' meeting a resolution is moved for the appointment of some person other than the nominee to be supervisor of the arrangement, there must be produced to the chairman, at or before the meeting –

(a) that person's written consent to act (unless he is present and then and there signifies his consent), and

(b) his written confirmation that he is qualified to act as an insolvency practitioner in relation to the debtor.

5.21 Hand-over of property, etc to supervisor (1) Forthwith after the approval of the voluntary arrangement, the debtor in Case 2, and the official receiver or trustee in Case 1, shall do all that is required for putting the supervisor into possession of the assets included in the arrangement.

(2) On taking possession of the assets in Case 1, the supervisor shall discharge any balance due to the official receiver and (if other) the trustee by way of remuneration or on account of –

(a) fees, costs, charges and expenses properly incurred and payable under the Act or the Rules, and

(b) any advances made in respect of the insolvent estate, together with interest on such advances at the official rate ruling at the date of the bankruptcy order.

(3) Alternatively in Case 1, the supervisor must, before taking possession, give the official receiver or the trustee a written undertaking to discharge any such balance out of the first realisation of assets.

(4) The official receiver and (if other) the trustee has in Case 1 a charge on the assets included in the voluntary arrangement in respect of any sums due as above until they have been discharged, subject only to the deduction from realisations by the supervisor of the proper costs and expenses of realisation.

Any sums due to the official receiver take priority over those due to a trustee.

(6) The supervisor shall from time to time out of the realisation of assets discharge all guarantees properly given by the official receiver or the trustee for the benefit of the estate, and shall pay all expenses of the latter.

5.22 Report of creditors' meeting (1) A report of the creditors' meeting shall be prepared by the chairman of the meeting.

(2) The report shall –

(a) state whether the proposal for a voluntary arrangement was approved or rejected and, if approved, with what (if any) modifications;

(b) set out the resolutions which were taken at the meeting, and the decision on each one;

(c) list the creditors (with their respective values) who were present or represented at the meeting, and how they voted on each resolution; and

(d) include such further information (if any) as the chairman thinks it appropriate to make known to the court.

(3) A copy of the chairman's report shall, within 4 days of the meeting being held, be filed in court; and the court shall cause that copy to be endorsed with the date of filing.

(4) The persons to whom notice of the result is to be given, under section 259(1), are all those who were sent notice of the meeting under this Part of the Rules.

The notice shall be sent immediately after a copy of the chairman's report is filed in court under paragraph (3).

5.23 Register of voluntary arrangements (1) The Secretary of State shall maintain a register of individual voluntary arrangements, and shall enter in it all such matters as are reported to him in pursuance of this Part of the Rules.

(2) The register shall be open to public inspection.

5.24 Reports to Secretary of State (1) Immediately after the chairman of the creditors' meeting has filed in court a report that the meeting has approved the voluntary arrangement, he shall report to the Secretary of State the following details of the arrangement –

(a) the name and address of the debtor;

(b) the date on which the arrangement was approved by the creditors;

(c) the name and address of the supervisor; and

(d) the court in which the chairman's report has been filed.

(2) A person who is appointed to act as supervisor of an individual voluntary arrangement (whether in the first instance or by way of replacement of another

person previously appointed) shall forthwith give written notice to the Secretary of State of his appointment.

If he vacates office as supervisor, he shall forthwith give written notice of that fact also to the Secretary of State.

5.25 Revocation or suspension of the arrangement (1) This Rule applies where the court makes an order of revocation or suspension under section 262.

(2) The person who applied for the order shall serve sealed copies of it –

(a) in Case 1, on the debtor, the official receiver and the trustee;

(b) in Case 2, on the debtor; and

(c) in either case on the supervisor of the voluntary arrangement.

(3) If the order includes a direction by the court under section 262(4)(b) for any further creditors' meeting to be summoned, notice shall also be given (by the person who applied for the order) to whoever is, in accordance with the direction, required to summon the meeting.

(4) The debtor (in Case 2) and the official receiver or the trustee (in Case 1) shall –

(a) forthwith after receiving a copy of the court's order, give notice of it to all persons who were sent notice of the creditors' meeting which approved the voluntary arrangement or who, not having been sent that notice, appear to be affected by the order,

(b) within 7 days of their receiving a copy of the order (or within such longer period as the court may allow), give notice to the court whether it is intended to make a revised proposal to creditors, or to invite re-consideration of the original proposal.

(5) The person on whose application the order of revocation or suspension was made shall, within 7 days after the making of the order, give written notice of it to the Secretary of State.

5.26 Supervisor's accounts and reports (1) Where the voluntary arrangement authorises or requires the supervisor –

(a) to carry on the debtor's business or to trade on his behalf or in his name, or

(b) to realise assets of the debtor or (in Case 1) belonging to the estate, or

(c) otherwise to administer or dispose of any funds of the debtor or the estate,

he shall keep accounts and records of his acts and dealings in and in connection with the arrangement, including in particular records of all receipts and payments of money.

(2) The supervisor shall, not less often than once in every 12 months beginning with the date of his appointment, prepare an abstract of such receipts and payments, and send copies of it, accompanied by his comments on the progress and efficacy of the arrangement, to –

(a) the court,

(b) the debtor, and

(c) all those of the debtor's creditors who are bound by the arrangement.

If in any period of 12 months he has made no payments and had no receipts, he shall at the end of that period send a statement to that effect to all who are specified in sub-paragraphs (a) to (c) above.

(3) An abstract provided under paragraph (2) shall relate to a period beginning with the date of the supervisor's appointment or (as the case may be) the day following the end of the last period for which an abstract was prepared under this Rule; and copies of the abstract shall be sent out, as required by paragraph (2), within the 2 months following the end of the period to which the abstract relates.

(4) If the supervisor is not authorised as mentioned in paragraph (1), he shall, not less often than once in every 12 months beginning with the date of this appointment,

send to all those specified in paragraph (2)(a) to (c) a report on the progress and efficacy of the voluntary arrangement.
(5) The court may, on application by the supervisor, vary the dates on which the obligation to send abstracts or reports arises.

5.27 Production of accounts and records to Secretary of State (1) The Secretary of State may at any time during the course of the voluntary arrangement or after its completion require the supervisor to produce for inspection –
(a) his records and accounts in respect of the arrangement, and
(b) copies of abstracts and reports prepared in compliance with Rule 5.26.
(2) The Secretary of State may require production either at the premises of the supervisor or elsewhere; and it is the duty of the supervisor to comply with any requirement imposed on him under this Rule.
(3) The Secretary of State may cause any accounts and records produced to him under this Rule to be audited; and the supervisor shall give to the Secretary of State such further information and assistance as he needs for the purposes of his audit.

5.28 Fees, costs, charges and expenses The fees, costs, charges and expenses that may be incurred for any purposes of the voluntary arrangement are –
(a) any disbursements made by the nominee prior to the approval of the arrangement, and any remuneration for his services as such agreed between himself and the debtor, the official receiver or the trustee;
(b) any fees, costs, charges or expenses which –
 (i) are sanctioned by the terms of the arrangement, or
 (ii) would be payable, or correspond to those which would be payable, in the debtor's bankruptcy.

5.29 Completion of the arrangement (1) Not more than 28 days after the final completion of the voluntary arrangement, the supervisor shall send to all creditors of the debtor who are bound by the arrangement, and to the debtor, a notice that the arrangement has been fully implemented.
(2) With the notice there shall be sent to each of those persons a copy of a report by the supervisor summarising all receipts and payments made by him in pursuance of the arrangement, and explaining any difference in the actual implementation of it as compared with the proposal as approved by the creditors' meeting.
(3) The supervisor shall, within the 28 days mentioned above, send to the Secretary of State and to the court a copy of the notice under paragraph (1), together with a copy of the report under paragraph (2).
(4) The court may, on application by the supervisor, extend the period of 28 days under paragraphs (1) and (3).

SECTION D: GENERAL

5.30 False representations, etc (1) The debtor commits an offence if he makes any false representation or commits any other fraud for the purpose of obtaining the approval of his creditors to a proposal for a voluntary arrangement under Part VIII of the Act.
(2) A person guilty of an offence under this Rule is liable to imprisonment or a fine, or both.

Part 6: Bankruptcy

CHAPTER 1: THE STATUTORY DEMAND

6.1 Form and content of statutory demand (1) A statutory demand under section

268 must be dated, and be signed either by the creditor himself or by a person stating himself to be authorised to make the demand on the creditor's behalf. [FORM 6.1 or FORM 6.2 or FORM 6.3]

(2) The statutory demand must specify whether it is made under section 268(1) (debt payable immediately) or section 268(2) (debt not so payable).

(3) The demand must state the amount of the debt, and the consideration for it (or, if there is no consideration, the way in which it arises) and –

(a) if made under section 268(1) and founded on a judgment or order of a court, it must give details of the judgment or order, and

(b) if made under section 268(2), it must state the grounds on which it is alleged that the debtor appears to have no reasonable prospect of paying the debt.

(4) If the amount claimed in the demand includes –

(a) any charge by way of interest not previously notified to the debtor as a liability of his, or

(b) any other charge accruing from time to time,

the amount or rate of the charge must be separately identified, and the grounds on which payment of it is claimed must be stated.

In either case the amount claimed must be limited to that which has accrued due at the date of the demand.

(5) If the creditor holds any security in respect of the debt, the full amount of the debt shall be specified, but –

(a) there shall in the demand be specified the nature of the security, and the value which the creditor puts upon it as at the date of the demand, and

(b) the amount of which payment is claimed by the demand shall be the full amount of the debt, less the amount specified as the value of the security.

6.2 Information to be given in statutory demand (1) The statutory demand must include an explanation to the debtor of the following matters –

(a) the purpose of the demand, and the fact that, if the debtor does not comply with the demand, bankruptcy proceedings may be commenced against him;

(b) the time within which the demand must be complied with, if that consequence is to be avoided;

(c) the methods of compliance which are open to the debtor; and

(d) his right to apply to the court for the statutory demand to be set aside.

(2) The demand must specify one or more named individuals with whom the debtor may, if he wishes, enter into communication with a view to securing or compounding for the debt to the satisfaction of the creditor or (as the case may be) establishing to the creditor's satisfaction that there is a reasonable prospect that the debt will be paid when it falls due.

In the case of any individual so named in the demand, his address and telephone number (if any) must be given.

6.3 Requirements as to service (1) Rule 6.11 in Chapter 2 below has effect as regards service of the statutory demand, and proof of that service by affidavit to be filed with a bankruptcy petition.

(2) The creditor is, by virtue of the Rules, under an obligation to do all that is reasonable for the purpose of bringing the statutory demand to the debtor's attention and, if practicable in the particular circumstances, to cause personal service of the demand to be effected.

(3) Where the statutory demand is for payment of a sum due under a judgment or order of any court and the creditor knows, or believes with reasonable cause –

(a) that the debtor has absconded or is keeping out of the way with a view to avoiding service, and

(b) there is no real prospect of the sum due being recovered by execution or other process,

the demand may be advertised in one or more newspapers; and the time limited for compliance with the demand runs from the date of the advertisement's appearance (or, as the case may be, its first appearance).

6.4 Application to set aside statutory demand (1) The debtor may, within the period allowed by this Rule apply to the appropriate court for an order setting the statutory demand aside. [FORM 6.4]

That period is 18 days from the date of the service on him of the statutory demand or, where the demand is advertised in a newspaper pursuant to Rule 6.3, from the date of the advertisement's appearance or (as the case may be) first appearance.

(2) Where the creditor issuing the statutory demand is a Minister of the Crown or Government Department, and –

(a) the debt in respect of which the demand is made, or a part of it equal to or exceeding the bankruptcy level (within the meaning of section 267), is the subject of a judgment or order of any court, and

(b) the statutory demand specifies the date of the judgment or order and the court in which it was obtained, but indicates the creditor's intention to present a bankruptcy petition against the debtor in the High Court,

the appropriate court under this Rule is the High Court; and in any other case it is that to which the debtor would, in accordance with paragraphs (1) and (2) of Rule 6.40 in Chapter 3 below, present his own bankruptcy petition.

(3) As from (inclusive) the date on which the application is filed in court, the time limited for compliance with the statutory demand ceases to run, subject to any order of the court under Rule 6.5(6).

(4) The debtor's application shall be supported by an affidavit –

(a) specifying the date on which the statutory demand came into his hands, and

(b) stating the grounds on which he claims that it should be set aside.

The affidavit shall have exhibited to it a copy of the statutory demand. [FORM 6.5]

6.5 Hearing of application to set aside (1) On receipt of an application under Rule 6.4, the court may, if satisfied that no sufficient cause is shown for it, dismiss it without giving notice to the creditor. As from (inclusive) the date on which the application is dismissed, the time limited for compliance with the statutory demand runs again.

(2) If the application is not dismissed under paragraph (1), the court shall fix a venue for it to be heard, and shall give at least 7 days' notice of it to –

(a) the debtor or, if the debtor's application was made by a solicitor acting for him, to the solicitor,

(b) the creditor, and

(c) whoever is named in the statutory demand as the person with whom the debtor may enter into communication with reference to the demand (or, if more than one person is so named, the first of them).

(3) On the hearing of the application, the court shall consider the evidence then available to it, and may either summarily determine the application or adjourn it, giving such directions as it thinks appropriate.

(4) The court may grant the application if –

(a) the debtor appears to have a counterclaim, set-off or cross demand which equals or exceeds the amount of the debt or debts specified in the statutory demand; or

(b) the debt is disputed on grounds which appear to the court to be substantial; or

(c) it appears that the creditor holds some security in respect of the debt claimed by the demand, and either Rule 6.1(5) is not complied with in respect of it, or the court is satisfied that the value of the security equals or exceeds the full amount of the debt; or

(d) the court is satisfied, on other grounds, that the demand ought to be set aside. [FORM 6.6]

(5) Where the creditor holds some security in respect of his debt, and Rule 6.1(5) is complied with in respect of it but the court is satisfied that the security is undervalued in the statutory demand, the creditor may be required to amend the demand accordingly (but without prejudice to his right to present a bankruptcy petition by reference to the original demand).

(6) If the court dismisses the application, it shall make an order authorising the creditor to present a bankruptcy petition either forthwith, or on or after a date specified in the order.

A copy of the order shall be sent by the court forthwith to the creditor.

CHAPTER 2: BANKRUPTCY PETITION (CREDITOR'S)

6.6 Preliminary The Rules in this Chapter relate to a creditor's petition, and the making of a bankruptcy order thereon; and in those Rules 'the debt' means, except where the context otherwise requires, the debt (or debts) in respect of which the petition is presented. [FORM 6.7 or FORM 6.8 or FORM 6.9 or FORM 6.10]

Those Rules also apply to a petition under section 264(1)(c) (supervisor of, or person bound by, voluntary arrangement), with any necessary modifications.

6.7 Identification of debtor (1) The petition shall state the following matters with respect to the debtor, so far as they are within the petitioner's knowledge –

(a) his name, place of residence and occupation (if any);

(b) the name or names in which he carries on business, if other than his true name, and whether, in the case of any business of a specified nature, he carries it on alone or with others;

(c) the nature of his business, and the address or addresses at which he carries it on;

(d) any name or names, other than his true name, in which he has carried on business at or after the time when the debt was incurred, and whether he has done so alone or with others;

(e) any address or addresses at which he has resided or carried on business at or after that time, and the nature of that business.

(2) The particulars of the debtor given under this Rule determine the full title of the proceedings.

(3) If to the petitioner's personal knowledge the debtor has used any name other than the one specified under paragraph (1)(a), that fact shall be stated in the petition.

6.8 Identification of debt (1) There shall be stated in the petition, with reference to every debt in respect of which it is presented –

(a) the amount of the debt, the consideration for it (or, if there is no consideration, the way in which it arises) and the fact that it is owed to the petitioner;

(b) when the debt was incurred or became due;

(c) if the amount of the debt includes –

(i) any charge by way of interest not previously notified to the debtor as a liability of his, or

(ii) any other charge accruing from time to time,

the amount or rate of the charge (separately identified) and the grounds on which it is claimed to form part of the debt;

(d) either –

(i) that the debt is for a liquidated sum payable immediately, and the debtor appears to be unable to pay it, or

(ii) that the debt is for a liquidated sum payable at some certain, future time (that time to be specified), and the debtor appears to have no reasonable prospect of being able to pay it,

and, in either case (subject to section 269) that the debt is unsecured.

(2) Where the debt is one for which, under section 268, a statutory demand must have been served on the debtor –

(a) there shall be specified the date and manner of service of the statutory demand, and

(b) it shall be stated that, to the best of the creditor's knowledge and belief –

(i) the demand has been neither complied with nor set aside in accordance with the Rules, and

(ii) no application to set it aside is outstanding.

(3) If the case is within section 268(1)(b) (debt arising under judgment or order of court; execution returned unsatisfied), the court from which the execution or other process issued shall be specified, and particulars shall be given relating to the return.

6.9 Court in which petition to be presented (1) In the following cases, the petition shall be presented to the High Court –

(a) if the petition is presented by a Minister or the Crown or a Government Department, and in any statutory demand on which the petition is based the creditor has indicated the intention to present a bankruptcy petition to that Court, or the petition is presented under section 268(1)(b), or

(b) if the debtor has resided or carried on business within the London insolvency district for the greater part of the 6 months immediately preceding the presentation of the petition, or for a longer period in those 6 months than in any other insolvency district, or

(c) if the debtor is not resident in England and Wales, or

(d) if the petitioner is unable to ascertain the residence of the debtor, or his place of business.

(2) In any other case the petition shall be presented to the country court for the insolvency district in which the debtor has resided or carried on business for the longest period during those 6 months.

(3) If the debtor has for the greater part of those 6 months carried on business in one insolvency district and resided in another, the petition shall be presented to the court for the insolvency district in which he has carried on business.

(4) If the debtor has, during those 6 months carried on business in more than one insolvency district, the petition shall be presented to the court for the insolvency district in which is, or has been for the longest period in those 6 months, his principal place of business.

(5) The petition shall contain sufficient information to establish that it is brought in the appropriate court.

6.10 Procedure for presentation and filing (1) The petition, verified by affidavit in accordance with Rule 6.12(1) below, shall be filed in court.

(2) No petition shall be filed unless there is produced with it the receipt for the deposit payable on presentation.

(3) The following copies of the petition shall also be delivered to the court with the petition –

(a) one for service on the debtor, and

(b) one to be exhibited to the affidavit verifying that service.

Each of these copies shall have applied to it the seal of the court, and shall be issued to the petitioner.

(4) The date and time of filing the petition shall be endorsed on the petition and on any copy issued under paragraph (3).

(5) The court shall fix a venue for hearing the petition, and this also shall be endorsed on the petition and on any copy so issued.

6.11 Proof of service of statutory demand (1) Where under section 268 the petition must have been preceded by a statutory demand, there must be filed in court, with the petition, an affidavit proving service of the demand.
(2) The affidavit must have exhibited to it a copy of the demand as served.
(3) Subject to the next paragraph, if the demand has been served personally on the debtor, the affidavit must be made by the person who effected that service. [FORM 6.11]
(4) If service of the demand (however effected) has been acknowledged in writing either by the debtor himself, or by some person stating himself in the acknowledgement to be authorised to accept service on the debtor's behalf, the affidavit must be made either by the creditor or by a person acting on his behalf, and the acknowledgement of service must be exhibited to the affidavit.
(5) If neither paragraph (3) nor paragraph (4) applies, the affidavit must be made by a person having direct personal knowledge of the means adopted for serving the statutory demand, and must –
(a) give particulars of the steps which have been taken with a view to serving the demand, and
(b) state the means whereby (those steps having been ineffective) it was sought to bring the demand to the debtor's attention, and
(c) specify a date by which, to the best of the knowledge, information and belief of the person making the affidavit, the demand will have come to the debtor's attention. [FORM 6.12]
(6) The steps of which particulars are given for the purposes of paragraph (5)(a) must be such as would have sufficed to justify an order for substituted service of a petition.
(7) If the affidavit specifies a date for the purposes of compliance with paragraph (5)(c), then unless the court otherwise orders, the date is deemed for the purposes of the Rules to have been the date on which the statutory demand was served on the debtor.
(8) Where the creditor has taken advantage of Rule 6.3(3) (newspaper advertisement), the affidavit must be made either by the creditor himself or by a person having direct personal knowledge of the circumstances; and there must be specified in the affidavit –
(a) the means of the creditor's knowledge or (as the case may be) belief required for the purposes of that Rule, and
(b) the date or dates on which, and the newspaper in which, the statutory demand was advertised under that Rule;
and there shall be exhibited to the affidavit a copy of any advertisement of the statutory demand.
(9) The court may decline to file the petition if not satisfied that the creditor has discharged the obligation imposed on him by Rule 6.3(2).

6.12 Verification of petition (1) The petition shall be verified by an affidavit that the statements in the petition are true, or are true to the best of the deponent's knowledge, information and belief. [FORM 6.13]
(2) If the petition is in respect of debts to different creditors, the debts to each creditor must be separately verified.
(3) The petition shall be exhibited to the affidavit verifying it.
(4) The affidavit shall be made –
(a) by the petitioner (or if there are two or more petitioners, any one of them), or
(b) by some person such as a director, company secretary or similar company officer, or a solicitor, who has been concerned in the matters giving rise to the presentation of the petition, or

(c) by some responsible person who is duly authorised to make the affidavit and has the requisite knowledge of those matters.
(5) Where the maker of the affidavit is not the petitioner himself, or one of the petitioners, he must in the affidavit identify himself and state –
(a) the capacity in which, and the authority by which, he makes it, and
(b) the means of his knowledge of the matters sworn to in the affidavit.
(6) The affidavit is prima facie evidence of the truth of the statements in the petition to which it relates.
(7) If the petition is based upon a statutory demand, and more than 4 months have elapsed between the service of the demand and the presentation of the petition, the affidavit must also state the reasons for the delay.

6.13 Notice to Chief Land Registrar When the petition is filed, the court shall forthwith send to the Chief Land Registrar notice of the petition together with a request that it may be registered in the register of pending actions. [FORM 6.14]

6.14 Service of petition (1) Subject as follows, the petition shall be served personally on the debtor by an officer of the court, or by the petitioning creditor or his solicitor, or by a person instructed by the creditor or his solicitor for that purpose; and service shall be effected by delivering to him a sealed copy of the petition.
(2) If the court is satisfied by affidavit or other evidence on oath that prompt personal service cannot be effected because the debtor is keeping out of the way to avoid service of the petition or other legal process, or for any other cause, it may order substituted service to be effected in such manner as it thinks fit.
(3) Where an order for substituted service has been carried out, the petition is deemed duly served on the debtor. [FORM 6.15, FORM 6.16]

6.15 Proof of service (1) Service of the petition shall be proved by affidavit.
(2) The affidavit shall have exhibited to it –
(a) a sealed copy of the petition, and
(b) if substituted service has been ordered, a sealed copy of the order;
and it shall be filed in court immediately after service. [FORM 6.17 or FORM 6.18]

6.16 Death of debtor before service If the debtor dies before service of the petition, the court may order service to be effected on his personal representatives, or on such other persons as it thinks fit.

6.17 Security for costs (s 268(2) only) (1) This Rule applies where the debt in respect of which the petition is presented is for a liquidated sum payable at some future time, it being claimed in the petition that the debtor appears to have no reasonable prospect of being able to pay it.
(2) The petitioning creditor may, on the debtor's application, be ordered to give security for the debtor's costs.
(3) The nature and amount of the security to be ordered is in the court's discretion.
(4) If an order is made under this Rule, there shall be no hearing of the petition until the whole amount of the security has been given.

6.18 Hearing of petition (1) Subject as follows, the petition shall not be heard until at least 14 days have elapsed since it was served on the debtor.
(2) The court may, on such terms as it thinks fit, hear the petition at an earlier date, if it appears that the debtor has absconded, or the court is satisfied that it is a proper case for an expedited hearing, or the debtor consents to a hearing within the 14 days.
(3) Any of the following may appear and be heard, that is to say, the petitioning creditor, the debtor and any creditor who has given notice under Rule 6.23 below.

6.19 Petition against two or more debtors Where two or more debtors are named in the petition, and the petition has not been served on both or all of them, the petition may be heard separately or collectively as regards any of those who have been served, and may subsequently be heard (separately or collectively) as regards the others, as and when service on them is effected.

6.20 Petition by moneylender A petition in respect of a moneylending transaction made before 27th January 1980 of a creditor who at the time of the transaction was a licensed moneylender shall at the hearing of the petition be supported by an affidavit incorporating a statement setting out in detail the particulars mentioned in section 9(2) of the Moneylenders Act 1927.

6.21 Petition opposed by debtor Where the debtor intends to oppose the petition, he shall not later than 7 days before the day fixed for the hearing –
(a) file in court a notice specifying the grounds on which he will object to the making of a bankruptcy order, and
(b) send a copy of the notice to the petitioning creditor or his solicitor. [FORM 6.19]

6.22 Amendment of petition With the leave of the court (given on such terms, if any, as the court thinks fit to impose), the petition may be amended at any time after presentation by the omission of any creditor or any debt.

6.23 Notice by persons intending to appear (1) Every creditor who intends to appear on the hearing of the petition shall give to the petitioning creditor notice of his intention in accordance with this Rule. [FORM 6.20]
(2) The notice shall specify –
(a) the name and address of the person giving it, and any telephone number and reference which may be required for communication with him or with any other person (to be also specified in the notice) authorised to speak or act on his behalf;
(b) whether his intention is to support or oppose the petition; and
(c) the amount and nature of his debt.
(3) The notice shall be sent so as to reach the addressee not later than 16.00 hours on the business day before that which is appointed for the hearing (or, where the hearing has been adjourned, for the adjourned hearing).
(4) A person failing to comply with this Rule may appear on the hearing of the petition only with the leave of the court.

6.24 List of appearances (1) The petitioning creditor shall prepare for the court a list of the creditors (if any) who have given notice under Rule 6.23, specifying their names and addresses and (if known to him) their respective solicitors. [FORM 6.21]
(2) Against the name of each creditor in the list it shall be stated whether his intention is to support the petition, or to oppose it.
(3) On the day appointed for the hearing of the petition, a copy of the list shall be handed to the court before the commencement of the hearing.
(4) If any leave is given under Rule 6.23(4), the petitioner shall add to the list the same particulars in respect of the person to whom leave has been given.

6.25 Decision on the hearing (1) On the hearing of the petition, the court may make a bankruptcy order if satisfied that the statements in the petition are true, and that the debt on which is is founded has not been paid, or secured or compounded for.
(2) If the petition is brought in respect of a judgment debt, or a sum ordered by any court to be paid, the court may stay or dismiss the petition on the ground that an appeal is pending from the judgment or order, or that execution of the judgment has been stayed. [FORM 6.22]

(3) A petition preceded by a statutory demand shall not be dismissed on the ground only that the amount of the debt was over-stated in the demand, unless the debtor, within the time allowed for complying with the demand, gave notice to the creditor disputing the validity of the demand on that ground; but, in the absence of such notice, the debtor is deemed to have complied with the demand if he has, within the time allowed, paid the correct amount.

6.26 Non-appearance of creditor If the petitioning creditor fails to appear on the hearing of the petition, no subsequent petition against the same debtor, either alone or jointly with any other person, shall be presented by the same creditor in respect of the same debt, without the leave of the court to which the previous petition was presented.

6.27 Vacating registration on dismissal of petition If the petition is dismissed or withdrawn by leave of the court, an order shall be made at the same time permitting vacation of the registration of the petition as a pending action; and the court shall send to the debtor two sealed copies of the order. [FORM 6.22]

6.28 Extension of time for hearing (1) The petitioning creditor may, if the petition has not been served, apply to the court to appoint another venue for the hearing.
(2) The application shall state the reasons why the petition has not been served.
(3) No costs occasioned by the application shall be allowed in the proceedings except by order of the court.
(4) If the court appoints another day for the hearing, the petitioning creditor shall forthwith notify any creditor who has given notice under Rule 6.23.

6.29 Adjournment (1) If the court adjourns the hearing of the petition, the following applies. [FORM 6.23]
(2) Unless the court otherwise directs, the petitioning creditor shall forthwith send –
(a) to the debtor, and
(b) where any creditor has given notice under Rule 6.23 but was not present at the hearing, to him,
notice of the making of the order of adjournment. The notice shall state the venue for the adjourned hearing. [FORM 6.24]

6.30 Substitution of petitioner (1) This Rule applies where a creditor petitions and is subsequently found not entitled to do so, or where the petitioner –
(a) consents to withdraw his petition or to allow it to be dismissed, or consents to an adjournment, or fails to appear in support of his petition when it is called on in court on the day originally fixed for the hearing, or on a day to which it is adjourned, or
(b) appears, but does not apply for an order in the terms of the prayer of his petition.
(2) The court may, on such terms as it thinks just, order that there be substituted as petitioner any creditor who –
(a) has under Rule 6.23 given notice of his intention to appear at the hearing,
(b) is desirous of prosecuting the petition, and
(c) was, at the date on which the petition was presented, in such a position in relation to the debtor as would have enabled him (the creditor) on that date to present a bankruptcy petition in respect of a debt or debts owed to him by the debtor, paragraphs (a) to (d) of section 267(2) being satisfied in respect of that debt or those debts.

6.31 Change of carriage and petition (1) On the hearing of the petition, any person who claims to be a creditor of the debtor, and who has given notice under Rule 6.23 of his intention to appear at the hearing, may apply to the court for an order giving him carriage of the petition in place of the petitioning creditor, but without requiring any amendment of the petition.

(2) The court may, on such terms as it thinks just, make a change of carriage order if satisfied that –

(a) the applicant is an unpaid and unsecured creditor of the debtor, and
(b) the petitioning creditor either –
  (i) intends by any means to secure the postponement, adjournment or withdrawal of the petition, or
  (ii) does not intend to prosecute the petition, either diligently or at all.

(3) The court shall not make the order if satisfied that the petitioning creditor's debt has been paid, secured or compounded for by means of –

(a) a disposition of property made by some person other than the debtor, or
(b) a disposition of the debtor's own property made with the approval of, or ratified by, the court.

(4) A change of carriage order may be made whether or not the petitioning creditor appears at the hearing.

(5) If the order is made, the person given the carriage of the petition is entitled to rely on all evidence previously adduced in the proceedings (whether by affidavit or otherwise).

6.32 Petitioner seeking dismissal or leave to withdraw (1) Where the petitioner applies to the court for the petition to be dismissed, or for leave to withdraw it, he must, unless the court otherwise orders, file in court an affidavit specifying the grounds of the application and the circumstances in which it is made.

(2) If, since the petition was filed, any payment has been made to the petitioner by way of settlement (in whole or in part) of the debt or debts in respect of which the petition was brought, or any arrangement has been entered into for securing or compounding it or them, the affidavit must state –

(a) what dispositions of property have been made for the purposes of the settlement or arrangement, and
(b) whether, in the case of any disposition, it was property of the debtor himself, or of some other person, and
(c) whether, if it was property of the debtor, the disposition was made with the approval of, or has been ratified by, the court (if so, specifying the relevant court order).

(3) No order giving leave to withdraw a petition shall be given before the petition is heard. [FORM 6.22]

6.33 Settlement and content of bankruptcy order (1) The bankruptcy order shall be settled by the court. [FORM 6.25]

(2) The order shall –

(a) state the date of the presentation of the petition on which the order is made, and the date and time of the making of the order, and
(b) contain a notice requiring the bankrupt, forthwith after service of the order on him, to attend on the official receiver at the place stated in the order.

(3) Subject to section 346 (effect of bankruptcy on enforcement procedures), the order may include provision staying any action or proceeding against the bankrupt.

(4) Where the petitioning creditor is represented by a solicitor, the order shall be endorsed with the latter's name, address, telephone number and reference (if any).

6.34 Action to follow making of order (1) At least two sealed copies of the

bankruptcy order shall be sent by the court to the official receiver, who shall forthwith send one of them to the bankrupt.
(2) Subject to the next paragraph, the official receiver shall –
(a) send notice of the making of the order to the Chief Land Registrar, for registration in the register of writs and orders affecting land,
(b) cause the order to be advertised in such local paper as the official receiver thinks fit, and
(c) cause the order to be gazetted. [FORM 6.26]
(3) The court may, on the application of the bankrupt or a creditor, order the official receiver to suspend action under paragraph (2), pending a further order of the court.
An application under this paragraph shall be supported by an affidavit stating the grounds on which it is made.
(4) Where an order is made under paragraph (3), the applicant for the order shall forthwith deliver a copy of it to the official receiver.

6.35 Amendment of title of proceedings (1) At any time after the making of a bankruptcy order, the official receiver of the trustee in bankruptcy may apply to the court for an order amending the full title of the proceedings.
(2) Where such an order is made, the official receiver shall forthwith send notice of it to the Chief Land Registrar, for corresponding amendment of the register; and, if the court so directs he shall also cause notice of the order to be gazetted, and to be advertised in such local newspaper as the official receiver thinks fit.

6.36 Old bankruptcy notices (1) Subject as follows, a person who has before the appointed day for the purposes of the Act served a bankruptcy notice under the Bankruptcy Act 1914 may, on or after that day, proceed on the notice as if it were a statutory demand duly served under Chapter 1 of this Part of the Rules.
(2) The conditions of the application of this Rule are that –
(a) the debt in respect of which the bankruptcy notice was served has not been paid, secured or compounded for in the terms of the notice and the Act of 1914;
(b) the date by which compliance with the notice was required was not more than 3 months before the date of presentation of the petition; and
(c) there has not, before the appointed day, been presented any bankruptcy petition with reference to an act of bankruptcy arising from non-compliance with the bankruptcy notice.
(3) If, before on or after the appointed day, application has been made (under the Act of 1914) to set the bankruptcy notice aside, that application is to be treated, on and after that day, as an application duly made (on the date on which it was in fact made) to set aside a statutory demand duly served on the date on which the bankruptcy notice was in fact served.

CHAPTER 3: BANKRUPTCY PETITION (DEBTOR'S)

6.37 Preliminary The rules in this Chapter relate to a debtor's petition, and the making of a bankruptcy order thereon. [FORM 6.27]

6.38 Identification of debtor (1) The petition shall state the following matters with respect to the debtor –
(a) his name, place of residence and occupation (if any);
(b) the name or names in which he carries on business, if other than his true name, and whether, in the case of any business of a specified nature, he carries it on alone or with others;

(c) the nature of his business, and the address or addresses at which he carries it on;
(d) any name or names, other than his true name, in which he has carried on business in the period in which any of his bankruptcy debts were incurred and, in the case of any such business, whether he has carried it on alone or with others; and
(e) any address or addresses at which he has resided or carried on business during that period, and the nature of that business.

(2) The particulars of the debtor given under this Rule determine the full title of proceedings.
(3) If the debtor has at any time used a name other than the one given under paragraph (1)(a), that fact shall be stated in the petition.

6.39 Admission of insolvency (1) The petition shall contain the statement that the petitioner is unable to pay his debts, and a request that a bankruptcy order be made against him.
(2) If within the period of 5 years ending with the date of the petition the petitioner has been adjudged bankrupt, or has made a composition with his creditors in satisfaction of his debts or a scheme of arrangement of his affairs, or he has entered into any voluntary arrangement or been subject to an administration order under Part VI of the County Courts Act 1984, particulars of these matters shall be given in the petition.

6.40 Court in which petition to be filed (1) In the following cases, the petition shall be presented to the High Court –
(a) if the debtor has resided or carried on business in the London insolvency district for the greater part of the 6 months immediately preceding the presentation of the petition, or for a longer period in those 6 months than in any other insolvency district, or
(b) if the debtor is not resident in England and Wales.

(2) In any other case, the petition shall (subject to paragraph (3) below), be presented to the debtor's own county court, which is –
(a) the county court for the insolvency district in which he has resided or carried on business for the longest period in those 6 months, or
(b) if he has for the greater part of those 6 months carried on business in one insolvency district and resided in another, the county court for that in which he has carried on business, or
(c) if he has during those 6 months carried on business in more than one insolvency district, the county court for that in which is, or has been for the longest period in those 6 months, his principal place of business.

(3) If, in a case not falling within paragraph (1), it is more expedient for the debtor with a view to expediting his petition, it may be presented to whichever county court is specified by Schedule 3 to the Rules as being, in relation to the debtor's own county court, the nearest full-time court.
(4) The petition shall contain sufficient information to establish that it is brought in the appropriate court.

6.41 Statement of affairs (1) The petition shall be accompanied by a statement of the debtor's affairs, verified by affidavit. [FORM 6.28]
(2) Section B of Chapter 5 below applies with respect to the statement of affairs.

6.42 Procedure for presentation and filing (1) The petition and the statement of affairs shall be filed in court, together with three copies of the petition, and two copies of the statement. No petition shall be filed unless there is produced with it the receipt for the deposit payable on presentation.

(2) The court may hear the petition forthwith. If it does not do so, it shall fix a venue for the hearing.
(3) Of the three copies of the petition delivered –
(a) one shall be returned to the petitioner, endorsed with any venue fixed;
(b) another, so endorsed, shall be retained by the court, to be sent to the official receiver if a bankruptcy order is made; and
(c) the remaining copy shall be retained by the court, to be sent to an insolvency practitioner (if appointed under section 273(2)).
(4) Of the two copies of the statement of affairs –
(a) one shall be retained by the court, to be sent to the official receiver if a bankruptcy order is made; and
(b) the other shall be retained by the court to be sent to the insolvency practitioner (if appointed).
(5) The affidavit verifying the debtor's statement of affairs may be sworn before an officer of the court duly authorised in that behalf.

6.43 Notice to Chief Land Registrar When the petition is filed, the court shall forthwith send to the Chief Land Registrar notice of the petition, for registration in the register of pending actions. [FORM 6.14]

6.44 Report of insolvency practitioner (1) If the court under section 273(2) appoints an insolvency practitioner to act in the debtor's case, it shall forthwith –
(a) send to the person appointed –
    (i) a sealed copy of the order of appointment, and
    (ii) copies of the petition and statement of affairs,
(b) fix a venue for the insolvency practitioner's report to be considered, and
(c) send notice of the venue to the insolvency practitioner and the debtor. [FORM 6.29]
(2) The insolvency practitioner shall file his report in court with one copy, and send one copy of it to the debtor, so as to be in his hands not less than 3 days before the date fixed for consideration of the report.
(3) The debtor is entitled to attend when the report is considered, and shall attend if so directed by the court. If he attends, the court shall hear any representations which he makes with respect to any of the matters dealt with in the report.
(4) If the official receiver is appointed interim receiver or a bankruptcy order is made, a copy of the insolvency practitioner's report, the debtor's petition and his statement of affairs shall be sent by the court to the official receiver.

6.45 Settlement and content of bankruptcy order (1) The bankruptcy order shall be settled by the court. [FORM 6.30]
(2) The order shall –
(a) state the date of the presentation of the petition on which the order is made, and the date and time of the making of the order, and
(b) contain a notice requiring the bankrupt, forthwith after the service of the order on him, to attend on the official receiver at the place stated in the order.
(3) Subject to section 346 (effect of bankruptcy on enforcement procedures), the order may include provision staying any action or proceeding against the bankrupt.
(4) Where the bankrupt is presented by a solicitor, the order shall be endorsed with the latter's name, address, telephone number and reference.

6.46 Action to follow making of order (1) At least two sealed copies of the

bankruptcy order shall be sent by the court to the official receiver. who shall forthwith send one of them to the bankrupt.
(2) Subject to the next paragraph, the official receiver shall –
(a) send notice of the making of the order to the Chief Land Registrar, for registration in the register of writs and orders affecting land,
(b) cause the order to be advertised in such local paper as the official receiver thinks fit, and
(c) cause notice of the order to be gazetted. [FORM 6.26]
(3) The court may, on the application of the bankrupt or a creditor, order the official receiver to suspend action under paragraph (2), pending a further order of the court.
An application under this paragraph shall be supported by an affidavit stating the grounds on which it is made.
(4) Where an order is made under paragraph (3), the debtor shall forthwith deliver a copy of it to the official receiver.

6.47 Amendment of title of proceedings (1) At any time after the making of the bankruptcy order, the official receiver or the trustee may apply to the court for an order amending the full title of the proceedings.
(2) Where such an order is made, the official receiver shall forthwith send notice of it to the Chief Land Registrar, for corresponding amendment of the register, and, if the court so directs, he shall also –
(a) cause notice of the order to be gazetted, and
(b) cause notice of the order to be advertised in such local paper as the official receiver thinks appropriate.

6.48 Certificate of summary administration (1) If the court under section 275 issues a certificate for the summary administration of the bankrupt's estate, the certificate may be included in the bankruptcy order. [FORM 6.30]
(2) If the certificate is not so included, the court shall forthwith send copies of it to the official receiver and the bankrupt.

6.49 Duty of official receiver in summary administration (1) Where a trustee has been appointed, the official receiver shall send a copy of the certificate of summary administration (whether or not included in the bankruptcy order) to him.
(2) Within 12 weeks after the issue of the certificates the official receiver shall (insofar as he has not already done so) give notice to creditors of the making of the bankruptcy order.

6.50 Revocation of certificate for summary administration (1) The court may under section 275(3) revoke a certificate for summary administration, either of its own motion or on the application of the official receiver. [FORM 6.31]
(2) If the official receiver applies for the certificate to be revoked, he shall give at least 14 days' notice of the application to the bankrupt.
(3) If the court revokes the certificate, it shall forthwith give notice to the official receiver and the bankrupt.
(4) If at the time of revocation there is a trustee other than the official receiver, the official receiver shall send a copy of the court's notice to him.

CHAPTER 4: THE INTERIM RECEIVER

6.51 Application for appointment of interim receiver (1) An application to the court for the appointment of an interim receiver under section 286 may be made by a

creditor or by the debtor, or by an insolvency practitioner appointed under section 273(2).
(2) The application must be supported by an affidavit stating –
(a) the grounds on which it is proposed that the interim receiver should be appointed.
(b) whether or not the official receiver has been informed of the application and, if so, has been furnished with a copy of it,
(c) whether to the applicant's knowledge there has been proposed or is in force a voluntary arrangement under Part VIII of the Act, and
(d) the applicant's estimate of the value of the property or business in respect of which the interim receiver is to be appointed.
(3) If an insolvency practitioner has been appointed under section 273, and it is proposed that he (and not the official receiver) should be appointed interim receiver, and it is not the insolvency practitioner himself who is the applicant under this Rule, the affidavit under paragraph (2) must state that he has consented to act.
(4) The applicant shall send copies of the application and the affidavit to the person proposed to be appointed interim receiver. If that person is the official receiver and an insolvency practitioner has been appointed under section 273 (and he is not himself the applicant), copies of the application and affidavit shall be sent by the applicant to the insolvency practitioner.
If, in any case where a copy of the application is to be sent to a person under this paragraph, it is for any reason not practicable to send a copy, that person must be informed of the application in sufficient time to enable him to be present at the hearing.
(5) The official receiver and (if appointed) the insolvency practitioner may attend the hearing of the application and make representations.
(6) The court may on the application, if satisfied that sufficient grounds are shown for the appointment, make it on such terms as it thinks fit.

6.52 Order of appointment (1) The order appointing the interim receiver shall state the nature and a short description of the property of which the person appointed is to take possession, and the duties to be performed by him in relation to the debtor's affairs. [FORM 6.32]
(2) The court shall, forthwith after the order is made, send 2 sealed copies of it to the person appointed interim receiver (one of which shall be sent by him forthwith to the debtor).

6.53 Deposit (1) Before an order appointing the official receiver as interim receiver is issued, the applicant for it shall deposit with him, or otherwise secure to his satisfaction, such sum as the court directs to cover his remuneration and expenses.
(2) If the sum deposited or secured subsequently proves to be insufficient, the court may, on application by the official receiver, order that an additional sum be deposited or secured. If the order is not complied with within 2 days after service on the person to whom the order is directed, the court may discharge the order appointing the interim receiver.
(3) If a bankruptcy order is made after an interim receiver has been appointed, any money deposited under this Rule shall (unless it is required by reason of insufficiency of assets for payment of remuneration and expenses of the interim receiver, or the deposit was made by the debtor out of his own property) be repaid to the person depositing it (or as that person may direct) out of the bankrupt's estate, in the prescribed order of priority.

6.54 Security (1) The following applies where an insolvency practitioner is appointed to be interim receiver under section 286(2).

(2) The cost of providing the security required under the Act shall be paid in the first instance by the interim receiver; but –
(a) if a bankruptcy order is not made, the person so appointed is entitled to be reimbursed out of the property of the debtor, and the court may make an order on the debtor accordingly, and
(b) if a bankruptcy order is made, he is entitled to be reimbursed out of the estate in the prescribed order of priority.

6.55 Failure to give or keep up security (1) If the interim receiver fails to give or keep up his security the court may remove him, and make such order as it thinks fit as to costs.
(2) If an order is made under this Rule removing the interim receiver, or discharging the order appointing him, the court shall give directions as to whether any, and if so what, steps should be taken for the appointment of another person in his place.

6.56 Remuneration (1) The remuneration of the interim receiver (whether the official receiver or another) shall be fixed by the court from time to time on his application.
(2) In fixing the interim receiver's remuneration, the court shall take into account –
(a) the time properly given by him (as interim receiver) and his staff in attending to the debtor's affairs,
(b) the complexity (or otherwise) of the case,
(c) any respects in which, in connection with the debtor's affairs, there falls on the interim receiver any responsibility of an exceptional kind or degree.
(d) the effectiveness with which the interim receiver appears to be carrying out, or to have carried out, his duties as such, and
(e) the value and nature of the property with which he has to deal.
(3) The interim receiver's remuneration shall be paid to him, and the amount of any expenses incurred by him reimbursed –
(a) if a bankruptcy order is not made, out of the property of the debtor (and the court may make an order on the debtor accordingly), and
(b) if a bankruptcy order is made, out of the estate in the prescribed order of priority,
or, in either case (the relevant funds being insufficient), out of the deposit under Rule 6.53.

6.57 Termination of appointment (1) The appointment of the interim receiver may be terminated by the court on his application, or on that of the official receiver, the debtor or any creditor.
(2) If the interim receiver's appointment terminates, in consequence of the dismissal of the bankruptcy petition or otherwise, the court may give such directions as it thinks fit with respect to the account of his administration and any other matters which it thinks appropriate.
(3) The court may under paragraph (2) –
(a) direct that any expenses properly incurred by the interim receiver during the period of his appointment, and any remuneration to which he is entitled, be paid out of property of the debtor, and
(b) authorise him to retain out of that property such sums as are required for meeting his expenses and remuneration.

Alternatively, the court may make such order as it thinks fit with respect to those matters.

CHAPTER 5: DISCLOSURE BY BANKRUPT WITH RESPECT TO THE STATE OF HIS AFFAIRS

Section A: Creditor's Petition

6.58 Preliminary The Rules in this Section apply with respect to the statement of affairs required by section 288(1) to be submitted by the bankrupt, following a bankruptcy order made on a creditor's petition, and the further and other disclosure which is required of him in that case.

6.59 The statement of affairs The bankrupt's statement of affairs shall be in Form 6.33, and contain all the particulars required by that form. [FORM 6.33]

6.60 Verification and filing (1) The bankrupt shall be furnished by the official receiver with instructions for the preparation of his statement of affairs, and the forms required for that purpose.
(2) The statement of affairs shall be verified by affidavit and delivered to the official receiver, together with one copy.
(3) The official receiver shall file the verified statement in court.
(4) The affidavit may be sworn before an official receiver or a deputy official receiver, or before an officer of the Department or the court duly authorised in that behalf.

6.61 Limited disclosure (1) Where the official receiver thinks that it would prejudice the conduct of the bankruptcy for the whole or part of the statement of affairs to be disclosed, he may apply to the court for an order of limited disclosure in respect of the statement, or any specified part of it.
(2) The court may on application order that the statement or, as the case may be, the specified part of it be not filed in court, or that it is to be filed separately and not be open to inspection otherwise than with the leave of the court.

6.62 Release from duty to submit statement of affairs; extension of time (1) The power of the official receiver under section 288(3) to release the bankrupt from his duty to submit a statement of affairs, or to grant an extension of time, may be exercised at the official receiver's own discretion, or at the bankrupt's request.
(2) The bankrupt may, if he requests a release or extension of time and it is refused by the official receiver, apply to the court for it.
(3) The court may, if it thinks that no sufficient cause is shown for the application, dismiss it; but it shall not do so unless the bankrupt has had an opportunity to attend the court for an ex parte hearing, of which he has been given at least 7 days' notice.

If the application is not dismissed under this paragraph, the court shall fix a venue for it to be heard, and give notice to the bankrupt accordingly.
(4) The bankrupt shall, at least 14 days before the hearing, send to the official receiver a notice stating the venue and accompanied by a copy of the application, and of any evidence which he (the bankrupt) intends to adduce in support of it.
(5) The official receiver may appear and be heard on the application; and, whether or not he appears, he may file a written report of any matters which he considers ought to be drawn to the court's attention.

If such a report is filed, a copy of it shall be sent by the official receiver to the bankrupt, not later than 5 days before the hearing.
(6) Sealed copies of any order made on the application shall be sent by the court to the bankrupt and the official receiver.
(7) On any application under this Rule the bankrupt's costs shall be paid in any event by him and, unless the court otherwise orders, no allowance towards them shall be made out of the estate.

6.63 Expenses of statement of affairs (1) If the bankrupt cannot himself prepare a proper statement of affairs, the official receiver may, at the expense of the estate employ some person or persons to assist in the preparation of the statement.
(2) At the request of the bankrupt, made on the grounds that he cannot himself prepare a proper statement, the official receiver may authorise an allowance payable out of the estate (in accordance with the prescribed order of priority) towards expenses to be incurred by the bankrupt in employing some person or persons to assist him in preparing it.
(3) Any such request by the bankrupt shall be accompanied by an estimate of the expenses involved; and the official receiver shall only authorise the employment of a named person or a named firm, being in either case approved by him.
(4) An authorisation given by the official receiver under this Rule shall be subject to such conditions (if any) as he thinks fit to impose with respect to the manner in which any person may obtain access to relevant books and papers.
(5) Nothing in this Rule relieves the bankrupt from any obligation with respect to the preparation, verification and submission of his statement of affairs, or to the provision of information to the official receiver or the trustee.

6.64 Requirement to submit accounts (1) The bankrupt shall, at the request of the official receiver, furnish him with accounts relating to his affairs of such nature, as at such date and for such period as he may specify.
(2) The period specified may begin from a date up to 3 years preceding the date of the presentation of the bankruptcy petition.
(3) The court may, on the official receiver's application, require accounts in respect of any earlier period.
(4) Rule 6.63 applies (with the necessary modifications) in relation to accounts to be furnished under this Rule as it applies in relation to the statement of affairs.

6.65 Submission and filing of accounts (1) The accounts to be furnished under Rule 6.64 shall, if the official receiver so requires, be verified by affidavit, and (whether or not so verified) delivered to him within 21 days of the request under Rule 6.64(1), or such longer period as he may allow.
(2) Two copies of the accounts and (where required) the affidavit shall be delivered by the bankrupt to the official receiver, who shall file one copy in court (with the affidavit, if any).

6.66 Further disclosure (1) The official receiver may at any time require the bankrupt to submit (in writing) further information amplifying, modifying or explaining any matter contained in his statement of affairs, or in accounts submitted in pursuance of the Act or the Rules.
(2) The information shall, if the official receiver so directs, be verified by affidavit, and (whether or not so verified) delivered to him within 21 days of the requirement under this Rule, or such longer period as he may allow.
(3) Two copies of the documents containing the information and (where verification is directed) the affidavit shall be delivered by the bankrupt to the official receiver, who shall file one copy in court (with the affidavit, if any).

Section B: Debtor's Petition

6.67 Preliminary The Rules in this Section apply with respect to the statement of affairs required in the case of a person petitioning for a bankruptcy order to be made against him, and the further disclosure which is required of him in that case.

6.68 Contents of statement The statement of affairs required by Rule 6.41 to accompany the debtor's petition shall be in Form 6.28, and contain all the particulars required by that form. [FORM 6.28]

6.69 Requirement to submit accounts (1) The bankrupt shall, at the request of the official receiver, furnish him with accounts relating to his affairs of such nature, as at such date and for such period as he may specify.
(2) The period specified may begin from a date up to 3 years preceding the date of the presentation of the bankruptcy petition.
(3) The court may, on the official receiver's application, require accounts in respect of any earlier period.

6.70 Submission and filing of accounts (1) The accounts to be furnished under Rule 6.69 shall, if the official receiver so requires, be verified by affidavit, and (whether or not so verified) delivered to him within 21 days of the request under Rule 6.69, or such longer period as he may allow.
(2) Two copies of the accounts and (where required) the affidavit shall be delivered by the bankrupt to the official receiver, who shall file one copy in court (with the affidavit, if any).

6.71 Expenses of preparing accounts (1) If the bankrupt cannot himself prepare proper accounts under Rule 6.69, the official receiver may, at the expense of the estate, employ some person or persons to assist in their preparation.
(2) At the request of the bankrupt, made on the grounds that he cannot himself prepare the accounts, the official receiver may authorise an allowance payable out of the estate (in accordance with the prescribed order of priority) towards expenses to be incurred by the bankrupt in employing some person or persons to assist him in their preparation.
(3) Any such request by the bankrupt shall be accompanied by an estimate of the expenses involved; and the official receiver shall only authorise the employment of a named person or a named firm, being in either case approved by him.
(4) An authorisation given by the official receiver under this Rule shall be subject to such conditions (if any) as he thinks fit to impose with respect to the manner in which any person may obtain access to relevant books and papers.
(5) Nothing in this Rule relieves the bankrupt from any obligation with respect to the preparation and submission of accounts, or to the provision of information to the official receiver or the trustee.

6.72 Further disclosure (1) The official receiver may at any time require the bankrupt to submit (in writing) further information amplifying, modifying or explaining any matter contained in his statement of affairs, or in accounts submitted in pursuance of the Act or the Rules.
(2) The information shall, if the official receiver so directs, be verified by affidavit, and (whether or not so verified) delivered to him within 21 days from the date of the requirement under paragraph (1), or such longer period as he may allow.
(3) Two copies of the documents containing the information and (where verification is directed) the affidavit shall be delivered by the bankrupt to the official receiver, who shall file one copy in court, with the affidavit (if any).

CHAPTER 6: INFORMATION TO CREDITORS

6.73 General duty of official receiver In accordance with this Chapter, the official receiver shall, at least once after the making of the bankruptcy order, send a report to creditors with respect to the bankruptcy proceedings, and the state of the bankrupt's affairs.

6.74 Those entitled to be informed Any reference in this Chapter to creditors is to creditors of the bankrupt who are known to the official receiver or, where the bankrupt has submitted a statement of affairs, are identified in the statement.

6.75 Report where statement of affairs lodged (1) Where the bankrupt has submitted a statement of affairs, and it has been filed in court, the official receiver shall send out to creditors a report containing a summary of the statement and such observations (if any) as he thinks fit to make with respect to it or to the bankrupt's affairs generally.
(2) The official receiver need not comply with paragraph (1) if he has previously reported to creditors with respect to the bankrupt's affairs (so far as known to him) and he is of opinion that there are no additional matters which ought to be brought to their attention.

6.76 Statement of affairs dispensed with (1) This Rule applies where the bankrupt has been released from the obligation to submit a statement of affairs.
(2) As soon as may be after the release has been granted, the official receiver shall send to creditors a report containing a summary of the bankrupt's affairs (so far as within his knowledge), and his observations (if any) with respect to it or the bankrupt's affairs generally.
(3) The official receiver need not comply with paragraph (2) if he has previously reported to creditors with respect to the bankrupt's affairs (so far as known to him) and he is of opinion that there are no additional matters which ought to be brought to their attention.

6.77 General rule as to reporting (1) The court may, on the official receiver's application, relieve him of any duty imposed on him by this Chapter of the Rules, or authorise him to carry out the duty in a way other than there required.
(2) In considering whether to act as above, the court shall have regard to the cost of carrying out the duty, to the amount of the funds available in the estate, and to the extent of the interest of creditors or any particular class of them.

6.78 Bankruptcy order annulled If the bankruptcy order is annulled, the duty of the official receiver to send reports under the preceding Rules in this Chapter ceases.

CHAPTER 7: CREDITORS' MEETING

6.79 First meeting of creditors (1) If under section 293(1) the official receiver decides to summon a meeting of creditors, he shall fix a venue for the meeting, not more than 4 months from the date of the bankruptcy order.
(2) When a venue has been fixed, notice of the meeting shall be given –
(a) to the court, and
(b) to every creditor of the bankrupt who is known to the official receiver or is identified in the bankrupt's statement of affairs.
(3) Notice to the court shall be given forthwith, and the notice to creditors shall be given at least 21 days before the date fixed for the meeting.
(4) The notice to creditors shall specify a time and date, not more than 4 days before the date fixed for the meeting, by which they must lodge proofs and (if applicable) proxies, in order to be entitled to vote at the meeting.
(5) Notice of the meeting shall also be given by public advertisement.
(6) Where the official receiver receives a request by a creditor under section 294 for a meeting of creditors to be summoned, and it appears to him that the request is properly made in accordance with the Act, he shall –

(a) withdraw any notice already given by him under section 293(2) (that he has decided not to summon such a meeting), and
(b) fix the venue of the meeting for not more than 3 months from his receipt of the creditor's request, and
(c) act in accordance with paragraphs (2) to (5) above, as if he had decided under section 293(1) to summon the meeting. [FORM 6.34]
(7) A meeting summoned by the official receiver under section 293 or 294 is known as 'the first meeting of creditors'.

6.80 Business at first meeting (1) At the first meeting of creditors, no resolutions shall be taken other than the following –
(a) a resolution to appoint a named insolvency practitioner to be trustee in bankruptcy or two or more named insolvency practitioners as joint trustees;
(b) a resolution to establish a creditors' committee;
(c) (unless it has been resolved to establish a creditor's committee) a resolution specifying the terms on which the trustee is to be remunerated, or to defer consideration of that matter;
(d) (if, and only if, two or more persons are appointed to act jointly as trustee) a resolution specifying whether acts are to be done by both or all of them, or by only one;
(e) (where the meeting has been requisitioned under section 294), a resolution authorising payment out of the estate, as an expense of the bankruptcy, of the cost of summoning and holding the meeting;
(f) a resolution to adjourn the meeting for not more than 3 weeks;
(g) any other resolution which the chairman thinks it right to allow for special reasons.
(2) No resolution shall be proposed which has for its object the appointment of the official receiver as trustee.

6.81 General power to call meetings (1) The official receiver or the trustee may at any time summon and conduct meetings of creditors for the purpose of ascertaining their wishes in all matters relating to bankruptcy.

In relation to any meeting of creditors, the person summoning it is referred to as 'the convener'.
(2) When a venue for the meeting has been fixed, notice of the meeting shall be given by the convener to every creditor who is known to him or is identified in the bankrupt's statement of affairs.

The notice shall be given at least 21 days before the date fixed for the meeting. [FORM 6.35]
(3) The notice to creditors shall specify the purpose for which the meeting is summoned, and a time and date (not more than 4 days before the meeting) by which creditors must lodge proxies and those who have not already lodged proofs must do so, in order to be entitled to vote at the meeting.
(4) Additional notice of the meeting may be given by public advertisement if the convener thinks fit, and shall be so given if the court so orders.

6.82 The chairman at a meeting (1) Where the convener of a meeting is the official receiver, he, or a person nominated by him, shall be chairman.

A nomination under this paragraph shall be in writing, unless the nominee is another official receiver or a deputy official receiver.
(2) Where the convener is other than the official receiver, the chairman shall be he, or a person nominated by him in writing to act.

A person nominated under this paragraph must be either –
(a) one who is qualified to act as an insolvency practitioner in relation to the bankrupt, or
(b) an employee of the trustee or his firm who is experienced in insolvency matters.

6.83 Requisitioned meetings (1) A request by creditors to the official receiver for a meeting of creditors to be summoned shall be accompanied by –
(a) a list of the creditors concurring with the request and the amount of their respective claims in the bankruptcy.
(b) from each creditor concurring, written confirmation of his concurrence, and
(c) a statement of the purpose of the proposed meeting.
Sub-paragraphs (a) and (b) do not apply if the requisitioning creditor's debt is alone sufficient, without the concurrence of other creditors. [FORM 6.34]
(2) The official receiver, if he considers the request to be properly made in accordance with the Act, shall –
(a) fix a venue for the meeting, to take place not more than 35 days from the receipt of the request, and
(b) give 21 days' notice of the meeting, and of the venue for it, to creditors.
(3) Where a request for a creditors' meeting is made to the trustee, this Rule applies to him as it does to the official receiver.

6.84 Attendance at meetings of bankrupt, etc (1) Whenever a meeting of creditors is summoned, the convener shall give at least 21 days' notice of the meeting to the bankrupt. [FORM 6.36]
(2) If the meeting is adjourned, the chairman of the meeting shall (unless for any reason it appears to him to be unnecessary or impracticable) give notice of the fact to the bankrupt, if the latter was not himself present at the meeting.
(3) The convener may, if he thinks fit, give notice to the bankrupt that he is required to be present, or in attendance.
(4) In the case of any meeting, the bankrupt or any other person may, if he has given reasonable notice of his wish to be present, be admitted; but this is at the discretion of the chairman.
The chairman's decision is final as to what (if any) intervention may be made by the bankrupt, or by any other person admitted to the meeting under this paragraph.
(5) If the bankrupt is not present, and it is desired to put questions to him, the chairman may adjourn the meeting with a view to obtaining his attendance.
(6) Where the bankrupt is present at a creditors' meeting, only such questions may be put to him as the chairman may in his discretion allow.

6.85 Notices of meetings by advertisement only (1) In the case of any meeting to be held under the Act or the Rules, the court may order that notice of it be given by public advertisement, and not by individual notice to the persons concerned.
(2) In considering whether to act under this Rule, the court shall have regard to the cost of public advertisement, to the amount of the funds available in the estate, and to the extent of the interest of creditors or any particular class of them.

6.86 Venue of meetings (1) In fixing the venue for a meeting of creditors, the person summoning the meeting shall have regard to the convenience of the creditors.
(2) Meetings shall in all cases be summoned for commencement between the hours of 10.00 and 16.00 hours on a business day, unless the court otherwise directs.
(3) With every notice summoning a creditors' meeting there shall be sent out forms of proxy. [FORM 8.5]

6.87 Expenses of summoning meetings (1) Subject to paragraph (3) below, the

expenses of summoning and holding a meeting of creditors at the instance of any person other than the official receiver or the trustee shall be paid by that person, who shall deposit security for their payment with the trustee or, if no trustee has been appointed, with the official receiver.
(2) The sum to be deposited shall be such as the trustee or (as the case may be) the official receiver determines to be appropriate; and neither shall act without the deposit having been made.
(3) Where a meeting is so summoned, it may vote that the expenses of summoning and holding it shall be payable out of the estate, as an expense of the bankruptcy.
(4) To the extent that any deposit made under this Rule is not required but for payment of expenses of summoning and holding the meeting, it shall be repaid to the person who made it.

6.88 Resolutions (1) At a meeting of creditors, a resolution is passed when a majority (in value) of those present and voting, in person or by proxy, have voted in favour of the resolution.
(2) In the case of a resolution for the appointment of a trustee –
(a) if on any vote there are two nominees for appointment, the person who obtains the most support is appointed;
(b) if there are three or more nominees, and one of them has a clear majority over both or all the others together, that one is appointed; and
(c) in any other case the chairman shall continue to take votes (disregarding at each vote any nominee who has withdrawn and, if no nominee was withdrawn, the nominee who obtained the least support last time), until a clear majority is obtained for any one nominee.
(3) The chairman may at any time put to the meeting a resolution for the joint appointment of any two or more nominees.
(4) Where a resolution is proposed which affects a person in respect of his remuneration or conduct as trustee, or as proposed or former trustee, the vote of that person, and of any partner or employee of his, shall not be reckoned in the majority required for passing the resolution.

This paragraph applies with respect to a vote given by person either as creditor or as proxy for a creditor (but subject to Rule 8.6 in Part 8 of the Rules).

6.89 Chairman of meeting as proxy-holder Where the chairman at a meeting holds a proxy for a creditor, which requires him to vote for a particular resolution, and no other person proposes that resolution –
(a) he shall himself propose it, unless he considers that there is good reason for not doing so, and
(b) if he does not propose it, he shall forthwith after the meeting notify his principal of the reason why not.

6.90 Suspension of meeting Once only in the course of any meeting, the chairman may, in his discretion and without an adjournment, declare the meeting suspended for any period up to one hour.

6.91 Adjournment (1) The chairman at any meeting may, in his discretion, and shall if the meeting so resolves, adjourn it to such time and place as seems to him to be appropriate in the circumstances.

This is subject to Rule 6.129(3) in a case where the trustee or his nominee is chairman and a resolution has been proposed for the trustee's removal.
(2) If within a period of 30 minutes from the time appointed for the commencement of a meeting a quorum is not present, then by virtue of this Rule the meeting stands adjourned to such time and place as may be appointed by the chairman.

(3) An adjournment under this Rule shall not be for a period of more than 21 days; and Rule 6.86(1) and (2) applies with regard to the venue of the adjourned meeting.
(4) If there is no person present to act as chairman, some other person present (being entitled to vote) may make the appointment under paragraph (2), with the agreement of others present (being persons so entitled).

Failing agreement, the adjournment shall be to the same time and place in the next following week or, if that is not a business day, to the business day immediately following.
(5) Where a meeting is adjourned under this Rule, proofs and proxies may be used if lodged at any time up to midday on the business day immediately before the adjourned meeting.

6.92 Quorum (1) A creditor's meeting is not competent to act for any purpose, except –
(a) the election of a chairman,
(b) the admission by the chairman of creditors' proofs, for the purpose of their entitlement to vote, and
(c) the adjournment of the meeting,
unless there are present in person or by proxy at least 3 creditors, or all the creditors, if their number does not exceed 3, being in either case persons entitled to vote.
(2) One person present constitutes a quorum if –
(a) he is himself a creditor with entitlement to vote and he holds a number of proxies sufficient to ensure that, with his own vote, paragraph (1) of this Rule is complied with, or
(b) being the chairman or any other person, he holds that number of proxies.

6.93 Entitlement to vote (1) Subject as follows, at a meeting of creditors a person is entitled to vote as a creditor only if –
(a) there has been duly lodged a proof of the debt claimed to be due to him from the bankrupt, and the claim has been admitted under Rule 6.94 for the purpose of entitlement to vote, and
(b) there has been lodged, by the time and date stated in the notice of the meeting, any proxy requisite for that entitlement,
(2) The court may, in exceptional circumstances, by order declare the creditors, or any class of them, entitled to vote at creditors' meetings, without being required to prove their debts.

Where a creditor is so entitled, the court may, on the application of the trustee, make such consequential orders as it thinks fit (as for example an order treating a creditor as having proved his debt for the purpose of permitting payment of dividend).
(3) A creditor shall not vote in respect of a debt for an unliquidated amount, or any debt whose value is not ascertained, except where the chairman agrees to put upon the debt an estimated value for the purpose of entitlement to vote and admits his proof for that purpose.
(4) A secured creditor is entitled to vote only in respect of the balance (if any) of his debt after deducting the value of his security as estimated by him.
(5) A creditor shall not vote in respect of a debt on, or secured by, a current bill of exchange or promisory note, unless he is willing –
(a) to treat the liability to him on the bill or note of every person who is liable on it antecedently to the bankrupt, and against whom a bankruptcy order has not been made (or, in the case of a company, which has not gone into liquidation), as a security in his hands, and
(b) to estimate the value of the security and (for the purpose of entitlement to vote, but not for dividend) to deduct it from his proof.

6.94 Admission and rejection of proof (1) At any creditors' meeting the chairman has power to admit or reject a creditor's proof for the purpose of his entitlement to vote; and the power is exercisable with respect to the whole or any part of the proof.
(2) The chairman's decision under this Rule, or in respect of any matter arising under Rule 6.93, is subject to appeal to the court by any creditor, or by the bankrupt.
(3) If the chairman is in doubt whether a proof should be admitted or rejected, he shall mark it as objected to and allow the creditor to vote, subject to his vote being subsequently declared invalid if the objection to the proof is sustained.
(4) If on an appeal the chairman's decision is reversed or varied, or a creditor's vote is declared invalid, the court may order that another meeting be summoned, or make such other order as it thinks just.
(5) Neither the official receiver nor any person nominated by him to be chairman is personally liable for costs incurred by any person in respect of an application to the court under this Rule; and the chairman (if other than the official receiver or a person so nominated) is not so liable unless the court makes an order to that effect.

6.95 Record of proceedings (1) The chairman at any creditors' meeting shall cause minutes of the proceedings at the meeting, signed by him, to be retained by him as part of his records of the bankruptcy.
(2) He shall also cause to be made up and kept a list of all the creditors who attended the meeting.
(3) The minutes of the meeting shall include a record of every resolution passed; and it is the chairman's duty to see to it that particulars of all such resolutions, certified by him, are filed in court not more than 21 days after the date of the meeting.

CHAPTER 8: PROOF OF BANKRUPTCY DEBTS

Section A: Procedure for Proving

6.96 Meaning of 'prove' (1) A person claiming to be a creditor of the bankrupt and wishing to recover his debt in whole or in part must (subject to any order of the court under Rule 6.93(2)) submit his claim in writing to the official receiver, where acting as receiver and manager, or to the trustee.
(2) The creditor is referred to as 'proving' for his debt; and the document by which he seeks to establish his claim is his 'proof'.
(3) Subject to the next two paragraphs, the proof must be in the form known as 'proof of debt' (whether the form prescribed by the Rules, or a substantially similar form), which shall be made out by or under the directions of the creditor, and signed by him or a person authorised in that behalf. [FORM 6.37]
(4) Where a debt is due to a Minister of the Crown or a Government Department, the proof need not be in that form, provided that there are shown all such particulars of the debt as are required in the form used by other creditors, and as are relevant in the circumstances.
(5) Where an existing trustee proves in a later bankruptcy under section 335(5), the proof must be in Form 6.38.
(6) In certain circumstances, specified below in this Chapter, the proof must be in the form of an affidavit. [FORM 6.39]

6.97 Supply of forms (1) Forms to be used for the purpose of proving bankruptcy debts shall be sent out by the official receiver or the trustee to every creditor of the bankrupt who is known to the sender, or is identified in the bankrupt's statement of affairs.
(2) The forms shall accompany (whichever is first) –
(a) the notice to creditors under section 293(2) (official receiver's decision not to call meeting of creditors), or

(b) the first notice calling a meeting of creditors, or
(c) where a certificate of summary administration has been issued by the court, the notice sent by the official receiver under Rule 6.49(2), or
(d) where a trustee is appointed by the court, the notice of his appointment sent by him to creditors.

(3) Where, with the leave of the court under section 297(7), the trustee advertises his appointment, he shall send proofs to the creditors within 4 months after the date of the bankruptcy order.

(4) The above paragraphs of this Rule are subject to any order of the court dispensing with the requirement to send out forms of proof, or altering the time at which the forms are to be sent.

6.98 Contents of proof (1) The following matters shall be stated in a creditor's proof of debt –
(a) the creditor's name and address;
(b) the total amount of his claim as at the date of the bankruptcy order;
(c) whether or not that amount includes outstanding uncapitalised interest;
(d) whether or not the claim includes value added tax;
(e) whether the whole or any part of the debt falls within any (and if so which) of the categories of preferential debts under section 386 of, and Schedule 6 to, the Act (as read with Schedule 3 of the Social Security Pensions Act 1975);
(f) particulars of how and when the debt was incurred by the debtor;
(g) particulars of any security held, the date when it was given and the value which the creditor puts upon it; and
(h) the name, address and authority of the person signing the proof (if other than the creditor himself).

(2) There shall be specified in the proof any documents by reference to which the debt can be substantiated; but (subject as follows) it is not essential that such documents be attached to the proof or submitted with it.

(3) The trustee, or the convener or chairman of any meeting, may call for any document or other evidence to be produced to him, where he thinks it necessary for the purpose of substantiating the whole or any part of the claim in the proof.

6.99 Claim established by affidavit (1) The trustee may, if he thinks it necessary, require a claim of debt to be verified by affidavit, for which purpose there shall be used the form known as 'affidavit of debt'. [FORM 6.39]

(2) An affidavit may be required notwithstanding that a proof of debt has already been lodged.

(3) The affidavit may be sworn before an official receiver or a deputy official receiver, or before an officer of the Department or of the court duly authorised in that behalf.

6.100 Cost of proving (1) Subject as follows, every creditor bears the cost of proving his own debt, including such as may be incurred in providing documents or evidence under Rule 6.98(3).

(2) Costs incurred by the trustee in estimating the value of a bankruptcy debt under section 322(3) (debts not bearing a certain value) fall on the estate, as an expense of the bankruptcy.

(3) Paragraphs (1) and (2) apply unless the court otherwise orders.

6.101 Trustee to allow inspection of proofs The trustee shall, so long as proofs lodged with him are in his hand, allow them to be inspected, at all reasonable times on any business day, by any of the following persons –

(a) any creditor who has submitted his proof of debt (unless his proof has been wholly rejected for purposes of dividend or otherwise),
(b) the bankrupt, and
(c) any person acting on behalf of either of the above.

6.102 Proof of licensed moneylender A proof of debt in respect of a moneylending transaction made before 27 January 1980, where the creditor was at the time of the transaction a licensed moneylender, shall have endorsed on or annexed to it a statement setting out in detail the particulars mentioned in section 9(2) of the Moneylenders Act 1927.

6.103 Transmission of proofs to trustee (1) Where a trustee is appointed, the official receiver shall forthwith transmit to him all the proofs which he has so far received, together with an itemised list of them.
(2) The trustee shall sign the list by way of receipt for the proofs, and return it to the official receiver.
(3) From then on, all proofs of debt shall be sent to the trustee and retained by him.

6.104 Admission and rejection of proofs for dividend (1) A proof may be admitted for dividend either for the whole amount claimed by the creditor, or for part of that amount.
(2) If the trustee rejects a proof in whole or in part, he shall prepare a written statement of his reasons for doing so, and send it forthwith to the creditor.

6.105 Appeal against decision on proof (1) If a creditor is dissatisfied with the trustee's decision with respect to his proof (including any decision on the question of preference), he may apply to the court for the decision to be reversed or varied.
The application must be made within 21 days of his receiving the statement sent under Rule 6.104(2).
(2) The bankrupt or any other creditor may, if dissatisfied with the trustee's decision admitting or rejecting the whole or any part of a proof, make such an application within 21 days of becoming aware of the trustee's decision.
(3) Where application is made to the court under this Rule, the court shall fix a venue for the application to be heard, notice of which shall be sent by the applicant to the creditor who lodged the proof in question (if it is not himself) and to the trustee.
(4) The trustee shall, on receipt of the notice, file in court the relevant proof, together (if appropriate) with a copy of the statement sent under Rule 6.104(2).
(5) After the application has been heard and determined, the proof shall, unless it has been wholly disallowed, be returned by the court to the trustee.
(6) The official receiver is not personally liable for costs incurred by any person in respect of an application under this Rule; and the trustee (if other than the official receiver) is not so liable unless the court makes an order to that effect.

6.106 Withdrawal or variation of proof A creditor's proof may at any time, by agreement between himself and the trustee, be withdrawn or varied as to the amount claimed.

6.107 Expunging of proof by the court (1) The court may expunge a proof or reduce the amount claimed –
(a) on the trustee's application, where he thinks that the proof has been improperly admitted, or ought to be reduced; or
(b) on the application of a creditor, if the trustee declines to interfere in the matter.
(2) Where application is made to the court under this Rule, the court shall fix a venue for the application to be heard, notice of which shall be sent by the applicant –

(a) in the case of an application by the trustee, to the creditor who made the proof, and
(b) in the case of an application by a creditor, to the trustee and to the creditor who made the proof (if not himself).

Section B: Quantification of Claim

6.108 Negotiable instruments, etc Unless the trustee allows, a proof in respect of money owed on a bill of exchange, promissory note, cheque or other negotiable instrument or security cannot be admitted unless there is produced the instrument or security itself or a copy of it, certified by the creditor or his authorised representative to be a true copy.

6.109 Secured creditors (1) If a secured creditor realises his security, he may prove for the balance of his debt, after deducting the amount realised.
(2) If a secured creditor voluntarily surrenders his security for the general benefit of creditors, he may prove for his whole debt, as if it were unsecured.

6.110 Discounts There shall in every case be deducted from the claim all trade and other discounts which would have been available to the bankrupt but for his bankruptcy, except any discount for immediate, early or cash settlement.

6.111 Debt in foreign currency (1) For the purpose of proving a debt incurred or payable in a currency other than sterling, the amount of the debt shall be converted into sterling at the official exchange rate prevailing on the date of the bankruptcy order.
(2) 'The official exchange rate' is the middle market rate at the Bank of England, as published for the date in question. In the absence of any such published rate, it is such rate as the court determines.

6.112 Payments of a periodical nature (1) In the case of rent and other payments of a periodical nature, the creditor may prove for any amounts due and unpaid up to the date of the bankruptcy order.
(2) Where at that date any payment was accruing due, the creditor may prove for so much as would have fallen due at that date, if accruing from day to day.

6.113 Interest (1) In the following circumstances the creditor's claim may include interest on the debt for periods before the bankruptcy order, although not previously reserved or agreed.
(2) If the debt is due by virtue of a written instrument and payable at a certain time, interest may be claimed for the period from that time to the date of the bankruptcy order.
(3) If the debt is due otherwise, interest may only be claimed if, before the presentation of the bankruptcy petition, a demand for payment was made in writing by or on behalf of the creditor, and notice given that interest would be payable from the date of the demand to the date of payment.

In that case interest may be claimed under this Rule for the period from the date of the demand to that of the bankruptcy order.
(4) The rate of interest to be claimed under this Rule is the rate specified in section 17 of the Judgments Act 1838 on the date of the bankruptcy order; except that, where the case falls within paragraph (3), the rate is that specified in the notice there referred to, not exceeding the rate under the Judgments Act as mentioned above.

6.114 Debt payable at future time A creditor may prove for a debt of which payment was not yet due at the date of the bankruptcy order, but subject to Rule 11.13 in Part 11 of the Rules (adjustment of dividend where payment made before time).

CHAPTER 9: SECURED CREDITORS

6.115 Value of security (1) A secured creditor may, with the agreement of the trustee or the leave of the court, at any time alter the value which he has, in his proof of debt, put upon his security.
(2) However, if a secured creditor –
(a) being the petitioner, has in the petition put a value on his security, or
(b) has voted in respect of the unsecured balance of his debt,
he may re-value his security only with leave of the court.

6.116 Surrender for non-disclosure (1) If a secured creditor omits to disclose his security in his proof of debt, he shall surrender his security for the general benefit of creditors, unless the court, on application by him, relieves him from the effect of this Rule on the ground that the omission was inadvertent or the result of honest mistake.
(2) If the court grants that relief, it may require or allow the creditor's proof of debt to be amended, on such terms as may be just.

6.117 Redemption by trustee The trustee may at any time give notice to a creditor whose debt is secured that he proposes, at the expiration of 28 days from the date of the notice, to redeem the security at the value put upon it in the creditor's proof.
(2) The creditor then has 21 days (or such longer period as the trustee may allow) in which, if he so wishes, to exercise his right to re-value his security (with the leave of the court, where Rule 6.115(2) applies).

If the creditor re-values his security, the trustee may only redeem at the new value.
(3) If the trustee redeems the security, the cost of transferring it is borne by the estate.
(4) A secured creditor may at any time, by a notice in writing, call on the trustee to elect whether he will or will not exercise his power to redeem the security at the value then placed on it; and the trustee then has 6 months in which to exercise the power or determine not to exercise it.

6.118 Test of security's value (1) Subject as follows, the trustee, if he is dissatisfied with the value which a secured creditor puts on his security (whether in his proof or by way of re-valuation under Rule 6.117), may require any property comprised in the security to be offered for sale.
(2) The terms of sale shall be such as may be agreed, or as the court may direct; and if the sale is by auction, the trustee on behalf of the estate, and the creditor on his own behalf, may appear and bid.
(3) This Rule does not apply if the security has been re-valued and the re-valuation has been approved by the court.

6.119 Realisation of security by creditor If a creditor who has valued his security subsequently realises it (whether or not at the instance of the trustee) –
(a) the net amount realised shall be substituted for the value previously put by the creditor on the security, and

(b) that amount shall be treated in all respects as an amended valuation made by him.

CHAPTER 10: THE TRUSTEE IN BANKRUPTCY

Section A: Appointment and Associated Formalities

6.120 Appointment by creditors' meeting (1) This Rule applies where a person has been appointed trustee by resolution of a creditors' meeting.
(2) The chairman of the meeting shall certify the appointment, but not unless and until the person to be appointed has provided him with a written statement to the effect that he is an insolvency practitioner, duly qualified under the Act to act as trustee in relation to the bankrupt, and that he consents so to act. [FORM 6.40 or FORM 6.41]
(3) The chairman (if not himself the official receiver) shall send the certificate to the official receiver.
(4) The official receiver shall in any case file a copy of the certificate in court; and the trustee's appointment is effective as from the date on which the official receiver files the copy certificate in court, that date to be endorsed on the copy certificate.
The certificate, so endorsed, shall be sent by the official receiver to the trustee.

6.121 Appointment by the court (1) This Rule applies where the court under section 297(3), (4) or (5) appoints the trustee. [FORM 6.42 or FORM 6.43]
(2) The court's order shall not issue unless and until the person appointed has filed in court a statement to the effect that he is an insolvency practitioner, duly qualified under the Act to be the trustee, and that he consents so to act.
(3) Thereafter, the court shall send 2 copies of the order to the official receiver. One of the copies shall be sealed, and this shall be sent by him to the person appointed as trustee.
(4) The trustee's appointment takes effect from the date of the order.

6.122 Appointment by Secretary of State (1) This Rule applies where the official receiver –
(a) under section 295 or 300, refers to the Secretary of State the need for an appointment of a trustee, or
(b) under section 296, applies to the Secretary of State to make the appointment.
(2) If the Secretary of State makes an appointment he shall send two copies of the certificate of appointment to the official receiver, who shall transmit one such copy to the person appointed, and file the other copy in court.
The certificate shall specify the date from which the trustee's appointment is to be effective.

6.123 Authentication of trustee's appointment Where a trustee is appointed under any of the 3 preceding Rules, a sealed copy of the order of appointment or (as the case may be) a copy of the certificate of his appointment may in any proceedings be adduced as proof that he is duly authorised to exercise the powers and perform the duties of trustee of the bankrupt's estate.

6.124 Advertisement of appointment (1) Where the trustee is appointed by a creditors' meeting, he shall, forthwith after receiving his certificate of appointment, give notice of his appointment in such newspaper as he thinks most appropriate for ensuring that it comes to the notice of the bankrupt's creditors.
(2) The expense of giving the notice shall be borne in the first instance by the trustee; but he is entitled to be reimbursed by the estate, as an expense of the bankruptcy.

The same applies also in the case of the notice or advertisement under section 296(4) (appointment of trustee by Secretary of State), and of the notice or advertisement under section 297(7) (appointment by the court).

6.125 Hand-over of estate to trustee (1) This Rule applies only where –
(a) the bankrupt's estate vests in the trustee under Chapter IV of part IX of the Act, following a period in which the official receiver is the receiver and manager of the estate according to section 287, or
(b) the trustee is appointed in succession to the official receiver acting as trustee.
(2) When the trustee's appointment takes effect, the official receiver shall forthwith do all that is required for putting him into possession of the estate.
(3) On taking possession of the estate, the trustee shall discharge any balance due to the official receiver on account of –
(a) expenses properly incurred by him and payable under the Act or the Rules, and
(b) any advances made by him in respect of the estate, together with interest on such advances at the rate specified in section 17 of the Judgments Act 1838 on the date of the bankruptcy order.
(4) Alternatively, the trustee may (before taking office) give to the official receiver a written undertaking to discharge any such balance out of the first realisation of assets.
(5) The official receiver has a charge on the estate in respect of any sums due to him under paragraph (3). But, where the trustee has realised assets with a view to making those payments, the official receiver's charge does not extend in respect of sums deductible by the trustee from the proceeds of realisation, as being expenses properly incurred therein.
(6) The trustee shall from time to time out of the realisation of assets discharge all guarantees properly given by the official receiver for the benefit of the estate, and shall pay all the official receiver's expenses.
(7) The official receiver shall give to the trustee all such information, relating to the affairs of the bankrupt and the course of the bankruptcy, as he (the official receiver) considers to be reasonably required for the effective discharge by the trustee of his duties in relation to the estate.
(8) The trustee shall also be furnished with any report of the official receiver under Chapter 6 of this Part of the Rules.

Section B: Resignation and Removal; Vacation of Office

6.126 Creditors' meeting to receive trustee's resignation (1) Before resigning his office, the trustee must call a meeting of creditors for the purpose of receiving his resignation. Notice of the meeting shall be sent to the official receiver at the same time as it is sent to creditors.
(2) The notice to creditors must be accompanied by an account of the trustee's administration of the bankrupt's estate, including –
(a) a summary of his receipts and payments and
(b) a statement by him that he has reconciled his account with that which is held by the Secretary of State in respect of the bankruptcy.
(3) Subject as follows, the trustee may only proceed under this Rule on grounds of ill health or because –
(a) he intends ceasing to be in practice as an insolvency practitioner, or
(b) there is some conflict of interest or change of personal circumstances which precludes or makes impracticable the further discharge by him of the duties of trustee.
(4) Where two or more persons are acting as trustee jointly, any one of them may proceed under this Rule (without prejudice to the continuation in office of the other

or others) on the ground that, in his opinion and that of the other or others, it is no longer expedient that there should continue to be the present number of joint trustees.

6.127 Action following acceptance of resignation (1) Where a meeting of creditors is summoned for the purpose of accepting the trustee's resignation, the notice summoning it shall indicate that that is the purpose, or one of the purposes, of the meeting; and the notice shall draw the attention of creditors to Rule 6.135 with respect to the trustee's release.
(2) A copy of the notice shall at the same time also be sent to the official receiver.
(3) Where the chairman of the meeting is other than the official receiver, and there is passed at the meeting any of the following resolutions –
(a) that the trustee's resignation be accepted,
(b) that a new trustee be appointed,
(c) that the resigning trustee be not given his release.
the chairman shall, within 3 days, send to the official receiver a copy of the resolution.

If it has been resolved to accept the trustee's resignation, the chairman shall send to the official receiver a certificate to that effect. [FORM 6.44]
(4) If the creditors have resolved to appoint a new trustee, the certificate of his appointment shall also be sent to the official receiver within that time; and Rule 6.120 above shall be complied with in respect of it.
(5) If the trustee's resignation is accepted, the notice of it required by section 298(7) shall be given by him forthwith after the meeting; and he shall send a copy of the notice to the official receiver.

The notice shall be accompanied by a copy of the account sent to creditors under Rule 6.126(2).
(6) The official receiver shall file a copy of the notice in court.
(7) The trustee's resignation is effective as from the date on which the official receiver files the copy notice in court, that date to be endorsed on the copy notice.

6.128 Leave to resign granted by the court (1) If at a creditors' meeting summoned to accept the trustee's resignation it is resolved that it be not accepted, the court may, on the trustee's application, make an order giving him leave to resign. [FORM 6.45]
(2) The court's order under this Rule may include such provision as it thinks fit with respect to matters arising in connection with the resignation, and shall determine the date from which the trustee's release is effective.
(3) The court shall send two sealed copies of the order to the trustee, who shall send one of the copies forthwith to the official receiver.
(4) On sending notice of his resignation to the court, as required by section 298(7), the trustee shall send a copy of it to the official receiver. [FORM 6.46]

6.129 Meeting of creditors to remove trustee (1) Where a meeting of creditors is summoned for the purpose of removing the trustee, the notice summoning it shall indicate that that is the purpose, or one of the purposes, of the meeting; and the notice shall draw the attention of creditors to section 299(3) with respect to the trustee's release. [FORM 6.35]
(2) A copy of the notice shall at the same time also be sent to the official receiver.
(3) At the meeting, a person other than the trustee or his nominee may be elected to act as chairman; but if the trustee or his nominee is chairman and a resolution has been proposed for the trustee's removal, the chairman shall not adjourn the meeting without the consent of at least one-half (in value) of the creditors present (in person or by proxy) and entitled to vote.

(4) Where the chairman of the meeting is other than the official receiver, and there is passed at the meeting any of the following resolutions:
(a) that the trustee be removed,
(b) that a new trustee be appointed,
(c) that the removed trustee be not given his release,
the chairman shall, within 3 days, send to the official receiver a copy of the resolution.

If it has been resolved to remove the trustee, the chairman shall send to the official receiver a certificate to that effect. [FORM 6.47]
(5) If the creditors have resolved to appoint a new trustee, the certificate of his appointment shall also be sent to the official receiver within that time; and Rule 6.120 shall be complied with in respect of it.

6.130 Court's power to regulate meeting under Rule 6.129 Where a meeting under Rule 6.129 is to be held, or is proposed to be summoned, the court may on the application of any creditor give directions as to the mode of summoning it, the sending out and return of forms of proxy, the conduct of the meeting, and any other matter which appears to the court to require regulation or control.

6.131 Procedure on removal (1) Where the creditors have resolved that the trustee be removed, the official receiver shall file the certificate of removal in court.
(2) The resolution is effective as from the date on which the official receiver files the certificate of removal in court, and that date shall be endorsed on the certificate.
(3) A copy of the certificate, so endorsed, shall be sent by the official receiver to the trustee who has been removed and, if a new trustee has been appointed, to him.
(4) The official receiver shall not file the certificate in court until the Secretary of State has certified to him that the removed trustee has reconciled his account with that held by the Secretary of State in respect of the bankruptcy.

6.132 Removal of trustee by the court (1) This Rule applies where application is made to the court for the removal of the trustee, or for an order directing the trustee to summon a meeting of creditors for the purpose of removing him. [FORM 6.48]
(2) The court may, if it thinks that no sufficient cause is shown for the application, dismiss it; but it shall not do so unless the applicant has had an opportunity to attend the court for an ex parte hearing, of which he has been given at least 7 days' notice.

If the application is not dismissed under this paragraph, the court shall fix a venue for it to be heard.
(3) The applicant shall, at least 14 days before the hearing, send to the trustee and the official receiver notice stating the venue so fixed; and the notice shall be accompanied by a copy of the application, and of any evidence which the applicant intends to adduce in support of it.
(4) Subject to any contrary order of the court, the costs of the application do not fall on the estate.
(5) Where the court removes the trustee –
(a) it shall send copies of the order of removal to him and to the official receiver;
(b) the order may include such provision as the court thinks fit with respect to matters arising in connection with the removal; and
(c) if the court appoints a new trustee, Rule 6.121 applies.

6.133 Removal of trustee by Secretary of State (1) If the Secretary of State decides to remove the trustee, he shall before doing so notify the trustee and the official receiver of his decision and the grounds of it, and specify a period within which the trustee may make representations against implementation of the decision.

(2) If the Secretary of State directs the removal of the trustee, he shall forthwith –
(a) file notice of his decision in court, and
(b) send notice to the trustee and the official receiver.
(3) If the trustee is removed by direction of the Secretary of State, the court may make any such order in his case as it would have power to make if he had been removed by itself.

6.134 Advertisement of resignation or removal (1) Where a new trustee is appointed in place of one who has resigned or been removed, the new trustee shall, in the advertisement of this appointment, state that his predecessor has resigned or, as the case may be, been removed and (if it be the case) that he has been given his release.

6.135 Release of resigning or removed trustee (1) Where the trustee's resignation is accepted by a meeting of creditors which has not resolved against his release, he has his release from when his resignation is effective under Rule 6.127.
(2) Where the trustee is removed by a meeting of creditors which has not resolved against his release, the fact of his release shall be stated in the certificate of removal.
(3) Where –
(a) the trustee resigns, and the creditors' meeting called to receive his resignation has resolved against his release, or
(b) he is removed by a creditors' meeting which has so resolved, or is removed by the court.
he must apply to the Secretary of State for his release.
(4) When the Secretary of State gives the release, he shall certify it accordingly, and send the certificate to the official receiver, to be filed in court. [FORM 6.49]
(5) A copy of the certificate shall be sent by the Secretary of State to the former trustee, whose release is effective from the date of the certificate.

Section C: Release on Completion of Administration

6.136 Release of official receiver (1) The official receiver shall, before giving notice to the Secretary of State under section 299(2) (that the administration of the estate is for practical purposes complete), send out notice of his intention to do so to all creditors who have proved their debts, and to the bankrupt.
(2) The notice shall in each case be accompanied by a summary of the official receiver's receipts and payments as trustee.
(3) The Secretary of State, when he has under section 299(2) determined the date from which the official receiver is to have his release, shall give notice to the court that he has done so. The notice shall be accompanied by the summary referred to in paragraph (2).

6.137 Final meeting of creditors (1) Where the trustee is other than the official receiver, he shall give at least 28 days' notice of the final meeting of creditors to be held under section 331. The notice shall be sent to all creditors who have proved their debts, and to the bankrupt. [FORM 6.35]
(2) The trustee's report laid before the meeting under that section shall include –
(a) a summary of his receipts and payments.
(b) a statement by him that he has reconciled his account with that which is held by the Secretary of State in respect of the bankruptcy.
(3) At the final meeting, the creditors may question the trustee with respect to any matter contained in his report, and may resolve against him having his release.
(4) The trustee shall give notice to the court that the final meeting has been held; and the notice shall state whether or not he has been given his release, and be

accompanied by a copy of the report laid before the final meeting. A copy of the notice shall be sent by the trustee to the official receiver. [FORM 6.50]
(5) If there is no quorum present at the final meeting, the trustee shall report to the court that a final meeting was summoned in accordance with the Rules, but there was no quorum present; and the final meeting is then deemed to have been held, and the creditors not to have resolved against the trustee having his release.
(6) If the creditors at the final meeting have not so resolved, the trustee is released when the notice under paragraph (4) is filed in court, if they have so resolved, the trustee must obtain his release from the Secretary of State, as provided by Rule 6.135.

Section D: Remuneration

6.138 Fixing of remuneration (1) The trustee is entitled to receive remuneration for his services as such.
(2) The remuneration shall be fixed either –
(a) as a percentage of the value of the assets in the bankrupt's estate which are realised or distributed, or of the one value and the other in combination, or
(b) by reference to the time properly given by the insolvency practitioner (as trustee) and his staff in attending to matters arising in the bankruptcy.
(3) Where the trustee is other than the official receiver, it is for the creditors' committee (if there is one) to determine whether his remuneration is to be fixed under paragraph (2)(a) or (b) and, if under paragraph (2)(a), to determine any percentage to be applied as there mentioned.
(4) In arriving at that determination, the committee shall have regard to the following matters –
(a) the complexity (or otherwise) of the case,
(b) any respects in which, in connection with the administration of the estate, there falls on the insolvency practitioner (as trustee) any responsibility of an exceptional kind of degree,
(c) the effectiveness with which the insolvency practitioner appears to be carrying out, or to have carried out, his duties as trustee, and
(d) the value and nature of the assets in the estate with which the trustee has to deal.
(5) If there is no creditors' committee, or the committee does not make the requisite determination, the trustee's remuneration may be fixed (in accordance with paragraph (2)) by a resolution of a meeting of creditors; and paragraph (4) applies to them as it does to the creditors' committee.
(6) If not fixed as above, the trustee's remuneration shall be on the scale laid down for the official receiver by general regulations.

6.139 Other matters affecting remuneration (1) Where the trustee sells assets on behalf of a secured creditor, he is entitled to take for himself, out of the proceeds of sale, a sum by way of remuneration equivalent to the remuneration chargeable in corresponding circumstances by the official receiver under general regulations.
(2) Where there are joint trustees, it is for them to agree between themselves as to how the remuneration payable should be apportioned. Any dispute arising between them may be referred –
(a) to the court, for settlement by order, or
(b) to the creditors' committee or a meeting of creditors, for settlement by resolution.
(3) If the trustee is a solicitor and employs his own firm, or any partner in it, to act on behalf of the estate, profit costs shall not be paid unless this is authorised by the creditors' committee, the creditors or the court.

6.140 Recourse of trustee to meeting of creditors If the trustee's remuneration has been fixed by the creditors' committee, and he considers the rate or amount to be insufficient, he may request that it be increased by resolution of the creditors.

6.141 Recourse to the court (1) If the trustee considers that the remuneration fixed for him by the creditors' committee, or by resolution of the creditors, or as under Rule 6.138(6), is insufficient, he may apply to the court for an order increasing its amount or rate.
(2) The trustee shall give at least 14 days' notice of his application to the members of the creditors' committee; and the committee may nominate one or more members to appear or be represented, and to be heard, on the application.
(3) If there is no creditors' committee, the trustee's notice of his application shall be sent to such one or more of the bankrupt's creditors as the court may direct, which creditors may nominate one or more of their number to appear or be represented.
(4) The court may, if it appears to be a proper case, order the costs of the trustee's application, including the costs of any member of the creditors' committee appearing on it, or any creditor so appearing, to be paid out of the estate.

6.142 Creditor's claim that remuneration is excessive (1) Any creditor of the bankrupt may, with the concurrence of at least 25 per cent. in value of the creditors (including himself), apply to the court for an order that the trustee's remuneration be reduced, on the grounds that it is, in all the circumstances, excessive.
(2) The court may, if it thinks that no sufficient cause is shown for the application, dismiss it; but it shall not do so unless the applicant has had an opportunity to attend the court for an ex parte hearing, of which he has been given at least 7 days' notice.
If the application is not dismissed under this paragraph, the court shall fix a venue for it to be heard.
(3) The applicant shall, at least 14 days before the hearing, send to the trustee a notice stating the venue so fixed; and the notice shall be accompanied by a copy of the application, and of any evidence which the applicant intends to adduce in support of it.
(4) If the court considers the application to be well-founded, it shall make an order fixing the remuneration at a reduced amount or rate.
(5) Unless the court orders otherwise, the costs of the application shall be paid by the applicant, and do not fall on the estate.

Section E: Supplementary Provisions

6.143 Trustee deceased (1) Subject as follows, where the trustee (other than the official receiver) has died, it is the duty of his personal representatives to give notice of the fact to the official receiver, specifying the date of the death.
This does not apply if notice has been given under any of the following paragraphs of this Rule.
(2) If the deceased trustee was a partner in a firm, notice may be given to the official receiver by a partner in the firm who is qualified to act as an insolvency practitioner, or is a member of any body recognised by the Secretary of State for the authorisation of insolvency practitioners.
(3) Notice of the death may be given by any person producing to the official receiver the relevant death certificate or a copy of it.
(4) The official receiver shall give notice to the court, for the purpose of fixing the time of the deceased trustee's release in accordance with section 299(3)(a).

6.144 Loss of qualification as insolvency practitioner (1) This Rule applies where

the trustee vacates office, under section 298(6), on his ceasing to be qualified to act as an insolvency practitioner in relation to the bankrupt.
(2) The trustee vacating office shall forthwith give notice of his doing so to the official receiver, who shall give notice to the Secretary of State.
The official receiver shall file in court a copy of his notice under this paragraph. [FORM 6.51]
(3) Rule 6.135 applies as regard the trustee obtaining his release, as if he had been removed by the court.

6.145 Notice to official receiver of intention to vacate office (1) Where the trustee intends to vacate office, whether by resignation or otherwise, and there remain in the estate any unrealised assets, he shall give notice of his intention to the official receiver, informing him of the nature, value and whereabouts of the assets in question.
(2) Where there is to be a creditors' meeting to accept the trustee's resignation, or otherwise in respect of his vacation of office, the notice to the official receiver must be given at least 21 days before the meeting.

6.146 Trustee's duties on vacating office (1) Where the trustee ceases to be in office as such, in consequence of removal, resignation or cesser of qualification as an insolvency practitioner, he is under obligation forthwith to deliver up to the person succeeding him as trustee the assets of the estate (after deduction of any expenses properly incurred, and distributions made, by him) and further to deliver up to that person –
(a) the records of the bankruptcy, including correspondence, proofs and other related papers appertaining to the bankruptcy while it was within his responsibility, and
(b) the bankrupt's books, papers and other records.
(2) When the administration of the bankrupt's estate is for practical purposes complete, the trustee shall forthwith file in court all proofs remaining with him in the proceedings.

6.147 Power of court to set aside certain transactions (1) If in the administration of the estate the trustee enters into any transaction with a person who is an associate of his, the court may, on the application of any person interested, set the transaction aside and order the trustee to compensate the estate for any loss suffered in consequence of it.
(2) This does not apply if either –
(a) the transaction was entered into with the prior consent of the court, or
(b) it is shown to the court's satisfaction that the transaction was for value, and that it was entered into by the trustee without knowing, or having any reason to suppose, that the person concerned was an associate.
(3) Nothing in this Rule is to be taken as prejudicing the operation of any rule of law or equity with respect to a trustee's dealings with trust property, or the fiduciary obligations of any person.

6.148 Rule against solicitation (1) Where the court is satisfied that any improper solicitation has been used by or on behalf of the trustee in obtaining proxies or procuring his appointment, it may order that no remuneration out of the estate be allowed to any person by whom, or on whose behalf, the solicitation was exercised.
(2) An order of the court under this Rule overrides any resolution of the creditors' committee or the creditors, or any other provision of the Rules relating to the trustee's remuneration.

6.149 Enforcement of trustee's obligation to official receiver (1) The court may, on the application of the official receiver, make such orders as it thinks necessary for enforcement of the duties of the trustee under section 305(3) (information and assistance to be given; production and inspection of books and records relating to the bankruptcy).
(2) An order of the court under this Rule may provide that all costs of and incidental to the official receiver's application shall be borne by the trustee.

CHAPTER 11: THE CREDITORS' COMMITTEE

6.150 Membership of creditors' committee (1) The creditors' committee shall consist of at least 3, and not more than 5, members.
(2) All the members of the committee must be creditors of the bankrupt; and any creditor (other than one who is fully secured) may be a member, so long as –
(a) he has lodged a proof of his debt, and
(b) his proof has neither been wholly disallowed for voting purposes, nor wholly rejected for the purposes of distribution or dividend.
(3) A body corporate may be a member of the committee, but it cannot act as such otherwise than by a representative appointed under Rule 6.156.

6.151 Formalities of establishment (1) The creditors' committee does not come into being, and accordingly cannot act, until the trustee has issued a certificate of its due constitution. [FORM 6.52]
(2) If the chairman of the creditors' meeting which resolves to establish the committee is not the trustee, he shall forthwith give notice of the resolution to the trustee (or, as the case may be, the person appointed as trustee by that same meeting), and inform him of the names and addresses of the persons elected to be members of the committee.
(3) No person may act as a member of the committee unless and until he has agreed to do so; and the trustee's certificate of the committee's due constitution shall not issue before at least 3 persons elected to be members of it have agreed to act.
(4) As and when the others (if any) agree to act, the trustee shall issue an amended certificate. [FORM 6.52]
(5) The certificate, and any amended certificate, shall be filed in court by the trustee.
(6) If after the first establishment of the committee there is any change in its membership, the trustee shall report the change to the court. [FORM 6.53]

6.152 Obligations of trustee to committee (1) Subject as follows, it is the duty of the trustee to report to the members of the creditors' committee all such matters as appear to him to be, or as they have indicated to him as being, of concern to them with respect to the bankruptcy.
(2) In the case of matters so indicated to him by the committee, the trustee need not comply with any request for information where it appears to him that –
(a) the request is frivolous or unreasonable, or
(b) the cost of complying would be excessive, having regard to the relative importance of the information, or
(c) the estate is without funds sufficient for enabling him to comply.
(3) Where the committee has come into being more than 28 days after the appointment of the trustee, the latter shall report to them, in summary form, what actions he has taken since his appointment, and shall answer such questions as they may put to him regarding his conduct of the bankruptcy hitherto.
(4) A person who becomes a member of the committee at any time after its first establishment is not entitled to require a report to him by the trustee, otherwise than in summary form, of any matters previously arising.

(5) Nothing in this Rule disentitles the committee, or any member of it, from having access to the trustee's records of the bankruptcy, or from seeking an explanation of any matter within the committee's responsibility.

6.153 Meetings of the committee (1) Subject as follows, meetings of the creditors' committee shall be held when and where determined by the trustee.
(2) The trustee shall call a first meeting of the committee to take place within 3 months of his appointment or of the committee's establishment (whichever is the later); and thereafter he shall call a meeting –
(a) if so requested by a member of the committee or his representative (the meeting then to be held within 21 days of the request being received by the trustee), and
(b) for a specified date, if the committee has previously resolved that a meeting be held on that date.
(3) The trustee shall give 7 days' notice in writing of the venue of any meeting to every member of the committee (or his representative, if designated for that purpose), unless in any case the requirement of the notice has been waived by or on behalf of any member.
Waiver may be signified either at or before the meeting.

6.154 The chairman at meetings (1) The chairman at any meeting of the creditors' committee shall be the trustee, or a person appointed by him in writing to act.
(2) A person so nominated must be either –
(a) one who is qualified to act as an insolvency practitioner in relation to the bankrupt, or
(b) an employee of the trustee or his firm who is experienced in insolvency matters.

6.155 Quorum A meeting of the committee is duly constituted if due notice of it has been given to all the members and at least 2 of the members are present or represented.

6.156 Committee-members' representatives (1) A member of the creditors' committee may, in relation to the business of the committee, be represented by another person duly authorised by him for that purpose.
(2) A person acting as a committee-member's representative must hold a letter of authority entitling him so to act (either generally or specially). The letter must be signed by or on behalf of the committee-member.
(3) The chairman at any meeting of the committee may call on a person claiming to act as a committee-member's representative to produce his letter of authority, and may exclude him if it appears that his authority is deficient.
(4) No member may be represented by a body corporate, or by a person who is an undischarged bankrupt or is subject to a composition or arrangement with his creditors.
(5) No person shall –
(a) on the same committee, act at one and the same time as representative of more than one committee-member, or
(b) act both as a member of the committee and as representative of another member.
(6) Where the representative of a committee-member signs any document on the latter's behalf, the fact that he so signs must be stated below his signature.

6.157 Resignation A member of the creditors' committee may resign by notice in writing delivered to the trustee.

6.158 Termination of membership (1) A person's membership of the creditors' committee is automatically terminated if –
(a) he becomes bankrupt or compounds or arranges with his creditors, or
(b) at 3 consecutive meetings of the committee he is neither present nor represented (unless at the third of those meetings it is resolved that this Rule is not to apply in his case), or
(c) he ceases to be, or is found never to have been, a creditor.
(2) However, if the cause of termination is the member's bankruptcy, his trustee in bankruptcy replaces him as a member of the committee.

6.159 Removal A member of the creditor's committee may be removed by resolution at a meeting of creditors, at least 14 days notice having been given of the intention to move that resolution.

6.160 Vacancies (1) The following applies if there is a vacancy in the membership of the creditors' committee.
(2) The vacancy need not be filled if the trustee and a majority of the remaining committee-members so agree, provided that the number of members does not fall below the minimum required by Rule 6.150(1).
(3) The trustee may appoint any creditor (being qualified under the Rules to be a member of the committee) to fill the vacancy, if a majority of the other members of the committee agree to the appointment and the creditor concerned consents to act.
(4) Alternatively, a meeting of creditors may resolve that a creditor be appointed (with his consent) to fill the vacancy. In this case at least 14 days' notice must have been given of a resolution to make such an appointment (whether or not of a person named in the notice).
(5) Where the vacancy is filled by an appointment made by a creditors' meeting at which the trustee is not present, the chairman of the meeting shall report to the trustee the appointment which has been made.

6.161 Voting rights and resolutions (1) At any meeting of the committee, each member (whether present himself, or by his representative) has one vote; and a resolution is passed when a majority of the members present or represented have voted in favour of it.
(2) Every resolution passed shall be recorded in writing, either separately or as part of the minutes of the meeting. The record shall be signed by the chairman and kept with the records of the bankruptcy.

6.162 Resolutions by post (1) In accordance with this Rule, the trustee may seek to obtain the agreement of members of the creditors' committee to a resolution by sending to every member (or his representative designated for the purpose) a copy of the proposed resolution.
(2) Where the trustee makes use of the procedure allowed by this Rule, he shall send out to members of the committee or their representatives (as the case may be) a statement incorporating the resolution to which their agreement is sought, each resolution (if more than one) being set out in a separate document.
(3) Any member of the committee may, within 7 days from the date of the trustee sending out a resolution, require the trustee to summon a meeting of the committee to consider the matters raised by the resolution.
(4) In the absence of such a request, the resolution is deemed to have been carried in the committee if and when the trustee is notified in writing by a majority of the members that they concur with it.

(5) A copy of every resolution passed under this Rule, and a note that the concurrence of the committee was obtained, shall be kept with the records of the bankruptcy.

6.163 Trustee's reports (1) The trustee shall, as and when directed by the creditors' committee (but not more often than once in any period of 2 months), send a written report to every member of the committee setting out the position generally as regards the progress of the bankruptcy and matters arising in connection with it, to which he (the trustee) considers the committee's attention should be drawn.
(2) In the absence of any such directions by the committee, the trustee shall send a report not less often than once in every period of 6 months.
(3) The obligations of the trustee under this Rule are without prejudice to those imposed by Rule 6.152.

6.164 Expenses of members, etc The trustee shall defray out of the estate, in the forescribed order of priority, any reasonable travelling expenses directly incurred by members of the creditors' committee or their representatives in respect of their attendance at the committee's meetings, or otherwise on the committee's business.

6.165 Dealings by committee-members and others (1) This Rule applies to –
(a) any member of the creditors' committee,
(b) any committee-member's representative;
(c) any person who is an associate of a member of the committee or a committee-member's representative, and
(d) any person who has been a member of the committee at any time in the last 12 months.
(2) Subject as follows, a person to whom this Rule applies shall not enter into any transaction whereby he –
(a) receives out of the estate any payment for services given or goods supplied in connection with the estate's administration, or
(b) obtains any profit from the administration, or
(c) acquires any asset forming part of the estate.
(3) Such a transaction may be entered into by a person to whom this Rule applies –
(a) with the prior leave of the court, or
(b) if he does so as a matter of urgency, or by way of performance of a contract in force before the commencement of the bankruptcy, and obtains the court's leave for the transaction, having applied for it without undue delay, or
(c) with the prior sanction of the creditors' committee, where it is satisfied (after full disclosure of the circumstances) that the person will be giving full value in the transaction.
(4) Where in the committee a resolution is proposed that sanction be accorded for a transaction to be entered into which, without that sanction or the leave of the court, would be in contravention of this Rule, no member of the committee, and no representative of a member, shall vote if he is to participate directly or indirectly in the transaction.
(5) The court may, on the application of any person interested –
(a) set aside a transaction on the ground that it has been entered into in contravention of this Rule, and
(b) make with respect to it such other order as it thinks fit, including (subject to the following paragraph) an order requiring a person to whom this Rule applies to account for any profit obtained from the transaction and compensate the estate for any resultant loss.
(6) In the case of a person to whom this Rule applies as an associate of a member of the committee or of a committee-member's representative, the court shall not make

any order under paragraph (5), if satisfied that he entered into the relevant transaction without having any reason to suppose that in doing so he would contravene this Rule.
(7) The costs of an application to the court for leave under this Rule do not fall on the estate, unless the court so orders.

6.166 Committee's functions vested in Secretary of State (1) At any time when the functions of the creditors' committee are vested in the Secretary of State under section 302(1) or (2), requirements of the Act of the Rules about notices to be given, or reports to be made, to the committee by the trustee do not apply, otherwise than as enabling the committee to require a report as to any matter.
(2) Where the committee's functions are so vested under section 302(2), they may be exercised by the official receiver.

CHAPTER 12: SPECIAL MANAGER

6.167 Appointment and remuneration (1) An application made by the official receiver or trustee under section 370 for the appointment of a person to be special manager shall be supported by a report setting out the reasons for the application.
The report shall include the applicant's estimate of the value of the estate, property or business in respect of which the special manager is to be appointed.
(2) The court's order appointing the special manager shall specify the duration of his appointment, which may be for a period of time, or until the occurrence of a specified event. Alternatively, the order may specify that the duration of the appointment is to be subject to a further order of the court. [FORM 6.54]
(3) The appointment of a special manager may be renewed by order of the court.
(4) The special manager's remuneration shall be fixed from time to time by the court.

6.168 Security (1) The appointment of the special manager does not take effect until the person appointed has given (or, being allowed by the court to do so, undertaken to give) security to the person who applies for him to be appointed.
(2) It is not necessary that security shall be given for each separate bankruptcy; but it may be given either specially for a particular bankruptcy, or generally for any bankruptcy in relation to which the special manager may be employed as such.
(3) The amount of the security shall be not less than the value of the estate, property or business in respect of which he is appointed, as estimated by the applicant in his report under Rule 6.167(1).
(4) When the special manager has given security to the person applying for his appointment, that person's certificate as to the adequacy of the security shall be filed in court.
(5) The cost of providing the security shall be paid in the first instance by the special manager; but –
(a) if a bankruptcy order is not made, he is entitled to be reimbursed out of the property of the debtor, and the court may make an order on the debtor accordingly, and
(b) if a bankruptcy order is made, he is entitled to be reimbursed out of the estate in the prescribed order of priority.

6.169 Failure to give or keep up security (1) If the special manager fails to give the required security within the time stated for that purpose by the order appointing him, or any extension of that time that may be allowed, the official receiver or trustee (as the case may be) shall report the failure to the court, which may thereupon discharge the order appointing the special manager.

(2) If the special manager fails to keep up his security, the official receiver or trustee shall report his failure to the court, which may thereupon remove the special manager, and make such order as it thinks fit as to costs.
(3) If an order is made under this Rule removing the special manager, or discharging the order appointing him, the court shall give directions as to whether any, and if so what, steps should be taken for the appointment of another special manager in his place.

6.170 Accounting (1) The special manager shall produce accounts, containing details of his receipts and payments, for the approval of the trustee.
(2) The accounts shall be in respect of 3-month periods for the duration of the special manager's appointment (or for a lesser period, if his appointment terminates less than 3 months from its date, or from the date to which the last accounts were made up).
(3) When the accounts have been approved, the special manager's receipts and payments shall be added to those of the trustee.

6.171 Termination of appointment (1) The special manager's appointment terminates if the bankruptcy petition is dismissed or if, an interim receiver having been appointed, the latter is discharged without a bankruptcy order having been made.
(2) If the official receiver or the trustee is of opinion that the employment of the special manager is no longer necessary or profitable for the estate, he shall apply to the court for directions, and the court may order the special manager's appointment to be terminated.
(3) The official receiver or the trustee shall make the same application if a resolution of the creditors is passed, requesting that the appointment be terminated.

CHAPTER 13: PUBLIC EXAMINATION OF BANKRUPT

6.172 Order for public examination (1) If the official receiver applies to the court, under section 290, for the public examination of the bankrupt, a copy of the court's order shall, forthwith after its making, be sent by the official receiver to the bankrupt. [FORM 6.55]
(2) The order shall appoint a venue for the hearing, and direct the bankrupt's attendance thereat.
(3) The official receiver shall give at least 14 days' notice of the hearing –
(a) if a trustee has been nominated or appointed, to him;
(b) if a special manager has been appointed, to him; and
(c) subject to any contrary direction of the court, to every creditor of the bankrupt who is known to the official receiver or is identified in the bankrupt's statement of affairs.
(4) The official receiver may, if he thinks fit, cause notice of the order to be given, by public advertisement in one or more newspapers, at least 14 days before the day fixed for the hearing.

6.173 Order on request by creditors (1) A request by a creditor to the official receiver, under section 290(2), for the bankrupt to be publicly examined shall be made in writing and be accompanied by –
(a) a list of the creditors concurring with the request and the amount of their respective claims in the bankruptcy.

(b) from each creditor concurring, written confirmation of his concurrence, and
(c) a statement of the reasons why the examination is requested.

Sub-paragraphs (a) and (b) do not apply if the requisitioning creditor's debt is alone sufficient, without the concurrence of others. [FORM 6.56]

(2) Before an application to the court is made on the request, the requisitionist shall deposit with the official receiver such sum as the latter may determine to be appropriate by way of security for the expenses of the hearing of a public examination, if ordered.

(3) Subject as follows, the official receiver shall, within 28 days of receiving the request, make the application to the court required by section 290(2).

(4) If the official receiver is of opinion that the request is an unreasonable one in the circumstances, he may apply to the court for an order relieving him from the obligation to make the application otherwise required by that subsection.

(5) If the court so orders, and the application for the order was made ex parte, notice of the order shall be given forthwith by the official receiver to the requisitionist. If the application for an order is dismissed, the official receiver's application under section 290(2) shall be made forthwith on conclusion of the hearing of the application first mentioned.

6.174 Bankrupt unfit for examination (1) Where the bankrupt is suffering from any mental disorder or physical affliction or disability rendering him unfit to undergo or attend for public examination, the court may, on application in that behalf, either stay the order for his public examination or direct that it shall be conducted in such manner and at such place as it thinks fit. [FORM 6.57]

(2) Application under this Rule shall be made –

(a) by a person who has been appointed by a court in the United Kingdom or elsewhere to manage the affairs of, or to represent, the bankrupt, or
(b) by a relative or friend of the bankrupt whom the court considers to be a proper person to make the application, or
(c) by the official receiver.

(3) Where the application is made by a person other than the official receiver, then –

(a) it shall, unless the bankrupt is a patient within the meaning of the Mental Health Act 1983, be supported by the affidavit of a registered medical practitioner as to the bankrupt's mental and physical condition;
(b) at least 7 days' notice of the application shall be given to the official receiver and the trustee (if any); and
(c) before any order is made on the application, the applicant shall deposit with the official receiver such sum as the latter certifies to be necessary for the additional expenses of any examination that may be ordered on the application.

An order made on the application may provide that the expenses of the examination are to be payable, as to a specified proportion, out of the deposit under sub-paragraph (c), instead of out of the estate.

(4) Where the application is made by the official receiver, it may be made ex parte and may be supported by evidence in the form of a report by the official receiver to the court.

6.175 Procedure at hearing (1) The bankrupt shall at the hearing be examined on oath; and he shall answer all such questions as the court may put, or allow to be put, to him.

(2) Any of the persons allowed by section 290(4) to question the bankrupt may, with the approval of the court (made known either at the hearing or in advance of it), appear by solicitor or counsel; or he may in writing authorise another person to question the bankrupt on his behalf.

(3) The bankrupt may at his own expense employ a solicitor with or without counsel, who may put to him such questions as the court may allow for the purpose of enabling him to explain or qualify any answers given by him, and may make representations on his behalf.
(4) There shall be made in writing such record of the examination as the court thinks proper. The record shall be read over either to or by the bankrupt, signed by him, and verified by affidavit at a venue fixed by the court. [FORM 6.58]
(5) The written record may, in any proceedings (whether under the Act or otherwise) be used as evidence against the bankrupt of any statement made by him in the course of his public examination.
(6) If criminal proceedings have been instituted against the bankrupt, and the court is of opinion that the continuance of the hearing would be calculated to prejudice a fair trial of those proceedings, the hearing may be adjourned.

6.176 Adjournment (1) The public examination may be adjourned by the court from time to time, either to a fixed date or generally. [FORM 6.59]
(2) Where the examination has been adjourned generally, the court may at any time on the application of the official receiver or of the bankrupt –
(a) fix a venue for the resumption of the examination, and
(b) give directions as to the manner in which, and the time within which, notice of the resumed public examination is to be given to persons entitled to take part in it. [FORM 6.60]
(3) Where application under paragraph (2) is made by the bankrupt, the court may grant it on terms that the expenses of giving the notices required by that paragraph shall be paid by him and that, before a venue for the resumed public examination is fixed, he shall deposit with the official receiver such sum as the latter considers necessary to cover those expenses.
(4) Where the examination is adjourned generally, the official receiver may, there and then, make application under section 279(3) (suspension of automatic discharge).

6.177 Expenses of examination (1) Where a public examination of the bankrupt has been ordered by the court on a creditors' requisition under Rule 6.173, the court may order that the expenses of the examination are to be paid, as to a specified proportion, out of the deposit under Rule 6.173(2), instead of out of the estate.
(2) In no case do the costs and expenses of a public examination fall on the official receiver personally.

CHAPTER 14: DISCLAIMER

6.178 Trustee's notice of disclaimer (1) Where the trustee disclaims property under section 315, the notice of disclaimer shall contain such particulars of the property disclaimed as enable it to be easily identified. [FORM 6.61]
(2) The notice shall be signed by the trustee and filed in court, with a copy. The court shall secure that both the notice and the copy are sealed and endorsed with the date of filing.
(3) The copy notice, so sealed and endorsed, shall be returned by the court of the trustee as follows –
(a) if the notice has been delivered at the offices of the court by the trustee in person, it shall be handed to him,
(b) if it has been delivered by some person acting on the trustee's behalf, it shall be handed to that person, for immediate transmission to the trustee, and

(c) otherwise, it shall be sent to the trustee by first class post.

The court shall cause to be endorsed on the original notice, or otherwise recorded on the file, the manner in which the copy notice was returned to the trustee.

(4) For the purposes of section 315, the date of the prescribed notice is that which is endorsed on it, and on the copy, in accordance with this Rule.

6.179 Communication of disclaimer to persons interested (1) Within 7 days after the day on which a copy of the notice of disclaimer is returned to him, the trustee shall send or give copies of the notice (showing the date endorsed as required by Rule 6.18) to the persons mentioned in paragraphs (2) to (5) below.

(2) Where the property disclaimed is of a leasehold nature, he shall send or give a copy to every person who (to his knowledge) claims under the bankrupt as underlessee or mortgagee.

(3) Where the disclaimer is of property in a dwelling-house, he shall send or give a copy to every person who (to his knowledge) is in occupation of, or claims a right to occupy, the house.

(4) He shall in any case send or give a copy of the notice to every person who (to his knowledge) –

(a) claims an interest in the disclaimed property, or

(b) is under any liability in respect of the property, not being a liability discharged by the disclaimer.

(5) If the disclaimer is of an unprofitable contract, he shall send or give copies of the notice to all such persons as, to his knowledge, are parties to the contract or have interests under it.

(6) If subsequently it comes to the trustee's knowledge, in the case of any person, that he has such an interest in the disclaimed property as would have entitled him to receive a copy of the notice of disclaimer in pursuance of paragraphs (2) to (5), the trustee shall then forthwith send or give to that person a copy of the notice.

But compliance with this paragraph is not required if –

(a) the trustee is satisfied that, the person has already been made aware of the disclaimer and its date, or

(b) the court, on the trustee's application, orders that compliance is not required in that particular case.

6.180 Additional notices The trustee disclaiming property may, without prejudice to his obligations under sections 315 to 319 and Rules 6.178 and 6.179, at any time give notice of the disclaimer to any persons who in his opinion ought, in the public interest or otherwise, to be informed of it.

6.181 Duty to keep court informed The trustee shall notify the court from time to time as to the persons to whom he has sent or given copies of the notice of disclaimer under the two preceding Rules, giving their names and addresses, and the nature of their respective interests.

6.182 Application for leave to disclaim (1) Where under section 315(4) the trustee requires the leave of the court to disclaim property claimed for the bankrupt's estate under section 307 or 308, he may apply for that leave ex parte.

(2) The application must be accompanied by a report –

(a) giving such particulars of the property proposed to be disclaimed as enable it to be easily identified,

(b) setting out the reasons why, the property having been claimed for the estate, the court's leave to disclaim is now applied for, and

(c) specifying the persons (if any) who have been informed of the trustee's intention to make the application.

(3) If it is stated in the report that any person's consent to the disclaimer has been signified, a copy of that consent must be annexed to the report.
(4) The court may, on consideration of the application, grant the leave applied for, and it may, before granting leave –
(a) order that notice of the application be given to all such persons who, if the property is disclaimed, will be entitled to apply for a vesting or other order under section 320, and
(b) fix a venue for the hearing of the application under section 315(4).

6.183 Application by interested party under s 316 (1) The following applies where, in the case of any property, application is made to the trustee by an interested party under section 316 (request for decision whether the property is to be disclaimed or not).
(2) The application –
(a) shall be delivered to the trustee personally or by registered post, and
(b) shall be made in the form known as 'notice to elect', or a substantially similar form. [FORM 6.62]
(3) This paragraph applies in a case where the property concerned cannot be disclaimed by the trustee without the leave of the court.
If within the period of 28 days mentioned in section 316(1) the trustee applies to the court for leave to disclaim, the court shall extend the time allowed by that section for giving notice of disclaimer to a date not earlier than the date fixed for the hearing of the application.

6.184 Interest in property to be declared on request (1) If, in the case of property which the trustee has the right to disclaim, it appears to him that there is some person who claims, or may claim, to have an interest in the property, he may give notice to that person calling on him to declare within 14 days whether he claims any such interest and, if so, the nature and extent of it. [FORM 6.63]
[2] Failing compliance with the notice, the trustee is entitled to assume that the person concerned has no such interest in the property as will prevent or impede its disclaimer.

6.185 Disclaimer presumed valid and effective Any disclaimer of property by the trustee is presumed valid and effective, unless it is proved that he has been in breach of his duty with respect to the giving of notice of disclaimer, or otherwise under sections 315 to 319, or under this Chapter of the Rules.

6.186 Application for exercise of court's powers under s 320 (1) This Rule applies with respect to an application by any person under section 320 for an order of the court to vest or deliver disclaimed property.
(2) The application must be made within 3 months of the applicant becoming aware of the disclaimer, or of his receiving a copy of the trustee's notice of disclaimer sent under Rule 6.179, whichever is the earlier.
(3) The applicant shall with his application file an affidavit –
(a) stating whether he applies under paragraph (a) of section 320(2) (claim of interest in the property), under paragraph (b) (liability not discharged) or under paragraph (c) (occupation of dwelling house);
(b) specifying the date on which he received a copy of the trustee's notice of disclaimer, or otherwise became aware of the disclaimer; and
(c) specifying the grounds of his appalication and the order which he desires the court to make under section 320.
(4) The court shall fix a venue for the hearing of the application; and the applicant shall, not later than 7 days before the date fixed, give to the trustee notice of the

venue, accompanied by copies of the application and the affidavit under paragraph (3).
(5) On the hearing of the application, the court may give directions as to other persons (if any) who should be sent or given notice of the application and the grounds on which it is made.
(6) Sealed copies of any order made on the application shall be sent by the court to the applicant and the trustee.
(7) In a case where the property disclaimed is of a leasehold nature, or is property in a dwelling house, and section 317 or (as the case may be) section 318 applies to suspend the effect of the disclaimer, there shall be included in the court's order a direction giving effect to the disclaimer.
This paragraph does not apply if, at the time when the order is issued, other applications under section 320 are pending in respect of the same property.

CHAPTER 15: REPLACEMENT OF EXEMPT PROPERTY

6.187 Purchase of replacement property (1) A purchase of replacement property under section 308(3) may be made either before or after the realisation by the trustee of the value of the property vesting in him under the section.
(2) The trustee is under no obligation, by virtue of the section, to apply funds to the purchase of a replacement for property vested in him, unless and until he has sufficient funds in the estate for that purpose.

6.188 Money provided in lieu of sale (1) The following applies where a third party proposes to the trustee that he (the former) should provide the estate with a sum of money enabling the bankrupt to be left in possession of property which would otherwise be made to vest in the trustee under section 308.
(2) The trustee may accept that proposal, if satisfied that it is a reasonable one, and that the estate will benefit to the extent of the value of the property in question less the cost of a reasonable replacement.

CHAPTER 16: INCOME PAYMENTS ORDERS

6.189 Application for order (1) Where the trustee applies for an income payments order under section 310, the court shall fix a venue for the hearing of the application.
(2) Notice of the application, and of the venue, shall be sent by the trustee to the bankrupt at least 28 days before the day fixed for the hearing, together with a copy of the trustee's application and a short statement of the grounds on which it is made. [FORM 6.64]
(3) The notice shall inform the bankrupt that –
(a) unless at least 7 days before the date fixed for the hearing he sends to the court and to the trustee written consent to an order being made in the terms of the application, he is required to attend the hearing, and
(b) if he attends, he will be given an opportunity to show cause why the order should not be made, or an order should be made otherwise than as applied for by the trustee.

6.190 Action to follow making of order (1) Where the court makes an income payments order, a sealed copy of the order shall, forthwith after it is made, be sent by the trustee to the bankrupt. [FORM 6.65 or FORM 6.66]
(2) If the order is made under section 310(3)(b), a sealed copy of the order shall also be sent by the trustee to the person to whom the order is directed.

6.191 Variation of order (1) If an income payments order is made under section 310(3)(a), and the bankrupt does not comply with it, the trustee may apply to the

court for the order to be varied, so as to take effect under section 310(3)(b) as an order to the payor of the relevant income. [FORM 6.67]
(2) The trustee's application under this Rule may be made ex parte.
(3) Sealed copies of any order made on the application shall, forthwith after it is made, be sent by the court to the trustee and the bankrupt.
(4) In the case of an order varying or discharging an income payments order made under section 310(3)(b), an additional sealed copy shall be sent to the trustee, for transmission forthwith to the payor of the relevant income.

6.192 Order to payor of income: administration (1) Where a person receives notice of an income payments order under section 310(3)(b) with reference to income otherwise payable by him to the bankrupt, he shall make the arrangements requisite for immediate compliance with the order.
(2) When making any payment to the trustee, he may deduct the appropriate fee towards the clerical and administrative costs of compliance with the income payments order.
He shall give to the bankrupt a written statement of any amount deducted by him under this paragraph.
(3) Where a person receives notice of an income payments order imposing on him a requirement under section 310(3)(b), and either –
(a) he is then no longer liable to make to the bankrupt any payment of income, or
(b) having made payments in compliance with the order, he ceases to be so liable,
he shall forthwith give notice of that fact to the trustee.

6.193 Review of order (1) Where an income payments order is in force, either the trustee or the bankrupt may apply to the court for the order to be varied or discharged.
(2) If the application is made by the trustee, Rule 6.189 applies (with any necessary modification) as in the case of an application for an income payments order.
(3) If the application is made by the bankrupt, it shall be accompanied by a short statement of the grounds on which it is made.
(4) The court may, if it thinks that no sufficient cause is shown for the application, dismiss it; but it shall not do so unless the applicant has had an opportunity to attend the court for an ex parte hearing, of which he has been given at least 7 days' notice.
If the application is not dismissed under this paragraph, the court shall fix a venue for it to be heard.
(5) At least 28 days before the date fixed for the hearing, the applicant shall send to the trustee or the bankrupt (whichever of them is not himself the applicant) notice of the venue, accompanied by a copy of the application.
Where the applicant is the bankrupt, the notice shall be accompanied by a copy of the statement of grounds under paragraph (3).
(6) The trustee may, if he thinks fit, appear and be heard on the application; and, whether or not he intends to appear, he may, not less than 7 days before the date fixed for the hearing, file a written report of any matters which he considers ought to be drawn to the court's attention.
If such a report is filed, a copy of it shall be sent by the trustee to the bankrupt.
(7) Sealed copies of any order made on the application shall, forthwith after the order is made, be sent by the court to the trustee, the bankrupt and the payor (if other than the bankrupt). [FORM 6.66]

CHAPTER 17: ACTION BY COURT UNDER SECTION 369

Order to Inland Revenue Official

6.194 Application for order (1) An application by the official receiver or the

trustee for an order under section 369 (order to inland revenue official to produce documents) shall specify (with such particularity as will enable the order, if made, to be most easily compiled with) the documents whose production to the court is desired, naming the official to whom the order is to be addressed.
(2) The court shall fix a venue for the hearing of the application.
(3) Notice of the venue, accompanied by a copy of the application, shall be sent by the applicant to the Commissioners of Inland Revenue ('the Commissioners') at least 28 days before the hearing.
(4) The notice shall require the Commissioners, not later than 7 days before the date fixed for the hearing of the application, to inform the court whether they consent or object to the making of an order under the section.
(5) If the Commissioners consent to the making of an order, they shall inform the court of the name of the official to whom it should be addressed, if other than the one named in the application.
(6) If the Commissioners object to the making of an order, they shall secure that an officer of theirs attends the hearing of the application and, not less than 7 days before it, deliver to the court a statement in writing of their grounds of objection.
A copy of the statement shall be sent forthwith to the applicant.

6.195 Making and service of the order (1) If on the hearing of the application it appears to the court to be a proper case, the court may make the order applied for, with such modifications (if any) as appear appropriate having regard to any representations made on behalf of the Commissioners. [FORM 6.69]
(2) The order –
(a) may be addressed to an inland revenue official other than the one named in the application,
(b) shall specify a time, not less than 28 days after service on the official to whom the order is addressed, within which compliance is required, and
(c) may include requirements as to the manner in which documents to which the order relates are to be produced.
(3) A sealed copy of the order shall be served by the applicant on the official to whom it is addressed.
(4) If the official is unable to comply with the order because he has not the relevant documents in his possession, and has been unable to obtain possession of them, he shall deliver to the court a statement in writing as to the reasons for his non-compliance.
A copy of the statement shall be sent forthwith to the applicant.

6.196 Custody of documents Where in compliance with an order under section 369 original documents are produced, and not copies, any person who, by order of the court under section 369(2) (authorised disclosure to persons with right of inspection), has them in his possession or custody is responsible to the court for their safe keeping and return as and when directed.

CHAPTER 18: MORTGAGED PROPERTY

6.197 Claim by mortgagee of land (1) Any person claiming to be the legal or equitable mortgagee of land belonging to the bankrupt may apply to the court for an order directing that the land be sold.
'Land' includes any interest in, or right over, land.
(2) The court, if satisfied as to the applicant's title, may direct accounts to be taken and enquiries made to ascertain –

(a) the principal, interest and costs due under the mortgage, and
(b) where the mortgagee has been in possession of the land or any part of it, the rents and profits, dividends, interest, or other proceeds received by him or on his behalf.

Directions may be given by the court under this paragraph with respect to any mortgage (whether prior or subsequent) on the same property, other than that of the applicant.

(3) For the purpose of those accounts and enquiries, and of making title to the purchaser, any of the parties may be examined by the court, and shall produce on oath before the court all such documents in their custody or under their control relating to the estate of the bankrupt as the court may direct.

The court may under this paragraph authorise the service of interrogatories on any party.

(4) In any proceedings between a mortgagor and mortgagee, or the trustee of either of them, the court may order accounts to be taken and enquiries made in like manner as in the Chancery Division of the High Court.

6.198 Power of court to order sale (1) The court may order that the land, or any specified part of it, be sold; and any party bound by the order and in possession of the land or part, or in receipt of the rents and profits from it, may be ordered to deliver up possession or receipt to the purchaser or to such other person as the court may direct.

(2) The court may permit the person having the conduct of the sale to sell the land in such manner as he thinks fit. Alternatively, the court may direct that the land be sold as directed by the order.

(3) The court's order may contain directions –
(a) appointing the persons to have the conduct of the sale,
(b) fixing the manner of sale (whether by contract conditional on the court's approval, private treaty, public auction, or otherwise);
(c) settling the particulars and conditions of sale;
(d) obtaining evidence of the value of the property, and fixing a reserve or minimum price;
(e) requiring particular persons to join in the sale and conveyance;
(f) requiring the payment of the purchase money into court, or to trustees or others;
(g) if the sale is to be by public auction, fixing the security (if any) to be given by the auctioneer, and his remuneration.

(4) The court may direct that, if the sale is to be by public auction, the mortgagee may appear and bid on his own behalf.

6.199 Proceeds of sale (1) The proceeds of sale shall be applied –
(a) first, in payment of the expenses of the trustee, of and occasioned by the application of the court, of the sale and attendance thereat, and of any costs arising from the taking of accounts, and making of enquiries, as directed by the court under Rule 6.197; and
(b) secondly, in payment of the amount found due to any mortgagee, for principal, interest and costs;

and the balance (if any) shall be retained by or paid to the trustee.

(2) Where the proceeds of the sale are insufficient to pay in full the amount found due to any mortgagee, he is entitled to prove as a creditor for any deficiency, and to receive dividends rateably with other creditors, but not so as to disturb any dividend already declared.

CHAPTER 19: AFTER-ACQUIRED PROPERTY

6.200 Duties of bankrupt in respect of after-acquired property (1) The notice to be

given by the bankrupt to the trustee, under section 333(2), of property acquired by, or devolving upon, him, or of any increase of his income, shall be given within 21 days of his becoming aware of the relevant facts.
(2) Having served notice in respect of property acquired by or devolving upon him, the bankrupt shall not, without the trustee's consent in writing, dispose of it within the period of 42 days beginning with the date of the notice.
(3) If the bankrupt disposes of property before giving the notice required by this Rule or in contravention of paragraph (2), it is his duty forthwith to disclose to the trustee the name and address of the disponee, and to provide any other information which may be necessary to enable the trustee to trace the property and recover it for the estate.
(4) Subject as follows, paragraphs (1) to (3) do not apply to property acquired by the bankrupt in the ordinary course of a business carried on by him.
(5) If the bankrupt carries on a business, he shall, not less often than 6-monthly, furnish to the trustee information with respect to it, showing the total of goods bought and sold (or, as the case may be, services supplied) and the profit or loss arising from the business.

The trustee, may require the bankrupt to furnish fuller details (including accounts) of the business carried on by him.

6.201 Trustee's recourse to disponee of property (1) Where property has been disposed of by the bankrupt, before giving the notice required by Rule 6.200 or otherwise in contravention of that Rule, the trustee may serve notice on the disponee, claiming the property as part of the estate by virtue of section 307(3).
(2) The trustee's notice under this Rule must be served within 28 days of his becoming aware of the disponee's identity and an address at which he can be served.

6.202 Expenses of getting in property for the estate Any expenses incurred by the trustee in acquiring title to after-acquired property shall be paid out of the estate, in the prescribed order of priority.

CHAPTER 20: LEAVE TO ACT AS DIRECTOR, ETC

6.203 Application for leave (1) An application by the bankrupt for leave, under section 11 of the Company Directors Disqualification Act 1986 to act as director of, or to take part or be concerned in the promotion, formation or management of a company, shall be supported by an affidavit complying with this Rule.
(2) The affidavit must identify the company and specify –
(a) the nature of its business or intended business, and the place or places where that business is, or is to be, carried on,
(b) whether it is, or is to be, a private or a public company,
(c) the persons who are, or are to be, principally responsible for the conduct of its affairs (whether as directors, shadow directors, managers or otherwise),
(d) the manner and capacity in which the applicant proposes to take part or be concerned in the promotion or formation of the company or, as the case may be, its management, and
(e) the emoluments and other benefits to be obtained from the directorship.
(3) If the company is already in existence, the affidavit must specify the date of its incorporation and the amount of its nominal and issued share capital; and if not, it must specify the amount, or approximate amount, of its proposed commencing share capital, and the sources from which that capital is to be obtained.
(4) Where the bankrupt intends to take part or be concerned in the promotion or formation of a company, the affidavit must contain an undertaking by him that he will, within not less than 7 days of the company being incorporated, file in court a

copy of its memorandum of association and certificate of incorporation under section 13 of the Companies Act.
(5) The court shall fix a venue for the hearing of the bankrupt's application, and give notice to him accordingly.

6.204 Report to official receiver (1) The bankrupt shall, not less than 28 days before the date fixed for the hearing, give to the official receiver and the trustee notice of the venue, accompanied by copies of the application and the affidavit under Rule 6.203.
(2) The official receiver may, not less than 14 days before the date fixed for the hearing, file in court a report of any matters which he considers ought to be drawn to the court's attention. A copy of the report shall be sent by him, forthwith after it is filed, to the bankrupt and to the trustee.
(3) The bankrupt may, not later than 7 days before the date of the hearing, file in court a notice specifying any statements in the official receiver's report which he intended to deny or dispute.

If he gives notice under this paragraph, he shall send copies of it, not less than 4 days before the date of the hearing, to the official receiver and the trustee.
(4) The official receiver and the trustee may appear on the hearing of the application, and may make representations and put to the bankrupt such questions as the court may allow.

6.205 Court's order on application (1) If the court grants the bankrupt's application for leave under section 11 of the Company Director's Disqualification Act 1986, its order shall specify that which by virtue of the order the bankrupt has leave to do.
(2) The court may at the same time, having regard to any representations made by the trustee on the hearing of the application –
(a) include in the order provision varying an income payments order already in force in respect of the bankrupt, or
(b) if no income payments order is in force, make one.
(3) Whether or not the application is granted, copies of the order shall be sent by the court to the bankrupt, the trustee and the official receiver.

CHAPTER 21: ANNULMENT OF BANKRUPTCY ORDER

6.206 Application for annulment (1) An application to the court under section 282(1) for the annulment of a bankruptcy order shall specify whether it is made –
(a) under subsection (1)(a) of the section (claim that the order ought not to have been made), or
(b) under subsection (1)(b) (debts and expenses of the bankruptcy all paid or secured).
(2) The application shall, in either case, be supported by an affidavit stating the grounds on which it is made; and, where it is made under section 282(1)(b), there shall be set out in the affidavit all the facts by reference to which the court is, under the Act and the Rules, required to be satisfied before annulling the bankruptcy order.
(3) A copy of the application and supporting affidavit shall be filed in court; and the court shall give to the applicant notice of the venue fixed for the hearing.
(4) The applicant shall, not less than 28 days before the hearing, give to the official receiver and (if other) the trustee notice of the venue, accompanied by copies of the application and the affidavit under paragraph (2).

6.207 Report by trustee (1) The following applies where the application is made

under section 282(1)(b) (debts and expenses of the bankruptcy all paid or secured).
(2) Not less than 21 days before the date fixed for the hearing, the trustee or, if no trustee has been appointed, the official receiver shall file a report with respect to the following matters –
(a) the circumstances leading to the bankruptcy,
(b) (in summarised form) the extent of the bankrupt's assets and liabilities at the date of the bankruptcy order and at the date of the present application;
(c) details of creditors (if any) who are known to him to have claims, but have not proved; and
(b) such other matters as the person making the report considers to be, in the circumstances, necessary for the information of the court.
(3) The report shall include particulars of the extent (if any) to which, and the manner in which, the debts and expenses of the bankruptcy have been paid or secured.

In so far as debts and expenses are unpaid but secured, the person making the report shall state in it whether and to what extent he considers the security to be satisfactory.
(4) A copy of the report shall be sent to the applicant at least 14 days before the date fixed for the hearing; and he may, if he wishes, file further affidavits in answer to statements made in the report.

Copies of any such affidavits shall be sent by the applicant to the official receiver and (if other) the trustee.
(5) If the trustee is other than the official receiver, a copy of his report shall be sent to the official receiver at least 21 days before the hearing. The official receiver may then file an additional report, a copy of which shall be sent to the applicant at least 7 days before the hearing.

6.208 Power of court to stay proceedings (1) The court may, in advance of the hearing, make an interim order staying any proceedings which it thinks ought, in the circumstances of the application, to be stayed.
(2) Application for an interim order under this Rule may be made ex parte.

6.209 Notice to creditors who have not proved Where the application for annulment is made under section 282(1)(b) and it has been reported to the court under Rule 6.207 that there are known creditors of the bankrupt who have not proved, the court may –
(a) direct the trustee to send notice of the application to such of those creditors as the court thinks ought to be informed of it, with a view of their proving their debts (if they so wish) within 21 days, and
(b) direct the trustee to advertise the fact that the application has been made, so that creditors who have not proved may do so within a specified time, and
(c) adjourn the application meanwhile, for any period not less than 35 days.

6.210 The hearing (1) The trustee shall attend the hearing of the application.
(2) The official receiver, if he is not the trustee, may attend, but is not required to do so unless he has filed a report under Rule 6.207.
(3) If the court makes an order on the application, it shall send copies of the order to the applicant, the official receiver and (if other) the trustee. [FORM 6.71]

6.211 Matters to be proved under s 282(1)(b) (1) This rule applies with regard to the matters which must, in an application under section 282(1)(b), be proved to the satisfaction of the court.
(2) Subject to the following paragraph, all bankruptcy debts which have been proved must have been paid in full.

(3) If a debt is disputed, or a creditor who has proved can no longer be traced, the bankrupt must have given such security (in the form of money paid into court, or a bond entered into with approved sureties) as the court considers adequate to satisfy any sum that may subsequently be proved to be due to the creditor concerned and (if the court thinks fit) costs.
(4) Where under paragraph (3) security has been given in the case of an untraced creditor, the court may direct that particulars of the alleged debt, and the security, be advertised in such manner as it thinks fit.

If advertisement is ordered under this paragraph, and no claim on the security is made within 12 months from the date of the advertisement (or the first advertisement, if more than one), the court shall, on application in that behalf, order the security to be released.

6.212 Notice to creditors (1) Where the official receiver has notified creditors of the debtor's bankruptcy, and the bankruptcy order is annulled, he shall forthwith notify them of the annulment.
(2) Expenses incurred by the official receiver in giving notice under this Rule are a charge in his favour on the property of the former bankrupt, whether or not actually in his hands.
(3) Where any property is in the hands of a trustee or any person other than the former bankrupt himself, the official receiver's charge is valid subject only to any costs that may be incurred by the trustee or that other person in effecting realisation of the property for the purpose of satisfying the charge.

6.213 Other matters arising on annulment (1) In an order under section 282 the court shall include provision permitting vacation of the registration of the bankruptcy petition as a pending action, and of the bankruptcy order, in the register of writs and orders affecting land.
(2) The court shall forthwith give notice of the making of the order to the Secretary of State.
(3) The former bankrupt may require the Secretary of State to give notice of the making of the order –
(a) in the Gazette, or
(b) in any newspaper in which the bankruptcy order was advertised, or
(c) in both.
(4) Any requirement by the former bankrupt under paragraph (3) shall be addressed to the Secretary of State in writing. The Secretary of State shall notify him forthwith as to the cost of the advertisement, and is under no obligation to advertise until that sum has been paid.
(5) Where the former bankrupt has died, or is a person incapable of managing his affairs (within the meaning of Chapter 7 in Part 7 of the Rules), the references to him in paragraphs (3) and (4) are to be read as referring to his personal representative or, as the case may be, a person appointed by the court to represent or act for him.

6.214 Trustee's final account (1) Where a bankruptcy order is annulled under section 282, this does not of itself release the trustee from any duty or obligation, imposed on him by or under the Act or the Rules, to account for all his transactions in connection with the former bankrupt's estate.
(2) The trustee shall submit a copy of his final account to the Secretary of State, as soon as practicable after following the court's order annulling the bankruptcy order; and he shall file a copy of the final account in court.
(3) The final account must include a summary of the trustee's receipts and payments in the administration, and contain a statement to the effect that he has reconciled his

account with that which is held by the Secretary of State in respect of the bankruptcy.
(4) The trustee is released from such time as the court may determine, having regard to whether –
(a) paragraph (2) of this Rule has been complied with, and
(b) any security given under Rule 6.211(3) has been, or will be, released.

CHAPTER 22: DISCHARGE

6.215 Application for suspension of discharge (1) The following applies where the official receiver applies to the court for an order under section 279(3) (suspension of automatic discharge), but not where he makes that application, pursuant to Rule 6.176(4), on the adjournment of the bankrupt's public examination.
(2) The official receiver shall with his application file a report setting out the reasons why it appears to him that such an order should be made.
(3) The court shall fix a venue for the hearing of the application, and give notice of it to the official receiver, the trustee and the bankrupt.
(4) Copies of the official receiver's report under this Rule shall be sent by him to the trustee and the bankrupt, so as to reach them at least 21 days before the date fixed for the hearing.
(5) The bankrupt may, not later than 7 days before the date of the hearing, file in court a notice specifying any statements in the official receiver's report which he intends to deny or dispute.

If he gives notice under this paragraph, he shall send copies of it, not less than 4 days before the date of the hearing, to the official receiver and the trustee.
(6) If on the hearing the court makes an order suspending the bankrupt's discharge, copies of the order shall be sent by the court to the official receiver, the trustee and the bankrupt. [FORM 6.72]

6.216 Lifting of suspension of discharge (1) Where the court has made an order under section 279(3) that the relevant period (that is to say, the period after which the bankrupt may under that section have his discharge) shall cease to run, the bankrupt may apply to it for the order to be discharged.
(2) The court shall fix a venue for the hearing of the application; and the bankrupt shall, not less than 28 days before the date fixed for hearing, give notice of the venue to the official receiver and the trustee, accompanied in each case by a copy of the application.
(3) The official receiver and the trustee may appear and be heard on the bankrupt's application; and, whether or not he appears, the official receiver may file in court a report of any matters which he considers ought to be drawn to the court's attention.
(4) If the court's order under section 279(3) was for the relevant period to cease to run until the fulfilment of specified conditions, the court may request a report from the official receiver as to whether those conditions have or have not been fulfilled.
(5) If a report is filed under paragraph (3) or (4), copies of it shall be sent by the official receiver to the bankrupt and the trustee, not later than 14 days before the hearing.
(6) The bankrupt may, not later than 7 days before the date of the hearing, file in court a notice specifying any statements in the official receiver's report which he intends to deny or dispute.

If he gives notice under this paragraph, he shall send copies of it, not less than 4 days before the date of the hearing, to the official receiver and the trustee.
(7) If on the bankrupt's application the court discharges the order under section 279(3) (being satisfied that the relevant period should begin to run again), it shall issue

to the bankrupt a certificate that it has done so, with effect from a specified date. [FORM 6.73, FORM 6.74]

6.217 Application by bankrupt for discharge (1) If the bankrupt applies under section 280 for an order discharging him from bankruptcy, he shall give to the official receiver notice of the application, and deposit with him such sum as the latter may require to cover his costs of the application.
(2) The court, if satisfied that paragraph (1) has been complied with, shall fix a venue for the hearing of the application, and give at least 42 days' notice of it to the official receiver and the bankrupt.
(3) The official receiver shall give notice accordingly –
(a) to the trustee, and
(b) to every creditor who, to the official receiver's knowledge, has a claim outstanding against the estate which has not been satisfied.
(4) Notices under paragraph (3) shall be given not later than 14 days before the date fixed for the hearing of the bankrupt's application.

6.218 Report of official receiver (1) Where the bankrupt makes an application under section 280, the official receiver shall, at least 21 days before the date fixed for the hearing of the application, file in court a report containing the following information with respect to the bankrupt –
(a) any failure by him to comply with his obligations under Parts VIII to XI of the Act;
(b) the circumstances surrounding the present bankruptcy, and those surrounding any previous bankruptcy of his;
(c) the extent to which, in the present and in any previous bankruptcy, his liabilities have exceeded his assets; and
(d) particulars of any distribution which has been, or is expected to be, made to creditors in the present bankruptcy or, if such is the case, that there has been and is to be no distribution;

and the official receiver shall include in his report any other matters which in his opinion ought to be brought to the court's attention.
(2) The official receiver shall send a copy of the report to the bankrupt and the trustee, so as to reach them at least 14 days before the date of the hearing of the application under section 280.
(3) The bankrupt may, not later than 7 days before the date of the hearing, file in court a notice specifying any statements in the official receiver's report which he intends to deny or dispute.

If he gives notice under this paragraph, he shall send copies of it, not less than 4 days before the date of the hearing, to the official receiver and the trustee. [FORM 6.75]
(4) The official receiver, the trustee and any creditor may appear on the hearing of the bankrupt's application, and may make representations and put to the bankrupt such questions as the court may allow.

6.219 Order of discharge on application (1) An order of the court under section 280(2)(b) (discharge absolutely) or (c) (discharge subject to conditions with respect to income or property) shall bear the date on which it is made, but does not take effect until such time as it is drawn up by the court. [FORM 6.76]
(2) The order then has effect retrospectively to the date on which it was made.
(3) Copies of any order made by the court on an application by the bankrupt for discharge under section 280 shall be sent by the court to the bankrupt, the trustee and the official receiver.

6.220 Certificate of discharge (1) Where a bankrupt is discharged, whether by expiration of time or otherwise, the court shall, on his application, issue to him a certificate of his discharge, and the date from which it is effective. [FORM 6.77]
(2) The discharged bankrupt may require the Secretary of State to give notice of the discharge –
(a) in the Gazette, or
(b) in any newspaper in which the bankruptcy was advertised, or
(c) in both.
(3) Any requirement by the former bankrupt under paragraph (2) shall be addressed to the Secretary of State in writing. The Secretary of State shall notify him forthwith as to the cost of the advertisement, and is under no obligation to advertise until that sum has been paid.
(4) Where the former bankrupt has died, or is a person incapable of managing his affairs (within the meaning of Chapter 7 in Part 7 of the Rules), the references to him in paragraphs (2) and (3) are to be read as referring to his personal representative or, as the case may be, a person appointed by the court to represent or act for him.

6.221 Deferment of issue of order pending appeal An order made by the court on an application by the bankrupt for discharge under section 280 shall not be issued or gazetted until the time allowed for appealing has expired or, if an appeal is entered, until the appeal has been determined.

6.222 Costs under this Chapter In no case do any costs or expenses arising under this Chapter fall on the official receiver personally.

6.223 Bankrupt's debts surviving discharge Discharge does not release the bankrupt from any obligation arising under a confiscation order made under section 1 of the Drug Trafficking Offences Act 1986.

CHAPTER 23: ORDER OF PAYMENT OF COSTS, ETC OUT OF ESTATE

6.224 General rule as to priority (1) The expenses of the bankruptcy are payable out of the estate in the following order of priority –
(a) expenses properly chargeable or incurred by the official receiver or the trustee in preserving, realising or getting in any of the assets of the bankrupt, including those incurred in acquiring title to after-acquired property;
(b) any other expenses incurred or disbursements made by the official receiver or under his authority, including those incurred or made in carrying on the business of a debtor or bankrupt;
(c) the cost of any security provided by an interim receiver, trustee or special manager in accordance with the Act or the Rules;
(d) the fees payable under any order made under section 415, including those payable to the official receiver, and any remuneration payable to him under general regulations;
(e) any repayable deposit lodged by the petitioner pursuant to the Rules (except where the deposit is applied to the payment of the remuneration of an insolvency practitioner appointed under section 273 (debtor's petition));
(f) the remuneration of the interim receiver (if any);
(g) any deposit lodged on an application for the appointment of an interim receiver;
(h) the costs of the petitioner, and of any person appearing on the petition whose costs are allowed by the court;

(j) the remuneration of the special manager (if any);
(k) any amount payable to a person employed or authorised, under Chapter 5 of this Part of the Rules, to assist in the preparation of a statement of affairs or of accounts;
(l) any allowance made, by order of the court, toward costs on an application for release from the obligation to submit a statement of affairs, or for an extension of time for submitting such a statement;
(m) any necessary disbursements by the trustee in the course of his administration (not including any payment of capital gains tax in circumstances referred to in sub-paragraph (p) below);
(n) the remuneration or emoluments of any person (including the bankrupt) who has been employed by the trustee to perform any services for the estate, as required or authorised by or under the Act or the Rules;
(o) the remuneration of the trustee, up to any amount not exceeding that which is payable to the official receiver under general regulations;
(p) the amount of any capital gains tax on chargeable gains accruing on the realisation of any asset of the bankrupt (without regard to whether the realisation is effected by the trustee, a secured creditor, or a receiver or manager appointed to deal with a security);
(q) the balance, after payment of any sums due under sub-paragraph (o) above, of any remuneration due to the trustee;
(r) any expenses incurred by members of the creditors' committee or their representatives and allowed by the trustee under Rule 6.164.

(2) The costs of employing a shorthand writer, if appointed by an order of the court made at the instance of the official receiver in connection with an examination, rank in priority with those specified in paragraph (1)(a). The costs of employing a shorthand writer so appointed in any other case rank after the allowance mentioned in paragraph (1)(l) and before the disbursements mentioned in paragraph (1)(m).
(3) Any expenses incurred in holding an examination under Rule 6.174 (examinee unfit), where the application for it is made by the official receiver, rank in priority with those specified in paragraph (1)(a).

CHAPTER 24: SECOND BANKRUPTCY

6.225 Scope of this Chapter (1) The Rules in this Chapter relate to the manner in which, in the case of a second bankruptcy, the trustee in the earlier bankruptcy is to deal with property and money to which section 334(3) applies, until there is a trustee of the estate in the later bankruptcy.
(2) 'The earlier bankruptcy', 'the later bankruptcy' and 'the existing trustee' have the meanings given by section 334(1).

6.226 General duty of existing trustee (1) Subject as follows, the existing trustee shall take into his custody or under his control all such property and money, in so far as he has not already done so as part of his duties as trustee in the earlier bankruptcy.
(2) Where any of that property consists of perishable goods, or goods the value of which is likely to diminish if they are not disposed of, the existing trustee has power to sell or otherwise dispose of those goods.
(3) The proceeds of any such sale or disposal shall be held, under the existing trustee's control, with the other property and money comprised in the bankrupt's estate.

6.227 Delivery up to later trustee (1) The existing trustee shall, as and when requested by the trustee for the purposes of the later bankruptcy, deliver up to the latter all such property and money as is in his custody or under his control in pursuance of Rule 6.226.

6.228 Existing trustee's expenses Any expenses incurred by the existing trustee in compliance with section 335(1) and this Chapter of the Rules shall be defrayed out of, and are a charge on, all such property and money as is referred to in section 334(3), whether in the hands of the existing trustee or of the trustee for the purposes of the later bankruptcy.

CHAPTER 25: CRIMINAL BANKRUPTCY

6.229 Presentation of petition (1) In criminal bankruptcy, the petition under section 264(1)(d) shall be presented to the High Court, and accordingly Rule 6.9 in Chapter 2 (court in which other petitions to be presented) does not apply. [FORM 6.79]
(2) This does not affect the High Court's power to order that the proceedings be transferred.

6.230 Status and functions of Official Petitioner (1) Subject as follows, the Official Petitioner is to be regarded for all purposes of the Act and the Rules as a creditor of the bankrupt.
(2) He may attend or be represented at any meeting of creditors, and is to be given any notice under the Act or the Rules which is required or authorised to be given to creditors; and the requirements of the Rules as to the lodging or use of proxies do not apply.

6.231 Interim receivership Chapter 4 of this Part of the Rules applies in criminal bankruptcy only in so far as it provides for the appointment of the official receiver as interim receiver.

6.232 Proof of bankruptcy debts and notice of order (1) The making of a bankruptcy order on a criminal bankruptcy petition does not affect the right of creditors to prove for their debts arising otherwise than in consequence of the criminal proceedings.
(2) A person specified in a criminal bankruptcy order as having suffered loss or damage shall be treated as a creditor of the bankrupt; and a copy of the order is sufficient evidence of his claim, subject to its being shown by any party to the bankruptcy proceedings that the loss or damage actually suffered was more or (as the case may be) less than the amount specified in the order.
(3) The requirements of the Rules with respect to the proof of debts do not apply to the Official Petitioner.
(4) In criminal bankruptcy, the forms to be used by any person for the purpose of proving bankruptcy debts shall be sent out by the official receiver, not less than 12 weeks from the making of the bankruptcy order, to every creditor who is known to him, or is identified in the bankrupt's statement of affairs.
(5) The official receiver shall, within those 4 months, send to every such creditor notice of the making of the bankruptcy order.

6.233 Meetings under the Rules (1) The following Rules in Chapter 6 of this Part do not apply in criminal bankruptcy –

Rules 6.79 and 6.80 (first meeting of creditors, and business thereat);
Rule 6.82(2)*(the chairman, if other than the official receiver);
Rule 6.88(2) and (3) (resolution for appointment of trustee).

(2) Rule 6.97 (supply of forms for proof of debts) does not apply.

6.234 Trustee in bankruptcy; creditors' committee; annulment of bankruptcy order (1) Chapter 11 of this Part of the Rules does not apply in criminal bankruptcy, except Rules 6.136 (release of official receiver) and 6.147 (power of court to set aside transactions).

(2) Chapter 12 (creditors' committee) does not apply.

(3) Chapter 21 (annulment of bankruptcy order) applies to an application to the court under section 282(2) as it applies to an application under section 282(1), with any necessary modifications.

CHAPTER 26: MISCELLANEOUS RULES IN BANKRUPTCY

6.235 Bankruptcy of solicitors Where a bankruptcy order is made against a solicitor, or such an order made against a solicitor is rescinded or annulled, the court shall forthwith give notice to the Secretary of the Law Society of the order that it has made.

6.236 Consolidation of petitions Where two or more bankruptcy petitions are presented against the same debtor, the court may order the consolidation of the proceedings, on such terms as it thinks fit.

6.237 Bankrupt's dwelling-house and home (1) This Rule applies where the trustee applies to the court under section 313 for an order imposing a charge on property consisting of an interest in a dwelling house.

(2) The bankrupt's spouse or former spouse shall be made respondents to the application; and the court may, if it thinks fit, direct other persons to be made respondents also, in respect of any interest which they may have in the property.

(3) The trustee shall make a report to the court, containing the following particulars: –

(a) the extent of the bankrupt's interest in the property which is the subject of the application; and

(b) the amount which, at the date of the application, remains owing to unsecured creditors of the bankrupt.

(4) The terms of the charge to be imposed shall be agreed between the trustee and the bankrupt or, failing agreement, shall be settled by the court.

(5) The rate of interest applicable under section 313(2) is the rate specified in section 17 of the Judgments Act 1838 on the day on which the charge is imposed, and the rate so applicable shall be stated in the court's order imposing the charge.

(6) The court's order shall also: –

(a) describe the property to be charged;

(b) state whether the title to the property is registered and, if it is, specify the title number;

(c) set out the extent of the bankrupt's interest in the property which has vested in the trustee.

(d) indicate, by reference to the amount which remains owing to unsecured creditors of the bankrupt, the amount of the charge to be imposed;

(e) set out the conditions (if any) imposed by the court under section 3(1) of the Charging Orders Act 1979;

(f) provide for any property comprised in the charge to vest again in the bankrupt as from a specified date.

(7) Unless the court is of the opinion that a different date is appropriate, the date under paragraph (6)(f) shall be that of the registration of the charge in accordance with section 3(2) of the Charging Orders Act 1979.
(8) The trustee shall, forthwith after the making of the court's order, send notice of it and its effect to the Chief Land Registrar.

THE THIRD GROUP OF PARTS

Part 7: Court Procedure and Practice

CHAPTER 1: APPLICATIONS

7.1 Preliminary This Chapter applies to any application made to the court under the Act or Rules except a petition for –
(a) an administration order under Part II,
(b) a winding-up order under Part IV, or
(c) a bankruptcy order under Part IX
of the Act.

7.2 Interpretation (1) In this Chapter, except in so far as the context otherwise requires –

'originating application' means an application to the court which is not an application in pending proceedings before the court; and
'ordinary application' means any other application to the court. [FORM 7.1, FORM 7.2]

(2) Every application shall be in the form appropriate to the application concerned.

7.3 Form and contents of application (1) Each application shall be in writing and shall state –
(a) the names of the parties;
(b) the nature of the relief or order applied for or the directions sought from the court;
(c) the names and addresses of the persons (if any) on whom it is intended to serve the application or that no person is intended to be served;
(d) where the Act or Rules require that notice of the application is to be given to specified persons, the names and addresses of all those persons (so far as known to the applicant); and
(e) the applicant's address for service.
(2) An originating application shall set out the grounds on which the applicant claims to be entitled to the relief or order sought.
(3) The application must be signed by the applicant if he is acting in person or, when he is not so acting, by or on behalf of his solicitor.

7.4 Filing and service of application (1) The application shall be filed in court, accompanied by one copy and a number of additional copies equal to the number of persons who are to be served with the application.
(2) Subject as follows in this Rule and the next, or unless the Rule under which the application is brought provides otherwise, or the court otherwise orders, upon the presentation of the documents mentioned in paragraph (1) above, the court shall fix a venue for the application to be heard.

(3) Unless the court otherwise directs, the applicant shall serve a sealed copy of the application, endorsed with the venue for the hearing, on the respondent named in the application (or on each respondent if more than one).
(4) The court may give any of the following directions –
(a) that the application be served upon persons other than those specified by the relevant provision of the Act or Rules;
(b) that the giving of notice to any person may be dispensed with;
(c) that notice be given in some way other than that specified in paragraph (3).
(5) Unless the provision of the Act or Rules under which the application is made provides otherwise, and subject to the next paragraph, the application must be served at least 14 days before the date fixed for the hearing.
(6) Where the case is one of urgency, the court may (without prejudice to its general power to extend or abridge time limits) –
(a) hear the application immediately, either with or without notice to, or the attendance of, other parties, or
(b) authorise a shorter period of service than that provided for by paragraph (5);
and any such application may be heard on terms providing for the filing or service of documents, or the carrying out of other formalities, as the court thinks fit.

7.5 Other hearings ex parte (1) Where the relevant provisions of the Act or Rules do not require service of the application on, or notice of it to be given to, any person, the court may hear the application ex parte.
(2) Where the application is properly made ex parte, the court may hear it forthwith, without fixing a venue as required by Rule 7.4(2).
(3) Alternatively, the court may fix a venue for the application to be heard, in which case Rule 7.4 applies (so far as relevant).

7.6 Hearing of application (1) Unless allowed or authorised to be made otherwise, every application before the registrar shall, and every application before the judge, may, be heard in chambers.
(2) Unless either –
(a) the judge has given a general or special direction to the contrary, or
(b) it is not within the registrar's power to make the order required,
the jurisdiction of the court to hear and determine the application may be exercised by the registrar, and the application shall be made to the registrar in the first instance.
(3) Where the application is made to the registrar he may refer to the judge any matter which he thinks should properly be decided by the judge, and the judge may either dispose of the matter or refer it back to the registrar with such directions as he thinks fit.
(4) Nothing in this Rule precludes an application being made directly to the judge in a proper case.

7.7 Use of affidavit evidence (1) In any proceedings evidence may be given by affidavit unless by any provision of the Rules it is otherwise provided or the court otherwise directs; but the court may, on the application of any party, order the attendance for cross-examination of the person making the affidavit.
(2) Where, after such an order has been made, the person in question does not attend, his affidavit shall not be used in evidence without the leave of the court.

7.8 Filing and service of affidavits (1) Unless the provision of the Act or Rules under which the application is made provides otherwise, or the court otherwise allows –
(a) if the applicant intends to rely at the first hearing on affidavit evidence, he shall file the affidavit or affidavits (if more than one) in court and serve a copy or

copies on the respondent, not less than 14 days before the date fixed for the hearing, and

(b) where a respondent to an application intends to oppose it and to rely for that purpose on affidavit evidence, he shall file the affidavit or affidavits (if more than one) in court and serve a copy or copies on the applicant, not less than 7 days before the date fixed for the hearing.

(2) Any affidavit may be sworn by the applicant or by the respondent or by some other person possessing direct knowledge of the subject matter of the application.

7.9 Use of reports (1) A report may be filed in court instead of an affidavit –

(a) in any case, by the official receiver (whether or not he is acting in any capacity mentioned in sub-paragraph (b)), or a deputy official receiver, or

(b) unless the application involves other parties or the court otherwise orders, by –
   (i) an administrator, a liquidator or a trustee in bankruptcy,
   (ii) a provisional liquidator or an interim receiver,
   (iii) a special manager, or
   (iv) an insolvency practitioner appointed under section 273(2).

(2) In any case where a report is filed instead of an affidavit, the report shall be treated for the purposes of rule 7.8(1) and any hearing before the court as if it were an affidavit.

(3) Any report filed by the official receiver in accordance with the Act or the Rules is prima facie evidence of any matter contained in it.

7.10 Adjournment of hearing; directions (1) The court may adjourn the hearing of an application on such terms (if any) as it thinks fit.

(2) The court may at any time give such directions as it thinks fit as to –

(a) service or notice of the application on or to any person, whether in connection with the venue of a resumed hearing or for any other purpose;

(b) whether particulars of claim and defence are to be delivered and generally as to the procedure on the application;

(c) the manner in which any evidence is to be adduced at a resumed hearing and in particular (but without prejudice to the generality of this sub-paragraph) as to –
   (i) the taking of evidence wholly or in part by affidavit or orally;
   (ii) the cross-examination either before the judge or registrar on the hearing in court or in chambers, of any deponents to affidavits;
   (iii) any report to be given by the official receiver or any person mentioned in rule 7.9(1)(b);

(d) the matters to be dealt with in evidence.

CHAPTER 2: TRANSFER OF PROCEEDINGS BETWEEN COURTS

7.11 General power of transfer (1) Where winding-up or bankruptcy proceedings are pending in the High Court, the court may order them to be transferred to a specified county court.

(2) Where winding-up or bankruptcy proceedings are pending in a county court, the court may order them to be transferred either to the High Court or to another county court.

(3) In any case where proceedings are transferred to a county court, the transfer must be to a court which has jurisdiction to wind up companies or, as the case may be, jurisdiction in bankruptcy.

(4) Where winding-up or bankruptcy proceedings are pending in a county court, a judge of the High Court may order them to be transferred to that Court.
(5) A transfer of proceedings under this Rule may be ordered –
(a) by the court of its own motion, or
(b) on the application of the official receiver, or
(c) on the application of a person appearing to the court to have an interest in the proceedings.

7.12 Proceedings commenced in wrong court Where winding-up or bankruptcy proceedings are commenced in a court which is, in relation to those proceedings, the wrong court, that court may –
(a) order the transfer of the proceedings to the court in which they ought to have been commenced;
(b) order that the proceedings be continued in the court in which they have been commenced; or
(c) order the proceedings to be struck out.

7.13 Applications for transfer (1) An application by the official receiver for proceedings to be transferred shall be made with a report by him –
(a) setting out the reasons for the transfer, and
(b) including a statement either that the petitioner consents to the transfer, or that he has been given at least 14 days' notice of the official receiver's application.
(2) If the court is satisfied from the official receiver's report that the proceedings can be conducted more conveniently in another court, the proceedings shall be transferred to that court.
(3) Where an application for the transfer of proceedings is made otherwise than by the official receiver, at least 14 days' notice of the application shall be given by the applicant –
(a) to the official receiver attached to the court in which the proceedings are pending, and
(b) to the official receiver attached to the court to which it is proposed that they should be transferred.

7.14 Procedure following order for transfer (1) Subject as follows, the court making an order under Rule 7.11 shall forthwith send to the transferee court a sealed copy of the order, and the file of the proceedings.
(2) On receipt of these, the transferee court shall forthwith send notice of the transfer to the official receivers attached to that court and the transferor court respectively.
(3) Paragraph (1) does not apply where the order is made by the High Court under Rule 7.11(4). In that case –
(a) the High Court shall send sealed copies of the order to the county court from which the proceedings are to be transferred, and to the official receivers attached to that court and the High Court respectively, and
(b) that county court shall send the file of the proceedings to the High Court.
(4) Following compliance with this Rule, the official receiver attached to the court to which the proceedings are ordered to be transferred becomes, in relation to those proceedings, the official receiver in place of the official receiver attached to the other court concerned.

7.15 Consequential transfer of other proceedings (1) This Rule applies where –
(a) an order for the winding up of a company, or a bankruptcy order in the case of an individual, has been made by the High Court, or

(b) in either such case, a provisional liquidator or (as the case may be) an interim receiver has been appointed, or
(c) winding-up or bankruptcy proceedings have been transferred to that Court from a county court.

(2) A judge of any Division of the High Court may, of his own motion, order the transfer to that Division of any such proceedings as are mentioned below and are pending against the company or individual concerned ('the insolvent') either in another Division of the High Court or in a court in England and Wales other than the High Court.

(3) Proceedings which may be so transferred are those brought by or against the insolvent for the purpose of enforcing a claim against the insolvent estate, or brought by a person other than the insolvent for the purpose of enforcing any such claim (including in either case proceedings of any description by a debenture-holder or mortgagee).

(4) Where proceedings are transferred under this Rule, the registrar may (subject to general or special directions of the judge) dispose of any matter arising in the proceedings which would, but for the transfer, have been disposed of in chambers or, in the case of proceedings transferred from a county court, by the registrar of that court.

CHAPTER 3: SHORTHAND WRITERS

7.16 Nomination and appointment of shorthand writers (1) In the High Court the judge and, in a county court, the registrar may in writing nominate one or more persons to be official shorthand writers to the court. [FORM 7.3]

(2) The court may, at any time in the course of insolvency proceedings, appoint a shorthand writer to take down the evidence of a person examined under section 133, 236, 290 or 366. [FORM 7.4]

(3) Where the official receiver applies to the court for an order appointing a shorthand-writer, he shall name the person he proposes for appointment; and that appointment shall be made, unless the court otherwise orders.

7.17 Remuneration (1) The fees of a shorthand writer appointed in insolvency proceedings shall be paid by the party at whose instance the appointment was made, or out of the insolvent estate, or otherwise, as the court may direct.

(2) The fees payable shall be those set out in Schedule 3 to the Rules.

7.18 Cost of shorthand note Where in insolvency proceedings the court appoints a shorthand writer on the application of the official receiver, in order that a written record may be taken of the evidence of a person to be examined, the cost of a written record is deemed an expense of the official receiver in the proceedings.

CHAPTER 4: ENFORCEMENT PROCEDURES

7.19 Enforcement of court orders (1) In any insolvency proceedings, orders of the court may be enforced in the same manner as a judgment to the same effect.

(2) Where an order in insolvency proceedings is made, or any process is issued, by a county court ('the primary court'), the order or process may be enforced, executed and dealt with by any other county court ('the secondary court'), as if it had been made or issued for the enforcement of a judgment or order to the same effect made by the secondary court.

This applies whether or not the secondary court has jurisdiction to take insolvency proceedings.

7.20 Orders enforcing compliance with the Rules (1) The court may, on application

by the competent person, make such orders as it thinks necessary for the enforcement of obligations falling on any person in accordance with –
(a) section 22, 47 or 131 (duty to submit statement of affairs in administration, administrative receivership or winding up),
(b) section 143(2) (liquidator to furnish information, books, papers, etc), or
(c) section 235 (duty of various persons to co-operate with office-holder).
(2) The competent person for this purpose is –
(a) under section 22, the administrator,
(b) under section 47, the administrative receiver,
(c) under section 131 or 143(2), the official receiver, and
(d) under section 235, the official receiver, the administrator, the administrative receiver, the liquidator or the provisional liquidator, as the case may be.
(3) An order of the court under this Rule may provide that all costs of and incidental to the application for it shall be borne by the person against whom the order is made.

7.21 Warrants (general provisions) (1) A warrant issued by the court under any provision of the Act shall be addressed to such officer of the High Court or of a county court (whether or not having jurisdiction in insolvency proceedings) as the warrant specifies, or to any constable.
(2) The persons referred to in sections 134(2), 236(5), 364(1), 365(3) and 366(3) (court's powers of enforcement) as the prescribed officer of the court are –
(a) in the case of the High Court, the tipstaff and his assistants of the court, and
(b) in the case of a county court, the registrar and the bailiffs.
(3) In this Chapter references to property include books, papers and records.

7.22 Warrants under s 134, 364 When a person is arrested under a warrant issued by the court under section 135 (officer of company failing to attend for public examination), or section 364 (arrest of debtor or bankrupt) –
(a) the officer apprehending him shall give him into the custody of the governor of the prison named in the warrant, who shall keep him in custody until such time as the court otherwise orders and shall produce him before the court as it may from time to time direct; and
(b) any property in the arrested person's possession which may be seized shall be –
   (i) lodged with, or otherwise dealt with as instructed by, whoever is specified in the warrant as authorised to receive it, or
   (ii) kept by the officer seizing it pending the receipt of written orders from the court as to its disposal,

as may be directed by the court in the warrant. [FORM 7.6, FORM 7.7]

7.23 Warrants under ss 236, 366 (1) When a person is arrested under a warrant issued under section 236 (inquiry into insolvent company's dealings) or 366 (the equivalent in bankruptcy), the officer arresting him shall forthwith bring him before the court issuing the warrant in order that he may be examined. [FORM 7.8]
(2) If he cannot immediately be brought up for examination, the officer shall deliver him into the custody of the governor of the prison named in the warrant, who shall keep him in custody and produce him before the court as it may from time to time direct. [FORM 7.9]
(3) After arresting the person named in the warrant, the officer shall forthwith report to the court the arrest or delivery into custody (as the case may be) and apply to the court to fix a venue for the person's examination.
(4) The court shall appoint the earliest practicable time for the examination, and shall –
(a) direct the governor of the prison to produce the person for examination at the time and place appointed, and

(b) forthwith give notice of the venue to the person who applied for the warrant. [FORM 7.9]

(5) Any property in the arrested person's possession which may be seized shall be –

(a) lodged with, or otherwise dealt with as instructed by, whoever is specified in the warrant as authorised to receive it, or

(b) kept by the officer seizing it pending the receipt of written orders from the court as to its disposal,

as may be directed by the court.

7.24 Execution of warrants outside court's district (1) This Rule applies where a warrant for a person's arrest has been issued in insolvency proceedings by a county court ('the primary court') and is addressed to another county court ('the secondary court') for execution in its district. [FORM 7.10]

(2) The secondary court may send the warrant to the registrar of any other county court (whether or not having jurisdiction to take insolvency proceedings) in whose district the person to be arrested is or is believed to be, with a notice to the effect that the warrant is transmitted to that court under this Rule for execution in its district at the request of the primary court.

(3) The court receiving a warrant transmitted by the secondary court under this Rule shall apply its seal to the warrant, and secure that all such steps are taken for its execution as would be appropriate in the case of a warrant issued by itself.

7.25 Warrants under s 365 (1) A warrant issued under section 365(3) (search of premises not belonging to the bankrupt) shall authorise any person executing it to seize any property of the bankrupt found as a result of the execution of the warrant.

(2) Any property seized under a warrant issued under section 365(2) or (3) shall be –

(a) lodged with, or otherwise dealt with as instructed by, whoever is specified in the warrant as authorised to receive it, or

(b) kept by the officer seizing it pending the receipt of written orders from the court as to its disposal,

as may be directed by the warrant. [FORM 7.12, FORM 7.13]

CHAPTER 5: COURT RECORDS AND RETURNS

7.26 Title of proceedings (1) Every proceeding under Parts I to VII of the Act shall, with any necessary additions, be intituled 'IN THE MATTER OF . . .' (naming the company to which the proceedings relate) AND IN THE MATTER OF THE INSOLVENCY ACT 1986'.

(2) Every proceeding under Parts IX to XI of the Act shall be intituled 'IN BANKRUPTCY'.

7.27 Court records The court shall keep records of all insolvency proceedings, and shall cause to be entered in the records the taking of any step in the proceedings, and such decisions of the court in relation thereto, as the court thinks fit.

7.28 Inspection of records (1) Subject as follows, the court's records of insolvency proceedings shall be open to inspection by any person.

(2) If in the case of a person applying to inspect the records the registrar is not satisfied as to the propriety of the purpose for which inspection is required, he may refuse to allow it. The person may then apply forthwith and ex parte to the judge, who may refuse the inspection, or allow it on such terms as he thinks fit.

(3) The judge's decision under paragraph (2) is final.

7.29 Returns to Secretary of State (1) The court shall from time to time send to the

Secretary of State the following particulars relating to winding-up and bankruptcy proceedings –
(a) the full title of the proceedings, including the number assigned to each case;
(b) where a winding-up or bankruptcy order has been made, the date of the order.
(2) The Secretary of State may, on the request of any person, furnish him with particulars sent by the court under this Rule.

7.30 File of court proceedings (1) In respect of all insolvency proceedings, the court shall open and maintain a file for each case; and (subject to directions of the registrar) all documents relating to such proceedings shall be placed on the relevant file.
(2) No proceedings shall be filed in the Central Office of the High Court.

7.31 Right to inspect the file (1) In the case of any insolvency proceedings, the following have the right, at all reasonable times, to inspect the court's file of the proceedings –
(a) the person who, in relation to those proceedings, is the responsible insolvency practitioner;
(b) any duly authorised officer of the Department; and
(c) any person stating himself in writing to be a creditor of the company to which, or the individual to whom, the proceedings relate.
(2) The same right of inspection is exercisable –
(a) in proceedings under Parts I to VII of the Act, by every person who is, or at any time has been, a director or officer of the company to which the proceedings relate, or who is a member of the company or a contributory in its winding up;
(b) in proceedings with respect to a voluntary arrangement proposed by a debtor under Part VIII of the Act, by the debtor,
(c) in bankruptcy proceedings, by –
 (i) the bankrupt,
 (ii) any person against whom, or by whom, a bankruptcy petition has been presented, and
 (iii) any person who has been served, in accordance with Chapter 1 of Part 6 of the Rules, with a statutory demand.
(3) The right of inspection conferred as above on any person may be exercised on his behalf by a person properly authorised by him.
(4) Any person may, by special leave of the court, inspect the file.
(5) The right of inspection conferred by this Rule is not exercisable in the case of documents, or parts of documents, as to which the court directs (either generally or specially) that they are not to be made open to inspection without the court's leave.
An application for a direction of the court under this paragraph may be made by the official receiver, by the person who in relation to any proceedings is the responsible insolvency practitioner, or by any party appearing to the court to have an interest.
(6) If, for the purpose of powers conferred by the Act or the Rules, the Secretary of State, the Department or the official receiver requires to inspect the file of any insolvency proceedings, and requests the transmission of the file, the court shall comply with the request (unless the file is for the time being in use for the court's own purposes).
(7) Paragraphs (2) and (3) of Rule 7.28 apply in respect of court records.

7.32 Filing of Gazette notices and advertisements (1) In any court in which insolvency proceedings are pending, an officer of the court shall file a copy of every issue of the Gazette which contains an advertisement relating to those proceedings.

(2) Where there appears in a newspaper an advertisement relating to insolvency proceedings pending in any court, the person inserting the advertisement shall file a copy of it in that court.

The copy of the advertisement shall be accompanied by, or have endorsed on it, such particulars as are necessary to identify the proceedings and the date of the advertisement's appearance.

(3) An officer of any court in which insolvency proceedings are pending shall from time to time file a memorandum giving the dates of, and other particulars relating to, any notice published in the Gazette, and any newspaper advertisements, which relate to proceedings so pending.

The officer's memorandum is prima facie evidence that any notice or advertisement mentioned in it was duly inserted in the issue of the newspaper or the Gazette which is specified in the memorandum.

CHAPTER 6: COSTS AND TAXATION

7.33 Application of Rules of Supreme Court and County Court Rules Subject to provision to inconsistent effect made as follows in this Chapter –

(a) Order 62 of the Rules of the Supreme Court applies to insolvency proceedings in the High Court, and

(b) Order 38 of the County Court Rules applies to such proceedings in a county court,

in either case, with any necessary modifications.

7.34 Requirement to tax costs (1) Subject as follows, where any costs, charges or expenses of any person are payable out of the insolvent estate, the responsible insolvency practitioner may agree them with the person entitled to payment or may require them to be taxed by the court to which the insolvency proceedings are allocated, or where in relation to a company there is no such court, by a court having jurisdiction to wind up the company.

(2) If a liquidation or creditors' committee established in insolvency proceedings (except administrative receivership) resolves that any such costs, charges or expenses be taxed, the insolvency practitioner shall require taxation.

(3) Where the costs, charges or expenses of any person employed by an insolvency practitioner in insolvency proceedings are required to be taxed, this does not preclude the insolvency practitioner from making payments on account to such person on the basis of an undertaking by that person to repay immediately any money which may, on taxation, prove to have been overpaid, with interest at the rate specified in section 17 of the Judgments Act 1838 on the date payment was made and for the period from the date of payment to that of repayment.

(4) In any proceedings before the court, including proceedings on a petition, the court may order costs to be taxed.

7.35 Procedure where taxation required (1) Before taxing the costs of any person employed in insolvency proceedings by a responsible insolvency practitioner, the taxing officer shall require a certificate of employment, which shall be endorsed on the bill and signed by the insolvency practitioner.

(2) The certificate shall include –

(a) the name and address of the person employed,

(b) details of the functions to be carried out under the employment, and

(c) a note of any special terms of remuneration which have been agreed.

(3) Every person whose costs are required to be taxed in insolvency proceedings shall, on being required in writing to do so by the insolvency practitioner, deliver his bill of costs to the taxing officer for taxation.

(4) If that person does not so deliver his bill within 14 days of the requirement under paragraph (3), or within such further time as the court, on application, may grant, the insolvency practitioner may deal with the insolvent estate without regard to any claim by that person, whose claim is forfeited.
(5) Where in any such case such claim lies additionally against a insolvency practitioner in his personal capacity, that claim is also forfeited.

7.36 Costs of sheriff (1) Where a sheriff –
(a) is required under section 184(2) or 346(2) to deliver up goods or money or,
(b) has under section 184(3) or 346(3) deducted costs from the proceeds of an execution or money paid to him,
the responsible insolvency practitioner may require in writing that the sheriff's bill of costs be taxed.
(2) Where such a requirement is made, Rule 7.35(4) applies.
(3) Where, in the case of a deduction under paragraph (1)(b), any amount is disallowed on taxation, the sheriff shall forthwith pay a sum equal to that amount to the insolvency practitioner for the benefit of the insolvent estate.

7.37 Petitions presented by insolvents (1) In any case where a petition is presented by a company or individual ('the insolvent') against himself, any solicitor acting for the insolvent shall in his bill of costs give credit for any sum or security received from the insolvent as a deposit on account of the costs and expenses to be incurred in respect of the filing and prosecution of the petition; and the deposit shall be noted by the taxing officer on the taxing certificate.
(2) Paragraph (3) applies where a petition is presented by a person other than the insolvent to whom the petition relates and before it is heard the insolvent presents a petition for the same order, and that order is made.
(3) Unless the court considers that the insolvent estate has benefited by the insolvent's conduct, or that there are otherwise special circumstances justifying the allowance of costs, no costs shall be allowed to the insolvent or his solicitor out of the insolvent estate.

7.38 Costs paid otherwise than out of the insolvent estate Where a bill of costs is taxed under an order of the court directing that the costs are to be paid otherwise than out of the insolvent estate, the taxing officer shall note on the certificate of taxation by whom, or the manner in which, the costs are to be paid.

7.39 Award of costs against official receiver or responsible insolvency practitioner Without prejudice to any provision of the Act or Rules by virtue of which the official receiver is not in any event to be liable for costs and expenses, where the official receiver or a responsible insolvency practitioner is made a party to any proceedings on the application of another party to the proceedings, he shall not be personally liable for costs unless the court otherwise directs.

7.40 Applications for costs (1) This rule applies where a party to, or person affected by, any proceedings in an insolvency –
(a) applies to the court for an order allowing his costs, or part of them, incidental to the proceedings, and
(b) that application is not made at the time of the proceedings.
(2) The person concerned shall serve a sealed copy of his application on the responsible insolvency practitioner, and, in a winding up by the court or bankruptcy, on the official receiver.
(3) The insolvency practitioner and, where appropriate, the official receiver may appear on the application.

(4) No costs of or incidental to the application shall be allowed to the applicant unless the court is satisfied that the application could not have been made at the time of the proceedings.

7.41 Costs and expenses of witness (1) Except as directed by the court, no allowance as a witness in any examination or other proceedings before the court shall be made to the bankrupt or officer of the insolvent company to which the proceedings relate.
(2) A person presenting any petition in insolvency proceedings shall not be regarded as a witness on the hearing of the petition, but the taxing officer may allow his expenses of travelling and subsistence.

7.42 Certificate of taxation (1) A certificate of taxation of the taxing officer is final and conclusive as to all matters which have not been objected to in the manner provided for under the rules of the court.
(2) Where it is proved to the satisfaction of a taxing officer that a certificate of taxation has been lost or destroyed, he may issue a duplicate.
(3) 'Certificate of taxation' includes, for the purposes of the Rules, an order of the registrar in a county court.

CHAPTER 7: PERSONS INCAPABLE OF MANAGING THEIR AFFAIRS

7.43 Introductory (1) The Rules in this Chapter apply where in insolvency proceedings it appears to the court that a person affected by the proceedings is one who is incapable of managing and administering his property and affairs either –
(a) by reason of mental disorder within the meaning of the Mental Health Act 1983, or
(b) due to physical affliction or disability.
(2) The person concerned is referred to as 'the incapacitated person'.

7.44 Appointment of another person to act (1) The court may appoint such person as it thinks fit to appear for, represent or act for the incapacitated person. [FORM 7.19]
(2) The appointment may be made either generally or for the purpose of any particular application or proceeding, or for the exercise of particular rights or powers which the incapacitated person might have exercised but for his incapacity.
(3) The court may make the appointment either of its own motion or on application by –
(a) a person who has been appointed by a court of competent jurisdiction to manage the affairs of, or to represent, the incapacitated person, or
(b) any relative or friend of the incapacitated person who appears to the court to be a proper person to make the application, or
(c) the official receiver, or
(d) the person who, in relation to the proceedings, is the responsible insolvency practitioner.
(4) Application under paragraph (3) may be made ex parte, but the court may require such notice of the application as it thinks necessary to be given to the person alleged to be incapacitated, or any other person, and may adjourn the hearing of the application to enable the notice to be given.

7.45 Affidavit in support of application (1) Except where made by the official receiver, an application under Rule 7.44(3) shall be supported by an affidavit of a registered medical practitioner as to the mental or physical condition of the incapacitated person.

(2) In the excepted case, a report made by the official receiver is sufficient.

7.46 Service of notices following appointment Any notice served on, or sent to, a person appointed under Rule 7.44 has the same effect as if it has been served on, or given to, the incapacitated person.

CHAPTER 8: APPEALS IN INSOLVENCY PROCEEDINGS

7.47 Appeals and reviews of court orders (winding up) (1) Every court having jurisdiction under the Act to wind up companies may review, rescind or vary any order made by it in the exercise of that jurisdiction.
(2) An appeal from a decision made in the exercise of that jurisdiction by a county court or by a registrar of the High Court lies to a single judge of the High Court; and an appeal from a decision of that judge on such an appeal lies, with the leave of that judge or the Court of Appeal, to the Court of Appeal.
(3) A county court is not, in the exercise of its jurisdiction to wind up companies, subject to be restrained by the order of any other court, and no appeal lies from its decision in the exercise of that jurisdiction except as provided by this Rule.
(4) Any application for the rescission of a winding-up order shall be made within 7 days after the date on which the order was made.

7.48 Appeals in bankruptcy (1) In bankruptcy proceedings, an appeal lies at the instance of the Secretary of State from any order of the court made on an application for the rescission or annulment of a bankruptcy order, or for a bankrupt's discharge.
(2) In the case of an order made by a county court or by a registrar of the High Court, the appeal lies to a single judge of the High Court; and an appeal from a decision of that judge on such an appeal lies, with the leave of that judge or the Court of Appeal, to the Court of Appeal.

7.49 Procedure on appeal (1) Subject as follows, the procedure and practice of the Supreme Court relating to appeals to the Court of Appeal apply to appeals in insolvency proceedings.
(2) In relation to any appeal to a single judge of the High Court under section 375(2) of the Act (individual insolvency) or Rule 7.47(2) above (company insolvency), any reference in the Rules of the Supreme Court to the Court of Appeal is replaced by a reference to that judge.
(3) In insolvency proceedings, the procedure under Order 59 of the Rules of the Supreme Court (appeal to the Court of Appeal) is by application, and not by summons.

7.50 Appeal against decision of Secretary of State or official receiver An appeal under the Act or the Rules against a decision of the Secretary of State or the official receiver shall be brought within 28 days of the notification of the decision.

CHAPTER 9: GENERAL

7.51 Principal court rules and practice to apply Except so far as inconsistent with the Insolvency Rules, the Rules of the Supreme Court and the practice of the High Court apply to insolvency proceedings in the High Court, and the County Court Rules and the practice of the county court apply to insolvency proceedings in a county court, in either case with any necessary modifications.

7.52 Right of audience (1) Official receivers and duputy official receivers have right of audience in insolvency proceedings, whether in the High Court or a county court.

(2) Subject as above, rights of audience in insolvency proceedings are the same as obtained before the coming into force of the Rules.

7.53 Right of attendance (company insolvency) (1) Subject as follows, in company insolvency proceedings any person stating himself in writing, in records kept by the court for that purpose, to be a creditor or member of the company or, where the company is being wound up, a contributory, is entitled, at his own cost, to attend in court or in chambers at any stage of the proceedings.
(2) Attendance may be by the person himself, or his solicitor.
(3) A person so entitled may request the court in writing to give him notice of any step in the proceedings; and, subject to his paying the costs involved and keeping the court informed as to his address, the court shall comply with the request.
(4) If the court is satisfied that the exercise by a person of his rights under this Rule has given rise to costs for the insolvent estate which would not otherwise have been incurred and ought not, in the circumstances, to fall on that estate, it may direct that the costs be paid by the person concerned, to an amount specified.

The person's rights under this Rule are in abeyance so long as those costs are not paid.
(5) The court may appoint one or more persons to represent the creditors, the members or the contributories of an insolvent company, or any class of them, to have the rights conferred by this Rule, instead of the rights being exercisable by any or all of them individually.

If two or more persons are appointed under this paragraph to represent the same interest, they must (if at all) instruct the same solicitor.

7.54 Insolvency practitioner's solicitor Where in any proceedings the attendance of the responsible insolvency practitioner's solicitor is required, whether in court or in chambers, the insolvency practitioner himself need not attend, unless directed by the court.

7.55 Formal defects No insolvency proceedings shall be invalidated by any formal defect or by any irregularity, unless the court before which objection is made considers that substantial injustice has been caused by the defect or irregularity, and that the injustice cannot be remedied by any order of the court.

7.56 Restriction on concurrent proceedings and remedies Where in insolvency proceedings the court makes an order staying any action, execution or other legal process against the property of a company, or against the property or person of an individual debtor or bankrupt, service of the order may be effected by sending a sealed copy of the order to whatever is the address for service of the plaintiff or other party having the carriage of the proceedings to be stayed.

7.57 Affidavits (1) Subject as follows, the rules and practice obtaining in the High Court with regard to affidavits, their form and contents, and the procedure governing their use, are to be taken as applicable in all insolvency proceedings in any court.
(2) In applying RSC Order 41 (which relates to affidavits generally), there are to be disregarded provisions which are inconsistent with, or necessarily excluded by, the following paragraphs of this Rule.
(3) Where in insolvency proceedings an affidavit is made by the official receiver or the responsible insolvency practitioner, the deponent shall state the capacity in which he makes it, the position which he holds, and the address at which he works.
(4) Notwithstanding RSC Order 41 Rule 8 (affidavit not to be sworn before party's own solicitor), a creditor's affidavit of debt may be sworn before his own solicitor.

(4) The official receiver, any deputy official receiver, or any officer of the court duly authorised in that behalf, may take affidavits and declarations.

7.58 Security in court (1) Where security has to be given to the court (otherwise than in relation to costs), it may be given by guarantee, bond or the payment of money into court.
(2) A person proposing to give a bond as security shall give notice to the party in whose favour the security is required, and to the court, naming those who are to be sureties to the bond.
(3) The court shall forthwith give notice to both the parties concerned of a venue for the execution of the bond and the making of any objection to the sureties.
(4) The sureties shall make an affidavit of their sufficiency (unless dispensed with by the party in whose favour the security is required) and shall, if required by the court, attend the court to be cross-examined.

7.59 Payment into court The Rules of the Supreme Court and the County Court Rules relating to payment into and out of court of money lodged in court as security for costs apply, in the High Court and a county court respectively, to money lodged in court under the Rules.

7.60 Discovery (1) Any party to insolvency proceedings may, with the leave of the court, administer interrogatories to, or obtain discovery from, any other party to those proceedings.
(2) Application under this Rule may be made ex parte.

7.61 Office copies of documents (1) Any person who has under the Rules the right to inspect the court file of insolvency proceedings may require the court to provide him with an office copy of any document from the file.
(2) A person's rights under this Rule may be exercised on his behalf by his solicitor.
(3) An office copy provided by the court under this Rule shall be in such form as the registrar thinks appropriate, and shall bear the court's seal.

Part 8: Proxies and Company Representation

8.1 Definition of 'proxy' (1) For the purposes of the Rules, a proxy is an authority given by a person ('the principal') to another person ('the proxy-holder') to attend a meeting and speak and vote as his representative. [FORMS 8.1 to 8.5]
(2) Proxies are for use at creditors', company or contributories' meetings under the Act or the Rules.
(3) Only one proxy may be given by a person for any one meeting at which he desires to be represented; and it may only be given to one person, being an individual aged 18 or over. But the principal may specify one or more other such individuals to be proxy-holder in the alternative, in the order in which they are named in the proxy.
(4) Without prejudice to the generality of paragraph (3), a proxy for a particular meeting may be given to whoever is to be the chairman of the meeting; and for a meeting held as part of the proceedings in a winding up by the court, or in a bankruptcy, it may be given to the official receiver.
(5) A proxy requires the holder to give the principal's vote on matters arising for determination at the meeting, or to abstain, either as directed or in accordance with the holder's own discretion; and it may authorise or require the holder to propose, in the principal's name, a resolution to be voted on by the meeting.

8.2 Issue and use of forms (1) When notice is given of a meeting to be held, in insolvency proceedings, and forms of proxy are sent out with the notice, no form so

sent out shall have inserted in it the name or description of any person as proxy-holder.
(2) No form of proxy shall be used at any meeting except that which is sent out with the notice summoning the meeting, or a substantially similar form.
(3) A form of proxy shall be signed by the principal, or by some person authorised by him (either generally or with reference to a particular meeting). If the form is signed by a person other than the principal, the nature of the person's authority shall be stated.

8.3 Use of proxies at meetings (1) A proxy given for a particular meeting may be used at any adjournment of that meeting.
(2) Where the official receiver holds proxies for use at any meeting, his deputy, or any other official receiver, may act as proxy-holder in his place.
Alternatively, the official receiver may in writing authorise another officer of the Department to act for him at the meeting and use the proxies as if that other officer were himself proxy-holder.
(3) Where the responsible insolvency practitioner holds proxies to be used by him as chairman of a meeting, and some other person acts as chairman, the other person may use the insolvency practitioner's proxies as if he were himself proxy-holder.

8.4 Retention of proxies (1) Subject as follows, proxies used for voting at any meeting shall be retained by the chairman of the meeting.
(2) The chairman shall deliver the proxies, forthwith after the meeting, to the responsible insolvency practitioner (where that is someone other than himself).

8.5 Right of inspection (1) The responsible insolvency practitioner shall, so long as proxies lodged with him are in his hands, allow them to be inspected, at all reasonable times on any business day, by –
(a) the creditors, in the case of proxies used at a meeting of creditors, and
(b) a company's members or contributories, in the case of proxies used at a meeting of the company or of its contributories.
(2) The reference in paragraph (1) to creditor is –
(a) in the case of a company in liquidation or of an individual's bankruptcy, those creditors who have proved their debts, and
(b) in any other case, persons who have submitted in writing a claim to be creditors of the company or individual concerned;
but in neither case does it include a person whose proof or claim has been wholly rejected for purposes of voting, dividend or otherwise.
(3) The right of inspection given by this Rule is also exercisable –
(a) in the case of an insolvent company, by its directors, and
(b) in the case of an insolvent individual, by him.

8.6 Proxy-holder with financial interest (1) A proxy-holder shall not vote in favour of any resolution which would directly or indirectly place him, or any associate of his, in a position to receive any remuneration out of the insolvent estate, unless the proxy specifically directs him to vote in that way.
(2) This Rule applies also to any person acting as chairman of a meeting and using proxies in that capacity; and in its application to him, the proxy-holder is deemed an associate of his.

8.7 Company representation (1) Where a person is authorised under section 375 of the Companies Act to represent a corporation at a meeting of creditors or of the company or its contributories, he shall produce to the chairman of the meeting a copy of the resolution from which he derives his authority.

(2) The copy resolution must be under the seal of the corporation, or certified by the secretary or a director of the corporation to be a true copy.

Part 9: Examination of Persons Concerned in Company and Individual Insolvency

9.1 Preliminary (1) The Rules in this Part relate to applications to the court for an order under –
(a) section 236 (inquiry into company's dealings when it is, or is alleged to be, insolvent), or
(b) section 366 (inquiry in bankruptcy, with respect to the bankrupt's dealings). [FORM 9.1]
(2) The following definitions apply –
(a) the person in respect of whom an order is applied for is 'the respondent';
(b) 'the applicable section' is section 236 or section 366, according to whether the affairs of a company or those of a bankrupt or (where the application under section 366 is made by virtue of section 368) a debtor are in question;
(c) the company or, as the case may be, the bankrupt or debtor concerned is 'the insolvent';

9.2 Form and contents of application (1) The application shall be in writing, and be accompanied by a brief statement of the grounds on which it is made.
(2) The respondent must be sufficiently identified in the application.
(3) It shall be stated whether the application is for the respondent –
(a) to be ordered to appear before the court, or
(b) to answer interrogatories (if so, particulars to be given of the matters in respect of which answers are required), or
(c) to submit affidavits (if so, particulars to be given of the matters to which he is required to swear), or
(d) to produce books, papers or other records (if so, the items in question to be specified),
or for any two or more of those purposes.
(4) The application may be made ex parte.

9.3 Order for examination etc (1) The court may, whatever the purpose of the application, make any order which it has power to make under the applicable section.
(2) The court, if it orders the respondent to appear before it, shall specify a venue for his appearance, which shall be not less than 14 days from the date of the order.
(3) If he is ordered to submit affidavits, the order shall specify –
(a) the matters which are to be dealt with in his affidavits, and
(b) the time within which they are to be submitted to the court.
(4) If the order is to produce books, papers or other records, the time and manner of compliance shall be specified.
(5) The order must be served forthwith on the respondent; and it must be served personally, unless the court otherwise orders.

9.4 Procedure for examination (1) At any examination of the respondent, the applicant may attend in person, or be represented by a solicitor with or without counsel, and may put such questions to the respondent as the court may allow.
(2) Any other person who could have applied for an order under the applicable section in respect of the insolvent's affairs may, with the leave of the court and if the applicant does not object, attend the examination and put questions to the respondent (but only through the applicant).

(3) If the respondent is ordered to answer by interrogatories, the court shall direct him as to the questions which he is required to answer, and as to whether his answers (if any) are to be made on affidavit.
(4) Where application has been made under the applicable section on information provided by a creditor of the insolvent, that creditor may, with the leave of the court and if the applicant does not object, attend the examination and put questions to the respondent (but only through the applicant).
(5) The respondent may at his own expense employ a solicitor with or without counsel, who may put to him such questions as the court may allow for the purpose of enabling him to explain or qualify any answers given by him, and may make representations on his behalf.
(6) There shall be made in writing such record of the examination as the court thinks proper. The record shall be read over either to or by the respondent and signed by him at a venue fixed by the court.
(7) The written record may, in any proceedings (whether under the Act or otherwise) be used as evidence against the respondent of any statement made by him in the course of his examination.

9.5 Record of examination (1) Unless the court otherwise directs, the written record of the respondent's examination, and any answer given by him to interrogatories, and any affidavits submitted by him in compliance with an order of the court under the applicable section, shall not be filed in court.
(2) The written record, answers and affidavits shall not be open to inspection, without an order of the court, by any person other than –
(a) the applicant for an order under the applicable section, or
(b) any person who could have applied for such an order in respect of the affairs of the same insolvent.
(3) Paragraph (2) applies also to so much of the court file as shows the grounds of the application for an order under the applicable section and to any copy of proposed interrogatories.
(4) The court may from time to time give directions as to the custody and inspection of any documents to which this Rule applies, and as to the furnishing of copies of, or extracts from, such documents.

9.6 Costs of proceedings under ss 236, 366 (1) Where the court has ordered an examination of any person under the applicable section, and it appears to it that the examination was made necessary because information had been unjustifiably refused by the respondent, it may order that the costs of the examination be paid by him.
(2) Where the court makes an order against a person under –
(a) section 237(1) or 367(1) (to deliver up property in his possession which belongs to the insolvent), or
(b) section 237(2) or 367(2) (to pay any amount in discharge of a debt due to the insolvent),
the costs of the application for the order may be ordered by the court to be paid by the respondent.
(3) Subject to paragraphs (1) and (2) above, the applicant's costs shall, unless the court otherwise orders, be paid out of insolvent estate.
(4) A person summoned to attend for private examination shall be tendered a reasonable sum in respect of travelling expenses incurred in connection with his attendance. Other costs falling on him are at the court's discretion.
(5) Where the examination is on the application of the official receiver otherwise than in the capacity of liquidator or trustee, no order shall be made for the payment of costs by him.

Part 10: Official Receivers

10.1 Appointment of official receivers Judicial notice shall be taken of the appointment under sections 399 to 401 of official receivers and deputy official receivers.

10.2 Persons entitled to act on official receiver's behalf (1) In the absence of the official receiver authorised to act in a particular case, an officer authorised in writing for the purpose by the Secretary of State, or by the official receiver himself, may, with the leave of the court, act on the official receiver's behalf and in his place –
(a) in any examination under section 133, 236, 290 or 366, and
(b) in respect of any application to the court.
(2) In case of emergency, where there is no official receiver capable of acting, anything to be done by, to or before the official receiver may be done by, to or before the registrar of the court.

10.3 Application for directions The official receiver may apply to the court for directions in relation to any matter arising in insolvency proceedings.

10.4 Official receiver's expenses (1) Any expenses incurred by the official receiver (in whatever capacity he may be acting) in connection with proceedings taken against him in insolvency proceedings are to be treated as expenses of the insolvency proceedings.
'Expenses' includes damages.
(2) In respect of any sums due to him under paragraph (1), the official receiver has a charge on the insolvent estate.

Part 11: Declaration and Payment of Dividend (Winding up and Bankruptcy)

11.1 Preliminary (1) The Rules in this Part relate to the declaration and payment of dividends in companies winding up and in bankruptcy.
(2) The following definitions apply –
(a) 'the insolvent' means the company in liquidation or, as the case may be, the bankrupt; and
(b) 'creditors' means those creditors of the insolvent of whom the responsible insolvency practitioner is aware, or who are identified in the insolvent's statement of affairs.

11.2 Notice of intended dividend (1) Before declaring a dividend, the responsible insolvency practitioner shall give notice of his intention to do so to all creditors who have not proved their debts.
(2) The notice shall specify a date ('the last date for proving') up to which proofs may be lodged. The date shall be the same for all creditors, and not less than 21 days from that of the notice.
(3) The insolvency practitioner shall in the notice state his intention to declare a dividend (specified as interim or final, as the case may be) within the period of 4 months from the last date for proving.

11.3 Final admission/rejection of proofs (1) The responsible insolvency practitioner shall, within 7 days from the last date for proving, deal with every creditor's proof (in so far as not already dealt with) by admitting or rejecting it in whole or in part, or by making such provision as he thinks fit in respect of it.
(2) The insolvency practitioner is not obliged to deal with proofs lodged after the last date for proving; but he may do so, if he thinks fit.

11.4 Postponement or cancellation of dividend If in the period of 4 months referred to in Rule 11.2(3) –
(a) the responsible insolvency practitioner rejected a proof in whole or in part and application is made to the court for his decision to be reversed or varied, or
(b) application is made to the court for the insolvency practitioner's decision on a proof to be reversed or varied, or for a proof to be expunged, or for a reduction of the amount claimed,
the insolvency practitioner may postpone or cancel the dividend.

11.5 Decision to declare dividend (1) If the responsible insolvency practitioner has not, in the 4-month period referred to in Rule 11.2(3), had cause to postpone or cancel the dividend, he shall within that period proceed to declare the dividend of which he gave notice under that Rule.
(2) Except with the leave of the court, the insolvency practitioner shall not declare the dividend so long as there is pending any application to the court to reverse or vary a decision of his on a proof, or to expunge a proof or to reduce the amount claimed.
If the court gives leave under this paragraph, the insolvency practitioner shall make such provision in respect of the proof in question as the court directs.

11.6 Notice of declaration (1) The responsible insolvency practitioner shall give notice of the dividend to all creditors who have proved their debts.
(2) The notice shall include the following particulars relating to the insolvency and the administration of the insolvent estate –
(a) amounts realised from the sale of assets, indicating (so far as practicable) amounts raised by the sale of particular assets;
(b) payments made by the insolvency practitioner in the administration of the insolvent estate;
(c) provision (if any) made for unsettled claims, and funds (if any) retained for particular purposes;
(d) the total number to be distributed, and the rate of dividend;
(e) whether, and if so when, any further dividend is expected to be declared.
(3) The dividend may be distributed simultaneously with the notice declaring it.
(4) Payment of dividend may be made by post, or arrangements may be made with any creditor for it to be paid to him in another way, or held for his collection.
(5) Where a dividend is paid on a bill of exchange or other negotiable instrument, the amount of the dividend shall be endorsed on the instrument, or on a certified copy of it, if required, to be produced by the holder for that purpose.

11.7 Notice of no, or no further, dividend If the responsible insolvency practitioner gives notice to creditors that he is unable to declare any dividend or (as the case may be) any further dividend, the notice shall contain a settlement to the effect either –
(a) that no funds have been realised, or
(b) that the funds realised have already been distributed or used or allocated for defraying the expenses of administration.

11.8 Proof altered after payment of dividend (1) If after payment of dividend the amount claimed by a creditor in his proof is increased, the creditor is not entitled to disturb the distribution of the dividend; but he is entitled to be paid, out of any money for the time being available for the payment of any further dividend, any dividend or dividends which he has failed to receive.
(2) Any dividend or dividends payable under paragraph (1) shall be paid before the money there referred to is applied to the payment of any such further dividend.
(3) If, after a creditor's proof has been admitted, the proof is withdrawn or expunged, or the amount of it is reduced, the creditor is liable to repay to the

responsible insolvency practitioner, for the credit of the insolvent estate, any amount overpaid by way of dividend.

11.9 Secured creditors (1) The following applies where a creditor revalues his security at a time when a dividend has been declared.
(2) If the revaluation results in a reduction of his unsecured claim ranking for dividend, the creditor shall forthwith repay to the responsible insolvency practitioner, for the credit of the insolvent estate, any amount received by him as dividend in excess of that to which he would be entitled having regard to the revaluation of the security.
(3) If the revaluation results in an increase of his unsecured claim, the creditor is entitled to receive from the insolvency practitioner, out of any money for the time being available for the payment of a further dividend, before any such further dividend is paid, any dividend or dividends which he has failed to receive, having regard to the revaluation of the security.
However, the creditor is not entitled to disturb any dividend declared (whether or not distributed) before the date of the revaluation.

11.10 Disqualification from dividend If a creditor contravenes any provision of the Act or the Rules relating to the valuation of securities, the court may, on the application of the responsible insolvency practitioner, order that the creditor be wholly or partly disqualified from participation in any dividend.

11.11 Assignment of right to dividend (1) If a person entitled to a dividend gives notice to the responsible insolvency practitioner that he wishes the dividend to be paid to another person, or that he has assigned his entitlement to another person, the insolvency practitioner shall pay the dividend to that other accordingly.
(2) A notice given under this Rule must specify the name and address of the person to whom payment is to be made.

11.12 Preferential creditors (1) Subject as follows, the Rules in this Part apply with respect to any distribution made in the insolvency to preferential creditors, with such adaptations as are appropriate considering that such creditors are of a limited class.
(2) The notice by the responsible insolvency practitioner under Rule 11.2, where a dividend is to be declared for preferential creditors, need only be given to those creditors in whose case he has reason to believe that their debts are preferential.

11.13 Debt payable at future time (1) Where a creditor has proved for a debt of which payment is not due at the date of the declaration of dividend, he is entitled to dividend equally with other creditors, but subject as follows.
(2) For the purpose of dividend (and for no other purpose), the amount of the creditor's proof shall be reduced by an amount calculated as follows –

$$\frac{I \times M}{12}$$

where I is the rate of interest specified in section 17 of the Judgments Act 1838 on the day on which the company went into liquidation or the relevant bankruptcy order was made, and M is the number of months (expressed, if need be, as, or as including, fractions of months) between the declaration of dividend and the date when payment of the creditor's debt would otherwise be due.
(3) Other creditors are not entitled to interest out of surplus funds under section 189(2) or (as the case may be) 328(4) until any creditor to whom paragraphs (1) and (2) apply has been paid the full amount of his debt.

Part 12: Miscellaneous and General

12.1 Power of Secretary of State to regulate certain matters Pursuant to paragraph 27 of Schedule 8 to the Act, and paragraph 30 of Schedule 9 to the Act, the Secretary of State may make regulations with respect to the following matters arising in companies winding up and individual bankruptcy –
(a) the preparation and keeping by liquidators, trustees, provisional liquidators, interim receivers and the official receiver, of books, accounts and other records, and their production to such persons as may be authorised or required to inspect them;
(b) the auditing of liquidators' and trustees' accounts;
(c) the manner in which liquidators and trustees are to act in relation to the insolvent company's or bankrupt's books, papers and other records, and the manner of their disposal by the responsible insolvency practitioner or others;
(d) the supply –
 (i) in company insolvency, by the liquidator to creditors and members of the company, contributories in its winding up and the liquidation committee, and
 (ii) in individual insolvency, by the trustee to creditors and the creditors' committee,
of copies of documents relating to the insolvency and the affairs of the insolvent company or individual (on payment, in such cases as may by specified by the regulations, of the specified fee);
(e) the manner in which insolvent estates are to be distributed by liquidators and trustees, including provision with respect to unclaimed funds and dividends;
(f) the manner in which moneys coming into the hands of a liquidator or trustee in the course of his administration are to be handled and, in the case of a liquidator, invested;
(g) the amount (or the manner of determining the amount) to be paid to the official receiver by way of remuneration when acting as provisional liquidator, liquidator, interim receiver or trustee.
(2) Regulations made pursuant to paragraph (1) may –
(a) confer a discretion on the court;
(b) make non-compliance with any of the regulations a criminal offence;
(c) make different provision for different cases, including different provision for different areas.

12.2 Costs, expenses, etc All fees, charges and other expenses incurred in the course of winding up or bankruptcy proceedings are to be regarded as expenses of the winding up or, as the case may be, of the bankruptcy.

12.3 Provable debts (1) Subject as follows, in both winding up and bankruptcy, all claims by creditors are provable as debts against the company or, as the case may be, the bankrupt, whether they are present or future, certain or contingent, ascertained or sounding only in damages.
(2) The following are not provable –
(a) in bankruptcy, any fine imposed for an offence, and any obligation arising under an order made in family or domestic proceedings;
(b) in winding up or bankruptcy, any obligation arising under a confiscation order made under section 1 of the Drug Trafficking Offences Act 1986.
'Fine', 'domestic proceedings' and 'family proceedings' have the meanings given by section 281(8) of the Act (which applies the Magistrates' Courts Act 1980 and the Matrimonial and Family Proceedings Act 1984).

(3) Nothing in this Rule prejudices any enactment or rule of law under which a particular kind of debt is not provable, whether on grounds of public policy or otherwise.

12.4 Notices (1) All notices required or authorised by or under the Act or the Rules to be given must be in writing, unless it is otherwise provided, or the court allows the notice to be given in some other way.
(2) Where in any proceedings a notice is required to be sent or given by the official receiver or by the responsible insolvency practitioner, the sending or giving of it may be proved by means of a certificate –
(a) in the case of the official receiver, by him or a member of his staff, and
(b) in the case of the insolvency practitioner, by him, or his solicitor, or a partner or an employee of either of them,
that the notice was duly posted.
(3) In the case of a notice to be sent or given by a person other than the official receiver or insolvency practitioner, the sending or giving of it may be proved by means of a certificate by that person that he posted the notice, or instructed another person (naming him) to do so.
(4) A certificate under this Rule may be endorsed on a copy or specimen of the notice to which it relates.

12.5 Evidence of proceedings at meetings (1) A minute of proceedings at a meeting (held under the Act or the Rules) of a person's creditors, or of the members of a company, or of the contributories in a company's liquidation, signed by a person describing himself as, or appearing to be, the chairman of that meeting is admissible in insolvency proceedings without further proof.
(2) The minute is prima facie evidence that –
(a) the meeting was duly convened and held,
(b) all resolutions passed at the meeting were duly passed, and
(c) all proceedings at the meeting duly took place.

12.6 Documents issuing from Secretary of State (1) Any document purporting to be, or to contain, any order, directions or certificate issued by the Secretary of State shall be received in evidence and deemed to be or (as the case may be) contain that order or certificate, or those directions, without further proof, unless the contrary is shown.
(2) Paragraph (1) applies whether the document is signed by the Secretary of State himself or an officer on his behalf.
(3) Without prejudice to the foregoing, a certificate signed by the Secretary of State or an officer on his behalf and confirming –
(a) the making of any order,
(b) the issuing of any document, or
(c) the exercise of any discretion, power or obligation arising or imposed under the Act or the Rules,
is conclusive evidence of the matters dealt with in the certificate.

12.7 Forms for use in insolvency proceedings (1) The forms contained in Schedule 4 to the Rules shall be used in and in connection with, insolvency proceedings, whether in the High Court or a county court.
(2) The forms shall be used with such variations, if any, as the circumstances may require.
(3) Where any form contained in Schedule 4 is substantially the same as one used for a corresponding purpose under the law and practice obtaining before the coming into

force of the Rules, the latter may continue to be used (with the necessary modifications) until the Lord Chancellor otherwise directs.

12.8 Insolvency practitioner's security (1) Wherever under the Rules any person has to appoint, or certify the appointment of, an insolvency practitioner to any office, he is under a duty to satisfy himself that the person appointed or to be appointed has sufficient security for the proper performance of his functions.
(2) It is the duty –
(a) of the creditors' committee in companies administration, administrative receivership and bankruptcy,
(b) of the liquidation committee in companies winding up, and
(c) of any committee of creditors established for the purposes of a voluntary arrangement under Part I or VIII of the Act,
to review from time to time the adequacy of the responsible insolvency practitioner's security.
(3) In any insolvency proceedings the cost of the responsible insolvency practitioner's security shall be defrayed as an expense of the proceedings.

12.9 Time-limits The provisions of Order 3 of the Rules of the Supreme Court, except Rules 3 and 6, apply as regards computation of time in respect of anything required or authorised by the Rules to be done.

12.10 Service by post (1) For a document to be properly served by post, it must be contained in an envelope addressed to the person on whom service is to be effected, and pre-paid for either first or second class post.
(2) Where first class post is used, the document is treated as served on the second business day after the date of posting, unless the contrary is shown.
(3) Where second class post is used, the document is treated as served on the fourth business day after the date of posting, unless the contrary is shown.
(4) The date of posting is presumed, unless the contrary is shown, to be the date shown in the post-mark on the envelope in which the document is contained.

12.11 General provisions as to service (1) Subject as follows, Order 65 of the Rules of the Supreme Court applies as regards any matter relating to the service of documents and the giving of notice in insolvency proceedings.
(2) In Order 65 Rule 7, the expression 'other originating process' does not include any application in insolvency proceedings.
(3) Order 65 Rule 9 does not apply.
(4) In Order 65 Rule 10, the expression 'process' includes any application in insolvency proceedings.

12.12 Service outside the jurisdiction (1) Order 11 of the Rules of the Supreme Court, and the corresponding County Court Rules, do not apply in insolvency proceedings.
(2) A bankruptcy petition may, with the leave of the court, be served outside England and Wales in such manner as the court may direct.
(3) Where for the purposes of insolvency proceedings any process or order of the court, or other document, is required to be served on a person who is not in England and Wales, the court may order service to be effected within such time, on such person, at such place and in such manner as it thinks fit, and may also require such proof of service as it thinks fit.

(4) An application under this Rule shall be supported by an affidavit stating –
(a) the grounds on which the application is made, and
(b) in what place or country the person to be served is, or probably may be found.

12.13 Confidentiality of documents (1) Where in insolvency proceedings the responsible insolvency practitioner considers, in the case of a document forming part of the records of the insolvency, that –
(a) it should be treated as confidential, or
(b) it is of such a nature that its disclosure would be calculated to be injurious to the interests of the insolvent's creditors or, in the case of a company's insolvency, its members or the contributories in its winding up,

he may decline to allow it to be inspected by a person who would otherwise be entitled to inspect it.

(2) The persons to whom the insolvency practitioner may under this Rule refuse inspection include the members of a liquidation committee or a creditor's committee.

(3) Where under this Rule the insolvency practitioner determines to refuse inspection of a document, the person wishing to inspect it may apply to the court for that determination to be overruled; and the court may either overrule it altogether, or sustain it subject to such conditions (if any) as it thinks fit to impose.

12.14 Notices sent simultaneously to the same person Where under the Act or the Rules a document of any description is to be sent to a person (whether or not as a member of a class of persons to whom that same document is to be sent), it may be sent as an accompaniment to any other document or information which the person is to receive, with or without modification or adaptation of the form applicable to that document.

12.15 Right to copy documents Where the Rules confer a right for any person to inspect documents, the right includes that of taking copies of those documents, on payment –
(a) in the case of documents on the court's file of proceedings, of the fee chargeable under any order made under section 130 of the Supreme Court Act 1981 or under section 128 of the County Courts Act 1984, and
(b) otherwise, of the appropriate fee.

12.16 Non-receipt of notice of meeting Where in accordance with the Act or the Rules a meeting of creditors or other persons is summoned by notice, the meeting is presumed to have been duly summoned and held, notwithstanding that not all those to whom the notice is to be given have received it.

12.17 Right to have list of creditors (1) This Rule applies in any of the following proceedings –
(a) proceedings under Part II of the Act (company administration),
(b) a creditors' voluntary winding up, or a winding up by the court, and
(c) proceedings in bankruptcy.

(2) In any such proceedings a creditor who under the Rules has the right to inspect documents on the court file also has a right to require the responsible insolvency practitioner to furnish him with a list of the insolvent's creditors and the amounts of their respective debts.

This does not apply if a statement of the insolvent's affairs has been filed in court or, in the case of a creditors' voluntary winding up, been delivered to the registrar of companies.

(3) The insolvency practitioner, on being required by any person to furnish the list, shall send it to him, but is entitled to charge the appropriate fee for doing so.

12.18 False claim of status as creditor, etc (1) Where the Rules provide for creditors, members of a company or contributories in a company's winding up a right to inspect any documents, whether on the court's file or in the hands of a responsible insolvency practitioner or other person, it is an offence for a person, with the intention of obtaining a sight of documents which he has not under the Rules any right to inspect, falsely to claim a status which would entitle him to inspect them.
(2) A person guilty of an offence under this Rule is liable to imprisonment or a fine, or both.

12.19 Execution overtaken by judgment debtor's insolvency (1) This Rule applies where execution has been taken out against property of a judgment debtor, and notice is given to the sheriff or other officer charged with the execution –
(a) under section 184(1) (that a winding-up order has been made against the debtor, or that a provisional liquidator has been appointed, or that a resolution for voluntary winding up has been passed); or
(b) under section 184(4) (that a winding-up petition has been presented or a winding-up order made, or that a meeting has been called at which there is to be proposed a resolution for voluntary winding up, or that such a resolution has been passed); or
(c) under section 346(2) (that the judgment debtor has been adjudged bankrupt); or
(d) under section 346(3)(b) (that a bankruptcy petition has been presented in respect of him).
(2) Subject as follows, the notice shall be in writing and be delivered by hand at, or sent by recorded delivery to, the office of the under-sheriff or (as the case may be) of the officer charged with the execution.
(3) Where the execution is in a county court, and the officer in charge of it is the registrar of the court, then if –
(a) there is filed in that court in respect of the judgment debtor a winding-up or bankruptcy petition, or
(b) there is made by that court in respect of him a winding-up order or an order appointing a provisional liquidator, or a bankruptcy order or an order appointing an interim receiver,
section 184 or (as the case may be) 346 is deemed satisfied as regards the requirement of a notice to be served on, or given to, the officer in charge of the execution.

12.20 The Gazette (1) A copy of the Gazette containing any notice required by the Act or the Rules to be gazetted is evidence of any facts stated in the notice.
(2) In the case of an order of the court notice of which is required by the Act or the Rules to be gazetted, a copy of the Gazette containing the notice may in any proceedings be produced as conclusive evidence that the order was made on the date specified in the notice.
(3) Where an order of the court which is gazetted has been varied, and where any matter has been erroneously or inaccurately gazetted, the person whose responsibility it was to procure the requisite entry in the Gazette shall forthwith cause the variation of the order to be gazetted or, as the case may be, a further entry to be made in the Gazette for the purpose of correcting the error or inaccuracy.

12.21 Punishment of offences (1) Schedule 5 to the Rules has effect with respect to the way in which contraventions of the Rules are punishable on conviction.

(2) In relation to an offence under a provision of the Rules specified in the first column of the Schedule (the general nature of the offence being described in the second column), the third column shows whether the offence is punishable on conviction on indictment, or on summary conviction, or either in the one way or the other.
(3) The fourth column shows, in relation to an offence, the maximum punishment by way of fine or imprisonment which may be imposed on a person convicted of the offence in the way specified in relation to it in the third column (that is to say, on indictment or summarily), a reference to a period of years or months being to a term of imprisonment of that duration.
(4) The fifth column shows (in relation to an offence for which there is an entry in that column) that a person convicted of the offence after continued contravention is liable to a daily default fine; that is to say, he is liable on a second or subsequent conviction of the offence to the fine specified in that column for each day on which the contravention is continued (instead of the penalty specified for the offence in the fourth column of the Schedule).
(5) Section 431 (summary proceedings), as it applies to England and Wales, has effect in relation to offences under the Rules as to offences under the Act.

Part 13: Interpretation

13.1 Introductory This Part of the Rules has effect for their interpretation; and any definition given in this Part applies except, and in so far as, the context otherwise requires.

13.2 'The court'; 'the registrar' (1) Anything to be done under or by virtue of the Act or the Rules by, to or before the court may be done by, to or before a judge or the registrar.
(2) The registrar may authorise any act of a formal or administrative character which is not by statute his responsibility to be carried out by the chief clerk or any other officer of the court acting on his behalf, in accordance with directions given by the Lord Chancellor.
(3) In individual insolvency proceedings, 'the registrar' means a Registrar in Bankruptcy of the High Court, or the registrar or deputy registrar of a county court.
(4) In a company insolvency proceedings in the High Court, 'the registrar' means –
(a) subject to the following paragraph, a Registrar in Bankruptcy of the High Court;
(b) where the proceedings are in the District Registry of Birmingham, Bristol, Cardiff, Leeds, Liverpool, Manchester, Newcastle-upon-Tyne or Preston, the District Registrar.
(5) In company insolvency proceedings in a county court, 'the registrar' means the officer of the court whose duty it is to exercise the functions which in the High Court are exercised by a registrar.

13.3 'Give notice', etc (1) A reference in the Rules to giving notice, or to delivering, sending or serving any document, means that the notice or document may be sent by post, unless under a particular Rule personal service is expressly required.
(2) Any form of post may be used, unless under a particular Rule a specified form is expressly required.
(3) Personal service of a document is permissible in all cases.
(4) Notice of the venue fixed for an application may be given by service of the sealed copy of the application under Rule 7.4(3).

13.4 Notice, etc to solicitors Where under the Act or the Rules a notice or other document is required or authorised to be given to a person, it may, if he has indicated that his solicitor is authorised to accept service on his behalf, be given instead to the solicitor.

13.5 Notice to joint liquidators, joint trustees, etc Where two or more persons are acting jointly as the responsible insolvency practitioner in any proceedings, delivery of a document to one of them is to be treated as delivery to them all.

13.6 'Venue' (1) References to the 'venue' for any proceeding or attendance before the court, or for a meeting, are to the time, date and place for the proceeding, attendance or meeting.

13.7 'Insolvency proceedings' 'Insolvency proceedings' means any proceedings under the Act or the Rules.

13.8 'Insolvent estate' References to 'the insolvent estate' are –
(a) in relation to a company insolvency, the company's assets, and
(b) in relation to an individual insolvency, the bankrupt's estate or (as the case may be) the debtor's property.

13.9 'Responsible insolvency practitioner' etc (1) In relation to any insolvency proceedings, 'the responsible insolvency practitioner' means
(a) the person acting in a company insolvency, as supervisor of a voluntary arrangement under Part I of the Act, or as administrator, administrative receiver, liquidator or provisional liquidator;
(b) the person acting in an individual insolvency, as the supervisor of a voluntary arrangement under Part VIII of the Act, or as trustee or interim receiver;
(c) the official receiver acting as receiver and manager of a bankrupt's estate.
(2) Any reference to the liquidator, provisional liquidator, trustee or interim receiver includes the official receiver when acting in the relevant capacity.

13.10 'Petitioner' In winding up and bankruptcy, references to 'the petitioner' or 'the petitioning creditor' include any person who has been substituted as such, or been given carriage of the petition.

13.10 'The appropriate fee' 'The appropriate fee' means –
(a) in Rule 6.192(2) (payor under income payments order entitled to clerical etc. costs) 50 pence; and
(b) in other cases, 15 pence per A4 or A5 page, and 30 pence per A3 page.

13.12 'Debt', 'liability' (winding up) (1) 'Debt', in relation to the winding up of a company, means (subject to the next paragraph) any of the following –
(a) any debt or liability to which the company is subject at the date on which it goes into liquidation;
(b) any debt or liability to which the company may become subject after that date by reason of any obligation incurred before that date; and
(c) any interest provable as mentioned in Rule 4.93(1).
(2) In determining for the purposes of any provision of the Act or the Rules about winding up, whether any liability in tort is a debt provable in the winding up, the company is deemed to become subject to that liability by reason of an obligation incurred at the time when the cause of action accrued.
(3) For the purposes of references in any provision of the Act or the Rules about winding up to a debt or liability, it is immaterial whether the debt or liability is present or future, whether it is certain or contingent, or whether its amount is fixed or liquidated, or is capable of being ascertained by fixed rules or as a matter of opinion;

and references in any such provision to owing a debt are to be read accordingly.
(4) In any provision of the Act or the Rules about winding up, except in so far as the context otherwise requires, 'liability' means (subject to paragraph (3) above) a liability to pay money or money's worth, including any liability under an enactment, any liability for breach of trust, any liability in contract, tort or bailment, and any liability arising out of an obligation to make restitution.

13.13 Expressions used generally (1) 'Business day' means any day other than a Saturday, a Sunday, Christmas Day, Good Friday or a day which is a bank holiday in any part of Great Britain.
(2) 'The Department' means the Department of Trade and Industry.
(3) 'File in court' means deliver to the court for filing.
(4) 'The Gazette' means the London Gazette.
(5) 'General regulations' means regulations made by the Secretary of State under Rule 12.1.
(6) 'Prescribed order of priority' means the order of priority of payments laid down by Chapter 20 of Part 4 of the Rules, or Chapter 23 of Part 6.

Appendix 3

Selected forms from the Insolvency Rules 1986

Part 6: Bankruptcy

Part 7: Court procedure and practice

Rule 6.1 **Form 6.1**

Statutory Demand under section 268(1)(a) of the Insolvency Act 1986
Debt for Liquidated Sum Payable Immediately

(TITLE)

Warning:

- This is an important document. You **must** deal with this demand within 21 days of its service upon you or you could be made bankrupt and your property and goods taken away from you. Please read this demand and notes carefully.
- If you are in any doubt about your position, you should seek advice **immediately** from a solicitor or your nearest Citizens Advice Bureau.
- There are additional notes overleaf.

Demand

To ______________________________

Address ______________________________

____

This demand is served on you by the creditor:

Name ______________________________

Address ______________________________

____

The creditor claims that you owe the following debt and that it is payable immediately and, to the extent of the sum demanded, is unsecured:

When Incurred (1)	Description of Debt (2)	Amount due as at the date of this demand (3)

Amount of Debt £ [ ]

If creditor issuing this demand is a Minister of the Crown or a Government Department, is it intended to present a bankruptcy petition in the High Court?

- Yes/No

The creditor demands that you pay the above debt or secure or compound for it to the creditor's satisfaction

Signature ______________________________

Name (BLOCK LETTERS) ______________________________

Date ______________________________

Position with or relationship to creditor: ______________________________

______________________________ duly authorised

Address ______________________________

Tel. No. ______________________________

Ref. ______________________________

N.B. The person making this demand must complete the whole of this page and parts A, B and C on page 2

Notes for Creditor

- If the creditor is entitled to the debt by way of assignment, details of the original creditor and any intermediary assignees should be given in part C on page 2.
- If the amount of debt includes interest, details should be given in column (2), including the grounds upon which interest is charged. The amount of interest must be shown separately in column (3).
- Any other charge accruing due from time to time may be claimed. The amount **or** rate of the charge must be identified and the grounds on which it is claimed must be stated.
- In either case the amount claimed must be limited to that which has accrued due at the date of the demand.
- If the creditor holds any security the amount of debt should be the sum the creditor is prepared to regard as unsecured for the purposes of this demand. Brief details of the total debt should be included in column (2), and the nature of the security and the value put upon it by the creditor, as at the date of the demand, must be specified.
- If signatory is a solicitor or other agent of the creditor the name of his/her firm should be given.

Form 6.1 contd.

Part A

Appropriate Court for setting aside demand

Rule 6.4(2) of the Insolvency Rules 1986 states that the appropriate court is the court to which you would have to present your own bankruptcy petition in accordance with Rule 6.40(1) and (2). In accordance with these rules on present information the appropriate Court is [the High Court of Justice] [court] (address)

Any application by you to set aside this demand should be made to that court.

Part B

The person or persons to whom any communication regarding this demand may be addressed is/are:

____

Address ____

____

Tel. No. ____

Part C

For completion if the creditor is entitled to the debt by way of assignment

	Name	Date(s) of Assignment
Original creditor		
Assignees		

How to comply with a statutory demand or have it set aside

If you wish to avoid a bankruptcy petition being presented against you, you must pay the debt set out on page 1 of this notice within the period of 21 days of service upon you. Alternatively, you can attempt to come to a settlement with the creditor. To do this you should:

- inform the person or persons (or one of the persons) named in part B above immediately that you are willing and able to offer security for the debt to the creditor's satisfaction; or
- inform the person or persons (or one of the persons) named in part B immediately that you are willing and able to compound for the debt to the creditor's satisfaction.

If you dispute the demand in whole or in part you should:

- contact the person or persons (or one of the persons) named in part B immediately

If you consider that you have grounds to have this notice set aside or if you do not receive a satisfactory written reply from the person or persons (or one of the persons) named in part B before the expiration of 18 days after the service you should:

- apply without delay to the appropriate court shown in part A above to have the notice set aside.

Remember: You have only 21 days from the date of service on you of this document before the creditor may present a bankruptcy petition.

Rule 6.1 **Form 6.2**

Statutory Demand under section 268(1)(a) of the Insolvency Act 1986
Debt for Liquidated Sum Payable Immediately Following a Judgment or Order of the Court

(TITLE)

Warning

- This is an important document. You **must** deal with this demand within 21 days of the service upon you or you could be made bankrupt and your property and goods taken away from you. Please read this demand and notes carefully.
- If you are in any doubt about your position, you should seek advice **immediately** from a solicitor or your nearest Citizens Advice Bureau
- There are additional notes overleaf

Demand

To ____________________

Address ____________________

____

This demand is served on you by the creditor:

Name ____________________

Address ____________________

____

The creditor claims that you owe the following debt and that it is payable immediately and, to the extent of the sum demanded, is unsecured:

When Incurred (1)	Description of Debt (2)	Amount due as at the date of this demand (3)

Amount of Debt £ [ ]

*By a Judgment/Order of the ____________ Court in proceedings entitled (Plaint) Number ______ between Plaintiff and ____________ Defendant it was adjudged/ordered that you pay to the Plaintiff creditor the sum of £ ______ and £ ______ for costs

If creditor issuing this demand is a Minister of the Crown or a Government Department, is it intended to present a bankruptcy petition in the High Court?

- Yes/No

The creditor demands that you pay the above debt or compound for it to the creditor's satisfaction.

Signature ____________________

Name (BLOCK LETTERS) ____________________

Date ____________________

Position with or relationship to creditor: ____________________

____

Address ____________________

____

Tel. No. ____________________

Ref. No. ____________________

NB. The person making this demand must complete the whole of this page and parts A, B and C on page 2

Notes for Creditor

- If the creditor is entitled to the debt by way of assignment, details of the original creditor and any intermediary assignees should be given in part C on page 2.
- If the amount of debt includes interest, details should be given in column (2), including the grounds upon which interest is charged. The amount of interest must be shown separately in column (3).
- Any other charge accruing due from time to time may be claimed. The amount **or** rate of the charge must be identified and the grounds on which it is claimed must be stated.
- In either case the amount claimed must be limited to that which has accrued due at the end of the demand.
- If the creditor holds any security the amount of debt should be the sum the creditor is prepared to regard as unsecured for the purposes of this demand. Brief details of the total debt should be included in column (2), and the nature of the security and the value put upon it by the creditor, as at the date of the demand, must be specified.
- *Here set out details of Judgement
- If signatory is a solicitor or other agent of the creditor the name of his/her firm should be given.

Form 6.2 contd.

Part A
Appropriate Court for setting aside demand

Rule 6.4(2) of the Insolvency Rules 1986 states that the appropriate court is the court to which you would have to present your own bankruptcy petition in accordance with Rule 6.40(1) and (2). In accordance with these rules on present information the appropriate Court is [the High Court of Justice] [court] (address)

Any application by you to set aside this demand should be made to that court, or, if this demand is issued by a Minister of the Crown or a Government Department, you **must** apply to the High Court to set aside if it is intended to present a bankruptcy petition against you in the High Court.

Part B

The person or persons to whom any communication regarding this demand may be addressed is/are:

____

Address ______________________________

____

Tel. No. ______________________________

Part C

For completion if the creditor is entitled to the debt by way of assignment

	Name	Date(s) of Assignment
Original creditor		
Assignees		

How to comply with a statutory demand or have it set aside

If you wish to avoid a bankruptcy petition being presented against you, you must pay the debt set out on page 1 of this notice within the period of 21 days of service upon you. However if the demand follows a Judgement or order of a County Court any payment must be made to that County Court. Alternatively, you can attempt to come to a settlement with the creditor. To do this you should:

- inform the person or persons (or one of the persons) named in part B above immediately that you are willing and able to offer security for the debt to the creditor's satisfaction; or
- inform the person or persons (or one of the persons) named in part B immediately that you are willing and able to compound for the debt to the creditor's satisfaction.

If you dispute the demand in whole or in part you should:

- Contact the person or persons (or one of the persons) named in part B immediately

If you consider that you have grounds to have this notice set aside or if you do not receive a satisfactory written reply from the person or persons (or one of the persons) named in part B before the expiration of 18 days after the service you should:

- apply without delay to the appropriate court shown in part A above to have the notice set aside.

Remember: You have only 21 days from the date of service on you of this document before the creditor may present a bankruptcy petition.

Rule 6.1 **Form 6.3**

Statutory Demand under section 268(2) of the Insolvency Act 1986
Debt Payable at Future Date

(TITLE)

Warning

- This is an important document. You **must** deal with this demand within 21 days of its service upon you or you could be made bankrupt and your property and goods taken away from you. Please read this demand and notes carefully.
- If you are in any doubt about your position, you should seek advice **immediately** from a solicitor or your nearest Citizens Advice Bureau.
- There are additional notes overleaf.

Demand

To ________________________________

Address ________________________________

____

This demand is served on you by the creditor:

Name ________________________________

Address ________________________________

____

The creditor claims that you will owe the following when payment falls due on ________________________________

When Incurred (1)	Description of Debt (2)	Amount of future debt (3)
		£

The creditor is of the opinion that you have no reasonable prospect of paying this debt when it falls due because*

____

____

____

If creditor issuing this demand is a Minister of the Crown or a Government Department, is it intended to present a bankruptcy petition in the High Court?

- Yes/No

Signature ________________________________

Name ________________________________

Date ________________________________

Position with or relationship to creditor ________________________________

____

Address ________________________________

Tel. No. ________________________________

Ref. No. ________________________________

NB The person making the demand must complete the whole of this page and parts A, B and C on page 2.

Notes for Creditor.

- If the creditor is entitled to the debt by way of assignment, details of the original creditor and any assignees should be given in part C on page 2.
- If the amount of debt when due will include interest, details should be given in column (2), including the grounds upon which interest is charged.
- Any other charge accruing due from time to time may be claimed. The amount **or** rate of the charge must be identified and the grounds on which it is claimed must be stated.
- In either case the amount claimed must be limited to that which will have accrued due when payment falls due on the date specified.
- If the creditor holds any security the amount of debt should be the sum the creditor is prepared to regard as unsecured for the purposes of this demand. Brief details of the total debt should be included in column (2), and the nature of the security and the value put upon it by the creditor, as at the date of the demand, must be specified.
- *Here set out the grounds for this opinion.
- If signatory is a solicitor or other agent of the creditor the name of his/her firm should be given.

Form 6.3 contd.

Part A

Appropriate Court for setting aside demand

Rule 6.4(2) of the Insolvency Rules 1986 states that the appropriate court is the court to which you would have to present your own bankruptcy petition in accordance with Rule 6.40 (1) and (2). In accordance with these rules on present information the appropriate court is [the High Court of Justice] [court] (address).

Any application by you to set aside this demand should be made to that court.

Part B

The person or persons to whom any communication regarding the demand may be addressed is/are:

____

Address ______________________________

____

Tel. No. ______________________________

Part C

For completion if the creditor is entitled to the debt by way of assignment

	Name	Date(s) of Assignment
Original creditor		
Assignees		

How to comply with a statutory demand or have it set aside

If you wish to avoid a bankruptcy petition being presented against you, you must within the period of 21 days of service upon you, satisfy the creditor that you are able to meet the debt demanded when it is due.

If you dispute that the debt will be due in whole or in part or if you dispute the allegation that you will be unable to pay the debt when it falls due or if you consider that you may be able to offer security for the debt or to compound for it you should:

- contact the person or persons (or one of the persons) named in part B immediately.

If you consider that you have grounds to have this notice set aside or if you do not receive a satisfactory written reply from the person or persons (or one of the persons) in part B before the expiration of 18 days after service you should

- apply without delay to the appropriate court shown in part A above to have the notice set aside.

Remember: You have only 21 days from the date of service on you of this document before the creditor may present a bankruptcy petition.

Rule 6.4 **Form 6.4**

Application to Set Aside a Statutory Demand

(TITLE)

(a) Insert name and address of person to attend hearing

Let (a)

attend before the Registrar as follows:—

Date ____________________

Time ____________________ hours

Place ____________________

(b) Insert name of debtor

on the hearing of an application by (b)

the applicant for an order that the statutory demand dated be set aside.

(c) Insert date

The grounds on which the applicant claims to be entitled to the order are set out in the affidavit of the applicant sworn on (c) a copy of which affidavit accompanies this application.

(d) State the names and addresses of the persons to be served

The names and addresses of the persons upon whom this application should be served are:— (d)

(e) State the applicant's address for service

The applicant's address for service is:— (e)

Dated ____________________

Signed ____________________
(Solicitor for the) Applicant

If you do not attend, the Court may make such order as it thinks fit

Rule 6.6 **Form 6.7**

Creditor's Bankruptcy Petition on Failure to Comply with a Statutory Demand for a Liquidated Sum Payable Immediately

(TITLE)

(a) Insert full name(s) and address(es) of petitioner(s).

I/We (a) ______________________________

____

____

(b) Insert full name, place of residence and occupation (if any) of debtor

petition the court that a bankruptcy order may be made against (b) ______________

____

(c) Insert in full any other name(s) by which the debtor is or has been known

[also known as (c) ______________________________]

(d) Insert trading name (adding "with another or others", if this is so), business address and nature of business

[and carrying on business as (d) ______________________________

____

______________________________]

(e) Insert any other address or addresses at which the debtor has resided at or after the time the petition debt was incurred

[and lately residing at (e) ______________________________

____

______________________________]

(f) Give the same details as specified in note (d) above for any other businesses which have been carried on at or after the time the petition debt was incurred

[and lately carrying on business as (f) ______________________________

____

______________________________]

and say as follows:—

1. The debtor has for the greater part of six months immediately preceding

(g) Delete as applicable

the presentation of this petition (g) [resided at] [carried on business at]

____

(h) Or as the case may be following the terms of Rule 6.9.

within the district of this court (h)

(j) Please give the amount of debt(s), what they relate to and when they were incurred. Please show separately the amount or rate of any interest or other charge not previously notified to the debtor **and the reasons why you are claiming it**

2. The debtor is justly and truly indebted to me[us] in the aggregate sum of

£(j) ______

3. The above-mentioned debt is for a liquidated sum payable immediately and the debtor appears to be unable to pay it.

(k) Insert date of service of a statutory demand

4. On (k) ______________________ a statutory demand was served upon the debtor by

(l) State manner of service of demand

(l) ______________________

in respect of the above-mentioned debt. To the best of my knowledge and belief the demand has neither been complied with nor set aside in accordance with the Rules and no application to set it aside is outstanding

(m) If 3 weeks have not elapsed since service of statutory demand give reasons for earlier presentation of petition

(m)

5. I/We do not, nor does any person on my/our behalf, hold any security on the debtor's estate, or any part thereof, for the payment of the above-mentioned sum

OR

(n) Delete as applicable

I/We hold security for the payment of (n) [part of] the above-mentioned sum. I/We will give up such security for the benefit of all the creditors in the event of a bankruptcy order being made.

OR

I/We hold security for the payment of part of the above-mentioned sum and I/we estimate the value of such security to be £ . This petition is not made in respect of the secured part of my/our debt.

Endorsement

This petition having been presented to the court on ______________________
it is ordered that the petition shall be heard as follows:—

Date ______________________

Time ______________________ hours

Place ______________________

(p) Insert name of debtor

and you, the above-named (p) ______________________, are to take notice that if you intend to oppose the petition you must not later than 7 days before the day fixed for the hearing:

(i) file in court a notice (in Form 6.19) specifying the grounds on which you object to the making of a bankruptcy order; and

(ii) send a copy of the notice to the petitioner or his solicitor.

(q) Only to be completed where the petitioning creditor is represented by a solicitor

The solicitor to the petitioning creditor is:— (q)

Name ______________________

Address ______________________

____

Telephone Number ______________________

Reference ______________________

Rule 6.6 **Form 6.8**

Creditor's Bankruptcy Petition on Failure to Comply with a Statutory Demand for a Liquidated Sum Payable at a Future Date

(TITLE)

(a) Insert full name(s) and address(es) of petitioner(s).

I/We (a) ____

____

____

(b) Insert full name, place of residence and occupation (if any) of debtor

petition the court that a bankruptcy order may be made against (b) ________

____

____

(c) Insert in full any other name(s) by which the debtor is or has been known

[also known as (c) ____]

____

(d) Insert trading name (adding "with another or others", if this is so), business address and nature of business

[and carrying on business as (d)

____

____]

(e) Insert any other address or addresses at which the debtor has resided at or after the time the petition debt was incurred.

[and lately residing at (e) ____

____]

(f) Give the same details as specified in note (d) above for any other businesses which have been carried on at or after the time the petition debt was incurred.

[and lately carrying on business as (f) ____

____]

and say as follows:—

(g) Delete as applicable

1. The debtor has for the greater part of six months immediately preceding the presentation of this petition (g) [resided at] [carried on business at] ________

____

(h) Or as the case may be following the terms of Rule 6.9.

within the district of this court (h)

(j) Please give the amount of debt(s), what they relate to and when they were incurred. Please show separately the amount or rate of any interest or other charge not previously notified to the debtor **and the reasons why you are claiming it.**

2. The debtor is justly and truly indebted to me[us] in the aggregate sum of

£(j) ______

(k) Insert date or dates when the debt becomes payable.

3. The above-mentioned debt is for a liquidated sum payable on (k) ______________________ and the debtor appears to have no reasonable prospect of being able to pay it.

(l) Insert date of service of statutory demand

4. On (l) ______________________ a statutory demand was served upon the debtor by

(m) State manner of service of the demand

(m) ______________________
in respect of the above-mentioned debt. To the best of my knowledge and belief the demand has neither been complied with nor set aside in accordance with the Rules and no application to set it aside is outstanding.

(n) If 3 weeks have not elapsed since service of statutory demand give reasons for earlier presentation of petition

(n)

5. I/We do not, nor does any person on my/our behalf, hold any security on the debtor's estate, or any part thereof, for the payment of the above-mentioned sum.

OR

(p) Delete as applicable

I/We hold security for the payment of (p) [part of] the above-mentioned sum. I/We will give up such security for the benefit of all the creditors in the event of a bankruptcy order being made.

OR

I/We hold security for the payment of part of the above-mentioned sum and I/we estimate the value of such security to be £ . This petition is not made in respect of the secured part of my/our debt.

Endorsement

This petition having been presented to the court on ______________________

it is ordered that the petition shall be heard as follows:—

Date ______________________

Time ______________________ hours

Place ______________________

(q) Insert name of debtor

and you, the above-named (q) ______________________ are to take notice that if you intend to oppose the petition you must not later than 7 days before the day fixed for the hearing:

(i) file in court a notice (in Form 6.19) specifying the grounds on which you object to the making of a bankruptcy order; and

(ii) send a copy of the notice to the petitioner or his solicitor.

(r) Only to be completed where the petitioning creditor is represented by a solicitor.

The solicitor to the petitioning creditor is:— (r)

Name ______________________

Address ______________________

____

Telephone Number ______________________

Reference ______________________

Rule 6.6 **Form 6.9**

Creditor's Bankruptcy Petition Where Execution or Other Process on a Judgment has been Returned in Whole or Part

(TITLE)

(a) Insert full name(s) and address(es) of petitioner(s).

I/We (a) ______________________________

____

(b) Insert full name, place of residence and occupation (if any) of debtor

petition the court that a bankruptcy order may be made against (b) __________

____

____

(c) Insert in full any other name(s) by which the debtor is or has been known

(d) Insert trading name (adding "with another or others", if this is so), business address and nature of business

(e) Insert any other address or addresses at which the debtor has resided at or after the time the petition debt was incurred

(f) Give the same details as specified in note (d) above for any other businesses which have been carried on at or after the time the petition debt was incurred

(g) Delete as applicable

(h) Or as the case may be following the terms of Rule 6.9.

[also known as (c) ______________________________]

[and carrying on business as (d) ______________________________

______________________________]

[and lately residing at (e) ______________________________

______________________________]

[and lately carrying on business as (f) ______________________________

____

______________________________]

and say as follows:—

1. The debtor has for the greater part of six months immediately preceding the presentation of this petition (g) [resided at] [carried on business at] _

____

within the district of this court (h)

2. The debtor is justly and truly indebted to me[us] in the aggregate sum of

(j) Please give the amount of debt(s), what they relate to and when they were incurred. Please show separately the amount or rate of any interest or other charge not previously notified to the debtor **and the reasons why you are claiming it.**

£(j) ______

3. The above mentioned debt is for a liquidated sum payable immediately and the debtor appears to be unable to pay it.

(k) Insert date on which judgment was obtained

4. On (k) ______________________ judgment was obtained in (g) [the High Court of Justice ____________ Division] [__________________ County Court]. [or as the case may be] on an action the short title and reference to the record whereof is "A " V. "B " Number ________ in the sum of £ ____________ following which execution was issued at the ______________ court in respect of the debt and on (l) ______________ the sheriff/county court (g) [made a return] [endorsed upon the writ a statement] to the effect that the execution was unsatisfied (g) [as to the whole] [as to part] and the above-mentioned debt represents the amount by which the execution was returned unsatisified.

(l) Insert date of execution

5. I/We do not, nor does any person on my/our behalf, hold any security on the debtor's estate, or any part thereof, for the payment of the above-mentioned sum.

OR

I/We hold security for the payment of (g) [part of] the above-mentioned sum. I/We will give up such security for the benefit of all the creditors in the event of a bankruptcy order being made

OR

I/We hold security for the payment of part of the above-mentioned sum and I/we estimate the value of such security to be £ . This petition is not made in respect of the secured part of my/our debt.

Endorsement

This petition having been presented to the court on ______________________

it is ordered that the petition shall be heard as follows:—

Date ____

Time ______________________________________ hours

Place ____

(m) Insert name of debtor

and you, the above-named (m) ______________________ are to take notice that if you intend to oppose the petition you must not later than 7 days before the day fixed for the hearing:

(i) file in court a notice (in Form 6.19) specifying the grounds on which you object to the making of a bankruptcy order; and

(ii) send a copy of the notice to the petitioner or his solicitor.

(n) Only to be completed where the petitioning creditor is represented by a solicitor.

The solicitor to the petitioning creditor is:— (n)

Name ____

Address ____

____

Telephone Number ___________________________________

Reference ____

Rule 6.6 **Form 6.10**

Bankruptcy Petition for Default in Connection with Voluntary Arrangement

(TITLE)

(a) Insert full name(s) and address(es) of petitioner(s).

I/We (a) ____

____

____

(b) Insert full name, place of residence and occupation (if any) of debtor

petition the court that a bankruptcy order may be made against (b) ____________

____

____

(c) Insert in full any other name(s) by which the debtor is or has been known

[also known as (c) ____

____

____]

(d) Insert trading name (adding "with another or others", if this is so), business address and nature of business

[and carrying on business as (d) ____

____

____]

(e) Insert any other address or addresses at which the debtor has resided at or after the time the petition debt was incurred

[and lately residing at (e) ____

____

____]

(f) Give the same details as specified in note (d) above for any other businesses which have been carried on at or after the time the petition debt was incurred

[and lately carrying on business as (f) ____

____

____]

and say as follows:—

(g) Delete as applicable

1. That the debtor has for the greater part of six months immediately preceding the presentation of this petition (g) [resided at] [carried on business at] _

____

(h) Or as the case may be following the terms of Rule 6.9.

within the district of this court (h)

(j) Insert date the debtor entered into voluntary arrangement

(k) Insert name of supervisor.

2. On (j) ____________ a voluntary arrangement proposed by the debtor was approved by his creditors and I am (g) [a person who is for the time being bound by the said voluntary arrangement and (k) ____________ is the supervisor] [(k) ____________ the supervisor of the said voluntary arrangement]

(l) Give details of the default in connection with the composition or scheme, being the grounds under section 276(1) IA86 upon which the bankruptcy order is sought

3. (l)

Endorsement

This petition having been presented to the court on ________________

it is ordered that the petition shall be heard as follows:—

Date ________________

Time ________________ hours

Place ________________

(m) Insert name of debtor

and you, the above-named (m) ________________ are to take notice that if you intend to oppose the petition you must not later than 7 days before the day fixed for the hearing:

(i) file in court a notice (in Form 6.19) specifying the grounds on which you object to the making of a bankruptcy order; and

(ii) send a copy of the notice to the petitioner or his solicitor.

(n) Only to be completed where the petitioning creditor is represented by a solicitor.

The solicitor to the petitioning creditor is:— (n)

Name ________________

Address ________________

____

Telephone Number ________________

Reference ________________

Rule 6.33 **Form 6.25**

Bankruptcy Order on Creditor's Petition

(TITLE)

(a) Insert name and address of petitioning creditor

Upon the petition of (a)

a creditor, which was presented on

and upon hearing

and upon reading the evidence

(b) Insert full description of debtor as set out in the petition

It is ordered that (b)

be adjudged bankrupt.

Dated ____________________________

Time ____________________________ hours

Important Notice to Bankrupt

*Delete as appropriate

(c) Insert address of Official Receiver's office

[The] [One of the] official receiver(s) attached to the court is by virtue of this order receiver and manager of the bankrupt's rebate. You are required to attend upon the Official Receiver of the court at (c) ____________________

____

____

____

immediately after you have received this order.

The Official Receiver's offices are open Monday to Friday (except on Holidays) from 10.00 to 16.00 hours.

(d) Order to be endorsed where petitioning creditor is represented by a solicitor

Endorsement on Order (d)

The solicitor to the petitioning creditor is:—

Name ____________________________

Address ____________________________

____

Telephone No. ____________________________

Reference ____________________________

Rule 6.37 **Form 6.27**

Debtor's Bankruptcy Petition

(TITLE)

(a) Insert full name, address and occupation (if any) of debtor

(b) Insert in full any other name(s) by which the debtor is or has been known

(c) Insert former address or addresses at which the debtor may have incurred debts or liabilities still unpaid or unsatisfied

(d) Insert trading name (adding "with another or others", if this is so), business address and nature of the business.

(e) Insert any former trading names (adding "with another or others", if this is so), business address and nature of the business in respect of which the debtor may have incurred debts or liabilities still unpaid or unsatisfied

(f) Delete as applicable

(g) State reasons

(h) Insert date

(j) Insert name of court

I (a) ______________________________

____

______________________________]

also known as (b) ______________________________

[lately residing at (c) ______________________________]

[and carrying on business as (d) ______________________________

____

______________________________]

[and lately carrying on business as (e) ______________________________

____

____

____

______________________________]

request the court that a bankruptcy order be made against me and say as follows:—

1. I have for the greater part of six months immediately preceding the presentation of this petition (f) [resided at] [carried on business at] ______________

____

within the district of (f) [this court] [(j) county court. I am presenting my petition to this court, as it is the nearest full-time county court to (j) county court, for the following reasons:

(g)

]

2. I am unable to pay my debts.

3. (f) That within the period of five years ending with the date of this petition:—

(i) I have not been adjudged bankrupt

OR

I was adjudged bankrupt on (h) in the (j)

(k) Insert number of bankruptcy proceedings

Court No. (k)

(ii) I have not (f) [made a composition with my creditors in satisfaction of my debts] or (f) [entered into a scheme of arrangement with creditors] (S.16 BA1914)

OR

On (h) I (f) [made a composition] [entered into a scheme of arrangement] with my creditors.

(iii) I have not entered into a voluntary arrangement

OR

On (h) I entered into a voluntary arrangement

(iv) I have not been subject to an administration order under Part VI of the County Courts Act 1984

OR

On (h) an administration order was made against me in the (j) county court.

4. A statement of my affairs is filed with this petition.

Date ______________________

Signature ______________________

Complete only if petition not heard immediately

Endorsement

This petition having been presented to the court on ______________ it is ordered that the petition shall be heard as follows:—

Date ______________________

Time ______________ hours

Place ______________________

Rule 6.96 **Form 6.37**

Proof of Debt–General Form

(TITLE)

Date of Bankruptcy Order No

1	Name of Creditor	
2	Address of Creditor	
3	Total amount of claim, including any Value Added Tax and outstanding uncapitalised interest as at the date of the bankruptcy order	£
4	Details of any documents by reference to which the debt can be substantiated. [Note: the official receiver or trustee may call for any document or evidence to substantiate the claim at his discretion]	
5	If the total amount shown above includes Value Added Tax, please show:— (a) amount of Value Added Tax (b) amount of claim NET of Value Added Tax	 £ £
6	If total amount above includes outstanding uncapitalised interest please state amount	£
7	If you have filled in both box 3 and box 5, please state whether you are claiming the amount shown in box 3 or the amount shown in box 5(b)	
8	Give details of whether the whole or any part of the debt falls within any (and if so which) of the categories of preferential debts under section 386 of, and schedule 6 to, the Insolvency Act 1986 (as read with schedule 3 to the Social Security Pensions Act 1975)	Category Amount(s) claimed as preferential £

9	Particulars of how and when debt incurred	
10	Particulars of any security held, the value of the security, and the date it was given	
11	Signature of creditor or person authorised to act on his behalf	
	Name in BLOCK LETTERS	
	Position with or relation to creditor	

Admitted to vote for

£

Date

Official Receiver/Trustee

Admitted preferentially for

£

Date

Trustee

Admitted non-preferentially for

£

Date

Trustee

Rule 6.96, 6.99 **Form 6.39**

Affidavit of Debt

(TITLE)

(a) Insert full name, address and description of person making oath

I (a)

make oath and say:

(b) Delete as applicable

(1) That (b) [I am a creditor of the above-named bankrupt] [I am (c)

(c) State capacity eg director, secretary, solicitor etc

of (d)

(d) Insert full name and address of creditor

a creditor of the above-named bankrupt.

(e) State means of knowledge of matters sworn to in affidavit

I have been concerned in this matter (e)

and am authorised by the creditor to make this affidavit on its/his behalf]

(f) Insert name of bankrupt

(2) That the said (f)

(g) Insert date

on (g) the date of the bankruptcy order, was and still is justly and truly indebted (b) [to me] [to the said creditor] in the sum of £ as shown in the proof of debt exhibited hereto marked "A".

Sworn at

Rule 6.173 **Form 6.56**

Request by Creditor(s) for the Holding of a Public Examination of the Bankrupt

(TITLE)

(a) Insert full name(s) and address(es) of creditor(s) making the request, whether an individual, firm or company

I/We (a)

of the above-named bankrupt request that you apply to the court for the holding of a public examination of the bankrupt under Section 290 of the Insolvency Act 1986.

My/Our claim in the bankruptcy is £ and attached is a list of other creditors who concur in this request together with confirmation by them of their concurrence. Their claims total £ which together with my/our claim makes a total of £ , and which, it is believed, represents not less than one-half in value of the debts of the above-named bankrupt.

I/We understand that I/we will be required to deposit with you such sum as you may determine to be appropriate by way of security for the expenses of holding a public examination.

(b) Insert reason why public examination required

I/We believe that a public examination is required because (b)

Signed ______________________________

Dated ______________________________

(c) Insert name and address of official receiver

To (c) ______________________________

____

Rule 6.178 **Form 6.61**

Notice of Disclaimer under Section 315 of the Insolvency Act 1986

(TITLE)

PART 1

(a) Insert date — On (a)

(b) Insert name of trustee — I (b) ______________________________,

the trustee of the above-named bankrupt's estate disclaimed all my interest in:

(c) Insert full particulars of property — (c)

Dated ______________________________

Signed ______________________________

Address ______________________________

____

____

Name in BLOCK LETTERS ______________________________

____

PART 2

(d) Insert name of court — This is a copy of a notice filed at the (d) Court on (a)

Seal of the Court

____

PART 3 This is a copy of a notice of disclaimer filed by me at the (d) Court

Signed ______________________________
Trustee

NOTE: 1. Part 1 is to be completed by the trustee and filed in court with a copy
Part 2 is to be completed by the court and returned to the trustee
Part 3 is to be completed by the trustee when sending out copy notice under Rule 6.179 or 6.180
2. The attention of a recipient of this notice is drawn to sections 315–321 of the Insolvency Act 1986.

Rule 6.183 **Form 6.62**

Notice to Elect

(TITLE)

(a) Insert name, address and particulars of interest in property (e.g landlord etc)

I (a)

(b) Insert details

of property comprising (b)

require the trustee to decide within 28 days of receiving this notice whether he will disclaim the above property or not and to notify me of his decision.

Dated ______________________

Signed ______________________

Name in BLOCK LETTERS ______________________

To the trustee of the above-named bankrupt's estate.

Address

Rule 6.184 **Form 6.63**

Notice of Intended Disclaimer to Interested Party

(TITLE)

(a) Insert full particulars of property

I intend to disclaim (a)

If you claim an interest in this property, you must declare to me the nature and extent of your claim within 14 days of receiving this notice
If you fail to do so, I am entitled to assume that you do not have any interest in the property which will prevent or impede my disclaimer

Dated ____________________

Signed ____________________
Trustee

Address ____________________

Name in BLOCK LETTERS ____________________

Rule 6.210 **Form 6.71**

Order of Annulment Under Section 282 of the Insolvency Act 1986

(TITLE)

Mr Registrar in chambers

(a) Insert full name, address and description of applicant

Upon the application of (a)

And upon hearing

And upon reading the evidence filed

(b) Delete as applicable

And it appearing that (b) [the bankruptcy order ought not to have been made] [the bankruptcy debts and the expenses of the bankruptcy have all been paid or secured to the satisfaction of the court] [under Section 282(2) of the Insolvency Act 1986 the bankruptcy order ought to be annulled].

(c) Insert bankrupt's full title as set out in the bankruptcy order

It is ordered that the bankruptcy order dated against (c)

is hereby annulled.

(d) Insert date

And it is ordered that the petition filed on (d) be dismissed.

(e) Insert date of registration/reference number

And it is ordered that the registration of the petition as a pending action at the Land Charges Department of HM Land Registry on (e) under reference number (e) and of the bankruptcy order on the register of writs and orders affecting land at that department on (e) under reference number (e) be vacated upon application made by the bankrupt.

Dated ______________________________

Notice to Bankrupt

1. Should you, the bankrupt, require advertisement of this order in a local newspaper and/or the Gazette, you should, within ________ days, notify the Secretary of State, enclosing the prescribed fee, details of which can be obtained by contacting the official receiver.
2. It is your responsibility and it is in your interest to ensure that the registration of the petition and of the bankruptcy order at HM Land Registry is cancelled.

Rule 7.2 **Form 7.1**

Originating Application

(TITLE)

Between

Applicant ____

and

Respondent ____

(a) Insert name and address of respondent

Let (a)

attend

before the Judge/Registrar on:—

Date ____

Time ________________________ hours

Place ____

(b) Insert name of applicant

On the hearing of an application by (b)
the applicant for an order in the following terms:—

(c) State the terms of the order to which the applicant claims to be entitled

(c)

The grounds on which the applicant claims to be entitled to the order are:—

(d) Set out grounds or refer to an affidavit in support

(d)

The names and addresses of the persons upon whom it is intended to serve this application are:—

(e) State the names and addresses of the persons intended to be served

(e)

OR

It is not intended to serve any person with this application.

(f) State the applicant's address for service

The applicant's address for service is: (f)

Dated ____

Signed: ______________________________
(SOLICITOR FOR THE) APPLICANT

If you do not attend, the court may make such order as it thinks fit.

Rule 7.2 **Form 7.2**

Ordinary Application

(TITLE)

Between

Applicant ______________________________

and

Respondent ______________________________

Take notice that I intend to apply to the Judge/Registrar on:

Date ______________________________

Time ____________________ hours

Place ______________________________

(a) State nature and grounds of application

for (a)

Signed: ______________________________

(SOLICITOR FOR THE) APPLICANT

My/Our address for service is:—

(b) Give the name(s) and address(es) of the person(s) (including the respondent) on whom it is intended to serve the application

To: (b)

OR

It is not intended to serve any person with this application

If you do not attend, the court will make such order as it thinks fit

Index